Koren Talmud Bavli
THE NOÉ EDITION

YEVAMOT

Steinsaltz Center

KOREN

תלמוד בבלי

KOREN TALMUD BAVLI

THE NOÉ EDITION

יבמות

YEVAMOT

Daf 17a through Daf 35a

COMMENTARY BY

Rabbi Adin Even-Israel Steinsaltz

EDITOR-IN-CHIEF

Rabbi Dr Tzvi Hersh Weinreb

SENIOR CONTENT EDITOR

Rabbi Dr Shalom Z Berger

EXECUTIVE EDITOR

Rabbi Joshua Schreier

STEINSALTZ CENTER

KOREN PUBLISHERS JERUSALEM

Supported by the Matanel Foundation

Koren Talmud Bavli, The Noe Edition
Vol. 14b: Tractate Yevamot, Daf 17a through Daf 35a
Paperback, ISBN, 978-965-7765-65-4

First Hebrew/English paperback edition, 2021

Koren Publishers Jerusalem Ltd.
PO Box 4044, Jerusalem 91040, ISRAEL
PO Box 8531, New Milford, CT 06776, USA
www.korenpub.com

Steinsaltz Center

Steinsaltz Center is the parent organization of institutions established by Rabbi Adin Even-Israel Steinsaltz

PO Box 45187, Jerusalem 91450 ISRAEL
Telephone: +972 2 646 0900, Fax +972 2 624 9454
www.steinsaltz-center.org

This book was published in cooperation with the Israel Institute for Talmudic Publications.

הִנֵּה יָמִים בָּאִים, נְאֻם אֲדֹנָי יֱהוִה, וְהִשְׁלַחְתִּי רָעָב בָּאָרֶץ,
לֹא־רָעָב לַלֶּחֶם וְלֹא־צָמָא לַמַּיִם, כִּי אִם־לִשְׁמֹעַ אֵת דִּבְרֵי יהוה.

Behold, days are coming – says the Lord God – I will send a hunger to the land, not a hunger for bread nor a thirst for water, but to hear the words of the Lord. (AMOS 8:11)

The Noé edition of the Koren Talmud Bavli
with the commentary of Rabbi Adin Even-Israel Steinsaltz
is dedicated to all those who open its covers
to quench their thirst for Jewish Knowledge,
in our generation of Torah renaissance.

This beautiful edition is for the young, the aged,
the novice and the savant alike,
as it unites the depth of Torah knowledge
with the best of academic scholarship.

Within its exquisite and vibrant pages,
words become worlds.

It will claim its place in the library of classics,
in the bookcases of the Beit Midrash,
the classrooms of our schools,
and in the offices of professionals and business people
who carve out precious time to grapple with its timeless wisdom.

For the Student and the Scholar

DEDICATED BY LEO AND SUE NOÉ

Steinsaltz Center

Executive Director, Steinsaltz Center

Rabbi Meni Even-Israel

Managing Editor

Rabbi Jason Rappoport

Senior Content Editor

Rabbi Dr. Shalom Z. Berger

Editors

Rabbi Joshua Amaru, *Coordinating Editor*
Amy Kaplan Benoff
Menucha Chwat
Rabbi Yoel Domb
Rabbi Yonatan Shai Freedman
Rabbi Alan Haber
Rabbi Tzvi Chaim Kaye
Catriel Lev
Elisha Loewenstern
Adina Luber
Rabbi Avishai Magence, *Content Curator*
Gavriel Reiss
Rabbi David Sedley
Shira Shmidman
Rabbi Michael Siev
Avi Steinhart
Rabbi Binyamin Zimmerman

Copy Editors

Aliza Israel, *Coordinator*
Bracha Hermon
Ita Olesker
Debbie Ismailoff
Shira Finson
Ilana Sobel
Deena Nataf
Eliana Kurlantzick Yorav
Nava Wieder

Language Consultants

Dr. Stephanie E. Binder, *Greek & Latin*
Rabbi Yaakov Hoffman, *Arabic*
Dr. Shai Secunda, *Persian*
Shira Shmidman, *Aramaic*

KOREN

Design & Typesetting

Raphaël Freeman, *Design & Typography*
Dena Landowne Bailey, *Typesetting*
Tani Bayer, *Jacket Design*

Images

Eliahu Misgav, *Illustration & Image Acquisition*

Introduction by the Publisher

The Talmud has sustained and inspired Jews for thousands of years. Throughout Jewish history, an elite cadre of scholars has absorbed its learning and passed it on to succeeding generations. The Talmud has been the fundamental text of our people.

Beginning in the 1960s, Rabbi Adin Even-Israel Steinsaltz שליט״א created a revolution in the history of Talmud study. His translation of the Talmud, first into modern Hebrew and then into other languages, as well the practical learning aids he added to the text, have enabled millions of people around the world to access and master the complexity and context of the world of Talmud.

It is thus a privilege to present the *Koren Talmud Bavli*, an English translation of the talmudic text with the brilliant elucidation of Rabbi Steinsaltz. The depth and breadth of his knowledge are unique in our time. His rootedness in the tradition and his reach into the world beyond it are inspirational.

Working with Rabbi Steinsaltz on this remarkable project has been not only an honor, but a great pleasure. Never shy to express an opinion, with wisdom and humor, Rabbi Steinsaltz sparkles in conversation, demonstrating his knowledge (both sacred and worldly), sharing his wide-ranging interests, and, above all, radiating his passion. I am grateful for the unique opportunity to work closely with him, and I wish him many more years of writing and teaching.

Our intentions in publishing this new edition of the Talmud are threefold. First, we seek to fully clarify the talmudic page to the reader – textually, intellectually, and graphically. Second, we seek to utilize today's most sophisticated technologies, both in print and electronic formats, to provide the reader with a comprehensive set of study tools. And third, we seek to help readers advance in their process of Talmud study.

To achieve these goals, the *Koren Talmud Bavli* is unique in a number of ways:

- The classic *tzurat hadaf* of Vilna, used by scholars since the 1800s, has been reset for great clarity, and opens from the Hebrew "front" of the book. Full *nikkud* has been added to both the talmudic text and Rashi's commentary, allowing for a more fluent reading with the correct pronunciation; the commentaries of *Tosafot* have been punctuated. Upon the advice of many English-speaking teachers of Talmud, we have separated these core pages from the translation, thereby enabling the advanced student to approach the text without the distraction of the translation. This also reduces the number of volumes in the set. At the bottom of each *daf*, there is a reference to the corresponding English pages. In addition, the Vilna edition was read against other manuscripts and older print editions, so that texts which had been removed by non-Jewish censors have been restored to their rightful place.
- The English translation, which starts on the English "front" of the book, reproduces the *menukad* Talmud text alongside the English translation (in bold) and commentary and explanation (in a lighter font). The Hebrew and Aramaic text is presented in logical paragraphs. This allows for a fluent reading of the text for the non-Hebrew or non-Aramaic reader. It also allows for the Hebrew reader to refer easily to the text alongside. Where the original text features dialogue or poetry, the English text is laid out in a manner appropriate to the genre. Each page refers to the relevant *daf*.

- Critical contextual tools surround the text and translation: personality notes, providing short biographies of the Sages; language notes, explaining foreign terms borrowed from Greek, Latin, Persian, or Arabic; and background notes, giving information essential to the understanding of the text, including history, geography, botany, archaeology, zoology, astronomy, and aspects of daily life in the talmudic era.
- Halakhic summaries provide references to the authoritative legal decisions made over the centuries by the rabbis. They explain the reasons behind each halakhic decision as well as the ruling's close connection to the Talmud and its various interpreters.
- Photographs, drawings, and other illustrations have been added throughout the text – in full color in the Standard and Electronic editions, and in black and white in the Daf Yomi edition – to visually elucidate the text.

This is not an exhaustive list of features of this edition, it merely presents an overview for the English-speaking reader who may not be familiar with the "total approach" to Talmud pioneered by Rabbi Steinsaltz.

Several professionals have helped bring this vast collaborative project to fruition. My many colleagues are noted on the Acknowledgments page, and the leadership of this project has been exceptional.

RABBI MENACHEM EVEN-ISRAEL, DIRECTOR OF THE STEINSALTZ CENTER, was the driving force behind this enterprise. With enthusiasm and energy, he formed the happy alliance with Koren and established close relationships among all involved in the work.

RABBI DR. TZVI HERSH WEINREB שליט״א, EDITOR-IN-CHIEF, brought to this project his profound knowledge of Torah, intellectual literacy of Talmud, and erudition of Western literature. It is to him that the text owes its very high standard, both in form and content, and the logical manner in which the beauty of the Talmud is presented.

RABBI JOSHUA SCHREIER, EXECUTIVE EDITOR, assembled an outstanding group of scholars, translators, editors, and proofreaders, whose standards and discipline enabled this project to proceed in a timely and highly professional manner.

RABBI MEIR HANEGBI, EDITOR OF THE HEBREW EDITION OF THE STEINSALTZ TALMUD, lent his invaluable assistance throughout the work process, supervising the reproduction of the Vilna pages.

RAPHAËL FREEMAN, EXECUTIVE EDITOR OF KOREN, created this Talmud's unique typographic design which, true to the Koren approach, is both elegant and user friendly.

It has been an enriching experience for all of us at Koren Publishers Jerusalem to work with the Steinsaltz Center to develop and produce the *Koren Talmud Bavli*. We pray that this publication will be a source of great learning and, ultimately, greater *avodat Hashem* for all Jews.

Matthew Miller, Publisher
Koren Publishers Jerusalem
Jerusalem 5772

Contents

For the vocalized Vilna Shas layout, please open as a Hebrew book.

Explanation of Diagrams in **Yevamot**

Man Woman

Married couple

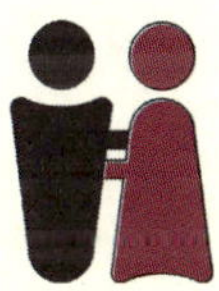

Siblings are indicated by identical patterning:

Members of the same generation are usually on the same horizontal row:

Parents and their offspring are either connected by a vertical line, indicated by identical shading on their heads, or both:

For the offspring of an unmarried couple, the shading on the head reflects that of both the father and the mother:

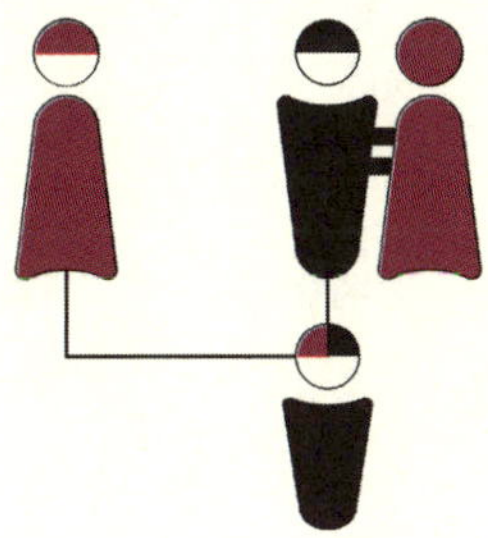

A deceased individual is indicated by an X on his head:

If more than one individual has died, each subsequent death is indicated by an additional X above the deceased's head. When more than one event is described in a single diagram, an arrow points to the later event.

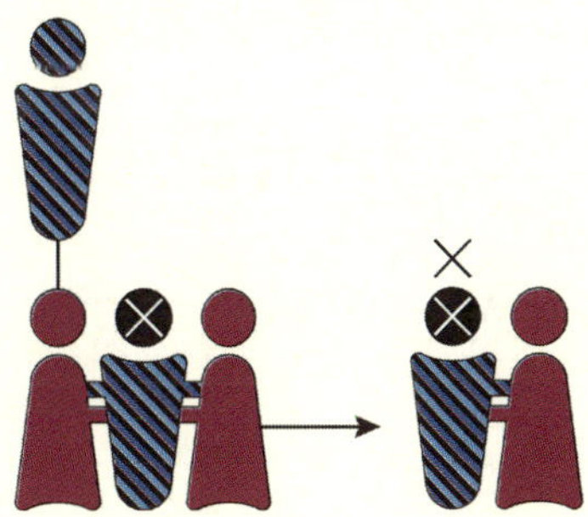

Introduction to **Perek II**

If brothers dwell together and one of them dies and he has no child, the wife of the dead man shall not be married outside of the family to one not of his kin; her brother-in-law will have intercourse with her and take her to him to be his wife and consummate the levirate marriage.

(Deuteronomy 25:5)

In the first chapter, the Gemara discussed women who are prohibited from entering into levirate marriage due to their being close relatives of, and therefore severely forbidden to, their *yavam*, together with the rival wives of such women. It was explained that these women are exempt from both levirate marriage and *ḥalitza*. However, there are other problems that can arise in cases of levirate marriage. Some women are not forbidden to their *yavam* with a prohibition of *karet* but are forbidden due to another prohibition or by rabbinic law. In these instances does the mitzva of levirate marriage override the prohibition?

Another issue discussed in this chapter is the definition of some fundamental concepts in levirate marriage. The Torah states that the brother must perform the levirate marriage, but the question of who exactly is considered a brother requires clarification. The first chapter mentioned the concept of: A brother with whom he did not coexist, to whom the *halakhot* of levirate marriage and *ḥalitza* do not apply. In such a case the exemption from levirate marriage is not due to a forbidden union but rather from the *halakhot* of levirate marriage themselves, as the verse states: "If brothers dwell together." This chapter defines this concept, and clarifies the details and application of the *halakha*.

Another issue discussed in this chapter is what the Torah means when it uses the term "brother." Does it refer to any brother or only the eldest, and does it apply equally to paternal and maternal half brothers? Must the brother performing levirate marriage be legitimate, or are illegitimate brothers included as well?

Another topic clarified in this chapter is the term "child" used in the verse. Since the Torah uses the masculine word for "child" does it also include a daughter? Does it include grandchildren and descendants? Does it refer only to legitimate children or also to illegitimate children? In cases of doubt as to whether or not there is a surviving child when the *yavam* dies is there an obligation to perform levirate marriage and *ḥalitza*?

These questions, along with several other corollary issues, constitute the primary substance of this chapter.

Perek **II**
Daf **17** Amud **a**

מתני׳ כֵּיצַד אֵשֶׁת אָחִיו שֶׁלֹּא הָיָה בְּעוֹלָמוֹ? שְׁנֵי אַחִים, וּמֵת אֶחָד מֵהֶן; וְנוֹלַד לָהֶן אָח, וְאַחַר כָּךְ יִיבֵּם הַשֵּׁנִי אֶת אֵשֶׁת אָחִיו וָמֵת. הָרִאשׁוֹנָה יוֹצְאָה מִשּׁוּם אֵשֶׁת אָחִיו שֶׁלֹּא הָיָה בְּעוֹלָמוֹ, וְהַשְּׁנִיָּה מִשּׁוּם צָרָתָהּ.

MISHNA Each of the women enumerated in the first chapter causes exemption from levirate marriage and *ḥalitza* for her rival wives. This is due to the close family relationship she has with her brother-in-law, making her forbidden to him. The single exception is the case explained in this mishna. **What is** the case of **the wife of a brother**[N] **with whom he did not coexist?**[H] For example: If there were **two brothers, and one of them died** childless, **and** subsequently **a brother of theirs was born, after which the second brother**, the elder, **took his** deceased **brother's wife in levirate marriage, and** then **died** as well. Consequently, two women require levirate marriage: The widow of the first brother who had been taken in levirate marriage by the second brother, and the widow of the second brother, the first widow's rival wife. **The first** widow, who had been the wife of the first brother to die, **goes out** without any obligation to be taken in levirate marriage by the youngest brother who was born later, **since** she is **the wife of a brother with whom he did not coexist.** The first deceased brother never lived at the same time as the newly born brother. **The second** widow, who had been married to the second brother, is exempt **due to her rival wife.**

עָשָׂה בָּהּ מַאֲמָר וָמֵת – שְׁנִיָּה חוֹלֶצֶת וְלֹא מִתְיַיבֶּמֶת.

The mishna discusses an additional situation: If the second brother had **performed** only **levirate betrothal**[B] **with her,** meaning that he had not yet consummated the marriage, **and then died,** both the wife betrothed by a levirate betrothal to the second brother and the wife of the second brother fall before the youngest brother born after the death of the first brother. In that case, the first wife certainly goes out and is exempt from both *ḥalitza* and levirate marriage, since she is to him the wife of a brother with whom he did not coexist. **The second,** however, was never effectively the rival wife of the first brother's wife, as the first brother's wife had only been betrothed by levirate betrothal and was not fully married to the second brother. Therefore, **she performs *ḥalitza* and may not enter into levirate marriage.**

גמ׳ אָמַר רַב נַחְמָן: מַאן דְּתָנֵי רִאשׁוֹנָה לָא מִשְׁתַּבֵּשׁ, מַאן דְּתָנֵי שְׁנִיָּה לָא מִשְׁתַּבֵּשׁ. מַאן דְּתָנֵי

GEMARA **Rav Naḥman said: He who taught** the version of the mishna which reads: **The first** widow goes out, **is not mistaken** in his version, and **he who taught** a variant version of the mishna which reads: **The second** widow goes out, **is not mistaken** either, since it is possible to understand the mishna both ways. Both versions of the text can refer to the same woman, i.e., the wife of the first brother, by different titles. The Gemara explains that **he who taught:**

Perek **II**
Daf **17** Amud **b**

רִאשׁוֹנָה לָא מִשְׁתַּבֵּשׁ. מַאי רִאשׁוֹנָה – רִאשׁוֹנָה לִנְפִילָה, וּמַאן דְּתָנֵי שְׁנִיָּה לָא מִשְׁתַּבֵּשׁ: מַאי שְׁנִיָּה – שְׁנִיָּה לִנְשׂוּאִין. מִי לָא עָסְקִינַן דְּיִיבֵּם וְאַחַר כָּךְ כָּנַס? אֶלָּא: מַאי שְׁנִיָּה – שְׁנִיָּה בִּנְשׂוּאִין.

The first, is not mistaken, as **what is** the meaning of **first?** It means **the first to fall** before her *yavam* for levirate marriage. **And he who taught** referring to her as **the second is not mistaken** either, as **what is** the meaning of **second?** It means **the second to enter marriage.** Since the second deceased brother was already married to one woman, this *yevama* whom he took in levirate marriage was his second wife. The Gemara wonders: Is this the necessary order of events? **Are we not** also **dealing with** a scenario **in which** the second brother **took** the wife of the first brother **in levirate marriage and then later took** another wife? Would such a situation not merit the same ruling? **Rather, what is** the meaning of calling the wife of the first brother **the second?** It means **she who had been married for a second time.** She had already been married twice, whereas the wife of the second brother had been married only once.

NOTES

What is the case of the wife of a brother, etc. – כֵּיצַד אֵשֶׁת אָחִיו וכו׳: The mishna comes to clarify the fundamental principle concerning the *halakha* of the wife of his brother with whom he did not coexist, and not to discuss all of its details, since those were already discussed in the previous chapter (Rashba).

HALAKHA

The wife of a brother with whom he did not coexist – אֵשֶׁת אָחִיו שֶׁלֹּא הָיָה בְּעוֹלָמוֹ: The levirate bond does not apply at all to the wife of a brother with whom one did not coexist. Therefore, she is exempt from levirate marriage and consequently forbidden to the *yavam*, and also causes exemption for her rival wives. In fact, she causes exemption for the rival wives of her rival wives as well, as per the ruling concerning all forbidden relations (Rambam *Sefer Nashim, Hilkhot Yibbum VaḤalitza* 6:16–17; *Shulḥan Arukh, Even HaEzer* 173:12).

BACKGROUND

Levirate betrothal [*ma'amar*] – מַאֲמָר: The betrothal performed by a *yavam* based on his levirate bond with his *yevama* is called *ma'amar*. A levirate betrothal does not have the halakhic status of an ordinary betrothal, since the levirate bond between *yavam* and widow is not dependent upon betrothal. Rather, it is a sort of continuation of the previous marriage to her deceased husband. Full marriage with one's sister-in-law comes into effect by intercourse alone. However, the Sages instituted this type of betrothal with a *yevama* for reasons of modesty, so that the *yavam* would not have intercourse with her without betrothal.

אֵשֶׁת אָחִיו שֶׁלֹּא הָיָה בְּעוֹלָמוֹ הֵיכָא כְּתִיבָא? אֲמַר רַב יְהוּדָה אֲמַר רַב: אָמַר קְרָא ״כִּי יֵשְׁבוּ אַחִים יַחְדָּו״ – שֶׁהָיְתָה לָהֶם יְשִׁיבָה אַחַת בָּעוֹלָם, פְּרָט לְאֵשֶׁת אָחִיו שֶׁלֹּא הָיָה בְּעוֹלָמוֹ. ״יַחְדָּו״ – מְיוּחָדִים בְּנַחֲלָה, פְּרָט לְאָחִיו מִן הָאֵם.

§ The Gemara turns from a review of the language used in the mishna to a discussion of the *halakhot* of a wife of a brother with whom one did not coexist. **Where is it written** that the mitzva of levirate marriage does not apply in the case of **the wife of a brother with whom he did not coexist?**[N] **Rav Yehuda said** that **Rav said: The verse states "If brothers dwell together** and one of them dies" (Deuteronomy 25:5), meaning **that they had a common dwelling** together **in the world.** This **excludes the wife of a brother with whom he did not coexist.** Furthermore, it is derived: **"Together"** means that they were **united** together **in an inheritance;**[N] i.e., they are united in that they inherit together. In other words, since property is inherited by sons from their father, it can be inferred that the verse is speaking specifically of brothers from the same father. This **excludes his maternal** half **brother,**[H] with whom he is not united by inheritance, since only brothers who share the same father inherit from each other.

רַבָּה אֲמַר: אַחִין מִן הָאָב – יָלֵיף ״אַחֲוָה״ ״אַחֲוָה״ מִבְּנֵי יַעֲקֹב, מַה לְּהַלָּן מִן הָאָב וְלֹא מִן הָאֵם, אַף כָּאן מִן הָאָב וְלֹא מִן הָאֵם.

Rabba said: One learns the ruling that levirate marriage applies only to **brothers from the** same **father** by the verbal analogy between the term **brotherhood** used in the context of levirate marriage and the term **brotherhood from the children of Jacob. Just as there,** with regard to the children of Jacob, they are all brothers **from the father and not from the mother,** since they were from four different mothers, **so too, here,** in the case of levirate marriage, it is referring specifically to brothers **from the father and not from the mother.**

וְלֵילַף ״אַחֲוָה״ ״אַחֲוָה״ מֵעֲרָיוֹת! דָּנִין ״אַחִים״ מֵ״אַחִים״, וְאֵין דָּנִין אַחִים מֵ״אָחִיךָ״.

The Gemara raises an objection: Why should we learn from the children of Jacob? **Let it derive** the meaning of the term **brotherhood** by verbal analogy to the term **brotherhood from** the verses discussing **those with whom relations are forbidden.** In the *halakhot* of forbidden relations, both paternal and maternal half brothers are considered brothers, and are thereby subject to such prohibitions as those against relations with a brother's wife. The Gemara answers: The first analogy is preferable, as **we infer "brothers" from "brothers."** The word "brothers" is stated both with regard to the children of Jacob and with regard to the *halakhot* of levirate marriage, **whereas** with regard to forbidden relations it says "your brother," and **one cannot make an inference to "brothers" from "your brother."**

מַאי נָפְקָא מִינָּהּ? הָא תָּנָא דְּבֵי רַבִּי יִשְׁמָעֵאל: ״וְשָׁב הַכֹּהֵן״ ״וּבָא הַכֹּהֵן״ זוֹ הִיא שִׁיבָה זוֹ הִיא בִּיאָה! הָנֵי מִילֵּי הֵיכָא דְּלֵיכָּא מִידֵּי דְּדָמֵי לֵיהּ, אֲבָל הֵיכָא דְּאִיכָּא מִידֵּי דְּדָמֵי לֵיהּ – מִדְּדָמֵי לֵיהּ יָלְפִינַן.

The Gemara objects: **What difference does it make** if there is a minor difference between the words being compared? **As the school of Rabbi Yishmael taught** a verbal analogy with regard to leprosy of houses between the verse **"and the priest shall return [*veshav*]"** (Leviticus 14:39) and the verse **"and the priest shall come [*uva*]"** (Leviticus 14:44), from which it is derived that **this is** the *halakha* with regard to **returning,** i.e., it is after seven days, and **this is** the same *halakha* with regard to **coming,** that it is after seven days. Consequently, a less pronounced difference of one letter between the Hebrew words for "brothers" and "your brother" should certainly not prevent the teaching of a verbal analogy. The Gemara responds: **This applies when nothing** else **was** more **similar, but where there is something similar we infer from that which is more similar.** In such situations, it is preferable to learn from the word that bears greater similarity.

וְלֵילַף ״אַחֲוָה״ ״אַחֲוָה״ מִלּוֹט, דִּכְתִיב ״כִּי אֲנָשִׁים אַחִים אֲנַחְנוּ״! מִסְתַּבְּרָא, מִבְּנֵי יַעֲקֹב הֲוָה לֵיהּ לְמֵילַף, מִשּׁוּם דְּמוּפְנֵי. מִדַּהֲוָה לֵיהּ לְמִכְתַּב ״שְׁנֵים עָשָׂר עֲבָדֶיךָ בְּנֵי אָבִינוּ״ וּכְתִיב ״אַחִים״ – שְׁמַע מִינָּהּ לְאַפְנוּיֵי.

The Gemara objects on another count: **Let** the *halakha* **derive** the meaning of the term **brotherhood** from the term **brotherhood from Lot, as it is written** that Abraham said to Lot: **"For we are brothers"** (Genesis 13:8). From here one could conclude that the word brothers means relatives and not necessarily brothers. The Gemara rejects this: **It is more reasonable to derive from the children of Jacob, due to** the fact that the word "brothers" **is free** in its context and is therefore available to be used in a verbal analogy: **Since it could have written: We your servants are twelve children of our father,** but instead it **writes:** "Twelve **brothers,** the children of one man" (Genesis 42:13), **learn from here** that this comes **to render** the word "brothers" **free** so that it may be allocated to another matter, i.e., the definition of brothers.

NOTES

Wife of a brother with whom he did not coexist – אֵשֶׁת אָחִיו שֶׁלֹּא הָיָה בְּעוֹלָמוֹ: *Tosafot* ask: Why doesn't the Gemara employ the principle that the Torah's ways are pleasant (see Proverbs 3:17), used in several other areas of *halakha*, and say that it would not be appropriate for a woman to wait her entire life for a brother to possibly be born to her late husband? In the Jerusalem Talmud the applicability of this concept is discussed. *Tosafot* answer that the verse comes to exclude even the case where the mother-in-law was pregnant at the time of the husband's death, so that the wait would be finite. The Rashba adds that the verse is necessary to teach the case when several *yevamin* were alive, in which case the principle of the Torah's ways of pleasantness would not apply, as well as to exclude any later born brother from the obligation of levirate marriage.

United in an inheritance – מְיוּחָדִים בְּנַחֲלָה: The Rashba challenges this explanation, as there are certain situations in which maternal half brothers inherit a common inheritance from their mother. He answers that since such a case occurs only infrequently, that cannot be the criterion used to determine brotherhood with regard to levirate marriage.

HALAKHA

Excludes his maternal half brother – פְּרָט לְאָחִיו מִן הָאֵם: Maternal half brothers are not considered brothers for purposes of levirate marriage. If a man dies and has brothers only by his mother, then his widow is permitted to marry anyone (Rambam *Sefer Nashim, Hilkhot Yibbum VaḤalitza* 1:7; *Shulḥan Arukh, Even HaEzer* 157:1).

וְאִיצְטְרִיךְ לְמִכְתַּב "אַחִים", וְאִיצְטְרִיךְ לְמִכְתַּב "יַחְדָּו". דְּאִי כָּתַב רַחֲמָנָא "אַחִים" הֲוָה אָמִינָא: לֵילַף "אַחֲוָה" "אַחֲוָה" מִלּוֹט. וְכִי תֵּימָא לָא מְפַנֵּי – לָאֵיי, אַפְנוּיֵי מְפַנֵּי, מִדַּהֲוָה לֵיהּ לְמִכְתַּב "רֵעִים" וּכְתִיב "אַחִים", שְׁמַע מִינָּהּ לְאַפְנוּיֵי – כָּתַב רַחֲמָנָא "יַחְדָּו", הַמְיוּחָדִים בְּנַחֲלָה.

The Gemara comments: **And** although Rav Yehuda and Rabba learned the same ruling from two different passages, according to both **it was necessary to write "brothers"**[N] **and it was necessary to write "together"** in the verses discussing levirate marriage, **as, if the Merciful One had written** only **"brothers," I would say that one should infer** the meaning of the term **"brothers"** from the term **"brothers" from Lot. And if you would say it is not free**[N] there in the same way that the word "brothers" is free in the passage concerning the children of Jacob, this is **not so;** in fact, **it is free.** With regard to Lot **it could have written: Friends,** as they were not actual brothers but relatives, **and** yet **"brothers" is written.** One might **learn from** here **that this is free** to be allocated elsewhere and teach that such relatives are called brothers even for levirate marriage. Therefore, **the Torah wrote "together"** to teach that this applies specifically to **those** brothers who are **united in an inheritance.**

וְאִי כָּתַב רַחֲמָנָא "יַחְדָּו", הֲוָה אָמִינָא: דְּמִייַחֲדִי בְּאַבָּא וּבְאִמָּא, צְרִיכָא.

And if the Merciful One had written "together" alone and not added "brothers," **I would say that** they must **have** both **the same father and mother together,** and that otherwise the mitzva of levirate marriage would not apply. Therefore, "brothers" is written to compare this to the children of Jacob, who were brothers from the same father but not the same mother. It is for this reason, then, that **it is necessary** to write both.

וְהָא מֵהֵיכָא תֵּיתֵי? יִבּוּם בְּנַחֲלָה תְּלָא רַחֲמָנָא, וְנַחֲלָה מִן הָאָב וְלֹא מִן הָאֵם הִיא! אִיצְטְרִיךְ, סָלְקָא דַּעְתָּךְ אָמִינָא: הוֹאִיל וְחִידּוּשׁ הוּא, דְּקָמִשְׁתְּרֵי עֶרְוָה גַּבֵּיהּ – אֵימָא עַד דְּמִיַּיחֲדִי בְּאַבָּא וּבְאִמָּא, צְרִיכָא.

The Gemara asks about the last supposition: **But from where would it be derived** that perhaps levirate marriage would apply only if they are full brothers, sharing both a father and mother? Why should one assume that maternal brotherhood is also of import here? Doesn't **the Merciful One make levirate marriage dependent upon inheritance?** The Torah states that the *yavam* who performs the levirate marriage will establish the name of his deceased brother, meaning that he inherits from him, **and inheritance** comes **from the father and not from the mother.** Nevertheless, this **was necessary,** as **it could enter your mind to say that since this** *halakha* of levirate marriage **is a novelty** in **that** a woman who was a **forbidden relation to him** as a brother's wife **is** now **rendered permitted, say** that this permissibility will be limited **only to** cases of brothers **with the same father and same mother together.** It is due to this possibility that the verbal analogy to the brothers who were the children of Jacob is **necessary.**

אָמַר רַב הוּנָא אָמַר רַב: שׁוֹמֶרֶת יָבָם שֶׁמֵּתָה – מוּתָּר בְּאִמָּהּ. אַלְמָא קָסָבַר: אֵין זִיקָה. וְלֵימָא: הֲלָכָה כְּדִבְרֵי הָאוֹמֵר אֵין זִיקָה!

§ **Rav Huna said** that **Rav said:** In the case of a **widow** whose husband had died childless and who is **waiting for her** *yavam* to perform levirate marriage or set her free with *ḥalitza*, **who** then **died** before her *yavam* could take her in levirate marriage, the *yavam* **is permitted to** marry **her mother.** The levirate obligation does not create a familial relation between them. **Apparently,** Rav Huna says that Rav **holds** that **the** levirate **bond** [*zikka*][BL] **is not substantial.** In other words, the bond formed between the *yevama* and her *yavam* requiring levirate marriage does not create a halakhic connection between the two. The Gemara asks: **Then let him say** explicitly: The ***halakha* is in accordance with the statement of he who says** that **the** levirate **bond is not substantial,** as this issue is in fact a matter of dispute between *tanna'im*. Why did he not simply conclude that the *halakha* is in accordance with the opinion of the *tanna* who held that the levirate bond is not substantial?

אִי הֲוָה אָמַר הָכִי הֲוָה אָמִינָא: הָנֵי מִילֵּי בִּתְרֵי, אֲבָל בְּחַד יֵשׁ זִיקָה.

The Gemara answers: **If he had said that, I would say: This** statement that the levirate bond is not substantial **applies** only in reference **to two** brothers, each of whom has the possibility to take her in levirate marriage. In such cases the levirate bond between either one of the brothers and the *yevama* is not absolute, as it is always possible for the other brother to marry her instead. **But in** cases of **one** brother, then since the obligation to the *yevama* is exclusively his, I would say that **the** levirate **bond is substantial.**

NOTES

It was necessary to write brothers, etc. – **אִיצְטְרִיךְ לְמִכְתַּב אַחִים וכו׳**: *Tosafot Yeshanim* raise the question: Would it not have been possible to omit the word "brothers" in reference to Lot and to omit "together" in the verses that discuss levirate marriage? If so, they are both unnecessary. Ramban answers that if the word "brothers" had not been written, the word "brother" might have been interpreted in the widest sense as referring to fellow men and not necessarily to relatives, just as many times in the Torah the words "your brother" refer to any Jewish person. Consequently, it was necessary to write "brothers" in reference to Lot to teach that the "brothers" referred to in the context of levirate marriage are specifically relatives (see Ritva).

Free – **מְפַנֵּי**: There is a tannaitic dispute with regard to the authority of a verbal analogy [*gezera shava*] where the key words are not superfluous in their respective contexts. In the Jerusalem Talmud, even in the case of a verbal analogy where the key words are not at all superfluous, the analogy may be expounded, with the caveat that it is open to refutation. This type of verbal analogy is really an enhanced analogy [*binyan av*] and is essentially nothing more than a logical connection based on the idea that identical expressions in two *halakhot* indicate that the Torah intended to emphasize the connection between them. However, in the Babylonian Talmud, a verbal analogy may be expounded only if the key word is superfluous in at least one of the verses. According to Rabbi Yishmael, the superfluity of the key word in one verse is sufficient proof that the Torah intended that this verbal analogy should be derived, and it cannot be refuted. The Sages who disagree with him hold that even that type of verbal analogy can be logically refuted.

BACKGROUND

Levirate bond – **זִיקָה**: This refers to the relationship between a *yevama* and her deceased husband's brothers, from the time of the husband's death until one of the brothers performs levirate marriage or *ḥalitza* with the widow. The precise nature of the relationship between the *yevama* and her *yevamin* during this period is the subject of much talmudic debate. In certain respects they are already considered to be betrothed from the time of the husband's death. For this reason, for example, a *yavam* may not marry a close relative of his *yevama*. The bond is either transformed into marriage by levirate marriage or nullified and severed by *ḥalitza*.

LANGUAGE

Levirate bond [*zikka*] – **זִיקָה**: From the root *z-k-k*, meaning connected or tied. The modern Hebrew words *zikim* or *azikim*, meaning handcuffs, come from the same source. While this root is also used literally in certain contexts, most of its usage by the Sages is abstract or metaphorical and represents legal, psychological, or sometimes sexual bonds. The word *zikka* is an abstract noun meaning a tie or a connection, and it indicates that an element is lacking.

וְלֵימָא: הֲלָכָה כְּדִבְרֵי הָאוֹמֵר אֵין זִיקָה אֲפִילּוּ בְּחַד?! אִי אֲמַר הָכִי הֲוָה אָמִינָא אֲפִילּוּ מֵחַיִּים, קָמַשְׁמַע לָן: לְאַחַר מִיתָה – אִין, מֵחַיִּים – לָא, מִשּׁוּם דְּאָסוּר לְבַטֵּל מִצְוַת יְבָמִין.

The Gemara asks: **Then let him say: The** ***halakha*** **is in accordance with the statement of the one who says that the** levirate **bond is not substantial, even in** the case of **one** brother. The Gemara answers: **If he had said that, I would say: Even** if his *yevama* were **alive** and required levirate marriage with him, he would be allowed to take her mother in marriage. Therefore, **this comes to teach us** that **after death, yes, he is** permitted to marry her mother; but **while** she is **alive,** he is **not.** Why not? This is **because it is prohibited to nullify the mitzva of levirate marriage.** Were he to marry her mother, he would no longer be able to take the daughter in levirate marriage because his wife's daughter is forbidden to him. As a result of his marriage, he would cancel the mitzva of levirate marriage so that it could no longer apply to him.

תְּנַן: יְבִמְתּוֹ שֶׁמֵּתָה – מוּתָּר בַּאֲחוֹתָהּ. בַּאֲחוֹתָהּ אִין, בְּאִמָּהּ לָא!

The Gemara raises an objection to the statement of Rav Huna: **We learned** in a mishna (49a): If **his** ***yevama*** **dies, he is permitted to** marry **her sister.** A precise reading of this phrase leads to the implication that with regard to **her sister, yes,** it is permitted, as even if it had been his wife who had died he would be permitted to marry her sister. But with regard to **her mother, no,** it is not permitted.

הוּא הַדִּין דַּאֲפִילּוּ בְּאִמָּהּ, וְאַיְּידֵי דִּתְנָא רֵישָׁא אִשְׁתּוֹ שֶׁמֵּתָה מוּתָּר בַּאֲחוֹתָהּ, בַּאֲחוֹתָהּ – אִין, אֲבָל בְּאִמָּהּ – לָא, דְּהָוְיָא לָהּ אִיסּוּרָא דְּאוֹרָיְיתָא, תָּנָא נַמִי סֵיפָא מוּתָּר בַּאֲחוֹתָהּ.

The Gemara rejects this: No evidence can be derived from here, as it is possible to say that **the same is true even for her mother,** that she too is permitted. **But since it taught in the first clause** of this mishna: If **his wife dies he is permitted to take her sister,** and there the language is precise and implies: **Her sister, yes, but her mother, no, as she is forbidden by Torah** law because it is prohibited for a man to marry both a woman and her daughter even after one of them dies, therefore he used the same language when **he taught the latter clause** of the same mishna that **he is permitted to** take **her sister.** However, in the latter clause it is not an exact reading, and in actuality one is allowed to marry any of her relatives. This completes the Gemara's explanation of Rav Huna's opinion.

וְרַב יְהוּדָה אָמַר: שׁוֹמֶרֶת יָבָם שֶׁמֵּתָה – אָסוּר בְּאִמָּהּ. אַלְמָא קָסָבַר: יֵשׁ זִיקָה. וְלֵימָא: הֲלָכָה כְּדִבְרֵי הָאוֹמֵר יֵשׁ זִיקָה!

And Rav Yehuda said: In the case of **a widow who dies** while **waiting for her brother-in-law** to perform *ḥalitza* or levirate marriage, **he is prohibited from** marrying **her mother.**[H] The Gemara comments: **Apparently** Rav Yehuda **holds** that **the levirate bond is substantial;** this would mean that the attachment between the *yevama* and the *yavam* is like that of marriage and that the *yavam* is therefore prohibited from marrying her relatives. **But** it must be asked: Why does Rav Yehuda say it in such a way? **Let him say:** The ***halakha*** **is in accordance with the statement of the one who says that the** levirate **bond is substantial.**

אִי הֲוָה אָמַר הָכִי הֲוָה אָמִינָא: הָנֵי מִילֵּי בְּחַד, אֲבָל בִּתְרֵי אֵין זִיקָה. וְהָא כִּי פְּלִיגִי – בִּתְרֵי פְּלִיגִי! אֶלָּא, אִי אֲמַר הָכִי

The Gemara responds: **If he would have said that, I would say that** with regard to the levirate bond, **this applies in** the case of **one** brother, **but** if there were **two** brothers then **the** levirate **bond is not substantial.** The Gemara objects: **But when** the *tanna'im* **disagree,** they **disagree in** a case of **two** brothers, so how could one think that Rav Yehuda is speaking only in the case of a single brother? **Rather,** one must say: **If he were to say that** the conclusive halakhic ruling is that the bond is substantial,

HALAKHA

A widow who dies while waiting for her bother-in-law, he is prohibited from marrying her mother – שׁוֹמֶרֶת יָבָם שֶׁמֵּתָה אָסוּר בְּאִמָּהּ: If one's *yevama* dies before he performs *ḥalitza*, then her relatives are forbidden to him as though she had been his wife.

This *halakha* is ruled in accordance with the opinion of Rav Yehuda in the name of Shmuel (18b), because it seems from the talmudic discussion that the *amora'im* made great efforts to resolve the difficulties in accordance with his opinion, and this implies that the *halakha* is ruled in accordance with his opinion (*Beit Yosef*). Although this contradicts the principle that the *halakha* is ruled in accordance with the opinion of Rav in his disputes with Shmuel, some versions of the text show that Rav Yehuda's statement was in fact said in the name of Rav. In that case, there is an amoraic dispute with regard to his opinion, and the *halakha* is ruled in accordance with the more certain opinion (Rabbeinu Ḥananel; Rambam *Sefer Nashim*, *Hilkhot Yibbum VaḤalitza* 1:13; *Shulḥan Arukh*, *Even HaEzer* 159:5).

הוה אמינא: מחיים, אבל לאחר מיתה פקעה לה זיקה, קא משמע לן דזיקה בכדי לא פקעה. לימא מסייע ליה: יבמתו שמתה מותר באחותה, באחותה – אין, באמה – לא.

I would say that the levirate bond applies as long as the *yevama* requiring levirate marriage **is alive but** that **after** her **death the bond was terminated.** In other words, after the *yevama* died any relationship between the two dissolved. **This comes to teach us that the bond is not terminated without cause** but instead requires an actual act, such as *ḥalitza* or levirate marriage. Until one of these acts is performed, the bond remains in place. **Let us say that it supports** Rav Yehuda's opinion from that which was taught: If **his** *yevama* **dies, he is permitted to** marry **her sister.** From here the Gemara deduces: **Her sister, yes; her mother, no,** in accordance with the opinion of Rav Yehuda.

הוא הדין דאפילו באמה, ואיידי דתנא רישא אשתו שמתה מותר באחותה, דוקא באחותה אבל באמה לא, דהויא לה איסורא דאורייתא – תנא נמי סיפא מותר באחותה.

The Gemara rejects this: **The same is true, that even her mother** is permitted. **And** this language was used only **since he taught in the first clause** of the *baraita*: **If his wife dies he is permitted to take her sister; specifically her sister but not her mother, as she is forbidden by Torah** law. Therefore, **he also taught in the latter clause** that **he is permitted to** marry **her sister.**

מתיב רב הונא בר חייא: עשה בה מאמר ומת – שניה חולצת ולא מתייבמת. טעמא – דעבד בה מאמר, הא לא עבד בה מאמר – שניה נמי יבומי מייבמה. ואי אמרת יש זיקה, הויא לה צרת אשת אחיו שלא היה בעולמו בזיקה!

Rav Huna bar Ḥiyya raised an objection to this from the mishna: If **he performed levirate betrothal with her and** then **died, the second** woman **performs *ḥalitza* and may not enter into levirate marriage.** This implies that **the reason is** specifically **that he performed levirate betrothal with her.** Had the brother **not performed levirate betrothal with her, the second** woman **would also** be permitted to **enter into levirate marriage. And if you say that the** levirate **bond is substantial,** then she would be considered **a rival wife of the wife of a brother with whom** the third brother **did not coexist by that bond.**[H] Since the wife of a brother with whom he did not coexist is prohibited from entering into levirate marriage, her rival wife would likewise be forbidden from doing so.

אמר רבה: הוא הדין דאף על גב דלא עבד בה מאמר – שניה מחלץ חליצה, יבומי לא מייבמה,

Rabba said: This should not be read precisely, as **the same is true even if** the second brother **did not perform levirate betrothal; the second** woman **must perform *ḥalitza* but may not enter into levirate marriage,** as the levirate bond renders her a rival wife of the wife of a brother with whom the third brother did not coexist.

והא דקתני מאמר – לאפוקי מבית שמאי, דאמרי: מאמר קונה קנין גמור, קא משמע לן.

And the reason **that** it **teaches** the case of **levirate betrothal** specifically was **in order to exclude** the opinion of **Beit Shammai,**[N] **who said:** The legal status of **levirate betrothal** with a *yevama* eligible for levirate marriage **is** that of **a full-fledged acquisition,** and it is legally binding to the same degree as an actual betrothal. Therefore, even *ḥalitza* would be unnecessary, similar to the case of a rival wife of a forbidden relation. This is what **it comes to teach us:** Even if he performed levirate betrothal she is not truly considered the rival wife of a forbidden relation; the prohibition concerning her is by rabbinic law, and she is therefore required to perform *ḥalitza*.

איתיביה אביי: שני אחין בעולם אחד, ומת אחד מהן בלא ולד, ועמד השני הזה לעשות מאמר ביבמתו, ולא הספיק לעשות בה מאמר עד שנולד לו אח, ומת, הראשונה יוצאה משום אשת אחיו שלא היה בעולמו, ושניה – או חולצת או מתייבמת. ואי אמרת יש זיקה – הויא לה צרת אשת אחיו שלא היה בעולמו בזיקה!

Abaye raised an objection to this from that which was taught: In the case of **two brothers who coexisted, and one died childless and the second arose to perform levirate betrothal with his *yevama* but did not manage to perform levirate betrothal before** a third **brother was born, and** then the second brother, who also had a wife, **died,** whereby both women would fall before the newly born brother for levirate marriage, then **the first goes out** and is not obligated in levirate marriage **because** she is **the wife of his brother with whom he did not coexist, and the second** woman, who was the wife of the second brother, **either performs *ḥalitza* or enters into levirate marriage. But if you say that the** levirate **bond is substantial,** then the wife of the second brother **would be rendered a rival wife of the wife of a brother with whom he did not coexist** by that **bond.**

HALAKHA

A rival wife of the wife of a brother with whom he did not coexist by that bond – צרת אשת אחיו שלא היה בעולמו בזיקה: If there were two brothers and one died childless, and subsequently a third brother was born, then if the second brother dies, even if he had not yet performed levirate betrothal to the widow of the first brother, the third brother must nevertheless perform *ḥalitza* for the wife of the second brother, and she may not enter into levirate marriage with him, since they ruled that the levirate bond is substantial. Accordingly, the levirate bond rendered the wife of the second brother a rival wife of the wife of the first brother, with whom the third brother did not coexist, as per Shmuel's opinion.

Rambam explains that this *halakha* applies only if the second brother had performed levirate betrothal. The author of the *Maggid Mishne* challenges this, since Rambam himself concludes explicitly that there is a levirate bond even if there was no levirate betrothal (Rambam *Sefer Nashim, Hilkhot Yibbum VaḤalitza* 6:18; *Shulḥan Arukh, Even HaEzer* 173:12).

NOTES

In order to exclude the opinion of Beit Shammai – לאפוקי מבית שמאי: *Tosafot Yeshanim* raise the question: Isn't it already known that when Beit Shammai express an opinion and Beit Hillel disagree, the opinion of Beit Shammai is considered as though it were not in the mishna at all and is completely disregarded? If so, why would it be necessary to explicitly exclude the opinion of Beit Shammai? The answer given is that in fact, the opinion that levirate betrothal constitutes a fully effective acquisition is not exclusive to Beit Shammai but is actually the opinion of several other *tanna'im*, and so it was necessary to exclude that opinion.

HALAKHA

Two brothers married to two sisters – שְׁנֵי אַחִים נְשׂוּאִים לִשְׁתֵּי אֲחָיוֹת: If two brothers were married to two sisters and both died childless, since both women would require levirate marriage but cannot both be married to the same man because they are sisters, both perform *ḥalitza* and neither may enter into levirate marriage, as stated in the mishna (Rambam *Sefer Nashim, Hilkhot Yibbum VaḤalitza* 7:1; *Shulḥan Arukh, Even HaEzer* 175:3).

הָא מַנִּי – רַבִּי מֵאִיר הִיא, דְּאָמַר: אֵין זִיקָה. וּמִי סְבִירָא לֵיהּ לְרַבִּי מֵאִיר אֵין זִיקָה? וְהָתְנַן: אַרְבָּעָה אַחִים, שְׁנַיִם מֵהֶן נְשׂוּאִים שְׁתֵּי אֲחָיוֹת, וּמֵתוּ הַנְּשׂוּאִין הָאֲחָיוֹת – הֲרֵי אֵלּוּ חוֹלְצוֹת וְלֹא מִתְיַיבְּמוֹת.

The Gemara rejects that: In accordance with **whose** opinion **is this? It is** the opinion of **Rabbi Meir, who said: The** levirate **bond is not substantial.** The Gemara asks: **Does Rabbi Meir hold that the** levirate **bond is not substantial?** After all, unattributed *mishnayot* are in accordance with the opinion of Rabbi Meir, and **didn't we learn** in a mishna (26a): In the case of **four brothers, two of whom are married to two sisters,**[H] if **those married to the sisters died,** whereby both sisters fall before the surviving brothers for levirate marriage, **then** those two sisters **must perform *ḥalitza* and may not enter into levirate marriage.** It would seem that the reason for this is that each of the sisters has a levirate bond to both remaining brothers.

וְאִי סָלְקָא דַּעְתָּךְ סָבַר רַבִּי מֵאִיר אֵין זִיקָה – הָנֵי מִתְּרֵי בָּתֵּי קָאָתְיָין, הַאי לְיַיבֵּם חֲדָא וְהַאי לְיַיבֵּם חֲדָא!

And if it enters your mind to say that **Rabbi Meir held that the** levirate **bond is not substantial,** didn't **these** two sisters **come from two** different **houses,** as each was married to a different brother? If so, **one** brother **should take one in levirate marriage and the other should take one in levirate marriage.**

לְעוֹלָם אֵין זִיקָה, מִשּׁוּם דְּקָסָבַר: אָסוּר לְבַטֵּל מִצְוַת יְבָמִין, דְּדִלְמָא אַדְּמְיַיבֵּם חַד מָיֵית אִידַּךְ, וְקָא בָּטְלַתְּ מִצְוַת יְבָמִין.

The Gemara answers: **Actually,** in Rabbi Meir's opinion **the** levirate **bond is not substantial.** The mishna states that they perform *ḥalitza* and do not enter into levirate marriage **because he held that it is prohibited to nullify the mitzva of levirate marriage.** That is to say, it is prohibited to act in such a way that the mitzva of levirate marriage becomes obviated. Under these circumstances there is concern that **perhaps as one** brother **performs levirate marriage** to one of the sisters **the other** brother **dies** before he manages to perform levirate marriage to the other. If that were to happen, **you** would thereby **nullify the mitzva of levirate marriage** since the sister that would now fall before the remaining brother would be his wife's sister and therefore prohibited from entering into levirate marriage with him.

וְאִי אֵין זִיקָה – תִּיבָּטֵל, דְּהָא רַבָּן גַּמְלִיאֵל אָמַר אֵין זִיקָה, וּמוּתָּר לְבַטֵּל מִצְוַת יְבָמִין.

The Gemara objects: **But if the** levirate **bond is not substantial,** then **let** the mitzva of levirate marriage **be nullified.** That is, if the levirate bond does not carry any real obligation, then the mitzva itself never truly came into effect. **As Rabban Gamliel said: The** levirate **bond is not substantial, and it is permitted to nullify the mitzva of levirate marriage.**

דִּתְנַן: רַבָּן גַּמְלִיאֵל אוֹמֵר: אִם מֵאֲנָה – מֵאֲנָה, וְאִם לֹא מֵאֲנָה – תַּמְתִּין עַד שֶׁתַּגְדִּיל וְתֵצֵא הַלֵּזוּ מִשּׁוּם אֲחוֹת אִשָּׁה!

As we learned in a mishna (109a): That mishna discusses a case of two brothers who were married to two sisters. One sister is an adult and therefore her marriage was fully effectual, and one sister is still a minor, and she was orphaned from her father, and her marriage was valid only by rabbinic ordinance. If the brother who was married to the elder sister died, then that sister falls for levirate marriage before the brother married to the minor. Under these circumstances, the Sages suggested directing the minor to refuse her marriage to her husband so that he would be able to take his brother's wife in levirate marriage. If the minor does not do so, he would be unable to take her sister in marriage, as she would be the sister of his minor wife and thereby fully exempt from the levirate obligation. **Rabban Gamliel said:** If the minor **refused**[N] in the meantime of her own accord, **then she refused, but if she did not refuse, let her wait until she reaches** the age of **maturity,**[N] **and** then **that other** adult sister **will be exempt** from performing *ḥalitza* or levirate marriage **due to** the fact that she is his **wife's sister.** Here it is apparent that Rabban Gamliel is not concerned about nullifying the mitzva of levirate marriage from one of them.

NOTES

Refusal – מֵיאוּן: A girl under the age of twelve can be married off by her father. However, if her father is no longer alive then by Torah law she cannot marry while still a minor. Nevertheless, the Sages ordained that her mother or brothers may marry her off with her consent. Since her consent is not legally valid until she reaches the age of maturity, the girl may terminate this marriage once she reaches twelve years of age by performing an act of refusal, i.e., declaring that she does not desire this marriage. In such cases, no bill of divorce is necessary. When a girl performs the act of refusal, the marriage is nullified retroactively, and it is considered as though she had never been married at all.

Let her wait until she reaches the age of maturity – תַּמְתִּין עַד שֶׁתַּגְדִּיל: Rashi understands this to mean that the adult sister must wait until her minor sister matures before she marries anyone else. *Tosafot* interpret this to mean that the minor must wait and not engage in intercourse until she becomes fully mature.

אֲמַר לֵיהּ: דְּרַבָּן גַּמְלִיאֵל אַדְּרַבִּי מֵאִיר קָרָמֵית? לָא, הָכִי קָאָמְרִינַן: רַבִּי מֵאִיר חָיֵישׁ אֲפִילּוּ לִסְפֵיקָא, רַבָּן גַּמְלִיאֵל – אֲפִילּוּ לְוַדַּאי לָא חָיֵישׁ?! דִּלְמָא, מַאן דְּלָא חָיֵישׁ אֲפִילּוּ לְוַדַּאי לָא חָיֵישׁ, וּמַאן דְּחָיֵישׁ – אֲפִילּוּ לִסְפֵיקָא חָיֵישׁ.

Rabba **said to** Abaye: Do you wish to **raise a contradiction between** the words of **Rabban Gamliel and Rabbi Meir?** This would imply that the contradiction needs to be resolved, but statements from two different *tanna'im* do not need to agree or to be resolved. Abaye responded: **No,** in fact **this is what we meant to say:** How could one possibly say that **Rabbi Meir is concerned** lest there be nullification of the mitzva of levirate marriage **even when it is uncertain** because perhaps the first brother will not die, whereas **Rabban Gamliel is not concerned** that the mitzva be nullified **even when it is certain?** It is surprising that there should be such a great difference between the tannaitic opinions. Rabba answered: **Perhaps the one who is not concerned** about nullification of the mitzva of levirate marriage **is not concerned even if** nullification is **certain, and the one who is concerned is concerned even if** nullification **is uncertain.**

אֲמַר לֵיהּ אַבַּיֵי לְרַב יוֹסֵף: הָא דְּרַב יְהוּדָה – דִּשְׁמוּאֵל הִיא, דִּתְנַן:

With regard to the actual dispute between Rav Huna and Rav Yehuda, **Abaye said to Rav Yosef: This** *halakha* stated **by Rav Yehuda,** that even if a woman waiting for levirate marriage dies her mother is still forbidden to the *yavam*, is from his teacher **Shmuel** and not from Rav, who was also one of his teachers. Evidence for this can be found in **that** which **we learned** in a mishna (41a):

שׁוֹמֶרֶת יָבָם שֶׁקִּידֵּשׁ אָחִיו אֶת אֲחוֹתָהּ, מִשּׁוּם רַבִּי יְהוּדָה בֶּן בְּתֵירָה אָמְרוּ: אוֹמְרִים לוֹ, הַמְתֵּן עַד שֶׁיַּעֲשֶׂה אָחִיךָ מַעֲשֶׂה. וְאָמַר שְׁמוּאֵל: הֲלָכָה כְּרַבִּי יְהוּדָה בֶּן בְּתֵירָה.

In the case of **a widow waiting for her** *yavam* to take her in levirate marriage or perform *ḥalitza*, if **his brother betrothed**[H] her **sister**[N] **they said in the name of Rabbi Yehuda ben Beteira: They say to** the brother who betrothed her: **Wait** and do not marry your betrothed **until your brother performs** the required **action,** either *ḥalitza* or levirate marriage. This is because until that time the levirate bond is still applicable and the woman betrothed to you is forbidden to you as the sister of a woman bonded to you. **And Shmuel said:** The *halakha* **is in accordance with** the opinion of **Rabbi Yehuda ben Beteira.** From here one may infer that Shmuel holds that the levirate bond is substantial.

אֲמַר לֵיהּ: דְּאִי דְּרַב מַאי? (אֲמַר לֵיהּ): קַשְׁיָא דְּרַב אַדְּרַב! דִּלְמָא אָמוֹרָאֵי נִינְהוּ, וְאַלִּיבָּא דְּרַב? כֵּיוָן דְּאִיתְּמַר מִשְּׁמֵיהּ דִּשְׁמוּאֵל בְּהֶדְיָא, וּמִשְּׁמֵיהּ דְּרַב כְּאָמוֹרָאֵי – לָא שָׁבְקִינַן מִשְּׁמֵיהּ דִּשְׁמוּאֵל בְּהֶדְיָא וּמוֹקְמִינַן כְּאָמוֹרָאֵי וְאַלִּיבָּא דְּרַב.

Rav Yosef **said to him: And if** it were the opinion **of Rav, what** problem would there be? Abaye **said to him: It is difficult** because there would be a contradiction between the opinion **of Rav** and another statement **of Rav,** since Rav Huna cited Rav, and the conclusion from his statements was that the levirate bond is not substantial. He said to him: Rav Huna and Rav Yehuda each cited Rav. **Perhaps they are** ***amora'im*** **and** disagree **in accordance with** the opinion **of Rav,** i.e., with regard to his opinion? The Gemara answers: **Since that which was stated in the name of Shmuel was explicit, while that** said **in the name of Rav** must be explained **as an amoraic dispute, we will not leave** that statement said **explicitly in the name of Shmuel and explain it as an amoraic** dispute **according to** the opinion **of Rav.**

אֲמַר רַב כָּהֲנָא, אָמְרִיתָהּ לִשְׁמַעְתָּא קַמֵּיהּ דְּרַב זְבִיד מִנְּהַרְדְּעָא, אֲמַר: אַתּוּן הָכִי מַתְנִיתוּ לָהּ, אֲנַן בְּהֶדְיָא מַתְנִינַן: אָמַר רַב יְהוּדָה אָמַר שְׁמוּאֵל: שׁוֹמֶרֶת יָבָם שֶׁמֵּתָה – אָסוּר בְּאִמָּהּ. אַלְמָא קָסָבַר: יֵשׁ זִיקָה. וְאַזְדָּא שְׁמוּאֵל לְטַעְמֵיהּ, דַּאֲמַר שְׁמוּאֵל: הֲלָכָה כְּרַבִּי יְהוּדָה בֶּן בְּתֵירָה.

Rav Kahana said: I reported this discussion before Rav Zevid of Neharde'a. He said: That is how you teach this, without knowing for certain that Rav Yehuda was stating the *halakha* in the name of Shmuel. **We learn it explicitly: Rav Yehuda said** that **Shmuel said:** In the case of **a widow waiting for her** *yavam* who **died** before he could perform *ḥalitza* or levirate marriage, **he is prohibited from** marrying **her mother. Apparently** Shmuel **holds** that **the levirate bond is substantial.**[H] **And Shmuel** conforms **to his** standard line of **reasoning, as Shmuel** also **said:** The *halakha* **is in accordance with** the opinion **of Rabbi Yehuda ben Beteira.**

HALAKHA

A widow waiting for her ***yavam*****, if his brother betrothed, etc.** – **שׁוֹמֶרֶת יָבָם שֶׁקִּידֵּשׁ אָחִיו וכו׳**: If a woman happened before several brothers for levirate marriage, and one of the brothers betrothed the sister of this woman who was bound to him, he is prohibited from marrying his betrothed until one of the brothers takes the widow in levirate marriage or performs *ḥalitza* for her, in accordance with the opinion of Rabbi Yehuda ben Beteira and Shmuel. Some say that if he already married her he is permitted to engage in intercourse even before another brother releases the widow (*Tosafot*), whereas others disagree (*Nimmukei Yosef*). The later commentaries say that if there is another brother who can perform *ḥalitza*, the brother who is married to the widow's sister should wait to consummate the marriage until after *ḥalitza* has been performed (*Pitḥei Teshuva*; *Shulḥan Arukh, Even HaEzer* 159:5).

The levirate bond is substantial – **יֵשׁ זִיקָה**: Where the mitzva of levirate marriage applies, the relatives of the *yevama* are forbidden to the *yavam* whether there is a single *yavam* or there are many. Even if she dies, her close relatives are forbidden to him (*Shulḥan Arukh, Even HaEzer* 159:5).

NOTES

His brother betrothed her sister – **קִדֵּשׁ אָחִיו אֶת אֲחוֹתָהּ**: The early commentaries discuss the reasons for this *halakha*, as one might have thought that the brother's betrothal of the sister effectively terminated the levirate bond between him and his brother's widow. *Tosafot* explain that the reason that he must wait is as a penalty because it was prohibited for him to betroth the sister of a woman with whom he has a levirate bond. However, Ramban challenges this answer, and suggests that the levirate bond lessens the validity of the betrothal to her sister, as the existence of a levirate bond renders this case similar to that of one who betroths the sister of his betrothed.

Some authorities hold that even if he actually married his betrothed he is told to wait and not engage in intercourse with her (Ritva; Meiri; *Nimmukei Yosef*; see Halakha section).

HALAKHA

The wife of a brother with whom he did not coexist – אשת אחיו שלא היה בעולמו: The wife of a brother with whom a newly born brother did not coexist is forbidden to him, whether this youngest brother was born before or after another brother took her in levirate marriage. This ruling is in accordance with the opinion of the first *tanna* in the mishna (Rambam *Sefer Nashim, Hilkhot Yibbum VaḤalitza* 6:17; *Shulḥan Arukh, Even HaEzer* 173:12).

וצריכי, דאי אשמעינן יש זיקה – הוה אמינא: הני מילי – בחד, אבל בתרי – לא, קא משמע לן. ואי אשמעינן הלכה כרבי יהודה בן בתירה – הוה אמינא הני מילי מחיים, אבל לאחר מיתה – פקעה לה זיקה, קא משמע לן: דזיקה בכדי לא פקעה.

The Gemara comments: Both statements by Shmuel on the subject **are necessary** and there was no redundancy here, **as, if he were to teach us** only the principle that **the** levirate **bond is substantial, I would say that this applies** only **to** the case of **one** *yavam* **but not to** a case of **two** *yevamin*, where the levirate bond is not as strong. **This comes to teach us** that even in the case of two *yevamin* there is a bond, and that is the conclusive *halakha* put forth by Rabbi Yehuda ben Beteira. **And if he were to teach us** only that the ***halakha*** **is in accordance with** the opinion of **Rabbi Yehuda ben Beteira, I would say that this applies** only in the case **where** the woman awaiting levirate marriage **is living, but after her death the** levirate **bond is terminated** and he is permitted to marry her relatives. **This comes to teach us that the** levirate **bond is not terminated without cause** but rather it is necessary to perform some act in order to exempt her from it.

מתני׳ שני אחים ומת אחד מהן, ויבם השני את אשת אחיו, ואחר כך נולד להן אח ומת – הראשונה יוצאה משום אשת אחיו שלא היה בעולמו, והשניה משום צרתה, עשה בה מאמר, ומת – השניה חולצת ולא מתייבמת.

MISHNA If there were **two brothers, and one died, and the second entered into levirate marriage with his brother's wife** while he was already married to another woman, **and subsequently** a third **brother was born to them, and** the second brother then **died,** whereby both of his wives happened before the third brother for levirate marriage, then **the first woman,** who was the wife of the first brother, **is exempt due to** the fact that she is **the wife of a brother with whom** the third brother **did not coexist,**[H] **and the second** woman, who was the first wife of the second brother, is exempt **due to her rival wife.** If the second brother had **performed** only **levirate betrothal with her and then died** before fully marrying her, **the second** woman **performs *ḥalitza* and may not enter into levirate marriage,** as the levirate betrothal is not considered a sufficiently valid marriage so as to render her the rival wife of a relation forbidden to the third brother.

רבי שמעון אומר: מייבם לאיזו מהן שירצה, או חולץ לאיזו מהן שירצה.

Rabbi Shimon says with regard to the first clause of the mishna: The third brother either **enters into levirate marriage with whichever one he wishes, or he performs *ḥalitza* with whichever one he wishes.** Since he was born after his second brother had already entered into levirate marriage with the first brother's widow, she is considered the wife of a brother with whom he did coexist, not the wife of a brother with whom he did not coexist. Therefore, he may enter into levirate marriage with her.

גמ׳ אמר רב אושעיא: חלוק היה רבי שמעון אף בראשונה. ממאי – מדקתני משנה יתירה –

GEMARA **Rav Oshaya**[N] **said: Rabbi Shimon's opinion differed even on the first** mishna. That is, Rabbi Shimon disagreed not only in the case stated explicitly in this mishna, in which the newly born brother came into the world after the widow of his first brother had already married his second brother, but he also disagreed in the case of the first mishna in the chapter, where the third brother was born prior to his second brother entering into levirate marriage with the widow. **From where** is this derived? Rav Oshaya came to this conclusion **from** the fact **that it teaches a superfluous mishna.**

NOTES

Rav Oshaya – רב אושעיא: *Masoret HaShas* emends the text here to read: Rabbi Oshaya. The reason for this is that later (19a) the Gemara cites a *baraita* which challenges this opinion, and states: This is a conclusive refutation of the opinion of Rabbi Oshaya. Rabbi Oshaya, also known as Rabbi Hoshaya, was a first generation *amora* who lived in Eretz Yisrael.

However, elsewhere in this discussion, Rav Oshaya is also mentioned. Rav Oshaya, also known as Rav Hoshaya, was a third generation *amora* who was born and lived in Babylonia. He was a student of Rav Yehuda and Rav Huna, and a friend of Rava. He eventually moved to Eretz Yisrael, where he received ordination.

בָּבָא דְּרֵישָׁא לְמַאן קָתָנֵי לַהּ? אִילֵימָא לְרַבָּנַן – הָשְׁתָּא יִבֵּם וּלְבַסּוֹף נוֹלַד, דְּכִי אַשְׁכַּחָהּ בְּהֶתֵּירָא אַשְׁכַּחָהּ, אָסְרִי רַבָּנַן – נוֹלַד וְאַחַר כָּךְ יִבֵּם מִיבַּעְיָא? אֶלָּא לָאו – לְרַבִּי שִׁמְעוֹן אִיצְטְרִיךְ,

How so? **In accordance with whose** opinion **is it teaching the section of the first clause,** i.e., the previous mishna? **If we say** it is the opinion of **the Rabbis,** who prohibit marriage to the wife of a brother with whom one did not coexist in all cases, then let us look at the second mishna. **Now** that even in the case where the second brother **entered into levirate marriage and afterward** the third brother **was born,**[B] such that **when he found her,** i.e., when he was born, she had a **permitted** status, as she was already married to the second brother, she was never in his lifetime the wife of a brother with whom he did not coexist but was in fact for him the wife of a living brother. Nevertheless, even under such circumstances, **the Rabbis prohibit** him from entering into levirate marriage with her. **Is it necessary,** then, to teach the case presented in the first mishna of a third brother who was **born and subsequently** the second brother **entered into levirate marriage** with the wife of the first brother?[B] According to the opinion of the Rabbis, this first mishna is redundant. **Rather, is it not** that it **was necessary** to state this first mishna **for** the opinion of **Rabbi Shimon?**

וְתָנָא רֵישָׁא לְהוֹדִיעֲךָ כֹּחוֹ דְּרַבִּי שִׁמְעוֹן, וְתָנָא סֵיפָא לְהוֹדִיעֲךָ כֹּחָן דְּרַבָּנַן. וּבְדִין הוּא דְּנִפְלוֹג רַבִּי שִׁמְעוֹן בְּרֵישָׁא, אֶלָּא נָטַר לְהוּ לְרַבָּנַן עַד דִּמְסַיְּימִי לְמִילְּתַיְיהוּ, וַהֲדַר פָּלֵיג עֲלַיְיהוּ.

If so, this is how it must be understood: **The first** mishna **was taught in order to convey to you the far-reaching nature** of the opinion of **Rabbi Shimon,** which allows even the case specified in the first mishna, **and the latter clause,** i.e., the present mishna, **was taught to convey the far-reaching nature** of the opinion of **the Rabbis,** that even if the third brother was born after levirate marriage to the second brother she remains forbidden to the third brother. **And by right it** should have explained **that Rabbi Shimon disagrees** even **in the first** mishna, **but** the author of the mishna **waited until the Rabbis finished their words, and then he went back** and wrote that Rabbi Shimon **disagreed with them.**

אֶלָּא, אֵשֶׁת אָחִיו שֶׁלֹּא הָיָה בְּעוֹלָמוֹ, לְרַבִּי שִׁמְעוֹן הֵיכִי מַשְׁכַּחַתְּ לַהּ? בְּחַד אַחָא, וּמִית, וְנוֹלַד לוֹ אָח. אִי נַמִי: בִּתְרֵי, וְלֹא יִבֵּם וְלֹא מִית.

The Gemara asks: **But according to** the opinion of **Rabbi Shimon, how can you find**[N] this case of **the wife of a brother with whom he did not coexist?** The Gemara answers: It is in the case of a **single brother who died and** subsequently another **brother was born to him.** Here, the widow would be the wife of a brother with whom he did not coexist, and she would not be required to perform *ḥalitza* or enter into levirate marriage with him. **Alternatively,** it can be found in the case of **two** brothers, one of whom died, **and** the remaining brother **did not take** the deceased brother's wife **in levirate marriage, and did not die,**[N] and in the meantime a third brother was born. She still has the levirate bond due to the deceased brother, who was a brother with whom the newly born brother did not coexist.

BACKGROUND

Died, then taken in levirate marriage, then born – מֵת יִבֵּם וְנוֹלַד: Reuven and Shimon were brothers from the same father, and Reuven was married to Peninna. Reuven died childless and Shimon entered into levirate marriage with Peninna. Later, a third brother, Levi, was born. According to Rabbi Shimon, since at the time that Levi was born Peninna was already the wife of Shimon, a brother with whom he did coexist, when Shimon dies Peninna is permitted to Levi.

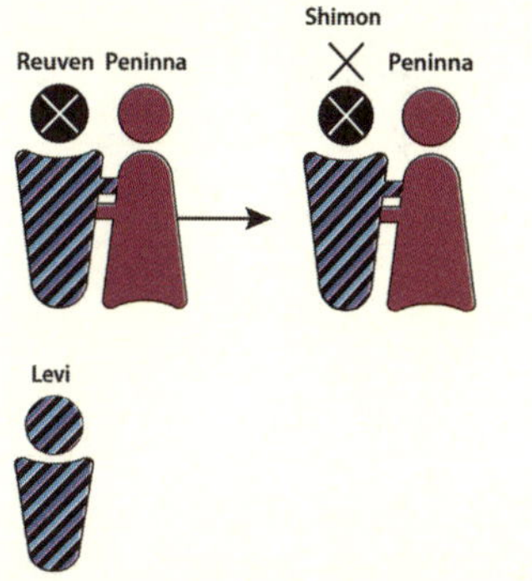

Died, then born, and then taken in levirate marriage – מֵת נוֹלַד וְיִבֵּם: Reuven and Shimon were brothers from the same father. Reuven was married to Peninna and subsequently died. After his death, a third brother, Levi, was born. To Levi, Peninna is a wife of a brother with whom he did not coexist. Therefore, even if Shimon later enters into levirate marriage with her and then dies childless, Peninna remains forbidden to Levi. According to most authorities, in the Gemara Rabbi Shimon agrees that in this case, Peninna is forbidden to Levi because for the period of time between Levi's birth and the levirate marriage to Shimon she was forbidden to Levi as the wife of a brother with whom he did not coexist.

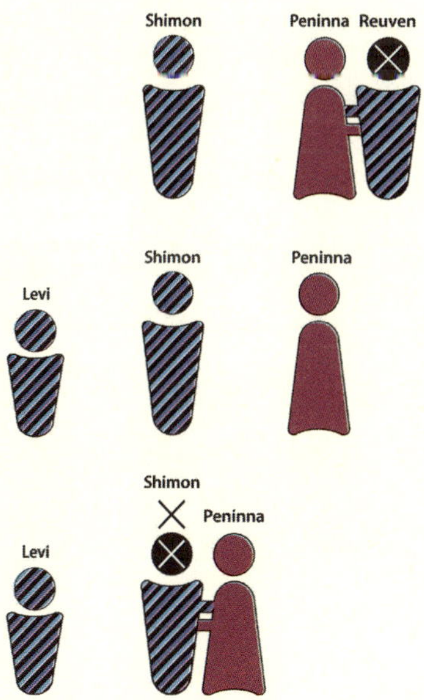

NOTES

According to the opinion of Rabbi Shimon how can you find – לְרַבִּי שִׁמְעוֹן הֵיכִי מַשְׁכַּחַתְּ לַהּ: One may ask how the Gemara knew that Rabbi Shimon holds that the wife of a brother with whom one did not coexist is in fact forbidden. It seems that it was clear to the Gemara that the fifteen women enumerated in the mishna (2a–2b) are agreed on by all opinions, and that even Rabbi Shimon agreed with this *halakha* in principle (Ritva).

Two brothers and the remaining brother…did not die – בִּתְרֵי...וְלֹא מִית: If the levirate bond is like marriage, then the widow of the first brother should be forbidden to any newly born brother, since she is the wife of the living brother, even if that brother has not yet performed levirate marriage. If so, then in Rabbi Shimon's opinion why was it necessary for the verse to state the word "together" specifically to render the *yevama* forbidden to a newly born brother? Perhaps his reasoning can be explained simply by saying that after another brother is born, the bond with the living brother was retroactively never absolute (see Ritva).

NOTES

Rav Yosef strongly objects to this – **מַתְקִיף לָהּ רַב יוֹסֵף**: The early commentaries ask why the Gemara did not state that Rabbi Shimon held the levirate bond to be like marriage specifically in the case where she later entered into levirate marriage, and why it sufficed to mention only that he performed a levirate betrothal. The Ramban answers that the principle that a levirate bond renders her like a married woman fully applies only if she ultimately marries. But if he does not take her in levirate marriage, she is not considered like a married woman (see Meiri). The Ritva explains that the Sages relied here upon the common sense reasoning that a bond to two brothers cannot render her like a married woman, even in Rabbi Shimon's opinion. Additionally, from the continuation of the discussion it would seem that this difficulty was not pertinent to the matter of the levirate bond but rather related to the validity of the levirate betrothal (Meiri).

בִּשְׁלָמָא יִבֵּם וְאַחַר כָּךְ נוֹלַד – כִּי אַשְׁכְּחָהּ בְּהֶתֵּירָא אַשְׁכְּחָהּ, אֶלָּא נוֹלַד וְאַחַר כָּךְ יִבֵּם – מַאי טַעְמָא? קָסָבַר: יֵשׁ זִיקָה, וְזִיקָה כִּכְנוּסָה דָּמְיָא.

The Gemara proceeds to clarify Rabbi Shimon's position: **Granted,** in the case when the second brother first **performed levirate marriage** and **subsequently** the third brother **was born,** it is possible to explain **that when** the third brother **found her,** i.e., when he was born, **he found her in a permitted** state because when he was born she was already the wife of a living brother with whom he coexisted. **But if he was born and subsequently** the second brother **performed levirate marriage, what is the reason** that Rabbi Shimon renders her permitted? The Gemara answers: One must say that Rabbi Shimon **holds that the** levirate **bond is substantial,** and that the bond itself created a tie of kinship. Moreover, a woman with a levirate **bond is considered like a married woman.** Since there is a bond between the *yevama* and the living brother it is as though she were already married to him. Accordingly, she is, for the new brother, like the wife of his brother with whom he coexisted.

מַתְקִיף לָהּ רַב יוֹסֵף: הָשְׁתָּא זִיקָה וּמַאֲמָר מְסַפְּקָא לֵיהּ לְרַבִּי שִׁמְעוֹן אִי כִּכְנוּסָה דָּמְיָא אִי לָאו כִּכְנוּסָה דָּמְיָא, זִיקָה לְחוּדַהּ מִיבַּעְיָא?

Rav Yosef strongly objects to this:[N] **Now** that in the case of a levirate **bond and a levirate betrothal** together **Rabbi Shimon is uncertain as to whether she is similar to a married woman or an unmarried woman, is it necessary** to say that by levirate **bond alone** she is not like a married woman? If so, how can the Gemara assume that for Rabbi Shimon, the levirate bond alone gives her the status of a married woman?

מַאי הִיא? דִּתְנַן: שְׁלֹשָׁה אַחִין נְשׂוּאִין שָׁלֹשׁ נָשִׁים נָכְרִיּוֹת, וּמֵת אֶחָד מֵהֶם וְעָשָׂה בָּהּ שֵׁנִי מַאֲמָר, וָמֵת – הֲרֵי אֵלּוּ חוֹלְצוֹת וְלֹא מִתְיַיבְּמוֹת,

What is the proof that this is Rabbi Shimon's opinion? **As we learned** in a mishna (31b): In the case of **three brothers** who were **married**[H] **to three unrelated women, and one of the** brothers **died, and the second** brother **performed levirate betrothal** with the widow **and** subsequently **died, then these** women, both the first wife of the second brother and the betrothed widow of the first brother, **must perform *ḥalitza* and may not enter into levirate marriage** with the third brother.

שֶׁנֶּאֱמַר ״וּמֵת אַחַד מֵהֶם יְבָמָהּ יָבֹא עָלֶיהָ״ – מִי שֶׁעָלֶיהָ זִיקַת יָבָם אֶחָד, וְלֹא שֶׁעָלֶיהָ זִיקַת שְׁנֵי יְבָמִין.

What is the reason that the wife of the first brother is not eligible for levirate marriage? **As it is stated: "And one of them dies… her brother-in-law will have intercourse with her** and will take her to him to be his wife and consummate the levirate marriage" (Deuteronomy 25:5). From here it is derived: **She who is subject to** a levirate **bond with a single *yavam*** enters levirate marriage **and not she who is subject to** a levirate **bond with two *yevamin*.** This woman requires levirate marriage due to the death of the first brother, and also, due to the subsequent levirate betrothal, requires levirate marriage following the death of the second brother.

רַבִּי שִׁמְעוֹן אוֹמֵר: מְיַיבֵּם לְאֵיזוֹ מֵהֶן שֶׁיִּרְצֶה, וְחוֹלֵץ לַשְּׁנִיָּה. יַבּוֹמֵי תַּרְוַיְיהוּ לָא – דִּלְמָא יֵשׁ זִיקָה, וְהָווּ שְׁנֵי יְבָמוֹת הַבָּאוֹת

However, **Rabbi Shimon says: Let him enter into levirate marriage** with **whichever he wishes and perform *ḥalitza* with the second.** Rabbi Shimon does not accept the homiletical interpretation forbidding a woman who is subject to two levirate bonds. The Gemara explains his opinion: Rabbi Shimon does **not** allow him to **take both in levirate marriage.** Why not? **Perhaps the** levirate **bond is substantial,** and combined with the levirate bond to the second brother the woman might be considered to be already married to the second brother, **and** then **these** two women **would be two *yevamot* who come**

HALAKHA

Three brothers married, etc. – **שְׁלֹשָׁה אַחִין נְשׂוּאִין וכו׳**: If three brothers were married to three unrelated women and one died childless, and the second brother performed a levirate betrothal with his *yevama* and then died before he could consummate the marriage, whereby both his wife and the *yevama* fall before the third brother, those women must perform *ḥalitza* and may not enter into levirate marriage. This is because the wife of the first deceased brother is subject to two levirate bonds and therefore cannot enter into levirate marriage, and the second, as her rival wife, performs *ḥalitza* but may not enter into levirate marriage, as she is forbidden to the third brother by rabbinic law (Rambam *Sefer Nashim, Hilkhot Yibbum VaḤalitza* 6:27; *Shulḥan Arukh, Even HaEzer* 174:4).

מִבַּיִת אֶחָד, יַבּוּמֵי חֲדָא וְאִיפְּטוֹר אִידָּךְ – לָא, דְּדִלְמָא אֵין זִיקָה כִּכְנוּסָה וַהֲווּ לְהוּ שְׁתֵּי יְבָמוֹת הַבָּאוֹת מִשְּׁנֵי בָתִּים. אַלְמָא: מְסַפְּקָא לֵיהּ.

from a single household, i.e., husband, and everyone agrees that only one wife from each household may be taken in levirate marriage, as the verse states: "To build his brother's house," which is interpreted to mean that the remaining brother may perform levirate marriage with only one wife of his late brother and not with two. To **take one in levirate marriage and exempt the other** without any procedure, he may **not** do, **as perhaps** the levirate **bond is not substantial** enough to make the first brother's widow **like a married woman** to the second brother. In that case this woman whose husband died first remains the wife of the first brother, and the second woman is the wife of the second brother. Then there would be two separate levirate obligations, and one could not exempt the other; **they would be two** *yevamot* **who come from two households.** Therefore, **apparently** even when levirate betrothal was performed Rabbi Shimon **is uncertain** whether or not the levirate bond is substantial.

וְכִי תֵּימָא: מִדְּאוֹרַיְיתָא הָכִי נַמִי דְּמִיַּיבְּמָא חֲדָא, וּמִפַּטְרָא חֲדָא, וּמִדְּרַבָּנַן הוּא דְּאָסוּר, גְּזֵירָה מִשּׁוּם שֶׁמָּא יֹאמְרוּ: שְׁתֵּי יְבָמוֹת הַבָּאוֹת מִשְּׁנֵי בָתִּים, חֲדָא מִיַּיבְּמָא וְאִידָּךְ מִיפַּטְרָא בְּלֹא כְלוּם,

And if you would say that **by Torah law, indeed, one** of them **may be taken in levirate marriage and** thereby **exempt the other,** and **this was prohibited** only **by rabbinic law,** this would be a rabbinic **decree due to** the concern **lest those** who were not aware of the details mistakenly **say** that in general if **two** *yevamot*[N] **come from two households** then **one is taken in levirate marriage and the other is exempt without anything.** One might have thought that the reason Rabbi Shimon required the other woman to perform *ḥalitza* is to avoid the possibility of such a mistake.

וְהָא טַעֲמָא דְּרַבִּי שִׁמְעוֹן מִשּׁוּם מַאֲמָר וְלָאו מַאֲמָר הוּא! דְּתַנְיָא, אָמַר לָהֶם רַבִּי שִׁמְעוֹן לַחֲכָמִים: אִם מַאֲמָרוֹ שֶׁל שֵׁנִי מַאֲמָר – אֵשֶׁת שֵׁנִי הוּא בּוֹעֵל,

But this cannot be, **as Rabbi Shimon's reason** is mentioned explicitly in the *baraita*, and there he does not state that this is a decree of the Sages. Rather, his reason **is due to** the question with regard to the strength of levirate betrothal, specifically whether the status of marriage is achieved by **levirate betrothal or not** achieved by **levirate betrothal. As it is taught** in a *baraita*: **Rabbi Shimon said to the Rabbis** in explanation of his opinion that one of the women could enter into levirate marriage: **If the levirate betrothal of the second** brother **is indeed levirate betrothal and** is considered as a fully valid marriage, then the third brother **is engaging in relations with the wife of the second** brother when he takes her in levirate marriage. That is, if the levirate betrothal by the second brother has the same status as full marriage, then she becomes the wife of this second brother, and all previous connections are no longer relevant.

וְאִם מַאֲמָרוֹ שֶׁל שֵׁנִי אֵינוֹ מַאֲמָר – אֵשֶׁת רִאשׁוֹן הוּא בּוֹעֵל.

But if the levirate betrothal of the second brother **is not levirate betrothal,** i.e., it does not have the full status **of** marriage, then there was never in fact any connection between the two. If she is then taken by the third brother in levirate marriage, **he would be engaging in relations with the wife of the first** brother. From here one can conclude that the basis for Rabbi Shimon's uncertainty is related to the questions concerning the strength of the levirate betrothal.

אֲמַר לֵיהּ אַבַּיֵי: וְלָא שָׁנֵי לָךְ בֵּין זִיקַת יָבָם אֶחָד לְזִיקַת שְׁנֵי יְבָמִים? דִּלְמָא, כִּי אָמַר רַבִּי שִׁמְעוֹן זִיקָה כִּכְנוּסָה דָּמְיָא – בְּיָבָם אֶחָד, אֲבָל בִּשְׁנֵי יְבָמִין – לָא.

Abaye said to him: From here you cannot prove what Rabbi Shimon's opinion was. **Is there no difference to you between a** levirate **bond to a single** *yavam* **and a bond to two** *yevamim*?[N] **Perhaps when Rabbi Shimon said** that a levirate **bond** is substantial enough to render her **like a married woman,** this applies only **when** there is **a single** *yavam*. If these were the circumstances of the case discussed, that when one brother died there remained only one *yavam*, then because the obligation of levirate marriage would apply only to him, she would be considered his wife. **But** perhaps he held that if there were **two** *yevamin*, then **no,** she would not be considered a married woman, as here the bond would apply to both at once. Accordingly, Rabbi Shimon's uncertainty is with regard to the case of a levirate bond with two *yevamin*.

NOTES

Lest those say two ***yevamot*****, etc.** – **שֶׁמָּא יֹאמְרוּ שְׁתֵּי יְבָמוֹת וכו׳**: Several early commentaries discuss a fundamental question that arises from this Gemara: Since Rabbi Shimon's opinion is that a woman subject to a levirate bond is considered like a married woman, then if two *yevamot* came from two households, it would have been appropriate for one to enter into levirate marriage and the second to be exempt. Rashi explains that the case involves two *yevamot* who fell simultaneously for levirate marriage. Some early commentaries consider this proposal far-fetched, since it is difficult to assume that a decree was made for such a rare occurrence (see Rashba).

A levirate bond to one or to two ***yevamin*** – **זִיקַת יָבָם אֶחָד וּשְׁנַיִם**: Certainly the opinion that a levirate bond to two *yevamin* is not substantial is more easily understood, as a woman cannot be married to two brothers simultaneously. However, it is possible to explain that the levirate bond to two *yevamin* is substantial by saying that provided neither has performed levirate betrothal, both brothers may potentially marry her and the levirate bond applies. If so, all prohibitions connected to marriage apply to both brothers at once (see Ramban).

HALAKHA

Three brothers, two of whom…married…sisters – שְׁלֹשָׁה אַחִין, שְׁנַיִם...נְשׂוּאִין...אֲחָיוֹת: If there were three brothers, two of whom married two sisters, and those brothers died consecutively, then both sisters are forbidden to the third brother, as due to the levirate bond they become rival wives to each other. They must perform *ḥalitza* and may not enter into levirate marriage, in accordance with the opinion of the unattributed mishna and contrary to the opinion of Rabbi Shimon (*Shulḥan Arukh, Even HaEzer* 175:6).

וּמִי שָׁנֵי לֵיהּ לְרַבִּי שִׁמְעוֹן? וְהָתַנְיָא, כְּלָל אָמַר רַבִּי שִׁמְעוֹן: כׇּל שֶׁהַלֵּידָה קוֹדֶמֶת לַנִּשּׂוּאִין – לֹא חוֹלֶצֶת וְלֹא מִתְיַיבֶּמֶת, נִשּׂוּאִין קוֹדֶם לַלֵּידָה – אוֹ חוֹלֶצֶת אוֹ מִתְיַיבֶּמֶת.

The Gemara challenges: **Does Rabbi Shimon differentiate** between the case of one *yavam* and the case of two *yevamin* in the matter of a wife of a brother with whom he did not coexist? **But it is taught** in a *baraita* with regard to the wife of a brother with whom he did not coexist: **Rabbi Shimon stated a principle: Whenever the birth** of the third brother **precedes the** levirate **marriage** of the second brother, if this second brother dies and the *yevama* falls before the third brother, **she does not perform *ḥalitza* and she does not enter into levirate marriage.** In such circumstances she is the wife of a brother with whom he did not coexist. But if **the** levirate **marriage preceded his birth, she either performs *ḥalitza* or enters into levirate marriage.**

מַאי לָאו בְּיָבָם אֶחָד, וְקָתָנֵי: לֹא חוֹלֶצֶת וְלֹא מִתְיַיבֶּמֶת! לֹא, בִּשְׁנֵי יְבָמִים.

What, is it not referring to the case of **a single *yavam*, and it is taught** in a *baraita*: **She does not perform *ḥalitza* and she does not enter into levirate marriage.** Even if there is only a single *yavam* this is not considered full marriage, and she remains forbidden as the wife of a brother with whom he did not coexist. Consequently, she who is subject to a levirate bond is not like a married woman. The Gemara answers: **No.** it refers to a case of **two *yevamin*.**

אֲבָל בְּיָבָם אֶחָד מַאי, הָכִי נַמִי אוֹ חוֹלֶצֶת אוֹ מִתְיַיבֶּמֶת? אִי הָכִי, אַדְּתָנֵי נִשּׂוּאִין קוֹדְמִין לַלֵּידָה אוֹ חוֹלֶצֶת אוֹ מִתְיַיבֶּמֶת – לִיפְלוֹג וְלִיתְנֵי בְּדִידָהּ: בַּמֶּה דְּבָרִים אֲמוּרִים – בִּשְׁנֵי יְבָמִים, אֲבָל בְּיָבָם אֶחָד – אוֹ חוֹלֶצֶת אוֹ מִתְיַיבֶּמֶת!

The Gemara asks: **But what,** then, is the ruling for **a single *yavam*? So too,** one should say **she either performs *ḥalitza* or enters into levirate marriage,** as the woman who requires levirate marriage is like the wife of the second brother for all purposes. **If so, rather than teaching** the case when **the marriage** of the second brother **precedes the birth** of the third brother, that if this second brother dies and she falls before the third brother, **she either performs *ḥalitza* or enters into levirate marriage, let** Rabbi Shimon **distinguish and teach** the distinction **within** the situation **itself** and say: **In what** case **is this statement said? When** there are **two *yevamin*. But** if there is **one *yavam*, she either performs *ḥalitza* or enters into levirate marriage.**

כּוּלָּהּ בִּשְׁנֵי יְבָמִין קָמַיְירֵי. וְאֶלָּא מַאי כְּלָלָא?

The Gemara rejects this: No, **the entire *baraita* is in reference to two *yevamin*** and differentiates between various cases involving two *yevamin*, namely, the case where the birth of the third brother preceded the marriage of the second brother and the case where the marriage of the second brother preceded the birth of the third brother. The Gemara asks: **Rather, what is the principle** in this matter? If Rabbi Shimon is speaking of two *yevamin* and not a single *yavam*, then it makes no sense to speak of a principle, as the *halakha* is different in the case of a single *yavam*.

וְעוֹד, מְתִיב רַב אוֹשַׁעְיָא: שְׁלֹשָׁה אַחִין, שְׁנַיִם מֵהֶן נְשׂוּאִין שְׁתֵּי אֲחָיוֹת, אוֹ אִשָּׁה וּבִתָּהּ, אוֹ אִשָּׁה וּבַת בִּתָּהּ, אוֹ אִשָּׁה וּבַת בְּנָהּ – הֲרֵי אֵלּוּ חוֹלְצוֹת וְלֹא מִתְיַיבְּמוֹת, וְרַבִּי שִׁמְעוֹן פּוֹטֵר.

Moreover, Rav Oshaya raised an objection from that which was taught in a mishna (28b): If there were **three brothers, two of whom were married to two sisters,**[H] **or to a woman and her daughter, or a woman and her daughter's daughter, or a woman and her son's daughter,** who are, in each case, two women who may not be married to the same person simultaneously, and subsequently these brothers who were married to relatives died, **then those** two women **must perform *ḥalitza* and may not enter into levirate marriage.** Since they both have a levirate bond to the third brother at the same time and he is prohibited from marrying both, they cause one another to be unable to perform levirate marriage. **And Rabbi Shimon exempts** them even from *ḥalitza*.

וְאִי סָלְקָא דַּעְתָּךְ קָסָבַר רַבִּי שִׁמְעוֹן זִיקָה כִּכְנוּסָה דָּמְיָא – לְיַיבֵּם לְקַמַּיְיתָא וְתִיפָּטַר אִידָּךְ!

And if it enters your mind that Rabbi Shimon held that a levirate **bond is substantial** enough to make her **like a married woman,** then **let** the third brother **consummate the levirate marriage to the** widow of the **first** husband to die, since as soon as her husband dies she has a levirate bond with the other brothers and should be considered to be like his wife, **and let the other be exempt** as a result, as her levirate bond began only with the death of the second husband.

אֲמַר רַב עַמְרָם: מַאי פּוֹטֵר נַמִי – פּוֹטֵר בִּשְׁנִיָּה. וְהָתַנְיָא: רַבִּי שִׁמְעוֹן פּוֹטֵר בִּשְׁתֵּיהֶן!

Rav Amram said: What is **really** the meaning of the word **exempt** used by Rabbi Shimon? Only **the second is exempt.** The Gemara objects: **But it is taught** in a *baraita*: **Rabbi Shimon exempts both.** From here it is clear that in his opinion a woman subject to a levirate bond does not have the same status as a married woman.

אָמַר רָבָא: שְׁנִיָּה שֶׁבְּזוּג זֶה וְהַשְּׁנִיָּה שֶׁבְּזוּג זֶה.

Rava said: In the case mentioned in that *baraita*, there were three brothers, two of whom died. Each of the deceased brothers had four wives who were related to the wives of the other brother as described in the mishna. One wife of the first brother was the sister of a wife of the second brother. Another wife was the mother of a wife of the second brother. Another was the daughter of the daughter of a wife of the second brother. And another was the daughter of the son of a wife of the second brother. When these brothers died, all eight women happened before the remaining brother for levirate marriage. When Rabbi Shimon deemed both of them exempt, he was referring to **the second from this pair and the second from that pair.** That is, since one of them was bound to the third brother her relative became exempt as a forbidden relative, and the other of the pair was her rival wife in each of the cases.

קָא טָעֵי רָבָא בְּאַרְבָּעָה זוּגֵי, חֲדָא: דְּ״אוֹ״ ״אוֹ״ קָתָנֵי. וְעוֹד: ״רַבִּי שִׁמְעוֹן פּוֹטֵר בְּאַרְבַּעְתָּן״ מִיבְּעֵי לֵיהּ.

The Gemara comments: **Rava was mistaken about** there being **four pairs.**[B] He mistakenly understood that the mishna spoke of two brothers who married four pairs of relatives. Why does the Gemara assume that he was mistaken? **One** piece of evidence **is that** the mishna **teaches** the case using the expression: **Or, or.** The mishna teaches: Or to a woman and her daughter, or to a woman and her daughter's daughter, or a woman and her son's daughter, meaning that not all of the pairs happened before a single *yavam* for levirate marriage. **And further,** the *baraita* **should have said: Rabbi Shimon exempts all four of them,**[N] i.e., the four women married to the second brother.

וְעוֹד: תַּנְיָא, רַבִּי שִׁמְעוֹן פּוֹטֵר בִּשְׁתֵּיהֶן מִן הַחֲלִיצָה וּמִן הַיִּיבּוּם, שֶׁנֶּאֱמַר ״וְאִשָּׁה אֶל אֲחוֹתָהּ לֹא תִקָּח לִצְרוֹר״ בְּשָׁעָה שֶׁנַּעֲשׂוּ צָרוֹת זוֹ לָזוֹ לֹא יְהֵא לְךָ לִיקּוּחִין אֲפִילּוּ בְּאַחַת מֵהֶן.

And further, it is taught explicitly in a *baraita* that **Rabbi Shimon exempts both of them from** both ***ḥalitza* and levirate marriage, as it is stated: "And you shall not take a woman to her sister, to be a rival to her"** (Leviticus 18:18). From here it is derived that **when** two sisters are about to **become rival wives one to the other,** that is, at the moment they fall before one brother for levirate marriage, **you do not have** the option of **taking even one of them.** In other words, levirate marriage to either of them is not permitted, and therefore both are exempt and not only the second. Thus Rava's explanation is rejected.

אֶלָּא אָמַר רַב אָשֵׁי: אִי דִּנְפוּל בָּזֶה אַחַר זֶה – הָכִי נָמֵי. הָכָא בְּמַאי עָסְקִינַן – דִּנְפוּל בְּבַת אַחַת, וְרַבִּי שִׁמְעוֹן סָבַר לָהּ כְּרַבִּי יוֹסֵי הַגְּלִילִי, דְּאָמַר: אֶפְשָׁר לְצַמְצֵם.

Rather, Rav Ashi said an alternative answer to the Gemara's challenge: **If these** *yevamot* **happened** before him for levirate marriage **one after the other, indeed it is so** that the first woman bound is like a married woman, and she exempts the second, who is her close relative. However, **here we are dealing with** a case when both brothers died at once and so both women **happened** before him **at once. And Rabbi Shimon holds in accordance with** the opinion of **Rabbi Yosei HaGelili, who said: It is possible to be precise.**[N] He held, contrary to the opinion of the Rabbis, that it was possible to be exact about measurements of time. Therefore, it is possible for two things to truly occur at once, and it is possible that both brothers died simultaneously.

BACKGROUND

Mistaken about there being four pairs – טָעֵי...בְּאַרְבָּעָה זוּגֵי: There were nine brothers by the same father. Shimon and Levi married the sisters Ḥogla and Milka, respectively; Yehuda married Dina, and Yissakhar married her daughter Osnat; Gad married Miriam, and Asher married Miriam's daughter's daughter, Tzila; Dan married Ruth and Naftali married her son's daughter, Adda. If these eight brothers were to die and all of the women were to fall before Binyamin for levirate marriage, clearly for each pair there are two women who cannot be taken in marriage at once. According to *Tosafot Yeshanim*, this is the description of the case at hand. According to Rashi, however, the situation is that Shimon married Ḥogla, Dina, Miriam, and Ruth, while his brother Levi married Milka, Osnat, Tzila, and Adda, and all of these women happened before Binyamin for levirate marriage.

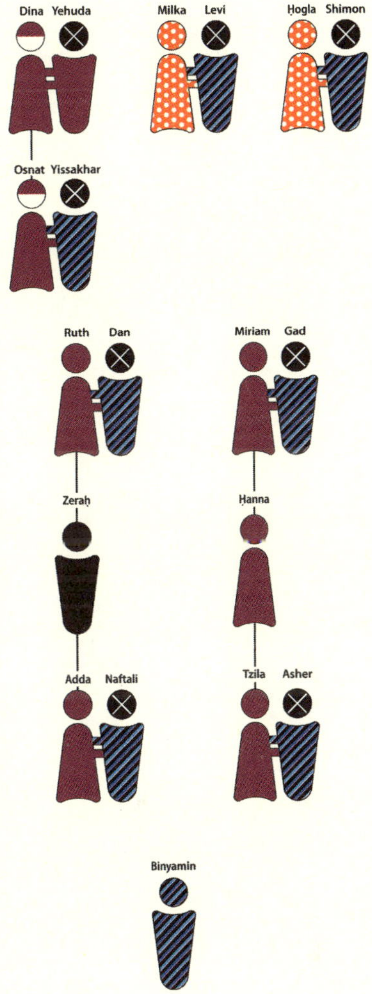

NOTES

Exempts all four of them – פּוֹטֵר בְּאַרְבַּעְתָּן: *Tosafot Yeshanim* raise the following objection: In actuality, it is not four wives who are exempt, but seven. He can perform levirate marriage on only one woman from each household, so that three women are exempt from the first household, and the four from the other household include a forbidden relation and her rival wives who are also forbidden. For this reason, an alternate explanation is suggested: The reference here is not to two brothers but to nine brothers, eight of whom were married in such a way that one was married to a woman and another to her daughter, and one was married to a woman and another to her sister, and so on. When they all happened before the ninth brother for levirate marriage, four were exempt (see *Tosefot HaRosh*).

It is possible to be precise – אֶפְשָׁר לְצַמְצֵם: This opinion, held by Rabbi Yosei HaGelili, relates to several areas in *halakha* and refers in essence to the question of whether or not in reality two entities can ever be absolutely equal, be it in questions of exact size or time of occurrence. According to the Rabbis, even if it appears that two things occurred simultaneously, this is only because humans are not able to measure precisely; in reality there must have been some gap between them.

רַב פַּפָּא אָמַר: בְּיִיבֵּם וְאַחַר כָּךְ נוֹלַד – פְּלִיג רַבִּי שִׁמְעוֹן, בְּנוֹלַד וְאַחַר כָּךְ יִיבֵּם – לָא פְּלִיג,

Until this point the Gemara dealt with Rav Oshaya's opinion stating that according to Rabbi Shimon's statement, even in the case of one who was born before his brother's levirate marriage the ruling of a wife of a brother with whom one did not coexist would not apply. However, **Rav Pappa said: Rabbi Shimon disagreed** in the case where the second brother **performed levirate marriage and after that** the third brother **was born;** however, **where** the third brother **was born** after the death of the first brother **and after that** the second brother **performed levirate marriage** Rabbi Shimon **did not disagree.** He agreed that in this case she would be forbidden to the newly born brother as the wife of a brother with whom he did not coexist.

וְתַרְוַיְיהוּ לְרַבָּנַן אִיצְטְרִיךְ, וְ"לֹא זוֹ אַף זוֹ" קָתָנֵי.

As for the question that Rav Oshaya raised with regard to the apparent redundancy of the similar rulings in both the first mishna of the chapter and the mishna on 18b, it can be explained that **both were necessary for** the opinion of **the Rabbis** who prohibited marriage to the wife of a brother with whom one did not coexist in every case. The difficulty raised concerning the apparent redundancy of the first mishna, given the greater scope of the opinion revealed in the second mishna, can be explained by saying that the *tanna* **teaches** the mishna employing the style: **Not** only **this** but **also that.** That is, the mishna follows the stylistic principle of first teaching the obvious case and continues by saying that this principle applies not only in the obvious case but even in the less obvious case. If so, there is no need to assume that there is an additional dispute with Rabbi Shimon.

תַּנְיָא כְּווֹתֵיהּ דְּרַב פַּפָּא, וּתְיוּבְתָּא דְּרַבִּי אוֹשַׁעְיָא: שְׁנֵי אַחִים בָּעוֹלָם אֶחָד, וּמֵת אֶחָד מֵהֶם בְּלֹא וָלָד, וְעָמַד הַשֵּׁנִי הַזֶּה לַעֲשׂוֹת מַאֲמָר בִּיבִמְתּוֹ, וְלֹא הִסְפִּיק לַעֲשׂוֹת בָּהּ מַאֲמָר עַד שֶׁנּוֹלַד לוֹ אָח, וּמֵת. הָרִאשׁוֹנָה יוֹצְאָה מִשּׁוּם אֵשֶׁת אָחִיו שֶׁלֹּא הָיָה בְּעוֹלָמוֹ, וּשְׁנִיָּה אוֹ חוֹלֶצֶת אוֹ מִתְיַיבֶּמֶת.

The Gemara continues: **It is taught** in a *baraita* **in accordance with the opinion of Rav Pappa, and this is a conclusive refutation of** the opinion of **Rabbi Oshaya:** If there were **two coexisting brothers, and one died childless, and the second was about to perform levirate betrothal with his** *yevama* **but did not manage to perform levirate betrothal before his brother was born, and** then the second brother **died,** then **the first** woman **goes out** and is free to remarry without *ḥalitza* or levirate marriage **due to** the fact that **she was the wife of a brother with whom** the third brother **did not coexist, and the second either performs** *ḥalitza* **or enters into levirate marriage.** She was never the rival wife of the widow of the first brother.

עָשָׂה בָּהּ מַאֲמָר, וְאַחַר כָּךְ נוֹלַד אָח, אוֹ שֶׁנּוֹלַד לוֹ אָח וְאַחַר כָּךְ עָשָׂה בָּהּ מַאֲמָר, וּמֵת – הָרִאשׁוֹנָה יוֹצְאָה מִשּׁוּם אֵשֶׁת אָחִיו שֶׁלֹּא הָיָה בְּעוֹלָמוֹ, וּשְׁנִיָּה חוֹלֶצֶת וְלֹא מִתְיַיבֶּמֶת.

If the second brother **performed levirate betrothal with her and afterward his brother was born, or if his brother was born and then he performed the levirate betrothal, and then he died, the first goes out** and is free to remarry **as the wife of a brother with whom he did not coexist, and the second,** the wife of the second brother, **must perform** ***ḥalitza*** **and may not enter into levirate marriage.** This is because, due to the levirate betrothal, she is considered by the Rabbis to be the rival wife of a wife of a brother with whom he did not coexist.

Perek **II**
Daf **19** Amud **b**

NOTES

Intercourse or *ḥalitza*, etc. – בִּיאָתָהּ אוֹ חֲלִיצָתָהּ וכו׳: The early commentaries asked why the rival wife requires *ḥalitza*. If Rabbi Shimon holds that the levirate bond is significant, she would be considered the rival wife of a wife of a brother with whom he did not coexist through the bond, and therefore totally exempt. *Tosafot* claim that according to Rabbi Shimon's opinion there is no bond. The Meiri explains that the bond is not significant enough to completely exempt the rival wife. Ramban explains that Rabbi Shimon holds that a woman subject to a levirate bond is considered like a married woman retroactively only in cases where she later actually married. But if she did not eventually marry her *yavam*, the bond is not considered significant (see *Tosafot Yeshanim* and *Tosefot HaRosh*).

רַבִּי שִׁמְעוֹן אוֹמֵר: בִּיאָתָהּ אוֹ חֲלִיצָתָהּ שֶׁל אַחַת מֵהֶם פּוֹטֶרֶת צָרָתָהּ, חָלַץ לְבַעֲלַת מַאֲמָר לֹא נִפְטְרָה צָרָה. כְּנָסָהּ וָמֵת, וְאַחַר כָּךְ נוֹלַד לוֹ אָח, אוֹ שֶׁנּוֹלַד לוֹ אָח וְאַחַר כָּךְ כְּנָסָהּ וָמֵת – שְׁתֵּיהֶן פְּטוּרוֹת מִן הַחֲלִיצָה וּמִן הַיִּיבּוּם.

Rabbi Shimon says: Intercourse or ***ḥalitza*****[N] with one of them,** i.e., the wife of the second brother, **exempts her rival wife,** but **if he performed** ***ḥalitza*** **with** the one **who received the levirate betrothal, then** her **rival wife,** i.e., the wife of the second brother, **is not** thereby **exempt,** since possibly levirate betrothal does not have the same strength as marriage. If the second brother **married** his deceased brother's wife **and then died** himself, **and afterward a brother was born, or if a brother was born and then he married her and died,** the two wives **are both exempt from** ***ḥalitza*** **and levirate marriage.** In this case, one was the wife of a brother with whom he did not coexist and the other her rival wife.

כְּנָסָהּ וְנוֹלַד לוֹ אָח, וְאַחַר כָּךְ מֵת – שְׁתֵּיהֶן פְּטוּרוֹת מִן הַחֲלִיצָה וּמִן הַיִּיבּוּם, דִּבְרֵי רַבִּי מֵאִיר. וְרַבִּי שִׁמְעוֹן אוֹמֵר: הוֹאִיל וּבָא וּמְצָאָהּ בְּהֶיתֵּר, וְלֹא עָמְדָה עָלָיו שָׁעָה אַחַת בְּאִיסּוּר – מְיַיבֵּם לְאֵיזוֹ מֵהֶן שֶׁיִּרְצֶה, אוֹ חוֹלֵץ לְאֵיזוֹ מֵהֶן שֶׁיִּרְצֶה.

The *baraita* continues: If he **married** his *yevama* **and** then a **brother was born, and then he died, both** the wife of the first deceased brother and the original wife of the *yavam* **are exempt from *ḥalitza* and levirate marriage;** this is **the statement of Rabbi Meir. And Rabbi Shimon says: Since** the third brother **came and found her in a permitted state, and she was never for a moment prohibited to him,** as when he was born she was already the wife of the second brother, who was still alive, **he** therefore **takes whichever he wishes in levirate marriage, or performs *ḥalitza* with whichever he wishes.**

הָא בָּבָא דְּסֵיפָא לְמַאן קָתָנֵי לַהּ? אִילֵימָא לְרַבִּי מֵאִיר קָתָנֵי לַהּ – מִכְּדִי, לָא שָׁנֵי לֵיהּ לְרַבִּי מֵאִיר בֵּין יִיבֵּם וְאַחַר כָּךְ נוֹלַד, בֵּין נוֹלַד וְאַחַר כָּךְ יִיבֵּם – לְעָרְבִינְהוּ וְלִתְנִינְהוּ.

The Gemara clarifies: **The section of the latter clause** of the *baraita*, which refers to the case of a brother born after the levirate marriage, **according to whom is it taught? If we say it is taught for** the purpose of clarifying the opinion of **Rabbi Meir,** it does not make sense, **since it makes no difference to Rabbi Meir whether the levirate marriage preceded the birth or the birth preceded the levirate marriage.** In his opinion under both circumstances she is the wife of a brother with whom he did not coexist. And if this were in fact taught for the purpose of clarifying his opinion **it should have combined** the cases **and taught them**[N] together.

אֶלָּא, לָאו רַבִּי שִׁמְעוֹן, וּבְיִיבֵּם וְאַחַר כָּךְ נוֹלַד – פָּלֵיג, בְּנוֹלַד וְאַחַר כָּךְ יִיבֵּם – לָא פָּלֵיג, שְׁמַע מִינָּהּ.

Rather, is it not that the latter segment was meant to clarify the opinion of **Rabbi Shimon,** since the different parts of the *baraita* enumerate different possibilities? **And** Rabbi Shimon **disagrees in** the case when the brother first **performed levirate marriage and afterward** his brother **was born,** but he **does not disagree in** the case where the younger brother **was born and afterward** the second brother performed **levirate marriage.** The Gemara summarizes: **Conclude from this** that Rabbi Shimon disagrees only here, as Rav Pappa explained.

אֲמַר מָר: עָמַד הַשֵּׁנִי לַעֲשׂוֹת מַאֲמָר בִּיבִמְתּוֹ, וְלֹא הִסְפִּיק לַעֲשׂוֹת מַאֲמָר בִּיבִמְתּוֹ עַד שֶׁנּוֹלַד לוֹ אָח, וָמֵת – רִאשׁוֹנָה יוֹצְאָה מִשּׁוּם אֵשֶׁת אָחִיו שֶׁלֹּא הָיָה בְּעוֹלָמוֹ, וּשְׁנִיָּה – אוֹ חוֹלֶצֶת אוֹ מִתְיַיבֶּמֶת. מַאי עָמַד וּמַאי לֹא הִסְפִּיק? אִי עֲבַד – עֲבַד, וְאִי לֹא עֲבַד – לָא עֲבַד!

§ The Gemara proceeds to discuss the *baraita* itself. **The Master said: The second was about to perform levirate betrothal with his *yevama*, but did not manage to perform levirate betrothal with his *yevama* before his brother was born, and** then the **second brother died. The first woman goes out** and is free to remarry without *ḥalitza* or levirate marriage **due to** the fact that **she was the wife of a brother with whom** the third brother **did not coexist, and the second** woman **performs *ḥalitza* or enters into levirate marriage.** The Gemara asks: **What is** the meaning of the phrase: **Was about to, and what is** the meaning of: **Did not manage** to perform levirate betrothal? The important issue is not his intention but his actions. **If he did it, he did it; and if he did not do it, he did not do it.**

אֶלָּא: עָמַד – מִדַּעְתָּהּ, וְלֹא הִסְפִּיק מִדַּעְתָּהּ, אֶלָּא בְּעַל כׇּרְחָהּ. וּדְלָא כְּרַבִּי, דְּתַנְיָא: הָעוֹשֶׂה מַאֲמָר בִּיבִמְתּוֹ שֶׁלֹּא מִדַּעְתָּהּ, רַבִּי אוֹמֵר: קָנָה, וַחֲכָמִים אוֹמְרִים: לֹא קָנָה.

Rather, the correct interpretation is: **Was about to** means that he was about to perform levirate betrothal **with her consent. Did not manage** means that he did not manage to perform it **with her consent, but instead** did it **against her will.** Consequently, it is understood that this *baraita* **is not in accordance with** the opinion of **Rabbi** Yehuda HaNasi, **as it is taught** in a *baraita*: With regard to **one who performs levirate betrothal with his *yevama* without her consent, Rabbi** Yehuda HaNasi **says: He acquired** her and the betrothal is fully valid, like a consensual levirate betrothal with his *yevama*; **and the Rabbis say: He did not acquire** her.[H]

NOTES

It should have combined and taught them – **לְעָרְבִינְהוּ וְלִיתְנִינְהוּ**: This objection could not be derived from the mishna itself, because the mishna detailed each ruling separately, which is the linguistic style of the Mishna. The *baraita*, on the other hand, does combine some rulings, and so the question is based on the fact that not all the rulings were combined here (Rivan; *Tosafot*). Also, it could be said that the *baraita* is clearly teaching by employing the style of: Not only this but also that, unlike the mishna. Rav Oshaya was of the opinion that it was preferable to explain each phrase in the mishna and not resort to saying that it is employing the style of: Not only this but also that. However, once it is clear that the *baraita* uses that style, it is reasonable to assume that the mishna also employs that style (*Tosefot HaRosh*).

HALAKHA

A levirate betrothal performed against her will – **מַאֲמָר בְּעַל כׇּרְחָהּ**: If one performs a non-consensual levirate betrothal, it is wholly ineffectual. The *halakha* is ruled in accordance with the opinion of the Rabbis, who are the majority, against the opinion of Rabbi Yehuda HaNasi (Rambam *Sefer Nashim*, *Hilkhot Yibbum VaḤalitza* 2:1; *Shulḥan Arukh*, *Even HaEzer* 166:3).

מַאי טַעֲמָא דְּרַבִּי? גָּמַר מִבִּיאָה דִּיבָמָה, מַה בִּיאָה דִּיבָמָה בְּעַל כָּרְחָהּ, אַף קִדּוּשִׁין דִּיבָמָה בְּעַל כָּרְחָהּ. וְרַבָּנַן גָּמְרִי מִקִּדּוּשִׁין דְּעָלְמָא, מַה קִּדּוּשִׁין דְּעָלְמָא – מִדַּעְתָּהּ, אַף קִדּוּשִׁין דִּיבָמָה – מִדַּעְתָּהּ.

The Gemara explains: **What is the reason for Rabbi Yehuda** HaNasi's opinion? **He learned** this **from** the case of a *yavam* engaging in **intercourse with a *yevama*.**[N] **Just as** even **non-consensual intercourse with the *yevama*** renders her his wife, as the matter does not require her consent, **so too, betrothal of a *yevama*** can be **non-consensual. But the Rabbis learned from** the *halakhot* of **betrothal in general; just as betrothal in general requires consent**[N] by the woman, **so too, betrothal of a *yevama*** for purposes of levirate marriage **requires consent.**

בְּמַאי קָמִיפַּלְגִי? מָר סָבַר: מִילֵּי דִּיבָמָה מִמִּילֵּי דִּיבָמָה הֲוָה לֵיהּ לְמֵילַף, וּמָר סָבַר: מִילֵּי דְּקִדּוּשִׁין מִמִּילֵּי דְּקִדּוּשִׁין הֲוָה לֵיהּ לְמֵילַף.

The Gemara explains: **With regard to what** principle do Rabbi Yehuda HaNasi and the Rabbis **disagree? One Sage,** Rabbi Yehuda HaNasi, **holds that** halakhic **matters concerning *yevamot* must be inferred from matters concerning *yevamot*** and not from other areas of *halakha*. **And one Sage,** the Rabbis, **holds** that halakhic **matters concerning** levirate **betrothal must be inferred from matters concerning betrothal.**

עָשָׂה בָּהּ מַאֲמָר וְאַחַר כָּךְ נוֹלַד לוֹ אָח, אוֹ שֶׁנּוֹלַד לוֹ אָח וְאַחַר כָּךְ עָשָׂה בָּהּ מַאֲמָר, וּמֵת, רִאשׁוֹנָה יוֹצְאָה מִשּׁוּם אֵשֶׁת אָחִיו שֶׁלֹּא הָיָה בְּעוֹלָמוֹ, וּשְׁנִיָּה חוֹלֶצֶת וְלֹא מִתְיַיבֶּמֶת. רַבִּי שִׁמְעוֹן אוֹמֵר: בִּיאָתָהּ אוֹ חֲלִיצָתָהּ שֶׁל אַחַת מֵהֶן פּוֹטֶרֶת צָרָתָהּ.

The Gemara clarifies another segment of the *baraita*. It is taught: If the second brother **performed levirate betrothal with her, and afterward his brother was born, or if his brother was born and then he performed levirate betrothal and died, the first** woman **goes out** and is free to remarry **because** she is **the wife of a brother with whom he did not coexist, and the second,** the wife of the second brother, **performs *ḥalitza* but does not enter into levirate marriage. Rabbi Shimon says: Intercourse or *ḥalitza* with one of them exempts her rival wife.**

רַבִּי שִׁמְעוֹן אַהַיָּיא קָאֵי? אִילֵימָא אַנּוֹלַד לוֹ אָח וְאַחַר כָּךְ עָשָׂה בָּהּ מַאֲמָר – הָא אָמְרַתְּ בְּנוֹלַד וּלְבַסּוֹף יִיבֵּם לָא פָּלֵיג רַבִּי שִׁמְעוֹן! אֶלָּא – אַעָשָׂה בָּהּ מַאֲמָר וְאַחַר כָּךְ נוֹלַד לוֹ אָח.

The Gemara asks: **To which** case is **Rabbi Shimon referring? If we say** that he is referring to the case when **his brother was born and then he performed levirate betrothal with her, didn't you** already **say** that **Rabbi Shimon did not dispute** the case where the brother **was born and then ultimately he performed a levirate marriage,** and she would be forbidden as the wife of a brother with whom he did not coexist. **Rather,** one must say that Rabbi Shimon disputed the case where **he performed levirate betrothal with her and afterward his brother was born.**

חָלַץ לְבַעֲלַת מַאֲמָר לֹא נִפְטְרָה צָרָה, מַאי טַעְמָא? מִשּׁוּם דַּהֲוַאי צָרָה וַדַּאי וּבַעֲלַת מַאֲמָר סָפֵק, וְאֵין סָפֵק מוֹצִיא מִידֵי וַדַּאי.

Later in the *baraita* it is taught: If the third brother **performed *ḥalitza* with** the wife of the first brother, **to whom** the second brother **performed levirate betrothal, her rival wife is not exempt.** The Gemara clarifies: **What is the reason** for this? It is **because the rival wife,** the widow of the second brother, has a **definite** legal status that requires an act to free her to remarry, as she is the wife of a brother with whom he did coexist, **whereas** the widow of the first brother **with whom** the second brother **performed levirate betrothal** had only **an uncertain** legal status, as it is not clear if she is to be considered truly the wife of the second brother by means of the levirate betrothal or not. **And** the principle is that **an uncertainty does not override a certainty.** Therefore, even if the third brother performs *ḥalitza*, since the status of the first woman's obligation is uncertain, the status of the *ḥalitza* itself is uncertain, as it is possible that she did not require *ḥalitza* at all. Consequently, this *ḥalitza* is not sufficient to exempt her rival wife. This teaches that he must perform *ḥalitza* or levirate marriage with the woman who is definitely obligated, and then the other will be exempt.

יָתֵיב רַב מְנַשֶּׁה בַּר זְבִיד קַמֵּיהּ דְּרַב הוּנָא, וְיָתֵיב וְקָאָמַר: מַאי טַעֲמָא דְּרַבִּי שִׁמְעוֹן? מַאי טַעֲמָא דְּרַבִּי שִׁמְעוֹן?! כְּדְאָמַר טַעֲמָא: הוֹאִיל וּבָא וּמְצָאָהּ בְּהֶיתֵּר, וְלֹא עָמְדָה עָלָיו שָׁעָה אַחַת בְּאִיסּוּר!

Rav Menashe bar Zevid sat before Rav Huna. He sat and said: What is the reason that Rabbi Shimon allows the third brother to marry the wife of his brother with whom he did not coexist where she was taken in levirate marriage prior to his birth? The Gemara also wonders: **What is Rabbi Shimon's reason? The reason is as he stated** in that same *baraita*: **Since** the third brother **came and found her in a permitted state, and she was never for a moment prohibited to him** he may perform levirate marriage with her.

NOTES

He learned this from the case of intercourse with a *yevama* – גָּמַר מִבִּיאָה דִּיבָמָה: *Tosafot* ask how Rabbi Yehuda HaNasi can derive the *halakha* pertaining to levirate betrothal, which is by rabbinic law, from the laws of levirate marriage, which is by Torah law. They answer that rabbinic enactments were often established as though they were Torah law. In the Jerusalem Talmud there is an opinion that considers levirate betrothal to be a Torah law itself, and if so, the laws of a levirate betrothal can certainly be derived from the laws of levirate marriage (see *Keren Ora*).

Betrothal in general requires consent – קִדּוּשִׁין דְּעָלְמָא מִדַּעְתָּהּ: Some early commentaries point out that there is an exception to this rule: A minor may be married off against her will if her father accepts the betrothal. Nevertheless, even in that case the father must give consent, and so it still requires some form of consent (Rivan).

אֶלָּא: מַאי טַעְמָא דְּרַבָּנַן? אָמַר קְרָא "וּלְקָחָהּ לוֹ לְאִשָּׁה וְיִבְּמָהּ" – עֲדַיִין יִבּוּמִים הָרִאשׁוֹנִים עָלֶיהָ. אֶלָּא, הָא דִּתְנַן: כְּנָסָהּ – הֲרֵי הִיא כְּאִשְׁתּוֹ לְכָל דָּבָר, וְאָמַר רַבִּי יוֹסֵי בַּר חֲנִינָא: מְלַמֵּד

Rather, the question was as follows: Rabbi Shimon gave such a persuasive explanation of his opinion that it raises the question: **What is the reason for the Rabbis'** opinion? The Gemara answers that **the verse states:** "Her brother-in-law will… **take her to him to be his wife and consummate the levirate marriage** [***veyibbema***]" (Deuteronomy 25:5). This means that **the first levirate bond is still upon her.**[N] Even after she is taken as a wife by the second brother, her earlier status as wife of her late first husband is still in effect. The Gemara challenges this: **But** what about **that which we learn** in a mishna (38a): If **he took** his *yevama* **in marriage** as his wife, **then** her legal status is **that of his wife in every sense; and Rabbi Yosei bar Ḥanina said:** This **teaches**

NOTES

The first levirate bond [*yibbumin*] is still upon her – עֲדַיִין יִבּוּמִים הָרִאשׁוֹנִים עָלֶיהָ: The early authorities ask: If the levirate bond remains, why is he allowed to continue to live with his *yevama*? Once he performs *yibbum*, she apparently remains his brother's wife, who is forbidden to him now that he has already performed the mitzva. They answer that the Torah did not intend to prohibit relations with the *yevama* after the act of consummation, as it states: "He will take her to him to be his wife." However, she remains a *yevama* even after she is married, in that if the couple were to divorce, they would not be permitted to remarry (Rashba).

Perek **II**
Daf **20** Amud **a**

שֶׁמְּגָרְשָׁהּ בְּגֵט וּמַחֲזִירָהּ, הָתָם נָמֵי לֵימָא: "וְיִבְּמָהּ" עֲדַיִין יִבּוּמִין הָרִאשׁוֹנִים עָלֶיהָ, וְתִיבְּעֵי חֲלִיצָה!

that he must divorce his *yevama* **with a bill of divorce** and she does not also require *ḥalitza*. **And he may remarry her,** if he wishes, after the divorce; as the *halakha* is not ruled in accordance with the opinion that after he performs the mitzva she is once more forbidden to him as his brother's wife. Why? **There, too, let** the *halakha* **say**[N] that the verse states: **"And consummate the levirate marriage** [***veyibbema***]," as explained above, meaning that **the first levirate bond is still upon her and she should** also **require *ḥalitza*.**

שָׁאנֵי הָתָם, דְּאָמַר קְרָא "וּלְקָחָהּ לוֹ לְאִשָּׁה", כֵּיוָן שֶׁלְּקָחָהּ נַעֲשֵׂית כְּאִשְׁתּוֹ לְכָל דָּבָר. אִי הָכִי, הָכָא נָמֵי! הָא כְּתַב רַחֲמָנָא "וְיִבְּמָהּ".

The Gemara answers: **It is different there, as the verse states: "And take her to him to be his wife"** (Deuteronomy 25:5) to teach that **once he has taken her,** her legal status is **that of his wife in every sense.** The Gemara objects: **If so, here too,** in the case of a brother born after the levirate marriage, according to the opinion of the Rabbis this same principle should apply. The Gemara answers that **The Merciful One states: "And consummate the levirate marriage** [***veyibbema***]," that is, even after the marriage she is still considered to be the wife of the deceased brother [*yevama*] with respect to any brothers who are born later.

וּמָה רָאִיתָ? מִסְתַּבְּרָא: שְׁדִי הֶיתֵּירָא אַהֶיתֵּירָא, וּשְׁדִי אִיסּוּרָא אַאִיסּוּרָא.

The Gemara asks: **What did you see** to distinguish in this way and say that once she is married the levirate obligation is totally abrogated with regard to *ḥalitza*, but that she remains prohibited as the wife of a brother with whom one did not coexist with respect to any brothers born in the future? The Gemara answers: **It stands to reason** to say: **Toss that which is permitted on that which is permitted, and toss that which is prohibited on that which is prohibited.** In other words, in cases where the woman becomes permitted to her *yavam* through levirate marriage, it stands to reason that this permitted state is absolute, but with regard to the prohibition against taking the wife of a brother with whom one did not coexist, it stands to reason that the verse comes to teach that she retains her prohibited status with respect to any brothers born in the future.

וּלְרַבִּי שִׁמְעוֹן, דְּאָמַר: הוֹאִיל וּבָא וּמְצָאָהּ בְּהֶיתֵּר וְלֹא עָמְדָה עָלָיו שָׁעָה אַחַת בְּאִיסּוּר, אֶלָּא מֵעַתָּה, אֲחוֹתוֹ מֵאִמּוֹ שֶׁנְּשָׂאָהּ אָחִיו מֵאָבִיו, וְאַחַר כָּךְ נוֹלַד אָח, וּמֵת – תִּתְיַבֵּם, הוֹאִיל וּבָא וּמְצָאָהּ בְּהֶיתֵּר!

The Gemara suggests: **But according to Rabbi Shimon, who said** that **since he came and found her in a permitted state** a brother born subsequently may perform levirate marriage **since she was never for a single moment prohibited to him; however, if** that is **so,** consider the case of **one's maternal** half **sister,** who **married his paternal** half **brother;** their marriage was fully permissible since the husband and wife were in no way related to each other. **And then his brother was born and** the married brother **died;** in that case, **let** the sister **enter into levirate marriage** with her newly born half brother for the same reason, i.e., **since he came and found her in a permitted state,** as when he was born she was already his brother's wife.

NOTES

There, too, let the *halakha* say, etc. – הָתָם נָמֵי לֵימָא וכו׳: Rabbeinu Ḥananel had a different version of the text here, and many early commentaries preferred his version. According to his text, the Gemara is discussing two challenges to the concept of the first levirate bond still being upon her: First, if a *yavam* performs levirate marriage and subsequently divorces his *yevama*, he may remarry her afterward. Since he has already performed levirate marriage, she is no longer forbidden to him as his brother's wife, even if he divorces her. This indicates that the original levirate bond is completely removed. Second, if he divorces his *yevama* he does so only with a bill of divorce and does not perform *ḥalitza*. This also indicates that the levirate bond is removed. Although Rashi has a different version of the text, his explanation accords with that of Rabbeinu Ḥananel.

אִיסּוּר אֲחוֹתוֹ לְהֵיכָן אֲזַל?! הָכָא נַמִי, אִיסּוּר אָחִיו שֶׁלֹּא הָיָה בָּעוֹלָם לְהֵיכָן אֲזַל! הַאי, אִיסּוּרָא דְּלֵית לֵיהּ הֶיתֵּירָא, הַאי – אִיסּוּרָא דְּאִית לֵיהּ הֶיתֵּירָא.

The Gemara challenges this suggestion: How can you say that? What happened to **the prohibition against** marrying **his sister, to where did it go?** This widow is the maternal sister of the newly born brother and is therefore forbidden to him. The Gemara objects: If so, **here too,** one could have said: What happened to **the prohibition** against marrying the wife of **a brother with whom one did not coexist, to where did it go?** In this case as well, the prohibition against marrying the wife of a brother with whom he did not coexist already applied from the first brother, so why does Rabbi Shimon see this as abrogated by marriage? The Gemara answers that the comparison is unsound. **This prohibition** against marrying one's sister **has no** case where it is **permitted** and so in this case is also not canceled, whereas **that prohibition** against marrying a brother's wife **has** a case where it is **permitted,**[N] when the mitzva of levirate marriage applies to a second brother and is therefore removed completely before the third brother is born.

מתני׳ כְּלָל אָמְרוּ בַּיְבָמָה: כׇּל שֶׁהִיא אִיסּוּר עֶרְוָה, לֹא חוֹלֶצֶת וְלֹא מִתְיַיבֶּמֶת. אִיסּוּר מִצְוָה וְאִיסּוּר קְדוּשָּׁה – חוֹלֶצֶת וְלֹא מִתְיַיבֶּמֶת.

MISHNA The Sages **stated a principle about a** *yevama*: **Whoever is** forbidden **by a prohibition of forbidden relations** to her *yavam* **neither performs** ***ḥalitza*** **nor enters into levirate marriage** and is completely exempt. If she is forbidden by **a prohibition** resulting from **a mitzva** or by **a prohibition** stemming from **sanctity,**[H] as will be explained later, then since in these cases the obligation of levirate marriage is not fundamentally nullified **she performs** ***ḥalitza*** in order to become free of the levirate bond, **and** due to her prohibition **she does not enter into levirate marriage.**

אֲחוֹתָהּ שֶׁהִיא יְבִמְתָּהּ – חוֹלֶצֶת אוֹ מִתְיַיבֶּמֶת.

The Sages stated another principle: If two sisters who had been married to two brothers who subsequently died happened before the third brother for levirate marriage, and one of those sisters is a close relation to this third brother and is therefore forbidden to him, she is exempt from levirate marriage. But the other, **her sister who is her** ***yevama,***[H] i.e., her sister-in-law, **performs** ***ḥalitza*** **or enters into levirate marriage.** In this case, they are not ruled to be two sisters who happened before him simultaneously for levirate marriage, since one of them is prohibited to him as a forbidden relation, and therefore she never actually happened before him at all.

אִיסּוּר מִצְוָה: שְׁנִיּוֹת מִדִּבְרֵי סוֹפְרִים. אִיסּוּר קְדוּשָּׁה: אַלְמָנָה לְכֹהֵן גָּדוֹל, גְּרוּשָׁה וַחֲלוּצָה לְכֹהֵן הֶדְיוֹט, מַמְזֶרֶת וּנְתִינָה לְיִשְׂרָאֵל, וּבַת יִשְׂרָאֵל לְנָתִין וּמַמְזֵר.

The mishna explains: **A prohibition** resulting from **a mitzva** is referring to **secondary** forbidden **relationships,** which are prohibited **by rabbinic law.** The Sages prohibited marriage to certain women who were not forbidden by the Torah but were nevertheless deemed forbidden incestuous relations. **A prohibition** stemming from **sanctity** is referring to marriage of **a widow to a High Priest, a divorcée or a woman who has performed** ***ḥalitza*** **[*ḥalutza*] to a common priest, a daughter born from an incestuous or adulterous relationship [*mamzeret*]** or **a Gibeonite woman to an Israelite, and also an Israelite woman to a Gibeonite** or to **a son born from an incestuous or adulterous relationship [*mamzer*].**

גמ׳ כְּלָל לְאַתּוּיֵי מַאי? אָמַר רָפְרָם בַּר פַּפָּא: לְאַתּוּיֵי צָרַת אַיְלוֹנִית, וְכִדְרַב אַסִּי.

GEMARA The Gemara asks: This **principle** stated in the mishna about *yevamot*, **what** other cases does it **add?** Since the entire list of cases involving a forbidden relation was already detailed in the first chapter, what is this mishna adding? **Rafram bar Pappa said: It comes to include the** case of a **rival wife of a sexually underdeveloped woman [*aylonit*],** who is incapable of bearing children. Not only does an *aylonit* herself not enter into levirate marriage, since she is unable to give birth, but her rival wife is exempt as well. **And** this is **like** the principle **of Rav Asi,** who said that the rival wife of an *aylonit* is forbidden because the *aylonit* herself remains prohibited to the *yavam* as the wife of his brother, as she was never rendered permitted by the obligation of levirate marriage. Therefore, her rival wife is the rival wife of someone prohibited as a forbidden relation.

NOTES

That prohibition has a case where it is permitted – אִיסּוּרָא דְּאִית לֵיהּ הֶיתֵּירָא: Rashi explains that the case where the prohibition is lifted is when the *yevama* is permitted to marry her *yavam*. According to *Tosafot*, however, the Gemara here is referring to the fact that the prohibition against marrying a brother's wife is totally nullified after levirate marriage, and the *yavam* may remarry her if he divorces her (see Ritva).

HALAKHA

A prohibition resulting from a mitzva or a prohibition stemming from sanctity – אִיסּוּר מִצְוָה וְאִיסּוּר קְדוּשָּׁה: A *yevama* who is forbidden to her *yavam* by a prohibition, or as a secondary forbidden relation, must perform *ḥalitza* and may not enter into levirate marriage, as explained in the mishna (Rambam *Sefer Nashim, Hilkhot Yibbum VaḤalitza* 6:7, 10; *Shulḥan Arukh, Even HaEzer* 174:1).

Her sister who is her ***yevama*** **– אֲחוֹתָהּ שֶׁהִיא יְבִמְתָּהּ:** If two sisters happened before their *yavam* for levirate marriage and one of them was prohibited to him as a forbidden relation, he may either perform *ḥalitza* with the other or take her in levirate marriage, as stated in the mishna and explained in the Gemara (Rambam *Sefer Nashim, Hilkhot Yibbum VaḤalitza* 7:1; 10; *Shulḥan Arukh, Even HaEzer* 175:2).

וְאִיכָּא דְּאָמְרִי: "כׇּל שֶׁאִיסּוּרָהּ אִיסּוּר עֶרְוָה" הוּא דַּאֲסִירָא צָרָתָהּ, הָא לֹא אִיסּוּרָהּ אִיסּוּר עֶרְוָה – צָרָתָהּ לֹא אֲסִירָא. לְמַעוּטֵי מַאי? אֲמַר רַפְרָם: לְמַעוּטֵי צָרַת אַיְלוֹנִית, וּדְלָא כְּרַב אַסִי.

And there are those who say that Rafram bar Pappa's statement was made in a different context. It was taught in the mishna: **Whoever is forbidden** to her *yavam* **by a prohibition of forbidden relations** is completely exempt, which implies that **it is** specifically in such a case **that her rival wife is forbidden. But** any case when one wife **is not forbidden by a prohibition of forbidden relations** but is instead forbidden for some other reason, then **her rival wife is not forbidden.** This case comes **to exclude what? Rafram said: It excludes the rival wife of an *aylonit*,** who requires levirate marriage or *ḥalitza* because the *aylonit* is not prohibited as a forbidden relation.[H] **And** this statement is **not in accordance with** the opinion of **Rav Asi.**

"אֲחוֹתָהּ שֶׁהִיא יְבִמְתָּהּ". אֲחוֹתָהּ דְּמַאן? אִילֵימָא דְּאִיסּוּר מִצְוָה, כֵּיוָן דְּמִדְּאוֹרַיְיתָא רַמְיָא קַמֵּיהּ פָּגַע בַּאֲחוֹת זְקוּקָתוֹ! אֶלָּא: אֲחוֹתָהּ דְּאִיסּוּר עֶרְוָה.

The mishna states: **Her sister who is her *yevama*** performs *ḥalitza* or enters into levirate marriage. The Gemara clarifies this: **Whose sister? If we say** it is the sister of one **who is** forbidden due to a **prohibition** resulting **from a mitzva, since by Torah** law **she is cast before him** for levirate marriage, then this would in fact simply be a case of two sisters who fell simultaneously before him, both requiring levirate marriage, since according to Torah law there is no prohibition against entering into levirate marriage with such a woman. If so, it turns out that **he encounters the sister of the woman with whom he has** a levirate **bond; but** that case has already been taught. **Rather,** it must refer to **the sister of** a woman who is forbidden to him by a **prohibition of forbidden relations,** and since he may not enter into levirate marriage with a forbidden relation, her sister is not considered to be the sister of a woman with whom he has a levirate bond. Therefore, the sister may be taken in levirate marriage.

"אִיסּוּר מִצְוָה שְׁנִיּוֹת". אַמַּאי קָרֵי לֵיהּ אִיסּוּר מִצְוָה? אָמַר אַבָּיֵי: מִצְוָה לִשְׁמוֹעַ דִּבְרֵי חֲכָמִים.

The mishna states that **a prohibition** resulting **from a mitzva** is referring to **secondary** forbidden **relationships,** which are prohibited by rabbinic law. The Gemara asks: **Why is this called a prohibition** resulting **from a mitzva? Abaye said:** This is because **it is a mitzva to listen to** and obey **the words of the Sages.**[N]

"אִיסּוּר קְדוּשָּׁה אַלְמָנָה לְכֹהֵן גָּדוֹל גְּרוּשָׁה וַחֲלוּצָה לְכֹהֵן הֶדְיוֹט", וְאַמַּאי קָרֵי לְהוּ אִיסּוּר קְדוּשָּׁה? דִּכְתִיב "קְדוֹשִׁים יִהְיוּ לֵאלֹהֵיהֶם".

The mishna states: **A prohibition** stemming from **sanctity** is referring to a marriage of **a widow to a High Priest, a divorcée or a *ḥalutza* to a common priest.** The Gemara asks: **Why are these called a prohibition** stemming from **sanctity? As it is written** with regard to the priests: **"They shall be sacred**[N] **to their God…** they shall not take a woman that is a harlot, or profaned; neither shall they take a woman divorced by her husband" (Leviticus 21:6–7).

תַּנְיָא, רַבִּי יְהוּדָה מַחֲלִיף: אִיסּוּר מִצְוָה – אַלְמָנָה לְכֹהֵן גָּדוֹל, גְּרוּשָׁה וַחֲלוּצָה לְכֹהֵן הֶדְיוֹט. וְאַמַּאי קָרֵי לֵיהּ אִיסּוּר מִצְוָה? דִּכְתִיב "אֵלֶּה הַמִּצְוֹת".

It is taught in a *baraita*: **Rabbi Yehuda switches** the terms: **A prohibition** resulting **from a mitzva** is referring to **a widow to the High Priest,** or **a divorcée or a *ḥalutza* to a common priest. And why is this called a prohibition** resulting **from a mitzva? As it is written** in summarization at the end of Leviticus: **"These are the *mitzvot*** that the Lord commanded Moses for the children of Israel in Mount Sinai" (Leviticus 27:34).

HALAKHA

The rival wife of a sexually underdeveloped woman [*aylonit*], etc. – צָרַת אַיְלוֹנִית: If the two wives of one man fall before his brother for levirate marriage and one of them is an *aylonit*, then her rival wife may either perform *ḥalitza* or enter into levirate marriage. This is in accordance with the opinion cited in the Gemara as: And there are those who say, and contrary to the opinion of Rav Asi (Rambam *Sefer Nashim, Hilkhot Yibbum VaḤalitza* 6:20; *Shulḥan Arukh, Even HaEzer* 172:1).

NOTES

It is a mitzva to listen to the words of the Sages – מִצְוָה לִשְׁמוֹעַ דִּבְרֵי חֲכָמִים: The *Nimmukei Yosef* notes that this mitzva is explicit in the Torah: "And you shall come…to the judge that shall be in those days…and you shall act according to the tenor of the sentence, which they shall declare…do not turn aside from the sentence that they shall declare" (Deuteronomy 17:9–11).

A prohibition stemming from sanctity…they shall be sacred, etc. – אִיסּוּר קְדוּשָּׁה...קְדוֹשִׁים יִהְיוּ וכו׳: The Rivan adds that although this verse refers specifically to priests, there is another verse that refers to Israelites: "Sanctify yourselves and be holy" (Leviticus 20:7). From here it is derived that there are prohibitions stemming from sanctity for Israelites as well, which are those forbidden sexual relations that are pertinent to them.

Some commentaries point out that included among those relationships enumerated as prohibitions due to sanctity is a woman who has performed *ḥalitza* [*ḥalutza*] marrying a priest, which is prohibited by rabbinic law, and a Gibeonite woman marrying an Israelite, which according to many opinions is also prohibited by rabbinic law and not by Torah law. Some commentaries explain that since these women are prohibited to all Jews these relationships can be called prohibitions due to sanctity, and the prohibition in these cases is unlike the safeguards established by the Sages, e.g., secondary forbidden relations (*Yosef Lekaḥ*).

NOTES

Whoever fulfills the words of the Sages – כָּל הַמְקַיֵּים דִּבְרֵי חֲכָמִים: The Rivan writes that this is alluded to in the verse: "And it shall come to pass that he that is left in Zion, and he that remains in Jerusalem, shall be called sacred" (Isaiah 4:3).

You must sanctify yourself by refraining from that which is permitted to you – קַדֵּשׁ עַצְמְךָ בַּמּוּתָּר לָךְ: The Ramban explains that this is the true meaning of the mitzva: "You shall be sacred" (Leviticus 19:2). Sanctity requires one to refrain from even that which the Torah permitted. The Ramban explains that it is possible for one to be vile without violating any other explicit Torah prohibitions. The Torah does not limit how much one may eat or how frequently one may engage in intercourse; a hedonist could spend all his time indulging in sensual pleasures. Therefore the Torah stressed: "You shall be sacred" (see Rashi on *Sanhedrin* 53a; Ritva).

HALAKHA

A widow to a High Priest – אַלְמָנָה לְכֹהֵן גָּדוֹל: If the brother of a High Priest dies childless and leaves a widow, even a widow from betrothal, then she must perform *ḥalitza* and not enter into levirate marriage. If he engages in intercourse with her, her rival wife is not exempt from *ḥalitza* (Rambam *Sefer Nashim, Hilkhot Yibbum VaḤalitza* 6:11 and *Sefer Kedusha, Hilkhot Issurei Bia* 17:12).

אִיסּוּר קְדוּשָּׁה – ״שְׁנִיּוֹת מִדִּבְרֵי סוֹפְרִים״, וְאַמַּאי קָרֵי לֵיהּ אִיסּוּר קְדוּשָּׁה? אֲמַר אַבַּיֵי: כׇּל הַמְקַיֵּים דִּבְרֵי חֲכָמִים נִקְרָא קָדוֹשׁ. אֲמַר לֵיהּ רָבָא: וְכׇל שֶׁאֵינוֹ מְקַיֵּים דִּבְרֵי חֲכָמִים, קָדוֹשׁ הוּא דְּלָא מִיקְּרֵי, רָשָׁע נַמִי לָא מִיקְּרֵי?! אֶלָּא אָמַר רָבָא: קַדֵּשׁ עַצְמְךָ בַּמּוּתָּר לָךְ.

A prohibition stemming from **sanctity** is referring to **secondary relationships** forbidden **by rabbinic law. And why is this called a prohibition** stemming from **sanctity? Abaye said: Whoever fulfills the words of the Sages**[N] **is called sacred. Rava said to him:** The language you use is not precise, since if so, **whoever does not fulfill the words of the Sages is not called sacred,** which implies that **he is also not called wicked.** However, anyone who transgresses the words of the Sages is in fact referred to as wicked. **Rather, Rava said** that the reason why this is called a prohibition stemming from sanctity is that the term sanctity indicates differentiation or separation, and there is a principle that **you must sanctify yourself** by refraining from that **which is permitted to you**[N] by Torah law. The Sages decreed against secondary forbidden relations so that one would not eventually come to transgress Torah law.

״אַלְמָנָה לְכֹהֵן גָּדוֹל״. קָפְסֵיק וְתָנֵי, לָא שְׁנָא מִן הַנִּשּׂוּאִין וְלָא שְׁנָא מִן הָאֵירוּסִין.

The mishna states that the levirate bond of **a widow to a High Priest**[H] requires her to perform *ḥalitza*, and she may not enter into levirate marriage. The Gemara comments: The *halakha* that a widow does not enter into levirate marriage with a High Priest is **taught categorically,** merely in a general manner. **It is no different** whether she is a widow **from marriage or** she is a widow **from betrothal** alone.

בִּשְׁלָמָא מִן הַנִּשּׂוּאִין – עֲשֵׂה וְלֹא תַעֲשֶׂה, וְאֵין עֲשֵׂה דּוֹחֶה לֹא תַעֲשֶׂה וַעֲשֵׂה. אֶלָּא מִן הָאֵירוּסִין, לֹא תַעֲשֶׂה גְּרֵידָא הוּא, יָבֹא עֲשֵׂה וְיִדְחֶה לֹא תַעֲשֶׂה!

Granted, she certainly may not enter into levirate marriage if she is a widow **from marriage,** since she is forbidden to the High Priest by the **positive mitzva** stated in the verse: "And he shall take a wife in her virginity" (Leviticus 21:13), **and** by the **prohibition** stated in the verse: "A widow, or one divorced…these he shall not take" (Leviticus 21:14). **And a positive mitzva,** levirate marriage, **does not override** both a **prohibition,** not marrying a widow, **and a positive mitzva,** marrying a virgin, together. **However,** if she is a widow **from betrothal,** then **there is only a prohibition,** as she is still a virgin. In that case, why not say that **the positive mitzva** of levirate marriage should **come and override the prohibition** against marrying a widow from betrothal?

אֲמַר רַב גִּידֵּל אֲמַר רַב: אָמַר קְרָא ״וְעָלְתָה יְבִמְתּוֹ הַשַּׁעְרָה״ שֶׁאֵין תַּלְמוּד לוֹמַר ״יְבִמְתּוֹ״, מַה תַּלְמוּד לוֹמַר יְבִמְתּוֹ – יֵשׁ לָךְ יְבָמָה אַחַת שֶׁעוֹלָה לַחֲלִיצָה וְאֵינָהּ עוֹלָה לְיִיבּוּם. וְאֵיזוֹ – זוֹ חַיָּיבֵי לָאוִין.

Rav Giddel said that **Rav said** in response: **The verse states: "His *yevama* shall ascend to the gate** to the Elders and say: My brother-in-law refused to establish a name for his brother in Israel, he did not wish to consummate the levirate marriage" (Deuteronomy 25:7). **As** there is **no need** for **the verse to state: "His *yevama*,"** since it is clear to whom the verse refers and no new information is added by this word, **what** is the meaning when **the verse states: "His *yevama*"?** It comes to teach that **there is one *yevama* who ascends for *ḥalitza* but may not ascend for levirate marriage,** and her brother-in-law is not given a choice. **Who is this? This is** a woman with whom it is prohibited for her *yavam* to enter into levirate marriage, as he would be **liable** for the violation of a **prohibition,** and the positive mitzva of levirate marriage does not override the prohibition.

וְאֵימָא חַיָּיבֵי כָּרֵיתוֹת! אֲמַר קְרָא ״וְאִם לֹא יַחְפּוֹץ הָאִישׁ לָקַחַת״ הָא חָפֵץ – מְיַיבֵּם, כׇּל הָעוֹלָה לְיִיבּוּם עוֹלָה לַחֲלִיצָה וְכׇל שֶׁאֵין עוֹלָה לְיִיבּוּם – אֵינוֹ עוֹלָה לַחֲלִיצָה.

The Gemara asks: **Say** that this is referring to **those** women who are forbidden and would be **liable** to receive the penalty of *karet* as well, i.e., that these too may not enter into levirate marriage but nevertheless require *ḥalitza*. The Gemara answers: **The verse states: "And if the man does not wish to take** his *yevama*" (Deuteronomy 25:7). This **implies** that if **he wishes, he takes her in levirate marriage;** it depends upon his wishes. However, **one who is eligible for levirate marriage is eligible for *ḥalitza*. And** conversely, **one who is ineligible for levirate marriage is ineligible for *ḥalitza*** and therefore does not require *ḥalitza* at all. Since those relations that carry a penalty of *karet* have no possibility of entering into levirate marriage, they do not require *ḥalitza* either.

אִי הָכִי, חַיָּיבֵי לָאוִין נַמִי! הָא רַבֵּי רַחֲמָנָא ״יְבִמְתּוֹ״. וּמָה רָאִיתָ?

The Gemara asks: **If so, those** relations who are forbidden as he would be **liable** for the violation of **a** standard **prohibition** also should not require *ḥalitza*, as they may not enter into levirate marriage. The Gemara answers: **But the Merciful One included** one category of *yevama* who is eligible for *ḥalitza* alone and not levirate marriage through the term: **"His *yevama*."** The Gemara asks: **And what did you see** to conclude that the additional term is referring to relations who are forbidden and with whom he would be liable for the violation of a prohibition and not those who are liable to receive *karet*?

מִסְתַּבְּרָא, חַיָּיבֵי לָאוִין תָּפְסִי בְּהוּ קִדּוּשִׁין, חַיָּיבֵי כָּרֵיתוֹת לָא תָּפְסִי בְּהוּ קִדּוּשִׁין.

The Gemara answers: That **stands to reason,** since **betrothal takes effect** with those women who are forbidden and with whom he would be **liable** for the violation of **a prohibition.**[N] That is, if a man betroths a woman who is forbidden to him and with whom he would be liable for the violation of a prohibition, then although he violates a prohibition in doing so, the betrothal is valid and cannot be ended without a bill of divorce. Therefore, such a woman also requires *ḥalitza*. In contrast, **betrothal does not take effect** at all with **those** who are forbidden and would be **liable** to receive the punishment of ***karet***, and therefore in these cases the laws of levirate marriage and *ḥalitza* do not apply at all.

מְתִיב רָבָא: אִיסּוּר מִצְוָה וְאִיסּוּר קְדוּשָּׁה, בָּא עָלֶיהָ אוֹ חָלַץ לָהּ – נִפְטְרָה צָרָתָהּ. וְאִי סָלְקָא דַּעְתָּךְ חַיָּיבֵי לָאוִין מִדְּאוֹרַיְיתָא לַחֲלִיצָה רַמְיָא, לְיִיבּוּם לָא רַמְיָא – כִּי בָּא עָלֶיהָ אַמַּאי נִפְטְרָה צָרָתָהּ?

Rava raised an objection to the explanation of Rav: It is taught in a *baraita* with regard to **a prohibition** resulting from **a mitzva and a prohibition** stemming from **sanctity** that **if he engages in intercourse with** such a woman[H] **or performs *ḥalitza* with her,**[H] **her rival wife is exempt,** even though it was prohibited for him to have engaged in intercourse with her in the first place. **If it enters your mind** that women who are forbidden, as he would be **liable** for the violation of **a prohibition, require *ḥalitza*** by Torah law **but do not require levirate marriage,** then **when he engages in intercourse with** his *yevama* **why is her rival wife exempt?** If there is no biblical mitzva to engage in intercourse with her, his action would carry no halakhic validity and the rival wife should not be exempt.

הוּא מוֹתִיב לָהּ וְהוּא מְפָרֵק לָהּ: לִצְדָדִין קָתָנֵי, בָּא עָלֶיהָ – אַאִיסּוּר מִצְוָה, חָלַץ לָהּ – אַאִיסּוּר קְדוּשָּׁה.

Rava **raised the objection and he resolved it:** The *baraita* **teaches it disjunctively;** it did not all deal with the same case. When the *baraita* says: **Engages in intercourse with her,** it is referring **to a prohibition** resulting from **a mitzva.** If one engages in intercourse with a *yevama* prohibited to him by rabbinic law, since by Torah law levirate marriage with her is valid, then although his act involved the transgression of a rabbinic decree, he nevertheless fulfilled the Torah mitzva and the rival wife is thereby exempt. When the *baraita* says: **Performs *ḥalitza* with her, it is referring to a prohibition** stemming from **sanctity,** and by Torah law there is no option of levirate marriage because of the prohibited relation; therefore, only *ḥalitza* exempts her rival wife.

מְתִיב רָבָא: פְּצוּעַ דַּכָּא וּכְרוּת שָׁפְכָה, סְרִיס אָדָם וְהַזָּקֵן – אוֹ חוֹלְצִין אוֹ מְיַיבְּמִין. כֵּיצַד? מֵתוּ, וְלָהֶם אַחִים וְלָהֶם נָשִׁים, וְעָמְדוּ אַחִין וְעָשׂוּ מַאֲמָר בִּנְשׁוֹתֵיהֶן, וְנָתְנוּ גֵּט, וְחָלְצוּ, מַה שֶּׁעָשׂוּ עָשׂוּ, וְאִם בְּעָלוּ קָנוּ.

Rava raised an objection from that which was taught in the *Tosefta* (*Yevamot* 11:3): **A man with crushed testicles**[H] or with other wounds to his genitals **or one whose penis has been severed, one who is a eunuch**[H] caused **by man** and not from birth or by disease, or **an elderly man,**[H] all of whom are incapable of fathering children, **one either performs *ḥalitza* or levirate marriage. How so?** If any of these infertile men **died, and they had brothers and they** also **had wives,** and they then died childless, **and the brothers proceeded to perform levirate betrothal with their wives, or gave them a bill of divorce, or performed *ḥalitza*, whatever they did is done;** i.e., their act was effective. **And if** any one of the brothers **engaged in intercourse** with the widow of one of those infertile men, he thereby **acquired** the woman as a wife according to the laws of levirate marriage.

HALAKHA

Intercourse with one's *yevama* who is prohibited due to a mitzva or sanctity – הַבָּא עַל יְבִמְתּוֹ אִיסּוּר מִצְוָה וְאִיסּוּר קְדוּשָּׁה: In cases where a *yevama* is forbidden to her *yavam* due to a prohibition or a positive mitzva, or where she is a secondary relation forbidden by rabbinic law, if he transgressed and engaged in intercourse with her she is considered married to him for all purposes; he must divorce her with a bill of divorce, and her rival wife is exempt from levirate marriage and *ḥalitza* (Rambam *Sefer Nashim, Hilkhot Yibbum VaḤalitza* 6:10; *Arukh HaShulḥan, Even HaEzer* 174:8).

One who performs *ḥalitza* with a *yevama* who is prohibited due to a mitzva or sanctity – הַחוֹלֵץ לְאִיסּוּר מִצְוָה וּקְדוּשָּׁה: In a case where two women were married to a brother and one of them was forbidden to her *yavam* by a prohibition or positive mitzva or by being a secondary forbidden relation, if he performs *ḥalitza* with this forbidden woman, then her rival wife is not exempt from levirate marriage or *ḥalitza* (Rambam *Sefer Nashim, Hilkhot Yibbum VaḤalitza* 7:10). However, in the opinion of the *Halakhot Gedolot* and many others, if he wishes to perform levirate marriage he should do so with the woman who is permitted to him, and if he wishes to perform *ḥalitza* he should do so with the woman who is forbidden to him, and her rival wife is thereby exempt; *Shulḥan Arukh, Even HaEzer* 170:18, 174:1).

The wife of a man with crushed testicles – אֵשֶׁת פְּצוּעַ דַּכָּא: If a woman had been prohibited to marry her husband due to a positive mitzva or prohibition, e.g., if he had been castrated by a person, etc., but this prohibition does not apply to her *yavam*, then she is permitted to enter into levirate marriage (Rambam *Sefer Nashim, Hilkhot Yibbum VaḤalitza* 6:13; *Shulḥan Arukh, Even HaEzer* 174:2).

A *yavam* who is a eunuch – יָבָם סָרִיס: If a woman falls for levirate marriage before one who was castrated by a person but who had previously been fit to marry, then he must perform *ḥalitza* and may not take her in levirate marriage, as he is prohibited from entering into the congregation, i.e., marrying a Jew. If he transgressed and engaged in intercourse with her he acquires her as his wife, but he must divorce her with a bill of divorce (Rambam *Sefer Nashim, Hilkhot Yibbum VaḤalitza* 6:4; *Shulḥan Arukh, Even HaEzer* 172:3).

An elderly man – הַזָּקֵן: The Rambam states that if the *yavam* is elderly then he should not take the woman in levirate marriage but rather should perform *ḥalitza* (*Sefer Nashim, Hilkhot Yibbum VaḤalitza* 6:4). However, most authorities hold differently, and this ruling does not appear in the *Shulḥan Arukh*.

NOTES

Betrothal takes effect with those women who are forbidden, and with whom he would be liable for the violation of a prohibition – חַיָּיבֵי לָאוִין תָּפְסִי בְּהוּ קִדּוּשִׁין: Rashi explains that the inference connecting betrothal to levirate marriage is from the term "to take" in the verse: "And if the man does not wish to take his *yevama*" (Deuteronomy 25:7), which means taking in marriage. Marriage, even through intercourse, is not valid in cases where one would be liable to receive *karet* for marrying such a woman and is therefore not considered taking in marriage. However, in the case of relations forbidden by a standard prohibition, although one transgresses Torah law, the betrothal nevertheless comes into effect and they are considered married for all purposes (see Rashba and Ritva).

מתו אחים, ועמדו הם ועשו מאמר בנשותיהן, ונתנו גט, או שחלצו – מה שעשו עשו. ואם בעלו – קנו ואסור לקיימן, משום שנאמר "לא יבא פצוע דכא". ואי סלקא דעתך חייבי לאוין מדאורייתא לחליצה רמיא, לייבום לא רמיא, אם בעלו – אמאי קנו?

The inverse is also true: If **the brothers died** childless, **and** the infertile men **proceeded to perform levirate betrothal with their wives,** or **gave a bill of divorce, or performed *ḥalitza*, whatever they did is done** and took effect. **And if they engaged in intercourse** with their *yevama*, **they** thereby **acquired** the *yevama* as their wife. However, **it is forbidden to maintain them,** i.e., allow them to continue to live as husband and wife, **because it is stated: "One with crushed testicles** or whose penis has been severed shall not enter into the assembly of the Lord" (Deuteronomy 23:2); they are prohibited from entering the congregation, i.e., marrying a Jew. **And if it enters your mind** that women who are forbidden, as he would be **liable** for the violation **a prohibition, require *ḥalitza*** by **Torah** law **but do not require levirate marriage, then** one could ask: **if they engaged in intercourse why are they acquired** as wives even though there would be no mitzva of levirate marriage because the men are prohibited from marrying them?

אלא אמר רבא: אלמנה מן האירוסין נמי עשה ולא תעשה הוא, דכתיב "קדושים יהיו לאלהיהם".

Rather, Rav's opinion is rejected, and **Rava said** an alternative explanation: The reason why a High Priest does not take **a widow from betrothal** in levirate marriage is because that relationship is **also** a violation of both **a positive mitzva and a prohibition** and therefore a different positive mitzva does not override it. How so? **As it is written: "They shall be sacred to their God"** (Leviticus 21:6), which teaches that there is a positive mitzva of sanctity associated with all prohibitions applying to priests. Therefore, any such prohibition contains both a positive and a negative mitzva.

ממזרת ונתינה מאי איכא למימר? כתיב "והתקדשתם"

The Gemara asks: This resolves the issue of priestly prohibitions, but **what is there to say** about **a daughter born from an incestuous or adulterous relationship [*mamzeret*] or a Gibeonite woman,** who are prohibited from entering the congregation due to considerations of sanctity? They too may not enter into levirate marriage despite the positive mitzva, which would ordinarily override a prohibition. The Gemara answers: **It is written** with regard to all of the mitzvot: **"Sanctify yourselves,** therefore, and be sacred" (Leviticus 11:44). This teaches that in addition to the prohibition, there is the positive mitzva of sanctity.

אי הכי, כל התורה כולה נמי עשה ולא תעשה הוא, דכתיב "והתקדשתם"! אלא אמר רבא: גזירה אלמנה מן האירוסין אטו אלמנה מן הנשואין.

The Gemara raises an objection: **If so,** then every single prohibition in **the entire Torah** contains both **a positive mitzva and a prohibition, as it is written: "Sanctify yourselves"** (Leviticus 11:44). **Rather,** this reasoning must be rejected, and **Rava stated** a different reason: While in essence the mitzva of levirate marriage does apply here, nevertheless, **a widow from betrothal** is prohibited from entering into levirate marriage with the High Priest **by** rabbinic **decree, due to** the case of **a widow from marriage.**

ממזרת ונתינה מאי איכא למימר? גזירה במקום מצוה אטו שלא במקום מצוה.

The Gemara asks: **What is there to say** about the case of **a *mamzeret* or a Gibeonite woman?** There appears to be no reason for a rabbinic decree in such cases. The Gemara answers: There, one must say that intercourse with a *mamzeret* even **when the mitzva** of levirate marriage **applies** was prohibited by rabbinic **decree due to** cases **when the mitzva** of levirate marriage **does not apply.** The decree was issued lest one come to think that since in the case of levirate marriage a *mamzeret* is permitted, even in cases when there is no levirate marriage a *mamzeret* is similarly permitted.

אלא מעתה, אשת אחיו מאביו לא תתייבם, גזירה משום אשת אחיו מאמו! ייבום בנחלה תלא רחמנא, מידע ידיע.

The Gemara asks: **However, if** that **is so,** and the levirate marriage is prohibited lest it become confused with another case, then **the wife of a paternal brother**[N] **should not enter into levirate marriage;** i.e., by the same logic, although the Torah allowed it, the Sages should have established a **rabbinic decree** requiring that she perform *ḥalitza* **due to** the case of **the wife of a maternal brother,** who always remains prohibited as a brother's wife. The Gemara answers: **The Merciful One made levirate marriage dependent upon inheritance,** and it **is well known** by everyone that only patrilineal relatives inherit, so there is no likelihood of confusion.

NOTES

However, if that is so, the wife of a paternal brother, etc. – **אלא מעתה, אשת אחיו מאביו וכו׳**: *Tosafot* explain this section as not referring to typical cases, as that would undermine the entire concept of levirate marriage. Rather, it is referring to particular examples, each of which is similar enough to the topic of the Gemara that it might deserve a rabbinic decree (see Ritva and *Tosafot Yeshanim*). The Ramban sees this explanation as far-fetched and objects on various grounds. He holds that the Gemara must be understood in a straightforward manner, and that the purpose of these challenges is to illustrate the absurdity of issuing a rabbinic decree to defer the mitzva of levirate marriage in favor of *ḥalitza*.

אִשָּׁה שֶׁאֵין לָהּ בָּנִים לֹא תִּתְיַיבֵּם, גְּזֵירָה מִשּׁוּם אִשָּׁה שֶׁיֵּשׁ לָהּ בָּנִים! בְּבָנִים תְּלָא רַחֲמָנָא, מֵידַע יְדִיעַ.

The Gemara objects further: Then **a childless woman should not enter into levirate marriage** even though the mitzva applies to her; there should be a rabbinic **decree due to** the case of **a woman who has children.** The Gemara answers: **The Merciful One made levirate marriage dependent upon children;** it **is well known** by everyone that the entire purpose of levirate marriage is to establish one's brother's name and that levirate marriage applies only when there are no children. Here, too, there is no likelihood of error.

אֵשֶׁת אָחִיו שֶׁהָיָה בְּעוֹלָמוֹ לֹא תִּתְיַיבֵּם, גְּזֵירָה מִשּׁוּם אֵשֶׁת אָחִיו שֶׁלֹּא הָיָה בְּעוֹלָמוֹ! בִּישִׁיבָה תְּלָא רַחֲמָנָא, מֵידַע יְדִיעַ.

The Gemara challenges further: **The wife of a brother with whom one did coexist should not enter into levirate marriage;** there should be a rabbinic **decree due to** the case of **the wife of a brother with whom he did not coexist.** The Gemara responds: **The Merciful One made levirate marriage dependent upon** a common **dwelling** together and coexistence of brothers, and this **is well known** by everyone since the matter is explicit in the Torah.

כָּל הַנָּשִׁים לֹא תִּתְיַיבֵּמְנָה, גְּזֵירָה מִשּׁוּם אַיְלוֹנִית! לָא שְׁכִיחָא. מַמְזֶרֶת וּנְתִינָה נַמִי לָא שְׁכִיחָא!

The Gemara continues to object: **No woman should enter into levirate marriage;** there should be a rabbinic **decree due to** the case of **an *aylonit*.** Since an *aylonit* may not enter into levirate marriage, all other women should be prohibited by rabbinic decree from doing so to avoid confusion. The Gemara answers: The case of an *aylonit* is **not commonplace,** and the Sages did not institute rabbinic decrees on matters that are not common. The Gemara asks: If so, **neither a *mamzeret* nor a Gibeonite woman is commonplace either.** Therefore, since the likelihood of taking a *mamzeret* in levirate marriage is so small, there is no danger that one might think it is permitted to marry a *mamzeret* even where the mitzva does not apply.

אֶלָּא אֲמַר רָבָא: גְּזֵרָה בִּיאָה רִאשׁוֹנָה אַטּוּ בִּיאָה שְׁנִיָּה.

Rather, Rava said that it is necessary to reject the previous suggestion and to offer a different reason: **The first** act of **intercourse** is prohibited by rabbinic **decree**[H] **due to** the likelihood of **a second** act of **intercourse.** Although intercourse the first time with the *yevama* is the fulfillment of a positive mitzva, which does override the prohibition, once the mitzva is fulfilled with that act there is no longer any positive mitzva involved. Afterward, this *yevama* becomes prohibited because there is no longer a positive mitzva to override the prohibition. Therefore, due to the possibility that one might engage in intercourse a second time with this woman, the Sages decreed that even the first act is prohibited.

תַּנְיָא נַמִי הָכִי: אִם בָּעֲלוּ – קָנוּ בְּבִיאָה רִאשׁוֹנָה, וְאָסוּר לְקַיְּימָן בְּבִיאָה שְׁנִיָּה.

The Gemara comments: **This is also taught** in a *baraita*: **If** one of those *yevamin* who may not marry their *yevama* due to a prohibition **engaged in intercourse** with her, **he acquired** her **with the first** act of **intercourse; however, it is prohibited to retain her for a second act of intercourse.**

הֲדַר אֲמַר רָבָא, וְאִיתֵּימָא רַב אַשִׁי: לָאו מִילְּתָא הִיא דַּאֲמַרִי, דְּאָמַר רֵישׁ לָקִישׁ: כָּל מָקוֹם שֶׁאַתָּה מוֹצֵא עֲשֵׂה וְלֹא תַעֲשֶׂה, אִם אַתָּה יָכוֹל לְקַיֵּים שְׁנֵיהֶם מוּטָב, וְאִם לָאו יָבֹא עֲשֵׂה וְיִדְחֶה אֶת לֹא תַעֲשֶׂה, הָכָא נַמִי אֶפְשָׁר בַּחֲלִיצָה דִּמְקַיֵּים עֲשֵׂה וְלֹא תַעֲשֶׂה.

The Gemara continues with a retraction from Rava: **Rava then said, and some say** it was actually **Rav Ashi** who said: **That which I said,** that the reason for the rabbinic decree was to prevent a second act of intercourse, **is not correct,** as there is a simpler explanation. **As Reish Lakish said** about the same matter: **In every place that you find a positive mitzva and a prohibition**[H] applying to the same matter, **if you can fulfill both of them** together, **this is best,** and the positive mitzva does not override the prohibition. **And if** there is **not** any possibility of fulfilling both, then **let the positive mitzva come and override the prohibition. Here, too,** in the case of levirate marriage, **it is possible, by way of *ḥalitza*, to fulfill the positive mitzva and** not to transgress **the prohibition** prohibiting marriage to these women.

מֵיתִיבִי: וְאִם בָּעֲלוּ קָנוּ! תְּיוּבְתָּא.

The Gemara **raises an objection** to this last statement by Rava from that which is taught in a *baraita*: **And if** one of those *yevamin* **engaged in intercourse,**[N] **he acquired** her as a wife. This shows that although it is possible to perform the mitzva by way of *ḥalitza*, if he nevertheless performs levirate marriage then the positive mitzva overrides the prohibition and the *yevama* is thereby acquired as his wife. The Gemara concludes: This is **a conclusive refutation,** and Rava's last explanation is rejected. The previous explanation is the correct one: The prohibition is due to rabbinic decree.

HALAKHA

The first act of intercourse is prohibited by rabbinic decree – גְּזֵירָה בִּיאָה רִאשׁוֹנָה וכו׳: Although the *halakhot* of levirate marriage apply to a woman whom one is prohibited from marrying due to a positive mitzva or a prohibition, the Sages decreed that she should not be taken in levirate marriage. They prohibited the first act of intercourse, which fulfills a mitzva, due to the second act, which involves a prohibition and no mitzva. Therefore, one who transgressed and engaged in intercourse with a *yevama* who was forbidden to him fully acquired her as his wife. However, he must divorce her with a bill of divorce, in accordance with the opinion of Rava (Rambam *Sefer Nashim, Hilkhot Yibbum VaḤalitza* 6:10; *Shulḥan Arukh, Even HaEzer* 174:1).

A positive mitzva and a prohibition – עֲשֵׂה וְלֹא תַעֲשֶׂה: In every case where a positive mitzva and a prohibition contradict one another, if it is possible to find a way to fulfill both, this is best. If not, the positive mitzva overrides the negative one, in accordance with the opinion of Reish Lakish (Rambam *Sefer Ahava, Hilkhot Tzitzit* 3:6).

NOTES

The Gemara raises an objection: And if one of those *yevamin* engaged in intercourse, etc. – מֵיתִיבִי וְאִם בָּעֲלוּ וכו׳: *Tosafot* point out that Rava himself cited this *baraita* earlier and ask how it could be that he did not notice this difficulty with his own words. Some commentaries answer that for this reason the Gemara presented alternate versions attributing this *halakha* to different names, to either Rava or Rav Ashi, in order to explain that the Sage who cited the *baraita* is not the same as Rava to whom the objection was directed.

אִיתְּמַר: בִּיאַת כֹּהֵן גָּדוֹל בְּאַלְמָנָה, רַבִּי יוֹחָנָן וְרַבִּי אֶלְעָזָר: חַד אָמַר: אֵינָהּ פּוֹטֶרֶת צָרָתָהּ, וְחַד אָמַר פּוֹטֶרֶת צָרָתָהּ.

§ On the same subject, **it was stated** with regard to the case of **a High Priest who engaged in intercourse with a widow** who was his *yevama* requiring levirate marriage that the *amora'im* **Rabbi Yoḥanan and Rabbi Elazar** disputed the matter. **One said** that intercourse **does not exempt her rival wife** who had also been married to the High Priest's brother, since the act was prohibited, **and one said** that it does **exempt her rival wife**, because although intercourse was forbidden, it is nevertheless a valid enactment of levirate marriage, and so her rival wife is thereby exempt.

Perek **II**
Daf **21** Amud **a**

HALAKHA

A High Priest who engaged in intercourse with a widow from marriage – בִּיאַת כֹּהֵן גָּדוֹל בִּיבִמְתּוֹ אַלְמָנָה: If a High Priest engaged in intercourse with his *yevama* who had been widowed from marriage, her rival wife is not thereby exempt, as a positive mitzva does not override both a negative and a positive mitzva together, as the Gemara states here (Rambam *Sefer Nashim, Hilkhot Yibbum VaḤalitza* 6:11).

בְּאַלְמָנָה מִן הַנִּשּׂוּאִין כּוּלֵּי עָלְמָא לָא פְּלִיגִי דְּלָא פָּטְרָה, דְּאֵין עֲשֵׂה דּוֹחֶה לֹא תַעֲשֶׂה וַעֲשֵׂה. כִּי פְּלִיגִי – בְּאַלְמָנָה מִן הָאֵרוּסִין. מַאן דְּאָמַר פּוֹטֶרֶת, אָתֵי עֲשֵׂה וְדָחֵי אֶת לֹא תַעֲשֶׂה, וּמַאן דְּאָמַר אֵינָהּ פּוֹטֶרֶת – לָא אָתֵי עֲשֵׂה וְדָחֵי אֶת לֹא תַעֲשֶׂה, כֵּיוָן דְּאֶפְשָׁר בַּחֲלִיצָה.

As for **a widow from marriage,**[H] **everyone agrees that this does not exempt** the rival wife, **as a positive mitzva does not override a prohibition and a positive mitzva** together. **When they disagree,** it is in the case of **a widow from betrothal. The one who said that it exempts** the rival wife holds that **the positive mitzva** of levirate marriage **comes and overrides** the **prohibition** against a High Priest marrying a widow. **And the one who said that it does not exempt** the rival wife held that **a positive mitzva does not come and override a prohibition, since it is possible** to perform ***ḥalitza***.

מֵיתִיבִי: וְאִם בָּעֲלוּ – קָנוּ! תְּיוּבְתָּא.

The Gemara **raises an objection** to the opinion that the rival wife would not be exempt, from the previously cited *baraita*: **If** one of those *yevamin* **engaged in intercourse, he acquired** her as a wife. This shows that the act of levirate marriage is valid, even when prohibited. If so, in the case of the High Priest and a widow as well, her rival wife should be exempt. **This is a conclusive refutation,** and that opinion is rejected.

לֵימָא תֶּיהֱוֵי נַמִי תְּיוּבְתָּא דְּרֵישׁ לָקִישׁ! אָמַר לָךְ רֵישׁ לָקִישׁ: כִּי אָמִינָא אֲנָא – הֵיכָא דְּמִקַּיְּימִי מִצְוָה, אֲבָל הָכָא, חֲלִיצָה בִּמְקוֹם יִיבּוּם לָאו מִצְוָה הִיא.

The Gemara asks: **Shall we say that** this is **also a conclusive refutation** of the opinion of **Reish Lakish** and therefore reject his principle? The Gemara answers: **Reish Lakish** could have **said to you: When I say** that in every place that you find a positive mitzva and a prohibition applying to the same matter, if you can fulfill both of them together without transgressing the prohibition, this is best, and the positive mitzva does not override the prohibition, this is applicable only **when the mitzva is fulfilled** properly; **but here, *ḥalitza* in place of levirate marriage is not** considered a proper fulfillment of the **mitzva.**[N]

אָמַר רָבָא: רֶמֶז לִשְׁנִיּוֹת מִן הַתּוֹרָה מִנַּיִן? שֶׁנֶּאֱמַר ״כִּי אֶת כָּל הַתּוֹעֵבוֹת הָאֵל עָשׂוּ אַנְשֵׁי הָאָרֶץ״. ״הָאֵל״ קָשׁוֹת, מִכְּלָל דְּאִיכָּא רַכּוֹת, וּמַאי נִינְהוּ – שְׁנִיּוֹת.

§ **Rava said: Where** is the prohibition against **secondary** forbidden **relationships hinted at in the Torah? As it is stated** at the end of the portion discussing forbidden incestuous relations: **"For all these abominations have the men of the land done"** (Leviticus 18:27). **"These"** must be understood to mean **the harsh ones,** i.e., the severe transgressions. This proves **by inference that there are** also lesser transgressions that are, as it were, **soft ones. And what are those** soft ones? They are **secondary** forbidden **relationships.**

וּמַאי מַשְׁמַע דְּ״הָאֵל״ לִישָּׁנָא דְּקָשֶׁה הוּא? דִּכְתִיב ״וְאֶת אֵילֵי הָאָרֶץ לָקָח״.

The Gemara asks: **From where** may it **be inferred** that the word **"these"** [*ha'el*] **is an expression** meaning **harsh? As it is written: "And the mighty** [*eilei*] **of the land he took away"** (Ezekiel 17:13). The similarity of these words implies that "these" also has connotations of mighty or harsh.

NOTES

Ḥalitza in place of levirate marriage is not a mitzva – חֲלִיצָה בִּמְקוֹם יִיבּוּם לָאו מִצְוָה: In the *Yosef Lekaḥ* it is explained that *ḥalitza* is a less than ideal option; it is valid but not preferred. Therefore, the positive mitzva of *ḥalitza* is not considered perfect performance of the mitzva. The *Me'a Kesita* explains that the positive mitzva of levirate marriage is similar to a mitzva whose lack of fulfillment can be rectified by fulfillment of another mitzva, i.e., *ḥalitza*. This is similar to the idea that the positive mitzva of returning a lost item rectifies the prohibition against theft. Therefore, *ḥalitza* is equivalent in importance to levirate marriage, but only when levirate marriage is not possible. Consequently, it is not considered a mitzva when levirate marriage is possible.

לֵימָא פְּלִיגָא דְּרַבִּי לֵוִי, דְּאָמַר רַבִּי לֵוִי: קָשֶׁה עוֹנָשִׁין שֶׁל מִדּוֹת יוֹתֵר מֵעוֹנָשִׁין שֶׁל עֲרָיוֹת, שֶׁזֶּה נֶאֱמַר בָּהֶן "אֵל" וְזֶה נֶאֱמַר בָּהֶן "אֵלֶּה". "אֵל" – קָשֶׁה; "וְאֵלֶּה" – קָשֶׁה מֵ"אֵל".

The Gemara asks: **Shall we say** that this statement **contradicts** the opinion of **Rabbi Levi? As Rabbi Levi said: The harshness of the punishment for** using dishonest **measures**[H] **is more than the punishment for** transgressing the prohibition of **forbidden relationships, as** with regard to **this,** forbidden relations, it **is stated** only: **"These** [*el*]," **whereas** with regard to **that,** dishonest measures, it **is stated: "These** [*eleh*]" with an additional letter *heh* as a suffix: "For all that do these [*eleh*] things, even all that do unrighteously, are an abomination unto the Lord your God" (Deuteronomy 25:16). This implies that the word *eleh* indicates harshness and not the word *el*. The Gemara answers: This does not contradict his opinion. The word ***el*** has the connotation of **harsh, but *eleh*** has the connotation of even **harsher than *el*.**

גַּבֵּי עֲרָיוֹת נַמִי, הָא כְּתִיב "אֵלֶּה". הַהוּא לְמַעוּטֵי מִדּוֹת מִכָּרֵת.

The Gemara asks: **With regard to forbidden relationships** the word ***eleh*** **is also written:** "For whosoever shall do any of these [*eleh*] abominations, even the souls that do them shall be cut off from among their people" (Leviticus 18:29). If so, why is the punishment for using dishonest measures considered harsher? The Gemara answers: **That** expression meaning these [*eleh*] in the context of forbidden relations does not emphasize their severity; rather, it comes **to exclude** one who uses deception in **measures from** the penalty of ***karet*.**

אֶלָּא, מַאי חוּמְרַיְיהוּ? הָנֵי אֶפְשָׁר בִּתְשׁוּבָה, הָנֵי – לָא אֶפְשָׁר בִּתְשׁוּבָה.

The Gemara asks: **Rather,** in **what** way is deception in measurements more **severe** than forbidden relations? The Gemara answers: **Those** who engage in forbidden relations have the **possibility of repentance.**[N] If one engaged in relations with a forbidden relative he can rectify the sin through repentance. In the case of **those** who deceive the public with dishonest measures, **it is not possible to repent** fully because, having deceived the general public, they have no way of returning the money. Whereas generally a thief can return stolen property to its rightful owner, one who used dishonest measures with multiple customers has no way to track them all down in order to return the money.

רַב יְהוּדָה אָמַר מֵהָכָא: "וְאִזֵּן וְחִקֵּר תִּקֵּן מְשָׁלִים הַרְבֵּה" וְאָמַר עוּלָּא אָמַר רַבִּי אֶלְעָזָר: קוֹדֶם שֶׁבָּא שְׁלֹמֹה הָיְתָה תּוֹרָה דּוֹמָה לִכְפִיפָה שֶׁאֵין לָהּ אׇזְנַיִם, עַד שֶׁבָּא שְׁלֹמֹה וְעָשָׂה לָהּ אׇזְנַיִם.

Rav Yehuda said that the prohibition of secondary forbidden relationships is learned **from here:** As it says with regard to King Solomon: **"He weighed** [*izzen*] **and sought out,**[N] **and set in order many proverbs"** (Ecclesiastes 12:9), **and Ulla said** that **Rabbi Elazar said: Before Solomon came, the Torah was like a basket** [***kefifa***][B] **without handles** [***oznayim***]**, until Solomon came and made handles for it.** By means of his explanation and proverbs he enabled each person to understand and take hold of the Torah, fulfill its mitzvot, and distance himself from transgressions.

רַבִּי אוֹשַׁעְיָא אָמַר מֵהָכָא: "פְּרָעֵהוּ אַל תַּעֲבׇר בּוֹ שְׂטֵה מֵעָלָיו וַעֲבוֹר".

Rabbi Oshaya said that the prohibition of secondary forbidden relationships is learned **from here: "Avoid it, pass not by it; turn from it, and pass on"** (Proverbs 4:15). One must distance oneself from any prohibited act and not pass near a place of forbidden objects or situations.

HALAKHA

The punishment for using dishonest measures – עוֹנָשִׁין שֶׁל מִדּוֹת: The punishment for deception in weights and measures is harsher than the punishment for transgressing the prohibition against forbidden relationships, based on the opinion of Rabbi Levi (Rambam *Sefer Nezikim, Hilkhot Geneiva* 7:12; *Shulḥan Arukh, Ḥoshen Mishpat* 231:19).

BACKGROUND

Basket [*kefifa*] – כְּפִיפָה: A *kefifa* was generally made from palm leaves and was used for carrying various items. It occasionally served to hold animal feed. These baskets would have handles attached to them after they were woven.

Basket with handles that were added after the initial weaving

NOTES

Those have the possibility of repentance – הָנֵי אֶפְשָׁר בִּתְשׁוּבָה: In the *Tosafot Yeshanim* it is written that full repentance for such people is possible only if their forbidden union has not produced a *mamzer*. However, if a *mamzer* has been born, this is considered a situation described by the verse: "That which is crooked cannot be made straight" (Ecclesiastes 1:15). However, the *Tosefot HaRosh* and the Meiri explain that even if a *mamzer* is born, repentance is still possible. If, on the other hand, one deceived others about measurements, full repentance is possible only if he returns that which was stolen. Since it is impossible to return the stolen money if he deceived the general public, because the sinner does not know from whom he stole, complete repentance is impossible.

He weighed and sought out – וְאִזֵּן וְחִקֵּר: The Rivan explains that the verses were interpreted as stating that King Solomon made safeguards around the Torah, as it says: "The words of the wise are as goads…and more than them, my son, beware" (Ecclesiastes 12:11–12). That is, one must be additionally cautious beyond the words of the Torah themselves.

It would seem from this Gemara that King Solomon instituted the decree against secondary forbidden relationships (see *Tosafot*; *Tosafot Yeshanim*). Alternatively, the author of *Ramat Shmuel* explains that the Gemara here does not propose that it was Solomon who instituted this decree, but that when they made a safeguard around the words of the Torah the Sages acted in accordance with the principle that Solomon laid down.

אמר רב אשי: משל דרבי אושעיא למה הדבר דומה – לאדם משמר פרדס, משמרו מבחוץ – כולו משתמר, משמרו מבפנים – שלפניו משתמר, שלאחריו – אינו משתמר. והא דרב אשי בדותא היא: התם, שלפניו מיהא משתמר, הכא, אי לאו שניות – פגע בערוה גופה.

Rav Ashi said a parable: To what is this matter, the opinion of **Rabbi Oshaya, comparable?** It is comparable **to a man guarding an orchard;** if he **guards it from the outside, all of it is guarded.** But if **he guards it from the inside,** only **that which is in front of him** that he can see **is guarded,** while **that which is behind him is unguarded.** The Gemara comments: **And this** parable **of Rav Ashi is a mistake** [*beduta*][N] and is not accurate. **There,** in his metaphor, **that which is in front of him at least is guarded; here,** in the case of forbidden relationships, **were it not for** the rabbinic decree against **secondary** forbidden **relationships one would** eventually **encounter** and transgress **the** biblically **forbidden relationship itself.** Guarding from the outside is not only preferable, it is essential.

רב כהנא אמר מהכא: "ושמרתם את משמרתי" – עשו משמרת למשמרתי.

Rav Kahana said that the prohibition of secondary forbidden relationships is alluded to **from here,** in the verse stated at the conclusion of the verses discussing the *halakhot* of forbidden relationships: **"Therefore shall you protect** [*ushmartem*] **My prized possession** [*mishmarti*], that you do not any of these abominable customs" (Leviticus 18:30). This means: **Establish a safeguard** [*mishmeret*] **for My prized possession.**[N]

אמר ליה אביי לרב יוסף: הא – דאורייתא, היא דאורייתא ופירשו רבנן. כל התורה נמי פירשו רבנן! אלא: מדרבנן, וקרא – אסמכתא בעלמא.

Abaye said to Rav Yosef: If the prohibition against secondary forbidden relationships is learned from here **then it would be by Torah** law, yet the prohibition against secondary forbidden relationships is by rabbinic law. He answered him: The requirement to add an additional safeguard itself is in fact **by Torah law, and the Sages interpreted** and defined where and when to apply this law. Abaye objected: But isn't **all of the Torah also interpreted by the Sages** and yet has the force of Torah law? In that case, why are these laws considered to be rabbinic? **Rather,** the prohibition of secondary forbidden relationships was decreed **by rabbinic** law, **and the verse is a mere support**[B] but does not indicate a Torah law.

תנו רבנן: מה הם שניות? אם אמו, ואם אביו, ואשת אבי אביו, ואשת אבי אמו, ואשת אחי האב מן האם, ואשת אחי האם מן האב, וכלת בנו, וכלת בתו. ומותר אדם באשת חמיו ובאשת חורגו, ואסור בבת חורגו. וחורגו מותר באשתו ובתו.

§ **The Sages taught** in a *baraita*: **What are the secondary** forbidden **relationships**[B] that were prohibited? **His mother's mother, and his father's mother, and his father's father's wife,**[H] **and his mother's father's wife, and the wife of his father's maternal** half **brother, and the wife of his mother's paternal** half **brother,**[H] **and his son's daughter-in-law,**[H] **and his daughter's daughter-in-law.**[H] **A man is permitted to take his father-in-law's** former **wife,**[H] provided she is not the mother of his wife, **and his stepson's wife,**[H] if the stepson died or divorced her. **And he is prohibited from** marrying **the daughter of his stepson.**[H] **And it is permitted for one's stepson** to marry the stepfather's **wife or daughter.**[H]

NOTES

Mistake [*beduta*] – בדותא: This term appears in several places in the Talmud, usually in the context of a complete rejection of statements attributed to later *amora'im*, e.g., Rav Ashi. There are two versions of the Gemara text. According to the first version, the statement is erroneous and unfounded. In other words, Rav Ashi could never have issued this statement, and it must have been attributed to him erroneously. According to a variant reading found in several sources the word is: External [*berota*]. According to this reading, when the Sages wanted to suggest that a certain opinion was without basis, they would do so in a respectful manner, saying: It is external, indicating that it is an outside opinion and should not be introduced into the study hall (*Arukh*).

Establish a safeguard for My prized possession – עשו משמרת למשמרתי: The author of the *Sefer Halakhot Gedolot* explains that although the Sages learned from this verse that they should make safeguards around the entire Torah, the verse itself is referring to the *halakhot* of forbidden relations. For this reason they made more safeguards around the *halakhot* of forbidden relationships than any others. This is a fulfillment of the mitzva of: "You shall be sacred" (Leviticus 19:2), which the Sages interpreted to mean: Separate yourselves from forbidden relationships.

BACKGROUND

Mere support – אסמכתא בעלמא: Sometimes the Gemara states that a verse cited as the basis for a *halakha* is merely an allusion to the *halakha* rather than its actual source. In such cases, the verse is called a support for the *halakha*. Since *halakhot* of this kind are not actually derived from the biblical text, which serves instead as a mnemonic device, they are generally rabbinic decrees. This is indicated in the Talmud by the phrase: The law is rabbinic, and the verse is a mere support.

Secondary forbidden relationships – שניות: See diagram following this chapter, p. 160.

HALAKHA

His mother's mother, and his father's mother, and his father's father's wife – אם אמו, ואם אביו, ואשת אבי אביו: One's mother's mother and one's father's mother and their mothers going back all generations, as well as the wife of his father's father and the wives of his fathers going back all generations are forbidden as secondary forbidden relationships by rabbinic law (Rambam *Sefer Nashim*, *Hilkhot Ishut* 1:6; *Shulḥan Arukh*, *Even HaEzer* 15:2, 4–6).

His mother's father's wife and his uncles' wives – אשת אבי אמו ונשי דודיו: His mother's father's wife is prohibited as a secondary forbidden relationship, as are the wife of his father's maternal half brother and the wife of his mother's maternal or paternal half brother. This prohibition applies only to these women themselves and not to their progenitors or descendants in accordance with the opinion of Ze'eiri (Rambam *Sefer Nashim*, *Hilkhot Ishut* 1:6; *Shulḥan Arukh*, *Even HaEzer* 15:7–9, 18).

His son's daughter-in-law – כלת בנו: The daughter-in-law of one's son is prohibited as a secondary forbidden relationship, as is his son's son's daughter-in-law, and daughters-in-law of all later generations (Rambam *Sefer Nashim*, *Hilkhot Ishut* 1:6; *Shulḥan Arukh*, *Even HaEzer* 15:19).

His daughter's daughter-in-law – כלת בתו: The daughter-in-law of one's daughter is prohibited as a forbidden secondary relationship, but this prohibition applies only to her alone and not to her descendants (Rambam *Sefer Nashim*, *Hilkhot Ishut* 1:6; *Shulḥan Arukh*, *Even HaEzer* 15:20).

His father-in-law's wife – אשת חמיו: One's father-in-law's wife who is not his wife's mother is permitted to him (Rif), based on the conclusion in the Gemara. Some hold that she is forbidden to him (*Sefer Halakhot Gedolot*; *Tosafot*) and follow the Jerusalem Talmud, which prohibits a relationship with her because it appears like a prohibition. Due to this dispute, marriage to her should not be allowed *ab initio*, but if he takes her in marriage he need not divorce her (*Be'er Heitev* on *Shulḥan Arukh*, *Even HaEzer* 15:24).

His stepson's wife – אשת חורגו: One is permitted to marry the former wife of his stepson (*Shulḥan Arukh*, *Even HaEzer* 15:21).

The daughter of his stepson – בת חורגו: It is prohibited by Torah law to marry one's stepson's daughter, i.e., the daughter of his wife's son (*Shulḥan Arukh*, *Even HaEzer* 15:13).

It is permitted for one's stepson to marry the stepfather's… daughter – חורגו מותר...ובתו: A woman is permitted to marry her stepbrother, the son of her mother's husband by another woman. So too, a man is permitted to marry the daughter of his mother's husband by another woman, even if they grew up together in the same household, as is stated explicitly in *Sota* 43b (*Shulḥan Arukh*, *Even HaEzer* 15:11).

וְאֵשֶׁת חוֹרְגוֹ אוֹמֶרֶת לוֹ: אֲנִי מוּתֶּרֶת לְךָ, וּבִתִּי אֲסוּרָה לְךָ.

Due to these rabbinic decrees concerning stepsons, unusual situations might arise. For example: **And his stepson's wife says to** him, i.e., her husband's stepfather, **I am permitted to you, but my daughter is forbidden to you,** since she is your stepson's daughter.

בַּת חוֹרְגוֹ – דְּאוֹרַיְיתָא הִיא, דִּכְתִיב "אֶת בַּת בְּנָהּ וְאֶת בַּת בִּתָּהּ"! מִשּׁוּם דְּקָבָעֵי לְמִיתְנֵי סֵיפָא: אֵשֶׁת חוֹרְגוֹ אוֹמֶרֶת לוֹ: אֲנִי מוּתֶּרֶת לְךָ וּבִתִּי אֲסוּרָה לְךָ, וְאַף עַל גַּב דְּבִתִּי אֲסוּרָה לְךָ מִדְּאוֹרַיְיתָא – בְּדִידִי לָא גְּזוּר בֵּיהּ רַבָּנַן, תָּנָא רֵישָׁא נַמִי בַּת חוֹרְגוֹ.

The Gemara challenges that which is stated in the *baraita*: **His stepson's daughter** is not a secondary relation by rabbinic law. **She is** forbidden **by Torah** law, since the daughter of his stepson is the daughter of his wife's son, **as it is written:** "You shall not take **her son's daughter or her daughter's daughter**" (Leviticus 18:17). The Gemara answers: This case was included **because** the *baraita* **wanted to teach the latter clause,** which states: **His stepson's wife says to him: I am permitted to you, but my daughter is forbidden to you. And although my daughter is forbidden to you by Torah** law, nevertheless **the Sages did not issue a decree** forbidding **me.** Therefore, the case of **his stepson's daughter was also taught in the first clause,** even though she is forbidden by Torah law and is not a secondary relation.

אִי הָכִי, אֵשֶׁת חָמִיו נַמִי תֵּימָא: אֲנִי מוּתֶּרֶת לְךָ וּבִתִּי אֲסוּרָה לְךָ, דְּהָוְיָא אֲחוֹת אִשְׁתּוֹ! הָא – פְּסִיקָא לֵיהּ, הָא – לָא פְּסִיקָא לֵיהּ.

The Gemara raises an objection: **If so,** that the *baraita* wished to teach this peculiarity, then why did it not teach: **His father-in-law's wife also says: I am permitted to you and my daughter is forbidden to you, as she is his wife's sister.** The Gemara answers: **This** matter **is conclusive for him.** In other words, his stepson's wife is forever permitted and his stepson's daughter is always forbidden to him. But as for the matter of his father-in-law's wife's daughter, **this is not conclusive for him.** This ruling is not final and might change, since if his wife dies her sister is permitted to him.

אָמַר רַב: אַרְבַּע נָשִׁים יֵשׁ לָהֶן הֶפְסֵק. נָקֵיט רַב בִּידֵיהּ תְּלָת: אֵשֶׁת אֲחִי הָאֵם מִן הָאָב, וְאֵשֶׁת אֲחִי הָאָב מִן הָאֵם, וְכַלָּתוֹ. וּזְעֵירִי מוֹסִיף אַף אֵשֶׁת אֲבִי אִמּוֹ. אָמַר רַב נַחְמָן בַּר יִצְחָק, וְסִימָנִיךְ: דְּעִילָּאֵי דְּרַב.

Rav said that he received a tradition with regard to secondary forbidden relationships that **four women have a conclusion;**[H] i.e., the prohibition does not continue to later generations but applies only to those women who were mentioned explicitly. **Rav held three** of them **in his hand;** he knew with certainty three of the four categories. They were: **The wife of his mother's paternal** half **brother, and the wife of his father's maternal** half **brother, and his daughter-in-law. And Ze'eiri adds: Also the wife of his mother's father. Rav Naḥman bar Yitzḥak said: And your mnemonic** for remembering who said what is as follows: Ze'eiri adds an extra generation **on top** of the prohibitions **of Rav,**[N] i.e., the wife of his mother's father, which Rav did not mention.

וְרַב, מַאי טַעֲמָא לָא חָשֵׁיב לֵיהּ? מִיחַלְּפָא לֵיהּ בְּאֵשֶׁת אֲבִי אָבִיו.

The Gemara asks: **And what is the reason** that **Rav did not reckon this** category mentioned by Ze'eiri to be among those who have a conclusion? The Gemara answers: In his opinion, this category might be mistakenly **switched with** the category of **the wife of his father's father,** which does not have a conclusion. With regard to the wife of his father, the prohibition applies equally to the wife of all ancestors in the father's line. Therefore, according to Rav, the Sages also included the ancestors of the mother's father's wife as secondary forbidden relationships.

וּזְעֵירִי: לְהָתָם שְׁכִיחַ וְאָזֵיל, לְהָכָא – לָא שְׁכִיחַ וְאָזֵיל.

The Gemara asks: **And** why is **Ze'eiri** not concerned that the two categories will become confused? The Gemara answers: **He is** often **found there,** in his father's father's home, **and goes** there frequently, but **here,** to his mother's household, **he is not commonly found to go.** Since he goes to his father's home frequently, he knows that his father's relatives are forbidden to him, and he will not confuse them with his mother's relatives.

כַּלָּתוֹ

Among the women enumerated by Rav is **his daughter-in-law.**

HALAKHA

Secondary forbidden relations that have a conclusion – שְׁנִיּוֹת שֶׁיֵּשׁ לָהֶם הֶפְסֵק: The four women listed by Rav and Ze'eiri: The wife of one's mother's paternal half brother, the wife of one's father's maternal half brother, the wife of one's mother's father, and one's daughter's daughter-in-law, while forbidden as secondary relations, see an end to their prohibition, as it applies to them alone and not to their descendants. There are other secondary forbidden relations that have a conclusion, but only those listed in the *baraita* were mentioned (*Yam shel Shlomo*; Rambam *Sefer Nashim, Hilkhot Ishut* 1:6; *Shulḥan Arukh, Even HaEzer* 15:18, 20).

NOTES

On top of Rav – עִילָּאֵי דְּרַב: The mnemonic refers to the names of the Rabbis: The word *rav* means large and the word *ze'eir* means small. Normally a small item is placed on top of a larger one.

HALAKHA

His daughter-in-law and his son's daughter-in-law – כַּלָּתוֹ וְכַלַּת בְּנוֹ: One's son's wife is forbidden to him by Torah law, and his son's son's wife is forbidden by rabbinic law. This prohibition has no conclusion (Rambam *Sefer Nashim, Hilkhot Ishut* 1:6; *Shulḥan Arukh, Even HaEzer* 15:19).

The wife of a mother's brother – אֵשֶׁת אֲחִי הָאֵם: The wife of one's mother's maternal or paternal brother is forbidden by rabbinic law, as per the conclusion of the Gemara's discussion according to the statement of Rav Yehuda bar Sheila (Rambam *Sefer Nashim, Hilkhot Ishut* 1:6; *Shulḥan Arukh, Even HaEzer* 15:9, 18).

BACKGROUND

Chaldean – כַּלְדָּאֵי: The term Chaldean is a synonym for Chasdean, one of the names for the Babylonian people. This term is used in the Bible as a synonym for stargazers or astrologers, as in the following verse: "Then the king commanded to call the magicians, and the enchanters, and the sorcerers, and the Chaldeans, to tell the king his dreams" (Daniel 2:2).

Some Sages prohibited consulting astrologers to discern the future, based on the Torah injunction: "You shall be wholehearted with the Lord your God" (Deuteronomy 18:13). Nevertheless, many people did consult with them. Although the Sages accepted the belief that astrologers had certain powers to foretell the future, they advised that astrologers should be neither consulted nor overly trusted.

NOTES

For example, the daughters-in-law of the house of bar Tzitai – כְּגוֹן כַּלָּתָה דְּבֵי בַּר צִיתַאי: The *Arukh* explains that Tzitai was an important man in his generation, and for this reason all his daughters-in-law would boast of their family connection to him, including his son's daughters-in-law and his daughter's daughters-in-law.

דְּאוֹרַיְיתָא הִיא, דִּכְתִיב "עֶרְוַת כַּלָּתְךָ לֹא תְגַלֶּה"! אֵימָא: כַּלַּת בְּנוֹ. וְכַלַּת בְּנוֹ יֵשׁ לָהּ הֶפְסֵק? וְהָא תַּנְיָא: כַּלָּתוֹ – עֶרְוָה, כַּלַּת בְּנוֹ – שְׁנִיָּה, וְכֵן אַתָּה אוֹמֵר בִּבְנוֹ, וּבֶן בְּנוֹ, עַד סוֹף כָּל הַדּוֹרוֹת! אֶלָּא אֵימָא: כַּלַּת בִּתּוֹ.

The Gemara asks: Is this relationship not forbidden **by Torah law? As it is written: "You shall not uncover the nakedness of your daughter-in-law"** (Leviticus 18:15). The Gemara emends: **Say** instead **his son's daughter-in-law.**[H] The Gemara asks: **And does** the prohibition against having a relationship with **his son's daughter-in-law indeed have a conclusion? Isn't it taught** in a *baraita*: **His daughter-in-law is a forbidden relation** by Torah law, **his son's daughter-in-law is a secondary** forbidden **relation, and similarly, you say** the daughter-in-law of **his son and** the daughter-in-law of **his son's son until the end of all generations** are secondary forbidden relationships. **Rather, say** instead that Rav was referring to **his daughter's daughter-in-law.**

דְּאָמַר רַב חִסְדָּא: הָא מִילְּתָא מִגַּבְרָא רַבָּה שְׁמִיעַ לִי, וּמַנּוּ – רַבִּי אַמִי: לֹא אָסְרוּ כַּלָּה אֶלָּא מִפְּנֵי כַּלָּה. וְאָמְרוּ לִי כַּלְדָּאֵי: מַלְפָנָא הָוֵית.

As Rav Ḥisda said: I heard this matter from a great man, and who was that great man? It was **Rabbi Ami,**[P] and he said: **They prohibited a daughter-in-law only due to** the **daughter-in-law.** Rav Ḥisda heard this in his youth but did not understand the meaning. **The Chaldean** astrologers[B] **said to me: You will be a teacher.**

אָמִינָא: אִי גַּבְרָא רַבָּה הָוֵינָא – אַסְבְּרָא מִדַּעְתִּי, אִי מַקְרֵי דַרְדְּקֵי הָוֵינָא – אַשַׁיְּילָהּ מֵרַבָּנַן דְּאָתוּ לְבֵי כְנִישְׁתָּא. הַשְׁתָּא סְבַרְתָּהּ מִדַּעְתִּי: לֹא אָסְרוּ כַּלַּת בִּתּוֹ אֶלָּא מִשּׁוּם כַּלַּת בְּנוֹ.

Rav Ḥisda further said: **I said** to myself: **If** the astrologers meant that **I will become a great man** and one who teaches the public, **I will** certainly be able to **reason** and understand this matter **with my knowledge. If** the astrologers meant that **I will become the teacher of children, I will ask it of the Sages who come to the synagogue** and in that way I will learn the meaning of Rabbi Ami's teaching. **Now I understand** the matter **on my own.** Rabbi Ami meant: **They prohibited his daughter's daughter-in-law only due to his son's daughter-in-law,** to avoid confusion between these daughters-in-law. The rabbinic decree prohibited one's daughter's daughter-in-law but did not extend to subsequent generations.

אֲמַר לֵיהּ אַבַּיֵי לְרָבָא: אַסְבְּרָהּ לָךְ, כְּגוֹן כַּלָּתָה דְּבֵי בַּר צִיתַאי. רַב פַּפָּא אָמַר: כְּגוֹן כַּלָּתָה דְּבֵי רַב פַּפָּא בַּר אַבָּא. רַב אַשִׁי אָמַר: כְּגוֹן כַּלָּתָה דְּבֵי מָרִי בַּר אִיסַק.

Various Sages proceed to give contemporary examples of families where the halakhic status of the daughters-in-law of the sons and the daughters-in-law of the daughters could be confused with each other. **Abaye said to Rava: I will explain to you** with an example how one might become confused about these daughters-in-law. **For example,** this would be possible in the case of **the daughter-in-law of the house of bar Tzitai,**[N] as there the children of the sons and the daughters of the same family lived together, and it was possible to confuse the halakhic status of the sons' daughters-in-law and the daughters' daughters-in-law. **Rav Pappa said: For example, the daughter-in-law of the house of Rav Pappa bar Abba. Rav Ashi said: For example, the daughter-in-law of the house of Mari bar Isak.**

אִיבַּעֲיָא לְהוּ: אֵשֶׁת אֲחִי הָאֵם מִן הָאֵם, מַהוּ? אֵשֶׁת אֲחִי הָאָב מִן הָאֵם, וְאֵשֶׁת אֲחִי הָאֵם מִן הָאָב, דְּאִיכָּא צַד אָב – הוּא דִּגְזַרוּ רַבָּנַן, אֲבָל הֵיכָא דְּלֵיכָּא צַד אָב לָא גְּזַרוּ בְּהוּ רַבָּנַן, אוֹ דִלְמָא לֹא שְׁנָא?

§ **A dilemma was raised before** the Sages: **What is** the *halakha* with regard to **the wife of** one's **mother's maternal** half **brother?**[H] The Gemara presents the different sides of the question: Both **the wife of** one's **father's maternal** half **brother and the wife of** one's **mother's paternal** half **brother contain** some **aspect of a father, and** perhaps **this** is the reason that **the Sages enacted** a prohibition. That is, they were both forbidden rabbinically to avoid confusion with the case of the wife of one's father's paternal half brother, who is forbidden by Torah law. **But** in the case of the wife of one's mother's maternal half brother, **where there is no aspect of a father** whatsoever, perhaps **the Sages did not make a decree? Or perhaps** this case **is no different?**

PERSONALITIES

A great man…Rabbi Ami – גַּבְרָא רַבָּה...רַבִּי אַמִי: Rabbi Ami was a well-known third-generation *amora* who lived in Eretz Yisrael at the end of the third century CE. He headed the yeshiva in Tiberias together with his colleague Rabbi Asi after the deaths of Rabbi Yoḥanan and Rabbi Elazar. Rabbi Ami considered Rabbi Yoḥanan to be his primary teacher, although he also studied under Reish Lakish, Rabbi Elazar, Rabbi Oshaya, and Rabbi Yehoshua ben Levi. During Rav Huna's lifetime Rabbi Ami deferred to his halakhic decisions, but after his death Rabbi Ami was considered the foremost authority. It may have been for this reason that he was known as a great man. In answer to one of the questions he received, he wrote: From me, Ami bar Natan, Torah emanates to all of Israel (*Gittin* 44a). Among those who sent him their queries were Rabbi Abbahu, Rav Naḥman, and Rava.

אָמַר רַב סָפְרָא: הִיא גּוּפָהּ גְּזֵירָה, וַאֲנַן נֵיקוּם וְנִגְזוֹר גְּזֵירָה לִגְזֵירָה?! אָמַר רָבָא: אַטּוּ כּוּלְּהוּ לָאו גְּזֵירָה לִגְזֵירָה נִינְהוּ? אִמּוֹ – עֶרְוָה, אֵם אִמּוֹ – שְׁנִיָּה, וְגָזְרוּ עַל אֵם אָבִיו מִשּׁוּם אֵם אִמּוֹ. וְטַעְמָא מַאי? כּוּלְּהוּ "דְּבֵי אִימָּא רַבְּתִי" קָרוּ לֵיהּ.

Rav Safra said: She herself, the wife of the mother's paternal half brother, **is** forbidden **by rabbinic decree,** and **will we then proceed to issue a decree to** prevent violation of **a decree?**[B] **Rava said: Is that to say that all of these** rabbinic decrees with regard to secondary relations **are not decrees** to prevent violation of **a decree?** For example, **his mother** is **a forbidden relation** by Torah law, and the Sages decreed that **his mother's mother is a secondary** forbidden **relationship. And they decreed** that **his father's mother** is also a secondary forbidden relationship **due to his mother's mother.**[H] **And what is the reason? They are all called the house of the grandmother,** and therefore people may confuse their halakhic status.

אֵשֶׁת אָבִיו – עֶרְוָה, אֵשֶׁת אֲבִי אָבִיו – שְׁנִיָּה, וְגָזְרוּ עַל אֵשֶׁת אֲבִי אִמּוֹ מִשּׁוּם אֵשֶׁת אֲבִי אָבִיו, וְטַעְמָא מַאי? כּוּלְּהוּ "דְּבֵי אַבָּא רַבָּה" קָרוּ לֵיהּ.

Rava continues: Similarly, **his father's wife is a forbidden relation** by Torah law, and the Sages decreed that **his father's father's wife is a secondary** forbidden **relationship. And they decreed** that **his mother's father's wife** is also a secondary forbidden relationship **due to his father's father's wife.**[H] **And what is the reason? They are all called the house of the grandfather.**

אֵשֶׁת אֲחִי הָאָב מִן הָאָב – עֶרְוָה, אֵשֶׁת אֲחִי הָאָב מִן הָאֵם – שְׁנִיָּה, וְגָזְרוּ עַל אֵשֶׁת אֲחִי הָאֵם מִן הָאָב מִשּׁוּם אֵשֶׁת אֲחִי הָאָב מִן הָאֵם, וְטַעְמָא מַאי – מִשּׁוּם דְּכוּלְּהוּ "דְּבֵי דּוֹדֵי" קָרֵי לְהוּ.

Also, **the wife of his father's paternal** half **brother,** his uncle, who is mentioned explicitly in the Torah (Leviticus 18:16), **is a forbidden relation** by Torah law, and the Sages decreed that **the wife of his father's maternal** half **brother**[H] **is a secondary** forbidden **relationship. And they decreed** that **the wife of his mother's paternal** half **brother** is also a secondary forbidden relationship **due to the wife of his father's maternal** half **brother. And what is the reason?** It is **because they are all called the house of the uncle;** it seems that in the realm of forbidden relations the Sages did issue decrees to prevent violation of a decree, and Rav Safra's claim is incorrect.

מַאי? תָּא שְׁמַע: דְּכִי אֲתָא רַב יְהוּדָה בַּר שֵׁילָא אֲמַר: אָמְרִי בְּמַעְרְבָא: כׇּל שֶׁבִּנְקֵבָה עֶרְוָה – בְּזָכָר גָּזְרוּ עַל אִשְׁתּוֹ מִשּׁוּם שְׁנִיָּה.

If so, then **what is the** *halakha* in this case of the wife of his mother's maternal half brother? **Come and hear: As when Rav Yehuda bar Sheila came** from Eretz Yisrael to Babylonia, **he said: In the West,** Eretz Yisrael, **they say** this principle: For **every female** relative who is **a forbidden relation**[N] by Torah law, the Sages **decreed on the wife** of the equivalent **male** relative **due to** her similarity to **a secondary** forbidden **relationship.**

וְאָמַר רָבָא: וּכְלָלָא הוּא? חֲמוֹתוֹ – עֶרְוָה, אֵשֶׁת חָמִיו מוּתֶּרֶת. בַּת חֲמוֹתוֹ – עֶרְוָה, אֵשֶׁת בֶּן חֲמוֹתוֹ מוּתֶּרֶת. בַּת חָמִיו – עֶרְוָה, אֵשֶׁת בֶּן חָמִיו – מוּתֶּרֶת. חוֹרְגְתּוֹ – עֶרְוָה, אֵשֶׁת חוֹרְגוֹ – מוּתֶּרֶת! בַּת חוֹרְגְתּוֹ עֶרְוָה אֵשֶׁת בֶּן חוֹרְגוֹ מוּתֶּרֶת.

And Rava said: Is this really an established **principle?** Isn't **his mother-in-law a forbidden relation** by Torah law, while **his father-in-law's wife is permitted?** Also, **his mother-in-law's daughter is a forbidden relation** by Torah law, as she is his wife's sister, yet **his mother-in-law's son's wife is permitted. His father-in-law's daughter is a forbidden relation** by Torah law, yet **the wife of his father-in-law's son is permitted. His stepdaughter is a forbidden relation** by Torah law, yet **his stepson's wife**[H] **is permitted. His stepdaughter's daughter,** i.e., his wife's granddaughter, **is a forbidden relation,** yet **the wife of his stepson's son is permitted.**

וְהָא דְּרַב יְהוּדָה בַּר שֵׁילָא לְאֵיתוּיֵי מַאי? לָאו לְאֵיתוּיֵי אֵשֶׁת אֲחִי הָאֵם מִן הָאֵם, דְּכׇל שֶׁבִּנְקֵבָה עֶרְוָה – בְּזָכָר גָּזְרוּ אִשְׁתּוֹ מִשּׁוּם שְׁנִיָּה!

The Gemara continues: If so, **what did that** statement **of Rav Yehuda bar Sheila come to include?** Since his principle is not true in every case, it must be intended to include a specific *halakha*. **Does it not come to include** the case of **the wife of** one's **mother's maternal** half **brother, since** for **every female** relative **who is a forbidden relation** by Torah law, such as his mother's maternal half sister, the Sages **decreed on the wife of** the equivalent **male** relative, in this case his mother's maternal half brother's wife, **due to** her similarity to **a secondary relation.**

מַאי שְׁנָא הָנֵי וּמַאי שְׁנָא הָא? הָא – בְּחַד קִידּוּשִׁין מִקְּרַב לַהּ, הָנֵי – עַד דְּאִיכָּא תְּרֵי קִידּוּשִׁין לָא מִקְּרַב לְהוּ.

The Gemara asks: **What is different** with regard to **these** cases, the wife of his father-in-law or the wife of his mother-in-law's son, who are permitted, **and this** case of the wife of a mother's maternal half brother, who is prohibited? The Gemara answers: **This,** the wife of a mother's maternal half brother, **is related by a single act of betrothal.** One's mother's brother is a blood relative, and his wife is therefore a secondary relation. In contrast, **these** other cases with regard to which the Sages did not issue a decree **are related** only **when there are two acts of betrothal.** For example, one's father-in-law is related to one through one's marriage to his own wife, and his father in law's wife is related to him through his father-in-law's marriage.

BACKGROUND

Decree to prevent violation of a decree – גְּזֵירָה לִגְזֵירָה: The reason that the Sages did not issue decrees to prevent violation of a decree is because although the Torah says that they must establish a fence around the mitzvot, they were not instructed to make a fence around that fence because, if that were to be done, it could continue ad infinitum. In some cases, however, the Gemara discusses a decree to prevent violation of another decree, and in those cases the Gemara explains that all the decrees were part of one original decree.

HALAKHA

His mother's mother and his father's mother – אֵם אִמּוֹ וְאֵם אָבִיו: One's mother is forbidden by Torah law, and one's mother's mother is forbidden by rabbinic law. The Sages decreed that one's father's mother is forbidden as well (Rambam *Sefer Nashim, Hilkhot Ishut* 1:6; *Shulḥan Arukh, Even HaEzer* 15:2, 4).

The wife of one's father's father and of one's mother's father – אֵשֶׁת אֲבִי הָאָב וַאֲבִי הָאֵם: One's father's wife is forbidden by Torah law, and one's father's father's wife and one's mother's father's wife are forbidden as secondary relations by rabbinic law (*Shulḥan Arukh, Even HaEzer* 15:5–7).

The wife of one's father's brother – אֵשֶׁת אֲחִי הָאָב: The wife of one's father's paternal half brother is forbidden by Torah law, and the wife of one's father's maternal half brother is forbidden by rabbinic law (*Shulḥan Arukh, Even HaEzer* 15:18)

His stepdaughter and his stepson's wife – חוֹרְגְתּוֹ וְאֵשֶׁת חוֹרְגוֹ: One's stepdaughter is forbidden by Torah law, but one's stepson's wife is permitted (*Shulḥan Arukh, Even HaEzer* 15:13, 21).

NOTES

Every female relative who is a forbidden relation, etc. – כׇּל שֶׁבִּנְקֵבָה עֶרְוָה וכו׳: According to the Gemara's conclusion, this principle applies in only a few cases. The Gemara is not stating a principle with regard to all forbidden relations but only with regard to aunts. Since one's father's sisters and mother's sisters and the wife of one's father's paternal half brother are forbidden by Torah law, the Sages decreed that anyone who is called an aunt is also forbidden, to avoid confusion between them (Ritva).

NOTES

The wife of a father's father's brother, etc. – אשת אחי אבי האב וכו׳: The early commentaries ask why the Gemara did not similarly inquire about the sister of one's mother's mother, as she is an equally close relative. They answered that the Gemara did not ask about every possible case, but took these two cases as examples. These specific cases were used because the Gemara's question is based on the fact that one generation below them is a forbidden relation by Torah law.

HALAKHA

The wife of one's father's father's brother, etc. – אשת אחי אבי אביו וכו׳: The wife of one's father's father's paternal half brother is permitted as well as both the maternal and paternal half sisters of one's father's father, in accordance with the statement of Ameimar. This is the *halakha* according to *She'iltot deRav Aḥai Gaon* and Rabbeinu Ḥananel and is also the opinion of the Rambam and the Rif. There is an opinion that these relations are forbidden (*Tur*, citing Ri; Rosh on *Yevamot* 40b). The *halakha* is ruled in accordance with the first opinion (*Shulḥan Arukh, Even HaEzer* 15:18).

PERSONALITIES

Mar, son of Rabbana – מר בריה דרבנא: Mar, son of Rabbana, was also known as Mar, son of Ravina. He was one of the outstanding fourth-generation Babylonian *amora'im* and the son of Ravina I. He was renowned in the Talmud as an extremely God-fearing man, and others derived proper behavior for a God-fearing individual from his conduct. He was vigilant in avoiding excessive levity or any matter that lessened the appropriate deference to God. He was particularly careful in his choice of words in order to avoid any possibility of affronting his teachers. He studied primarily with Rav Naḥman bar Yitzḥak as a disciple-colleague. The Talmud relates that he left halakhic notes that served as the basis for discussion in subsequent generations.

שלח ליה רב משרשיא מתוסנייא לרב פפי: ילמדנו רבינו, אשת אחי אבי האב, ואחות אבי האב, מהו? מדלמטה ערוה – למעלה נמי גזרו ביה, או דלמא, הא איתפליג דרתא?

§ **Rav Mesharshiyya from Tusneya sent** a message **to Rav Pappi: Let our Master teach us: What is** the *halakha* with regard to **the wife of a father's father's brother**[N] **and the sister of a father's father?** Did the Sages prohibit these as secondary forbidden relations? The Gemara presents the different sides of the dilemma: Since one generation **below is a forbidden relation,** i.e., a father's sister and the wife of a father's paternal brother, who are both forbidden by Torah law, perhaps the Sages **also decreed** about the women one generation **above. Or, perhaps the generations are separate** and the women in the generation above are not considered to be forbidden relatives.

תא שמע: ״מה הן שניות״, ולא קחשיב להו בהדייהו.

The Gemara attempts to answer: **Come and hear** from that *baraita* cited above, which taught: **What are the secondary** forbidden **relationships** that were prohibited? **And these** women, i.e., the wife of one's father's father's brother and the sister of his father's father **were not reckoned among them.** This implies that these women are permitted.

תנא ושייר. מאי שייר דהאי שייר? שייר שניות דבי רבי חייא.

The Gemara replies that this is not conclusive. Perhaps the *tanna* of the *baraita* **taught** some examples **and omitted** other examples of secondary forbidden relations; i.e., perhaps the list is not exhaustive. The Gemara asks: **What** else **did he omit that he omitted this?** It cannot be that the *tanna* had an exhaustive list except for one case. He either left out more than one case or he included all possible cases. The Gemara answers: **He omitted** the list of **secondary** forbidden **relationships** that were enumerated by **the school of Rabbi Ḥiyya,** which is listed later. Therefore, this *baraita* is not conclusive, as the *tanna* left out many cases.

אמימר אכשר באשת אחי אבי אביו, ובאחות אבי אביו. אמר ליה רב הלל לרב אשי: לדידי חזיא לי שניות מר בריה דרבנא, וכתיבן שיתסרי לאיסורא. מאי לאו תמני דמתניתא ושית דבי רבי חייא, והנך תרתי – הא שיתסרי!

The Gemara states that **Ameimar permitted the wife of one's father's father's brother**[H] **and the sister of one's father's father. Rav Hillel said to Rav Ashi,** challenging Ameimar's statement: **I myself saw** a list of **secondary** forbidden **relationships** written by **Mar, son of Rabbana,**[P] **and it was written** there that **sixteen** women **were forbidden. What, is it not** that these sixteen must be the **eight** cases listed **in the *baraita*, and six from the school of Rabbi Ḥiyya, and these two** cases of the wife of one's father's father's brother and one's father's father's sister, and **this** totals **sixteen?**

ולטעמיך שיבסרי הויין, דהא איכא אשת אחי האם מן האם, דפשטינן לאיסורא! הא לא קשיא,

Rav Ashi defended Ameimar's opinion: **And according to your reasoning,** Rav Hillel, that these cases should be included, **there are seventeen** cases, **as there is** the additional case of **the wife of a mother's maternal** half **brother, whose status was resolved** earlier, concluding **that she is forbidden.** If it is as you say, then there should be seventeen cases. The Gemara answers on behalf of Rav Hillel: **This is not difficult.**

הנך תרתי דדמיין להדדי – כחדא חשיב להו, והא שיתסרי. והא מכל מקום לדידי חזיין לן דכתיבן לאיסורא! אמר ליה: וליטעמיך, אי הוה כתיב להיתירא – מי הוות סמכת עלייהו? דמר בריה דרבנא – מי חתים עלייהו? השתא נמי דכתיב לאיסורא – לאו מר בריה דרבנא חתים עלייהו.

Those two, the wife of a father's father's brother and the sister of a father's father, **are similar to each other** and **are counted as a single** case, **and** so **there are sixteen.** The Gemara restates Rav Hillel's challenge to Ameimar's opinion: **But in any case I myself saw them written as prohibited.** Rav Ashi **said to** Rav Hillel: **And according to your reasoning, if** in the list **it was written that they were permitted, would you have relied on that?** Is the signature of **Mar, son of Rabbana, signed on it?** Although you saw the list, you don't know for certain who wrote it. **Now too, that it is written that they are prohibited,** the same holds true; the signature of **Mar, son of Rabbana, is not signed on it,** and so it cannot be relied upon to reject the opinion of Ameimar.

תָּנֵי דְּבֵי רַבִּי חִיָּיא: שְׁלִישֵׁי שֶׁבִּבְנוֹ וְשֶׁבְּבִתּוֹ, וְשֶׁבְּבֶן אִשְׁתּוֹ וְשֶׁבְּבַת אִשְׁתּוֹ – שְׁנִיָּה, וּרְבִיעִי שֶׁבַּחֲמָיו וְשֶׁבַּחֲמוֹתוֹ – שְׁנִיָּה.

§ One of the Sages **of the school of Rabbi Ḥiyya taught: The third** generation **from one's son and one's daughter,**[H] i.e., one's great-grandchildren, **and the** third generation **from his wife's son and his wife's daughter,**[H] i.e., one's wife's great-grandchildren, are all forbidden as **secondary** forbidden **relationships.** So too, **the fourth** generation **from his father-in-law and from his mother-in-law,**[H] i.e., his wife's great-grandmothers, are prohibited as **secondary** forbidden **relationships.**

אָמַר לֵיהּ רָבִינָא לְרַב אָשֵׁי: מַאי שְׁנָא לְמַעְלָה, דְּקָחָשֵׁיב לַהּ לְאִשְׁתּוֹ, וּמַאי שְׁנָא לְמַטָּה, דְּלָא קָחָשֵׁיב לַהּ לְאִשְׁתּוֹ? לְמַעְלָה, דְּאִיסּוּרָא מִכֹּחַ אִשְׁתּוֹ קָא אָתֵי, חָשֵׁיב לַהּ. לְמַטָּה, דְּאִיסּוּרָא לָאו מִכֹּחַ אִשְׁתּוֹ קָאָתֵי – לָא קָחָשֵׁיב לַהּ.

Ravina said to Rav Ashi: What is different between the generations **above,** referring to his wife's great-grandmothers, such **that** the Sage **counts his wife** as one of the generations and refers to them as the fourth generation, **and what is different** with regard to the generations **below,** referring to his great-granddaughters, such **that he did not count his wife** and referred to them as only the third generation? The Gemara answers: When counting **above, the prohibition stems from his wife,** as they are not his blood relatives but his wife's. Therefore, **she is counted.** When counting **below,** however, **the prohibition does not stem from his wife,** as they are his own blood relatives, **and so she was not counted.**

וְהָא בֶּן אִשְׁתּוֹ וּבַת אִשְׁתּוֹ, דְּאִיסּוּרָא מִכֹּחַ אִשְׁתּוֹ קָאָתֵי וְלָא חָשֵׁיב לַהּ! אַיְּידֵי דִּתְנָא שְׁלֹשָׁה דּוֹרוֹת לְמַטָּה דִּידֵיהּ, וְלָא חֲשָׁבָהּ, תְּנָא נַמִּי שְׁלֹשָׁה דּוֹרוֹת לְמַטָּה דִּידָהּ וְלָא חֲשָׁבָהּ.

The Gemara objects: **But** he includes the granddaughter of **his wife's son and his wife's daughter** in his list of those **forbidden due to his wife, yet he does not count her** and refer to this as the fourth generation. The Gemara answers: **Since he** already **taught three generations below himself,** i.e., his own great-granddaughter, **and** there **he did not count** from his wife because it is his own blood relative, **he taught three generations below** his wife **and did not count her.** Instead, he referred to her great-granddaughter also as three generations below to maintain the uniform style of his words.

אָמַר לֵיהּ רַב אָשֵׁי לְרַב כָּהֲנָא: שְׁנִיּוֹת דְּבֵי רַבִּי חִיָּיא יֵשׁ לָהֶן הֶפְסֵק אוֹ אֵין לָהֶם הֶפְסֵק?

Rav Ashi said to Rav Kahana: Do those **secondary** forbidden **relationships** taught by one of the Sages **of the school of Rabbi Ḥiyya have a conclusion,**[H] **or do they not have a conclusion?** Are those specified cases alone forbidden, or are all generations above and below also forbidden?

תָּא שְׁמַע דְּאָמַר רַב: אַרְבַּע נָשִׁים יֵשׁ לָהֶם הֶפְסֵק. וְתוּ לָא. דִּלְמָא, כִּי קָאָמַר רַב – לְהָהִיא מַתְנִיתָא: תָּא שְׁמַע, שְׁלִישִׁי וּרְבִיעִי. שְׁלִישִׁי וּרְבִיעִי – אִין, טְפֵי – לָא! דִּלְמָא מִשְּׁלִישִׁי וְאֵילָךְ, מֵרְבִיעִי וְאֵילָךְ.

Come and **hear** that **which Rav said: Four women have a conclusion.** This implies that it is only these four **and no more.** The Gemara rejects this: **Perhaps when Rav said this he was referring** only **to** the relationships listed in **the *baraita*** and not to all cases of secondary relationships. The Gemara suggests: **Come** and **hear** from the *baraita* itself, which states: **The third** generation from his son and his daughter **and the fourth** generation from his father-in-law and mother-in-law. This implies that with regard to **the third and the fourth** generations, **yes,** they are forbidden; but **more** than that, **no.** The Gemara rejects this: **Perhaps** this means **from the third onward and from the fourth onward.** The Gemara does not resolve this issue.

אֲמַר לֵיהּ רָבָא לְרַב נַחְמָן: חֲזֵי מָר הַאי מֵרַבָּנַן דַּאֲתָא מִמַּעַרְבָא וַאֲמַר: בָּעוּ בְּמַעַרְבָא, גָּזְרוּ שְׁנִיּוֹת בְּגֵרִים אוֹ לָא גָּזְרוּ שְׁנִיּוֹת בְּגֵרִים?

§ **Rava said to Rav Naḥman: Did the Master see this one of the Sages who came from the West,** Eretz Yisrael, **who said: In the West they asked** whether the Sages **issued a decree** prohibiting **secondary** forbidden **relationships for converts, or** whether **they did not issue a decree** prohibiting **secondary** forbidden **relationships for converts?**[N]

HALAKHA

The third generation from one's son and one's daughter – שְׁלִישֵׁי שֶׁבִּבְנוֹ וְשֶׁבְּבִתּוֹ: One's great-granddaughter is forbidden as a secondary relation (Rambam *Sefer Nashim, Hilkhot Ishut* 1:6; *Shulḥan Arukh, Even HaEzer* 15:12).

The third generation from the son and daughter of his wife – שְׁלִישֵׁי שֶׁבְּבֶן וְשֶׁבְּבַת אִשְׁתּוֹ: One's wife's great-granddaughter is forbidden as a secondary relation (*Shulḥan Arukh, Even HaEzer* 15:14; and see Rambam *Sefer Nashim, Hilkhot Ishut* 1:6 and *Kesef Mishne* there).

The fourth generation from his father-in-law and from his mother-in-law – רְבִיעִי שֶׁבַּחֲמָיו וְשֶׁבַּחֲמוֹתוֹ: One's wife's great-grandmother is forbidden as a secondary relation (Rambam *Sefer Nashim, Hilkhot Ishut* 1:6; *Shulḥan Arukh, Even HaEzer* 15:15).

A conclusion for the secondary forbidden relationships of Rabbi Ḥiyya – הֶפְסֵק בִּשְׁנִיּוֹת דְּרַבִּי חִיָּיא: The Rosh holds that the secondary relations enumerated by Rabbi Ḥiyya do not end but continue upward and downward for all generations (see Ramban). According to the Rambam they do end, since the Gemara does not give a definitive answer, and in cases of uncertainty with regard to rabbinic decrees, the *halakha* is ruled in accordance with the lenient opinion (Rambam *Sefer Nashim, Hilkhot Ishut* 1:6; *Shulḥan Arukh, Even HaEzer* 15:15).

NOTES

Secondary forbidden relationships for converts – שְׁנִיּוֹת בְּגֵרִים: The reason for the rabbinic prohibition against marriage of converts to their relatives is lest the converts say that they came from a more stringent sanctity as gentiles to a state of lesser sanctity as Jews, since previously forbidden relationships would then be permitted to them. The Ritva writes that by this rationale, in the case of one who converts to Judaism from a religion that is more stringent with regard to forbidden relationships, these relations should remain forbidden to the convert even after his conversion to Judaism.

אמר ליה: השתא, ומה ערוה גופה, אי לאו שלא יאמרו באין מקדושה חמורה לקדושה קלה לא גזרו בהו רבנן – שניות מיבעיא?!

Rav Naḥman did not answer whether he had seen this Sage, but **said to him: Now, with regard to** all the **forbidden relationships themselves, were it not** for the fact that if converts would find that as Jews they were permitted to enter into relationships that were forbidden to them as gentiles and **would say** that they went from **a state of more stringent sanctity** as gentiles **to a state of lesser sanctity** as Jews, **then the Sages would not have decreed** to prohibit these relationships.[H] Without the rabbinic decree it would have been permitted for a convert to marry even a close female relative, even his twin sister, who also converted. This is because a convert has the legal status of a newborn, with no family ties. **Is it necessary** to state that the Sages did not extend that decree to include **secondary** forbidden **relationships?**[H] The purpose of the rabbinic prohibitions is to protect the Torah prohibitions, but in the case of converts this particular Torah prohibition does not apply.

אמר רב נחמן: גרים, הואיל ואתו לידן נימא בהו מלתא: אחין מן האם לא יעידו, ואם העידו – עדותן עדות. אחין מן האב מעידין לכתחלה. אמימר אמר: אפילו אחין מן האם נמי מעידין לכתחלה.

Rav Naḥman said: Since the issue of **converts** and their relatives **has come to hand** and is the topic of discussion, **let us say a matter** of *halakha*: **Maternal** half **brothers** who both convert **may not testify** together as a pair of witnesses before the court, **but if they did testify, their testimony is valid.** Although blood relatives are invalid as witnesses, converts are considered as though they have no relations. **Paternal** half **brothers** who both convert **may testify** together *ab initio*, since the *halakha* does not consider paternal half brothers of gentiles to be true relatives. **Ameimar said: Even maternal** half **brothers may also testify** together *ab initio*.[H]

ומאי שנא מעריות? ערוה לכל מסורה, עדות – לבית דין מסורה, וגר שנתגייר כקטן שנולד דמי.

In **what** way **is this case different from forbidden relations,**[N] where a convert may not marry his maternal sister due to rabbinic decree? The *halakhot* of **forbidden relations are handed over to all,** and every individual chooses his own wife. Therefore, the Sages issued a decree to prevent confusion between the status of a convert and that of a born Jew. However, **testimony is handed over to the court,** and the court knows to distinguish between the status of a born Jew and that of a convert. **And** the legal status of **a convert who** just **converted is like** that of **a child** just **born,**[HB] and all previous family ties become irrelevant.

מתני׳ מי שיש לו אח מכל מקום – זוקק את אשת אחיו ליבום, ואחיו הוא לכל דבר, חוץ ממי שיש לו אח מן השפחה ומן הגויה. מי שיש לו בן מכל מקום – פוטר אשת אביו מן היבום, וחייב על מכתו ועל קללתו, ובנו לכל דבר – חוץ ממי שיש לו בן מן השפחה ומן הגויה.

MISHNA In the case of **anyone who has a brother of any kind,**[HN] that brother **creates a levirate bond** causing his *yevama* **to** be required to **perform levirate marriage** if the first brother dies childless. **And he is his brother in all respects, except for one who has a brother** born **from** a Canaanite **maidservant or from a gentile woman,** as these do not have the legal status of brothers. Similarly, in the case of **anyone who has a child of any kind,**[H] that child **exempts his father's wife from levirate marriage,** since his father did not die childless. **And** that child **is liable** to receive capital punishment **if he strikes** his father **or curses him. And he is his child in all respects, except for whoever has a child** born **from** a Canaanite **maidservant or from a gentile woman,** as these do not have the halakhic status of children.

HALAKHA

Forbidden relations for a convert – איסור עריות בגר: By Torah law it is permitted for a convert to marry any of his relatives who converted, even his mother or sister. However, the Sages decreed it prohibited for converts to marry close relatives so that one who converted would not think that he came from a greater state of sanctity, before he was Jewish, into a state of lesser sanctity (Rambam *Sefer Kedusha, Hilkhot Issurei Bia* 14:12; *Shulḥan Arukh, Yoreh De'a* 269:1).

Secondary relationships for a convert – שניות בגר: The Sages did not render prohibited secondary relationships of converts. Therefore, a convert may marry his maternal grandmother. Similarly, a born Jew is permitted to marry a converted woman and her maternal grandmother, though marrying a woman and her grandmother who were born Jewish is a rabbinic prohibition (*Shulḥan Arukh, Yoreh De'a* 269:8).

Testimony of related converts – עדות גרים קרובים: Once a gentile converts, his biological relations no longer have the legal status of relations. Even if twin brothers convert, they may testify together as a pair of witnesses (Rambam *Sefer Shofetim, Hilkhot Edut* 13:2; *Shulḥan Arukh, Yoreh De'a* 269:10 and *Ḥoshen Mishpat* 33:11).

The legal status of a convert who just converted is like that of a child just born – גר שנתגייר כקטן שנולד דמי: A gentile who converts and a freed gentile slave have the legal status of newly born children, and any previous familial relationships are considered nonexistent (Rambam *Sefer Kedusha, Hilkhot Issurei Bia* 14:11; *Shulḥan Arukh, Yoreh De'a* 269:10 and *Ḥoshen Mishpat* 33:11).

A brother of any kind – אח מכל מקום: Every paternal half brother, even if he is of flawed lineage or a *mamzer*, causes his *yevama* to require levirate marriage or *ḥalitza*. A half brother whose mother is a gentile or a Canaanite maidservant is not considered a brother in this regard (Rambam *Sefer Nashim, Hilkhot Yibbum VaḤalitza* 1:6; *Shulḥan Arukh, Even HaEzer* 157:1).

A child of any kind – בן מכל מקום: If one dies and leaves a child or any descendants, whether of unflawed or flawed lineage, even a *mamzer*, his widow is exempt from levirate marriage. This holds true in all cases except for children from Canaanite maidservants or gentile women (Rambam *Sefer Nashim, Hilkhot Yibbum VaḤalitza* 1:3–4; *Shulḥan Arukh, Even HaEzer* 156:2).

NOTES

In what way is this case different from forbidden relations – ומאי שנא מעריות: *Tosafot* ask: The reason just given, i.e., lest it be said that the converts came from a more stringent level of sanctity to a more lenient level, should be sufficient to explain the difference between forbidden relations and testimony. With regard to the *halakhot* of testimony there is no disqualification for gentiles who are related. They explain that the primary reason for the rabbinic decree is to avoid confusion with regard to such relationships between Jews. This rationale fits with the opinion that maternal brothers may not testify together *ab initio*, as in such a case there is also a concern that it may lead to confusion (see Ritva; *Tosafot Yeshanim*).

A brother of any kind – אח מכל מקום: The Gemara explains that this expression was adopted in order to teach the additional case of a brother who is a *mamzer*. This discussion is also the basis for those early commentaries who rule that a brother who converts to another religion still causes his *yevama* to require levirate marriage. Some commentaries differentiated between a brother who had already converted to another religion at the time of his brother's marriage and one who converted after the marriage (see *Otzar HaGe'onim*; Ritva).

BACKGROUND

The legal status of a convert who just converted is like that of a child just born – גר שנתגייר שנולד דמי כקטן: This is a fundamental principle in *halakha*, and it means that through the act of conversion a convert becomes like a new person and all ties that he had with his previous gentile world are severed. Since he is considered like a newly born child, all his biological relations are consequently not considered by *halakha* to be related to him. Despite this, the Sages decreed that a gentile may not marry one of his blood relatives if they also converted. There are two reasons for this: (1) A convert might think that he has descended from a greater sanctity to a lesser sanctity. The Sages did not want him to think that what was forbidden to him as a gentile is now permitted. A convert intends to ascend to a higher sanctity and does not seek leniencies. (2) Others may not realize that this individual is a convert, and therefore when they see him marrying a woman who appears to be forbidden to him, this might lead them to erroneous conclusions.

גמ׳ מִכָּל מָקוֹם לְאָתוּיֵי מַאי? אָמַר רַב יְהוּדָה לְאָתוּיֵי מַמְזֵר. פְּשִׁיטָא, אָחִיו הוּא! מַהוּ דְּתֵימָא: לֵילַף אַחְוָה אַחְוָה מִבְּנֵי יַעֲקֹב, מָה לְהַלָּן כְּשֵׁרִין וְלֹא פְּסוּלִין, אַף כָּאן כְּשֵׁרִין וְלֹא פְּסוּלִין – קָא מַשְׁמַע לַן.

GEMARA The Gemara asks: With regard to the statement that a brother **of any kind** causes his *yevama* to be required to perform levirate marriage, **what** additional case does this come **to add? Rav Yehuda said: This adds** the case of a *mamzer*, who, notwithstanding his status, is considered a brother. The Gemara wonders: But **isn't** that **obvious? He is his brother.** The Gemara explains: This is necessary **lest you say: Let us derive** a verbal analogy between the word **"brother"** stated in the verse with regard to levirate marriage and **"brother"** stated with regard to **the children of Jacob. Just as there,** Jacob's children **are of unflawed** lineage **and not of flawed** lineage and are not *mamzerim*, **so too here,** one might think that only brothers of **unflawed** lineage **and not** brothers of **flawed** lineage, i.e., *mamzerim*, obligate the *yevama* in levirate marriage. Therefore, **this teaches us** that a *mamzer* is considered a brother for the purposes of levirate marriage.

וְאֵימָא הָכִי נַמִי! כֵּיוָן דִּלְעִנְיַן יִבּוּם מִיפְּטַר נָפְטַר

The Gemara asks: **And say that** is **indeed** the *halakha*. Perhaps a brother who is a *mamzer* does not obligate his *yevama* in levirate marriage. The Gemara answers: **Since with regard to levirate marriage,** if the husband had a child who was a *mamzer* he would **exempt** the wife from levirate marriage,

מִיזְקָק נַמִי זָקֵיק.

the husband's brother **also causes a levirate bond** with his *yevama* even if he is a *mamzer*.

״וְאָחִיו הוּא לְכָל דָּבָר״. לְמַאי הִלְכְתָא? לְיוֹרְשׁוֹ וְלִיטַּמֵּא לוֹ.

§ The mishna stated that **he is his brother in all respects.** The Gemara asks: **With regard to what** ***halakha*** was this said? The Gemara answers: **To inherit from him,**[H] **and to become ritually impure for him**[H] if he is a priest, as a brother is one of the relations for whom a priest is permitted to become ritually impure by attending his funeral.

פְּשִׁיטָא, אָחִיו הוּא! סָלְקָא דַּעְתָּךְ אָמִינָא: הוֹאִיל וּכְתִיב ״כִּי אִם לִשְׁאֵרוֹ הַקָּרוֹב אֵלָיו״ וְאָמַר מָר: שְׁאֵרוֹ – זוֹ אִשְׁתּוֹ, וּכְתִיב ״לֹא יִטַּמָּא בַּעַל בְּעַמָּיו לְהֵחַלּוֹ״. יֵשׁ בַּעַל שֶׁמִּטַּמֵּא וְיֵשׁ בַּעַל שֶׁאֵין מִטַּמֵּא, הָא כֵּיצַד? מִטַּמֵּא הוּא לְאִשְׁתּוֹ כְּשֵׁרָה, וְאֵין מִטַּמֵּא לְאִשְׁתּוֹ פְּסוּלָה,

The Gemara asks: **Isn't** this **obvious,** as **he is his brother?** The Gemara answers: It might **enter your mind to say** that a priest does not become impure for his brother of flawed lineage, **since it is written** with regard to priests: "None shall defile himself for the dead among his people **except for his kin, that is near unto him"** (Leviticus 21:1–2), **and the Master said "his kin"; this is his wife,** and a priest may defile himself for his wife. **But it is written: "He shall not defile himself, being a husband among his people, to profane himself"** (Leviticus 21:4), implying that he may not defile himself for his wife. This apparent contradiction is resolved as follows: **There is a husband who does become impure** for his wife, **and there is a husband who does not become impure. How so? He becomes impure for his wife if she was fit** and was permitted to a priest, **but he does not become impure for his wife** if she was **unfit**[H] to marry a priest.

הָכִי נַמִי מִטַּמֵּא הוּא לְאָח כָּשֵׁר וְאֵין מִטַּמֵּא לְאָח פָּסוּל, קָא מַשְׁמַע לַן. וְאֵימָא הָכִי נַמִי! הָתָם לְאַפּוּקֵי קַיְימָא, הָכָא – אָחִיו הוּא.

So too, one might have thought that a priest **becomes impure for a brother who is** of **unflawed** lineage and not a *mamzer*, **but he does not become impure for a brother** of **flawed** lineage. Therefore, **this comes to teach us** that he does become impure for a brother who is a *mamzer*. The Gemara asks: **Say this also,** that by the same reasoning by which a priest may not become impure for a wife who was unfit for him, he may not become impure for an unfit brother either. Just as he does not become impure for an unfit wife, he should not become impure for an unfit brother? The Gemara answers: The two cases are different, as **there,** with regard to the unfit wife, **she stands to be dismissed,**[N] since according to Torah law unfit women must be divorced. For this reason he does not become impure for her. **Here, he is his brother.**

HALAKHA

To inherit from him – לְיוֹרְשׁוֹ: All relatives, even those born through transgression, inherit just as those born in accordance with *halakha*. A *mamzer* brother or son inherits just like offspring of unflawed lineage (Rambam *Sefer Mishpatim, Hilkhot Naḥalot* 1:7; *Shulḥan Arukh, Ḥoshen Mishpat* 276:6).

To become ritually impure for him – לִיטַּמֵּא לוֹ: A priest becomes ritually impure for his father, his mother, his brother, his unmarried sister, his son, and his daughter, even if they are unfit or *mamzerim* (Rambam *Sefer Shofetim, Hilkhot Evel* 2:9; *Shulḥan Arukh, Yoreh De'a* 373:4).

His wife if she was unfit – אִשְׁתּוֹ פְּסוּלָה: A priest becomes ritually impure for his wife if she was permitted to marry him, but if it was prohibited for her to marry him he may not become impure for her (Rambam *Sefer Shofetim, Hilkhot Evel* 2:9; *Shulḥan Arukh, Yoreh De'a* 373:4).

NOTES

She stands to be dismissed – לְאַפּוּקֵי קַיְימָא: With regard to the exceptions when a priest may become ritually impure, the Torah states: "Except for his kin, that is near unto him" (Leviticus 21:2). The Gemara explains that "his kin" is referring to his wife. A wife who is prohibited to the priest is not considered to be "his kin."

"חוּץ מִמִּי שֶׁיֵּשׁ לוֹ אָח מִן הַשִּׁפְחָה וּמִן הַגּוֹיָה", מַאי טַעֲמָא? אָמַר קְרָא "הָאִשָּׁה וִילָדֶיהָ תִּהְיֶה לַאֲדוֹנֶיהָ".

§ The mishna says: **Except for whoever has a brother** born **from a** Canaanite **maidservant or from a gentile woman,** as in these cases he is not considered a brother. The Gemara asks: **What is the reason** for this *halakha*? The Gemara answers: **The verse states** with regard to a Jewish slave who has children with a Canaanite maidservant: **"The wife and her children shall be her master's"** (Exodus 21:4). This means that the children also have the status of Canaanite slaves, which implies that the lineage of a Canaanite maidservant's child comes from the mother and not from the father.

"מִי שֶׁיֵּשׁ לוֹ בֵּן מִכָּל מָקוֹם פּוֹטֵר" וכו׳. מִכָּל מָקוֹם לְאַתּוּיֵי מַאי? אָמַר רַב יְהוּדָה: לְאִיתּוּיֵי מַמְזֵר. מַאי טַעֲמָא? דְּאָמַר קְרָא "וּבֵן אֵין לוֹ" – עַיֵּין עָלָיו.

The mishna states: With regard to **anyone who has a son of any kind,**[N] that son **exempts** his father's wife from any levirate bond. The Gemara asks: **What is added** by the phrase: **Of any kind? Rav Yehuda said: It adds** a child who is a *mamzer*. **What is the reason** that a *mamzer* exempts a woman from any levirate bond? **As the verse states** with regard to levirate marriage: **"And he has no [*ain lo*] child"** (Deuteronomy 25:5). The phrase *ain lo* can be understood as *ayyen alav*, meaning **investigate him.**[N] That is to say, investigate whether he is indeed childless, because any child, even a *mamzer*, exempts the widow from a levirate bond.

"וְחַיָּיב עַל מַכָּתוֹ", אַמַּאי? קְרִי כָּאן "וְנָשִׂיא בְעַמְּךָ לֹא תָאוֹר" – בְּעוֹשֶׂה מַעֲשֵׂה עַמְּךָ!

It states in the mishna that a child who is a *mamzer* **is liable** to receive punishment **if he strikes** his father or curses him.[H] The Gemara asks: **Why** should he be liable? **Read here** the verse: **"You shall not curse a ruler of your people"** (Exodus 22:27), which is interpreted to imply that the prohibition against cursing applies only **to one who acts according to the deeds of your people.**[N] However, this father must have engaged in sexual relations with a woman who was forbidden to him in order to have a child who is a *mamzer*. Therefore, he did not act according to the deeds of the people. In that case, why should this son be liable to receive punishment for hitting him or cursing him?

כִּדְאָמַר רַב פִּנְחָס מִשְּׁמֵיהּ דְּרַב פָּפָּא: בְּעוֹשֶׂה תְּשׁוּבָה – הָכָא נַמִי כְּשֶׁעָשָׂה תְּשׁוּבָה.

The Gemara answers: **As Rav Pinehas said in the name of Rav Pappa** with regard to a different matter: This is referring to **one who performs repentance. Here too,** it is referring to **one who performed repentance** after the *mamzer* was born. He is thereafter considered to be living in accordance with *halakha*, and so his *mamzer* son is liable to receive punishment for cursing him.

וְהַאי בַּר תְּשׁוּבָה הוּא? וְהָתְנַן: שִׁמְעוֹן בֶּן מְנַסְיָא אוֹמֵר: אֵיזֶהוּ "מְעֻוָּת לֹא יוּכַל לִתְקוֹן", זֶה הַבָּא עַל הָעֶרְוָה וְהוֹלִיד מִמֶּנָּה מַמְזֵר! הָשְׁתָּא מִיהָא עוֹשֶׂה מַעֲשֵׂה עַמְּךָ הוּא.

The Gemara objects: **Is he in fact able to repent** after fathering a *mamzer*? **Didn't we learn** in a mishna that **Shimon ben Menasya says: Which is: "That which is crooked cannot be made straight"** (Ecclesiastes 1:15)? **This is** referring to **one who engaged in intercourse with a relative** who is **forbidden** to him **and fathered a *mamzer* with her.** This implies that he has no possibility of achieving total repentance. The Gemara responds: **At least now,** after repenting, **he** is considered as one who **acts according to the deeds of your people.** Although he cannot totally rectify his transgression, his child is liable to receive punishment for cursing or hitting him.

תָּנוּ רַבָּנַן: הַבָּא עַל אֲחוֹתוֹ וְהִיא בַּת אֵשֶׁת אָבִיו – חַיָּיב מִשּׁוּם אֲחוֹתוֹ, וּמִשּׁוּם בַּת אֵשֶׁת אָבִיו. רַבִּי יוֹסֵי בֶּן יְהוּדָה אוֹמֵר: אֵינוֹ חַיָּיב אֶלָּא מִשּׁוּם אֲחוֹתוֹ בִּלְבַד, וְלֹא מִפְּנֵי בַּת אֵשֶׁת אָבִיו.

§ **The Sages taught: He who** unwittingly **engages in sexual relations with his sister, who is the daughter of his father's** lawful **wife,**[H] **is liable** and must bring two sin-offerings. He must bring one sin-offering **because** she is **his sister**[H] and another **because** she is **the daughter of his father's wife,** which is mentioned in a separate verse in the Torah. **Rabbi Yosei ben Yehuda says: He is liable only because** she is **his sister alone, and not because** of the prohibition against engaging in sexual relations with **the daughter of his father's wife.**

מַאי טַעֲמַיְיהוּ דְּרַבָּנַן? אָמְרִי: מִכְּדִי כְּתִיב "עֶרְוַת אֲחוֹתְךָ בַת אָבִיךָ אוֹ בַת אִמֶּךָ" "עֶרְוַת בַּת אֵשֶׁת אָבִיךָ מוֹלֶדֶת אָבִיךָ אֲחוֹתְךָ הִיא" לָמָּה לִי? שְׁמַע מִינָּהּ: לְחַיְּיבוֹ מִשּׁוּם אֲחוֹתוֹ וּמִשּׁוּם בַּת אֵשֶׁת אָבִיו.

The Gemara asks: **What is the reason** for the opinion **of the Rabbis,** the first *tanna* of the *baraita*? **They said: Since it is written** in the Torah: **"The nakedness of your sister, the daughter of your father, or the daughter of your mother**…you shall not uncover" (Leviticus 18:9), then **why do I need** the verse: **"The nakedness of your father's wife's daughter, begotten of your father, she is your sister**…you shall not uncover" (Leviticus 18:11)? **Conclude from this** that the additional verse serves **to make him liable** separately **due to** the fact that she is **his sister and due to** the fact that she is **his father's wife's daughter.**

NOTES

A son of any kind – בֵּן מִכָּל מָקוֹם: In the Jerusalem Talmud the following point is added: Since he is considered his son in all regards, the father fulfills the mitzva to be fruitful and multiply through this son. Also, he is considered his son with regard to all matters of forbidden relations.

And he has no child, meaning investigate him – וּבֵן אֵין לוֹ, עַיֵּין עָלָיו: Rashi explains that the word "no [*ain*]" could have been written without the letter *yod*. The homiletical interpretation is derived from the additional letter; the word spelled in this way bears similarity to the word for eye [*ayyen*], which implies investigation (see *Tosefot Yom Tov*). In the *Sma* this interpretation is explained differently: The Torah's stress on the phrase "has no" indicates that he has absolutely no children of any kind in any place.

One who acts according to the deeds of your people – עוֹשֶׂה מַעֲשֵׂה עַמְּךָ: Rambam maintains that a *mamzer* son is still obligated to respect his father and to fear him even if he is exempt from punishment for cursing or striking him (*Sefer Shofetim, Hilkhot Mamrim* 6:11). However, other authorities disagree (*Tur*, *Yoreh De'a* 240).

HALAKHA

He is liable to receive punishment if he strikes his father or curses him – חַיָּיב עַל מַכָּתוֹ וְעַל קִלְלָתוֹ: According to the opinion of the Rambam and the Rif, even if parents were totally wicked and transgressors, and even if they were sentenced to death, it is prohibited for the son to strike them or curse them. However, *Tosafot* hold that in such a case there is no prohibition. If he did strike them or curse them in that case, then he is exempt from punishment. If they repented, even if they were sentenced to death, he is liable to receive punishment for striking or cursing them, even if he is acting as the agent of the court carrying out their punishment (Rambam *Sefer Shofetim, Hilkhot Mamrim* 5:12; *Shulḥan Arukh*, *Yoreh De'a* 241:4).

His sister…the daughter of his father's wife – אֲחוֹתוֹ...בַּת אֵשֶׁת אָבִיו: If one engages in sexual relations with his sister born of a woman married to his father, he is liable twice, once for his sister and once for the daughter of his father's wife, in accordance with the opinion of the first *tanna* and against the lone dissenting opinion (Rambam *Sefer Kedusha, Hilkhot Issurei Bia* 2:4).

Prohibition against relations with one's sister – אִיסּוּר אֲחוֹתוֹ: One's sister is forbidden to him by Torah law, whether she is his maternal or paternal half-sister, and whether she is fit or unfit for marriage, and even if she is a *mamzeret*, except for a sister born to his father by a gentile woman or a Canaanite maidservant, as then she is not considered his sister at all (*Shulḥan Arukh*, *Even HaEzer* 15:10).

וְרַבִּי יוֹסֵי בְּרַבִּי יְהוּדָה: אָמַר קְרָא ״אֲחוֹתְךָ הִיא״, מִשּׁוּם אֲחוֹתוֹ אַתָּה מְחַיְּיבוֹ וְאִי אַתָּה מְחַיְּיבוֹ מִשּׁוּם בַּת אֵשֶׁת אָבִיו –

And Rabbi Yosei, son of Rabbi Yehuda, says: **The verse states: "She is your sister,"** which comes to limit and emphasize that **you hold him liable due to** the fact that she is **his sister but you do not hold him liable** a second time **due to** the fact that she is also **his father's wife's daughter.**

וְרַבָּנַן, הַאי ״אֲחוֹתְךָ הִיא״ מַאי עָבְדִי לֵיהּ? מִיבְּעֵי לְהוּ לְחַיְּיבוֹ עַל אֲחוֹתוֹ בַּת אָבִיו וּבַת אִמּוֹ, לוֹמַר שֶׁאֵין מַזְהִירִין מִן הַדִּין.

The Gemara asks: **And what do the Rabbis do with this** verse: **"She is your sister"? They require it in order to hold him liable** to receive punishment **for** having relations with **his sister** who is both **the daughter of his father and the daughter of his mother, to say that** the Sages **do not** derive an additional Torah **prohibition by way of a logical derivation,** i.e., an *a fortiori* inference.[N] In other words, although it would seem that since he is liable to receive punishment for having relations with his father's daughter and also for his mother's daughter, this must be all the more true in a case where she is the daughter of both his father and his mother, yet nevertheless, there is no new prohibition here. Therefore, the matter was taught explicitly in the Torah, to teach that the Sages may not derive additional prohibitions by way of *a fortiori* inferences.

וְרַבִּי יוֹסֵי בְּרַבִּי יְהוּדָה? אִם כֵּן לִכְתּוֹב רַחֲמָנָא ״אֲחוֹתְךָ״, ״הִיא״ לָמָּה לִי – מִשּׁוּם אֲחוֹתְךָ אַתָּה מְחַיְּיבוֹ וְאִי אַתָּה מְחַיְּיבוֹ מִשּׁוּם בַּת אֵשֶׁת אָבִיו.

And Rabbi Yosei, son of Rabbi Yehuda, says: **If so,** that the matter was written for this purpose, **then the Merciful One should have written** only: **Your sister. Why do I need** the phrase **"she is"?** This limits the *halakha* and teaches that for unintentional intercourse with his sister who is also his father's wife's daughter **you hold him liable because** she is **his sister; you do not** additionally **hold him liable because** she is **his father's wife's daughter.**

וְרַבָּנַן? אַף עַל גַּב דִּכְתִיב ״אֲחוֹתְךָ״ אִיצְטְרִיךְ לְמִכְתַּב ״הִיא״, שֶׁלֹּא תֹּאמַר: בְּעָלְמָא מַזְהִירִין מִן הַדִּין.

And how do **the Rabbis** interpret the additional phrase "she is"? **Although "your sister" is written, it was necessary to write "she is" so that you not say** that **generally** the Sages may derive additional **prohibitions by way of a logical derivation,** i.e., an *a fortiori* inference.

וְכִי תֵּימָא: ״אֲחוֹתְךָ״ דִּכְתַב רַחֲמָנָא לָמָּה לִי – מִילְּתָא דְּאָתְיָא בְּקַל וָחוֹמֶר טָרַח וּכְתַב לָהּ קְרָא – כְּתַב רַחֲמָנָא ״הִיא״.

The Gemara explains how this principle is derived from the text. **As, if you would say: Why do I** need the term **"your sister" that the Merciful One writes** in the Torah, since it is possible to derive this by *a fortiori* inference and it therefore appears redundant? The answer is that the Torah wrote this apparently redundant term to teach the principle that with regard to **a matter that** could **be derived by** means of an ***a fortiori* inference, the verse unnecessarily wrote it** explicitly. **The Merciful One writes** the term **"she is"** in order to teach that just as in this case the Sages may not derive additional prohibitions by way of an *a fortiori* inference, so too, in all other cases they may not derive additional prohibitions that are not stated in the text.

וְרַבִּי יוֹסֵי בְּרַבִּי יְהוּדָה: אִם כֵּן לִיכְתְּבֵיהּ רַחֲמָנָא לְ״אֲחוֹתְךָ הִיא״ בְּאִידַּךְ קְרָא.

And Rabbi Yosei, son of Rabbi Yehuda, says: **If** this is the reason for the verse, **then let the Merciful One write: She is your sister, in the other verse,** which states: "The nakedness of your sister, the daughter of your father, or the daughter of your mother," and not in the verse that speaks of the daughter of one's father's wife.

וְרַבִּי יוֹסֵי בְּרַבִּי יְהוּדָה, הַאי ״בַּת אֵשֶׁת אָבִיךָ״ מַאי עָבֵיד לֵיהּ? מִיבְּעֵי לֵיהּ: מִי שֶׁיֵּשׁ לוֹ אִישׁוּת לְאָבִיךָ בָּהּ, פְּרָט לַאֲחוֹתוֹ מִשִּׁפְחָה וְגוֹיָה, שֶׁאֵין אִישׁוּת לְאָבִיךָ בָּהּ.

The Gemara asks: **And what does Rabbi Yosei, son of Rabbi Yehuda, do with this** verse, which states: **"The daughter of your father's wife"** (Leviticus 18:9)? **He requires it** to teach that one is liable only for relations with a half-sister whose mother is **someone with whom there is no** possibility of forging **marital** ties **with your father,** even if she was not in actuality his wife. This comes **to exclude his sister from** a Canaanite **maidservant or a gentile woman, with whom your father cannot have marital** ties, since betrothal does not take effect with these women.

וְאֵימָא: פְּרָט לַאֲחוֹתוֹ מֵאֲנוּסָה? הַהִיא לָא מָצֵית אָמְרַתְּ, מִדְּרָבָא.

The Gemara asks: **So say:** "Your father's wife's daughter" comes to teach specifically the case of a daughter from a woman married to his father, thereby **excluding from** the definition of: His sister, **his sister from a woman who had been raped.** Perhaps if she was born of a woman who was not married to his father she would not be considered his sister. The Gemara answers: **You cannot say that due to** the reason said by **Rava.**

NOTES

The Sages do not derive an additional prohibition by way of a logical derivation – אֵין מַזְהִירִין מִן הַדִּין: Some commentaries explain that according to all opinions, one is permitted in general to draw his own *a fortiori* inferences. Therefore, there is concern that one might err in his considerations on the matter, and consequently these inferences may not be relied upon in cases where it would lead to one being liable to receive lashes. On the other hand, the Maharsha in tractate *Sanhedrin* cites the *Sefer Mitzvot Gadol* and states that it is unknown whether the punishment derived by an *a fortiori* inference is severe enough to atone for the transgression performed. Others explain that this principle is a Torah decree, without reason (*Yosef Lekaḥ*).

HALAKHA

His sister by a woman his father raped – אחותו מאנוסתו: If a daughter was born from a woman his father raped, rather than married, then as that daughter's paternal half brother he is liable to receive punishment for relations with her only because she is his sister but not as the daughter of his father's wife (Rambam *Sefer Kedusha, Hilkhot Issurei Bia* 2:4).

דרבא רמי: כתיב "ערות בת בנך או בת בתך לא תגלה", הא בת בנה דידה ובת בתה דידה – שרי, וכתיב "ערות אשה ובתה לא תגלה את בת בנה ואת בת בתה". הא כיצד?

As Rava raised a contradiction: In one verse **it is written: "The nakedness of your son's daughter, or of your daughter's daughter, you shall not uncover"** (Leviticus 18:10), which implies, **consequently,** that her **son's daughter or her daughter's daughter is permitted. And it is written** elsewhere: **"You shall not uncover the nakedness of a woman and her daughter; you shall not take her son's daughter or her daughter's daughter"** (Leviticus 18:17), which states explicitly that her son's daughter and daughter's daughter are prohibited. **How can these** texts be reconciled?

כאן באונסין כאן בנשואין.

Here, it is referring to a daughter by a woman whom one **raped,** in which case he is allowed to marry her daughter provided she is not also his daughter. **There,** it is referring to a woman whom one **married,** in which case it is forbidden to marry her daughter under any circumstances. However, even in a case where one's father raped a woman, one is still permitted to marry the woman's daughter by another man. If one's father had a daughter with this woman, one would be prohibited from having a relationship with that daughter, as she is his paternal half-sister.[H]

Perek **II**
Daf **23** Amud **a**

HALAKHA

Betrothal comes into effect with women who are forbidden and one would be liable for violating prohibitions – חייבי לאוין תפשי בהו קדושין: If one betroths a woman forbidden to him by a prohibition, the betrothal is nevertheless fully effective (Rambam *Sefer Nashim, Hilkhot Ishut* 4:14; *Shulḥan Arukh, Even HaEzer* 44:7).

Prohibition against union with one's sister – איסור אחות: One's sister is forbidden to him by Torah law, whether she is a paternal or maternal sister, whether she is a sister from her father's marriage or outside of marriage. Even a sister born from a forbidden union is considered a sister and one is liable to receive punishment for having relations with her (Rambam *Sefer Kedusha, Hilkhot Issurei Bia* 2:1; *Shulḥan Arukh, Even HaEzer* 15:10).

ואימא פרט לחייבי לאוין? אמר רב פפא: חייבי לאוין תפשי בהו קדושין,

The Gemara raises a challenge: **And say** that the verse: "The daughter of your father's wife" comes to **exclude** women who were forbidden, as they are **liable** for violating **prohibitions** but were nevertheless married to his father, such as a *mamzeret*. If so, his sister from such a union would not be considered his sister. **Rav Pappa said: Betrothal comes into effect with** women who are forbidden, and one would be **liable** for violating **prohibitions**[H] despite the fact that union with them is forbidden, and so she is called the wife of your father.

דכתיב "כי תהיין לאיש שתי נשים האחת אהובה והאחת שנואה", וכי יש אהובה לפני המקום ויש שנואה לפני המקום? אלא: אהובה – אהובה בנישואיה, שנואה – שנואה בנישואיה, ואמר רחמנא: "כי תהיין".

This is derived from the verse in **which it is written: "If a man has two wives, the one beloved, and the other hated"** (Deuteronomy 21:15). **Is there one** who is **loved by the Omnipresent and one** who is **hated by the Omnipresent? Rather, "beloved"** means **her marriage is beloved,** as it was permitted for her to be married, in accordance with *halakha,* and **"hated"** means **her marriage is hated** because it was not permitted for her to be married, according to *halakha.* **And the Merciful One states: "If** a man **has** two wives," meaning that both are considered to be married.

ואימא פרט לחייבי כריתות – אמר רבא: אמר קרא "ערות אחותך בת אביך או בת אמך מולדת בית או מולדת חוץ", בין שאומרים לו לאביך: "קיים", בין שאומרים לו לאביך "הוצא", ואמר רחמנא: "אחותך היא" –

The Gemara asks: **Say** that this verse comes to **exclude** a union between one's father and a woman that is forbidden to him as they are **liable** to receive ***karet,*** and that since betrothal does not come into effect with her there is no marriage bond. Perhaps a sister born of such a woman would not be prohibited as the daughter of one's father's wife. **Rava said** that **the verse states: "The nakedness of your sister, the daughter of your father, or the daughter of your mother, whether born at home or born outside"** (Leviticus 18:9).[H] This includes all daughters, **whether** from a woman **for whom** the Sages **tell your father: Maintain** her within your home, or **whether** the Sages **tell your father** she is a woman who is forbidden to him and therefore: **Send her out** of your home. **And the Merciful One states** that nevertheless: **"She is your sister."** Even the daughter of a woman who was forbidden to your father such that both parties are liable to receive *karet* is called your sister.

אֵימָא: בֵּין שֶׁאוֹמֵר לוֹ אָבִיךָ ״קַיֵּים״ בֵּין שֶׁאוֹמֵר לוֹ אָבִיךָ ״הוֹצֵא״, וְאָמַר רַחֲמָנָא ״אֲחוֹתְךָ הִיא״ – לְרַבּוֹת אֲחוֹתוֹ מִשִּׁפְחָה וְגוֹיָה – אָמַר קְרָא ״בַּת אֵשֶׁת אָבִיךָ״, מִי שֶׁיֵּשׁ לוֹ אִישׁוּת לְאָבִיךָ בָּהּ, פְּרָט לַאֲחוֹתוֹ מִשִּׁפְחָה וְגוֹיָה.

The Gemara asks: **Say that whether** the Sages **say to your father: Maintain** her, **or whether** they **say to your father: Send her out, and the Merciful One states** that **"she is your sister,"** this comes **to include** the additional cases of **his sister from** a Canaanite **maidservant or a gentile woman.** The Gemara rejects this: **The verse states: "The daughter of your father's wife,"** and this means **whoever can enter a marriage bond with your father.** This **excludes his sister from** a Canaanite **maidservant or gentile woman,** with whom no marital bond is possible.

וּמָה רָאִיתָ? מִסְתַּבְּרָא, חַיָּיבֵי כְּרֵיתוֹת הֲוָה לֵיהּ לְרַבּוֹת, שֶׁכֵּן תָּפְסִי בָּהֶן קִדּוּשִׁין לְעָלְמָא.

The Gemara asks: Since the verse rendering his sister forbidden both includes and excludes cases, **what did you see** as a reason to include a daughter from a woman who is forbidden and both parties are liable to receive *karet*, and to exclude the daughter of a Canaanite maidservant or gentile woman? The Gemara answers: **It stands to reason** that those relationships that are forbidden because they render both parties **liable to receive *karet* should be included, since in general betrothal can come into effect with them.** This is because although this woman is forbidden to his father, she is nevertheless permitted to other men.

אַדְּרַבָּה, שִׁפְחָה וְגוֹיָה הֲוָה לֵיהּ לְרַבּוֹת, דְּאִי מִגַּיְּירָה – לְדִידֵיהּ נַמִי תָּפְסִי בָּהּ קִדּוּשִׁין! לְכִי מִגַּיְּירָה גּוּפָא אַחֲרִינָא הִיא.

The Gemara rejects this: **On the contrary, it should include** a Canaanite **maidservant or a gentile woman, as, if she converts, betrothal can come into effect with** the father **himself.** The Gemara answers: **When she converts, she is** considered like **a different body,** i.e., a new person, but when she was a gentile there was no possibility of marital relations with her. Therefore, the verse excludes her.

וְרַבָּנַן, לְמַעוּטֵי שִׁפְחָה וְגוֹיָה מְנָא לְהוּ? נָפְקָא לְהוּ מֵ״הָאִשָּׁה וִילָדֶיהָ תִּהְיֶה לַאֲדוֹנֶיהָ״.

The Gemara asks: **And** with regard to **the Rabbis,** who infer a different matter from the verse "your father's wife's nakedness," **from where do they** derive the *halakha* **to exclude** one's sister from a Canaanite **maidservant or gentile woman?** The Gemara answers: **They derive it** from that which was said with regard to a Canaanite maidservant who was married to a Hebrew slave: **"The wife and her children**[N] **shall be her master's"** (Exodus 21:4). From here they learn that the lineage of the maidservant's children is connected only to their mother and not at all connected to their Jewish father.

וְרַבִּי יוֹסֵי בְּרַבִּי יְהוּדָה: חַד – בְּשִׁפְחָה, וְחַד – בְּגוֹיָה. וּצְרִיכִי, דְּאִי אַשְׁמְעִינַן שִׁפְחָה – מִשּׁוּם דְּאֵין לָהּ חַיִּיס, אֲבָל גּוֹיָה דְּאִית לָהּ חַיִּיס – אֵימָא לָא.

The Gemara asks: **And** why does **Rabbi Yosei, son of Rabbi Yehuda,** not learn this from here? The Gemara responds: **One** verse was necessary to teach the case of a Canaanite **maidservant, and one** verse was necessary to teach the case of **a gentile woman. And** both verses **are necessary, as, if** the Torah **taught us** only about a Canaanite **maidservant,** one could say she is excluded only **because she does not have a pedigree,** since the Torah ascribes no family relationships to maidservants, **but** with regard to **a gentile woman who does have a pedigree,**[N] **say no.** It was therefore necessary to say that one's daughter by a gentile woman does not have the legal status of a daughter.

וְאִי אַשְׁמְעִינַן גּוֹיָה – מִשּׁוּם דְּלָא שַׁיְיכָא בְּמִצְוֹת, אֲבָל שִׁפְחָה, דְּשַׁיְיכָא בְּמִצְוֹת, אֵימָא לָא – צְרִיכָא.

Conversely, **if it would teach us** only the case of **a gentile woman,** one might say that this is **because she does not have any connection with the mitzvot** and therefore her children are in no way Jewish. **But** since a Canaanite **maidservant** has a **connection with the mitzvot,** as she is obligated to observe the prohibitions in the same way as a Jewish woman, **say no,**[H] i.e., her children should be considered children of their Jewish father. Therefore, this additional proof **is necessary.**

וְרַבָּנַן, אַשְׁכְּחַן שִׁפְחָה, גּוֹיָה מְנָא לְהוּ? וְכִי תֵּימָא: נֵילַף מִשִּׁפְחָה – הָנְהוּ מִצְרָךְ צְרִיכִי!

The Gemara asks: **And** according to the opinion of **the Rabbis, we found** a source that the children of a Canaanite **maidservant** are not considered the children of their Jewish father, but **from where** do we derive that children born to a Jewish father by **a gentile woman** are not considered his children? **And if you say: Let us derive** it **from** the case of the Canaanite **maidservant,** it has already been shown that **these are** both **necessary,** and one cannot be derived from the other.

NOTES

The wife and her children, etc. – **מֵהָאִשָּׁה וִילָדֶיהָ וכו׳:** Some commentaries explain that the status of the children is derived from a close reading of the text. Instead of stating: The wife and the children, it states: "The wife and her children." This implies that the children have the legal status of her children alone.

Does have a pedigree – **אִית לָהּ חַיִּיס:** The question of a pedigree here relates to paternal lineage. A child's status does not necessarily follow his father's lineage; rather, it depends on the specific *halakha*. For some realms of *halakha*, lineage follows the mother's family. Consequently, even when it is certain who the biological father is, the *halakha* does not necessarily consider the child a part of that family. The conclusion of the talmudic discussion here that *halakha* takes paternal lineage into account is not agreed upon by all. In the Jerusalem Talmud there is a dispute over whether gentiles follow their father's family lineage or not.

HALAKHA

A son from a Canaanite maidservant or a gentile woman – **בֵּן מִשִּׁפְחָה וְנָכְרִית:** A son born to a Jewish man from a Canaanite maidservant or from a gentile woman is not considered his son, neither for purposes of levirate marriage, nor inheritance, nor any other matter (Rambam *Sefer Nashim, Hilkhot Yibbum VaḤalitza* 1:4 and *Sefer Mishpatim, Hilkhot Naḥalot* 1:7).

NOTES

A son from a gentile woman – **בֵּן מִן הַנׇּכְרִית**: This *halakha* appears to be explicit in the verses: "We have broken faith with our God, and have married foreign women of the peoples of the land…Now therefore let us make a covenant with our God to put away all the wives, and such as are born of them…" (Ezra 10:2–3). Nevertheless, the Gemara sought to find a source for this *halakha* from the Torah (see Jerusalem Talmud).

She is called a Jew who is unfit – **יִשְׂרָאֵל פָּסוּל מִיקְרֵי**: According to most commentaries, being unfit refers to disqualification from the priesthood. A daughter of a gentile father and Jewish mother is unfit for marriage to a priest. Others hold that the disqualification mentioned here is not related to the priesthood but relates only to a defect in lineage (Ramban; *Yam shel Shlomo*).

HALAKHA

Offspring from a gentile or slave – **הַוּוֹלָד מִנׇּכְרִי וְעֶבֶד**: If a gentile or slave had relations with a Jewish woman and she gave birth to a child, that child is a Jew and is eligible to enter the congregation. If that offspring is a daughter, then she is unfit to marry a priest (*Shulḥan Arukh, Even HaEzer* 4:19; Rambam *Sefer Kedusha, Hilkhot Issurei Bia* 15:3).

אָמַר רַבִּי יוֹחָנָן מִשּׁוּם רַבִּי שִׁמְעוֹן בֶּן יוֹחַי: אָמַר קְרָא "כִּי יָסִיר אֶת בִּנְךָ מֵאַחֲרַי", בִּנְךָ מִיִּשְׂרְאֵלִית קָרוּי בִּנְךָ, וְאֵין בִּנְךָ הַבָּא מִן הַגּוֹיָה קָרוּי בִּנְךָ, אֶלָּא בְּנָהּ.

The Gemara answers: **Rabbi Yoḥanan said in the name of Rabbi Shimon ben Yoḥai:** The **verse states:** "Neither shall you make marriages with them: Your daughter you shall not give unto his son, nor his daughter shall you take unto your son, **for he will turn away your son from following Me**" (Deuteronomy 7:3–4). This teaches that **your son** born **from a Jewish woman is called your son, but your son** born **from a gentile woman is not called your son, but her son.**[N] The verse teaches that since the son of a gentile woman is her son alone, he is not considered related at all to his Jewish father.

אֲמַר רָבִינָא שְׁמַע מִינָּהּ: בֶּן בִּתְּךָ הַבָּא מִן הַגּוֹי – קָרוּי בִּנְךָ. לֵימָא קָסָבַר רָבִינָא גּוֹי וְעֶבֶד הַבָּא עַל בַּת יִשְׂרָאֵל הַוָּלָד כָּשֵׁר? נְהִי דְּמַמְזֵר לָא הָוֵי – כָּשֵׁר נַמִי לָא הָוֵי, יִשְׂרָאֵל פָּסוּל מִיקְּרֵי.

Ravina said: Conclude from here that **the son of your daughter by a gentile** father is nevertheless **called your son,** i.e., grandson. The Gemara asks: **Shall we say that Ravina holds that** if **a gentile or slave engaged in intercourse with a Jewish woman, the offspring is** of **unflawed** lineage?[H] The Gemara answers: There is no conclusive proof from here, because **granted, she is not a** ***mamzer,*** but nevertheless **she is still not** of **unflawed** lineage; rather, **she is called a Jew who is unfit**[N] to marry into the priesthood.

הַאי בְּשִׁבְעָה אוּמּוֹת כְּתִיב! "כִּי יָסִיר" לְרַבּוֹת כׇּל הַמְסִירִים.

The Gemara asks with regard to Rabbi Shimon's reasoning: Was **this** verse not **written in** relation to **the seven nations** who inhabited the land of Canaan when Joshua entered Eretz Yisrael but not with regard to other nations? The Gemara responds that the words **"He will turn away" comes to include all those who would turn** one's grandson **away** from God, i.e., any gentile.

הָנִיחָא לְרַבִּי שִׁמְעוֹן, דְּדָרֵישׁ טַעֲמָא דִּקְרָא, אֶלָּא לְרַבָּנַן מְנָא לְהוּ? מַאן תַּנָּא דְּפָלֵיג עֲלֵיהּ דְּרַבִּי יוֹסֵי בְּרַבִּי יְהוּדָה – רַבִּי שִׁמְעוֹן הִיא.

The Gemara asks: **This works out well for Rabbi Shimon, who interprets the rationale** behind the mitzva **in the verse** and draws halakhic conclusions based on that interpretation. Although the verse is stated with regard to the seven nations, the reason for the verse applies to all other gentile nations. **However, according to the** opinion of **the Rabbis,** who do not draw inferences from the rationale of the verse to apply this ruling to all other nations, **from where** do they derive **this** *halakha*? The Gemara answers: **Who is the** ***tanna*** **who disagrees with Rabbi Yosei, son of Rabbi Yehuda? It is Rabbi Shimon,** who applies the rationale of the verse to all other nations.

Perek **II**
Daf **23** Amud **b**

NOTES

Betrothed one of two sisters – **קִידֵּשׁ אַחַת מִשְּׁתֵּי אֲחָיוֹת**: There are several possible ways in which this could happen. He might have, e.g., betrothed one sister prior to some tumultuous event after which he did not remember which of them he betrothed and others offered conflicting opinions. Such an occurrence is recorded as having taken place and was brought before the *ge'onim* for a decision. If the mishna is referring to a case where the husband never knew to which sister he was betrothed, it must be a case where the two sisters appointed an emissary to accept their betrothals for them, and though the man intended to betroth one of them he did not explicitly designate which of them he desired.

מתני׳ מִי שֶׁקִּידֵּשׁ אַחַת מִשְּׁתֵּי אֲחָיוֹת וְאֵין יוֹדֵעַ אֵי זֶה מֵהֶן קִידֵּשׁ – נוֹתֵן גֵּט לָזוֹ וְגֵט לָזוֹ. מֵת, וְלוֹ אָח אֶחָד – חוֹלֵץ לִשְׁתֵּיהֶן.

MISHNA In the case of **one who betrothed one of two sisters**[NH] **and does not know which of them he betrothed,** so that both are forbidden to him, **he gives a bill of divorce to this one and a bill of divorce to that one** due to the uncertainty. If the man who had betrothed one of these women **died**[H] before he could give a bill of divorce, **and he had one brother,** that brother **performs** ***ḥalitza*** **with both of them,** but he may not take either in levirate marriage. This is because he does not know which woman is his *yevama* and which is forbidden to him as the sister of a woman with whom he has a levirate bond.

HALAKHA

Betrothed one of two sisters – **קִידֵּשׁ אַחַת מִשְּׁתֵּי אֲחָיוֹת**: One who betrothed one of two sisters and is uncertain as to which he betrothed may not consummate the marriage with either one of them. Rather, he must give a bill of divorce to each (Rambam *Sefer Nashim, Hilkhot Ishut* 9:3; *Shulḥan Arukh, Even HaEzer* 41:2, 176:1).

One who betroths one of two sisters and subsequently dies – **הַמְקַדֵּשׁ אַחַת הָאֲחָיוֹת וּמֵת**: If one betrothed one of two sisters and does not know which he betrothed, and then dies, his brother must perform *ḥalitza* with both of them in order to permit them to remarry. If the deceased had two brothers, one must perform *ḥalitza* with one sister, and the second is permitted to enter a levirate marriage with the other. One must not take one of the women in levirate marriage *ab initio*, as he would thereby encounter the sister of a woman with whom he has a levirate bond, as explained in the Gemara. If the two brothers both entered levirate marriage with the two sisters before consulting the court, they are not required to divorce (Rambam *Sefer Nashim, Hilkhot Yibbum VaḤalitza* 8:1; *Shulḥan Arukh, Even HaEzer* 176:1).

הָיוּ לוֹ שְׁנַיִם – אֶחָד חוֹלֵץ וְאֶחָד מְיַיבֵּם. קָדְמוּ וְכָנְסוּ – אֵין מוֹצִיאִין מִיָּדָם.

If the man who betrothed one of these women **had two** brothers, **one of them performs *ḥalitza*** with one of the sisters, but he may not enter into levirate marriage with her due to the possibility that she is the sister of a woman with whom he has a levirate bond. **And one takes** the other **in levirate marriage** if he so desires. If the two brothers **married** the two sisters **before** consulting the court, the court does not **remove them** from their marriage and they are permitted to remain married. The couple who performed levirate marriage second was even permitted to do so, since there was no longer any doubt about the levirate bond.

שְׁנַיִם שֶׁקִּדְּשׁוּ שְׁתֵּי אֲחָיוֹת, זֶה אֵינוֹ יוֹדֵעַ אֵי זוֹ קִידֵּשׁ, וְזֶה אֵינוֹ יוֹדֵעַ אֵיזוֹ קִידֵּשׁ – זֶה נוֹתֵן שְׁנֵי גִּיטִּין, וְזֶה נוֹתֵן שְׁנֵי גִּיטִּין. מֵתוּ, לָזֶה אָח וְלָזֶה אָח – זֶה חוֹלֵץ לִשְׁתֵּיהֶן, וְזֶה חוֹלֵץ לִשְׁתֵּיהֶן.

Furthermore, in the case of **two** unrelated men **who betrothed two sisters:** If **this one does not know which** sister **he betrothed and that one does not know which** sister **he betrothed, this one gives two bills of divorce,** one to each of the women, **and that one gives two bills of divorce.** If the two men **died** before they divorced, and **this one had a brother and that one had a brother,** then **this** brother **performs *ḥalitza* with both of them, and that** brother **performs *ḥalitza* with both of them.**

לָזֶה אֶחָד וְלָזֶה שְׁנַיִם – הַיָּחִיד חוֹלֵץ לִשְׁתֵּיהֶן. וְהַשְּׁנַיִם – אֶחָד חוֹלֵץ וְאֶחָד מְיַיבֵּם. קָדְמוּ וְכָנְסוּ – אֵין מוֹצִיאִין מִיָּדָם. לָזֶה שְׁנַיִם וְלָזֶה שְׁנַיִם – אָחִיו שֶׁל זֶה חוֹלֵץ לְאַחַת וְאָחִיו שֶׁל זֶה חוֹלֵץ לְאַחַת, אָחִיו שֶׁל זֶה מְיַיבֵּם חֲלוּצָתוֹ שֶׁל זֶה וְאָחִיו שֶׁל זֶה מְיַיבֵּם חֲלוּצָתוֹ שֶׁל זֶה.

If **this one had one** brother **and that one had two** brothers, **the single** brother **performs *ḥalitza* with both of them, and** of **the two** brothers, **one performs *ḥalitza* and one performs levirate marriage** if he so desires. If **they married** the sisters **before** consulting the court, the court **does not remove them** from the marriage and they are not told to divorce them. If **this one had two** brothers **and that one had two** brothers, **the brother of this one performs *ḥalitza* with one** sister, **and the brother of that one performs *ḥalitza* with one** sister. **The brother of this** one who performed *ḥalitza* **may take the woman who performed *ḥalitza*** [*ḥalutza*] **of that** other's brother **in levirate marriage, and the brother of that** second one who performed *ḥalitza* **may take the *ḥalutza* of that** other's brother **in levirate marriage.**

קָדְמוּ שְׁנַיִם וְחָלְצוּ – לֹא יְיַבְּמוּ הַשְּׁנַיִם, אֶלָּא אֶחָד חוֹלֵץ וְאֶחָד מְיַיבֵּם. קָדְמוּ וְכָנְסוּ – אֵין מוֹצִיאִין מִיָּדָם.

If the two brothers **performed *ḥalitza*** with both wives **before** consulting the court, **the** two brothers of the second man **may not take** sisters **in levirate marriage** lest one marry the sister of a woman who with whom he had a levirate bond. **Rather, one performs *ḥalitza* and one performs levirate marriage** if he so desires. If **they married** their wives **before** consulting the court, the court **does not remove them** from the marriage.

גמ׳ שְׁמַע מִינָּהּ: קִדּוּשִׁין שֶׁאֵין מְסוּרִין לְבִיאָה – הָווּ קִדּוּשִׁין!

GEMARA **Learn from here** in the mishna that **betrothals that cannot** ultimately **lead to consummation**[N] **are nevertheless betrothals.** There is a dispute between Abaye and Rava in tractate *Kiddushin* with regard to a case of a betrothal that, due to some halakhic complication, can never be consummated. The cases in this mishna may not be consummated, since each of the two sisters is forbidden due to the uncertainty as to whether she is the woman he betrothed or the sister of the woman he betrothed. Therefore, both are forbidden to him. Nevertheless, the mishna instructs that he must give a bill of divorce to both of them. This implies that such betrothals are valid, in contrast to Rava's opinion that betrothals that cannot ultimately be consummated are not betrothals at all.

הָכָא בְּמַאי עָסְקִינַן – כְּשֶׁהוּכְּרוּ וּלְבַסּוֹף נִתְעָרְבוּ. דַּיְקָא נַמִי, דְּקָתָנֵי "וְאֵינוֹ יוֹדֵעַ", וְלֹא קָתָנֵי "וְאֵינוֹ יָדוּעַ", שְׁמַע מִינָּהּ.

The Gemara rejects this: **With what are we dealing here?** We are dealing with a case **when** at first both sisters **were recognized** and at the moment of betrothal he knew whom he betrothed; it was a betrothal destined for consummation. **But later** the two sisters **were mixed up** so that he was no longer certain which he betrothed. If so, there was not any flaw in the betrothal itself initially. The language of the mishna **is also precise, as it teaches: And he does not know** which of them he betrothed, **but it does not teach: It is unknown** completely. This implies that the matter was known at some time. The Gemara adds: **Conclude from** here that this is the case.

NOTES

Betrothals that cannot ultimately lead to consummation – קִידּוּשִׁין שֶׁאֵין מְסוּרִין לְבִיאָה: *Tosafot* clarify that this principle does not apply in cases where there is some halakhic obstacle preventing sexual relations, e.g., some prohibition. The Gemara here is referring only to cases where the act of betrothal itself prevents the consummation of the marriage.

מַאי קָא מַשְׁמַע לַן? סֵיפָא אִיצְטְרִיכָא לֵיהּ: מֵת וְלוֹ אָח אֶחָד – חוֹלֵץ לִשְׁתֵּיהֶן, הָיוּ לוֹ שְׁנַיִם – אֶחָד חוֹלֵץ וְאֶחָד מְיַיבֵּם. דַּוְקָא מִיחְלָץ וַהֲדַר יַבּוּמֵי, אֲבָל יַבּוּמֵי בְּרֵישָׁא – לָא, דְּקָא פָּגַע בַּאֲחוֹת זְקוּקָתוֹ.

The Gemara asks: If so, **what is** the mishna **teaching us** in the segment of the mishna referring to the giving of two bills of divorce? That is obvious. The Gemara answers: **It was necessary** to teach **the last clause** of the mishna, as there it teaches: If **he died and he had one brother,** that brother **performs *ḥalitza* with both of them;** if **he had two** brothers, **one performs *ḥalitza*** and the other **one enters into levirate marriage** if he so desires. **Specifically,** one brother must perform ***ḥalitza*** first, **and only subsequently** the other brother may perform **levirate marriage. But** one brother **may not enter levirate marriage first,** before the other brother has performed *ḥalitza*, **as he** would thereby **encounter the sister of a woman with whom he has a levirate bond.**

״שְׁנַיִם שֶׁקִּדְּשׁוּ שְׁתֵּי אֲחָיוֹת״ וכו׳. שְׁמַע מִינַּהּ: קִדּוּשִׁין שֶׁאֵין מְסוּרִין לְבִיאָה הָווּ קִדּוּשִׁין! הָכָא נַמִי: כְּשֶׁהוּכְּרוּ וּלְבַסּוֹף נִתְעָרְבוּ. דַּיְקָא נַמִי, דְּקָתָנֵי ״וְאֵין יוֹדֵעַ״ וְלָא קָתָנֵי ״וְאֵין יָדוּעַ״, שְׁמַע מִינַּהּ.

The mishna says: In the case of **two** unrelated men **who betrothed two sisters:**[H] If this one does not know which sister he betrothed and that one does not know which sister he betrothed, this one gives two bills of divorce, one to each of the women, and that one gives two bills of divorce. The Gemara asks: **Learn from here** that **betrothals that cannot** ultimately **lead to consummation**[H] **are** valid **betrothals.** The Gemara rejects this: **Here too,** this is referring to a case **where they were recognized and later mixed up.** The language **is also precise, as it teaches: And he does not know,** meaning that he does not know now whom he betrothed, **and it does not teach: It is unknown.** The Gemara summarizes: Indeed, **conclude this from here** that this is the case.

וּמַאי קָא מַשְׁמַע לַן? סֵיפָא אִיצְטְרִיכָא לֵיהּ: ״מֵתוּ, לָזֶה אֶחָד וְלָזֶה שְׁנַיִם – הַיָּחִיד, חוֹלֵץ לִשְׁתֵּיהֶן. וְהַשְּׁנַיִם, אֶחָד חוֹלֵץ וְאֶחָד מְיַיבֵּם״.

The Gemara asks: If so, **what does it come to teach us** in relating that both of them must give bills of divorce? The Gemara explains: **It was necessary** to teach **the last clause,** where it says: If **they died** and **this one had one** brother **and this one had two, the single** brother **performs *ḥalitza* with both of them. And of the two, one performs *ḥalitza* and one enters levirate marriage** if he so desires.

פְּשִׁיטָא, הַיְינוּ רֵישָׁא! מַהוּ דְּתֵימָא: לִיגְזוֹר תְּרֵי אַטּוּ חַד, קָא מַשְׁמַע לַן.

The Gemara asks: **That is obvious,** as **this is** identical to the *halakha* taught in **the first clause** of the mishna. Why should this case be different from the previous case of two brothers? The Gemara answers: It is necessary to teach this **lest you say** the Sages should **issue a decree** in the case of **two** brothers **due to** the case of **one** brother. In a case of one brother he may only perform *ḥalitza* but may not enter into levirate marriage. Without this mishna one may have thought the same should be true for two brothers. **This comes to teach us** that they did not issue such a decree, and in this case one of them is allowed to enter into levirate marriage.

וְדַוְקָא מִיחְלָץ וַהֲדַר יַבּוּמֵי, אֲבָל יַבּוּמֵי בְּרֵישָׁא – לָא, דְּקָא פָּגַע בִּיבָמָה לַשּׁוּק.

And this is specifically if the brother of one man first **performs *ḥalitza* and subsequently** the brother of the other man **consummates the levirate marriage, but if he consummated the levirate marriage first, then no,** that is prohibited. And why is that? He might **be encountering** the prohibition of **a *yevama* to** a member of the **public.** Possibly the woman he married was not his *yevama* but someone else's *yevama*, and until the other man's brother performs *ḥalitza* with her she is still forbidden to other men.

HALAKHA

Two who betrothed two sisters – שְׁנַיִם שֶׁקִּדְּשׁוּ שְׁתֵּי אֲחָיוֹת: With regard to the case of two unrelated men who betrothed two sisters but do not know who betrothed whom and then both men died, if each had one brother, each brother performs *ḥalitza* with both of the women, and they may not enter levirate marriage.

If one of the deceased had one brother and the other had two brothers, then the single brother performs *ḥalitza* with both sisters, and with regard to the two brothers of the second man, one must first perform *ḥalitza* with one of the wives and then the other may enter levirate marriage with the other if he so desires. However, if these two brothers both entered into levirate marriage with the sisters before consulting the court but after the brother of the other man had performed *ḥalitza*, they need not divorce.

If each of the deceased men had two brothers, then one brother of the first performs *ḥalitza* for one of the women, and one brother of the second performs *ḥalitza* with the other woman. Then the second brother of the first is permitted to enter into levirate marriage with the woman who performed *ḥalitza* with the brother of the second. Similarly, the second brother of the second may marry the woman who performed *ḥalitza* with the brother of the first.

If both brothers of one man performed *ḥalitza* with both sisters, then *ab initio* one brother of the second should perform *ḥalitza* with one of the women and the second may then take the other in levirate marriage. If, however, both brothers of the second entered into levirate marriage with the sisters after the sisters performed *ḥalitza* with the brothers of the first, then the men are not made to divorce them (Rambam *Sefer Nashim, Hilkhot Yibbum VaḤalitza* 8:2–3; *Shulḥan Arukh, Even HaEzer* 176:3).

Betrothals that cannot ultimately lead to consummation – קִידּוּשִׁין שֶׁאֵין מְסוּרִין לְבִיאָה: A betrothal that cannot ultimately be consummated due to a halakhic impediment is nevertheless a valid betrothal, and the bond can be broken only by a bill of divorce. This ruling is against the Gemara here, which attempts to resolve the matter in accordance with Rava's opinion as well. Rather, this ruling is the conclusion of the talmudic discussion in tractate *Kiddushin* (51b) and is one of six cases where the *halakha* is ruled in accordance with the opinion of Abaye and not Rava (Rambam *Sefer Nashim, Hilkhot Ishut* 9:3; *Shulḥan Arukh, Even HaEzer* 176:1).

"לזה שנים ולזה שנים" וכו׳. הא תו למה לי, היינו הך! מהו דתימא: ליגזור דלמא מייבם בלא חליצה, קא משמע לן.

The mishna taught: If **this one had two** brothers **and that one had two** brothers, the brother of this who performed *ḥalitza* may take the *ḥalutza* of that other's brother in levirate marriage, and the brother of that second one who performed *ḥalitza* may take the *ḥalutza* of that other's brother in levirate marriage. The Gemara asks: **Why do I need this as well? This** clause **is identical** to **that** previous *halakha*. The Gemara answers: It is necessary **lest you say: Let** the Sages **issue a decree lest he consummate the levirate marriage without** the other first **performing *ḥalitza*** at all. **This comes to teach us** that such a decree is not issued. Rather, one of each pair of brothers can enter a levirate marriage.

מאי שנא מהא דתנן: ארבעה אחין, שנים מהן נשואין שתי אחיות, ומתו הנשואין את האחיות – הרי אלו חולצות ולא מתייבמות?

The Gemara asks: In **what** way **is** this case **different from that which we learned** in a mishna (26a): If there were **four brothers,** and **two of them were married to two sisters, and those married to the sisters died, then those** two sisters **perform *ḥalitza* but may not enter into levirate marriage** with the remaining brothers, since each woman is the sister of a woman with a levirate bond to each of the brothers. Why not say here as well that each is the sister of a woman with a levirate bond?

הכי השתא?!

The Gemara rejects this: **How can** these cases **be compared?**

Perek **II**
Daf **24** Amud **a**

התם אי למאן דאמר יש זיקה – יש זיקה. ואי למאן דאמר אסור לבטל מצות יבמין – אסור לבטל מצות יבמין. הכא – כל חד וחד, אימור דידיה קא מתרמיא ליה.

There, in that mishna, **if** it is **according to the one who said** that the levirate **bond is substantial,** then **there is a bond** in that case, as two sisters were certainly married to the brothers and require levirate marriage. **And if** it is **according to the one who said that** it is **prohibited to nullify the levirate mitzva** through marrying the sister of the *yevama*, then the explanation of that mishna is that **it is prohibited to nullify the levirate mitzva** and for this reason they must perform *ḥalitza* and may not enter into levirate marriage. However, **here,** in this mishna, there is uncertainty concerning the betrothal such that with regard to **each one** of the brothers, one could **say that** possibly he **encountered his own** *yevama*. Perhaps each brother took his own brother's wife in levirate marriage, and for this reason the Sages did not issue a decree.

"קדמו וכנסו אין מוציאין" כו׳. תני שילא: ואפילו שניהם כהנים. מאי טעמא? חלוצה דרבנן היא, וספק חלוצה – לא גזרו בהו רבנן.

§ The mishna states that if **they married** their wives **before** consulting the court, the **court does not remove them**[N] from the marriage. **Sheila teaches** a *baraita* that clarifies the mishna: **And** this is the case **even** if **both of** the brothers were **priests.**[H] A woman who performed *ḥalitza* is normally forbidden to a priest, yet in this case, although the brother of the other man performed *ḥalitza,* they are not required to divorce. **What is the reason** for this *halakha*? It is as follows: **A *ḥalutza* is** forbidden to a priest by **rabbinic law** because her status is similar to that of a divorcée, who is forbidden to a priest by Torah law. **And** in a case of **uncertainty** as to whether she is a ***ḥalutza,*** since it may not have been her *yavam* who performed the ceremony, **the Sages did not issue a decree.**[N]

וחלוצה דרבנן היא? והתניא: "גרושה", אין לי אלא גרושה, חלוצה מנין? תלמוד לומר "ואשה"! מדרבנן הוא, וקרא אסמכתא בעלמא הוא.

The Gemara asks: **And is** the prohibition against a ***ḥalutza*** marrying a priest[H] really **by rabbinic law? But isn't it taught** in a *baraita*: "They shall not take a woman that is a harlot, or profaned; neither shall they take a woman **divorced** from her husband; for he is holy unto his God" (Leviticus 21:7). **I have** derived **only a divorcée; from where** do I derive that a priest may not marry **a *ḥalutza*? The verse states:** "Neither shall they take **a woman.**" The repetition of the word "woman" extends the *halakha* to include a *ḥalutza*. The Gemara answers: **This** prohibition **is by rabbinic** law, **and the verse is a mere support.**

NOTES

The court does not remove them – אין מוציאין : In this case they are not required to divorce, because it is uncertain whether each woman is the sister of a woman with whom he has a levirate bond or not. However, the early commentaries write that in a case where she is certainly the sister of a woman with whom one has a levirate bond, then although that prohibition is rabbinic, nevertheless, one who transgresses it and marries her is required to divorce her.

In a case of uncertainty whether she is a *ḥalutza* the Sages did not issue a decree – ספק חלוצה לא גזרו: *Tosafot* challenge this because later (36b) the Gemara implies that the Sages did indeed render it prohibited for a priest to marry a woman whose *ḥalitza* was uncertain. Ramah, cited by *Tosefot HaRosh*, explains that there is a distinction between a case of *ḥalitza* performed out of uncertainty and a case where it is uncertain whether or not *ḥalitza* was performed. In cases where there was an actual *ḥalitza*, even if it is not certain that the *ḥalitza* was necessary, the Sages decreed that the *ḥalutza* is forbidden to a priest. In the case where it is not certain whether or not there was a *ḥalitza*, the Sages did not decree that she is forbidden to a priest.

HALAKHA

They married their wives before consulting the court… even if both…were priests – קדמו וכנסו...אפילו שניהם כהנים: Once they are married they are not required to divorce, even if they are priests, as the *ḥalitza* performed by the single brother is an uncertain *ḥalitza*, and the Sages did not apply their decree to such a case (Rambam *Sefer Nashim, Hilkhot Yibbum VaḤalitza* 8:2 and *Sefer Kedusha, Hilkhot Issurei Bia* 17:7; *Shulḥan Arukh, Even HaEzer* 176:3).

A *ḥalutza* marrying a priest – חלוצה לכהן: A *ḥalutza* is forbidden to a priest by rabbinic law since she is considered similar to a divorcée (Rambam *Sefer Nashim, Hilkhot Yibbum VaḤalitza* 8:2; *Sefer Kedusha, Hilkhot Ishut* 1:6 and *Hilkhot Issurei Bia* 17:7; *Shulḥan Arukh, Even HaEzer* 6:1).

מתני׳ מצוה בגדול לייבם ואם קדם הקטן – זכה.

MISHNA **It is a mitzva for the eldest to consummate the levirate marriage,**[H] i.e., the eldest takes precedence over the other brothers, though they too are obligated. **But if the younger** brother consummated the levirate marriage **first, he acquires** the *yevama* as his wife.[H]

גמ׳ תנו רבנן: ״והיה הבכור״ – מיכן שמצוה בגדול לייבם: ״אשר תלד״ – פרט לאילונית שאין יולדת: ״יקום על שם אחיו״ – לנחלה.

GEMARA **The Sages taught** the following interpretation of the verse: **"And it shall be that the firstborn** that she bears shall be established in the name of his dead brother and his name will not be blotted out of Israel" (Deuteronomy 25:6). **From here** the Sages derive **that the mitzva to consummate the levirate marriage is upon the eldest.** The next phrase: **"That she bears,"** is interpreted **to exclude** levirate marriage in the case of a widow who is **an *aylonit*, who cannot bear children.** From the next phrase: **"Shall be established in the name of his dead brother,"** it is derived that the same brother who performs the mitzva of levirate marriage is established in his brother's name with regard **to inheritance,**[H] i.e., he inherits his brother's property.

אתה אומר לנחלה, או אינו אלא לשם, יוסף – קורין אותו יוסף, יוחנן – קורין אותו יוחנן? נאמר כאן ״יקום על שם אחיו״ ונאמר להלן ״על שם אחיהם יקראו בנחלתם״, מה ״שם״ האמור להלן – נחלה, אף ״שם״ האמור כאן – לנחלה.

The *baraita* continues and asks: Do **you say** that he succeeds in the name of his brother **for inheritance, or** perhaps **it is only to** inherit **his name?** If, e.g., the deceased brother was named **Yosef, they** must **call** the son born from levirate marriage **Yosef,** or if his name was **Yoḥanan,** then **they** must **call him Yoḥanan.** The *baraita* answers: **It is stated here: "He shall succeed in the name of his brother," and it is stated there: "They shall be called after the name of their brothers in their inheritance"** (Genesis 48:6). **Just as** the word **"name" stated there** in Genesis is referring explicitly to **inheritance, so too,** the word **"name" stated here** in Leviticus means with regard **to inheritance.**

״ולא ימחה שמו״ – פרט לסריס, ששמו מחוי.

The *baraita* continues to expound the next phrase of the verse: **"And his name will not be blotted out** of Israel" (Deuteronomy 25:6). This **excludes** the case where the deceased was **a eunuch,**[H] **as his name is** already **blotted out,** since it is impossible for him to have children.

אמר רבא: אף על גב דבכל התורה כולה אין מקרא יוצא מידי פשוטו, הכא אתאי גזרה שוה אפיקתיה מפשטיה לגמרי.

Rava said: Even though in the entire Torah a verse does not depart from its literal meaning,[B] and even if the Sages offer a homiletical interpretation of the verses, the literal meaning remains intact, **here the verbal analogy**[B] teaching that the word "name" is referring to inheritance **comes to remove** the verse **from its literal meaning altogether.**[N]

ואי לאו גזרה שוה הוה אמינא ״שם״ שם ממש?! למאן קמזהר רחמנא, ליבם – ״יקום על שם אחיך״ מיבעי ליה! אי לבי דינא – ״יקום על שם אחי אביו״ מיבעי ליה!

The Gemara asks: **Were it not for the verbal analogy, would I have said** that the meaning of the word **"name" is the actual name?** The verse would be incomprehensible according to the literal reading. **Whom is the Merciful One instructing** in this verse? To whom does the possessive pronoun in the phrase "his brother" apply? If He is speaking **to the *yavam*, He should have stated: Shall succeed in the name of your dead brother. And if** the verse is instructing **the court** about the *halakha* in general, **it should have said: Shall succeed in the name of his father's brother.**

ודלמא הכי קאמר להו רחמנא לבית דין: אמרו ליה ליבם ״יקום על שם אחיו!״. אלא, אתאי גזרה שוה אפיקתיה לגמרי.

The Gemara rejects this question: **And perhaps this is what the Merciful One is saying to the court: Say to the *yavam*** that the child born to him **shall be established in the name of his brother.** Were it not for the verbal analogy, the verse could have been understood according to its literal meaning. **Rather, the verbal analogy comes to remove it** from its literal meaning **altogether.**

השתא דאמרת קרא בגדול כתיב, אימא: בכור – לייבם, פשוט – לא לייבם.

The Gemara challenges the *baraita*: **Now that you say that the verse:** "And it shall be that the firstborn that she bears" **is written** in reference to **the eldest** brother, **say** that **the firstborn** brother **consummates the levirate marriage** but that **an ordinary** brother, i.e., not the firstborn, **may not consummate the levirate marriage,** and that if the firstborn son is unable to enter into levirate marriage or is no longer alive, no one else may perform the mitzva.

HALAKHA

It is a mitzva for the eldest to consummate the levirate marriage – מצוה בגדול לייבם: The primary obligation to consummate the levirate marriage or perform *ḥalitza* devolves upon the eldest of the brothers (Rambam *Sefer Nashim, Hilkhot Yibbum VaḤalitza* 2:6; *Shulḥan Arukh, Even HaEzer* 161:4).

If the younger consummated the levirate marriage first, he acquires her as his wife – ואם קדם הקטן זכה: Although the mitzva of levirate marriage devolves primarily upon the eldest of the brothers, if one of the others went ahead and entered into levirate marriage, then it is effective (Rambam *Sefer Nashim, Hilkhot Yibbum VaḤalitza* 2:6; *Shulḥan Arukh, Even HaEzer* 161:7).

Shall be established in the name of his dead brother, with regard to inheritance – יקום על שם אחיו לנחלה: The brother who consummates levirate marriage with his brother's widow inherits all of the property that is actually in his brother's possession (Rambam *Sefer Mishpatim, Hilkhot Naḥalot* 3:7; *Shulḥan Arukh, Even HaEzer* 163:1).

Excludes a eunuch – פרט לסריס: A man who became sexually impotent through illness is not eligible for *ḥalitza* or levirate marriage. If he performed *ḥalitza* or if others performed *ḥalitza* with his wife, it has no halakhic significance (Rambam *Sefer Nashim, Hilkhot Yibbum VaḤalitza* 6:2, 4; *Shulḥan Arukh, Even HaEzer* 172:1).

BACKGROUND

A verse does not depart from its literal meaning – אין מקרא יוצא מידי פשוטו: Even when the Bible is interpreted metaphorically, and even when halakhic conclusions are reached by means of a homiletic interpretation of a verse, these conclusions do not negate the literal meaning of the text (*Alfei Menashe*).

Verbal analogy – גזרה שוה: This is a fundamental talmudic principle of biblical exegesis appearing in all the standard lists of hermeneutical principles. If the same word or phrase appears in two places in the Torah, and a certain *halakha* is explicitly stated in one of these places, then on the basis of verbal analogy it is inferred that the same *halakha* applies in the other case as well.

Certain restrictions were placed on the use of this principle to prevent unfounded conclusions from being drawn. Most significantly: One cannot infer a verbal analogy on one's own, i.e., only a verbal analogy based on ancient tradition is valid.

NOTES

Remove the verse from its literal meaning altogether – אפיקתיה מפשטיה לגמרי: It is a transmitted tradition that there is no requirement to name the firstborn son of a levirate marriage after the deceased. Therefore, the verse cannot be read in accordance with its literal meaning (see Rashi).

The reason the Torah writes that the son will take the name of the deceased brother, even though that is not the *halakha*, is explained by the commentaries based on esoteric teachings. Through levirate marriage the soul of the deceased brother is reincarnated in the newborn son. This idea is elaborated upon in Ramban's Commentary on the Torah (Genesis, chapter 38; see *Sefer HaBoneh*).

אִם כֵּן, אֵשֶׁת אָחִיו שֶׁלֹּא הָיָה בְּעוֹלָמוֹ דְּמִיעֵט רַחֲמָנָא – לָמָּה לִי?

The Gemara answers: **If so** that the mitzva of levirate marriage applies only to the firstborn, then in the case of **a wife of a brother with whom he did not coexist,** which **the Merciful One excluded** by the verse: "If brothers dwell together," **why do I need** such an exclusion? If only the firstborn is obligated to perform levirate marriage, then there is no need to separately exclude the case of a wife of one's brother with whom one did not coexist, because by definition one in that position cannot be the firstborn.

פְּרֵיךְ רַב אַחָא: וְאֵימָא לְמַעוּטֵי בּוּכְרָא דְּאִמָּא! הַהוּא לָא מָצֵית אָמְרַתְּ, דְּיִבּוּם בְּנַחֲלָה תָּלָה רַחֲמָנָא, וְנַחֲלָה מִן הָאָב וְלֹא מִן הָאֵם.

Rav Aḥa refutes the Gemara's answer: **But say that** the verse comes **to exclude** the case of a brother with whom one did not coexist when one is nevertheless **the firstborn of the mother,** e.g., if the father had two wives. The Gemara rejects this: **You cannot say that, as the Merciful One made levirate marriage dependent upon inheritance,**[N] **and inheritance** comes **from the father**[H] **and not from the mother.**

וְאֵימָא: כִּי אִיכָּא בְּכוֹר תִּתְקַיֵּים מִצְוַת יִבּוּם, כִּי לֵיכָּא בְּכוֹר לָא תִּתְקַיֵּים מִצְוַת יִבּוּם! אָמַר קְרָא: "וּמֵת אֶחָד מֵהֶם", מִי לָא עָסְקִינַן דְּמִית בְּכוֹר, וְאָמַר רַחֲמָנָא לְיַיבֵּם קָטָן.

The Gemara again challenges the *baraita*: **Then say that when there is a firstborn the mitzva of levirate marriage can be fulfilled** by any of the brothers, **but that when there is no firstborn,** e.g., if he had already died, **the mitzva of levirate marriage may not be fulfilled** by any of the younger brothers. The Gemara answers: **The verse states: "And one of them dies"** (Deuteronomy 25:5), without specifying which brother dies. **Are we not dealing** even with the case **where the firstborn died, and** yet **the Merciful One states** that **the younger** brother **should consummate the levirate marriage?**

וְאֵימָא דְּמִית קָטָן, וְאָמַר רַחֲמָנָא לְיַיבֵּם בְּכוֹר! הָא מִיעֵט רַחֲמָנָא אֵשֶׁת אָחִיו שֶׁלֹּא הָיָה בְּעוֹלָמוֹ.

The Gemara refutes this answer: **Say that** the case in the Torah is referring to when **the younger** brother **died, and** only then **the Merciful One states that the firstborn must consummate the levirate marriage.** The Gemara answers: **Didn't the Merciful One** explicitly **exclude the wife of a brother with whom he did not coexist,** which can apply only to a brother who was not the firstborn?

וְאֵימָא: כִּי לֵיכָּא בְּכוֹר – קָדַם קָטָן זָכָה, וְאִי אִיכָּא בְּכוֹר – קָדַם קָטָן לֹא זָכָה! אָמַר קְרָא: "כִּי יֵשְׁבוּ אַחִים יַחְדָּו" – הוּקְשָׁה יְשִׁיבַת אַחִים זֶה לָזֶה.

The Gemara challenges the *halakha*: **Say** that **when there is no firstborn** brother, if **a younger** brother **went ahead** and consummated the levirate marriage, then **he acquires** his *yevama* as a wife. **But if there is a firstborn,** and **the younger** brother **went ahead** and performed levirate marriage first, then **he does not acquire** his *yevama* as a wife, because the Torah specifies that the firstborn brother must perform the mitzva. The Gemara rejects this: **The verse states: "If brothers dwell together"** (Deuteronomy 25:5), implying that **the brothers' dwellings were equated one with the other,** and all the brothers are equally obligated in this mitzva.

וְאֵימָא: כִּי אִיכָּא בְּכוֹר – לִיהֲדַר אַגָּדוֹל, כִּי לֵיכָּא בְּכוֹר – אֵין חוֹזְרִין אֵצֶל גָּדוֹל! אַלְמָה תָּנֵי אַבַּיֵּי קַשִּׁישָׁא: מִצְוָה בַּגָּדוֹל לְיַיבֵּם. לֹא רָצָה – הוֹלְכִים אֵצֶל אָחִיו הַקָּטָן, לֹא רָצָה – חוֹזְרִין אֵצֶל גָּדוֹל!

The Gemara challenges the *halakha* again: **Then say: When there is a firstborn, let** the mitzva **return to the eldest** brother if the other brothers refuse to perform levirate marriage. But **when there is no firstborn,** the court **does not return to the eldest,** as the mitzva primarily applies specifically to the firstborn, and if there is no firstborn, none of the brothers take precedence. **Why did Abaye the Elder teach: It is a mitzva for the eldest** of the brothers **to consummate the levirate marriage? If** the eldest **did not wish** to do so, then the court **goes to his younger brother.** If **he** also **did not wish** to do so, the court **returns** again **to the eldest.** This implies that the eldest, even if he is not the firstborn, has a greater mitzva than the younger brothers.

כִּבְכוֹר, מָה בְּכוֹר – בְּכוֹרָתוֹ גָּרְמָה לוֹ, אַף גָּדוֹל – גַּדְלוּתוֹ גָּרְמָה לוֹ.

The Gemara answers: Since it is derived that the eldest brother takes precedence from the verse about the firstborn, then **just as** with regard to **the firstborn, his status as firstborn causes him**[N] to take precedence, **so too,** with regard to **the eldest, his status as eldest causes him** to take precedence.[H]

NOTES

The Merciful One made levirate marriage dependent upon inheritance – יִבּוּם בְּנַחֲלָה תָּלָה רַחֲמָנָא: Rashi explains that this is referring only to the firstborn son, who inherits a double portion from his father. Therefore the firstborn of only the father has relevance, not the firstborn of the mother. See Rabbi Yehuda bar Natan, *Tosefot HaRosh*, and Rashba, who suggest an alternative explanation.

Just as with regard to the firstborn, his status as firstborn causes him, etc. – כִּבְכוֹר מָה בְּכוֹר בְּכוֹרָתוֹ גָּרְמָה לוֹ וכו׳: In other words, since the Gemara has explained that with regard to levirate marriage the firstborn status is irrelevant, it is clear that the key factor is that he is the eldest of the brothers. This implies that the eldest takes precedence in matters of levirate marriage (*Tosefot HaRosh*).

HALAKHA

Inheritance from the father – נַחֲלָה מִן הָאָב: One's mother's family is not called family with regard to inheritance, and inheritance is received only from one's father's family. Therefore, maternal half brothers do not inherit from one another (Rambam *Sefer Mishpatim, Hilkhot Naḥalot* 1:6; *Shulḥan Arukh, Ḥoshen Mishpat* 276:4).

Order of the obligation to enter levirate marriage – סֵדֶר הַמִּצְוֹת בְּיִבּוּם: The obligation of levirate marriage falls upon the eldest of the surviving brothers. If he does not wish to fulfill his mitzva, it devolves upon the next eldest. According to the Rambam it devolves equally on all of the remaining brothers. If none of the younger brothers fulfills the obligation, the obligation to perform the mitzva remains with the eldest (Rambam *Sefer Nashim, Hilkhot Yibbum VaḤalitza* 2:6; *Shulḥan Arukh, Even HaEzer* 161:4).

וְאֵימָא: כִּי מְיַיבֵּם בְּכוֹר – לִישְׁקוֹל נַחֲלָה, כִּי מְיַיבֵּם פָּשׁוּט לָא לִישְׁקוֹל נַחֲלָה! אָמַר קְרָא: "יָקוּם עַל שֵׁם אָחִיו" – וַהֲרֵי קָם.

The Gemara challenges the *halakha* again: **Then say** that **if the firstborn consummates the levirate marriage he receives** his deceased brother's **inheritance,** but **if an ordinary brother consummates the levirate marriage he does not receive the inheritance.** The Gemara answers that **the verse states:** "The firstborn that she bears **shall be established in the name of his** dead **brother"** (Deuteronomy 25:6), **and** if the younger brother performs levirate marriage he has **established** his brother's name and thereby earns the inheritance.

וְאֶלָּא בְּכוֹר דְּקַרְיֵיהּ רַחֲמָנָא,

The Gemara asks: **But** if there is no difference between the firstborn and the eldest, why does **the Merciful One call** the brother who enters levirate marriage the **firstborn?**

Perek **II**
Daf **24** Amud **b**

לְמַאי הִלְכְתָא? לְגָרִיעוּתָא, מָה בְּכוֹר אֵינוֹ נוֹטֵל בְּרָאוּי כְּבַמּוּחְזָק – אַף הַאי אֵינוֹ נוֹטֵל בְּרָאוּי כְּבַמּוּחְזָק.

With regard to what *halakha* was that word written in the Torah? **This is in order to limit**[N] the inheritance. **Just as a firstborn does not take** in inheritance property **due as** he does property **possessed,** but instead receives a double inheritance only from that property already in actual possession of their father, **so too, this** one who enters levirate marriage, whether firstborn or younger, **does not take** in inheritance property **due as** he does property **possessed.**[H]

מתני׳ הַנִּטְעָן עַל הַשִּׁפְחָה וְנִשְׁתַּחְרְרָה, אוֹ עַל הַגּוֹיָה וְנִתְגַּיְּירָה, הֲרֵי זֶה לֹא יִכְנוֹס. וְאִם כָּנַס – אֵין מוֹצִיאִין מִיָּדוֹ. הַנִּטְעָן עַל אֵשֶׁת אִישׁ וְהוֹצִיאוּהָ מִתַּחַת יָדוֹ, אַף עַל פִּי שֶׁכָּנַס – יוֹצִיא.

MISHNA **One suspected** by others of engaging in sexual relations **with a Canaanite maidservant**[N] **and she was** later **set free, or** one suspected of relations **with a gentile woman**[H] **and she** subsequently **converted, may not marry** that woman, since this will strengthen the suspicions against him. **But if he did marry her, they,** the judges of the court, **do not remove** her **from him,** i.e., they do not require him to divorce her. With regard to **one who is suspected of** illicit relations with **a married woman and they,** the judges of the court, **removed her from** her husband, i.e., required them to divorce due to this, **even if** the man suspected of the illicit relations subsequently **married** her, **he must divorce** her.

NOTES

In order to limit – לְגָרִיעוּתָא: *Tosafot* point out that equating the inheritance of one who performs levirate marriage with the inheritance of a firstborn is not solely a limitation, but also gives a benefit, as this additional inherited portion of land is not divided with the other brothers in the Jubilee Year. However, it is described as a limitation because Rabbi Elazar disagrees with regard to the benefit and holds that land inherited through levirate marriage does revert to be shared with the other brothers in the Jubilee Year (*Tosafot* on *Bekhorot* 52b and *Tosefot HaRosh*; see *Mei Neftoaḥ*).

One suspected of relations with a Canaanite maidservant, etc. – הַנִּטְעָן עַל הַשִּׁפְחָה וכו׳: This mishna and those following are not directly related to the main topic of this chapter. They appear here because the earlier mishna mentioned the distinction between cases where the court removes a wife from her husband and those where it permits her to remain married to him (*Yosef Lekaḥ*).

HALAKHA

One who enters levirate marriage does not take in inheritance property due – הַמְיַיבֵּם אֵינוֹ נוֹטֵל בְּרָאוּי: One who performs levirate marriage receives the property of his deceased brother and also receives his brother's portion in the inheritance from their father. However, this applies only to property in the brother's possession, as is the case when the father predeceased the brother but the inheritance had yet to be divided when the brother died. However, if the brother died prior to the father, the one who performed levirate marriage does not receive his brother's portion of the inheritance (Rambam *Sefer Mishpatim, Hilkhot Naḥalot* 3:7; *Shulḥan Arukh, Even HaEzer* 163:1).

One suspected of relations with a Canaanite maidservant… or with a gentile woman – הַנִּטְעָן עַל הַשִּׁפְחָה...אוֹ עַל הַגּוֹיָה: One who is suspected of relations with a Canaanite maidservant or a gentile woman may not marry her *ab initio* if the maidservant was set free or if the gentile woman converted. However, if he did marry her, the court does not require him to divorce her (Rambam *Sefer Nashim, Hilkhot Geirushin* 10:14; *Shulḥan Arukh, Even HaEzer* 11:5).

גמ׳ הָא גִּיּוֹרֶת מִיהָא הָוְיָא, וּרְמִינְהִי: אֶחָד אִישׁ שֶׁנִּתְגַּיֵּיר לְשׁוּם אִשָּׁה, וְאֶחָד אִשָּׁה שֶׁנִּתְגַּיְּירָה לְשׁוּם אִישׁ, וְכֵן מִי שֶׁנִּתְגַּיֵּיר לְשׁוּם שׁוּלְחַן מְלָכִים, לְשׁוּם עַבְדֵי שְׁלֹמֹה – אֵינָן גֵּרִים, דִּבְרֵי רַבִּי נְחֶמְיָה.

GEMARA The mishna teaches that one who is suspected of relations with a gentile woman who later converted may never marry her. **This** implies that **she is, however, a convert,** although it appears that she converted only in order that he might marry her. The Gemara **raises a contradiction** from a *baraita*: **Both a man who converted for the sake of a woman**[N] **and a woman who converted for the sake of a man, and similarly, one who converted for the sake of the king's table,**[N] so that he could serve in a prestigious capacity, or **for the sake of Solomon's servants,** who were also considered prestigious, in all of these cases **they are not converts;** this is **the statement of Rabbi Neḥemya.**

שֶׁהָיָה רַבִּי נְחֶמְיָה אוֹמֵר: אֶחָד גֵּירֵי אֲרָיוֹת וְאֶחָד גֵּירֵי חֲלוֹמוֹת, וְאֶחָד גֵּירֵי מָרְדֳּכַי וְאֶסְתֵּר – אֵינָן גֵּרִים עַד שֶׁיִּתְגַּיְּירוּ בַּזְּמַן הַזֶּה.

As Rabbi Neḥemya would say: With regard to **converts** by **lions,** i.e., forced converts such as the Samaritans [*Kutim*] described in II Kings (17:24–25); **and converts** who convert based on their **dreams; and converts of** the time of **Mordecai and Esther** described in the verse, "And many from among the peoples of the land became Jews; for the fear of the Jews was fallen upon them" (Esther 8:17); all of these **are not converts until they are converted at this** present **time.**

בַּזְּמַן הַזֶּה סָלְקָא דַּעְתָּךְ?! אֶלָּא, אֵימָא: כִּבַזְּמַן הַזֶּה.

The Gemara clarifies the meaning of the words: Could it **enter your mind** to say only **at this present time?** Since he mentioned the converts of Mordecai and Esther, who were deceased before Rabbi Neḥemya made this statement, he therefore cannot possibly mean this phrase literally. **Rather, say: Like at this** present **time,** when the Jewish people are in exile and there is no material benefit to conversion.

הָא אִיתְּמַר עֲלַהּ, אָמַר רַב יִצְחָק בַּר שְׁמוּאֵל בַּר מָרְתָא מִשְּׁמֵיהּ דְּרַב: הֲלָכָה כְּדִבְרֵי הָאוֹמֵר כּוּלָּם גֵּרִים הֵם.

Returning to the question above: How could a woman who converted for the sake of a man be considered a true convert? The Gemara answers: But **wasn't it stated with regard to** that *baraita* that **Rav Yitzḥak bar Shmuel bar Marta said in the name of Rav:** The ***halakha*** **is** in accordance with **the statement of the one who says that they are all converts.**[H]

אִי הָכִי לְכַתְּחִלָּה נָמֵי! מִשּׁוּם דְּרַב אַסִּי, דְּאָמַר רַב אַסִּי: ״הָסֵר מִמְּךָ עִקְּשׁוּת פֶּה וּלְזוּת שְׂפָתַיִם״ וגו׳.

The Gemara asks: **If so,** why is one suspected of relations with such a woman not permitted to enter into marriage with her ***ab initio*** **as well?** The Gemara answers: The reason for the prohibition is **due to** the following statement **of Rav Asi. As Rav Asi said** with regard to such cases: **"Put away from yourself**[N] **a twisted mouth, and perverse lips** put far from you" (Proverbs 4:24). If they were to marry, they would give substance to the prior suspicions.

תָּנוּ רַבָּנַן: אֵין מְקַבְּלִין גֵּרִים לִימוֹת הַמָּשִׁיחַ. כַּיּוֹצֵא בּוֹ לֹא קִבְּלוּ גֵּרִים לֹא בִּימֵי דָוִד וְלֹא בִּימֵי שְׁלֹמֹה. אָמַר רַבִּי אֱלִיעֶזֶר: מַאי קְרָא – ״הֵן גּוֹר יָגוּר אֶפֶס מֵאוֹתִי מִי גָר אִתָּךְ עָלַיִךְ יִפּוֹל״ אֲבָל אִידָּךְ – לָא.

The Sages taught: Converts are not accepted in the days of the Messiah. Similarly, they did not accept converts in the days of King **David or in the days of** King **Solomon.**[NH] **Rabbi Eliezer said: What is the verse** that hints at this *halakha*? **"Behold, they may gather together [*gor yagur*],**[N] **but without Me; whosoever shall gather together [*gar*] with you shall fall on yours"** (Isaiah 54:15). The word *gor* implies that only a convert [*ger*] who becomes part of the Jewish people when the Jews are living in exile, at a time when God is not clearly revealed, i.e., "without Me," are considered part of the Jewish people. **But another** who wishes to convert in a time when God is clearly revealed shall **not** be accepted.

HALAKHA

They are all converts – **כּוּלָּם גֵּרִים הֵם:** The court must examine the motivation of a potential convert to ensure that he wishes to convert solely for the sake of Heaven. If the court did not examine his motivation before converting him, and even if it subsequently became known that he converted for some ulterior motive, since he has been circumcised and immersed in a ritual bath before a court of three, he no longer has the status of a gentile but his status remains in doubt until it becomes clear that he accepted Judaism completely. He does not have the status of a Jew such that he should be trusted, e.g., in declaring food to be permitted, but nevertheless he is not considered a gentile, and if he marries a Jewish woman the marriage is valid. Even if he reverted to idol worship he is considered an apostate Jew, based on the opinion of Rav and the conclusion of the Gemara's discussion (Rambam *Sefer Kedusha, Hilkhot Issurei Bia* 13:14–17; *Shulḥan Arukh, Yoreh De'a* 268:12).

They did not accept converts in the days of King David or in the days of King Solomon – **לֹא קִבְּלוּ גֵּרִים לֹא בִּימֵי דָוִד וְלֹא בִּימֵי שְׁלֹמֹה:** The court did not accept converts in the eras of David and Solomon, as they feared that gentiles might convert due to the strength and glory of the Jewish kingdom (Rambam *Sefer Kedusha, Hilkhot Issurei Bia* 13:15).

NOTES

Who converted for the sake of a woman – **שֶׁנִּתְגַּיֵּיר לְשׁוּם אִשָּׁה:** *Mishpetei Uziel* derives from this Gemara that one can accept a convert *ab initio*, even if he intends to marry a Jewish woman at the time of his conversion, if it becomes clear that he would have married her anyway while remaining a gentile and instead chose of his own accord to become a Jew. He explains that the concern of the Sages is that a gentile who converts for the sake of a woman may still remain attached to his previous religion, and as soon as his love fades he will once again revert to his former religion. However, if it is apparent that he sincerely wants to become a Jew, even if there were other motives involved it can be assumed that the purer motives will prevail and he will maintain his principles even afterward. Moreover, it may be preferable to convert him in such a case so that the Jewish woman will not marry a gentile, since she would have been willing to marry him even if he did not convert. He bases this on the halakhic principle: "It is time to work for the Lord; they have made void Your Torah" (Psalms 119:126; see *Berakhot* 54a), which implies that when one needs to perform God's will, it is occasionally permitted to negate even a biblical precept or, in this case, a rabbinical decree (*Mishpetei Uziel, Yoreh De'a* 2:53).

For the sake of the king's table – **לְשׁוּם שׁוּלְחַן מְלָכִים:** In the minor tractate that discusses the *halakhot* of converts, known as tractate *Gerim*, there is a list of four different categories of converts. One of them is a convert for the sake of sustenance, which means that he saw poor Jews receiving sustenance from their brethren and converted so that he too could receive sustenance. He is therefore compared to a pauper, as it is written: "You shall leave them for the poor and the stranger [*ger*]" (Leviticus 19:10). It is possible that the king's table is also referring to this sustenance, as the poor would eat from the king's table (see Meiri).

The so-called minor tractates, some of which are rather long, were also called external tractates by the *ge'onim*. They deal with many subjects, but what they have in common is that their subject matter was generally not discussed in one specific tractate or chapter in the Mishna and Talmud, although many of them do refer to Torah laws and major halakhic principles. These tractates could be an indication that another order of the Mishna once existed.

As Rav Asi said, Put away from yourself, etc. – **דְּאָמַר רַב אַסִּי: הָסֵר מִמְּךָ וכו׳:** Since this is a biblical verse, why is it attributed to Rav Asi? *Tosafot* on *Ketubot* 72b explain that Rav Asi would frequently cite this verse, and it became associated with him. The Maharatz Hayyut writes that there are alternative interpretations of the verse; it is only due to Rav Asi's interpretation that actions are prohibited if they appear to give validity to prior rumors.

Not…in the days of King David or in the days of King Solomon – **לֹא בִּימֵי דָוִד וְלֹא בִּימֵי שְׁלֹמֹה:** Rambam explains that in each of these two eras there was a different reason for refusing converts: In the time of King David converts were not accepted lest their conversion stem from fear of King David; in the days of King Solomon the concern was that they may have converted due to his glory and wealth.

Behold, they may gather together – **הֵן גּוֹר יָגוּר:** The homiletical interpretation is based on the fact that the word gather [*gar*] is similar to the word convert [*ger*]. Rabbi Yehuda bar Natan gives an alternative explanation. He writes that the word *gur* also means terror, as in the verse: "For I have heard the whispering of many, terror [*magor*] on every side" (Psalms 31:14). Therefore, if one converted due to fear he is considered "without Me," i.e., not part of God's people.

״הַנִּטְעָן עַל אֵשֶׁת אִישׁ״ וכו׳. אֲמַר רַב: וּבְעֵדִים.

§ The mishna states that **one who was suspected of** relations with **a married woman** may not marry her even after she divorces her husband. Even if they marry without permission, they must divorce. **Rav said: This is** only in a case when there were **witnesses** to her infidelity, and because of their testimony the court required her first husband divorce her. However, if her first husband divorced her due to suspicion and rumors but without witnesses, her second husband would not be obligated to divorce her.

אֲמַר רַב שֵׁשֶׁת: אָמִינָא כִּי נָיֵים וְשָׁכֵיב רַב אֲמַר לְהַאי שְׁמַעְתְּתָא. דְּתַנְיָא: הַנִּטְעָן עַל אֵשֶׁת אִישׁ וְהוֹצִיאוּהָ עַל יָדוֹ, וְנִתְגָּרְשָׁה מִתַּחַת יְדֵי אַחֵר, אִם כָּנַס – לֹא יוֹצִיא.

Rav Sheshet said: I say that when Rav was dozing or sleeping[N] **he said that *halakha*,** and it is mistaken. **As it is taught** in a *baraita*: With regard to **one who was suspected of** adultery with **a married woman and** as a result the court requires her husband to **divorce her,** and later she married someone else[H] **and was then divorced by this other, if** the one who had been suspected of illicit relations with her then **married** her, **he need not divorce** her.

הֵיכִי דָּמֵי, אִי דְּאִיכָּא עֵדִים – כִּי אֲתָא אַחֵר וְאַפְסְקֵיהּ לְקָלָא מַאי הָוֵי? אֶלָּא לָאו דְּלֵיכָּא עֵדִים, וְטַעְמָא, דַּאֲתָא אַחֵר וְאַפְסְקֵיהּ לְקָלָא, הָא לָאו הָכִי – מַפְּקִינַן!

The Gemara clarifies this: **What are the circumstances** of this case? **If** it is referring to a case where **there are witnesses** to their adultery, **when another came and put an end to the rumor** of her misconduct by marrying her, **what of it?** If there were witnesses, the adulterers may never marry each other. **Rather, is it not** referring to a case **where there were no witnesses** to the adultery, **and the reason** she does not have to be divorced from her third husband, with whom she committed adultery while married to her first husband, is specifically **because another came** and, by marrying her, **put an end to the rumor? This** implies that **were it not so,** i.e., had she not married someone else before marrying the man suspected of committing adultery with her, the court **would have removed** her from him and required them to divorce, even without witnesses to their adultery. This contradicts Rav's statement above that they must divorce only if there were witnesses to the infidelity.

אָמַר לָךְ רַב: הוּא הַדִּין דְּאַף עַל גַּב דְּלָא אֲתָא אַחֵר וְאַפְסְקֵיהּ לְקָלָא. אִי אִיכָּא עֵדִים – מַפְּקִינַן, אִי לֵיכָּא עֵדִים – לָא מַפְּקִינַן, וְהָכִי קָאָמַר: דְּאַף עַל גַּב דַּאֲתָא אַחֵר וְאַפְסְקֵיהּ לְקָלָא – לְכַתְּחִלָּה לֹא יִכְנוֹס.

The Gemara responds: **Rav** could have **said to you** that **the same is true even if another did not come and put an end to the rumor** by marrying her. The same principle applies: **If there were witnesses** to the adultery the court **removes her** and requires them to divorce, but **if there were no witnesses,** the court **does not remove her. And this is what** the *baraita* **is saying:** The novelty in this *baraita* is **that even though another came and put an end to the rumor** by marrying her, nevertheless, the suspected adulterer may **not marry her *ab initio*** due to the original suspicions.

מֵיתִיבֵי: בַּמֶּה דְּבָרִים אֲמוּרִים – כְּשֶׁאֵין לָהּ בָּנִים, אֲבָל יֵשׁ לָהּ בָּנִים – לֹא תֵּצֵא. וְאִם בָּאוּ עֵדֵי טוּמְאָה – אֲפִילּוּ יֵשׁ לָהּ כַּמָּה בָּנִים תֵּצֵא.

The Gemara **raises an objection** from a different *baraita* that qualifies the previous one: **In what** case **is this statement,** that the court removes her from the suspected adulterer, **said?** It is **when she has no children** from her first husband. **But if she has children** from him, **she is not** required to be **divorced**[H] from the suspected adulterer. On the contrary, if they were required to divorce, it could strengthen the original rumor and others might suspect that her children are *mamzerim*. **However, if witnesses to** her **impurity,** i.e., her adultery, **came** and testified[H] that she had relations with this man while she was married, then **even if she has several children** from the first husband, **she** is required to be **divorced.** This implies that a woman without children from her first husband must separate from a man suspected of illicit relations with her on strength of suspicion alone.

רַב מוֹקֵי לָהּ לְמַתְנִיתִין בְּיֵשׁ לָהּ בָּנִים וְיֵשׁ לָהּ עֵדִים. וּמַאי דּוּחְקֵיהּ דְּרַב לְאוֹקְמֵי לְמַתְנִיתִין בְּיֵשׁ לָהּ בָּנִים וְיֵשׁ לָהּ עֵדִים, וְטַעְמָא דְּאִיכָּא עֵדִים – מַפְּקִינַן, וְאִי לֵיכָּא עֵדִים – לָא מַפְּקִינַן, לוֹקְמַהּ בְּשֶׁאֵין לָהּ בָּנִים, אַף עַל גַּב דְּלֵיכָּא עֵדִים?

The Gemara answers and explains that **Rav establishes the mishna** as referring only to a case **where she has children** by her first husband **and there are witnesses** to her adultery. In such a situation, she and the adulterer must divorce, but without witnesses they are not required to divorce. The Gemara asks: **What forced Rav to establish the mishna** as referring to a case **where she has children and there are witnesses** and explain that **the reason that** the court **removes her** from the suspected adulterer **is because there were witnesses, but that if there were no witnesses they do not remove her?** Why does he not **establish** the mishna as referring to a case **where there were no children** and that they must divorce **even if there were no witnesses?**

NOTES

When Rav was dozing or sleeping – כִּי נָיֵים וְשָׁכֵיב רַב: Some commentaries suggest that this is merely a polite way of saying that Rav's statement is incorrect.

HALAKHA

One who was suspected of adultery with a married woman and later she married someone else – הַנִּטְעָן עַל אֵשֶׁת אִישׁ וְנִשֵּׂאת לְאַחֵר: If one was suspected of committing adultery with a married woman, and due to this her husband divorced her and she married someone else and was later divorced from him, it is nevertheless prohibited for her to marry the suspected adulterer. However, if she transgressed and married him he need not divorce her, even if she had no children. The ruling applies even if there were witnesses to circumstantial evidence, provided they were not witnesses to the adultery itself, in which case the adulterer would be forced to divorce the adulteress (Rambam *Sefer Nashim, Hilkhot Sota* 2:15; *Shulḥan Arukh, Even HaEzer* 11:2).

If she has children she is not required to be divorced – יֵשׁ לָהּ בָּנִים לֹא תֵּצֵא: In the case of a husband who had not made a declaration of jealousy with regard to his wife, yet witnesses came forward and testified that she had been secluded with a man, if the husband then sent her away due to circumstantial evidence, she may not marry the man with whom she is suspected of misconduct. If the divorcée transgressed this *halakha* and married the suspected adulterer, the following distinction applies: If she had no children from the first husband, the court requires him to divorce her; if she had children from him she is not required to be divorced, based on the Rif's interpretation of the Gemara. If the first husband had made a declaration of jealousy with regard to his wife, then she must be divorced from the suspected adulterer even if she had children from him (Rambam *Sefer Nashim, Hilkhot Sota* 2:13; *Shulḥan Arukh, Even HaEzer* 11:1).

Witnesses to her impurity came and testified – בָּאוּ עֵדֵי טוּמְאָה: If witnesses testify that a married woman committed adultery, and consequently her husband divorces her, she may not marry the adulterer. If she transgressed and married him, even if she had children from the first husband, she must be divorced from him (Rambam *Sefer Nashim, Hilkhot Sota* 2:16; *Shulḥan Arukh, Even HaEzer* 11:2 and 178:18).

אָמַר רָבָא: מַתְנִיתִין קָשִׁיתֵיהּ: מַאי אִירְיָא דְּתָנֵי "הוֹצִיאוּהָ", לִיתְנֵי הוֹצִיאָהּ, אֶלָּא, כׇּל "הוֹצִיאוּהָ" בְּבֵית דִּין, וּבֵית דִּין – בְּעֵדִים הוּא דְּמַפְּקִי.

Rava said: The language of **the mishna was difficult for him;** due to that he deemed it necessary to interpret it as he did. **Why does the** *tanna* **specifically teach: They remove her** from him [*hotziuha*]**? Let it teach: He divorces her** [*hotziah*] in the singular. **Rather, every time** the plural form: **They remove her,** is used, it is referring **to the** judges of the **court. And a court removes** a woman from her suspected adulterer only **if there were witnesses,** and not due to suspicion alone.

וְאִי בָּעֵית אֵימָא: הָנֵי מַתְנְיָיתָא – רַבִּי הִיא, דְּתַנְיָא: רוֹכֵל יוֹצֵא וְאִשָּׁה חוֹגֶרֶת בְּסִינָר, אָמַר רַבִּי: הוֹאִיל וּמְכוֹעָר הַדָּבָר – תֵּצֵא. רוֹק לְמַעְלָה מִן הַכִּילָּה, אָמַר רַבִּי: הוֹאִיל וּמְכוֹעָר הַדָּבָר – תֵּצֵא.

If you wish, say a different answer for Rav's explanation: **Those** ***baraitot*** that require the wife and the suspected adulterer to divorce even without witnesses to the adultery are taught in accordance with the opinion of **Rabbi** Yehuda HaNasi. **As it is taught** in a *baraita*: With regard to a case where a husband saw **a peddler leaving**[N] the house, **and** when he entered he found his **wife retying her smock** [*sinar*],[L] i.e., putting her clothes back on, **Rabbi** Yehuda HaNasi **said: Since this is a distasteful matter**[H] because it looks as though she committed adultery with the peddler, **she** must be **divorced** by her husband. Alternatively, if the husband entered after the peddler had left and found **saliva above**[N] **the netting of the bed,** implying that someone had lain on the bed and spit upward, although no actual act was witnessed, **Rabbi** Yehuda HaNasi **said: Since this is a distasteful matter, she** must be **divorced.**

NOTES

A peddler leaving – רוֹכֵל יוֹצֵא: The Gemara refers to peddlers because they would frequently spend time selling their wares to women. Therefore, their actions were commonly suspected.

Saliva above – רוֹק לְמַעְלָה: The Meiri holds that this phrase is a euphemism meaning that signs of semen were found in the bed.

LANGUAGE

Smock [*sinar*] – סִינָר: The source of this word is not entirely clear, but some suggest that the word was borrowed from the Greek ζωνάριον, *zonariyon*, which comes from the term for belt and means a strap or girdle worn by women as an undergarment. However, the *sinar* described by the Sages is some kind of trousers worn as an undergarment.

HALAKHA

A distasteful matter – דָּבָר מְכוֹעָר: What is considered a distasteful matter? It is a case where, e.g., one entered the house of a married woman after some other man had left and found her standing next to the bed in her undergarments, or one saw the couple exiting from a secluded place, or one saw them lock themselves in a room, or any similar circumstance. Each case is judged at the judges' discretion (Rambam *Sefer Nashim, Hilkhot Sota* 2:13 and *Sefer Kedusha, Hilkhot Ishut* 24:15; *Shulḥan Arukh, Even HaEzer* 11:1, 178:18).

Perek **II**
Daf **25** Amud **a**

מִנְעָלִים הֲפוּכִים תַּחַת הַמִּטָּה, אָמַר רַבִּי: הוֹאִיל וּמְכוֹעָר הַדָּבָר – תֵּצֵא. מִנְעָלִים הֲפוּכִים? לֵיחְזֵי דְּמַאן נִינְהוּ! אֶלָּא: מְקוֹם מִנְעָלִים הֲפוּכִים (תַּחַת הַמִּטָּה. אָמַר רַבִּי: הוֹאִיל וּמְכוֹעָר הַדָּבָר – תֵּצֵא).

The same applies if the husband found **the shoes reversed under the bed,** so that the toe of the shoe faced the bed; this is a sign that a stranger came in and placed them like that. **Rabbi** Yehuda HaNasi **said: Since this is a distasteful matter, she** must be **divorced.** The Gemara questions this: **Shoes turned around? Let him see whose they are** and clarify who the stranger was and then find out what he was doing there. **Rather,** the case was that he found the **place of the shoes,** i.e., shoe prints, **reversed**[N] **under the bed** and cannot recognize whose shoe prints they are. **Rabbi** Yehuda HaNasi **said: Since this is a distasteful matter, she** must be **divorced.**

NOTES

The place of the shoes reversed – מְקוֹם מִנְעָלִים הֲפוּכִים: According to Rashi and Rabbi Yehuda bar Natan, this means that the husband found prints of shoes that had been turned upside down so that the sole of the shoe faced up. Rashi holds that they were overturned so as to hide the ownership of the shoes. On the other hand, Rabbi Yehuda bar Natan holds that they were upside down due to the peddler's great haste, so that he did not have time to place the shoes in the regular fashion. According to the Meiri, the shoe prints were not under the bed but at the foot of the bed, indicating that apparently the shoes fell off while they were engaged in adultery. The Meiri also gives a second explanation, that the husband found footprints of his wife's shoes next to his own bed, suggesting that she lay there with someone else. This opinion is similar to Rashi's second explanation.

וְהִלְכְתָא כְּווֹתֵיהּ דְּרַב, וְהִלְכְתָא כְּווֹתֵיהּ דְּרַבִּי. קַשְׁיָא הִלְכְתָא אַהִלְכְתָא! לָא קַשְׁיָא: הָא – בְּקָלָא דְּפָסֵיק, הָא – בְּקָלָא דְּלָא פָּסֵיק. קָלָא דְּלָא פָּסֵיק וְלֵיכָּא עֵדִים – כְּרַבִּי, קָלָא דְּפָסֵיק וְאִיכָּא עֵדִים – כְּרַב.

The Gemara concludes: **The *halakha* is in accordance with** the opinion **of Rav,** that they must divorce only if there were witnesses, **and the *halakha* is in accordance with** the opinion of **Rabbi** Yehuda HaNasi, that they must divorce if there is a matter that is distasteful.[HN] The Gemara challenges this: One ***halakha*** is **difficult,** as it contradicts **the** other ***halakha*.** The Gemara answers: This contradiction is **not difficult. This one** relates to a case **where the rumor ceases** and the woman is sent away only if there are witnesses, but **that one** relates to a case **where the rumor does not cease,** in which case he divorces her even if there are no witnesses. The Gemara elucidates the cases: In cases of **a rumor that does not cease,** even if **there are no witnesses** the *halakha* is **in accordance with** the opinion of **Rabbi** Yehuda HaNasi and he divorces her. If **the rumor ceases and there are witnesses,** the *halakha* is **in accordance with** the opinion of **Rav,** and he divorces her because there are witnesses.

וְקָלָא דְּלָא פָּסֵיק עַד כַּמָּה? אֲמַר אַבַּיֵי, אָמְרָה לִי אֵם: דּוּמֵי דְּמָתָא יוֹמָא וּפַלְגָא. וְלָא אֲמַרַן אֶלָּא דְּלָא פָּסַק בֵּינֵי וּבֵינֵי, אֲבָל פָּסַק בֵּינֵי וּבֵינֵי – הָא פָּסַק. וְלָא אֲמַרַן אֶלָּא דְּלָא פָּסַק מֵחֲמַת יִרְאָה, אֲבָל פָּסַק מֵחֲמַת יִרְאָה – מֵחֲמַת יִרְאָה הוּא. וְלָא אֲמַרַן אֶלָּא דְּלֵיכָּא אוֹיְבִים, אֲבָל אִיכָּא אוֹיְבִים – אוֹיְבִים הוּא דְּאַפְּקוּ לֵיהּ לְקָלָא.

The Gemara clarifies this: **At what point** is it considered to be **a persistent rumor?**[H] **Abaye said:** My **mother told me:**[B] **A rumor in the city** lasts **a day and a half.** The Gemara comments: **We said** that this is the length of time **only** if the rumor **did not cease in the meantime. But** if the rumor **did cease in the meantime,** even it was later renewed, **this is** considered a rumor that **has ceased** and is disregarded. **And we said** that a rumor that ceased is not considered persistent **only** if the reason it **ceased** was **not due to fear** of the individual about whom it is said. **But if it ceased due to fear, it is** only **due to fear** and is still considered a persistent rumor. **And we said** that a persistent rumor has validity **only** if the subject of the rumor **does not have any** known **enemies, but if he has enemies** it may be assumed that **it is the enemies who put out the rumor** about him.

HALAKHA

When does the court require a woman to be divorced from her husband or from a man suspected of adultery – מתי מוציאים אשה מבעלה ומנטען: In a case where the husband did not make a declaration of jealousy, if witnesses came forward that his wife was secluded alone with a certain man, and based on that testimony the husband divorces her, she may not marry the suspected adulterer. If the suspected adulterer ignored the *halakha* and married her anyway, and she bore him children, he is not required to divorce her. They may remain married if they had children together even if there was a persistent rumor in town that she had committed adultery with the suspected individual. This is in accordance with the opinion of Rabbi Yehuda HaNasi. However, if there was no rumor, or if the rumor ran its course and ended, then if she married the suspected individual she need not be divorced, even if she did not bear him any children. Even if a single witness came forward and testified that she had committed adultery with him she need not be divorced, according to the opinion of Rav.

Some say that if there was a persistent rumor along with witnesses to some distasteful matter the court requires her husband to divorce her, even though there are no witnesses that she actually committed adultery (Rema, citing Rashi; *Shulḥan Arukh, Even HaEzer* 11:1).

At what point is it a persistent rumor – איזהו קול שאינו פוסק: A persistent rumor is a rumor about a married woman and a suspected adulterer that is discussed in town continually for a day and a half or longer. Even if the rumor ceased in the middle, if it ceased due to fear, this is not considered a rumor that ended. All of this applies only if neither the woman, nor the suspected individual, nor the husband had any enemies who may have started the rumor (Ran; *Shulḥan Arukh, Even HaEzer* 11:1).

BACKGROUND

Mother told me – אמרה לי אם: Abaye's mother died when he was an infant, and he was raised by a foster mother whom he called mother (*Kiddushin* 31b). He usually quoted her on issues of health and remedies, as she had expertise in these fields.

NOTES

The opinions of Rabbi Yehuda HaNasi and Rav – שיטות רבי ורב: There are many explanations in the commentaries as to the opinions of Rabbi Yehuda HaNasi and Rav. Two main issues remain unresolved in the Gemara: Is the discussion over whether the woman must divorce her husband, or the suspected adulterer if she later married him, or both? Does the matter that is distasteful require witnesses? The following chart summarizes the various opinions:

Commentary	In order to require her to be divorced from her husband		In order to require her to be divorced from the suspected adulterer if she later married him	
	Rav requires	Rabbi Yehuda HaNasi requires	Rav requires	Rabbi Yehuda HaNasi requires
Rashi; Responsa of the Rashba	Witnesses to adultery	A distasteful matter	Witnesses to adultery	A distasteful matter
Rif; Rambam according to the understanding of Rashba	Witnesses to adultery	Witnesses to adultery	Witnesses to adultery	Witnesses to a distasteful matter
Rabbeinu Tam's initial opinion	Witnesses to adultery	Witnesses to adultery	Witnesses to adultery	A distasteful matter
Rabbeinu Tam's revised opinion	Witnesses to a distasteful matter	Witnesses to a distasteful matter	Witnesses to a distasteful matter	Witnesses to a distasteful matter
Ramban; Rambam according to the understanding of *Darkhei Moshe*	Witnesses to adultery	Witnesses to a distasteful matter	Witnesses to adultery	A persistent rumor
Rosh	Witnesses to adultery	Witnesses to a distasteful matter	Witnesses to adultery	Witnesses to a distasteful matter

תְּנַן הָתָם: הַמּוֹצִיא אֶת אִשְׁתּוֹ מִשּׁוּם שֵׁם רַע – לֹא יַחְזִיר. מִשּׁוּם נֶדֶר – לֹא יַחְזִיר. שְׁלַח לֵיהּ רַבָּה בַּר הוּנָא לְרַבָּה בַּר רַב נַחְמָן: יְלַמְּדֵנוּ רַבֵּינוּ, כָּנַס מַהוּ שֶׁיּוֹצִיא?

§ **We learned** in a mishna **there** (*Gittin* 45b): A man **who divorces his wife due to** her **bad reputation may not take** her **back** again, even if it turns out that the rumor was untrue. Likewise, if he divorced his wife **due to a vow**[H] of hers that is unbearable to him **he may not take** her **back** even if she is released from that vow. **Rabba bar Rav Huna sent** a question **to Rabba bar Rav Naḥman: Our teacher, instruct us.** If one of those men listed in that mishna divorced his wife due to her bad reputation or vow and it was therefore prohibited for him to take her back, yet he nevertheless **remarried** her, **what is the** *halakha*? **Must** he **divorce** her?[H]

אֲמַר לֵיהּ, תְּנֵינָא: הַנִּטְעָן עַל אֵשֶׁת אִישׁ וְהוֹצִיאָהּ מִתַּחַת יָדוֹ, אַף עַל פִּי שֶׁכָּנַס יוֹצִיא. אֲמַר לֵיהּ: מִי דָּמֵי? הָתָם "הוֹצִיאוּהָ" וְהָכָא "הוֹצִיאָהּ"! וְרַבָּה בַּר רַב נַחְמָן – מַתְנִיתִין נַמִי "הוֹצִיאָהּ" תְּנַן.

Rabba bar Rav Naḥman **said to him: We** already **learned** in the mishna (24b): With regard to **one who is suspected of** committing adultery with **a married woman, and he,** her husband, **divorced her, even if he** subsequently **remarried** her **he must divorce** her. Rabba bar Rav Huna **said to him: Is this comparable** to the case I asked about? **There,** in the mishna, it says: **They,** the court, **remove her** from him, **whereas here** (*Gittin* 45b), the mishna states: **He divorced her** of his own accord. Perhaps if the court requires them to divorce, the *halakha* is different. The Gemara explains: **And Rabba bar Rav Naḥman,** who held that the two *mishnayot* were comparable, had a text of **the mishna** that **also** read: **He divorced her,** instead of: They remove her.

וְאַכַּתִּי מִי דָּמֵי? הָכָא – בַּעַל, וְהָתָם – בּוֹעֵל! אֲמַר לֵיהּ: שַׁפִּיר דָּמֵי אַהֲדָדֵי: הָכָא אָמוּר רַבָּנַן לֹא יִכְנוֹס, וְאִם כָּנַס יוֹצִיא – הָכִי נַמִי אָמְרִי רַבָּנַן לֹא יַחְזִיר, וְאִם כָּנַס – יוֹצִיא.

Rabba bar Rav Huna asks: **Still, is this comparable? Here,** the question was raised in a case where **the** first **husband** remarried her, which will not strengthen the rumors of her bad reputation, **but there,** the mishna refers to **the man** with whom she committed **adultery** remarrying her, which strengthens those rumors. **He said to him: They are certainly comparable to each other: Here,** in the mishna discussing one who is suspected of committing adultery, **the Sages said that he may not marry** her **and if he did marry** her **he must divorce** her. **So too, the Sages said** in the case of one who divorced his wife due to her reputation or vow **that he may not take** her **back, and if he does remarry** her **he must divorce** her.

וְלָא הִיא, הָתָם – אַלּוּמֵי אַלְּמֵיהּ לְקָלָא, הָכָא אָמְרִינַן קָם בֵּיהּ בְּקָלָא וְלֵיתֵיהּ.

The Gemara rejects this: **That is not so,** as **there,** when the man suspected of committing adultery marries the woman, **he thereby strengthens the rumor** of adultery. For this reason he must divorce her. **Here, we say that he,** the husband, **established** the facts of **the rumor** and found that it **was not so** and the rumor was baseless. Therefore, there is no need for him to divorce her if he remarries her. Rabba bar Rav Huna's question remains unresolved.

מתני׳ הַמֵּבִיא גֵּט מִמְּדִינַת הַיָּם וְאָמַר "בְּפָנַי נִכְתַּב וּבְפָנַי נֶחְתַּם" לֹא יִשָּׂא אֶת אִשְׁתּוֹ. "מֵת", "הֲרַגְתִּיו", "הֲרַגְנוּהוּ" – לֹא יִשָּׂא אֶת אִשְׁתּוֹ. רַבִּי יְהוּדָה אוֹמֵר "הֲרַגְתִּיו" – לֹא תִּנָּשֵׂא אִשְׁתּוֹ: "הֲרַגְנוּהוּ" – תִּנָּשֵׂא אִשְׁתּוֹ.

MISHNA An agent **who brought a bill of divorce from a country overseas**[N] **and said: It was written in my presence and it was signed in my presence,** as required in order to establish the bill of divorce as valid, **may not marry the wife,**[H] i.e., the divorcée. Since the validity of the bill of divorce is based upon his testimony, marrying the divorcée creates the impression that he had an ulterior motive for his testimony. Similarly, a witness who testified that a certain man **died,**[H] or testified: **I killed him,** or: **We killed him,**[H] **may not marry** that man's **wife. Rabbi Yehuda says:** If he testified: **I killed him, his wife may not be married**[N] at all based on that evidence, as his testimony is unreliable, but if he said: **We killed him, his wife may be married** to anyone other than those witnesses.

גמ׳ טַעְמָא דְּמִמְּדִינַת הַיָּם – דַּעֲלֵיהּ קָסָמְכִינַן, אֲבָל מֵאֶרֶץ יִשְׂרָאֵל, דְּלָאו עֲלֵיהּ קָסָמְכִינַן, יִשָּׂא אֶת אִשְׁתּוֹ.

GEMARA The Gemara clarifies: **The reason that** the agent may not marry the divorcée applies specifically in a case where he brings the bill of divorce **from a country overseas, as** in this case **we,** the court, **rely upon his** testimony to validate the bill of divorce. **But** an agent who brings a bill of divorce **from Eretz Yisrael** need not make any verbal declaration, and **since we,** the court, **do not rely upon his** testimony but upon the written bill of divorce alone, **he may marry his wife,** i.e., the divorcée, since it does not arouse suspicion.

HALAKHA

One who divorces his wife due to her bad reputation or vows – הַמּוֹצִיא אִשְׁתּוֹ מִשּׁוּם שֵׁם רַע אוֹ נְדָרִים: One who divorced his wife because she made vows that were unbearable to him, or because she came to have a bad reputation may not remarry her. Some say that this applies only if he told her explicitly that this is the reason for the divorce and if he confirmed that were it not for the vows or the reputation he would not have divorced her (*Tur*, citing Rosh). Some say that even if he did not confirm this explicitly, he may not remarry her (*Tur*, citing Ramah). One opinion (Rambam) holds that even if he did not tell her why he divorced her he may not take her back (*Shulḥan Arukh, Even HaEzer* 10:3).

One who takes back a wife he divorced due to a bad reputation – הַמַּחְזִיר אִשָּׁה שֶׁגֵּרֵשׁ מִשּׁוּם שֵׁם רַע: If one divorces his wife due to her bad reputation or a similar issue, he may not remarry her. However, if he transgressed this prohibition and remarried her, he need not divorce her again, in accordance with the conclusion of the Gemara here (*Shulḥan Arukh, Even HaEzer* 11:5).

One who brings a bill of divorce and wishes to marry the divorcée – הַמֵּבִיא גֵּט וְרוֹצֶה לָשֵׂאת הַגְּרוּשָׁה: An agent who brings a woman her bill of divorce from a place for which he must testify: It was written in my presence and signed in my presence, may not marry her because this may arouse suspicions. However, if he brought the bill of divorce from a place for which he need not say this, he is permitted to marry the divorcée, based on the mishna and the conclusion of the Gemara (Rambam *Sefer Nashim, Hilkhot Geirushin* 10:14; *Shulḥan Arukh, Even HaEzer* 12:1).

One who testifies that the husband died – הַמֵּעִיד עַל הַבַּעַל שֶׁמֵּת: If a single witness came and testified to a woman that her husband died, she is allowed to marry by virtue of that testimony. However, she may not marry the witness, as this appears suspicious (Rambam *Sefer Nashim, Hilkhot Geirushin* 10:14; *Shulḥan Arukh, Even HaEzer* 17:3).

I killed him, we killed him – הֲרַגְתִּיו, הֲרַגְנוּהוּ: The testimony of one who testified that he killed a man, or that he was with the murderers, is accepted, and that man's wife is permitted to marry by virtue of that testimony (Rambam *Sefer Nashim, Hilkhot Geirushin* 13:10; *Shulḥan Arukh, Even HaEzer* 17:7).

NOTES

An agent who brought a bill of divorce from a country overseas – הַמֵּבִיא גֵּט מִמְּדִינַת הַיָּם: Two reasons are given in the Talmud to explain why an agent bringing a bill of divorce from overseas must testify that it was written and signed in his presence (*Gittin* 2a): First, the witnesses who signed the bill of divorce are not present and cannot establish its validity. The agent's testimony consequently prevents the husband from claiming that it is a forgery. Second, there was concern that in the Diaspora the scribes were not experts and might not write the bill correctly. If it was written and signed in the presence of the agent, the court can ask him, and verify, that the document was written correctly.

A witness who…testified: I killed him…his wife may not be married – הֲרַגְתִּיו לֹא תִּנָּשֵׂא אִשְׁתּוֹ: In Rambam's Commentary on the Mishna it is explained that Rabbi Yehuda does not accept the principle that an individual does not make himself wicked.

וְהָא מֵת, דְּלָאו עֲלֵיהּ קָסָמְכִינַן, דְּאָמַר מָר: אִשָּׁה דַּיְיקָא וּמִינַּסְבָא, וְקָתָנֵי: לֹא יִשָּׂא אֶת אִשְׁתּוֹ!

The Gemara challenges this: **But** also in the case of a witness who said that the husband **died, we,** the court, **do not rely** solely **upon** his testimony. **As the Master said: A woman is exacting** in her investigation of the truth of the testimony that her husband died before she **marries** again, and it is primarily on that basis that she is permitted to remarry. **Yet it is taught that he** still **may not marry his wife.**

הָתָם לֵיכָּא כְּתָבָא, הָכָא – אִיכָּא כְּתָבָא. דִּתְנַן: מַה בֵּין גֵּט לְמִיתָה – שֶׁהַכְּתָב מוֹכִיחַ.

The Gemara answers: The two cases are not comparable, as **there,** in the case when a witness testifies that the husband has died, **there is not anything written** as proof, and therefore he may not marry the widow. However, **here,** in a case where an agent brings a bill of divorce from Eretz Yisrael, **there is a written** document that is valid without any testimony. **As we learned** in a mishna (117a): **What is the difference between a bill of divorce and death?** Why does the court rely upon those men who are not trusted as witnesses to the death of a husband if they act as agents to bring a bill of divorce, even from overseas, such that they must give testimony that it was written and signed in their presence? The difference is **that** with regard to a bill of divorce **the writing proves** their testimony.

״מֵת״, ״הֲרַגְתִּיו״, ״הֲרַגְנוּהוּ״ – לֹא יִשָּׂא אֶת אִשְׁתּוֹ. הוּא נִיהוּ דְּלֹא יִשָּׂא אֶת אִשְׁתּוֹ, הָא לְאַחֵר – תִּנָּשֵׂא.

The mishna stated that if the witness said with regard to the husband that **he died,** or: **I killed him,** or: **We killed him,** then **he may not marry** the **wife** of the deceased. The Gemara infers that **he,** the witness **himself, may not marry** the **wife; this** implies that **to another she may be married** on the basis of his testimony.

וְהָאָמַר רַב יוֹסֵף: ״פְּלוֹנִי רְבָעַנִי לְאוֹנְסִי״ – הוּא וְאַחֵר מִצְטָרְפִין לְהָרְגוֹ. ״לִרְצוֹנִי״ – רָשָׁע הוּא, וְהַתּוֹרָה אָמְרָה: ״אַל תָּשֶׁת יָדְךָ עִם רָשָׁע לִהְיוֹת עֵד חָמָס״.

The Gemara challenges this: **Didn't Rav Yosef say:** With regard to one who testified that **so-and-so sodomized me**[H] **against my will,** then **he** who testified to being the victim of the sexual assault **and another** bystander witness can **combine** as a pair of witnesses in order **to put** the assailant **to death** for homosexual intercourse. But if he testified: I was **willingly** sodomized by so-and-so, then **he is wicked**[H] by his own admission, since he willingly transgressed. **And the Torah said: "Put not your hand with the wicked to be a corrupt witness"** (Exodus 23:1). If one renders himself unfit as a witness by admitting to murder, how can his testimony be accepted to permit the wife to remarry?

וְכִי תֵּימָא שָׁאנֵי עֵדוּת אִשָּׁה דְּאַקִּילוּ בָּהּ רַבָּנַן – וְהָאָמַר רַב מְנַשֶּׁה:

And if you would say that **testimony** that **a woman's** husband died **is different, as the Sages ruled leniently** in such matters and perhaps accepted testimony of a wicked witness in such cases, **didn't Rav Menashe say:**

HALAKHA

So-and-so sodomized me – **פְּלוֹנִי רְבָעַנִי**: One who testified that he was sodomized by another may combine his testimony with that of another witness in order to put the sodomizer to death. This is regardless of whether it was an act of rape or whether the witness participated willingly, in accordance with Rava's opinion in the dispute with Rav Yosef that we divide the statement. His statement includes both self-incriminating testimony and other information, so the court divides his assertion, accepting as evidence only information that is not self-incriminating. His report about being a willing partner is discarded, and the court accepts only that another sodomized him (Rambam *Sefer Shofetim*, *Hilkhot Edut* 12:2; *Shulḥan Arukh*, *Ḥoshen Mishpat* 34:26).

A wicked witness – **עֵד רָשָׁע**: Wicked individuals who willingly violate the words of the Torah are unfit for giving testimony by Torah law (Rambam *Sefer Shofetim*, *Hilkhot Edut* 10:1).

Perek **II**
Daf **25** Amud **b**

גַּזְלָן דְּדִבְרֵיהֶם – כָּשֵׁר לְעֵדוּת אִשָּׁה, גַּזְלָן דְּדִבְרֵי תוֹרָה – פָּסוּל לְעֵדוּת אִשָּׁה. נֵימָא רַב מְנַשֶּׁה דְּאָמַר כְּרַבִּי יְהוּדָה?

Although one who is considered **a robber according to the words of the Sages**[N] is unfit for other forms of testimony, **he is fit** as a witness **for testimony** that **a woman's** husband died. **A robber according to Torah law is unfit**[N] as a witness even **for testimony** that **a woman's** husband has died.[H] **Should we say that** what **Rav Menashe said is in accordance with** the opinion of **Rabbi Yehuda?** Rabbi Yehuda said in the mishna that one who is considered absolutely wicked because he admitted that he is a murderer is unfit for testifying to the death of a husband, but one who was merely present among a gang of murderers is not.

NOTES

A robber according to the words of the Sages – **גַּזְלָן דְּדִבְרֵיהֶם**: In tractate *Sanhedrin* (24b), there is a list of those who are unfit by rabbinic decree for giving testimony. This list includes those who take money from others but are not categorized as robbers according to Torah law.

A robber according to Torah law is unfit – **גַּזְלָן דְּדִבְרֵי תוֹרָה פָּסוּל**: According to the Rif, even though a wicked individual is unfit for testifying that a woman's husband has died, if he were to make an incidental remark about the matter, this evidence would be accepted by the court. In this respect he is no worse than a gentile, who is believed if he makes an incidental remark.

HALAKHA

A robber with regard to testimony rendering it permitted for a woman to remarry – **גַּזְלָן בְּעֵדוּת אִשָּׁה**: One who is unfit for giving testimony by Torah law is not believed when testifying that a woman's husband died, but one who is unfit by rabbinic law is believed in such instances (Rambam *Sefer Nashim*, *Hilkhot Geirushin* 12:17; *Shulḥan Arukh*, *Even HaEzer* 17:3).

אֲמַר לָךְ רַב מְנַשֶּׁה: אֲנָא דַּאֲמַרִי אֲפִילּוּ לְרַבָּנַן, וְטַעֲמָא דְּרַבָּנַן הָכָא – כִּדְרָבָא, דְּאָמַר רָבָא: אָדָם קָרוֹב אֵצֶל עַצְמוֹ, וְאֵין אָדָם מֵשִׂים עַצְמוֹ רָשָׁע.

The Gemara rejects this: **Rav Menashe** could have **said to you: I am speaking even according to** the opinion of **the Rabbis.** Although the Rabbis did not allow one who was wicked by Torah law to testify for a woman, a witness who admitted: I killed him, is nevertheless believed. **And the rationale of the Rabbis here is in accordance with** the opinion of **Rava, as Rava** disputed Rav Yosef's opinion and **said:** Even if one said that he was willingly sodomized by this man, he is not believed concerning his own actions, because **a person is his own relative.**[N] Consequently, he may not testify about himself, just as the testimony of any relative is disqualified. **And** furthermore, **a person does not make himself wicked.**[H] His testimony with regard to his own actions is inadmissible because he is his own relative, but his testimony is accepted both to put a sodomizer to death or to render it permitted for a woman to remarry by saying that he killed her husband.

לֵימָא רַב יוֹסֵף דְּאָמַר כְּרַבִּי יְהוּדָה?! אֲמַר לָךְ רַב יוֹסֵף: אֲנָא דַּאֲמַרִי אֲפִילּוּ לְרַבָּנַן, וְשָׁאנֵי עֵדוּת אִשָּׁה דְּאַקִּילוּ בָּהּ רַבָּנַן, וְרַב מְנַשֶּׁה דְּאָמַר כְּרַבִּי יְהוּדָה.

The Gemara asks: **Shall we say** according to this explanation that the opinion **that Rav Yosef spoke is in accordance with** the opinion of **Rabbi Yehuda?** The Gemara rejects this: **Rav Yosef** could have **said to you: I am speaking even according to** the opinion of **the Rabbis, as** in my opinion, **testimony** enabling a **woman** to remarry **is different in that the Rabbis ruled more leniently** and they even accept testimony from a completely wicked individual. However, **Rav Menashe, who** renders unfit one who is wicked by Torah law from testimony enabling a woman to remarry, **spoke in accordance with** the opinion of **Rabbi Yehuda,** who differentiates even in such testimony between one who is considered wicked according to Torah law and one who is considered wicked by rabbinic law.

״הֲרַגְתִּיו״ כו׳ ״הֲרַגְנוּהוּ״ תִּנָּשֵׂא כו׳. מַאי שְׁנָא הֲרַגְתִּיו וּמַאי שְׁנָא הֲרַגְנוּהוּ? אֲמַר רַב יְהוּדָה: בְּאוֹמֵר ״אֲנִי הָיִיתִי עִם הוֹרְגָיו״.

In the mishna it is taught that the court accepts testimony from one who said: **I killed him,** or: **We killed him,** while Rabbi Yehuda differentiates between one who said: I killed him, whose testimony is not accepted, and one who said: We killed him, whose testimony is accepted and the woman **may be married** to others. The Gemara asks: **What is different between: I killed him, and: We killed him?** Isn't he a murderer by his own admission as well when he testifies: We killed him? **Rav Yehuda said:** Do not understand that by saying: We killed him, he included himself among the murderers. Rather, it is referring to a case **where he said: I was with his murderers,** but he was not an active participant to the murder.

וְהָתַנְיָא: אָמְרוּ לוֹ לְרַבִּי יְהוּדָה, מַעֲשֶׂה בְּלִסְטִים אֶחָד שֶׁיָּצָא לֵיהָרֵג בִּמְגִיזַת קַפּוֹטְקִיָּא, וַאֲמַר לָהֶם ״לְכוּ אִמְרוּ לָהּ לְאֵשֶׁת שִׁמְעוֹן בֶּן כֹּהֵן: אֲנִי הָרַגְתִּי אֶת בַּעְלָהּ בִּכְנִיסָתִי לְלוֹד״ וְאָמְרִי לָהּ ״בִּכְנִיסָתוֹ לְלוֹד״ – וְהִשִּׂיאוּ אֶת אִשְׁתּוֹ. אֲמַר לָהֶם: מִשָּׁם רְאָיָה?! בְּאוֹמֵר: אֲנִי הָיִיתִי עִם הוֹרְגָיו –

And it is taught in a *baraita* that this is the basis for Rabbi Yehuda's distinction: **They told Rabbi Yehuda:** There was **an incident involving an armed bandit** [*listim*][L] **who was taken out to be executed in the passage** [*megizat*][L] **of Cappadocia,**[B] **and he said to** those present: **Go and tell the wife of Shimon the Priest** that **I killed her husband as I entered Lod. And some say** that he said: **As he entered Lod. And they married off his wife** on the basis of this testimony. This implies that the court accepts testimony from the murderer himself. Rabbi Yehuda **said to them:** You derive **proof from there?** The case was **that he said: I was with his murderers,** but not that he himself murdered the woman's husband.

Cappadocian rock formations

NOTES

A person is his own relative – אָדָם קָרוֹב אֵצֶל עַצְמוֹ: This concept is connected to the halakhic principle that the court divides the statement of a witness, allowing them to reject the part of the testimony wherein the witness incriminates himself while accepting the rest of his testimony as valid. The court accepts the testimony that the individual he claimed to have murdered is dead, without accepting that this witness is a murderer. The halakhic principle applied is that just as one may not testify about a close relative, one may not testify about oneself.

There are differences of opinion concerning the rationale for the principle of dividing the statement of a witness. According to the Rashba, the court applies this principle only in cases where the witness's testimony could be interpreted in another way without negating its validity. If, e.g., a witness said: I killed him, it could be interpreted to mean that he was with the murderers or that he killed the victim unwittingly, etc. However, if there is no other possible interpretation of his testimony, his testimony is inadmissible. Many commentaries disagree with this and hold that even in such cases the court may divide the statement and accept the testimony (see *Noda Bihuda* and *Kovetz He'arot*).

HALAKHA

A person does not make himself wicked – אֵין אָדָם מֵשִׂים עַצְמוֹ רָשָׁע: One is not rendered unfit by admitting his own transgression, because an individual does not make himself wicked (Rambam *Sefer Nashim, Hilkhot Geirushin* 13:10 and *Sefer Shofetim, Hilkhot Edut* 12:2; *Shulḥan Arukh, Ḥoshen Mishpat* 34:26).

LANGUAGE

An armed bandit [*listim*] – לִיסְטִים: From the Greek ληστής, *lestès*. Several Aramaic and Hebrew forms were based upon this word in the language of the Sages. The written form was corrupted slightly to *listim* rather than *listis*.

Passage [*megizat*] – מְגִיזַת: This word apparently comes from the Arabic مجاز, *majāz*, meaning crossing or way.

BACKGROUND

Passage of Cappadocia – מְגִיזַת קַפּוֹטְקִיָּא: Cappadocia is a country in Asia Minor west of the Euphrates River and north of the Taurus Mountains. The Hebrew name, Kappotkiyya, comes from the Greek Καππαδοκία, Kappadokia. At the time of the Talmud this was a Roman province with a large Jewish population, and there were Jewish scholars, mentioned in both the Jerusalem and Babylonian Talmuds, who came from Cappadocia to Eretz Yisrael. Today it is a popular tourist site famous for its unique rock formations, referred to as fairy chimneys.

Location of Cappadocia

וְהָא לִסְטִים קָתָנֵי! שֶׁנִּתְפַּס עַל יְדֵי לִסְטִיּוּת. וְהָא יָצָא לֵיהָרֵג קָתָנֵי! בֵּי דִינָא דְגוֹיִם דְּלָא דָּיְיקִי וְקָטְלִי.

The Gemara challenges: How could Rabbi Yehuda understand the incident in such a way? **But it is taught** in the *baraita* that the witness himself was **an armed bandit.** The Gemara answers: **He was captured for** a charge of **armed banditry.** The Gemara asks: **But it is taught that he was taken out to be executed,** implying that he was found guilty of murder. The Gemara answers: That was **a gentile court, and they execute without being precise.** One who is among a gang of bandits is executed by a gentile court regardless of whether or not he himself was a murderer. This *baraita* therefore provides evidence that Rabbi Yehuda admits the testimony of such a witness only if he says: I was with his murderers.

מתני׳ הֶחָכָם שֶׁאָסַר אֶת הָאִשָּׁה בְּנֶדֶר עַל בַּעְלָהּ – הֲרֵי זֶה לֹא יִשָּׂאֶנָּה, מֵיאֲנָה אוֹ שֶׁחָלְצָה בְּפָנָיו – יִשָּׂאֶנָּה, מִפְּנֵי שֶׁהוּא בֵּית דִּין.

MISHNA A **Sage who** refused to release a woman from a vow that **rendered the wife forbidden to her husband by** that **vow,**[H] resulting in her being divorced from her husband, **may not marry her,** so as to avoid suspicion that he rendered her forbidden to her husband in order to marry her himself. However, a judge before whom a woman **performed refusal** when she was a minor, declaring that she did not desire the husband chosen for her by her family, **or before whom** she **performed *ḥalitza*,**[H] **may marry her because** he was only one member of **the court,** thereby alleviating suspicion.

גמ׳ הָא הִתִּירָהּ יִשָּׂאֶנָּה, בְּמַאי עָסְקִינַן? אִילֵימָא בְּחַד – חַד מִי מָצֵי מַתִּיר? וְהָאָמַר (רַב אָמַר) רַבִּי חִיָּיא בַּר אָבִין אָמַר רַב עַמְרָם: תָּנָא, הַתָּרַת נְדָרִים בִּשְׁלֹשָׁה!

GEMARA The mishna taught that a Sage who rendered a woman forbidden to her husband may not then marry her. The Gemara deduces from here: **This** implies that if **he** rendered **her permitted** to her husband and she was later widowed or divorced, then **he may marry her.** The Gemara clarifies this: **With what are we dealing? If we say** that he was **a single** judge and not part of a court, **can a single** judge **dissolve** vows? **But didn't Rav say** that **Rabbi Ḥiyya bar Avin said** that **Rav Amram said: It is taught** in a *baraita*: **Dissolution of vows** requires a court of **three**[H] judges?

וְאֶלָּא בִּתְלָתָא – מִי חֲשִׁידִי? וְהָתְנַן: מֵיאֲנָה אוֹ שֶׁחָלְצָה בְּפָנָיו יִשָּׂאֶנָּה, מִפְּנֵי שֶׁהוּא בֵּית דִּין!

Rather, could it be a case **of three** judges rather than one? In such a case, **would they be suspect** of distorting judgment? **But didn't we learn** in the mishna: If **she performed refusal or performed *ḥalitza* before him, he may marry her because he** functioned as a member of **a court** of three? This teaches that there is no suspicion of a judge in a court of three.

לְעוֹלָם בְּחַד, וּכְדַאֲמַר רַב חִסְדָּא אָמַר רַבִּי יוֹחָנָן: בְּיָחִיד מוּמְחֶה, הָכָא נָמֵי – בְּיָחִיד מוּמְחֶה.

The Gemara answers: **Actually,** you should explain that this case is **that of a single** judge, **and** it is **as Rav Ḥisda said** that **Rabbi Yoḥanan said:** Vows may be dissolved even **by a single expert,**[B] and a three-member court is not always necessary. **Here too,** it is referring to **a single expert** refusing to nullify her vow.

״מֵיאֲנָה אוֹ שֶׁחָלְצָה״ וכו׳. טַעְמָא דְּבֵית דִּין, הָא בִּתְרֵי – לָא.

It is taught in the mishna that if a woman **performed refusal or performed *ḥalitza*** before a judge, he may still marry her, as he was part of a court. The Gemara deduces from here: **The reason is** specifically that he functioned on **the court** as one of three judges. The Gemara deduces: **Then, if there were** only **two** judges, **he would not** be permitted to marry her.

מַאי שְׁנָא מֵהָא דִּתְנַן: עֵדִים הַחֲתוּמִים עַל שְׂדֵה מִקָּח וְעַל גֵּט אִשָּׁה – לֹא חָשׁוּ חֲכָמִים לְדָבָר זֶה! הִיא גּוּפַהּ קָמַשְׁמַע לַן, לְאַפּוֹקֵי מִמַּאן דְּאָמַר מֵיאוּן בִּפְנֵי שְׁנַיִם, קָמַשְׁמַע לַן: מֵיאוּן בִּשְׁלֹשָׁה.

If so, in **what** way **is this** case **different from that which we learned** in a *baraita*: If **witnesses signed on the** document of **sale of a field or on a woman's bill of divorce, the Sages were not concerned about this matter** if one of the witnesses subsequently purchased the field or married the divorcée. Since there are two witnesses, there is no suspicion that they collaborated for the benefit of one of them. The Gemara answers: If there were two judges there would also be no concern; however, **this** mishna **itself** comes **to teach us** that a refusal must be performed before a full court, **to exclude** the opinion of **the one who said that refusal may be performed before two. This teaches us** that **refusal** must be performed before **three** judges.

HALAKHA

A Sage who rendered the wife forbidden to her husband by that vow – הֶחָכָם שֶׁאָסַר אֶת הָאִשָּׁה בְּנֶדֶר עַל בַּעְלָהּ: If a woman vowed not to receive any benefit from her husband and the husband did not nullify her vow, and she then came before a Sage but he did not find way to dissolve it, then that Sage may not subsequently marry her after she is divorced from her husband (Rambam *Sefer Nashim, Hilkhot Geirushin* 10:14; *Shulḥan Arukh, Even HaEzer* 12:2).

Before whom a woman performed refusal or… performed *ḥalitza* – מֵיאֲנָה אוֹ שֶׁחָלְצָה בְּפָנָיו: A woman who performed refusal or performed *ḥalitza* before a court may later marry one of the judges of the court (*Shulḥan Arukh, Even HaEzer* 12:2).

Dissolution of vows requires a court of three – הַתָּרַת נְדָרִים בִּשְׁלֹשָׁה: Dissolution of vows must be performed by an expert scholar or, if no expert can be found, by three ordinary men (Rambam *Sefer Hafla'a, Hilkhot Shevuot* 6:1; *Shulḥan Arukh, Yoreh De'a* 228:1).

BACKGROUND

A single expert – יָחִיד מוּמְחֶה: In general a Jewish court comprises three judges for monetary matters and other cases, aside from cases of capital punishment. This ensures that there will be a majority, as at least two judges will agree on the verdict. In tractate *Avot* (4:10) it is written: Do not judge alone, as only God can judge alone. However, *Tosafot* explain that this is meant merely as advice, but if an individual judge is an expert in certain matters he may adjudicate on those matters by himself.

איבעיא להו: כנס, מהו שיוציא? רב כהנא אמר: כנס – מוציא, רב אשי אמר: כנס – אינו מוציא. תני להו רב זוטי דבי רב פפי כדברי האומר כנס אינו מוציא.

§ **A dilemma was raised before** the Sages with regard to one who was prohibited from marrying a certain woman: If he nevertheless **married** her despite the prohibition, **what is the** *halakha* with regard to whether **he must divorce** her? **Rav Kahana said: If he married** her, **he must divorce** her. **Rav Ashi said: If he married** her, **he need not divorce** her.[H] **Rav Zuti from the school of Rav Pappi taught** the Sages a *baraita* **in accordance with the statement of the** one who **said** that if **he married** her, **he need not divorce** her.

אמרו ליה רבנן לרב אשי: גמרא או סברא? אמר להו: מתניתין היא: הנטען משפחה ונשתחררה, מגויה ונתגיירה, הרי זה לא יכנוס, ואם כנס – אין מוציא. אלמא

The Rabbis said to Rav Ashi: With regard to the *halakha* that you said, that if he married her he need not divorce her, was it based upon **tradition or** is it your own **conclusion? He said to them: It is the mishna.** I reached this conclusion from the wording of the mishna, which taught that **one suspected** by others of engaging in sexual relations **with a** Canaanite **maidservant and she** was subsequently **set free, or with a gentile woman and she** subsequently **converted may not marry** that woman. **But if he did marry her, they,** the judges of the court, **do not remove** her from him. **Apparently,**

ברננה לא מפקינן, הכא נמי ברננה לא מפקינן.

we do not remove her from her husband owing to suspicion **due to rumor** alone. **Here too, we do not remove her** from her husband **due to a rumor.**

מתני׳ וכולם שהיו להם נשים ומתו – מותרות לינשא להם.

MISHNA And for **all of these**[N] who were involved in permitting the wife to remarry, i.e., the judge, the agent who brought a bill of divorce, and the one who testified for a woman that her husband died, if **they had wives**[NH] at the time of the ruling or the testimony **and** their wives **died** thereafter, then those women they had set free **are permitted to be married to them.** There is no concern that while their wives were still alive these individuals set their eyes upon another woman.

וכולן שנישאו לאחרים, ונתגרשו או שנתאלמנו – מותרות לינשא להם. וכולן מותרות לבניהם או לאחיהם.

And with regard to **all of these** women who were prohibited from marrying a certain man due to some suspicion, if **they were** subsequently **married to others**[H] **and** then **were divorced or widowed** from the second husband, **they are permitted to be married to them,** i.e., to the judge, messenger, or witness who permitted her to remarry. **And all of these** women who were prohibited from marrying due to some suspicion **are permitted to the sons or to the brothers**[NH] of those who set them free.

גמ׳ מתו – אין, נתגרשו – לא.

GEMARA The mishna taught that if any of the men had wives who subsequently died, they may marry those women freed by them. The Gemara deduces from here: If the wives of those who rendered the woman permitted **died, yes,** they are permitted to marry the woman that they freed for marriage; but if the wives **were divorced, no,** it is prohibited. In such a case, marrying the woman that one had rendered permitted would raise suspicions that he had in fact planned to marry her all along.

HALAKHA

If he married her, he need not divorce her – כנס אינו מוציא: If a Sage declared a wife forbidden to her husband due to her vow, that Sage is forbidden from marrying her *ab initio.* If he nevertheless married her he is not forced to divorce her, in accordance with the conclusion of the Gemara (Rambam *Sefer Nashim, Hilkhot Geirushin* 10:14; *Shulḥan Arukh, Even HaEzer* 12:2).

NOTES

And for all of these, etc. – וכולם וכו׳: Rashi explains that the term: All of these, is referring only to a Sage or a witness who testified for a woman (see Rid). Rambam, however, interprets this ruling as applying to one who was under suspicion of misconduct with a maidservant or other woman as well.

They had wives, etc. – היו להם נשים וכו׳: At the time of the mishna, bigamy was permitted, yet it was extremely rare, and so there was no concern that one would free a woman in order to marry her as a second wife.

Are permitted to the sons or to the brothers – מותרות לבניהם או לאחיהם: In the Jerusalem Talmud this is explained by the statement that it is not common for one to sin for the benefit of his relative or his teacher.

HALAKHA

They had wives – היו להם נשים: It is permitted for one who was married when he rendered a woman free to marry that woman if his wife subsequently died (Rambam *Sefer Nashim, Hilkhot Geirushin* 10:15; *Shulḥan Arukh, Even HaEzer* 12:4).

And all of these women, if they were subsequently married to others – וכולן שנישאו לאחרים: It is permitted for all of these women who subsequently married others and were then widowed or divorced to marry one of those men who permitted them to remarry (Rambam *Sefer Nashim, Hilkhot Ishut* 10:15; *Shulḥan Arukh, Even HaEzer* 12:3).

Are permitted to the sons or to the brothers – מותרות לבניהם או לאחיהם: All of these women are permitted to marry the close relatives of the witness or the Sage who freed them (Rambam *Sefer Nashim, Hilkhot Ishut* 10:16; *Shulḥan Arukh, Even HaEzer* 12:4).

אֲמַר לֵיהּ רַב הִלֵּל לְרַב אַשִׁי: וְהָתַנְיָא אֲפִילּוּ נִתְגָּרְשׁוּ! לָא קַשְׁיָא; הָא – דַּהֲוַאי קְטָטָה, הָא – דְּלָא הֲוַאי קְטָטָה.

Rav Hillel said to Rav Ashi: Yet it is taught in a *baraita*: **Even if they were divorced**[H] from their first wives they are permitted to marry the women they freed. The Gemara responds: **This is not difficult: This** mishna is referring to a case **when there was a quarrel** between the husband and the wife at the time that he freed the other woman, as then there is legitimate concern that he was already interested in her. **That** case of the *baraita* **was when there was no quarrel**[N] between them at the time, and therefore the divorce clearly resulted from some other reason.

וְאִיבָּעֵית אֵימָא: הָא וְהָא דְּלָא הֲוַאי קְטָטָה, וְלָא קַשְׁיָא; הָא – דְּאַרְגִּיל הוּא, הָא – דְּאַרְגִּילָה הִיא.

And if you wish, say: Both this and that were said in cases **when there was no quarrel** between the one who freed the woman and his first wife, and only later did they quarrel and divorce. **And this is not difficult: This** case of the mishna **was when he started** the quarrel **himself,** as then there is legitimate concern that he had an interest in this other woman and therefore sought out a reason to divorce his wife. **And that** case of the *baraita* **was when** his wife **started** the quarrel, as then there would be no reason to suspect him of freeing the other woman in order to marry her.

״וְכוּלָּן שֶׁנִּישְּׂאוּ״ וכו׳. קָא סָלְקָא דַּעְתִּין מִיתָה אַמִּיתָה, וְגֵירוּשִׁין אַגֵּירוּשִׁין,

The mishna stated: **And** with regard to **all of these** women, **if they were married** to others and then were divorced or widowed, it is permitted for them to marry those who caused them to be free to marry in the first place. **It enters our mind to say** that the case referred to here was one of **death after death,** i.e., the case of a woman whose first husband's death had been substantiated by a single witness but whose second husband died as well, **and** also to the case of **divorce following** a bill of **divorce** that had been validated by a single witness.

נֵימָא מַתְנִיתִין דְּלָא כְּרַבִּי, דְּאִי כְּרַבִּי – הָאָמַר: בִּתְרֵי זִימְנֵי הָוְיָא חֲזָקָה!

Based on this, **should we say that the mishna,** which permits a woman to remarry even after her two previous husbands have died, **is not in accordance with** the opinion of **Rabbi** Yehuda HaNasi? **As, if it is in accordance with** the opinion of **Rabbi** Yehuda HaNasi, **didn't** Rabbi Yehuda HaNasi **say: After two times** a woman has the **presumptive status** to cause death to her husbands, and such a woman is considered murderous. Therefore, she may not remarry. Since there is no mention of such concern in the mishna, it appears that the mishna is not in accordance with the opinion of Rabbi Yehuda HaNasi.

לָא, מִיתָה אַגֵּירוּשִׁין וְגֵירוּשִׁין אַמִּיתָה.

The Gemara rejects this: **No** evidence can be derived from here, as the reference here may be to **death after divorce or divorce after death.** The mishna could be referring either to a woman who was at first divorced and then later widowed by her second husband's death, or to a woman whose first husband died and who was subsequently divorced, but not to a case where she was widowed by the death of two husbands.

״וְכוּלָּן מוּתָּרוֹת לִבְנֵיהֶם אוֹ לַאֲחֵיהֶם״. מַאי שְׁנָא מֵהָא דִּתְנַן: הַנִּטְעָן מִן הָאִשָּׁה – אָסוּר בְּאִמָּהּ וּבְבִתָּהּ וּבַאֲחוֹתָהּ!

§ The mishna taught: **And all of these** women who were prohibited from marrying the man who freed them due to some suspicion **are permitted to the sons or to the brothers** of those who set them free. The Gemara asks: In **what** way **is** this case **different from that which we learned** in the *Tosefta* (4:5) that **one suspected** of adultery **with** a specific **woman is prohibited** not only from marrying her, but also **from** marrying **her mother, and her daughter, and her sister.** Yet here we allow his sons and brothers to marry the woman despite the suspicion.

נָשֵׁי לְגַבֵּי נָשֵׁי – שְׁכִיחָן דְּאָזְלָן, גַּבְרֵי לְגַבֵּי – גַּבְרֵי לָא שְׁכִיחָן.

The Gemara answers: There is a distinction between the situations, for **it is common for women** to be at the house of other **women** and to stay overnight. Therefore, there is concern that a relative of the alleged adulterer's wife, with whom he was suspected of misconduct, might frequent his house and he might be tempted to repeat his transgression. On the other hand, **it is not common for men** to be at the house of other **men,** so that even if she was married to his relative, the one suspected of misconduct would not generally sleep at the house of the husband.

HALAKHA

They were divorced – נִתְגָּרְשׁוּ: If those who rendered these women permitted were married at the time and subsequently divorced because their wives started a quarrel, it is permitted for them to marry those women. If they themselves started the quarrel, they may not marry those women. There are those who render it prohibited for them to marry these women if their first wives were sick at the time they freed the women (Rema, citing *Nimmukei Yosef*; Rambam *Sefer Nashim*, *Hilkhot Ishut* 10:15; *Shulḥan Arukh*, *Even HaEzer* 12:4).

NOTES

That was when there was no quarrel – הָא דְּלָא הֲוַאי קְטָטָה: Rashi explains that if there was a quarrel between the Sage who permitted this woman and his wife before they divorced, it appears that the divorce resulted from the quarrel and not from interest in the other woman. However, in *Yam shel Shlomo* the opposite explanation is suggested: If there was a quarrel between them beforehand, there is suspicion that due to the quarrel he decided to divorce his wife and seek out another wife for himself. Meiri explains that if there was a quarrel, then the reason for the divorce is not clear, and so there is no room for suspicion. However, if he divorced his wife without another clear reason, there is concern that it appears that he did so due to his desire for the other woman.

אִי נַמִּי: נָשֵׁי דְּלָא אָסְרָן שְׁכִיבְתָן אַהֲדָדֵי – לָא קָפְדֵי אַהֲדָדֵי, גַּבְרֵי דְּאָסְרָן שְׁכִיבְתָן אַהֲדָדֵי – קָפְדֵי אַהֲדָדֵי.

Alternatively, a different argument could be made: **Women are not so strict with one another, as lying with them** and having sexual relations with them **does not render them mutually forbidden.** In other words, if a man commits adultery with his wife's close relative, his wife does not become forbidden to him, so she may not pay attention to his behavior with the woman under suspicion. However, **men are strict with one another, as lying with them** and having sexual relations with the other man's wife **does render them,** the husband and wife, **mutually forbidden.** In other words, if another man has relations with a married woman, she is forbidden to her husband, and so men pay close attention to what the others are doing.

אִי הָכִי אָבִיו נַמִּי! לָא מִיבַּעְיָא קָאָמַר, לָא מִיבַּעְיָא אָבִיו – דְּבָזִיז בְּנֵיה מִינֵּיהּ, אֲבָל בְּנוֹ דְּלָא בְּזִיז אָבִיו מִינֵּיהּ – אֵימָא לָא, קָא מַשְׁמַע לָן.

The Gemara asks: **If so, one's father** should be permitted to marry a woman set free by his son **as well.** So why does the mishna say: Their sons or their brothers, and not: Their fathers? The Gemara answers: Certainly his father is allowed as well, but the mishna **is speaking** utilizing the style of: **It is not necessary. It is not necessary** to mention the case of **his father** because he is most certainly permitted to marry a woman set free by his son, **as his son is embarrassed** [***baziz***][L] **before him** and so would not come to sleep with his father's wife. **But I might say that** since **the father is not embarrassed before his son,** she **may not** be married to the son of one for whom there is suspicion. Therefore, **this comes to teach us** that there is no such concern.

הדרן עלך כיצד אשת אחיו

LANGUAGE

Embarrassed [*keziz*] – **כְּזִיז:** Although this version of the text has *baziz*, the version of the text that reads *keziz* is more correct because it comes from the Aramaic root *k-u-z*, which means to be ashamed or fearful.

Rabbi Ḥiyya's Description of Forbidden Relationships According to Rambam

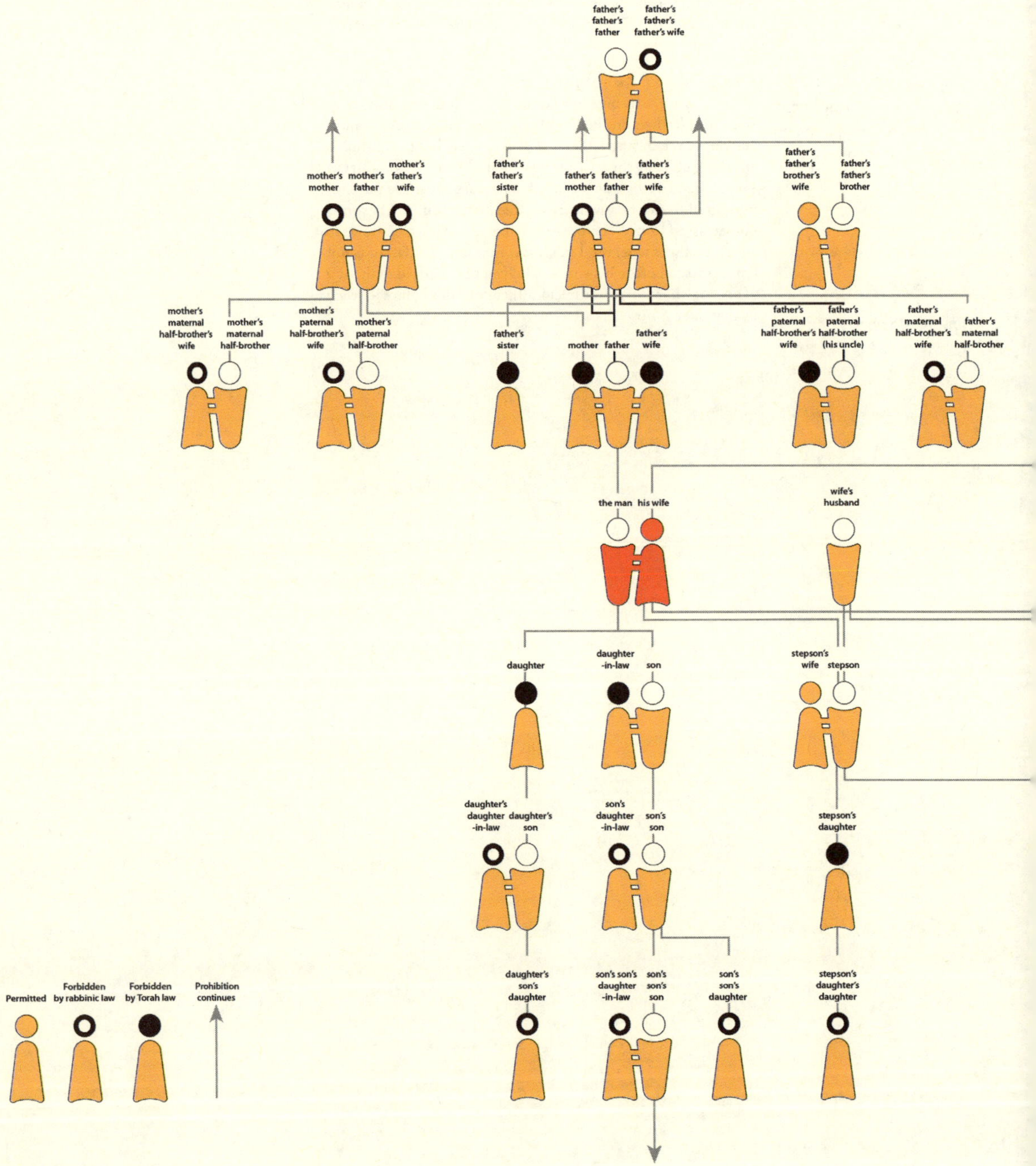

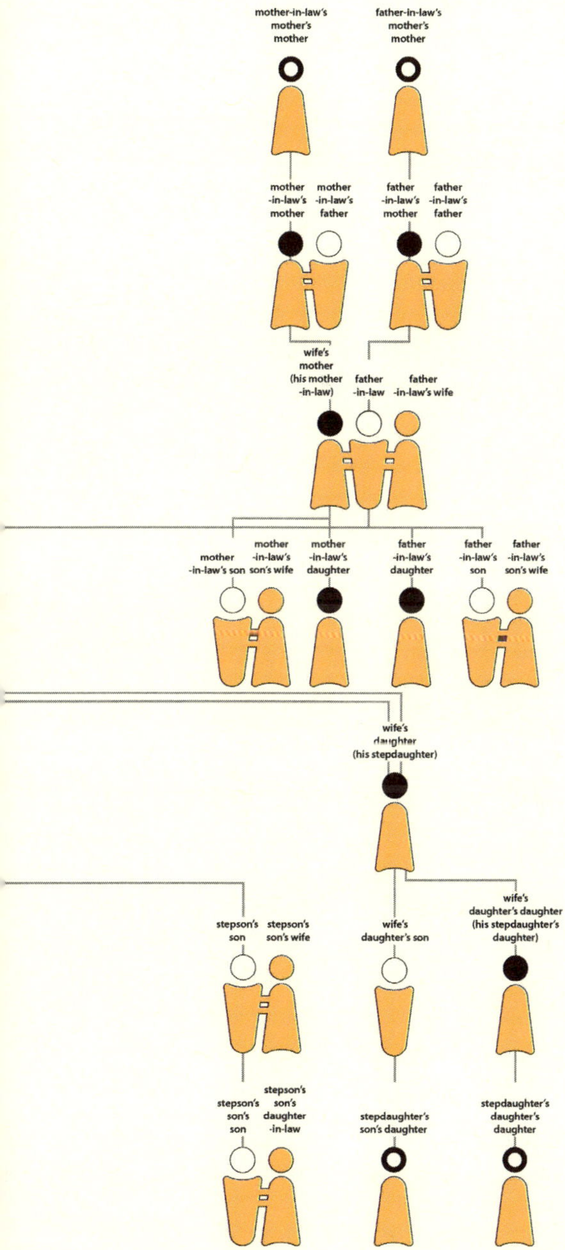
mother-in-law's mother's mother
father-in-law's mother's mother
mother -in-law's mother
mother -in-law's father
father -in-law's mother
father -in-law's father
wife's mother (his mother -in-law)
father -in-law
father -in-law's wife
mother -in-law's son
mother -in-law's son's wife
mother -in-law's daughter
father -in-law's daughter
father -in-law's son
father -in-law's son's wife
wife's daughter (his stepdaughter)
stepson's son
stepson's son's wife
wife's daughter's son
wife's daughter's daughter (his stepdaughter's daughter)
stepson's son's son
stepson's son's daughter -in-law
stepdaughter's son's daughter
stepdaughter's daughter's daughter

Summary of **Perek II**

This chapter, in addition to touching on a wide range of topics, primarily discusses several difficulties that arise in the *halakhot* of levirate marriage. It also deals with difficulties inherent in the general *halakhot* of marriage.

The *halakha* is that a brother is exempt from levirate marriage with the wife of a brother with whom he did not coexist. This means that if a brother was born after the death of the childless man whose wife requires levirate marriage, this newborn brother is exempt from performing levirate marriage. This applies even if the *yevama* had in the meantime been married to another brother who later died childless as well, whereby she would once again happen before a *yavam* for levirate marriage. She is exempt from both levirate marriage and *ḥalitza* and causes her rival wives to be exempt as well.

Although the eldest brother is specified by the Torah for the mitzva of levirate marriage, all of the brothers are eligible to perform the mitzva. The brother referred to by the Torah for the purposes of levirate marriage is specifically a paternal brother. Any paternal brother is included, even if he was born outside of marriage or is a *mamzer*. However, it does not include a brother whose mother was a gentile or a Canaanite maidservant.

The term "child" in the verse "If brothers dwell together and one of them dies and he has no child…" (Deuteronomy 25:5), is understood in the widest possible sense; it includes any descendants of the deceased brother. Whether it is a son, a daughter, or a grandchild, and whether that child is fit to enter the community or is disqualified, provided the descendant is not the child of a gentile woman or Canaanite maidservant, that child absolves the widow from the obligation of levirate marriage.

The Gemara concludes that in every case where the *yevama* is forbidden to the *yavam*, whether due to a prohibition resulting from a mitzva or a prohibition stemming from sanctity, including those prohibitions specific to the priestly class or those instituted by rabbinic law, even though she may not enter levirate marriage she must undergo *ḥalitza*. This is because the mitzva itself still applies to her by Torah law. If she had a rival wife who was not forbidden, then that rival wife is permitted to enter into levirate marriage. *Ḥalitza* rather than levirate marriage is also required in cases where it is uncertain whether the mitzva applies or to whom it applies.

As part of the deliberations over these issues, the matter of forbidden secondary relatives was also summarized in this chapter. These were defined as closely related women who did not fall under the category of forbidden relatives by Torah law, but were prohibited by rabbinic decree to create a safeguard, so that one not be confused between them and those women who are forbidden relatives by Torah law. The primary source for these *halakhot* is this chapter, and several issues were left unresolved, leading to disputes among halakhic authorities.

Another subject mentioned in this chapter is the general prohibition against marrying a woman if that marriage would raise suspicions of previous misconduct or cast doubt upon the veracity of testimony or the uprightness of judges.

Introduction to **Perek III**

If brothers dwell together and one of them dies and he has no child, the wife of the dead man shall not be married outside of the family to one not of his kin; her brother-in-law will have intercourse with her and take her to him to be his wife and consummate the levirate marriage.

(Deuteronomy 25:5)

The first two chapters of this tractate discussed the essential *halakhot* of levirate marriage in and of themselves. From Chapter Three onward, the Gemara's discussion concerns both how these *halakhot* apply to specific combinations of circumstances and the evaluation of different instructive examples. All of this is grounded in the principles that were clarified in the previous chapters. Based on these principles, the rulings are determined for situations where related women who were married to two or more brothers happen before their brothers-in-law, i.e., become candidates for levirate marriage with them, and the various possible relationships between these women and their brothers-in-law are evaluated as well. In the process it becomes clear that the relationship between brothers-in-law and *yevamot*, known in the Gemara as the levirate bond, requires further clarification.

From the verses, it is apparent that a sister-in-law requiring levirate marriage is bound to her brother-in-law and cannot marry another man until he releases her from the levirate bond via levirate marriage or *ḥalitza*. The Torah itself, however, does not provide any definition of this bond. Perhaps the bond can be understood simply as a one-sided obligation, whereby the sister-in-law is compelled to wait for her brother-in-law to perform some act. This opinion asserts that the levirate bond is not substantial. Alternatively, one could explain that the levirate bond is substantial, and the relationship between the parties obligated in levirate marriage is similar to that of those who are engaged, in that it would be prohibited for the *yavam* to marry the relatives of the *yevama*, in the same way that it would be prohibited for him to marry the relatives of his wife. Indeed, this perspective raises a certain difficulty, for there should apparently be some difference between the simple case of a *yevama* who is bonded to a single brother-in-law and the case where she is bonded to two brothers-in-law or more. However, by defining the levirate bond as a relationship that is substantial enough to create prohibitions for the parties involved, a fundamental contradiction arises in the case of a woman who is simultaneously bound to two different men.

Defining the parameters of the levirate relationship is also problematic when complex familial relations exist between the brothers-in-law and sisters-in-law. It must be determined precisely when the levirate bond is formed. Is it formed at the moment of the husband's death, following the opinion that a woman's status at the time of her husband's death determines her status with regard the levirate bond created between her and her brothers-in-law? Or, perhaps the original moment of marriage between the woman and her late husband created a levirate bond between her and her brothers-in-law, following the opinion that marriage determines a woman's status with regard to the levirate bond?

This chapter explores and clarifies these issues along with other questions that arise incidentally within the Gemara's discussions.

מתני׳ אַרְבָּעָה אַחִין, שְׁנַיִם מֵהֶם נְשׂוּאִים שְׁתֵּי אֲחָיוֹת, וּמֵתוּ הַנְּשׂוּאִים אֶת הָאֲחָיוֹת – הֲרֵי אֵלּוּ חוֹלְצוֹת וְלֹא מִתְיַיבְּמוֹת. וְאִם קָדְמוּ וְכָנְסוּ – יוֹצִיאוּ. רַבִּי אֱלִיעֶזֶר אוֹמֵר, בֵּית שַׁמַּאי אוֹמְרִים: יְקַיֵּים, וּבֵית הִלֵּל אוֹמְרִים: יוֹצִיאוּ.

MISHNA In the case of **four brothers,**[H] **two of whom were married to two sisters, and the ones married to the sisters died, then those** sisters must **perform *ḥalitza* and may not enter into levirate marriage.**[N] Since both sisters require levirate marriage with each of the surviving brothers, a levirate bond exists between each sister and the brothers. Each of them is considered the sister of a woman with whom each brother has a levirate bond and is therefore forbidden to him by rabbinic law. **And if they married** the sisters **before** consulting the court, **they should divorce** them, for the Sages decreed that in this situation they may not remain married. **Rabbi Eliezer says** that there is a dispute in this matter: **Beit Shammai**[N] **say: He may maintain** her as his wife, **while Beit Hillel say: They** must **divorce** them.

הָיְתָה אַחַת מֵהֶן אֲסוּרָה עַל הָאֶחָד אִיסּוּר עֶרְוָה – אָסוּר בָּהּ וּמוּתָּר בַּאֲחוֹתָהּ, וְהַשֵּׁנִי אָסוּר בִּשְׁתֵּיהֶן.

If **one of** the sisters **was forbidden**[H] **to one** of the brothers due to **a prohibition against forbidden relations** because she was a relative of his wife or a relative on his mother's side, then **he is forbidden to** marry **her but permitted to** marry **her sister.** Because she is his close relative, she is exempt from levirate marriage with him, and therefore she is not bound to him with a levirate bond. Consequently, her sister is not considered the sister of a woman with whom he has a levirate bond, and he is permitted to enter into levirate marriage with her. But **the second** brother, who is not a close relative of either sister, **is forbidden to** marry **both of them.** Indeed, for him each woman remains the sister of a woman with whom he has a levirate bond.

אִיסּוּר מִצְוָה וְאִיסּוּר קְדוּשָּׁה – חוֹלֶצֶת וְלֹא מִתְיַיבֶּמֶת.

If a **prohibition** resulting from **a mitzva**[N] or **a prohibition** stemming from **sanctity**[N] will be transgressed when one of the women marries one of the brothers, then her sister must **perform *ḥalitza* and may not enter into levirate marriage,** as she is considered the sister of a woman with whom he has a levirate bond. In this case, the sister who is forbidden to the brother due to a mitzva or due to sanctity is bound to the brother for the purpose of *ḥalitza*.

הָיְתָה אַחַת מֵהֶן אֲסוּרָה עַל זֶה אִיסּוּר עֶרְוָה, וְהַשְּׁנִיָּה אֲסוּרָה עַל זֶה אִיסּוּר עֶרְוָה – הָאֲסוּרָה לְזֶה מוּתֶּרֶת לְזֶה, וְהָאֲסוּרָה לְזֶה מוּתֶּרֶת לְזֶה.

If **one of those** women **was forbidden to this** one brother due to **a prohibition against forbidden relations and the second** woman **was forbidden to that** second brother due to **a prohibition against forbidden relations, then she who is forbidden to this** brother **is permitted to that** brother, **and she who is forbidden to that** brother **is permitted to this** one.

וְזוֹ הִיא שֶׁאָמְרוּ: אֲחוֹתָהּ כְּשֶׁהִיא יְבִמְתָּהּ – אוֹ חוֹלֶצֶת אוֹ מִתְיַיבֶּמֶת.

And this is the case that was referred to when **they said: When her sister is** also **her *yevama*,** i.e., in a case where two sisters are also *yevamot* and therefore happened for levirate marriage before two brothers, **she either performs *ḥalitza* or enters into levirate marriage.** This must be referring to a case where each sister is forbidden to one of the brothers due to a prohibition concerning forbidden relatives. In this case, each sister has a levirate bond only with the one brother to whom she is permitted, and the prohibition against marrying the sister of a woman with whom one has a levirate bond does not apply. Therefore, each brother can either perform the act of *ḥalitza* or consummate the levirate marriage with the sister to whom he is not related.

NOTES

Must perform *ḥalitza* and may not enter into levirate marriage – חוֹלְצוֹת וְלֹא מִתְיַיבְּמוֹת: One could suggest that one of the brothers performs *ḥalitza* with one sister and then afterward the second brother consummates the levirate marriage with the second sister, as she would then no longer be the sister of a woman with whom he has a levirate bond. This, however, is not allowed according to both explanations of the mishna. According to the opinion that it is prohibited to negate the mitzva of levirate marriage, there is a concern that they will confuse the order and perform the levirate marriage first. According to the opinion that the levirate bond is substantial, the second brother may not consummate the levirate marriage, as the woman was already forbidden to him once as the sister of a woman with whom he has a levirate bond, and she can no longer be rendered permitted (*Tosefot HaRosh*).

Rabbi Eliezer says, Beit Shammai, etc. – רַבִּי אֱלִיעֶזֶר אוֹמֵר, בֵּית שַׁמַּאי וכו׳: Although it is common for the Gemara to ask why a Sage saw fit to inform us of Beit Shammai's opinion when it does not accord with *halakha*, here there is an explanation. It seems that Rabbi Eliezer states this version of the dispute between Beit Shammai and Beit Hillel in order to exclude the opinion of Abba Shaul (*Yevamot* 28a), which sets forth an opposite tradition with regard to this dispute (*Tosefot HaRosh*).

A prohibition resulting from a mitzva – אִיסּוּר מִצְוָה: In addition to the sexual relationships prohibited on the basis of Torah prohibitions, there are additional relationships that are prohibited by rabbinic law. These are called prohibitions resulting from a mitzva, because the basis for the authority of rabbinic prohibitions is the Torah mitzva not to deviate from the words of the Sages, as it is stated: "According to the *halakha* that they shall teach you, and according to the judgment that they shall tell you, you shall do" (Deuteronomy 17:11).

A prohibition stemming from sanctity – אִיסּוּר קְדוּשָּׁה: This is referring to a marriage that is prohibited not because of the family relationship between the parties but because of the more elevated level of sanctity of one of the marriage partners. These include the prohibition against the marriage of a native-born Israelite to a *mamzer*, a priest to a divorcée, or a High Priest to a widow.

HALAKHA

Four brothers – אַרְבָּעָה אַחִין: In the case of four brothers, two of whom were married to two sisters and died childless, these sisters must perform *ḥalitza* and they may not enter into levirate marriage. If the brothers married the sisters before consulting with the court, they must divorce them (Rambam *Sefer Nashim*, *Hilkhot Yibbum* 7:1; *Shulḥan Arukh*, *Even HaEzer* 175:3).

If one was forbidden, etc. – הָיְתָה אַחַת אֲסוּרָה וכו׳: If one of the sisters was forbidden from marrying one of the brothers due to a prohibition against forbidden sexual relations, then he is permitted to marry her sister, and the other brother is prohibited from marrying both of them. If one of the sisters was forbidden to one brother and the second to another brother, each brother may marry the sister who is not forbidden to him (Rambam *Sefer Nashim*, *Hilkhot Yibbum* 7:1–2; *Shulḥan Arukh*, *Even HaEzer* 175:4–5).

גמ׳ שְׁמַע מִינָּהּ: יֵשׁ זִיקָה. דְּאִי אֵין זִיקָה, מִכְּדִי הָנֵי מִתְּרֵי בָּתֵּי קָאָתְיָין, הַאי לְיַיבֵּם חֲדָא וְהַאי לְיַיבֵּם חֲדָא!

GEMARA The Gemara deduces from the *halakha* cited in the mishna: **Conclude from here** that the **levirate bond**[H] **is substantial.** That is, the very obligation of levirate marriage creates a bond that is similar to marriage. **For if the levirate bond were not substantial,** why would these two women not enter into levirate marriage? **After all, these** two women **come from two households,** as each had a different husband, and they both require levirate marriage. **Let this** brother **consummate the levirate marriage with one** sister **and let that** brother **consummate the levirate marriage with** the **other** sister. The fact that the mishna requires *ḥalitza* in this situation indicates that the levirate bond is substantial and resembles marriage to the extent that each sister is forbidden to each brother due to the prohibition against marrying the sister of a woman to whom one has a levirate bond.

לְעוֹלָם אֵימָא לָךְ: אֵין זִיקָה, וּמִשּׁוּם דְּקָסָבַר אָסוּר לְבַטֵּל מִצְוַת יְבָמִין; דִּלְמָא אַדְּמְיַיבֵּם חַד – מָיֵית אִידָךְ, וְקָמְבַטֵּל מִצְוַת יְבָמִין.

The Gemara rejects this: **Actually, I** could **say to you** that according to this *tanna* **the levirate bond is not substantial,** and yet they are prohibited from entering levirate marriage for a different reason. It is **because** the *tanna* **holds that it is prohibited to negate the mitzva of levirate marriage.**[N] It is prohibited to act in a way that would lead to a situation where the mitzva to perform levirate marriage is negated. How would this situation arise? **Perhaps before one** brother **consummates the levirate marriage, the other** brother **dies,** and only one brother remains. In that case, the second sister would also happen before him for levirate marriage, **and** by performing levirate marriage with one sister **he would** thereby **negate the mitzva of levirate marriage** with the other sister. When the remaining brother marries one of the sisters, the mitzva to enter into levirate marriage or perform *ḥalitza* is automatically negated from the second sister, as she is then forbidden to him as his wife's sister.

אִי הָכִי, תְּלָתָא נַמִּי!

The Gemara asks: **If so,** if this is the rationale behind the ruling in the mishna, then the same concern would exist if there were **three**[N] brothers, **as well.** Why did the mishna specify four brothers? It could have cited the case of three brothers, two of whom were married to two sisters. In these circumstances, the concern for negating the mitzva of levirate marriage also exists.

לָא מִיבַּעְיָא קָאָמְרִינַן; לָא מִיבַּעְיָא תְּלָתָא, דְּוַדַּאי בָּטְלָה מִצְוַת יְבָמִין, אֲבָל אַרְבָּעָה, לְמִיתָה לָא חָיְישִׁינַן – קָא מַשְׁמַע לָן.

The Gemara answers: Indeed, the ruling would be the same in that case. However, the mishna **is speaking** utilizing the style of: **It is not necessary. It is not necessary**[N] to specify that the women must perform *ḥalitza* in a case involving **three** brothers, **as certainly the mitzva of levirate marriage is negated** with one of the sisters when the *yavam* marries the other sister. **But** in the case of **four** brothers, where there is concern only over the possibility that one of the brothers might die, we might have said that **we are not concerned over** the possibility of **the death** of a brother and therefore allow the brothers to consummate the levirate marriage. The mishna therefore **teaches us** that even in the case where there is concern only for the negation of the mitzva, they must perform *ḥalitza* and not consummate the levirate marriage.

אִי הָכִי,

The Gemara asks: **If so,** i.e., if we are concerned over the possibility that the remaining brother might die,

NOTES

Levirate bond or negation of the mitzva of levirate marriage – זִיקָה אוֹ בִּטּוּל מִצְוַת יִבּוּם: *Yosef Lekaḥ* elaborates on both sides of this ancient dispute. It appears in the Jerusalem Talmud and in other places and is formulated as follows: Is *ḥalitza* a mitzva in and of itself or is its purpose only to release one from the levirate bond?

According to the opinion that *ḥalitza* is indeed the fulfillment of a mitzva, one can understand the rationale against negating the mitzva of levirate marriage. By consummating the levirate marriage with one sister, the *yavam* prevents the other sister from performing both the mitzva of *ḥalitza* and of levirate marriage.

If, however, *ḥalitza* merely releases the woman from the levirate bond, it should not matter if that exemption comes from the act of *ḥalitza* or from his marriage to her relative. According to the opinion that *ḥalitza* serves only to release the woman from the levirate bond, it is apparent that the reason for requiring *ḥalitza* here must be due to the levirate bond. Although there is no mitzva involved in performing *ḥalitza*, it is nevertheless necessary, as there is a prohibition against consummating the levirate marriage due to the levirate bond.

If so, three – אִי הָכִי תְּלָתָא: This question is based on the assumption of the Gemara that this case should involve three brothers, as all the cases in the continuation of the chapter involve three brothers. For this reason, the Gemara wonders why the number of brothers was increased to four in this mishna (Rashba; Ritva).

It is not necessary, etc. – לָא מִיבַּעְיָא וכו׳: Many early commentaries ask: Why is this question raised specifically with regard to the opinion that the ruling is based on the prohibition against negating the mitzva of levirate marriage, but not with regard to the opinion that the levirate bond is substantial (see Rashi, Rivan, and *Tosafot*)?

The Ramban, in explanation of Rashi's comments, says: According to the opinion that the levirate bond is substantial, there is a novelty to be learned if the case involves specifically four brothers. This is because there is a dispute with regard to whether the levirate bond is substantial only if there is a single brother or even if there are two brothers. Accordingly, in order to teach that the levirate bond is significant even if there are multiple brothers, the case of four brothers is preferable to the case of three brothers.

However, according to the opinion that there is concern for the negation of the mitzva of levirate marriage, it stands to reason that the same concern should exist regardless of the number of brothers. Therefore, if the reasoning behind the ruling in the mishna is that the levirate bond is not substantial, it would have been appropriate to teach the case of three brothers, in order to indicate that although the levirate bond is not substantial, it is nevertheless prohibited to perform levirate marriage. It would then be clear that the rationale behind the ruling is based specifically on the idea that negating the mitzva of levirate marriage should be avoided. However, when the case involves four brothers the underlying rationale is not as clear (Ramban).

HALAKHA

The levirate bond – זִיקָה: In accordance with Shmuel's opinion here, the conclusive *halakha* is that the levirate bond is substantial. Although the halakha generally follows Rav's opinion in his disputes with Shmuel that pertain to prohibitions, the deliberation of the *amora'im* on Shmuel's opinion indicates that the *halakha* should be ruled according to him (Rosh; Rambam *Sefer Nashim*, *Hilkhot Yibbum* 1:13; *Shulḥan Arukh*, *Even HaEzer* 159:5).

חֲמִשָּׁה נַמִּי! לְמִיתָה דִּתְרֵי לָא חָיְישִׁינַן.

then this should **also** be true in a case of **five** brothers, two of whom were married to two sisters and died, and their wives happened before the three remaining brothers for levirate marriage. The Gemara answers: **We are not concerned over** the possibility of **the death of two**[N] brothers in such a short period of time.

אָמַר רָבָא בַּר רַב הוּנָא אָמַר רַב: שָׁלֹשׁ אֲחָיוֹת יְבָמוֹת שֶׁנָּפְלוּ לִפְנֵי שְׁנֵי אַחִין יְבָמִין, זֶה חוֹלֵץ לְאַחַת, וְזֶה חוֹלֵץ לְאַחַת, וְאֶמְצָעִית צְרִיכָה חֲלִיצָה מִשְּׁנֵיהֶם.

§ **Rava bar Rav Huna said** that **Rav said:** In a case where **three sisters** who were married to three brothers became ***yevamot*** and **happened before two** remaining **brothers** who were their ***yevamin*** for levirate marriage, then **this** one brother **performs *ḥalitza* with one** of the women, **and that** brother **performs *ḥalitza* with** another **one** of the women. **And the middle,** i.e., third, sister **requires *ḥalitza* with both of** the brothers.

אֲמַר לֵיהּ רַבָּה: מִדְּקָאָמְרַתְּ אֶמְצָעִית צְרִיכָה חֲלִיצָה מִשְּׁנֵיהֶם – קָסָבְרַתְּ יֵשׁ זִיקָה, וְהָוְיָא לָהּ חֲלִיצָה פְּסוּלָה, וַחֲלִיצָה פְּסוּלָה צָרִיךְ לַחֲזוֹר עַל כׇּל הָאַחִין.

Rabba said to them: From the fact **that you say** that **the middle one requires *ḥalitza* with both of** the brothers, it can be deduced that **you hold** that **the levirate bond is substantial** and creates a familial relationship, **and** similarly **this** *ḥalitza* performed by each of the brothers with the third sister **is invalid *ḥalitza*.**[NH] Since the third woman is the sister of a woman with whom he performed *ḥalitza*, it is not possible to consummate the levirate marriage with her. Therefore, the *ḥalitza* performed with her is not entirely valid and does not release her from the levirate bond between her and the two brothers. **And** there is a principle that **invalid *ḥalitza***[N] **must be repeated by all of the brothers;** each of them must perform an act of *ḥalitza* with this woman.

אִי הָכִי, קַמַּיְיתָא נַמִּי!

The Gemara asks: **If that is so, the first** two women should **also** require *ḥalitza* from each of the brothers because each act of *ḥalitza* was invalid, as each woman has the status of the sister of a woman with whom the man has a levirate bond, and it is therefore prohibited for the men to consummate the levirate marriage with them.

אִי דִּנְפוּל בְּבַת אַחַת – הָכִי נַמִּי, לָא צְרִיכָא דִּנְפוּל בְּזוֹ אַחַר זוֹ.

The Gemara responds: **If** the case is **that they,** i.e., the sisters, **happened** before the brothers **simultaneously,**[N] **it is indeed so** that the two brothers would each be obligated to perform *ḥalitza* with each of the three sisters. This *halakha* is **necessary only** in the case **where they happened** before the brothers, **one after the other.**

נָפְלָה חֲדָא – חָלַץ לָהּ רְאוּבֵן, נָפְלָה אִידַּךְ חָלַץ לָהּ שִׁמְעוֹן.

How so? **One** sister **happened** before the brothers for levirate marriage and then **Reuven,** one of the brothers, **performed** valid ***ḥalitza* with her. Another** sister **happened** before the brothers for levirate marriage, and the brother **Shimon performed *ḥalitza* with her.** In this case, Shimon was allowed to consummate the levirate marriage with her if he so desired, as she had no family relationship to him at all. When Reuven performed *ḥalitza* with the first sister, he removed the levirate bond between her and the other brothers, such that Shimon has no relationship with the first sister at all and is free to marry the second sister. Therefore, when he performed *ḥalitza*, the act was valid.

NOTES

We are not concerned over the possibility of the death of two – לְמִיתָה דִּתְרֵי לָא חָיְישִׁינַן: The Ritva writes that even according to those who hold that there might be legitimate concern over the possibility of two deaths, this is a case of a rabbinic decree that prohibits the negation of the mitzva of levirate marriage, where there need not be concerned for such a possibility.

Invalid *ḥalitza* – חֲלִיצָה פְּסוּלָה: The early commentaries dispute what constitutes invalid *ḥalitza*. According to one opinion, *ḥalitza* performed in a case where the *yavam* is prohibited from consummating the levirate marriage and the sister-in-law still requires *ḥalitza* is invalid *ḥalitza*. It must be performed by all the brothers before the *yevama* is permitted to remarry (Rashi; see Rambam).

According to *Tosafot*, however, invalid *ḥalitza* occurs only when the prohibition that precludes the possibility of performing levirate marriage directly weakens the levirate bond. The present case in the Gemara serves as an example: The woman requiring levirate marriage from the *yavam* is the sister of a woman who already underwent *ḥalitza* with him. If consummation of the levirate marriage is prohibited for a reason unrelated to her status as a *yevama*, such as when the initial marriage of the *yevama* was licentious due to her being her husband's remarried divorcée (see 11b), the proposed *ḥalitza* is not termed invalid and she needs to perform it only with one brother. The later commentaries discuss extensively how this dispute reflects a general question about the essence of *ḥalitza* (*Ḥiddushei Rav Shimon Shkop*; *Arza deVei Rav*).

The Ramban, following the Jerusalem Talmud, explains why invalid *ḥalitza* must be performed with all the brothers: Ordinary *ḥalitza* has two aspects. In one way it is similar to levirate marriage in that it a mitzva performed with one of the *yevamot* that concludes the levirate bond with both the *ḥalutza* and her rival wives. However, *ḥalitza* also bears resemblance to divorce in that it nullifies the connection between the *yavam* and the *yevama*. Invalid *ḥalitza* is limited in that it only operates in this second way and therefore the woman needs to sever her connection to each *yavam* separately.

The levirate bond is substantial…invalid *ḥalitza*, etc. – יֵשׁ זִיקָה...חֲלִיצָה פְּסוּלָה וכו׳: The Ritva and the Meiri explain that only if one maintains that the levirate bond is substantial is it possible to say that there was invalid *ḥalitza* and the *yevama* must repeat the *ḥalitza* with each of the *yevamin*. If, however, there is no levirate bond, then even invalid *ḥalitza* suffices to release the sister-in-law. However, from a discussion in the Jerusalem Talmud it would seem that these are two separate questions: First, is the *ḥalitza* an act of acquisition or release? Second, is the levirate bond an act of acquisition?

If the case is that they happened simultaneously – אִי דִּנְפוּל בְּבַת אַחַת: *Tosafot* comment that if the case is indeed referring to a situation where the two sisters became candidates for levirate marriage with the brothers simultaneously, then it would have been sufficient to state this ruling with regard to only two sisters. In this case, they would also need to repeat the *ḥalitza* with both brothers. Therefore, *Tosafot* raise the question as to why the Gemara specifically chose a case with three brothers. The Ramban writes that although, according to Rav's opinion, it would have sufficed to state this ruling with regard to two sisters, the case of three sisters was necessary according to Shmuel's statement later on. *Tosefot Ḥad MiKamma'ei* and the Meiri say that it was necessary to state the case of three sisters in order to inform us of a novel ruling: Even the third middle sister, whose levirate bond was weakened because she is the sister of a woman with whom he performed *ḥalitza*, requires *ḥalitza* from both of the brothers.

HALAKHA

Invalid *ḥalitza* – חֲלִיצָה פְּסוּלָה: The early authorities offer two definitions of invalid *ḥalitza*. The most common understanding is that in any case where the *yevama* is prohibited from consummating the levirate marriage but still requires *ḥalitza*, that *ḥalitza* is regarded as invalid and must be performed by all the brothers (Rashi; Rambam; see Vilna Gaon). The Rema, following *Tosafot*, writes that invalid *ḥalitza* occurs only when the relevant prohibition directly weakens the levirate bond, such as is the case when a *yavam* has a levirate bond with two sisters (Rambam *Sefer Nashim, Hilkhot Yibbum* 7:9; *Shulḥan Arukh, Even HaEzer* 170:5).

נָפְלָה אִידָךְ חָלַץ לָהּ הַאי מַפְקַע זִיקָתוֹ, חָלַץ לָהּ הַאי מַפְקַע זִיקָתוֹ.

Another third sister then **happened** before the brothers for levirate marriage. When **this** first brother **performs *ḥalitza* with her, he terminates his levirate bond, and** when **this** second brother **performs *ḥalitza* with her, he terminates his levirate bond.** However, neither brother can, by performing *ḥalitza*, terminate the other brother's levirate bond because each brother's *ḥalitza* is invalid, as each brother is unable to consummate the levirate marriage in this case. This is due to the woman's status as the sister of a woman with whom he performed *ḥalitza*.

וְהָאָמַר רַב: אֵין זִיקָה! לְדִבְרֵי הָאוֹמֵר יֵשׁ זִיקָה קָאָמַר.

The Gemara asks: How can this statement be cited in the name of Rav? **But didn't Rav say: The levirate bond is not substantial.** This *halakha*, however, was explained based on the assumption that the levirate bond is substantial. The Gemara answers: Indeed, according to Rav himself it is unnecessary to perform *ḥalitza* with multiple brothers. He, however, **states** this *halakha* **in accordance with the statement of the one who says that the levirate bond is substantial,**[N] despite the fact that he does not hold this himself.

וּשְׁמוּאֵל אָמַר: אֶחָד חוֹלֵץ לְכוּלָּן. מִכְּדִי שָׁמְעִינַן לֵיהּ לִשְׁמוּאֵל דְּאָמַר: חֲלִיצָה מְעַלְּיָא בָּעֵינַן, דְּאָמַר שְׁמוּאֵל:

And with regard to the above case **Shmuel said** a different halakhic ruling: It is sufficient if **one** brother **performs *ḥalitza* with each** of the sisters. The Gemara raises a difficulty: **But since we have heard that Shmuel said: We require a full-fledged *ḥalitza*,** and invalid *ḥalitza* does not result in complete exemption, this ruling is difficult. It is not clear why the invalid *ḥalitza* in this case would be sufficient, **as Shmuel said:**

NOTES

In accordance with the statement of the one who says that the levirate bond is substantial – לְדִבְרֵי הָאוֹמֵר יֵשׁ זִיקָה: Most of the early commentaries hold that Rav presented an opinion that was not his own and that he does not accept. Rivan, however, says that there is an amoraic dispute as to whether or not Rav holds that the levirate bond is substantial, and the opinion presented here follows that of the *amora* who maintains that Rav is of the opinion that the levirate bond is substantial (see *Yevamot* 18b).

Perek **III**
Daf **27** Amud **a**

חָלַץ לָאֲחָיוֹת לֹא נִפְטְרוּ צָרוֹת. הֵיכָא דְּקַיְימָא חֲלִיצָה דְּשִׁמְעוֹן חֲלִיצָה כְּשֵׁרָה, חָלֵיץ לָהּ רְאוּבֵן חֲלִיצָה פְּסוּלָה.

In the case of three brothers, two of whom were married to several women, including two sisters, and the two married brothers later died, and their wives happened before the *yavam* for levirate marriage, if the *yavam* **performed *ḥalitza* with the sisters** who were among the wives, **the rival wives are not** thereby **exempt.**[H] One can deduce from here that since the *yavam* cannot consummate the levirate marriage with the sisters, as each is the sister of a woman with whom he has a levirate bond, then the act of *ḥalitza* is invalid, and invalid *ḥalitza* is ineffective in exempting their rival wives. It is concluded from here that even Shmuel requires valid *ḥalitza*, i.e., *ḥalitza* that occurs when there is a possibility of consummating the levirate marriage. According to this rationale, however, Shmuel's ruling in the above case is difficult: With regard to the second sister, **when there exists** the possibility for **Shimon's *ḥalitza*,** i.e., the *ḥalitza* of the second brother who did not yet perform *ḥalitza*, to be **a valid *ḥalitza*,**[N] would it be allowed for **Reuven,** the brother who already did *ḥalitza* with one sister, **to perform invalid *ḥalitza*** with her?

מַאי "אֶחָד חוֹלֵץ לְכוּלָּן" נַמִי דְּקָאָמַר – אַאֶמְצָעִית. וְהָא כּוּלָּן קָאָמַר! כֵּיוָן דְּרוּבָּה גַּבֵּיהּ קָרֵי לֵיהּ "כּוּלָּן". וְאִיבָּעֵית אֵימָא: כִּי קָאָמַר שְׁמוּאֵל חֲלִיצָה מְעַלְּיָא בָּעֵינַן – הָנֵי מִילֵּי לְמִיפְטַר צָרָתָהּ, אֲבָל מִפְטְרָא נַפְשָׁהּ – פָּטְרָה.

The Gemara resolves this difficulty by reinterpreting Shmuel's statement. **What does it mean that it says: One performs *ḥalitza* with each of them, that** Shmuel **stated?** Shmuel **says that with regard to the middle one,** i.e., the third sister, one of the two brothers performs *ḥalitza* with her. The Gemara asks: **But didn't he say: Each of them,** indicating that one brother performs *ḥalitza* with all of the sisters? The Gemara answers: **Since** the brother who performed *ḥalitza* with one sister repeats the act with another, it turns out that **most** of the acts of *ḥalitza* **are** performed **with him,**[N] **and this is called:** With **each of them. And if you wish, say** a different answer: **When Shmuel said we require a full-fledged *ḥalitza*, this applies only to exempt her rival wife** by means of that *ḥalitza*. **But to exempt** the woman **herself,** even invalid *ḥalitza* would render her **exempt.**[H] In the case above, since no rival wives are involved, it would be sufficient for one brother to perform *ḥalitza* with each of the sisters.

HALAKHA

If he performed *ḥalitza* with the sisters the rival wives are not exempt – חָלַץ לָאֲחָיוֹת לֹא נִפְטְרוּ צָרוֹת: In the case of three brothers, two of whom were married to two sisters, where each had a rival wife, and the brothers died and their wives happened before the third brother for levirate marriage, if the *yavam* performs the act of *ḥalitza* with the rival wives then the sisters are thereby exempt as well. However, if he performs *ḥalitza* with the sisters, the rival wives do not become exempt, in accordance with the opinion of Shmuel as explained by Rav Ashi (Rambam *Sefer Nashim*, *Hilkhot Yibbum* 7:9; *Shulḥan Arukh*, *Even HaEzer* 170:17, 174:1).

To exempt the woman herself…exempt – מִפְטְרָא נַפְשָׁהּ, פָּטְרָה: It would seem that even according to those authorities who rule that in the case of invalid *ḥalitza* the woman must repeat the *ḥalitza* with the other brothers, this is required in order to completely nullify the levirate bond and exempt the rival wives. The woman who performed the invalid *ḥalitza*, however, is free of her bond and is permitted to the general public without repeating the *ḥalitza*. At the very least, she is permitted after the fact (see *Beit Shmuel*; Rambam *Sefer Nashim*, *Hilkhot Yibbum* 5:12; *Shulḥan Arukh*, *Even HaEzer* 170:19).

NOTES

Shimon's *ḥalitza*, a valid *ḥalitza* – חֲלִיצָה דְּשִׁמְעוֹן חֲלִיצָה כְּשֵׁרָה: Some commentaries say that when Reuven performed *ḥalitza* with the first sister, Shimon's bond with her was completely nullified, and therefore when Shimon performs *ḥalitza* with the second sister it is a completely valid *ḥalitza* (see Rashba). Others explain that even if some aspect of Shimon's original bond with the first sister remains intact, his act of *ḥalitza* with the second sister is nevertheless more efficacious than the *ḥalitza* performed by Reuven (Rivan).

Since most are with him – כֵּיוָן דְּרוּבָּה גַּבֵּיהּ: This follows the principle that in any matter, the majority is equivalent to the entirety (Ritva).

גּוּפָא, אָמַר שְׁמוּאֵל: חָלַץ לָאֲחָיוֹת – לֹא נִפְטְרוּ צָרוֹת, לַצָּרוֹת – נִפְטְרוּ אֲחָיוֹת. חָלַץ לְבַעֲלַת הַגֵּט – לֹא נִפְטְרָה צָרָה, לַצָּרָה – נִפְטְרָה בַּעֲלַת הַגֵּט.

§ Apropos of Shmuel's statement, the Gemara examines **the** matter **itself. Shmuel said:** In the case of three brothers, two of whom were married to several women, including two sisters, and the two married brothers later died, and their wives happened before the *yavam* for levirate marriage, if the *yavam* **performed *ḥalitza* with the sisters,**[B] **the rival wives are not** thereby **exempt.** But if he performed *ḥalitza* **with the rival wives, the sisters are exempt.**[N] Similarly, if he gave a bill of divorce to one of these women, whereby he would no longer be permitted to consummate the levirate marriage with them due to a rabbinic decree, and he then **performed *ḥalitza* with the woman who received a bill of divorce, the rival wife is not** thereby **exempt.** Since he was unable to consummate the levirate marriage with her, the *ḥalitza* performed with her was invalid, and invalid *ḥalitza* does not exempt the rival wife. If he performed the act of *ḥalitza* **with the rival wife,** then **the woman who received a bill of divorce is exempt.**[N]

חָלַץ לְבַעֲלַת הַמַּאֲמָר – לֹא נִפְטְרָה צָרָה, לַצָּרָה – נִפְטְרָה בַּעֲלַת מַאֲמָר.

The ruling is similar with regard to the case where the *yavam* performed *ma'amar*, i.e., levirate betrothal,[N] to one of the wives. If **he** then **performed *ḥalitza* with** the woman **who received** his **levirate betrothal** then **the rival wife is not exempt.** Indeed, this *ḥalitza* is invalid as well, for once the *yavam* performed levirate betrothal, this act can be rescinded only by means of a bill of divorce. Because the woman needs to receive a bill of divorce in addition to the *ḥalitza* in order to exempt her from her bond, the *ḥalitza* is considered invalid and is not sufficient to exempt the rival wife. But if the *yavam* performed *ḥalitza* **with the rival wife,** then **she who received** his **levirate betrothal is exempt**[N] from *ḥalitza* and requires only a bill of divorce.[H]

מַאי שְׁנָא לָאֲחָיוֹת דְּלָא נִפְטְרוּ צָרוֹת – דַּהֲוְיָא לוֹ אֲחוֹת אִשָּׁה בְּזִיקָה, חָלַץ לַצָּרוֹת נַמִּי לָא לִיפַּטְרוּ אֲחָיוֹת, דַּהֲוְיָא לְהוּ צָרוֹת אֲחוֹת אִשָּׁה בְּזִיקָה! קָסָבַר שְׁמוּאֵל: אֵין זִיקָה.

The Gemara asks: **What is different** in the two cases? Why, if he performed *ḥalitza* **with the sisters, are the rival wives not exempt?** This is because the sister **is** related **to him** as **the sister of a woman with whom he has a levirate bond.** Since, under these circumstances he would not be permitted to consummate the levirate marriage with her, her *ḥalitza* is then considered invalid *ḥalitza*. However, if that is so, when **he performed *ḥalitza* with the rival wives, the sisters should not be exempt either,** as **the** rival wives **are** related **to him as rival wives of the sister of a woman with whom he has a levirate bond.** If the woman is forbidden to him due to a relationship created by the levirate bond, then her rival wife is forbidden to him in the same way, and her *ḥalitza* would be invalid as well. The Gemara answers: **Shmuel holds** that **the levirate bond is not substantial,** and therefore the levirate bond does not create a relationship between the *yavam* and the sisters such that the prohibition would be extended to the rival wives as well.

NOTES

With the rival wives, the sisters are exempt – לַצָּרוֹת נִפְטְרוּ אֲחָיוֹת: Even though there is some small deficiency in the performance of *ḥalitza* with the rival wives, this deficiency is, according to all opinions, negligible (*Tosefot Rid*).

The woman who received a bill of divorce is exempt – נִפְטְרָה בַּעֲלַת הַגֵּט: It is preferable to perform *ḥalitza* with the rival wife, although she is not eligible to enter into levirate marriage because the *yavam* did not perform any previous act with her, unlike with the woman who received a bill of divorce (*Tosefot Rid*).

Levirate betrothal – מַאֲמָר: The Sages instituted that even in cases of levirate marriage, which can be effected by conjugal relations alone according to Torah law, the *yavam* should first perform betrothal by means of a legal document or a transfer of money accompanied by a verbal declaration of betrothal. As opposed to standard betrothal, this levirate betrothal is not binding by Torah law.

She who received levirate betrothal is exempt – נִפְטְרָה בַּעֲלַת מַאֲמָר: Although the rival wife of one who received levirate betrothal is also forbidden to the *yavam*, as he is allowed to build one household and not two, it is still preferable to perform *ḥalitza* with the rival wife. This is because a woman who received levirate betrothal is not exempt from her connection with him by the act of *ḥalitza* alone but would require a bill of divorce as well (see *Tosefot Rid*).

With regard to the deficiency in the *ḥalitza* of a woman who had received levirate betrothal, some commentaries explain that the performance of levirate betrothal renders this woman ineligible for levirate marriage with the other brothers, and even a slight deficiency in the levirate bond renders the *ḥalitza* deficient (see Rivan and Ramban).

Tosafot explain that the woman who received levirate betrothal is somewhat similar to a woman who entered into marriage. Marriage completely nullifies the levirate bond; levirate betrothal weakens the levirate bond.

HALAKHA

***Ḥalitza* with a woman who received a bill of divorce or levirate betrothal – חֲלִיצָה לְבַעֲלַת הַגֵּט אוֹ מַאֲמָר:** In the case of one who performed levirate betrothal with his *yevama* or gave her a bill of divorce, if she had a rival wife and he then came to perform *ḥalitza* with one of the women, *ḥalitza* with the woman who received the bill of divorce or levirate betrothal would not exempt her rival wife from performing *ḥalitza*. *Ḥalitza* with the rival wife, however, does render the woman who received a bill of divorce or levirate betrothal exempt from performing *ḥalitza*, in accordance with the statement of Shmuel (*Shulḥan Arukh, Even HaEzer* 170:17).

BACKGROUND

He performed *ḥalitza* with the sisters – חָלַץ לָאֲחָיוֹת: Reuven, Shimon, and Levi are paternal brothers. Shimon married Rachel and Ḥanna. Levi married Rachel's sister, Leah, and Miriam. When Shimon and Levi die childless, their wives happen before Reuven for levirate marriage. If Reuven first performs *ḥalitza* with Leah and then afterward with Rachel, Rachel's *ḥalitza* is considered invalid. Although Rachel herself is rendered exempt through this *ḥalitza*, her rival wife Ḥanna is not. However, Leah's *ḥalitza* is valid, and therefore her rival wife Miriam is rendered exempt by it.

וְהָא אֲמַר שְׁמוּאֵל: יֵשׁ זִיקָה! לְדִבְרֵי הָאוֹמֵר אֵין זִיקָה קָאָמַר.

The Gemara challenges: **But didn't Shmuel say** explicitly that **the levirate bond is substantial?** The Gemara responds: **He stated** this *halakha* **in accordance with the statement of those who say that the levirate bond is not substantial,**[N] although he himself maintains the opposite.

אִי הָכִי, חָלַץ לָאֲחָיוֹת אַמַּאי לֹא נִפְטְרוּ צָרוֹת? בִּשְׁלָמָא צָרָה דְּרָחֵל לָא תִּיפָּטֵר – דְּכֵיוָן דְּחָלַץ לָהּ לְלֵאָה וַהֲדַר חָלַץ לְרָחֵל – הָוְיָא לָהּ חֲלִיצָה דְּרָחֵל חֲלִיצָה פְּסוּלָה. אֶלָּא צָרָה דְּלֵאָה תִּיפָּטֵר!

The Gemara asks: **If that is** indeed **so,** that he stated this ruling in accordance with the opinion that the levirate bond is not substantial, then when the *yavam* **performed *ḥalitza* with the sisters, why were** their **rival wives not exempt? Granted,** Rachel's **rival wife,** i.e., the rival wife of the second sister, **would not be exempt, for once he performed *ḥalitza* with Leah,** the first sister, **and then** later **performed *ḥalitza* with Rachel,** it turns out that **Rachel's *ḥalitza* was invalid *ḥalitza*,**[H] as he could not consummate the levirate marriage with Rachel because she is the sister of a woman with whom he performed *ḥalitza,* and invalid *ḥalitza* does not exempt a rival wife. **However, the rival wife of Leah should be exempt** because if the levirate bond is not substantial, the *ḥalitza* with the first sister would have been completely valid.

מַאי "לֹא נִפְטְרוּ צָרוֹת" נַמִי דְּקָאָמַר – אַצָּרָה דְּרָחֵל, וְהָא "צָרוֹת" קָאָמַר! צָרוֹת דְּעָלְמָא.

The Gemara explains: **What** does it mean **that** it says: **The rival wives are not exempt, that** Shmuel **stated?** It is referring only **to the rival wife of Rachel,** the second sister, who is not exempt. The Gemara challenges: **But he said rival wives** in the plural, seeming to refer to both rival wives? The Gemara answers: He spoke of **rival wives in general.**[N] In other words, this is a general *halakha,* and for that reason it was stated in the plural. However, it does not mean that both the rival wife of the first sister and the rival wife of the second sister are not exempt.

אִי הָכִי, חָלַץ "לַצָּרוֹת נִפְטְרוּ אֲחָיוֹת", וְאַצָּרַת רָחֵל מִי מִיפַּטְרָא? וְהָא תְּנַן: אָסוּר אָדָם בְּצָרַת קְרוֹבַת חֲלוּצָתוֹ!

The Gemara challenges this: **If that is so,** that when Shmuel chose to speak in the plural he was referring only to the rival wife of Rachel, there arises a difficulty with the second half of the statement: If **he performed *ḥalitza* with the rival wives, the sisters are exempt. But would Rachel** become **exempt** by *ḥalitza* performed **with her rival wife? But didn't we learn** in a mishna: **A man is forbidden to** marry **the rival wife of a close relative of his *ḥalutza*?** Once the *yavam* performs *ḥalitza* with one sister, Leah, then her sister's rival wife, i.e., Rachel's rival wife, would be considered the rival wife of the sister of a woman with whom he performed *ḥalitza.* Being as she is forbidden to him, her *ḥalitza* is invalid and should not exempt Rachel.

שְׁמוּאֵל נַמִי, הִתְחִיל וְלֹא הִתְחִיל קָאָמַר: הִתְחִיל בָּאֲחָיוֹת – לֹא יִגְמוֹר בַּצָּרוֹת, דִּתְנַן: אָסוּר אָדָם בְּצָרַת קְרוֹבַת חֲלוּצָתוֹ, הִתְחִיל בַּצָּרוֹת – יִגְמוֹר אַף בָּאֲחָיוֹת, דִּתְנַן: מוּתָּר אָדָם בִּקְרוֹבַת צָרַת חֲלוּצָתוֹ.

The Gemara answers: **Shmuel also** meant to distinguish between a case where **he began**[N] **and** the case where **he did not begin.** This is how his statement should be understood: If **he began** by performing *ḥalitza* **with** one of **the sisters, he may not finish by** performing a second act of *ḥalitza* **with** any one of **the rival wives, as we learned** in a mishna (40b): **A man is forbidden** to marry **the rival wife of a close relative of his *ḥalutza*.**[H] Due to this prohibition, *ḥalitza* performed with the second rival wife is invalid *ḥalitza* and would not exempt the second sister. If, however, **he began with the rival wives** and performed the first *ḥalitza* with the rival wife of Leah, **he may finish with the sisters as well** and perform the second *ḥalitza* with Leah, **as we learned** in a mishna (40b): **A man is permitted to** marry **the close relative of the rival wife of his *ḥalutza*.**[H] Therefore, if he performed *ḥalitza* with Leah's rival wife, then Rachel, who is the sister of the rival wife of his *ḥalutza,* is permitted to him. He can therefore perform a completely valid *ḥalitza* with her and thereby exempt her rival wife.

NOTES

In accordance with the statement of those who say that the levirate bond is not substantial – לְדִבְרֵי הָאוֹמֵר אֵין זִיקָה: The early commentaries raise an objection: The Gemara maintains that the ruling that *ḥalitza* with a woman who received a bill of divorce does not exempt her rival wife was said only in accordance with the opinion that the levirate bond is substantial (*Yevamot* 51a). If so, how can the Gemara here explain that Shmuel stated this ruling in accordance with the opinion that the levirate bond is not substantial?

Tosafot, Ramban, and others hold that the present discussion is cited for the sake of the talmudic argumentation alone and does not represent a true summary of the issue. However, *Tosafot Yeshanim* say that the two *halakhot* mentioned follow two different opinions: The first *halakha*, which discusses *ḥalitza* with sisters, follows the opinion that the levirate bond is not substantial. The *halakha* that discusses *ḥalitza* with a woman who received a bill of divorce follows the opinion that the levirate bond is substantial.

Rival wives in general – צָרוֹת דְּעָלְמָא: This phrase indicates that this *halakha* applies to any case that is similar to this one. The Sages occasionally employ the plural forms in order to establish a general ruling (Rashi). The Rivan understands that this ruling extends to all instances of a rival wife of a woman who is forbidden to the *yavam* by rabbinic law. This includes not only women prohibited to the *yavam* due to the levirate bond, but also women who are secondary forbidden relationships by rabbinic law.

Shmuel…began, etc. – שְׁמוּאֵל...הִתְחִיל וכו׳: Some commentaries explain this passage specifically according to the opinion that the levirate bond is substantial, similar to the next answer suggested by the Gemara in the name of Rav Ashi. If so, the Gemara changes its assumption during the course of its discussion. Although this type of change would normally be noted by the word rather, as that word is generally employed to indicate the retraction of a previous explanation and the introduction of a new suggestion, this practice is not strictly adhered to if the first opinion is presented anonymously and not in the name of a specific *amora* (*Tosefot HaRosh*; Ramban).

HALAKHA

Invalid *ḥalitza* must be repeated – חֲלִיצָה פְּסוּלָה צְרִיכָה לַחֲזוֹר: There are a variety of opinions with regard to this *halakha*. Some authorities determined that in cases of invalid *ḥalitza*, if there are several *yevamin* the woman must repeat the *ḥalitza* with all of the *yevamin*. If, however, there are two sisters-in-law whose *ḥalitza* is considered invalid and only a single *yavam*, he can exempt them both through a single act of *ḥalitza*. Some say that if there are two sisters-in-law he must perform *ḥalitza* with each of them (Ramban). Other authorities hold that invalid *ḥalitza* does not necessitate that the woman repeat the *ḥalitza* with the other brothers, and even in the case of two *yevamin* and a single *yevama*, a single act of *ḥalitza* would suffice. It seems that most of the halakhic authorities hold in accordance with this opinion (Rambam *Sefer Nashim, Hilkhot Yibbum* 5:12; *Shulḥan Arukh, Even HaEzer* 170:5, 19).

Forbidden to marry the rival wife of a close relative of his *ḥalutza* – אָסוּר...בְּצָרַת קְרוֹבַת חֲלוּצָתוֹ: The Sages considered a woman with whom one performed *ḥalitza* to be like his wife, and therefore he is forbidden to marry her close relatives, including her sister, mother, etc. If a close relative of the woman with whom he performed *ḥalitza* is married to his brother, then her rival wife is likewise forbidden to him. If, however, she is married to another man, her rival wife is permitted to him, as per most halakhic authorities, but not in accordance with Rashi (Rambam *Sefer Nashim, Hilkhot Yibbum* 6:20; *Shulḥan Arukh, Even HaEzer* 162:5).

Permitted to marry the close relative of the rival wife of his *ḥalutza* – מוּתָּר...בִּקְרוֹבַת צָרַת חֲלוּצָתוֹ: A man is allowed to marry the sister, or any other relatives, of the rival wife of a woman with whom he performed *ḥalitza*, in accordance with the mishna cited here (Rambam *Sefer Nashim, Hilkhot Yibbum* 1:13; *Shulḥan Arukh, Even HaEzer* 162:4).

רַב אַשִׁי אֲמַר: לְעוֹלָם כִּדְקָאָמְרַתְּ, וּמִשּׁוּם דְּלָא אַלִּימָא זִיקָה לְשַׁוְּיֵי לַצָּרָה כְּעֶרְוָה.

Rav Ashi said: Actually, Shmuel's statement should be interpreted **as you** originally **said,** that Shmuel's rationale for these *halakhot* accords with his opinion that the levirate bond is substantial. As for the objection that was raised as to why the sisters would be exempted by *ḥalitza* performed with the rival wives if these rival wives were considered the rival wife of the sister of a woman with whom the *yavam* had a levirate bond, this can be resolved as follows: This **is because the levirate bond is not** so **strong**[N] **as to render the** status of **a rival wife like** an actual **forbidden relative.** The levirate bond is sufficient to prohibit levirate marriage with the sister of a woman with whom he has a levirate bond, but not sufficient to prohibit their rival wives to the *yavam*.

תַּנְיָא כְּוָותֵיהּ דְּרַב אַשִׁי: חָלַץ לָאֲחָיוֹת – לֹא נִפְטְרוּ צָרוֹת, הָא לַצָּרוֹת נִפְטְרוּ אֲחָיוֹת – מַאי טַעֲמָא, לָאו מִשּׁוּם דְּקָסָבַר יֵשׁ זִיקָה, וְלֹא אַלִּימָא זִיקָה לְשַׁוְּיֵיהּ לַצָּרָה כְּעֶרְוָה?!

The Gemara comments: It **is taught** in a *baraita* **in accordance with** the opinion **of Rav Ashi:**[N] **If he performed *ḥalitza* with the sisters, the rival wives are not exempt** from levirate marriage. From here one can deduce: **Consequently,** if he performed *ḥalitza* **with the rival wives, the sisters are exempt. What is the reason** for this? **Is it not because** this *tanna* **held** that **the levirate bond is substantial,** and therefore the rival wives were not rendered exempt by the *ḥalitza* of the sisters, **but** nevertheless **the levirate bond is not** so **strong as to render the rival wife equivalent to a forbidden relative** Therefore, the prohibition with regard to the rival wives in this case is less severe than the prohibition concerning the sisters themselves, and when they perform *ḥalitza*, the *ḥalitza* is valid and the sisters are exempt.

אָמַר רַבִּי אַבָּא בַּר מֶמֶל: הָא מַנִּי – בֵּית שַׁמַּאי הִיא, דִּתְנַן: בֵּית שַׁמַּאי מַתִּירִין הַצָּרוֹת לָאַחִין. אִי הָכִי, יַבּוּמֵי נַמִּי תִּתְיַיבֵּם!

Rabbi Abba bar Memel rejected this explanation and **said:** In accordance with **whose** opinion **is this** *baraita* taught? **It is** in accordance with the opinion of **Beit Shammai,**[N] **as we learned** in a mishna: **Beit Shammai permitted the rival wives to** marry **the brothers;** even if they are the rival wives of his actual relatives, they are permitted to enter into levirate marriage. In the case above, where they are merely rival wives of the sister with whom he has a levirate bond, all the more so they are permitted to enter into levirate marriage. The Gemara objects: **If that is so,** if this ruling is in accordance with the opinion of Beit Shammai, who say that the rival wives are permitted, then the rival wife **should enter into levirate marriage as well.** Why does it speak here only of *ḥalitza* but not of the possibility of entering levirate marriage?

כְּרַבִּי יוֹחָנָן בֶּן נוּרִי, דְּאָמַר: בּוֹאוּ וּנְתַקֵּן לָהֶם לַצָּרוֹת שֶׁיְּהוּ חוֹלְצוֹת וְלֹא מִתְיַיבְּמוֹת. וְהָאָמַר מָר לֹא הִסְפִּיקוּ לִגְמוֹר אֶת הַדָּבָר עַד שֶׁנִּטְרְפָה הַשָּׁעָה! אֲמַר רַב נַחְמָן בַּר יִצְחָק: אַחֲרָיו חָזְרוּ וְתִקְּנוּ.

The Gemara answers: The ruling is **in accordance with** the opinion of **Rabbi Yoḥanan ben Nuri, who said: Come and let us establish** a ruling **that the rival wives must perform *ḥalitza* and may not enter into levirate marriage,** thereby circumventing the dispute between Beit Shammai and Beit Hillel. Although Beit Shammai permitted the rival wives to the perform levirate betrothal, they should perform *ḥalitza* instead in order to conform to Beit Hillel's opinion as well. The Gemara objects: **But didn't the Master say** that **they did not succeed in finalizing the matter** and establishing Rabbi Yoḥanan ben Nuri's amendment **before the times of trouble**[B] **came** in the form of the anti-Jewish decrees, and so this ruling was never actually established? **Rav Naḥman bar Yitzḥak said: After his** time, other Sages **returned** to this issue and **established** this amendment in accordance with his opinion.[N]

אִיבַּעְיָא לְהוּ:

§ Apropos of the statement of Shmuel with regard to a woman who received a bill of divorce and a woman who received levirate betrothal, **a dilemma was raised before** the Sages:

NOTES

The levirate bond is not so strong – **לָא אַלִּימָא זִיקָה**: This assertion does not mean that the bond does not affect the rival wives at all, as rival wives may not enter into levirate marriage, even according to Rav Ashi's opinion. Rather, this means that the levirate bond is not so strong as to disqualify the rival wives in the same way that it disqualifies the sisters.

It is taught in accordance with the opinion of Rav Ashi – **תַּנְיָא כְּוָותֵיהּ דְּרַב אַשִׁי**: It is not possible to interpret this *baraita* as the words of Shmuel were interpreted, by adding: He began, and: He did not begin, since it would have been necessary for the *baraita* to add additional segments clarifying the matter (*Tosafot*; see Ritva).

Whose opinion is this? It is Beit Shammai – **הָא מַנִּי, בֵּית שַׁמַּאי הִיא**: This matter is also raised in the Jerusalem Talmud, and there, too, it was suggested that the *baraita* should be interpreted as the opinion of Rabbi Yoḥanan ben Nuri. There, however, the Gemara does not suggest the hard-pressed explanation that the Sages proceeded to established this amendment (see *Tosafot*). Instead, the Gemara establishes the *baraita* as one version of the opinion of Beit Shammai, which itself is the matter of a tannaitic dispute.

Summary of the talmudic discussion – **סִיכּוּם הַסּוּגְיָה**: In this complicated talmudic discussion, the Gemara assumes that Rav and Shmuel made statements opposing their own opinions and also suggests various interpretations of Shmuel's statements wherein it is unclear whether or not these interpretations concur with one another. This leads the commentaries and especially the halakhic authorities to arrive at vastly different conclusions. The Rema and the Ramban conclude that the *halakha* follows Rav with regard to invalid *ḥalitza*. Since Rav made his statement in accordance with the opinion that the levirate bond is substantial, as is the halakhic conclusion, we must follow the principle that the *halakha* is in accordance with the opinion of Rav in matters of prohibitions. Therefore, according to the Ramban and others, in cases of invalid *ḥalitza*, each sister must repeat the *ḥalitza* with all the other *yevamin*.

According to most authorities, the Rif concludes that the *halakha* is in accordance with the most straightforward explanation of Shmuel, which is the latter explanation of his words. Therefore, one *yavam* performs *ḥalitza* with each of the sisters. The Rif establishes the *halakha* in accordance with the opinion of Shmuel, in opposition to Rav, because the principle that the *halakha* follows Rav applies only if Rav employs his own opinion in the dispute but not when he offers an explanation of another opinion that is not his own (*Nimmukei Yosef*).

The early commentaries were divided over how to understand the Rambam's opinion here, for it would seem that his words support two different opinions. Most commentaries maintain that he establishes the *halakha* in accordance with Shmuel and the latter explanation in the Gemara (Ramban; Rashba; Meiri; *Tur*).

The Ra'avad, *Tosafot*, and the Rosh all establish the *halakha* in accordance with the opinion of Shmuel, but according to the first formulation. Accordingly, the middle woman does not require *ḥalitza* with all of the brothers but the second sister does require *ḥalitza* from the second brother. They reason that where it is possible to perform valid *ḥalitza*, invalid *ḥalitza* does not suffice to exempt the woman. There are, however, differences of opinion within these commentaries. It would seem that the Ra'avad holds that after the fact the latter explanation can be relied upon (see *Beit Shmuel*). However, *Tosafot* maintain that even after the fact the *halakha* is according to the first explanation.

BACKGROUND

Times of trouble – **נִטְרְפָה הַשָּׁעָה**: It would seem, according to the chronology of the generations, that this is referring to several times of distress that occurred successively over one period. This period extended from the polemic of Trajan and Kitos, also known as the Diaspora Revolt, which destroyed the Jewish settlement in several lands adjacent to Israel, through the bar Kokheva revolt, which caused total upheaval in Jewish life. These disturbances completely prevented the Sanhedrin's ability to take organized action, including instituting ordinances, e.g., obligatory *ḥalitza* for rival wives.

בַּעֲלַת הַגֵּט וּבַעֲלַת מַאֲמָר – אֵיזוֹ מֵהֶן קוֹדֶמֶת? בַּעֲלַת הַגֵּט עֲדִיפָא – מִשּׁוּם דְּאַתְחֵיל בָּהּ בַּחֲלִיצָה, אוֹ דִּלְמָא בַּעֲלַת מַאֲמָר עֲדִיפָא מִשּׁוּם דִּקְרוֹבָה לְבִיאָה?

If two women happened before a single *yavam* for levirate marriage, and one is **a woman who received a bill of divorce and** the other is **a woman who received levirate betrothal,**[H] **which has precedence** for *ḥalitza*? **Is the woman who received a bill of divorce preferred**[N] **because he began the** process of ***ḥalitza* with her,** as presenting a bill of divorce represents the first step separating the woman from him? **Or perhaps the woman who received levirate betrothal is preferred, because she is closest to** being able to enter into permitted **sexual intercourse.** The act of levirate betrothal is generally done just prior to levirate marriage and is equivalent to the act of betrothal in non-levirate contexts. As a result, levirate betrothal strengthens the connection between the woman and the *yavam*. For this reason, it may be preferable to perform *ḥalitza* with the woman who received levirate betrothal.

אָמַר רַב אָשֵׁי, תָּא שְׁמַע: וּמוֹדֶה רַבָּן גַּמְלִיאֵל שֶׁיֵּשׁ גֵּט אַחַר מַאֲמָר, וּמַאֲמָר אַחַר גֵּט.

Rav Ashi said: Come and hear: The Sages disputed the ruling with regard to a *yavam* who performed levirate betrothal with one sister-in-law and then performed it with her rival wife as well, or conversely, gave both women a bill of divorce. In such cases, would the second levirate betrothal or bill of divorce be effective? It was taught: **And Rabban Gamliel concedes that a bill of divorce is effective after levirate betrothal.** Therefore, the bill of divorce that the *yavam* gave to one *yevama* after having performed levirate betrothal with the other *yevama* is effective to some degree. Similarly, Rabban Gamliel concedes that **levirate betrothal** performed **after a bill of divorce is effective.**

אִי גֵּט עָדִיף – לָא לִיהֲנֵי מַאֲמָר אַבַּתְרֵיהּ, וְאִי מַאֲמָר עָדִיף – לָא לִיהֲנֵי גֵּט אַבַּתְרֵיהּ! אֶלָּא לָאו שְׁמַע מִינַּהּ כִּי הֲדָדֵי נִינְהוּ, שְׁמַע מִינַּהּ.

If the bill of divorce is preferred to levirate betrothal, then **levirate betrothal** performed **afterward should not be effective.** The opposite would hold true as well: **And if levirate betrothal is preferred,** then **a bill of divorce** given **afterward should not be effective. Rather,** must one **not conclude from** this statement **that the two are equivalent to each other?**[N] The Gemara summarizes: Indeed, **conclude from** this statement that they are equivalent. Therefore, neither the woman who received a bill of divorce nor the woman who received levirate betrothal has precedence for *ḥalitza*.

אָמַר רַב הוּנָא אָמַר רַב: שְׁתֵּי אֲחָיוֹת יְבָמוֹת שֶׁנָּפְלוּ לִפְנֵי יָבָם אֶחָד, חָלַץ לָרִאשׁוֹנָה – הוּתְּרָה, חָלַץ לַשְּׁנִיָּה – הוּתְּרָה.

§ **Rav Huna said** that **Rav said:** In a case of **two sisters** who became ***yevamot***, i.e., the two sisters were married to two brothers who died, **who happened before one *yavam*** for levirate marriage,[H] if **he performed *ḥalitza* with the first** sister, then **she is permitted** to marry any man. If **he performed *ḥalitza* with the second** sister, then **she is permitted** to do so as well.

HALAKHA

A woman who received a bill of divorce and a woman who received levirate betrothal – בַּעֲלַת הַגֵּט וּבַעֲלַת מַאֲמָר: If two *yevamot* from a single household happened before a *yavam* for levirate marriage, and he delivered a bill of divorce to one and performed levirate betrothal with the other, then he can perform the act of *ḥalitza* with whichever of them he choose and thereby exempt the second (*Shulḥan Arukh, Even HaEzer* 170:17).

Two sisters, *yevamot*, who happened before one *yavam* for levirate marriage – שְׁתֵּי אֲחָיוֹת יְבָמוֹת שֶׁנָּפְלוּ לִפְנֵי יָבָם אֶחָד: In the case of two sisters who happened before a *yavam* for levirate marriage one after the other, if the second sister died before he had performed any act the first sister is permitted to him. If, however, the first sister died, the second is forbidden. This ruling is in accordance with the opinion of Rabbi Yoḥanan, as the *halakha* follows him in disputes with Rav (Rambam *Sefer Nashim, Hilkhot Yibbum* 7:4; *Shulḥan Arukh, Even HaEzer* 175:1).

NOTES

Is the woman who received a bill of divorce preferred, etc. – בַּעֲלַת הַגֵּט עֲדִיפָא וכו׳: The use of the word preferred does not accurately represent the meaning here, and therefore the early commentaries diverge in their interpretation of it. According to the first suggestion of *Tosafot*, the word preferred simply clarifies the question of which woman underwent an act of more importance, and therefore this clarification does not decide the ruling of precedence with regard to *ḥalitza*.

From the words of the Rivan, however, it seems that being preferred indicates precedence for the purposes of *ḥalitza*. According to this explanation, the question at hand is: Once the *yavam* began the process of nullification with the woman who received a bill of divorce, would it be more appropriate for him to continue the process and do ḥalitza with her, or would the woman who received levirate betrothal hold precedence because her levirate bond is more complete? Alternatively, *Tosafot Yeshanim* explain that the question is: Which woman is it preferable to release from the levirate bond by performing *ḥalitza* with her rival wife; the woman who received a bill of divorce, because her bond was already weakened and therefore *ḥalitza* with her would be less powerful, or the woman who received levirate betrothal, because her levirate bond was weakened by the performance of levirate betrothal?

The two are equivalent to each other – הֲדָדֵי נִינְהוּ: Some commentaries hold that since the act of *ḥalitza* with either one of the women is equally flawed, both acts are considered invalid *ḥalitza*. Accordingly, the *ḥalitza* would have to be repeated with both women in order to release them from their levirate bonds (*Tosefot HaRosh*; see *Tosafot* and Ramban). However, according to Rashi and most halakhic authorities, since each act of *ḥalitza* is equally flawed, *ḥalitza* with one woman is sufficient to exempt the other. The Meiri adds another reason for this ruling, and states that invalid *ḥalitza* requires repetition only if there was some form of levirate bond in place. In this case, a single act of *ḥalitza* suffices, as there is no levirate bond.

מֵתָה רִאשׁוֹנָה מוּתָּר בַּשְּׁנִיָּיה, וְאֵין צָרִיךְ לוֹמַר מֵתָה שְׁנִיָּיה שֶׁמּוּתָּר בָּרִאשׁוֹנָה, מִשּׁוּם דְּהָוְיָא יְבָמָה שֶׁהוּתְּרָה וְנֶאֶסְרָה וְחָזְרָה וְהוּתְּרָה – תַּחֲזוֹר לְהֶיתֵּירָהּ הָרִאשׁוֹן.

If **the first** sister **died** before the *yavam* was able to perform *ḥalitza* with her, then he **is permitted to** take **the second**[N] sister in levirate marriage, for even if had actually been married to the first sister, one is permitted to marry the sister of his wife after his wife dies. **And needless to say, if the second** sister **died, then he is permitted to** take **the first** sister in levirate marriage **because she would be** considered **a *yevama* who was permitted** at the time that she happened before the *yavam* for levirate marriage; **and** then later **forbidden** as the sister of a woman with whom he has a levirate bond when the second sister happened before him for levirate marriage; **and subsequently became permitted** by the death of the second sister. Therefore, **she can return** completely **to her original permitted status.**

וְרַבִּי יוֹחָנָן אָמַר: מֵתָה שְׁנִיָּיה – מוּתָּר בָּרִאשׁוֹנָה. אֲבָל מֵתָה רִאשׁוֹנָה – אָסוּר בַּשְּׁנִיָּיה. מַאי טַעְמָא – שֶׁכָּל יְבָמָה שֶׁאֵין אֲנִי קוֹרֵא בָּהּ בִּשְׁעַת נְפִילָה "יְבָמָהּ יָבֹא עָלֶיהָ" הֲרֵי זוֹ כְּאֵשֶׁת אָח שֶׁיֵּשׁ לָהּ בָּנִים, וַאֲסוּרָה.

However, Rabbi Yoḥanan said: If the second sister **dies, he is permitted to** take **the first. But if the first** sister **dies, he is prohibited from** taking **the second** sister. **What is the reason** for this ruling? The reason is **that any *yevama* to whom the verse "her brother-in-law will have intercourse with her"** (Deuteronomy 25:5) **cannot be applied at the time that she happens** before him for levirate marriage because she was forbidden to him at that moment, **is then** forever considered to be **like the wife of a brother who has children, and she is forbidden** to him. Because the second sister was forbidden to the *yavam* at the time that she happened before him for levirate marriage, being the sister of a woman with whom he had a levirate bond, she can never again be permitted to him.

וְרַב לֵית לֵיהּ הַאי סְבָרָא? וְהָאָמַר רַב: כָּל אִשָּׁה שֶׁאֵין אֲנִי קוֹרֵא בָּהּ בִּשְׁעַת נְפִילָה "יְבָמָהּ יָבֹא עָלֶיהָ" הֲרֵי הִיא כְּאֵשֶׁת אָח שֶׁיֵּשׁ לוֹ בָּנִים וַאֲסוּרָה! הָנֵי מִילֵּי הֵיכָא דְּקָאֵי בְּאַפָּהּ אִיסּוּר אֲחוֹת אִשָּׁה דְּאוֹרָיְיתָא, אֲבָל הָכָא – זִיקָה דְּרַבָּנַן הִיא.

The Gemara asks: **And does Rav not accept that reason?**[N] **Didn't Rav** himself **say** the exact same words: **Any woman to whom the verse "her brother-in-law will have intercourse with her" cannot be applied at the time that she happens** before him for levirate marriage **is then** considered to be **like the wife of a brother who has children,**[N] **and she is forbidden** to him? The Gemara answers: **This applies only when** the prohibition **that stands before her** and prevents the levirate marriage **is the prohibition against marrying the sister of one's wife, which is prohibited by Torah** law. Therefore, if the woman who happens before the *yavam* for levirate marriage is his wife's sister, he is prohibited from performing levirate marriage even if his wife dies afterward. **But here** the prohibition to marry the sister stems from a relationship created by **a levirate bond.** This prohibition is **by rabbinic** law,[N] and therefore the bond does not render her forbidden to him forever.

NOTES

Rav said…the first died, he is permitted to take the second – אָמַר רַב...מֵתָה רִאשׁוֹנָה מוּתָּר בַּשְּׁנִיָּיה: There are several different opinions as to how to explain Rav's ruling. Rabbeinu Ḥananel holds that Rav is consistent with his opinion that the levirate bond is not substantial, and he apparently thought that those who maintain that the levirate bond is substantial hold that the levirate bond has the force of Torah law (see Rashba). Therefore, the *yavam* is not permitted to consummate the levirate marriage with one of the sisters *ab initio* due to the prohibition against negating the mitzva of levirate marriage (see *Tosafot*).

The Meiri analyzes the issue in a similar way. He states that although Rav holds that the levirate bond is not substantial, the *yavam* is nevertheless unable to consummate the levirate marriage with any one of the sisters *ab initio*, since both of them happened before him for levirate marriage, and marrying one would negate the mitzva of levirate marriage with the other. Similarly, the *yavam* cannot perform the act of *ḥalitza* with one sister *ab initio* and then consummate the levirate marriage with the other since, she would be rendered forbidden to him as the sister of a woman with whom he performed *ḥalitza*.

Alternatively, the Ramban says that Rav's ruling is also consistent with the opinion that the levirate bond is substantial. Accordingly, the reason why the *yavam* is permitted to take the second sister is that a levirate bond has the force of rabbinic law and is therefore not sufficiently binding to cause the *yevama* to be forbidden to him forever.

And does Rav not accept that reason – וְרַב לֵית לֵיהּ הַאי סְבָרָא: The commentaries ask why the Gemara did not object to Rav based on an explicit mishna that states: She is now forbidden to him forever since she was forbidden to him at one time (*Yevamot* 32a; see *Tosafot*). The Ramban explains that had the Gemara objected based on that mishna, Rav could have resolved the objection by noting that the mishna explicitly refers to a case involving a relationship forbidden by Torah law. Alternatively, he could have said that the *halakha* in the mishna, as later becomes clear, is in accordance with the opinion of Rabbi Eliezer, but that the Rabbis disagree with him.

Like the wife of a brother who has children – כְּאֵשֶׁת אָח שֶׁיֵּשׁ לוֹ בָּנִים: One must say that this means that she is like the wife of a brother who has children at the time of his death, such that even if the children later died she would not again require *ḥalitza* (see *Meromei Sadeh*).

Here a levirate bond by rabbinic law – הָכָא זִיקָה דְּרַבָּנַן הִיא: According to those who maintain that this ruling of Rav is consistent with his opinion that the levirate bond is not substantial, this resolution proves difficult because, according to this opinion, there should be no bond at all.

The Rashba explains that Rav agrees that there is a prohibition in place. However, it does not stem from the levirate bond, but rather it is a rabbinic prohibition against negating the mitzva of levirate marriage. He would therefore interpret this phrase to mean that there is a rabbinic prohibition not to negate the levirate bond of the second woman.

Tosafot Yeshanim ask about a different aspect of this ruling: Why doesn't Rav prohibit the second woman, as she was forbidden to the *yavam* at the time of her husband's death due to the possibility of negating the mitzva of levirate marriage, as becomes clear later in the Gemara? He answers that one must differentiate between an actual prohibition with regard to a specific woman and a decree stemming from concern lest the mitzva of levirate marriage be negated, for such a concern indeed becomes irrelevant with the death of the other woman.

אֵיתִיבֵיהּ רַבִּי יוֹסֵי בַּר חֲנִינָא לְרַבִּי יוֹחָנָן: אַרְבָּעָה אַחִין, שְׁנַיִם מֵהֶם נְשׂוּאִים שְׁתֵּי אֲחָיוֹת, וּמֵתוּ הַנְּשׂוּאִין אֶת הָאֲחָיוֹת – הֲרֵי אֵלּוּ חוֹלְצוֹת וְלֹא מִתְיַיבְּמוֹת. וְאַמַּאי? לֵיקוּ חַד מִינַּיְיהוּ לַחֲלוֹץ לָהּ לַשְּׁנִיָּיה, וְתֶיהֱוֵי רִאשׁוֹנָה לְגַבֵּי אִידָּךְ כִּיבָמָה שֶׁהוּתְּרָה וְנֶאֶסְרָה וְחָזְרָה וְהוּתְּרָה – תַּחֲזוֹר לְהֶיתֵּירָהּ הָרִאשׁוֹן!

Rabbi Yosei bar Ḥanina raised an objection to the opinion of Rabbi Yoḥanan[N] from the mishna: In the case of **four brothers, two of whom were married to two sisters, and those married to the sisters died, then those** sisters **must perform** ***ḥalitza*** **and may not enter into levirate marriage. And why** does the mishna require *ḥalitza*? **Let one of** the brothers **rise and perform** ***ḥalitza*** **with the second** sister, i.e., the sister whose husband died later. As a result, **the first would be like a** ***yevama*** **who was permitted** at the time of her husband's death but later became **forbidden** due to the bond that was created with her sister, **and** she then **subsequently became permitted** by means of *ḥalitza* performed with her sister, **insofar as the other** brother, i.e., he who did not perform *ḥalitza*, **is concerned.** Therefore, **she should return to her original permitted status.**

אָמַר לֵיהּ: אֲחָיוֹת אֵינִי יוֹדֵעַ מִי שְׁנָאָן. וְלֵימָא לֵיהּ: מַאי "חוֹלְצוֹת" נַמִי דְּקָתָנֵי – חוֹלֶצֶת חֲדָא! "חוֹלְצוֹת" קָתָנֵי.

Rabbi Yoḥanan **said to him: I do not know who taught: Sisters.** Rabbi Yoḥanan was in doubt as to the correct version of this mishna, as he could not find any reasonable explanation of this mishna according to any known opinion. The Gemara asks: Why did Rabbi Yoḥanan respond in such an extreme manner. **Let him say to him,** to Rabbi Yosei bar Ḥanina, an alternate solution: **What is** the meaning of the ruling that the sisters **perform** ***ḥalitza***, **which** the mishna **teaches?** The meaning is that **one** sister **performs** ***ḥalitza***. The Gemara answers: Such a solution is untenable, as the mishna **teaches** the ruling using the words: **Perform** ***ḥalitza***, in the plural.

וְלֵימָא לֵיהּ: מַאי "חוֹלְצוֹת" חוֹלְצוֹת דְּעָלְמָא! "הֲרֵי אֵלּוּ" קָתָנֵי. וְלֵימָא: דְּחָלֵיץ לֵיהּ לָרִאשׁוֹנָה בְּרֵישָׁא! "חוֹלְצוֹת"

The Gemara suggests: **And let** Rabbi Yoḥanan **say to him: What is** the meaning of the ruling to **perform** ***ḥalitza***? **They perform** ***ḥalitza*** **in general.** Accordingly, the mishna teaches that in such cases the second women performs *ḥalitza*. The Gemara responds: The mishna **teaches: Then those** women perform *ḥalitza*. The emphasis on the word: Those, indicates that it is specifically those two women who both perform *ḥalitza*. The Gemara asks further: **And let him say** that the mishna is referring only to the specific case **where** *the yavam* **performed** ***ḥalitza*** **with the first** sister **first.** As a result, there was no longer be any possibility of rendering the second sister permitted, as Rabbi Yoḥanan permitted levirate marriage only in the case where *ḥalitza* was performed with the second sister first. The Gemara answers: This cannot be suggested either, for the phrase: **Perform** ***ḥalitza***,

לְכַתְּחִלָּה קָתָנֵי. וְלֵימָא לֵיהּ גְּזֵירָה דִּלְמָא קָדֵים וְחָלֵיץ לָרִאשׁוֹנָה בְּרֵישָׁא! "וְלֹא מִתְיַיבְּמוֹת" קָתָנֵי, דְּלֵיכָּא דִּין יִבּוּם הָכָא כְּלָל.

implies that the mishna **teaches** a case in which *ḥalitza* is performed ***ab initio***. This indicates that this is the first course of action and the only way to resolve the situation. The Gemara asks further: And **let him say to him** the following: The mishna prohibits levirate marriage *ab initio* in this case, due to a rabbinic **decree lest he proceed**[N] **and perform the** ***ḥalitza*** **with the first**[H] sister **first**, whereby it would be prohibited to consummate the levirate marriage with the second. Perhaps for this reason the Sages decreed that it is prohibited to consummate the levirate marriage even if *ḥalitza* was performed with the second sister. The Gemara answers: **It teaches: They may not enter into levirate marriage.**[N] This indicates that **the** ***halakha*** **of levirate marriage does not apply here at all.** Accordingly, even after the fact, if he performed *ḥalitza* with the second sister, the *halakha* of levirate marriage would not apply to the first sister.

NOTES

Raised an objection to Rabbi Yoḥanan, etc. – אִיתִּיבֵיהּ...לְרַבִּי יוֹחָנָן וכו׳: Some commentaries suggest that Rabbi Yosei bar Ḥanina's objection poses a more significant difficulty to Rav's position, but it was not mentioned as an objection to Rav because Rav held that this mishna is in accordance with the opinion that the levirate bond is substantial, though Rav himself does not maintain that stance (*Tosafot*). The Meiri adds further that since there is a principle that Rav is considered like a *tanna*, in that he can disagree with a mishna, it is less compelling to challenge his ruling from a mishna. *Tosefot HaRosh* explains that in truth this objection applies to Rav as well, but since Rabbi Yosei bar Ḥanina was close to Rabbi Yoḥanan and from the same generation as him, he raised it against him specifically. Moreover, this issue is later resolved on its own in the process of the talmudic deliberations in accordance with Rav's opinion, as Rav is concerned lest the mitzva of levirate marriage be negated. Alternatively, the Rivan holds that there is no difficulty for Rav here at all because Rav holds that in cases of invalid *ḥalitza*, the woman must repeat the *ḥalitza* with all of the brothers. In that case, the second woman would be the sister of his *ḥalutza*, which would preclude the possibility of consummating the levirate marriage. The Rashba proves from the fact the Gemara did not resolve the issue in this way, according to Rabbi Yoḥanan's opinion, that Rabbi Yoḥanan agrees with Shmuel, both with regard to the question of whether the levirate bond is substantial as well as with regard to the issue of whether a woman who performed invalid *ḥalitza* must repeat it with all of the brothers.

NOTES

And let him say…lest he proceed, etc. – וְלֵימָא...דִּלְמָא קָדֵים וכו׳: One can ask with regard to this question: Doesn't Rabbi Yoḥanan himself hold that if the second sister dies the first is permitted? This indicates that he is not concerned that there might be confusion of this kind. This difficulty can be resolved by asserting that Rabbi Yoḥanan allows the first sister to enter into levirate marriage only in the case where one of the sisters died, as in such a situation there is no concern for confusion. However, in a case where both sisters are alive, perhaps there would be concern, and therefore this rabbinic decree would apply. The Gemara, however, did not assume this distinction when it raised the objection, but rather understood that the fear of confusing the women was a legitimate concern in all cases (Rashba).

It teaches they may not enter into levirate marriage – וְלֹא מִתְיַיבְּמוֹת קָתָנֵי: The Rivan explains that if the matter were prohibited by rabbinic decree, it would have sufficed to say: They perform *ḥalitza*. The fact that the mishna repeated the ruling and stressed that they may not enter into levirate marriage indicates that this matter was a conclusive halakhic ruling.

HALAKHA

Lest he proceed and perform the ***ḥalitza*** **with the first, etc.** – דִּלְמָא קָדֵים וְחָלֵיץ לָרִאשׁוֹנָה וכו׳: If there were four brothers, and two of them were married to two sisters, and the two married brothers died one after the other, and one of the surviving brothers proceeded to perform *ḥalitza* with the second sister, then the first sister is rendered permitted to the other brother. It seems that even Rabbi Yoḥanan is in agreement with this *halakha*, but he could not find a way to interpret the mishna to accord with this ruling (Rambam *Sefer Nashim, Hilkhot Yibbum* 7:1; *Shulḥan Arukh, Even HaEzer* 175:1).

וְלֵימָא לֵיהּ גְּזֵירָה שֶׁמָּא יָמוּת, וְאָסוּר לְבַטֵּל מִצְוַת יְבָמִין! רַבִּי יוֹחָנָן לְמִיתָה לָא חָיֵישׁ.

The Gemara asks: **And let him say to him** a different reason for the ruling of the mishna: It is due to a rabbinic **decree lest** the second brother **die, and it is prohibited to negate the mitzva of levirate marriage.** Perhaps for this reason it would be forbidden to consummate the levirate marriage in the case where two sisters happened before him for levirate marriage, and not due to the prohibition proscribing the sister of a woman with whom he has a levirate bond. The Gemara answers: **Rabbi Yoḥanan was not concerned over** the possibility of the **death**[N] of a brother, and in his opinion there is no need to make a decree to address such cases.

וְלֵימָא לֵיהּ רַבִּי אֶלְעָזָר הִיא, דְּאָמַר: כֵּיוָן שֶׁעָמְדָה עָלָיו שָׁעָה אַחַת בְּאִיסּוּר נֶאֶסְרָה עָלָיו עוֹלָמִית! מִדְּסֵיפָא רַבִּי אֶלְעָזָר רֵישָׁא לָאו רַבִּי אֶלְעָזָר.

The Gemara asks: **And let** Rabbi Yoḥanan **say to him** that this mishna **is** in accordance with the opinion of **Rabbi Elazar, who said: Once the** *yevama* **stood before him at one time as forbidden,** even if it was not at the time that she happened before him, **she remains forbidden to him forever.** Perhaps the mishna could be explained according to Rabbi Elazar's opinion. The Gemara answers: **Since** the opinion of **Rabbi Elazar** is cited explicitly **in the latter clause** of the mishna, it can be deduced that **the first clause is not** according to the opinion of **Rabbi Elazar.** Therefore, this ruling cannot be attributed to Rabbi Elazar.

וְנֵימָא לְהוּ דִּנְפוּל בְּבַת אַחַת וְרַבִּי יוֹסֵי הַגְּלִילִי הִיא, דְּאָמַר: אֶפְשָׁר לְצַמְצֵם! לָא סָתַם לָן תַּנָּא כְּרַבִּי יוֹסֵי הַגְּלִילִי.

The Gemara asks: **And let him say to him** that here the reference is to a situation **where** the two brothers died at once, and consequently both of the women **happened before** the *yevamin* for levirate marriage **at the same time. And** this mishna **is** in accordance with the opinion of **Rabbi Yosei HaGelili, who says: It is possible to be precise.**[N] It is possible to determine that two events occurred at exactly the same moment, both sisters were forbidden at the time that they happened before the brothers-in-law. The Gemara answers: **The *tanna* did not teach an unattributed** mishna **in accordance with** the opinion of **Rabbi Yosei HaGelili.** Any time the mishna is cited in accordance with Rabbi Yosei HaGelili's opinion, it is always attributed to him explicitly.

וְלֵימָא לֵיהּ דְּלָא יָדְעִינַן הֵי נְפוּל בְּרֵישָׁא!

The Gemara asks: **And let him say to him** a different explanation for the ruling: This mishna is indeed addressing a case where the brothers died one after the other, yet **we do not know which** sister **happened** before the *yevamin* for levirate marriage **first.**[H] In that case, it would be impossible to determine which sister would be permitted.

אִי הָכִי, הַיְינוּ דְּקָתָנֵי ״קָדְמוּ וְכָנְסוּ יוֹצִיאוּ״? בִּשְׁלָמָא רִאשׁוֹנָה אָמְרִינַן לֵיהּ: מַאן שַׁרְיָא לָךְ? אֶלָּא שְׁנִיָּה, אָמַר: חַבְרָאִי שְׁנִיָּה יִיבֵּם, אֲנָא רִאשׁוֹנָה מְיַיבֵּם!

The Gemara answers: **If so, that which** the mishna **teaches** in the latter clause: **And if they married** their wives **before** consulting the court **they should divorce them,** is difficult. Why must they divorce their wives in this situation? **Granted,** the brother who took **the first** sister in levirate marriage must divorce her, as **we say to him: Who permitted her to you?** Indeed, she was forbidden as the sister of a woman with whom he had a levirate bond, and so he must divorce her. **However,** the brother who took **the second** sister **could say: My fellow** brother **consummated the levirate marriage with the second**[N] sister, but **I am consummating the levirate marriage with the first** sister. It is possible that after the other brother consummated the levirate marriage with the second sister, the first sister would then be permitted to him after the fact, and he is not required to divorce her unless it is certain that he violated a prohibition.

הַיְינוּ דְּקָאָמַר לֵיהּ: אֲחָיוֹת אֵינִי יוֹדֵעַ מִי שְׁנָאָן.

The Gemara concludes: Indeed, **this is what** Rabbi Yoḥanan meant when he **said to** Rabbi Yosei bar Ḥanina: **I do not know who taught: Sisters,** for according to these considerations he cannot properly resolve the ruling of this mishna.

HALAKHA

We do not know which sister happened before the *yevamin* first – **דְּלָא יָדְעִינַן הֵי נְפוּל בְּרֵישָׁא**: If two brothers who were married to two sisters died, and it is unknown which died first, then both sisters must perform *ḥalitza* and may not enter into levirate marriage (Rambam *Sefer Nashim, Hilkhot Yibbum* 7:1; *Shulḥan Arukh, Even HaEzer* 175:2).

NOTES

He was not concerned over the possibility of the death – **לְמִיתָה לָא חָיֵישׁ**: The early commentaries object to this statement based on several sources, especially the discussion in the beginning of tractate *Yoma*, where the *tanna* Rabbi Yehuda is concerned that the wife of the High Priest might die. They point out that even if Rabbi Yoḥanan himself is not concerned over this eventuality, he could still interpret this mishna as following the opinion of those who are concerned for the possibility of death.

There are various suggestions as to how to resolve this difficulty. Some commentaries explain that Rabbi Yoḥanan held that although this opinion exists, it is the opinion of only a single Sage, and therefore it would not be presented in an unattributed manner in the mishna. This answer is similar to the one cited by the Gemara in the continuation of the discussion concerning the opinion of Rabbi Yosei HaGelili. The Gemara does not accept the suggestion that the mishna follows the opinion of Rabbi Yosei HaGelili, as his is the opinion of a single Sage.

Alternatively, since Rabbi Yoḥanan is not concerned about the possibility of death and because he always concludes the *halakha* follows the unattributed mishna, his opinion is that it is impossible for there to be an unattributed mishna that holds that there is no concern over the possibility of death (see Rashba and Ritva).

The Rashba explains that even if there is a concern over the possibility of death, such a concern would not be significant enough to negate the mitzva of levirate marriage, and this follows the opinion that *ḥalitza* is not considered a fulfillment of the mitzva of levirate marriage.

The Maharsha, in *Mahadura Batra*, states that there is concern about the possibility that the High Priest may die, despite the fact that it is an improbable scenario, only because all of Israel depend upon him for atonement on Yom Kippur. *Mitzpe Eitan* explains that there is concern over the possibility of death in cases where the death will cause the violation of a prohibition for which one is liable to receive the death penalty. This is not a concern in cases where death could prevent one from fulfilling a positive mitzva.

It is possible to be precise – **אֶפְשָׁר לְצַמְצֵם**: The Sages of the Mishna differ as to whether it is possible for two events to occur at precisely the same moment. The early commentaries differ in their understanding of this dispute. According to Rashi and the Rambam, it is physically impossible for two events to occur at the exact same moment. Therefore, the dispute between the *tanna'im* revolves around the question of how to relate to events that appear to occur simultaneously. According to the opinion that it is not possible to be precise, the assumption is that the events did not occur simultaneously. Because the order in which they took place cannot be ascertained, the instance is related to as a case of uncertainty. According to the opinion that it is possible to be precise, despite the fact that the events did not actually take place simultaneously, the *halakha* relates to them as if they had occurred at exactly the same time.

In contrast, *Tosafot* maintain that events can actually occur simultaneously. The dispute therefore relates to a situation where two events appear to occur simultaneously. In this case, is it assumed that the events indeed took place at the same time, or is it assumed that it is impossible to determine whether or not these events actually occurred simultaneously, and therefore this is a case of uncertainty?

My fellow brother consummated the levirate marriage with the second, etc. – **חַבְרָאִי שְׁנִיָּה יִיבֵּם וכו׳**: Some point out the following problem: According to this assertion, his brother transgressed and engaged in sexual relations with the sister of a woman with whom he had a levirate bond. However, according to the Gemara on 50b, licentious relations do not fully consummate levirate marriage, and the *yevama* under such circumstances still requires *ḥalitza*. Accordingly, in the case here, there is still a levirate bond connecting this sister to the second brother and the other sister remains forbidden as the sister of a woman with whom he has a levirate bond. This difficulty can be resolved by saying that the requirement for *ḥalitza* is a rabbinic decree, and even licentious relations between a *yavam* and *yevama* still uproot the levirate bond (*Ḥazon Ish*).

תְּנַן: הָיְתָה אַחַת מֵהֶן אֲסוּרָה עַל הָאֶחָד אִיסּוּר עֶרְוָה – אָסוּר בָּהּ וּמוּתָּר בַּאֲחוֹתָהּ, וְהַשֵּׁנִי אָסוּר בִּשְׁתֵּיהֶן. סָלְקָא דַּעְתָּךְ דְּנָפְלָה חֲמוֹתוֹ תְּחִלָּה.

We learned in the mishna: If one of the sisters was forbidden[H] to one of the brothers due to a prohibition against forbidden relatives because she was a relative of his wife or a relative from his mother's side, then **he is prohibited from** marrying **her but permitted to** marry **her sister. But the second** brother, who is not a close relative of either sister, **is prohibited from** marrying **both of them. It enters your mind** to say **that** a forbidden woman, such as **his mother-in-law, happened** before the *yavam* for levirate marriage **first.**[B]

וְאַמַּאי? לֵיקוּ חָתָן לְיַיבֵּם הַךְ דְּאֵינָהּ חֲמוֹתוֹ בְּרֵישָׁא, וְתֶהֱוֵי חֲמוֹתוֹ לְגַבֵּי אִידָךְ כִּיבָמָה שֶׁהוּתְּרָה וְנֶאֶסְרָה וְחָזְרָה וְהוּתְּרָה – תַּחֲזוֹר לְהֶיתֵּרָהּ הָרִאשׁוֹן.

Accordingly, the Gemara asks: **And why** would both women be forbidden to the second brother? **Let the son-in-law rise and consummate the levirate marriage with** the sister[N] **who is not his mother-in-law first. Consequently, with regard to the other** brother, **his mother-in-law would be** considered **a *yevama* who was permitted** to perform levirate marriage at the time that she happened before him, **and then forbidden** when her sister happened before him for levirate marriage as well, **and then subsequently became permitted** when his brother consummated the levirate marriage with her sister. If so, the mother-in-law **should return to her original permitted status** and may enter into levirate marriage with him.

אָמַר רַב פַּפָּא: כְּגוֹן דְּנָפְלָה הַךְ דְּאֵינָהּ חֲמוֹתוֹ בְּרֵישָׁא.

Rav Pappa said: The mishna is referring to a case **where** the woman **who was not his mother-in-law happened** before the brothers for levirate marriage **first,**[H] in which case she was permitted to both of them. When her sister, i.e., the mother-in-law, happened before them for levirate marriage as well, both women were rendered forbidden to the second brother, as each one is the sister of a woman with whom he has a levirate bond. Because the mother-in-law was forbidden from the time that she happened before the *yavam* for levirate marriage, she can never be permitted to him.

"רַבִּי אֱלִיעֶזֶר אוֹמֵר: בֵּית שַׁמַּאי אוֹמְרִים" וכו׳. תַּנְיָא: רַבִּי אֱלִיעֶזֶר אוֹמֵר בֵּית שַׁמַּאי אוֹמְרִים: יְקַיְּימוּ, וּבֵית הִלֵּל אוֹמְרִים: יוֹצִיאוּ. רַבִּי שִׁמְעוֹן אוֹמֵר: יְקַיְּימוּ. אַבָּא שָׁאוּל אוֹמֵר: קַל הָיָה לָהֶם לְבֵית הִלֵּל בְּדָבָר זֶה, שֶׁבֵּית שַׁמַּאי אוֹמְרִים יוֹצִיאוּ וּבֵית הִלֵּל אוֹמְרִים יְקַיְּימוּ.

§ With regard to the case of two brothers who married their wives before consulting the court,[H] the mishna states that the women should be divorced. **Rabbi Eliezer** disagrees and **says** that this is a matter of dispute between Beit Shammai and Beit Hillel, as **Beit Shammai say:** They may maintain them as their wives, and Beit Hillel say: They should divorce them. An expanded version of this discussion **is taught** in the *Tosefta* (5:1): **Rabbi Eliezer says** that **Beit Shammai say: They may maintain them** as their wives, **and Beit Hillel say: They should divorce them. Rabbi Shimon says: They may maintain them** as their wives. **Abba Shaul** disagrees with Rabbi Eliezer and **says: This was a matter of leniency for Beit Hillel.**[N] They were the ones who put forth a lenient ruling, **as Beit Shammai say: They should divorce them, and Beit Hillel say: They may maintain them** as their wives.

HALAKHA

If one of them was forbidden, etc. – הָיְתָה אַחַת מֵהֶן אֲסוּרָה וכו׳: If one of the sisters was the forbidden relative of one brother, then that brother is permitted to marry the second woman, and the second brother is forbidden to both women. If each was forbidden to a different brother, then she who is forbidden to one is permitted to the other. This applies only in cases of forbidden relatives, but in cases of prohibitions stemming from sanctity or a mitzva, both women must perform *ḥalitza* (Rambam *Sefer Nashim, Hilkhot Yibbum* 7:5; *Shulḥan Arukh, Even HaEzer* 175:1).

A case where the woman who was not his mother-in-law happened before them first – כְּגוֹן דְּנָפְלָה הַךְ דְּאֵינָהּ חֲמוֹתוֹ בְּרֵישָׁא: If the first sister who happened before the *yevamin* for levirate marriage was a relative forbidden to the *yavam*, such as his mother-in-law, and he consummated the levirate marriage with the second sister, then the first sister is permitted to the other brother (Rambam *Sefer Nashim, Hilkhot Yibbum* 7:5; *Shulḥan Arukh, Even HaEzer* 175:1).

Two brothers who married their wives before consulting the court – קָדְמוּ וְכָנְסוּ: If two sisters happened before two brothers for levirate marriage, and the two brothers proceeded to marry them before consulting the court, they must divorce them, as is stated explicitly in the mishna. This ruling is not in accordance with the statement of Abba Shaul, which opposes both the unattributed mishna and the opinion of Rabbi Eliezer (Rif; Rambam; Rosh).

Some say that they are not required to divorce their wives (*Tur*). They explain that because Beit Hillel is generally the more lenient opinion, we follow the opinion of Rabbi Shimon and Abba Shaul (Rambam's Commentary on the Mishna). The *Baḥ*, however, holds that this is a scribal error in the *Tur* (Rambam *Sefer Nashim, Hilkhot Yibbum* 7:5; *Shulḥan Arukh, Even HaEzer* 175:3).

NOTES

Let the son-in-law rise and consummate the levirate marriage with the sister, etc. – לֵיקוּ חָתָן לְיַיבֵּם הַךְ וכו׳: This objection could apparently be resolved according to the suggestion that appeared previously in the Gemara, that there is a rabbinic decree in these cases to prevent his brother from consummating the levirate marriage with the wrong woman. This suggestion arose only in passing during the talmudic deliberations and was rejected outright because there is no concern for confusion between the women (Rashba).

This was a matter of leniency for Beit Hillel – קַל הָיָה לָהֶם לְבֵית הִלֵּל: In the Jerusalem Talmud, a question is raised about this formulation: Did Abba Shaul intend to speak disparagingly of Beit Hillel by suggesting that they acted leniently where there should have been a prohibition? It is explained there that he intended to say that, according to Beit Hillel, there was not an actual prohibition in place at all, and so it would be permitted to consummate the levirate marriage.

BACKGROUND

His mother-in-law happened before him first – נָפְלָה חֲמוֹתוֹ תְּחִלָּה: There were four brothers from the same father: Reuven, Shimon, Levi, and Yehuda. Reuven and Shimon married the sisters Milka and Ḥogla, while Yehuda married Adda, the daughter of Milka, Reuven's wife. If Reuven and Shimon die childless, the sisters Milka and Ḥogla happen before the two brothers, Yehuda and Levi, for levirate marriage. With regard to Levi, both Milka and Ḥogla are sisters who are *yevamot* but are otherwise unrelated to him. Consequently, they are both forbidden to him. With regard to Yehuda, however, Milka is his mother-in-law as well, and he is prohibited from marrying her. This renders her ineligible for levirate marriage with him. If Reuven died before Shimon, Milka was never eligible for levirate marriage with Yehuda because she was forbidden to him as his mother-in-law. His obligation of levirate marriage applies only to Ḥogla. Consequently, if Yehuda consummates the levirate marriage with Ḥogla, Milka is eligible to consummate the levirate marriage with Levi. She was initially permitted to him when Reuven died, as she was the only *yevama*; then forbidden to him when Shimon died, since two sisters happened before him for levirate marriage at that time; and subsequently became permitted by means of Yehuda's marriage to Ḥogla.

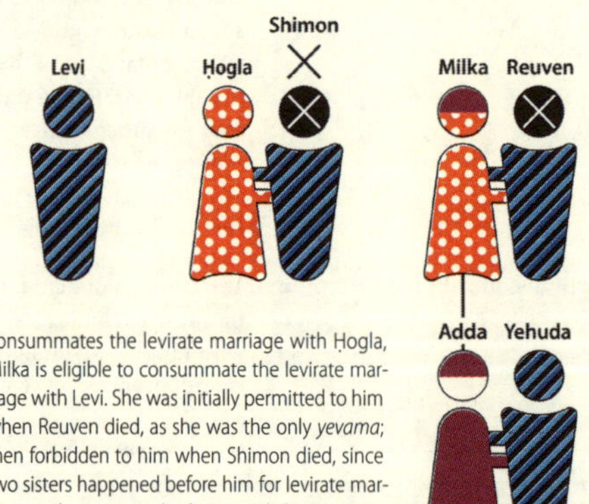

רַבִּי שמעון כמאן? אי כבית שמאי – היינו רבי אליעזר, אי כבית הלל – היינו אבא שאול! הכי קאמר לא נחלקו בית שמאי ובית הלל בדבר זה.

The Gemara asks about this *baraita*: **In accordance with whose opinion is** the statement of **Rabbi Shimon?**[N] This matter is a dispute between Beit Hillel and Beit Shammai, with different versions of their opinions, and therefore Rabbi Shimon should not have formulated the *halakha* in this manner. Indeed, **if** he holds **in accordance with** the opinion of **Beit Shammai,** then **that is** the same as the opinion of **Rabbi Eliezer.** He would thereby conclude that the *halakha* is in accordance with the opinion of Beit Shammai, as per Rabbi Eliezer's version. If so, he should have formulated his opinion in that way. **If,** however, he holds **in accordance with** the opinion of **Beit Hillel,** then **that is** the opinion of **Abba Shaul.** The Gemara responds: **This is what he is saying:** Rabbi Shimon actually maintains a third opinion: **Beit Shammai and Beit Hillel did not dispute this matter;** both agreed that the marriages may be maintained.

"היתה אחת מהם" כו׳. הא תנינא חדא זימנא: אחותה כשהיא יבמתה או חולצת או מתייבמת!

§ The mishna stated: If **one of** the sisters **was** forbidden to one of the brothers due to a prohibition against forbidden relations, then he is prohibited from marrying her but permitted to marry her sister. The Gemara asks: **We** already **learned** this **on one occasion: When her sister,** who is a forbidden relative to the *yavam*, **is her *yevama*** as well, **she either performs *ḥalitza* or enters into levirate marriage.**

צריכא, דאי אשמועינן התם משום דליכא למיגזר משום שני, אבל הכא דאיכא למיגזר משום שני – אימא לא.

The Gemara answers: It is **necessary** that this be said here as well, **for if it taught us** this *halakha* only **there** in its more general formulation (*Yevamot* 20a), then I might have said: The *yavam* is permitted to marry the sister **because there is no** reason **to issue** a rabbinic **decree due to a second** brother. There, there is only one *yavam*, to whom one sister is permitted and the other is forbidden. **Here, however,** in the case of two brothers, **where there is** reason **to issue** a rabbinic **decree due to the second** brother, lest he consummate the levirate marriage as well, **I would say** that we do **not** allow even the first brother to perform levirate marriage, and both sisters-in-law should be forbidden to both brothers.

ואי אשמועינן הכא – משום דאיכא שני דקא מוכח, אבל התם דליכא שני – אימא לא, צריכא.

And if the mishna **had taught us** the *halakha* only **here,** it would have been possible to say that the permissibility of levirate marriage here is **because there is** a second brother who **indicates,** by refraining from performing levirate marriage, that the sister of a woman bound by a levirate bond is forbidden. **However, there,** where there **is not a second** brother, **I would say no,** this *halakha* would not apply, due to a concern that people might wrongly conclude that the sister of a woman bound by a levirate bond is permitted. Therefore, it is **necessary** to state this *halakha* in both places.

"איסור מצוה" כו׳. הא נמי תנינא:

It was taught in the mishna: If one of the sisters was forbidden to one of the brothers due to **a prohibition** resulting from **a mitzva** or due to a prohibition stemming from sanctity, then her sister must perform *ḥalitza* and may not enter into levirate marriage. The Gemara wonders: **We** already **learned this as well:**

NOTES

In accordance with whose opinion is Rabbi Shimon – רבי שמעון כמאן: It would be difficult to say that Rabbi Shimon stated his own opinion, as he lived long after the period of Beit Shammai and Beit Hillel and was therefore not in a position to dispute them (Rivan).

In the Jerusalem Talmud, Abba Shaul distinguishes between the opinions of Rabbi Shimon and Beit Hillel. There, it is explained that Rabbi Shimon allows the brothers to maintain their wives after the fact only when consummation had already taken place and specifically when both brothers had relations concurrently. However, according to Abba Shaul's version of Beit Hillel's opinion, the brothers would be allowed to consummate the levirate marriage even *ab initio* (see *Penei Moshe*).

NOTES

Here there is a prohibition resulting from a mitzva and her sister – הָכָא אִיסּוּר מִצְוָה וַאֲחוֹתָהּ: The question arises: The Gemara has explained the reason for this *halakha* in the current mishna, but the first mishna that states a ruling with regard to a prohibition resulting from a mitzva remains superfluous. Why does the mishna state this ruling earlier (20a)? It would have sufficed to state it here alone?

A similar question arises later on the Gemara, and it is resolved as follows: Were this *halakha* stated only here, one might have thought that the rabbinic decree not to enter into levirate marriage was issued only where there was an additional brother to whom the *yevama* is permitted, for in that case the levirate marriage could be fulfilled with him. If, however, there is no other brother, and the mitzva of levirate marriage will be negated, perhaps the Sages did not issue a decree, and the *yavam* is permitted to consummate the levirate marriage with this woman. Therefore, the *halakha* was necessary in the previous mishna as well (*Arukh LaNer*).

אִיסּוּר מִצְוָה וְאִיסּוּר קְדוּשָּׁה חוֹלֶצֶת וְלֹא מִתְיַיבֶּמֶת! הָתָם אִיסּוּר מִצְוָה לְחוּדָהּ. הָכָא אִיסּוּר מִצְוָה וַאֲחוֹתָהּ.

If a **prohibition** resulting from **a mitzva** or a **prohibition** stemming from **sanctity** will be transgressed through the levirate marriage, then the woman must **perform *ḥalitza* and she may not enter into levirate marriage.** The Gemara answers: There is a novelty here: **There,** where the *halakha* is reviewed in general terms, it speaks of **a prohibition due to a mitzva alone.** One woman happened before the *yavam* for levirate marriage and it is only as a result of this prohibition that she is prevented from entering levirate marriage. **Here,** there is **a prohibition** resulting from **a mitzva and,** in addition, **her sister**[N] happened before the *yevamin* for levirate marriage together with her.

סָלְקָא דַּעְתָּךְ אָמִינָא: לֵיקוּם אִיסּוּר מִצְוָה בִּמְקוֹם אִיסּוּר עֶרְוָה, וְתִתְיַיבֵּם, קָא מַשְׁמַע לַן.

It might enter your mind to say: Let the prohibition resulting from **a mitzva stand in** the same **place,** i.e., level of severity, **as the prohibition against forbidden relatives.** Consequently, the woman who is forbidden to the *yavam* is considered a forbidden relative and her sister is permitted to him. Despite the fact that the prohibition resulting from a mitzva is not as severe, here is it is given equal status, **and** we might say: **Let** her sister **enter into levirate marriage.** Therefore, **this comes to teach us** that this is not the case.

וְתִתְיַיבֵּם! כֵּיוָן דְּמִדְּאוֹרַיְיתָא רַמְיָא קַמֵּיהּ קָא פָּגַע בַּאֲחוֹת זְקוּקָתוֹ, סָלְקָא דַּעְתָּךְ אָמִינָא: מִשּׁוּם מִצְוָה עֲבוּד רַבָּנַן – קָא מַשְׁמַע לַן.

The Gemara asks: **And** why in fact **does** her sister not **enter into levirate marriage?** The Gemara answers: Her sister is forbidden to him **because by Torah** law the prohibited woman **is** still **set before** *the yavam* for levirate marriage. Were he to take the sister in levirate marriage **he would** essentially **be encountering the sister of the woman with whom he has** a levirate bond. **It might enter your mind to say** that **due to the mitzva** of levirate marriage, **the Sages did as they did** and nullified their decree prohibiting the sister of a woman with whom the *yavam* has a levirate bond from entering levirate marriage, when the original sister is forbidden only as the result of a mitzva. Therefore, it **teaches us** that they did not cancel their decree in this situation.

״הָיְתָה אַחַת מֵהֶן״ כו׳. הָא תּוּ לָמָּה לִי? הַיְינוּ הָךְ, מַה לִּי לְחַד מַה לִּי לְתְרֵי!

It was taught in the mishna: If **one of those** women was forbidden to this one brother due to a prohibition against forbidden relatives and the second was forbidden to that second brother due to a prohibition against forbidden relatives, then she who is forbidden to this brother is permitted to that brother, and she who is forbidden to that brother is permitted to this one. The Gemara asks: **Why do I need this** *halakha* **as well, for this is** identical to **that** which was taught earlier, when the mishna stated that if one of the sisters was forbidden to one of the brothers due to a prohibition against forbidden relatives, then he is forbidden to marry her but permitted to marry her sister. However, the second brother, who is not a close relative of either sister, is prohibited from marrying both of them. Once the mishna taught that the *yavam* is permitted to marry the woman to whom he is not related, **what is the** difference **to me** if there is **one** brother **or two** brothers? If this happened to both brothers, clearly both should be allowed.

צְרִיכָא, דְּאִי אַשְׁמוּעִינַן הָתָם – מִשּׁוּם דְּאִיכָּא שֵׁנִי דְּמוֹכַח, אֲבָל הָכָא דְּלֵיכָּא שֵׁנִי דְּקָא מוֹכַח – אֵימָא לָא.

The Gemara answers: It is **necessary** to state this, **for if it taught us** the *halakha* only **there,** in the case where only one brother is permitted, one might have said: **This is because there is a second** brother **who indicates** that the sister of a woman bound by a levirate bond is forbidden to him by refraining from levirate marriage with her. **However, here,** where there **is not a second** brother **who indicates** this, as both brothers are performing levirate marriage, then **I would say no;** this *halakha* would not apply, due to the concern that people might wrongly conclude that the sister of a woman with whom the *yavam* has a levirate bond is permitted even in cases where the other woman is not a forbidden relative.

וְאִי אַשְׁמוּעִינַן הָכָא – אַדְּרַבָּה, תַּרְוַויְיהוּ מוֹכְחֵי אַהֲדָדֵי. אֲבָל אִידָּךְ לָא – צְרִיכָא.

And the opposite could also be said: **If it taught us** the ruling only **here,** in the case of two brothers, one might have said: **On the contrary, they both indicate** the nature of **each other's** status. Each of the brothers married a specific sister-in-law, i.e., the woman who was not his close relative, indicating he does not have a levirate bond with the other sister. **But in the other** case, where one brother is allowed to consummate the levirate marriage and the second brother is forbidden to both sisters, I might say that **no,** we would not allow marriage to the first brother either. Therefore, it is **necessary** to state the *halakha* in both instances.

״זוֹ הִיא שֶׁאָמְרוּ״ וכו׳. זוֹ הִיא לְמַעוּטֵי מַאי? לְמַעוּטֵי אִיסּוּר מִצְוָה לְזֶה וְאִיסּוּר מִצְוָה לְזֶה.

It was taught in the mishna: **And this is** the case that was referred to when **they said:** When her sister is also her *yevama,* she either performs *ḥalitza* or enters into levirate marriage. The Gemara asks: **What does** the expression: **This is,** come to **exclude?** The Gemara answers: **It excludes** the case where there is **a prohibition** resulting from **a mitzva for this** one **and a prohibition** resulting from **a mitzva for that** one. Although each woman is forbidden to a different brother due to a prohibition resulting from a mitzva, they may not both enter into levirate marriage.

הָא תּוּ לָמָּה לִי? הַיְינוּ הָךְ, מַה לִּי לְחַד מַה לִּי לִתְרֵי!

The Gemara asks: **Why do I need this as well? This is** identical to **that** which was taught previously, that if one of the sisters was forbidden to the *yavam* due to a prohibition resulting from a mitzva, then he is not permitted to consummate the levirate marriage with either of them. **What difference is** there **to me** if she happened before **one** brother **or two?**

מַהוּ דְּתֵימָא: כִּי לָא אָמְרִינַן אוֹקֵי אִיסּוּר מִצְוָה בִּמְקוֹם אִיסּוּר עֶרְוָה – הֵיכָא דְּאִיכָּא לְמִיגְזַר מִשּׁוּם שֵׁנִי, אֲבָל הֵיכָא דְּלֵיכָּא לְמִיגְזַר מִשּׁוּם שֵׁנִי – אֵימָא: לְהַאי אוֹקִימְנָא אִיסּוּר מִצְוָה בִּמְקוֹם אִיסּוּר עֶרְוָה וּלְהַאי [אוֹקִימְנָא] אִיסּוּר מִצְוָה בִּמְקוֹם אִיסּוּר עֶרְוָה, וְלַיְיבְּמוּ. קָא מַשְׁמַע לָן.

The Gemara answers: **Lest you say:** There is only one instance **when we do not say: Let the prohibition** resulting from **a mitzva stand in** the same **place,** i.e., level of severity, **as a prohibition against forbidden relatives.** It occurs in a case **where it is** appropriate **to issue** a rabbinic **decree due to the second** brother, who is prohibited from marrying both sisters. **But** in a case **where it is not** appropriate **to issue** a rabbinic **decree due to the second** brother, as the second sister is permitted to the second brother as well, I might **say: For this brother, let us stand the prohibition** resulting from **a mitzva in** the same **place as a prohibition against forbidden relatives, and for this** brother **let us stand the prohibition** resulting from **a mitzva in** the same **place as a prohibition against forbidden relatives, and** as a result both brothers may **consummate the levirate marriage.** Therefore, **it teaches us** that this is not so.

אָמַר רַב יְהוּדָה אָמַר רַב. וְכֵן תָּנֵי רַבִּי חִיָּיא: בְּכוּלָּן אֲנִי קוֹרֵא בָּהֶן הָאֲסוּרָה לְזֶה מוּתֶּרֶת לָזֶה, וַאֲחוֹתָהּ כְּשֶׁהִיא יְבִמְתָּהּ – אוֹ חוֹלֶצֶת אוֹ מִתְיַיבֶּמֶת.

§ Incidental to this *halakha,* the Gemara cites the following statement: **Rav Yehuda said that Rav said, and similarly Rabbi Ḥiyya teaches** in a *baraita*: **With regard to all of those** women enumerated in the first mishna of the tractate, who are forbidden to the *yevamin* as forbidden relatives, the following situation could arise: These women could also be two sisters who were married to two brothers who happen before their *yevamin* for levirate marriage while each one is a forbidden relative to one of the *yevamin.* In these situations, **I could apply** the ruling that **she who is forbidden to this** brother **is permitted to that** brother, **as well as** the ruling that **when her sister is also her *yevama* she may either perform *ḥalitza* or enter into levirate marriage.**

וְרַב יְהוּדָה מְתַרְגֵּם מֵחֲמוֹתוֹ וְאֵילָךְ, אֲבָל שִׁיתָּא בָּבֵי דְּרֵישָׁא – לָא.

But Rav Yehuda interprets these principles as applying only to those cases found in the list **from** the **mother-in-law of** the *yavam* **and onward, but not to the six cases at the beginning,** which include his daughter, and his wife's daughter, and their descendants.

מַאי טַעֲמָא? כֵּיוָן דְּבִתּוֹ בְּאוֹנָסִין הוּא דְּמַשְׁכַּחַתְּ לָהּ, בִּנְשׂוּאִין לָא מַשְׁכַּחַתְּ לָהּ,

What is the reason for Rav Yehuda's distinction? **This is because you find** the scenario where two women who are candidates for levirate marriage are both sisters as well as the daughters of the two *yevamin* only in a case where the women are the daughters of the *yevamin* **through rape, but you cannot find it** in a case where they are his daughters **through marriage.** If one brother married a woman and had a daughter with her, then this woman, the wife of a brother who has children, is forbidden to all of his brothers. Therefore, it would be impossible for another brother to have a daughter with that same woman, and therefore the two daughters could never be sisters. The scenario of daughters who are also sisters is possible only when the first brother raped a woman and gave birth to a daughter, such that the woman is not forbidden to his brothers. If one of the brothers then had a daughter with this woman and both daughters married other brothers who then died, it is possible that these daughters would happen before their fathers for levirate marriage.

בִּנְשׂוּאִין – קָמַיְירֵי, בְּאוֹנָסִין – לָא קָא מַיְירֵי.

Rav Yehuda maintains that the current mishna **deals with** cases of **marriage but does not deal with** cases of **rape,**[N] and therefore he does not apply the principles governing sisters to those cases.

וְאַבַּיֵי מְתַרְגֵּם אַף בִּתּוֹ (בָּאָה) מֵאֲנוּסָתוֹ, כֵּיוָן דְּאַשְׁכּוּחֵי מַשְׁכַּחַתְּ לָהּ, אִי בָּעֲיָא בְּאוֹנָסִין – תֶּיהֱוֵי, אִי בָּעֲיָא בִּנְשׂוּאִין – תֶּהֱוֵי. אֲבָל אֵשֶׁת אָחִיו שֶׁלֹּא הָיָה בְּעוֹלָמוֹ – לָא, כֵּיוָן דְּאַלִּיבָּא דְּרַבִּי שִׁמְעוֹן הוּא דְּמַשְׁכַּחַתְּ לָהּ – אַלִּיבָּא דְּרַבָּנַן לָא מַשְׁכַּחַתְּ לָהּ בִּפְלוּגְתָּא לָא קָמַיְירֵי.

And Abaye interprets these principles as applying **even to his daughter from a woman he raped. Since you can find this** scenario, if the statement **wants** to deal with cases of **rape, let it; if it wants** to deal with cases of **marriage, let it.** It is preferable to explain this matter with regard to cases of marriage, but if that is not possible, it can still be explained as dealing with cases of rape. **However, it cannot** be explained as referring to **the wife of a brother with whom he did not coexist.** Even according to the opinion of Abaye, this case cannot be included, **since you can find** a situation where two sisters happen before two brothers for levirate marriage while each woman is the wife of a brother with whom he did not coexist only **according to** the opinion of **Rabbi Shimon, while** such a case **cannot be found according to** the opinion of **the Rabbis.** And Rabbi Ḥiyya **does not deal with** cases that are subject to **dispute.**

וְרַב סָפְרָא מְתַרְגֵּם אַף אֵשֶׁת אָחִיו שֶׁלֹּא הָיָה בְּעוֹלָמוֹ, וּמַשְׁכַּחַתְּ לָהּ בְּשִׁיתָּא אָחֵי, וְאַלִּיבָּא דְּרַבִּי שִׁמְעוֹן. וְסִימָנִיךְ: מֵת נוֹלַד וְיִיבֵּם, מֵת נוֹלַד וְיִיבֵּם;

And Rav Safra interprets these principles as applying to the **wife of a brother with whom he did not coexist, and you can find this** scenario **in the case of the six brothers**[B] **and according to the** opinion of **Rabbi Shimon. And your mnemonic** to remember how this might come about **is** as follows: **Died, born, consummated the levirate marriage; died, born, consummated the levirate marriage.**[B]

NOTES

Does not deal with rape – בְּאוֹנָסִין לָא קָא מַיְירֵי: The reason why Rav Yehuda held that the mishna does not deal with cases of rape is not elaborated upon here at all. It is also unclear why he and Abaye do not assume that the mishna follows Rabbi Shimon's opinion. It seems that the opinions here relate to a question that was raised in Chapter One: Why was the case of his mother who was raped by his father not mentioned among the fifteen forbidden relatives? One of the answers is that the mishna there discusses only cases of marriage but not cases of rape. Alternatively, the mishna there does not list matters for which there are differing opinions. Therefore, these answers can be applied to the issue here. Rav Safra's opinion is that issues subject to dispute were cited in the mishna. The Gemara there (10a) raises objections to this opinion and proceeds to resolve the issues according to this opinion as well (*Arukh LaNer*).

BACKGROUND

Died, born, consummated the levirate marriage; died, born, consummated the levirate marriage – מֵת נוֹלַד וְיִיבֵּם, מֵת נוֹלַד וְיִיבֵּם: Originally, there were six brothers that were all the sons of one father: Reuven, Shimon, Levi, Yehuda, Gad, and Asher. Reuven and Shimon married two sisters, Ḥogla and Milka, and similarly Levi and Yehuda married two sisters, Rachel and Leah. Gad and Asher married women who were not related to each other or to any of the other wives. Gad married Adda and Asher married Miriam.

The order of events is as follows: Reuven dies without children, and his wife, Ḥogla, happens before the other brothers for levirate marriage. Before any of the brothers consummate the levirate marriage or perform *ḥalitza* with her, another brother, Yissakhar, is born. Yissakhar is prohibited from marrying Ḥogla, as she is considered the wife of a brother, Reuven, with whom he did not coexist. Consequently, Levi consummates the levirate marriage with Ḥogla, Reuven's wife. Afterward, Shimon dies without children and his wife, Milka, happens before all the brothers, including Yissakhar, for levirate marriage. Before any of the brothers act, another brother, Zevulun, is born, and he is prohibited from marrying Milka, as she is considered the wife of a brother to Shimon, with whom he did not coexist. Consequently, Yehuda consummates the levirate marriage with Milka. Afterward, both Levi and Yehuda die without children, and both sets of sisters, Ḥogla and Milka as well as Rachel and Leah, happen before the brothers for levirate marriage. At this point, Yissakhar is forbidden not only to Ḥogla, who is the wife of the brother Reuven, with whom he did not coexist, but also to Rachel, as she became the rival wife of Ḥogla and is therefore forbidden to Yissakhar as the rival wife of the wife of a brother with whom he did not coexist. These women, however, are not forbidden to Zevulun, according to the opinion of Rabbi Shimon, because at the time that he was born, they were both married to Levi, who is a brother with whom Zevulun did coexist. However, Zevulun is prohibited from marrying both Milka, who is the wife of the brother Shimon with whom he did not coexist, and her rival wife Leah.

If Gad and Asher consummate the levirate marriage with Rachel and Leah, thereby exempting Ḥogla and Milka from levirate marriage, and die afterward, it turns out that Adda, the wife of Gad, is the rival wife of Rachel, who is the rival wife of Ḥogla. Consequently, in relation to Yissakhar, Adda is considered the rival wife of the rival wife of the wife of a brother, Reuven, with whom he did not coexist. Similarly, Miriam is the rival wife of the rival wife of Milka, and she is forbidden to Zevulun because of Milka, who was the wife of a brother, Shimon, with whom he did not coexist. Therefore, the one who is permitted to this brother, i.e., Adda who is permitted to Zevulun, is forbidden to Yissakhar. Similarly, the one who is permitted to this brother, i.e., Miriam who is permitted to Yissakhar, is forbidden to Zevulun.

Additionally, with regard to Rachel and Leah, the ruling of: When her sister is also her *yevama* she can either perform *ḥalitza* or enter into the levirate marriage, applies as well. This is because Rachel and Leah are sisters who happen before the brothers for levirate marriage, and the one who is forbidden to one brother is permitted to the other. This ruling therefore applies in the case of a rival wife, as well in the case of the rival wife of a rival wife.

BACKGROUND

Six brothers – שִׁיתָּא אָחֵי:

רְאוּבֵן וְשִׁמְעוֹן נְשׂוּאִין שְׁתֵּי אֲחָיוֹת, לֵוִי וִיהוּדָה נְשׂוּאִין שְׁתֵּי נָכְרִיּוֹת. מֵת רְאוּבֵן נוֹלַד יִשָּׂשכָר וְיִיבֵּם לֵוִי, מֵת שִׁמְעוֹן נוֹלַד זְבוּלֻן וְיִיבֵּם יְהוּדָה. מֵתוּ לֵוִי וִיהוּדָה בְּלֹא בָּנִים, וְנָפְלוּ לְהוּ קַמֵּי יִשָּׂשכָר וּזְבוּלֻן,

How could this come about? There were two brothers, **Reuven and Shimon,** who were **married** to **two sisters.** And there were two other brothers, **Levi and Yehuda,** who were **married** to **two unrelated women. Reuven died, Yissakhar was born, and Levi consummated the levirate marriage** with Reuven's wife. Afterward, **Shimon died, Zevulun was born, and Yehuda consummated the levirate marriage** with Shimon's wife. Later, **Levi and Yehuda died childless and** these two sisters **happened before Yissakhar and Zevulun for levirate marriage.**

הָאֲסוּרָה לָזֶה מוּתֶּרֶת לָזֶה, וְהָאֲסוּרָה לָזֶה מוּתֶּרֶת לָזֶה, וַאֲחוֹתָהּ שֶׁהִיא יְבִמְתָּהּ.

In this scenario, the woman who had been Reuven's wife **is forbidden to this** brother, Yissakhar, as the wife of a brother with whom he did not coexist, because he was not alive at the same time as Reuven, and yet **she is** nevertheless **permitted to this** brother, Zevulun, because when Zevulun was born this woman was already the wife of Levi, a brother with whom he did coexist. According to Rabbi Shimon, the fact that she had previously been the wife of Reuven, a brother with whom he did not coexist, is not taken into account. Similarly, with regard to Shimon's wife, we find that **she who is forbidden to this** one **is permitted to that** one. Shimon's wife is forbidden to Zevulun as the wife of a brother with whom he did not coexist, but she is nevertheless permitted to Yissakhar. Accordingly, the situation of **her sister who is her *yevama*,** i.e., two sisters who are *yevamot* and yet are allowed to perform levirate marriage, can be applied to this case as well.

לָמָּה לִי יִיבֵּם יְהוּדָה? בְּלֹא יִיבֵּם יְהוּדָה נַמִי מַשְׁכַּחַתְּ לָהּ!

The Gemara asks: **Why do I** need to assume that this is referring to a scenario where **Yehuda consummated the levirate marriage? You can find this** possibility **in** a case where **Yehuda did not consummate the levirate marriage as well.** This scenario can also take place with only five brothers and without Yehuda: Reuven and Shimon were married to two sisters, Reuven died, Yissakhar was born, and Levi consummated the levirate marriage with Reuven's wife. Then Shimon died and Zevulun was born. If Levi then dies, Levi's wife is forbidden to Yissakhar as the wife of his brother Reuven, with whom he did not coexist, but she would be permitted to Zevulun because she was already the wife of Levi when Zevulun was born. Shimon's wife would be forbidden to Zevulun but permitted to Yissakhar.

מִשּׁוּם צָרָה. הָא תֵּינַח צָרָה, צָרָה דְּצָרָה מַאי אִיכָּא לְמֵימַר?

The Gemara responds: This is **due to the rival wife.** It was taught in this way in order to make the principle applicable not only to the wives, but also to their rival wives. In this scenario, Levi and Yehuda were previously married to two sisters who then became the rival wives of a wife of a brother with whom one did not coexist. This allows the ruling to apply to the case of rival wives as well. The Gemara notes: **This works out well** if the mishna comes to include only **a rival wife** herself, but **what can be said** about **the rival wife of a rival wife?** How can this case explained? If one aims to include all of the details of the mishna in Rabbi Ḥiyya's principle, then the mishna must be referring not only to a case involving the brothers' rival wives, but also to the rival wives of those rival wives mentioned in the mishna.

כְּגוֹן דַּהֲדַר וְיַבְּמִינְהוּ נַמִי גָּד וְאָשֵׁר.

The Gemara answers: Therefore, one must include a case **where Gad and Asher subsequently consummated the levirate marriage** with these women **as well.** That is, initially there were two other brothers, Gad and Asher, who consummated the levirate marriage with the previous wives of Levi and Yehuda, each of whom had taken one of the wives of Reuven and Shimon. Later, when Gad and Asher died, their previous wives, who are the rival wives of the rival wives of Reuven and Shimon's wives, happen before Yissakhar and Zevulun for levirate marriage.

מתני׳ שְׁלֹשָׁה אַחִין, שְׁנַיִם מֵהֶן נְשׂוּאִין שְׁתֵּי אֲחָיוֹת, אוֹ אִשָּׁה וּבִתָּהּ, אוֹ אִשָּׁה וּבַת בִּתָּהּ, אוֹ אִשָּׁה וּבַת בְּנָהּ – הֲרֵי אֵלּוּ חוֹלְצוֹת וְלֹא מִתְיַיבְּמוֹת, וְרַבִּי שִׁמְעוֹן פּוֹטֵר.

MISHNA In the case of **three brothers, two of whom** were **married to** close relatives, e.g., **two sisters; or a woman and her daughter; or a woman and her daughter's daughter; or a woman and her son's daughter,**[H] if the two brothers who were married to two close relatives died and their wives happened before a third brother for levirate marriage, **then these** two women must **perform *ḥalitza* and may not enter into levirate marriage,** as each of them is a relative of a woman with whom he has a levirate bond. **And Rabbi Shimon exempts**[N] them even from the obligation to perform *ḥalitza*.

הָיְתָה אַחַת מֵהֶן אֲסוּרָה עָלָיו אִיסּוּר עֶרְוָה – אָסוּר בָּהּ, וּמוּתָּר בַּאֲחוֹתָהּ. אִיסּוּר מִצְוָה אוֹ אִיסּוּר קְדוּשָּׁה – חוֹלְצוֹת וְלֹא מִתְיַיבְּמוֹת.

If **one of them was forbidden to him,** the third brother, due to a **prohibition against forbidden relatives,** then **he is prohibited from** marrying **her but is permitted to** marry **her sister.** Because the woman who is forbidden to him is not considered to be a woman who requires him for levirate marriage, there is only one woman who happens before him for levirate marriage. However, if one of the women was forbidden due to **a prohibition** resulting from **a mitzva or a prohibition** stemming from **sanctity,** then **they** must **perform *ḥalitza* and may not enter into levirate marriage.** This is because these prohibitions do not completely cancel the levirate bond.

גמ׳ תַּנְיָא: רַבִּי שִׁמְעוֹן פּוֹטֵר בִּשְׁתֵּיהֶן מִן הַחֲלִיצָה וּמִן הַיִּיבּוּם, שֶׁנֶּאֱמַר ״וְאִשָּׁה אֶל אֲחוֹתָהּ לֹא תִקָּח לִצְרוֹר״ – בְּשָׁעָה שֶׁנַּעֲשׂוּ צָרוֹת זוֹ לָזוֹ לֹא יְהֵא לְךָ לִיקּוּחִין אֲפִילּוּ בְּאַחַת מֵהֶן.

GEMARA It is taught in a *baraita*: **Rabbi Shimon exempts both of them from *ḥalitza* and from levirate marriage, as it is stated: "And you shall not take a woman to her sister, to be a rival to her"** (Leviticus 18:18). This indicates that **at the time that** a situation arises wherein **they are to become rival wives to each other,** e.g., two sisters happen before one *yavam* for levirate marriage, **you shall not have** the ability **to take even one of them** in marriage. In his opinion, both women are exempt from both levirate marriage and *ḥalitza* at the moment that they happen before the *yavam*, just as a forbidden relative is exempt from both levirate marriage and *ḥalitza*.

״הָיְתָה אַחַת מֵהֶן״ כו׳. הָא תּוּ לָמָּה לִי? הַיְינוּ הַךְ!

It was taught in the mishna: If **one of them was** forbidden to him due to a prohibition against forbidden relatives, he is prohibited from marrying her but is permitted to marry her sister. The Gemara asks: **Why do I need this** statement **as well? This is** identical to **that** which was taught in the previous mishna.

לְרַבִּי שִׁמְעוֹן אִיצְטְרִיךְ: סָלְקָא דַּעְתָּךְ אָמִינָא: הוֹאִיל וְאָמַר רַבִּי שִׁמְעוֹן שְׁתֵּי אֲחָיוֹת לֹא חוֹלְצוֹת וְלֹא מִתְיַיבְּמוֹת – לִגְזוֹר מִשּׁוּם שְׁתֵּי אֲחָיוֹת דְּעָלְמָא, קָמַשְׁמַע לָן.

The Gemara answers: **It was necessary** to state this again here according to the opinion of **Rabbi Shimon. It might enter your mind to say: Since Rabbi Shimon said** that **two sisters may not perform *ḥalitza* and may not enter into levirate marriage,** as the very fact that they require levirate marriage from the same man and stand to become rival wives to each other renders them forbidden, **we should issue** a rabbinic **decree** in this case as well. Although in this case only one of the sisters is eligible for levirate marriage, as the other is a forbidden relative, perhaps there should be a rabbinic decree prohibiting the *yavam* from marrying the permitted sister, **due to** the similarity to the case of **two sisters in general** who happen before him for levirate marriage. **This teaches us** that even Rabbi Shimon does not hold that there is a rabbinic decree in this case.

״אִיסּוּר מִצְוָה״ כו׳.

It was taught in the mishna that if the wives are forbidden to the *yavam* due to **a prohibition** resulting from **a mitzva** or sanctity, they must perform *ḥalitza* and may not enter into levirate marriage.

NOTES

And Rabbi Shimon exempts – **וְרַבִּי שִׁמְעוֹן פּוֹטֵר**: The Gemara here explains the rationale behind Rabbi Shimon's opinion by way of a homiletical interpretation of the verse "And you shall not take a woman to her sister, to be a rival to her" (Leviticus 18:18). From here he learns that if two sisters happen before the *yavam* for levirate marriage, they are both rendered exempt.

In the Jerusalem Talmud, however, Rabbi Oshaya explains that Rabbi Shimon maintains that only the sister who happened before the *yavam* second is exempt from *ḥalitza* and levirate marriage. Accordingly, the rationale behind Rabbi Shimon's opinion is that a woman with a levirate bond is considered to be married to the *yavam*. Therefore, the second sister is exempt from levirate marriage, as she is equivalent to his wife's sister. If this is the rationale behind Rabbi Shimon's opinion, then when the Gemara here asserts that both women are exempt, it must be referring to a situation where both women happened before the *yavam* simultaneously, and it must be in accordance with the opinion that it is possible to determine that two events occur simultaneously (see *Ḥiddushei Anshei Shem*).

Tosafot explain that this ruling applies specifically in a case where the women happened before a single *yavam*. However, if they happened before two *yevamin*, Rabbi Shimon himself rules that the marriages may be maintained after the fact (*Yevamot* 28a). This must be due to a distinction in the strength of the levirate bond with two *yevamin* and the levirate bond with only one *yavam*. In the case of a levirate bond with only one *yavam*, Rabbi Shimon maintains that the woman is considered married to the *yavam*, while in the case of two *yevamin*, the levirate bond is not exclusive and therefore does not have the strength to render the woman married to the *yavam* (Rabbi Yehuda al-Madari).

HALAKHA

Two close relatives who happened for levirate marriage – **שְׁתֵּי קְרוֹבוֹת שֶׁנָּפְלוּ לְיִיבּוּם**: In the case of three brothers, two of whom were married to two sisters, if one of the brothers married to a sister dies, and later the second dies, and both sisters happen before the third brother for levirate marriage, then both women are forbidden to him. This is also the case for any other two women that he is prohibited from marrying simultaneously, e.g., a woman and her daughter, or a woman and her daughter's daughter. The two women are considered rival wives due to the levirate bond. Consequently, they must perform *ḥalitza* and may not enter into levirate marriage (Rambam *Sefer Nashim*, *Hilkhot Yibbum* 6:25; *Shulḥan Arukh*, *Even HaEzer* 175:6).

וְהָא אָמַר רַבִּי שִׁמְעוֹן: שְׁתֵּי אֲחָיוֹת לֹא חוֹלְצוֹת וְלֹא מִתְיַיבְּמוֹת!

This *halakha* was also taught in the previous mishna (26a), and it is cited in this mishna according to the opinion of Rabbi Shimon. The Gemara asks: **But didn't Rabbi Shimon say: Two sisters neither perform *ḥalitza* nor enter into levirate marriage?** Because these women are eligible for levirate marriage according to Torah law, they are considered the sisters of a woman with whom he has a levirate bond. In this case, Rabbi Shimon exempts them from both *ḥalitza* and levirate marriage. Why, then, does the mishna require them to perform *ḥalitza*?

גְּזֵירָה מִשּׁוּם אִיסּוּר מִצְוָה דְּעָלְמָא.

The Gemara answers: It is **a rabbinic decree due to the general case of a prohibition** resulting from **a mitzva.** If they did not perform *ḥalitza* in this case, where they are sisters, there is a concern that people would assume that their exemption from *ḥalitza* stemmed not from their status as sisters but rather due to the prohibition. This would lead to the mistaken conclusion that women who are forbidden due to a mitzva do not require *ḥalitza*. Therefore, the Sages issued a rabbinic decree requiring *ḥalitza* in this case.

הָא תֵּינַח אִיהִי, אֲחוֹתָהּ מַאי אִיכָּא לְמֵימַר? גְּזֵירָה אֲחוֹתָהּ מִשּׁוּם לָתָא דִּידָהּ.

The Gemara asks: **This works out well** for her, as **she** is forbidden due to the prohibition resulting from a mitzva. It is appropriate to require *ḥalitza* with her, to demonstrate that *ḥalitza* is generally applied in cases where there is a prohibition resulting from a mitzva. But with regard to **her sister, what is there to say?** Why must she perform *ḥalitza* as well? The Gemara answers: There is **a rabbinic decree** with regard to **her sister due to her.**[N]

וְהָא גַּבֵּי עֶרְוָה לָא גָּזְרִינַן! שָׁאנֵי עֶרְוָה דְּמִגְמַר גְּמִירִי לַהּ אֱינָשֵׁי, וְקָלָא אִית לַהּ.

The Gemara asks: If Rabbi Shimon issues a decree in this case requiring *ḥalitza* for the sister, out of concern for confusion, then there is a difficulty: **But, with regard to a forbidden relative we do not issue a decree**[N] requiring *ḥalitza* due to her sister; why does Rabbi Shimon issue a rabbinic decree requiring *ḥalitza* with a woman forbidden due to a prohibition resulting from a mitzva and not with a woman who is a forbidden relative? The Gemara answers: **Forbidden relatives are different, as people learn** the *halakhot* pertaining to **them** because they are stated explicitly in the Torah and are well known to all, **and** the ruling **has publicity.** Therefore, there is no concern lest people mistakenly confuse this case with cases of *yevamot* who are not sisters. Prohibitions resulting from mitzvot are not, however, explicit in the Torah, nor are they generally known.

מתני׳ שְׁלֹשָׁה אַחִין, שְׁנַיִם נְשׂוּאִים שְׁתֵּי אֲחָיוֹת, וְאֶחָד מוּפְנֶה; מֵת אֶחָד מִבַּעֲלֵי אֲחָיוֹת וְעָשָׂה בָּהּ מוּפְנֶה מַאֲמָר, וְאַחַר כָּךְ מֵת אָחִיו הַשֵּׁנִי,

MISHNA In the case of **three brothers, two of** whom **were married to two sisters, and one who was single,**[N] the following occurred: **The husband of one of the sisters died** childless, leaving behind his wife, **and the single** brother **performed levirate betrothal** [*ma'amar*] to this wife.[H] The single brother performed an act of betrothal to the *yevama* but did not yet consummate the marriage by engaging in sexual intercourse. **Afterward, the second brother died,** and therefore the second brother's wife, the sister of the betrothed, happened before the single brother for levirate marriage as well.

NOTES

Due to her – מִשּׁוּם לָתָא דִּידָהּ: The Sages issued a decree requiring the sister of a woman forbidden as the result of a mitzva to perform *ḥalitza* in order to prevent people from permitting levirate marriage to the forbidden woman herself. This, however, would seem to be a decree to prevent the violation of another decree, which the Sages generally refrained from issuing. However, because this case is dealing with two sisters who are exempt primarily for the same reason, it is considered as if they are both included in one general decree (see Rivan and Rabbi Yehuda al-Madari).

But with regard to a forbidden relative we do not issue a decree – וְהָא גַּבֵּי עֶרְוָה לָא גָּזְרִינַן: Rashi interprets this question in a straightforward manner: Why is there not a similar decree in the cases of sisters of forbidden relatives (see Ritva)? There are, however, early commentaries who interpret the question as follows: If it turned out that the same woman was both a forbidden relative and forbidden as the result of a mitzva, why would the Sages not issue a decree in this case as well, so that others not come to allow cases where the woman is forbidden by a mitzva alone? They explain the Gemara's answer as asserting that everyone knows that she was exempt from levirate marriage as a forbidden relative. They would not come to think that there was also a prohibition resulting from a mitzva involved (Razah; Ramban; Rashba).

And one who was single – וְאֶחָד מוּפְנֶה: As far as the *halakha* is concerned, it makes no difference if the third brother was single or married to a woman who was not related to his brothers' wives. It states that he was single due to the subsequent *mishnayot*, which also include the rulings pertaining to rival wives. In those cases, it is important to mention that the third brother was married to an unrelated woman, which is not the case in the present mishna (Rivan; Rabbi Yehuda al-Madari; *Nimmukei Yosef*). Others explain that this is stated due to the wording: Woe unto him. If he was single at first, he ends up without any wife at all and is therefore unfortunate. This would not be so if he was married (*Tosafot Yeshanim*; Meiri).

HALAKHA

Levirate betrothal and the levirate bond in the case of two sisters – מַאֲמָר וְזִיקָה בִּשְׁתֵּי אֲחָיוֹת: There is a case of three brothers, two of whom were married to two sisters, and the husband of one of the sisters died. Afterward, the third brother performed levirate betrothal with the widowed sister, but before he could consummate the levirate marriage with her, the other sister's husband died as well, at which point this sister happened before the third brother for levirate marriage. In this case, the third brother must send both sisters away. She who received levirate betrothal is sent away with a bill of divorce and *ḥalitza*, and her sister must perform *ḥalitza*. This ruling is in accordance with the statement of Beit Hillel (Rambam *Sefer Nashim*, *Hilkhot Yibbum* 7:6; *Shulḥan Arukh*, *Even HaEzer* 175:6).

בֵּית שַׁמַּאי אוֹמְרִים: אִשְׁתּוֹ עִמּוֹ, וְהַלָּזוֹ תֵּצֵא מִשּׁוּם אֲחוֹת אִשָּׁה. וּבֵית הִלֵּל אוֹמְרִים: מוֹצִיא אֶת אִשְׁתּוֹ בְּגֵט וּבַחֲלִיצָה, וְאֵשֶׁת אָחִיו בַּחֲלִיצָה. זוֹ הִיא שֶׁאָמְרוּ: אוֹי לוֹ עַל אִשְׁתּוֹ, וְאוֹי לוֹ עַל אֵשֶׁת אָחִיו.

In this case, **Beit Shammai say: His wife remains with him.** The woman he betrothed is considered like his wife, and he is not required to divorce her. **And this other** woman **leaves** the *yavam* and is exempt from levirate marriage **as the sister of a wife. Beit Hillel say:** Being as he had not yet entered into marriage with the first woman, he is required to perform levirate marriage with both women. Therefore, **he divorces his wife,** i.e., the woman to whom he performed levirate betrothal, **with a bill of divorce,** which nullifies levirate betrothal, **and by *ḥalitza*,** which nullifies the levirate bond. **And,** he sends away **the wife of his** second **brother with *ḥalitza*** as well. They comment: **This is** the case **that** was referred to when the Sages **said: Woe unto him**[N] **for his wife and woe unto him for the wife of his brother.** Due to the combination of circumstances, he loses them both.

גמ׳ ״זוֹ הִיא״ לְמַעוּטֵי מַאי? לְמַעוּטֵי הָךְ דְּרַבִּי יְהוֹשֻׁעַ, דְּלָא עָבְדִינַן כְּוָותֵיהּ, אֶלָּא אִי כְּרַבָּן גַּמְלִיאֵל אִי כְּרַבִּי אֶלְעָזָר.

GEMARA The Gemara asks: **What** does the mishna's formulation of the term: **This is,** which indicates limitation and exactitude, come **to exclude?** The Gemara answers: **It excludes that** statement **of Rabbi Yehoshua** (109a). There, Rabbi Yehoshua holds that if a man is married to a minor when her sister happens before him for levirate marriage, he must send both of the women away. He said there: Woe unto him for his wife and woe unto him for the wife of his brother. From the language in the mishna here, we learn **that we do not act in accordance with his** opinion. **Rather,** we act **either in accordance with** the opinion of **Rabban Gamliel**[N] **or in accordance with** the opinion of **Rabbi Elazar.** According to the opinion of both of these *tanna'im* in the mishna (109a), despite the conflict between the brother's marriage to the minor and the levirate bond with her sister, there is still a way for him to marry one of the women.

אָמַר רַבִּי אֶלְעָזָר: לָא תֵּימָא מַאֲמָר לְבֵית שַׁמַּאי קוֹנֶה קִנְיָן גָּמוּר, דְּאִי בָּעֵי לְאַפּוֹקֵי סַגִּי לַהּ בְּגִיטָּא, אֶלָּא: מַאֲמָר לְבֵית שַׁמַּאי אֵינוֹ קוֹנֶה אֶלָּא לִדְחוֹת בְּצָרָה בִּלְבַד.

§ With regard to the main issue of levirate betrothal, it would seem from this mishna that Beit Shammai hold that levirate betrothal has the legal force of levirate marriage. However, **Rabbi Elazar said: Do not say** that **levirate betrothal acquires** the woman **as a full-fledged acquisition according to** the opinion of **Beit Shammai,**[N] such that the first woman becomes his wife to the extent **that if he wants to divorce** her **a bill of divorce would suffice** without an act of ***ḥalitza*. Rather, for Beit Shammai, levirate betrothal acquires** the woman **only** insofar **as it precludes a rival wife** from entering levirate marriage.[N] The legal force of levirate betrothal is limited to preventing the rival wife[N] of the sister from performing levirate marriage; she is exempt from both levirate marriage and *ḥalitza*.

NOTES

This is the case when they said woe unto him – זוֹ הִיא שֶׁאָמְרוּ אוֹי לוֹ: *Nimmukei Yosef* explains that the phrase: Woe unto him, related to the fact this man acquired at the time of levirate betrothal the usufruct property of the woman as well as his brother's property, but now he must return it all.

Tosafot explain that the phrase: Woe unto him, apply only to a situation where one performed an act that should not have led to complications, but events outside of his control caused him to lose everything he had acquired. The *Mei Naftoaḥ* raises an objection: How did the third brother lose out? Had he not performed levirate betrothal he would have been unable to marry either woman, being as they were sisters who happened before him at the same time. He answers that in a case where the brothers were married to other rival wives, were it not for levirate betrothal, he would have been allowed to marry one of the rival wives. After levirate betrothal, however, he may no longer marry any of them.

Either in accordance with Rabban Gamliel – אִי כְּרַבָּן גַּמְלִיאֵל: Although it is later proven that the opinion of Beit Hillel does not accord with that of Rabban Gamliel, and the *halakha* does not accord with his opinion either, here the only deduction that can be made is that the mishna is not in accordance with the opinion of Rabbi Yehoshua. It is only from a different source that that it can be proven that the *halakha* accords with the opinion of Rabbi Eliezer specifically (Ramban; Rashba).

Do not say that levirate betrothal…according to the opinion of Beit Shammai, etc. – לָא תֵּימָא מַאֲמָר לְבֵית שַׁמַּאי וכו׳: The Jerusalem Talmud presents the opinion of Rabbi Elazar ben Arakh, who does assert that levirate betrothal completely acquires the *yevama*. According to his opinion, levirate betrothal completely establishes the relationship between the *yavam* and the *yevama*, just like sexual intercourse. In the course of the discussion in the Jerusalem Talmud, however, it is proven that Beit Shammai do not accord with this opinion.

In the Jerusalem Talmud, it is explained that Beit Shammai's opinion about the strength of levirate betrothal is the same as Rabbi Shimon's opinion concerning the levirate bond: These bonds are sufficiently effective to prevent the creation of a bond with another woman, e.g., the sister of the *yevama*, but are not sufficient to nullify the levirate bond completely. Therefore, if the *yavam* later wants to divorce the *yevama*, she requires *ḥalitza* (see Ramban and Rashba).

Only insofar as it precludes a rival wife from entering levirate marriage – אֶלָּא לִדְחוֹת בְּצָרָה בִּלְבַד: The question arises: If levirate betrothal cannot establish the union with the same legal force as sexual relations, how can it completely preclude the rival wife from performing levirate marriage? One commentary explains that levirate betrothal is equivalent to betrothal in the following matter: If the *yavam* betrothed one sister and then the other happened before him for levirate marriage, he need not divorce his betrothed. Rather, her sister is precluded from levirate marriage and is therefore exempt from it. Nevertheless, levirate betrothal does not terminate the levirate bond with the first sister, and she requires *ḥalitza* if the *yavam* later choses to divorce this woman (*Tosafot Yeshanim*).

Precluding a rival wife from performing levirate marriage – דְּחִיַּית צָרָה: Rashi explains here and throughout this talmudic discussion that the rival wife that the Gemara is referring to is in fact the sister who happened before the *yavam* for levirate marriage. Although these women are not actually rival wives, as each was married to a different brother, the sister is considered a rival wife in this context. However, *Tosafot* and the Meiri explain that the Gemara is referring to an actual rival wife. If the brother was married to two women and the *yavam* performed levirate betrothal with one of them, the levirate betrothal prevents the other wife from entering levirate marriage with the *yavam*.

אֲמַר רַבִּי אָבִין, אַף אֲנַן נַמִּי תָּנֵינָא: בֵּית שַׁמַּאי אוֹמְרִים: יְקַיְּימוּ, יְקַיְּימוּ – אִין, לְכַתְּחִלָּה – לָא,

Rabbi Avin said: We, too, learn in the mishna a proof that levirate betrothal is not a full-fledged act of acquisition, even according to Beit Shammai. The mishna at the beginning of this chapter (26a) teaches that when two sisters who are *yevamot* happen before two brothers for levirate marriage, if the brothers married their wives before consulting the court, then **Beit Shammai say: They may maintain them** as their wives. From here it can be deduced: If they already married them, **yes, they may maintain them.** However, marrying them ***ab initio*, no,** this is prohibited due to the prohibition against marrying the sister of a woman with whom one has a levirate bond.

Perek **III**
Daf **29** Amud **b**

וְאִי סָלְקָא דַּעְתָּךְ מַאֲמָר לְבֵית שַׁמַּאי קוֹנֶה קִנְיָן גָּמוּר – זֶה יַעֲשֶׂה מַאֲמָר וְיִקְנֶה, וְזֶה יַעֲשֶׂה מַאֲמָר וְיִקְנֶה!

And if it enters your mind that according to Beit Shammai levirate betrothal acquires the woman **as a full-fledged acquisition,** then this matter could potentially have been resolved *ab initio*: **This** brother **should perform levirate betrothal**[N] **and acquire** one sister, **and that** brother **should perform levirate betrothal and acquire** the other sister. As there is no prohibition whatsoever involved in performing levirate betrothal, the concern for violating a prohibition by consummating the levirate marriage with a sister of a woman with whom he has a levirate bond is avoided; he only betroths her, but does not engage in sexual intercourse with her. After the betrothal, the levirate bond of her sister is dissolved and he can freely consummate the levirate marriage with her.

אֶלָּא מַאי – דּוֹחֶה דְּחִיָּיה גְּמוּרָה? זֶה יַעֲשֶׂה מַאֲמָר וְיִדְחֶה, וְזֶה יַעֲשֶׂה מַאֲמָר וְיִדְחֶה.

The Gemara objects: **Rather, what** then? If levirate betrothal does not serve to fully acquire the woman, what is the alternative? It must be that according to Beit Shammai levirate betrothal **precludes** the rival wife from entering levirate marriage with **a complete preclusion.** If so, there is an additional potential scenario: **This one should perform levirate betrothal** with one sister **and preclude** the second sister from entering levirate marriage, **and that one should perform**[N] **levirate** betrothal with the second sister **and preclude** the first sister from entering levirate marriage. In this way, the *yevamin* can consummate the levirate marriage with the sisters *ab initio* as well. Yet the mishna does not allow for this possibility.

אֶלָּא מַאי אִית לָךְ לְמֵימַר: מַאֲמָר דְּהֶיתֵּירָא – דָּחֵי, דְּאִיסּוּרָא – לָא דָּחֵי – הָכִי נַמִּי: מַאֲמָר, אֲפִילּוּ לְמַאן דְּאָמַר מַאֲמָר קוֹנֶה קִנְיָן גָּמוּר, מַאֲמָר דְּהֶיתֵּירָא – קָנֵי דְּאִיסּוּרָא – לָא קָנֵי.

Rather, what have you to say? One must assert that **levirate betrothal** performed **in** circumstances where it is **permitted** to perform levirate marriage, i.e. where there is no prohibition with regard to the close relative of a woman with whom the *yavam* has a levirate bond, completely **precludes** the rival wife from entering levirate marriage. However, levirate betrothal performed **in** circumstances where it is **forbidden** to perform levirate marriage, **does not preclude** entering levirate marriage.[N] Therefore, in the case of two sisters who happen simultaneously before two brothers for levirate marriage, the sisters cannot be precluded from entering levirate marriage via levirate betrothal. **So too here,** with regard to **levirate betrothal** performed by the third brother, the same distinction can be made. **Even according to the one who said that levirate betrothal acquires** a woman **as a full-fledged acquisition,** just like marriage, there is the following difference: **Levirate betrothal under permitted** circumstances **acquires** the woman, but levirate betrothal **under forbidden circumstances does not acquire** the woman. Therefore, there is no proof as to the nature of levirate betrothal according to the opinion of Beit Shammai from the first mishna in the chapter.

NOTES

This brother should perform levirate betrothal – זֶה יַעֲשֶׂה מַאֲמָר: Rashi writes that performing levirate betrothal does not violate a prohibition, but engaging in sexual intercourse does. Similarly, the Rambam holds that there is no prohibition involved in betrothing a woman who is forbidden; the prohibition is only violated by engaging in sexual intercourse. The Rashba adds that only with regard to the special prohibitions relating to priests could an act of betrothal constitute violation of a prohibition. However, the *Smag* and *Sefer HaḤinnukh* hold that one violates a Torah prohibition simply by performing betrothal with a forbidden woman. According to their opinion, one must explain that in situations where the mitzva of levirate marriage may be fulfilled, such betrothals are not prohibited (*Keren Ora*). Alternatively, one could explain that betrothals are prohibited only in cases where the sexual intercourse that would follow is forbidden. In this case, however, the sexual intercourse that follows the levirate betrothal would be permitted as the levirate betrothal served to cancel the prohibition (*Yosef Lekaḥ*).

This one should perform levirate betrothal…and that one should perform – זֶה יַעֲשֶׂה מַאֲמָר...וְזֶה יַעֲשֶׂה: Most of the early commentaries write that it is in fact sufficient for one of the brothers to perform levirate betrothal as this would eliminate the prohibition proscribing the second sister. In *Tosefot HaRosh*, however, it is explained that the Gemara here follows the opinion that we are concerned lest the mitzva of levirate marriage be negated. This concern can be allayed only by both brothers performing levirate betrothal at the same time via an agent. The later commentaries explain that although there is still concern that the levirate marriage may not be consummated, as the fulfillment of the mitzva primarily involves intercourse the levirate betrothal still represents the beginning of the performance of the mitzva, and that is sufficient to allay the concern (*Ḥiddushei Batra*).

In circumstances where it is forbidden to perform levirate marriage, it does not preclude levirate marriage – דְּאִיסּוּרָא לָא דָּחֵי: The question arises: If levirate betrothal is effective by Torah law, and there is no Torah prohibition against performing the levirate betrothal, why should it preclude the rival wife from levirate marriage? This can be resolved by stating that the Sages would not instruct one to perform levirate betrothal in order to preclude the possibility of levirate marriage in a case where rabbinic prohibitions are involved (*Tosefot HaRosh*).

רַב אַשִׁי מַתְנֵי הָכִי, אֲמַר רַבִּי אֶלְעָזָר: לָא תֵּימָא מַאֲמָר לְבֵית שַׁמַּאי דָּחֵי דְּחִיָּיה גְּמוּרָה, וְצָרָתָהּ חֲלִיצָה נַמִי לָא בָּעֲיָא, אֶלָּא דּוֹחֶה וּמְשַׁיֵּיר הוּא.

Rav Ashi teaches this discourse in **this** manner: **Rabbi Elazar said: Do not say** that **according to Beit Shammai levirate betrothal precludes** entering levirate marriage as **a complete preclusion,** so that **the rival wife** of the woman who received levirate betrothal **does not require even *ḥalitza*. Rather, it precludes** entering levirate marriage **and** yet **leaves a remnant** of the levirate bond in place. Accordingly, levirate betrothal precludes the rival wife's entering levirate marriage to the degree that the *yavam* is not required to divorce the woman he betrothed, but the levirate bond with the rival wife remains to the extent that he must still perform *ḥalitza* with her.

אָמַר רַבִּי אָבִין: אַף אֲנַן נַמִי תָּנֵינָא: בֵּית שַׁמַּאי אוֹמְרִים: יְקַיְּימוּ. יְקַיְּימוּ – אִין, לְכַתְּחִלָּה – לָא. וְאִי סָלְקָא דַּעְתָּךְ מַאֲמָר לְבֵית שַׁמַּאי דּוֹחֶה דְּחִיָּיה גְּמוּרָה – זֶה יַעֲשֶׂה מַאֲמָר וְיִדְחֶה, וְזֶה יַעֲשֶׂה מַאֲמָר וְיִדְחֶה! וְאֶלָּא הָא קָתָנֵי, בֵּית שַׁמַּאי אוֹמְרִים: אִשְׁתּוֹ עִמּוֹ, וְהַלֵּזוּ תֵּצֵא מִשּׁוּם אֲחוֹת אִשָּׁה!

Rabbi Avin said: We, too, learn this statement from the mishna, where it states: **Beit Shammai say: They may maintain them** as their wives. From here it can be deduced: **Yes, they may maintain them** as their wives after the fact; **no,** they are not allowed to marry them ***ab initio*. And if it enters your mind** to say that, **according to Beit Shammai, levirate betrothal precludes entering** levirate marriage as **a complete preclusion,** then **this** brother **should perform levirate betrothal and preclude** one sister from levirate marriage, **and that** brother **should perform levirate betrothal and preclude** the other sister from levirate marriage. The Gemara challenges this conclusion: **But didn't** the mishna **teach** that **Beit Shammai say: His wife remains with him, and this other is sent away due to** her status **as a sister of his wife?** This indicates that she is exempt from levirate marriage and does not even require *ḥalitza*.

אֶלָּא: יְבָמָה דַּחֲזְיָא לְכוּלְּהוּ – חַזְיָא לְמִקְצָתָהּ. יְבָמָה דְּלָא חַזְיָא לְכוּלְּהוּ – לָא חַזְיָא לְמִקְצָתָהּ.

Rather, one must resolve this by asserting that **a *yevama* who is suitable for all of** the aspects of levirate marriage **is** also **suitable for part of it.** If a *yevama* is eligible for both levirate marriage and *ḥalitza* when she happens before the brothers, as in the case cited in the present mishna where the woman who happened before the third brother was permitted to enter into levirate marriage, she is eligible for part of it. This indicates that if the *yavam* does not take her in levirate marriage but performs only levirate betrothal, the levirate betrothal has sufficient legal force to preclude the rival wife completely. However, **a *yevama* who is not suitable for all of the** aspects of levirate marriage **is** also **not suitable for a part of it.** If the *yevama* is not eligible for levirate marriage, such as in the case referred to in the first mishna of this chapter, where both women happened simultaneously so that the *yavam* is not permitted to consummate the levirate marriage with either woman, she is not suitable for part of it. In that case, if the *yavam* performs levirate betrothal, it does not have the legal force to affect a total preclusion.

בָּעֵי רַבָּה: מַאֲמָר, לְבֵית שַׁמַּאי, נִישּׂוּאִין עוֹשֶׂה אוֹ אֵירוּסִין עוֹשֶׂה? אֲמַר לֵיהּ אַבַּיֵּי: לְמַאי הִלְכְתָא?

§ With regard to Beit Shammai's opinion about levirate betrothal, **Rabba asks: Does levirate betrothal, according to** the opinion of **Beit Shammai, create** a full-fledged **marriage** bond? **Or, does it** merely **create betrothal,**[N] similar to all other acts of betrothal? **Abaye said to him: With regard to what *halakha*** do you ask this?

NOTES

Does it…create a marriage bond or does it create betrothal – נִישּׂוּאִין עוֹשֶׂה אוֹ אֵירוּסִין עוֹשֶׂה: The marriage process consists of two steps. The first is the act by which a woman becomes betrothed to a man. The bond created by betrothal is so strong that a betrothed woman requires a divorce before she can marry another man. Similarly, intercourse with other men is considered adulterous and is punishable by death. During the period of betrothal, a couple may not live together as man and wife, and most of the couple's mutual obligations do not yet apply.

The second step, marriage itself, is effected when the bride and groom enter the bridal canopy. This immediately confers upon the newlywed couple both the privileges and the responsibilities associated with marriage. In modern times, both betrothal and marriage take place during the wedding.

אִילֵימָא לְיוֹרְשָׁהּ וְלִיטַּמֵּא לָהּ וּלְהָפֵר נְדָרֶיהָ – הַשְׁתָּא אֲרוּסָה בְּעָלְמָא תָּנֵי רַבִּי חִיָּיא: אִשְׁתּוֹ אֲרוּסָה לֹא אוֹנֵן וְלֹא מִטַּמֵּא לָהּ, וְכֵן הִיא לֹא אוֹנֶנֶת וְלֹא מִטַּמְּאָה לוֹ, מֵתָה – אֵינוֹ יוֹרְשָׁהּ, מֵת הוּא – גּוֹבָה כְּתוּבָּתָהּ, עָבַד בָּהּ מַאֲמָר מִיבַּעְיָא?

If we say it pertains **to inheriting** from **her** when she dies, **and to becoming ritually impure for her**[N] if he is a priest, **and to nullifying her vows,**[N] all of which are rights and obligations acquired by marriage, this is difficult. **Now,** with regard to **a betrothed woman in general,** i.e., a woman who was betrothed by Torah law, **Rabbi Ḥiyya teaches** in a *baraita*: **One does not enter acute mourning**[N] on the day of the death of **his betrothed wife, nor can he become ritually impure for her** if she dies if he is a priest. **Similarly, she does not enter acute mourning for him and** is **not** obligated **to become ritually impure for him.**[NH] **If she dies, he does not inherit from her;**[H] **if he dies, she collects** the payment of **her marriage contract;**[H] In a case where **he performed** only **levirate betrothal with her, is it necessary to say**[N] that he does not inherit from her, nor does he become ritually impure for her? Therefore, this *halakha* is obvious and Rabba's question seems superfluous.

וְאֶלָּא לְעִנְיַן מְסִירָה לְחוּפָּה, מַאי? נִישּׂוּאִין עוֹשָׂה – וְלָא בָּעֲיָא מְסִירָה לְחוּפָּה, אוֹ דִלְמָא אֵירוּסִין עוֹשָׂה – וּבָעֲיָא מְסִירָה לְחוּפָּה!

Rather, the question must relate **to the matter of delivery** of the woman **to** the husband under **a wedding canopy.**[N] **What is** the ruling with regard to this? Is the *yavam* obligated to enter the wedding canopy in the manner that he would with any other betrothed woman, or not? This is the dilemma: Does levirate betrothal **create** a full-fledged **marriage** bond, whereby the *yevama* **would not require** further **delivery to a wedding canopy? Or,** does levirate betrothal **perhaps create** only **betrothal,** whereby **she would require delivery to a wedding canopy?**

HALAKHA

Mourning and impurity for a betrothed woman – אֲבֵלוּת וְטוּמְאָה בַּאֲרוּסָה: If a man's betrothed dies, he does not enter the state of acute mourning or regular mourning for her, nor does a woman enter acute or regular mourning over the death of her betrothed. If the man is a priest, he may not become ritually impure for her, and she is not obligated to become ritually impure for him (Rambam *Sefer Shofetim, Hilkhot Evel* 2:3; *Shulḥan Arukh, Yoreh De'a* 373:4, 374:4, *Even HaEzer* 55:5).

If she dies he does not inherit from her – מֵתָה אֵינוֹ יוֹרְשָׁהּ: If a man's betrothed dies, he does not inherit from her (Rambam *Sefer Nashim, Hilkhot Ishut* 22:2; *Shulḥan Arukh, Even HaEzer* 55:5).

If he dies she collects the payment of her marriage contract – מֵת הוּא, גּוֹבָה כְּתוּבָּתָהּ: If one betroths a woman, writes her a wedding contract, and then dies before he is able to bring her under the wedding canopy, then she may collect the primary dues that are a mandatory part of the contract from his available property, but not the voluntary additions that the husband added from his own accord.

Although some say that the Sages established that every betrothed woman should automatically receive a wedding contract, even if one was not actually written for her (Rosh; Ran), it is not the custom to act in accordance with this opinion, but rather according to the opinion that states that the automatic institution of a wedding contract only applies to married women (Rema; Rambam *Sefer Nashim, Hilkhot Ishut* 10:11; *Shulḥan Arukh, Even HaEzer* 55:6).

NOTES

To becoming ritually impure for her – לִיטַּמֵּא לָהּ: Priests are prohibited from contracting ritual impurity through proximity with a corpse. The exception to this principle is the funeral of certain relatives, including wives.

To nullifying her vows – לְהָפֵר נְדָרֶיהָ: The Torah authorizes a husband to nullify vows made by his wife (see Numbers, chapter 30). The vow must be nullified on the same day on which the husband hears of it. A husband is empowered to nullify only those vows which either directly or indirectly affect the personal relationship between him and his wife.

Enter into acute mourning – אוֹנֵן: The period of acute mourning begins on the day of the death of a close relative, i.e., a spouse, father, mother, son, daughter, brother, or sister. The mourner is exempt from all positive mitzvot from the time of the death of the close relative until after the burial. At that point, his status changes from that of an acute mourner to that of a mourner.

Not obligated to become ritually impure for him – לֹא מִיטַּמְּאָה לוֹ: There is a halakhic difficulty here, as there is no prohibition against a priestly woman becoming ritually impure for the dead. Why would she not become impure for her husband? Rashi maintains that this phrase is only cited in order to create a parallelism between the obligations of the man and the woman. Additionally he suggests perhaps this is referring to the period of the Festivals, where there is a general prohibition to become impure. The Ritva and other commentaries concur with the *Tosafot*, suggesting that this phrase indicates that the woman is not obligated to become impure for him.

He performed levirate betrothal with her, is it necessary to say – עָבַד בָּהּ מַאֲמָר מִיבַּעְיָא: It would seem from Rashi that even according to Beit Shammai levirate betrothal only has the force of rabbinic law. Many commentaries challenge this opinion from several different sources. For example, it is stated in the Jerusalem Talmud that Beit Shammai derive the obligation to perform levirate betrothal from an explicit verse in the Torah: "And he shall take her" (Deuteronomy 25, 5). The Rashba, therefore, understands that Rashi did not intend to propose that Beit Shammai held levirate betrothal to have the force of rabbinic law, but rather that even according to their opinion that levirate betrothal has the force of Torah law, it is still not equivalent to actual betrothal. For example, a *yevama* who received levirate betrothal is not sentenced to stoning if she commits adultery.

To the matter of delivery to a wedding canopy – לְעִנְיַן מְסִירָה לְחוּפָּה: *Tosefot HaRosh* explains, in accordance with *Tosafot*, that this discussion does not refer to a case where the *yavam* performed levirate betrothal alone, but rather to a case where he performed levirate betrothal and also engaged in sexual intercourse. Since a woman is normally not considered to be married unless she willingly enters the wedding canopy, a question arises: When the *yavam* engages in intercourse with her against her will, is there no longer any need for her to willingly enter the wedding canopy, as levirate marriage is effective even without the woman's consent? Or perhaps, as Rabba asserts, once she received levirate betrothal consensually, she is now rendered like any other woman and cannot become his full wife without consenting to marriage?

אָמַר לֵיהּ: הָשְׁתָּא, לָא עֲבַד בָּהּ מַאֲמָר כְּתִיב ״יְבָמָהּ יָבֹא עָלֶיהָ״, בְּעַל כָּרְחָהּ, עֲבַד בָּהּ מַאֲמָר מִיבַּעְיָא?

Abaye **said to him** that this question is not necessary, as well: **Now,** if **he did not perform levirate betrothal with her** at all, **it is written: "Her brother-in-law will have intercourse with her"** (Deuteronomy 25:5). It is deduced from this verse that he can take her even **against her will. Is it necessary** to say **that** if **he performed levirate betrothal with her,** even without a wedding canopy, that he is allowed to engage in sexual intercourse with her?

אָמַר לֵיהּ: שֶׁאֲנִי אוֹמֵר כׇּל הָעוֹשֶׂה מַאֲמָר בִּיבִמְתּוֹ – פָּרְחָה מִמֶּנּוּ זִיקַת יְבָמִין, וְחָלָה עֲלֵיהּ זִיקַת אֵירוּסִין. מַאי?

Rabba **said to him:** This question is relevant, as **I say** that **anyone who performs levirate betrothal with his** ***yevama*** **causes the levirate bond to be removed from him,** and he is no longer considered subject to the *halakhot* of levirate marriage. Instead, a standard **bond of betrothal applies to him.** Therefore, it is appropriate to ask if this act of levirate betrothal is similar to a standard betrothal insofar as the wedding canopy is concerned, and consequently the woman would be required to enter the wedding canopy. Alternatively, perhaps the *halakhot* of levirate marriage still apply somewhat, in which case the woman would not be required to enter a wedding canopy in order to become married, similar to a standard *yevama* to whom levirate betrothal was not performed. Does the performance of levirate betrothal weaken the capacity of intercourse to establish levirate marriage on its own? **What** is the halakhic ruling here?

תָּא שְׁמַע: שׁוֹמֶרֶת יָבָם, בֵּין יָבָם אֶחָד בֵּין שְׁנֵי יְבָמִין, רַבִּי אֱלִיעֶזֶר אוֹמֵר: יָפֵר, רַבִּי יְהוֹשֻׁעַ אוֹמֵר: לְאֶחָד וְלֹא לִשְׁנַיִם, רַבִּי עֲקִיבָא אוֹמֵר: לֹא לְאֶחָד וְלֹא לִשְׁנַיִם.

The Gemara suggests: **Come** and **hear** an answer from what is taught in a mishna (*Nedarim* 74a): What is the ruling with regard to the nullification of vows for **a widow** who is **waiting for her** ***yavam*****,**[H] **whether** she is waiting for a **single** ***yavam*** **or two** ***yevamin*****? Rabbi Eliezer says: Let him nullify** her vows. The *yavam* may nullify her vows as though he were her husband. **Rabbi Yehoshua says:** This holds true only if she is bonded to **a single** ***yavam*****, but not** to **two. Rabbi Akiva says:** It does **not** hold true, neither **to one** *yavam* **nor to two** *yevamin*. They may not they nullify her vows.

וְהָוֵינַן בָּהּ: בִּשְׁלָמָא רַבִּי עֲקִיבָא סָבַר: אֵין זִיקָה אֲפִילּוּ לְחַד, לְרַבִּי יְהוֹשֻׁעַ: לְחַד יֵשׁ זִיקָה, לִתְרֵי – אֵין זִיקָה. אֶלָּא לְרַבִּי אֱלִיעֶזֶר, נְהִי נַמִי דְּקָסָבַר יֵשׁ זִיקָה. בִּשְׁלָמָא לְחַד – מֵיפֵר, אֶלָּא לִתְרֵי – אַמַּאי?

And we discussed this issue, interpreting the various opinions: **Granted, Rabbi Akiva holds that the levirate bond is not substantial,**[N] **even in** the case of **one** *yavam*. In his opinion, the levirate obligation does not create a marriage bond at all, even if there is only a single *yavam*. And according **to Rabbi Yehoshua, the levirate bond with one** ***yavam*** **is substantial.** The *yevama* undoubtedly requires this *yavam* for levirate marriage, and therefore she is considered to be like his wife. **But with two** ***yevamin*****, the levirate bond is not substantial,**[N] since it is not clear which brother will consummate the levirate marriage with her. **However, Rabbi Eliezer,** if he **indeed holds that the levirate bond is substantial,** his opinion is difficult. **Granted,** if there is **one** *yavam*, **he can nullify** her vows, **but** if there are **two,** why should only one of them suffice to nullify her vows, as it is not yet clear which of them will eventually marry her?

וְאָמַר רַבִּי אַמִּי (בַּר אַהֲבָה): הָכָא בְּמַאי עָסְקִינַן – כְּגוֹן דַּעֲבַד בָּהּ מַאֲמָר, וּבֵית שַׁמַּאי הִיא, דְּאָמַר: מַאֲמָר קוֹנֶה קִנְיָן גָּמוּר.

And Rabbi Ami bar Ahava said: With what are we dealing here? This is a case **where** one of them **performed levirate betrothal with her, and** this **is** in accordance with **the opinion of Beit Shammai, who say: Levirate betrothal acquires** her **as a full-fledged acquisition.**

אִי אָמְרַתְּ בִּשְׁלָמָא נִישּׂוּאִין עוֹשֶׂה – מִשּׁוּם הָכִי מֵיפֵר, אֶלָּא אִי אָמְרַתְּ אֵירוּסִין עוֹשֶׂה – הֵיכִי מָצֵי מֵיפֵר? וְהָתְנַן: נַעֲרָה הַמְאוֹרָסָה אָבִיהָ וּבַעְלָהּ מְפִירִים נְדָרֶיהָ! אָמַר רַב נַחְמָן בַּר יִצְחָק: מַאי מֵיפֵר – מֵיפֵר בְּשׁוּתָּפוּת.

This interpretation can resolve Rabba's question. **Granted, if you say** levirate betrothal **creates** a full-fledged **marriage, it is due to that** reason that the *yavam* **can nullify** her vows just as a full-fledged husband does. **However, if you say** that levirate betrothal merely **creates betrothal,**[N] **how can he nullify** the vows? Even in standard cases of betrothal by Torah law the husband cannot nullify her vows, **for didn't we learn** in a mishna: With regard to **a betrothed young woman,** only **her father and her husband** together can **nullify her vows?**[H] How could a *yavam* nullify the vows without the father of the *yevama*, if he is not considered a full-fledged husband? **Rav Naḥman bar Yitzḥak said** that this proof can be rejected by interpreting the mishna as follows: **What is** the meaning of the phrase: He **nullifies? That he nullifies** her vows only **in conjunction** with her father.

HALAKHA

Nullification of vows for a widow waiting for her ***yavam*** **– הֲפָרַת נִדְרֵי שׁוֹמֶרֶת יָבָם:** With regard to a woman awaiting levirate marriage, the *yavam* may not nullify her vows, whether she is waiting for several *yevamin* or just one, in accordance with the statement of Rabbi Akiva (Rambam *Sefer Hafla'a, Hilkhot Nedarim* 11:23; *Shulḥan Arukh, Yoreh De'a* 234:7).

Nullification of vows for a betrothed young woman – הֲפָרַת נִדְרֵי נַעֲרָה מְאוֹרָסָה: With regard to a betrothed young woman, her father and betrothed nullify her vows together (Rambam *Sefer Hafla'a, Hilkhot Nedarim* 11:9; *Shulḥan Arukh, Yoreh De'a* 234:5).

NOTES

Rabbi Akiva holds that the levirate bond is not substantial – רַבִּי עֲקִיבָא סָבַר אֵין זִיקָה: According to Rashi, Rabbi Akiva holds that the levirate bond is not substantial on any level, and therefore this woman is not considered to be the wife of the *yavam*. Others explain that even Rabbi Akiva agrees that the levirate bond has the force of rabbinic law, but since the nullification of vows is a Torah law, the levirate bond is not effective with regard to these *halakhot* in this case (Rabbi Avraham min HaHar).

With two the levirate bond is not substantial – לִתְרֵי אֵין זִיקָה: Rashi states that in the case of multiple *yevamin*, the levirate bond is weakened. Other commentaries differ and explain that this ruling is due to the fact that nullification of vows entails a clear knowledge of the identity of the husband at the time of the nullification, as retroactive designation does not apply to the *halakhot* of vows. Even if the *yevama* is later married to the brother-in-law who nullified her vows, this clarification is not effectual after the fact.

However, if you say it creates betrothal, etc. – אֶלָּא אִי אָמְרַתְּ אֵירוּסִין עוֹשֶׂה וכו׳: Although Abaye and Rabba discussed only whether levirate betrothal is equivalent to a betrothal by Torah law, here the Gemara seems to entertain the notion that levirate betrothal might be more powerful than standard betrothal, in that the *yavam* would be able to nullify vows on his own (*Tosefot HaRosh*; see Rashba).

NOTES

Any woman who makes a vow, etc. – כָּל הַנּוֹדֶרֶת וכו׳: The commentaries ask: If providing a woman's sustenance is reason enough to justify the husband's ability to nullify his wife's vows, then why was it necessary for the Torah to write the passage on nullification of vows? It must be that this halakhic rationale was established after the Torah explicitly stated the primary ruling with regard to the nullification of vows (*Tosafot Yeshanim*). This idea can be found in a slightly different form in the Responsa of the Rosh, where he says that even though one does not generally interpret the *halakha* based on the underlying rationale of the verses, in the case of nullification of vows, one does utilize the underlying rationale in order to determine how to apply the *halakhot*.

וְלְרַבִּי אֶלְעָזָר, דְּאָמַר: מַאֲמָר לְבֵית שַׁמַּאי אֵינוֹ קוֹנֶה אֶלָּא לִדְחוֹת לַצָּרָה בִּלְבַד, אַמַּאי מֵיפֵר בְּשׁוּתָּפוּת? אָמַר לָךְ רַבִּי אֶלְעָזָר: אֵימַר דַּאֲמָרִי אֲנָא אֵינוֹ קוֹנֶה אֶלָּא לִדְחוֹת לַצָּרָה בִּלְבַד – דְּלָא סַגִּי לָהּ בְּגִיטָּא אֶלָּא בָּעֵי נַמִּי חֲלִיצָה, לְהָפֵר נְדָרֶיהָ – מִי אָמְרִינַן?

The Gemara questions this reading of the mishna: **And according to** the opinion of **Rabbi Elazar, who said** that **for Beit Shammai levirate betrothal acquires** the woman **only** insofar **as it precludes a rival wife** from entering levirate marriage, and it is not a full-fledged acquisition, **why should** the *yavam* **nullify** her vows, even if he does so **in conjunction** with her father? The Gemara answers: **Rabbi Eliezer** could have **said to you:** One can **say that** when **I said** that levirate betrothal **acquires** the woman **only** insofar **as it precludes the rival wife** from entering levirate marriage, it was to emphasize **that a bill of divorce would not suffice for her, but rather she also requires *ḥalitza*.** However, with regard **to** the matter of **nullifying her vows, do we say** that levirate betrothal is not effective, and that he cannot nullify her vows alone?

וְאִיבָּעֵית אֵימָא, אָמַר לָךְ רַבִּי אֶלְעָזָר: וּלְרַב נַחְמָן בַּר יִצְחָק מִי נִיחָא? מִי קָתָנֵי ״יָפֵרוּ״? ״יָפֵר״ קָתָנֵי. אֶלָּא הָכָא בְּמַאי עָסְקִינַן – שֶׁעָמְדָה בְּדִין וּפָסְקוּ לָהּ מְזוֹנוֹת מִשֶּׁלּוֹ,

And if you wish, say an alternate explanation: **Rabbi Elazar** could have **said to you: And as for Rav Naḥman bar Yitzḥak, does this** resolution that the mishna is only referring to a case where the father and the *yavam* can nullify her vows together **work out well? Did the** mishna **teach** that **they** can **nullify** her vows? **It teaches** that **he** can **nullify** her vows in the singular, implying that he nullifies the vows alone and not in conjunction with anyone else. **Rather,** the mishna must be explained differently: **With what are we dealing here?** It is a case where the *yavam*, regardless of whether or not he performed levirate betrothal, did not want to consummate the levirate marriage or perform *ḥalitza*. Therefore, the *yevama* **stood in court** so as to compel him to consummate the levirate marriage or perform *ḥalitza*, **and it ruled that he** must supply **her sustenance.** Because she is bound to him and cannot marry another, the court ruled that he was responsible for her livelihood.

וְכִדְרַב פִּנְחָס מִשְּׁמֵיהּ דְּרָבָא, דְּאָמַר רַב פִּנְחָס מִשְּׁמֵיהּ דְּרָבָא: כָּל הַנּוֹדֶרֶת – עַל דַּעַת בַּעְלָהּ הִיא נוֹדֶרֶת.

And this is in accordance with the statement that Rav Pineḥas said **in the name of Rava, as Rav Pineḥas said in the name of Rava: Any woman who makes a vow,**[N] **makes her vow with the consent of her husband.** Because she is dependent upon her husband for her livelihood, she does not act without his consent. In this case, because the *yavam* is responsible to supply the *yevama* with sustenance, it is assumed that her vows are also made with his consent. It is for this reason that he can nullify her vows without her father. Consequently, no conclusive proof can be derived from here with regard to the strength of acquisition through levirate betrothal.

Perek **III**
Daf **30** Amud **a**

מתני׳ שְׁלֹשָׁה אַחִין, שְׁנַיִם מֵהֶם נְשׂוּאִים שְׁתֵּי אֲחָיוֹת וְאֶחָד נָשׂוּי נָכְרִית. מֵת אֶחָד מִבַּעֲלֵי אֲחָיוֹת, וְכָנַס נְשׂוּי נָכְרִית אֶת אִשְׁתּוֹ, וָמֵת – הָרִאשׁוֹנָה יוֹצְאָה מִשּׁוּם אֲחוֹת אִשָּׁה, וּשְׁנִיָּה מִשּׁוּם צָרָתָהּ. עָשָׂה בָּהּ מַאֲמָר וָמֵת – נָכְרִית חוֹלֶצֶת וְלֹא מִתְיַיבֶּמֶת.

MISHNA In the case of **three brothers, two of whom were married to two sisters and one who was married to an unrelated woman,** the following occurred: **The husband of one of the sisters died** childless, **and** the brother **who was married to the unrelated woman married,** i.e., performed levirate marriage with, the deceased brother's **wife and** later **died** himself, childless. In this situation, both women happen for levirate marriage before the other, remaining, brother. **The first** woman **is dismissed due to** the prohibition proscribing **the sister of one's wife,** as she is the sister of this brother's wife, **and the second** woman is dismissed **due to** her status as the first woman's **rival wife.** Following the first levirate marriage, this second woman became the rival wife of the sister, and is therefore exempt from levirate marriage as well. If, however, the brother married to the unrelated woman **performed** only **levirate betrothal,** but had not yet consummated the levirate marriage with the sister, **and he died, the unrelated woman,** whose halakhic status with regard to *yibbum* is similar to that of a sister's rival wife, must **perform *ḥalitza* and may not enter into levirate marriage.**

גמ׳ טַעְמָא דְּעָבַד בָּהּ מַאֲמָר, הָא לָא עָבַד בָּהּ מַאֲמָר – נׇכְרִית יִבּוּמֵי נַמִי מִייַּבְּמָה. אָמַר רַב נַחְמָן: זֹאת אוֹמֶרֶת אֵין זִיקָה, וַאֲפִילּוּ בְּחַד אַחָא.

GEMARA The Gemara deduces the following *halakha* from the second clause of the mishna: **The reason** that the mishna requires *ḥalitza* is specifically **because he,** the brother who was married to the unrelated woman, **performed levirate betrothal with** the sister.[N] **Consequently, had he not performed levirate betrothal with her, the unrelated woman** would be permitted to **enter into levirate marriage as well.** This is true despite the fact that the levirate bond could potentially render her the rival wife of his wife's sister. **Rav Naḥman said: That is to say, the** levirate **bond is not substantial;**[N] the woman requiring levirate marriage is not considered married to the *yavam*. **And** this is true **even** if the levirate bond was **with a single brother,** as this widowed sister happened for levirate marriage only before the brother who was married to the unrelated woman; her levirate bond was with him alone.

מתני׳ שְׁלֹשָׁה אַחִים, שְׁנַיִם מֵהֶם נְשׂוּאִים שְׁתֵּי אֲחָיוֹת וְאֶחָד נָשׂוּי נׇכְרִית. מֵת הַנָּשׂוּי נׇכְרִית, וְכָנַס אֶחָד מִבַּעֲלֵי אֲחָיוֹת אֶת אִשְׁתּוֹ וָמֵת – הָרִאשׁוֹנָה יוֹצְאָה מִשּׁוּם אֲחוֹת אִשָּׁה, וּשְׁנִיָּה מִשּׁוּם צָרָתָהּ. עָשָׂה בָּהּ מַאֲמָר וָמֵת – נׇכְרִית חוֹלֶצֶת וְלֹא מִתְיַיבֶּמֶת.

MISHNA In the case of **three brothers, two of whom were married to two sisters and one who was married to an unrelated woman,** the following occurred: **He who was married to the unrelated woman died, and one of the husbands of the sisters married his wife, and** then **died** childless as well. **The first** woman, i.e., the sister who was originally married to the brother who performed levirate marriage, **is dismissed** and is exempt from levirate marriage **due to** her status as **the sister of his wife. And the second** woman, i.e., the unrelated woman who had entered into levirate marriage, is dismissed **as her rival wife.**[H] If, however, **he performed levirate betrothal** with the unrelated woman, **and** then **died,** then this **unrelated woman** must **perform *ḥalitza* and may not enter into levirate marriage,** as levirate betrothal rendered her status with regard to *yibbum* as similar to the rival wife of his wife's sister.

גמ׳ הָא תּוּ לָמָּה לִי? הַיְינוּ הָךְ! הַשְׁתָּא, וּמָה הָתָם דַּאֲחוֹת אִשָּׁה הָוְיָא צָרָה לְנׇכְרִית אָמְרַתְּ: נׇכְרִית אֲסוּרָה, הָכָא, דְּנׇכְרִית הָוְיָא צָרָה לַאֲחוֹת אִשָּׁה – לֹא כׇּל שֶׁכֵּן?

GEMARA The Gemara asks: **Why do I need this** mishna **as well? This** principle **is identical**[N] to the principle behind the ruling in the previous mishna, and therefore this ruling can easily be deduced from the previous ruling. **Now, just as there,**[N] **when his wife's sister became rival wife of the unrelated woman**[N] who was already the brother's wife, **you say** that **the unrelated woman is forbidden** despite the fact that the forbidden relative joined later, **here, where the unrelated woman became the rival wife of** his **wife's sister** afterward, is it **not all the more so** clear that she is exempt as a rival wife?

HALAKHA

Exemption for the rival wife of a forbidden relative – פְּטוֹר צָרַת עֶרְוָה: In the case where there were three brothers, two of whom were married to two sisters and one who was married to an unrelated woman, the following occurred: The brother who was married to the unrelated woman died, and the husband of the first sister married his wife, the unrelated woman, and then died childless as well. Two women now happen before the third brother, the husband of the second sister, for levirate marriage, and both are exempt from levirate marriage and *ḥalitza*, one as a sister of his wife and the other as the rival wife of that first sister. If the husband of a sister did not enter into marriage with the unrelated woman, whether or not he performed levirate betrothal with her, then the unrelated woman must perform *ḥalitza* and may not enter into levirate marriage, for she would be the rival wife of his wife's sister by levirate bond. This is the opinion of the Rif, the Rosh, and other halakhic authorities who conclude that the *halakha* is in accordance with the opinion of Rav Ashi, who states that the levirate bond is substantial, as appears later.

The Rambam, however, cites the language of the mishna, specifying that the husband performed levirate betrothal. According to the *Tur*, the Rambam holds that specifically if he performed levirate betrothal with the unrelated woman would she be required to perform *ḥalitza* (see *Or Same'aḥ*). The *Beit Yosef* holds, however, that the Rambam accepted the Rif's opinion but merely opted to copy the formulation found in the mishna rather than be precise (Rambam *Sefer Nashim, Hilkhot Yibbum* 7:7; *Shulḥan Arukh, Even HaEzer* 175:7).

NOTES

The reason is because he performed levirate betrothal with the sister – טַעְמָא דְּעָבַד בָּהּ מַאֲמָר: In the Jerusalem Talmud as well, both this mishna and the following one are understood as referring specifically to cases where he performed levirate betrothal. They explain there that the ruling in the mishna conforms with both the opinion of Rabbi Shimon, who is in doubt as to whether levirate betrothal effects a full-fledged acquisition or does not bring about acquisition at all, as well as according to the opinion of the Rabbis, who hold that levirate betrothal effects a partial acquisition. According to both opinions, albeit for different reasons, the woman performs *ḥalitza* but may not enter into levirate marriage.

That is to say, the levirate bond is not substantial – זֹאת אוֹמֶרֶת אֵין זִיקָה: *Tosafot* wonder: Why did Rav Naḥman not deduce this from the first mishna of the second chapter of the tractate? One commentary explains that it could be said that the purpose of that earlier mishna was only to exclude the statement of Beit Shammai with regard to levirate betrothal, and therefore one could not deduce the status of the levirate bond from there. However, it was necessary to say this only once, such that when the mishna repeated this ruling it perforce indicated that the levirate bond is not substantial (Rabbi Akiva Eiger). Additionally, since the previous mishna in this chapter mentioned the dispute between the houses of Shammai and Hillel with regard to the issue of levirate betrothal, it would not be appropriate for the next mishna to categorically exclude the opinion of Beit Shammai (*Melo HaRo'im*).

This is identical, etc. – הַיְינוּ הָךְ וכו׳: *Tosafot* point out that in other cases the Gemara might have resolved this question by invoking the structural principle: This, and it is unnecessary to say that. There are times when the mishna states two *halakhot* and the second one seems to be unnecessary and obvious once the first one is stated. This redundancy is resolved by attributing the repetition to the style of: this, and it is unnecessary to say that. In this case, however, that explanation does not suffice, because the entire mishna is superfluous. Furthermore, if that were the case it would have been possible to unite the two *mishnayot* with a single opening (Ritva).

Now just as there, etc. – הַשְׁתָּא וּמָה הָתָם וכו׳: Rashi and most of the commentaries hold that the question and answer revolve primarily around the fact that he performed levirate betrothal. However, the Rashash holds that this could be referring to the principal *halakha* itself: Is the rival wife of a forbidden relative prohibited only if she was the second wife, married after the forbidden relative herself?

His wife's sister became rival wife of the unrelated woman – אֲחוֹת אִשָּׁה הָוְיָא צָרָה לְנׇכְרִית: The later commentaries explain in various ways why there might be a difference between rulings in these cases. One commentary explains that if he married the forbidden relative first, the prohibition with regard to a wife's sister was already in place, and there was never any possibility for the rival wife to become eligible to enter into levirate marriage. If, however, he had married the rival wife first, it could be said that she was, by her very marriage, eligible to enter into levirate marriage, and that a forbidden relative cannot negate that original permitted status once it is in place (*Ḥiddushei Batra*; see *Or Same'aḥ*).

תנא הך תנא ברישא, והך חזיא להתירא, ושריא. והדר חזיא לאיסורא.

The Gemara answers: This mishna was unnecessary, and this is how the duplication occurred: **The *tanna* taught this** mishna **at first, and** with regard to **that** previous case **saw it** fitting to render her **permitted, and he permitted** her to the brother, for he held that if the forbidden relative joined the man's household later, then she would not render the first wife prohibited as the rival wife of a forbidden relative. **And then** the *tanna* subsequently retracted and **saw it** fitting **to** render the woman **forbidden.** He decided that this woman should be considered the rival wife of a forbidden relative as well, and therefore rendered her forbidden to the brother.

ואיידי דחביבה ליה – אקדמה, ומשנה לא זזה ממקומה.

And since that case was novel, **it was beloved to him and he taught it earlier.** In truth, it would have now been possible to eliminate the present mishna, for there was no longer any novelty in it; its ruling could be derived by an *a fortiori* argument from the previous ruling. **However, a mishna does not move from its place.**[B] Since this version of the mishna had already been fixed, it was deemed inappropriate to remove it completely, and it remained in place despite the fact that it was no longer necessary.

מתני׳ שלשה אחין, שנים מהם נשואים שתי אחיות ואחד נשוי נכרית. מת אחד מבעלי אחיות, וכנס נשוי נכרית את אשתו, ומתה אשתו של שני, ואחר כך מת נשוי נכרית – הרי זו אסורה עליו עולמית, הואיל ונאסרה עליו שעה אחת.

MISHNA In the case of **three brothers, two of whom were married to two sisters and one who was married to an unrelated woman,** the following occurred: **One of the husbands of the sisters died, and he who was married to the unrelated woman married** the deceased husband's **wife, and** then **the wife of the second** brother, the other one of the sisters, **died. Afterward,** the brother **who was married to the unrelated woman died,** leaving two women for levirate marriage before the remaining brother: The unrelated woman and the woman who was previously prohibited as the sister of his deceased wife. In this case, the sister **is forbidden to him**[N] **forever.** She is not forbidden due to her status as his wife's sister, as his wife already died and one's wife's sister is permitted after the wife's death. However, **since she was** already **forbidden to him at one time,**[H] she is forbidden to him forever. When she first happened before the brothers for levirate marriage, before the third brother married her, she was forbidden to the second brother as his wife's sister. Therefore, she is forbidden to him forever. In addition, she exempts her rival wife, the unrelated woman, from levirate marriage.

גמ׳ אמר רב יהודה אמר רב: כל יבמה שאין אני קורא בה בשעת נפילה ״יבמה יבא עליה״ הרי היא כאשת אח שיש לה בנים, ואסורה. מאי קא משמע לן? תנינא: הרי זו אסורה עליו עולמית, הואיל ונאסרה עליו שעה אחת!

GEMARA **Rav Yehuda said** that **Rav said** a principle on this matter: **Any *yevama* to whom the verse "Her brother-in-law will have intercourse with her"** (Deuteronomy 25:5) **cannot be applied at the time that she happens** before him for levirate marriage because she was forbidden to him at that moment, **is then** forever considered to be **like the wife of a brother** with whom **she has children, and she is forbidden** to him. The Gemara asks: **What is** Rav **teaching us** with this statement? **We** already **learned** this in the mishna: **She is forbidden to him forever, since she was forbidden to him at one time.**

מהו דתימא: הני מילי – היכא דלא איחזיא לה בנפילה ראשונה, אבל היכא דאיחזיא לה בנפילה ראשונה – אימא תישתרי, קא משמע לן.

The Gemara answers: This was necessary **lest you say that this** ruling **applies** only in cases **where she was not eligible** at all **during** the **first** time that she **happened** before the brothers for levirate marriage. Such is the case in the mishna, when she was forbidden to the *yavam* as his wife's sister the entire time that she was eligible for levirate marriage. Even though his wife died after the other *yavam* married this woman, because she was forbidden to him that entire time, she is forbidden to him forever. **But** in cases **where she was eligible** at some point **during** the **first** time she **happened** before the brothers for levirate marriage, such as in the scenario where the brother's wife died prior to the time when his other brother married her, one could **say** that **she would be permitted.** In that case, since the prohibition had in the meantime been canceled and she was indeed rendered eligible for levirate marriage with him during the period of the first time she happened before him, one might think that she would now be permitted. It is for this reason that Rav **teaches us** that even in this scenario she would be forbidden to him forever.

BACKGROUND

A mishna does not move from its place – משנה לא זזה ממקומה: There is a dispute among the early commentaries, as well as among modern scholars, as to whether Rabbi Yehuda HaNasi actually wrote the Mishna or if he merely edited it into its final form for the purposes of oral study. In either case, even according to those who say that he fixed the Mishna in writing, it was not commonly available, and its study primarily continued orally. Since students learned the *mishnayot* orally in their proper order, omitting a particular mishna and replacing it with a similar one, or combining two *mishnayot* into one, could cause confusion in the students' learning. It is for this reason that Rabbi Yehuda HaNasi left the original mishna in place, even if it was unnecessary (see Ritva).

NOTES

The sister is forbidden to him – הרי זו אסורה עליו: The Rambam in his Commentary on the Mishna writes that while the *halakha* with regard to a sister was explicit, the *halakha* with regard to the unrelated woman, her rival wife, was not, and in his opinion she must perform *ḥalitza* but may not enter into levirate marriage due to uncertainty. In contrast, the Rambam himself concludes in *Mishne Torah*, in accordance with the opinions of all the early commentaries, that this woman is released without *ḥalitza*. If we decide, as does Rav, that the sister is forbidden like the wife of a brother who has children, then her rival wife is the rival wife of a forbidden relative and is exempt. The later commentaries attempt to explain Rambam's uncertainty in this matter.

HALAKHA

She was forbidden to him at one time – נאסרה עליו שעה אחת: In the case of three brothers, two of whom were married to two sisters and one who was married to an unrelated woman, the following occurred: One of the husbands of the sisters died, and the brother who was married to the unrelated woman married his wife. Later, the wife of the other brother, i.e., the sister of the woman who entered into levirate marriage, died. Afterward, the brother who was married to the unrelated woman died. In this case, the widowed brother is not permitted to take his deceased brother's wife in levirate marriage because she was forbidden to him the first time she happened before him for levirate marriage. As she was forbidden to him at one time, she is forbidden to him forever (Rambam *Sefer Nashim*, *Hilkhot Yibbum* 7:11; *Shulḥan Arukh*, *Even HaEzer* 175:1).

הָא נַמִּי תָּנֵינָא: שְׁנֵי אַחִין נְשׂוּאִין שְׁתֵּי אֲחָיוֹת, מֵת אֶחָד מֵהֶם וְאַחַר כָּךְ מֵתָה אִשְׁתּוֹ שֶׁל שֵׁנִי – הֲרֵי זוֹ אֲסוּרָה עָלָיו עוֹלָמִית, הוֹאִיל וְנֶאֶסְרָה עָלָיו שָׁעָה אַחַת!

The Gemara raises an objection: **We learned** this **as well,** as a later mishna (32a) states: In the case of **two brothers who were married to two sisters,** if **one of them,** i.e., one of the brothers, **died and afterward the wife of the second** brother **died, then she,** the surviving wife, **is forbidden to him,** the surviving brother, **forever, since she was forbidden to him** during the period she happened before him **at one time.**

מַהוּ דְּתֵימָא: הָתָם הוּא דְּאִידַּחִי לַהּ מֵהַאי בֵּיתָא לְגַמְרֵי. אֲבָל הָכָא, דְּלָא אִידַּחֵי לַהּ מֵהַאי בֵּיתָא לְגַמְרֵי, אֵימָא: מִיגּוֹ דַּחֲזְיָא לְהַאי נְשׂוּי נָכְרִית חַזְיָא נַמִּי לְהַאי, קָא מַשְׁמַע לַן.

The Gemara answers: One cannot learn the halakhic principle from that case. **Lest you say that there** she is forbidden forever because of the following argument: When she was forbidden to the brother, **she was precluded from** entering **this household completely,** i.e., from the entire obligation of levirate marriage. She received total exemption from the mitzva of levirate marriage because this obligation applied only to the one remaining brother, and she was forbidden to him at the time that she happened before him for levirate marriage. But **here, however,** in the case Rav is referring to, **where she was not completely precluded from** entering **this household** because she still required levirate marriage with another brother, one could **say: Since she is eligible** and permitted **to this** brother, **who was married to the unrelated woman, she is eligible for this** second brother following the death of his wife **as well,** in other words, she was not rendered completely exempt from the obligation of levirate marriage. Lest one make this argument, Rav **teaches us** that under any circumstances she who was forbidden at one time is forbidden forever.

מתני׳ שְׁלֹשָׁה אַחִים, שְׁנַיִם מֵהֶם נְשׂוּאִין שְׁתֵּי אֲחָיוֹת וְאֶחָד נְשׂוּי נָכְרִית. גֵּירֵשׁ אֶחָד מִבַּעֲלֵי אֲחָיוֹת אֶת אִשְׁתּוֹ, וּמֵת נְשׂוּי נָכְרִית, וּכְנָסָהּ הַמְגָרֵשׁ וָמֵת – זוֹ הִיא שֶׁאָמְרוּ: וְכוּלָּן שֶׁמֵּתוּ אוֹ נִתְגָּרְשׁוּ – צָרוֹתֵיהֶן מוּתָּרוֹת.

MISHNA In the case of **three brothers,**[B] **two of whom were married to two sisters and one who was married to an unrelated woman,** the following occurred: Shimon, **the husband of one of the sisters, divorced**[NH] **his wife,** and then Levi, **who was married to the unrelated woman, died, and** Shimon, **the man who divorced** his wife, **married,** i.e., performed levirate marriage with, **her,**[N] i.e., this unrelated woman. **And** then Shimon himself later **died,** so that the unrelated woman happened for levirate marriage before Reuven, the third brother, who is married to the second sister. In this scenario, Reuven is allowed to consummate the levirate marriage with the unrelated woman. **This is** the case that was referred to when **they said: And** with regard to **all those** fifteen forbidden relatives **who died or were divorced, their rival wives are permitted** to enter into levirate marriage. This is because at the time that they happened before the *yavam* for levirate marriage they were no longer the rival wives of a forbidden relative.

NOTES

Three brothers…divorced, etc. – שְׁלֹשָׁה אַחִים...גֵּירֵשׁ וכו׳: *Tosafot* ask why it was necessary to state that there were three brothers, for this *halakha* could have been taught in a case with only two brothers. They explain this according to several different opinions. The Rashba writes that according to Rava's opinion cited later it was indeed not necessary to describe a case with three brothers. However, as the entire chapter is referring to cases of three brothers, that number was used in this case as well despite the fact that it is not necessary.

The man who divorced his wife married her – כְּנָסָהּ הַמְגָרֵשׁ: *Tosafot* ask how the man who divorced his wife could possibly marry this woman, for is she not the rival wife of his wife's sister due to the levirate bond with the third brother? They explain that while the husband who divorced his wife is alive, it is not relevant to consider the unrelated woman as the rival wife of his wife's sister. The issue of the rival wife of his wife's sister by levirate bond is relevant only when the other brother dies and both women happen before the third brother for levirate marriage (see *Tosefot HaRosh*).

HALAKHA

He who divorces the close relative of his *yevama* – הַמְגָרֵשׁ אֶת קְרוֹבַת יְבִמְתּוֹ: In the case of three brothers, two of whom were married to two sisters and one of whom was married to an unrelated woman, the following occurred: The husband of one of the sisters divorced his wife, and the one married to an unrelated woman died, and the man who divorced his wife married this unrelated woman and then died. This woman would be permitted to the third brother, as she had never been the rival wife of his wife's sister.

If, however, the brother who was married to the unrelated woman died first, and then the husband of one of the sisters divorced his wife, even if he did not manage to marry the unrelated woman, she would nevertheless be forbidden to the remaining brother because she was the rival wife of his wife's sister by levirate bond, prior to the divorce.

And if the husband of one of the sisters entered into marriage with the unrelated woman and divorced the sister (whether the divorce took place before or after the marriage to the unrelated woman), if this brother dies as well then the unrelated woman is permitted to the husband of the other sister, for he takes her in levirate marriage as a consequence of the latest marriage, and at the time that she happened before him she was no longer the rival wife of his wife's sister (Rambam *Sefer Nashim*, *Hilkhot Yibbum* 7:12; *Shulḥan Arukh*, *Even HaEzer* 175:8).

BACKGROUND

Three brothers – שְׁלֹשָׁה אַחִים: There were three paternal brothers, Reuven, Shimon, and Levi. Reuven and Shimon married two sisters, Ḥogla and Milka, respectively, while Levi married Miriam, who was not related to either of them. Eventually, Milka died, after which Levi died childless, and Shimon took Miriam in levirate marriage. If Shimon then dies childless, Reuven is allowed to take Miriam in levirate marriage, since she was never the rival wife of his wife's sister.

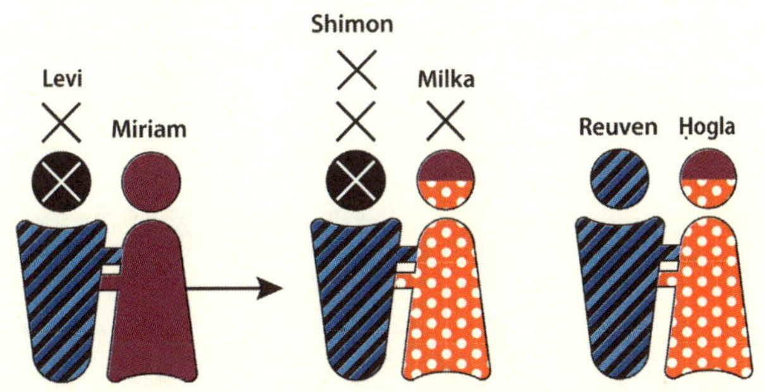

גמ׳ טַעֲמָא דְּגֵירֵשׁ וְאַחַר כָּךְ מֵת, אֲבָל מֵת וְאַחַר כָּךְ גֵּירֵשׁ – אֲסוּרָה. אָמַר רַב אַשִׁי: זֹאת אוֹמֶרֶת יֵשׁ זִיקָה, אֲפִילּוּ בִּתְרֵי אַחֵי.

GEMARA The Gemara deduces from here that **the reason** for this *halakha* is specifically **that** Shimon **divorced** his wife **and after that** Levi **died** and Shimon married the unrelated woman. **But** if Levi had **died** first, **and later** Shimon **divorced** his wife, then the unrelated woman would be **forbidden** to Reuven due to the levirate bond that existed between her and Shimon prior to the latter's divorce. She would be considered the rival wife of the divorced woman who is the sister of Reuven's wife. **Rav Ashi said: That is to say, the** levirate **bond is substantial, even with two brothers.** Although the unrelated woman required levirate marriage with two brothers, the levirate bond is substantial enough to create a relationship between the unrelated woman and Shimon such that the unrelated woman is considered the rival wife of the divorced woman, i.e., the sister of Reuven's wife.

וּלְרַב אַשִׁי קַשְׁיָא דְּרַב נַחְמָן! אָמַר לָךְ רַב אַשִׁי: הוּא הַדִּין דְּאַף עַל גַּב דְּלָא עֲבַד בָּהּ מַאֲמָר נׇכְרִית – מִיחֲלַץ חָלְצָה, יַבּוּמֵי לָא מִייַּבְּמָה. וְהָא דְּקָתָנֵי מַאֲמָר – לְאַפּוֹקֵי בֵּית שַׁמַּאי, דְּאָמְרִי: מַאֲמָר קוֹנֶה

The Gemara asks: **And according to Rav Ashi,** that which **Rav Naḥman** said is **difficult,** as Rav Naḥman deduced from the earlier mishna that the levirate bond is not substantial even in the case of a single brother. The Gemara answers: **Rav Ashi** could have **said to you:** Rav Naḥman's deduction in the first mishna was not logically necessary. With regard to that mishna, one could have said that when the mishna requires *ḥalitza* in the case of levirate betrothal, **the same is true even** in the case **where he** who was married to the unrelated woman **did not perform levirate betrothal with her.** In that case as well, **the unrelated woman must perform *ḥalitza* and may not enter into levirate marriage** since she was the rival wife of his wife's sister by levirate bond. **And** the reason **that it teaches** the ruling in the case of **levirate betrothal** was not in order to inform us that she was forbidden due to levirate betrothal, but rather **to exclude** the statement of **Beit Shammai,**[N] **who say** that through the act of **levirate betrothal** one **acquires** the *yevama*

NOTES

To exclude the statement of Beit Shammai – לְאַפּוֹקֵי בֵּית שַׁמַּאי: The question arises: If this mishna comes to exclude the statement of Beit Shammai, then why was it necessary to teach this twice, both here and in the second chapter? Alternatively, why was it necessary to teach in both places that the levirate bond is not substantial? Some commentaries explain that according to Rav Ashi, it is more reasonable to hold that the levirate bond is not substantial, and therefore it was necessary to repeat this in order to emphasize that the mishna is not teaching that the levirate bond is not substantial but rather that the mishna is excluding Beit Shammai's statement. Similarly, according to the opinion of Rav Naḥman, it is more reasonable to maintain that the levirate bond is substantial, and therefore the matter was taught twice in order to emphasize that it is not (*Tosefot HaRosh*; *Tosafot Yeshanim*).

קִנְיָן גָּמוּר, קָא מַשְׁמַע לָן דְּלָא כְּבֵית שַׁמַּאי.

as a **full-fledged acquisition.** According to that opinion, the unrelated woman does not even require *ḥalitza*, since she is considered to be a rival wife of a forbidden relative. This mishna **teaches us that the** *halakha* **is not in accordance with** the opinion of **Beit Shammai.**

וּלְרַב נַחְמָן קַשְׁיָא דְּרַב אַשִׁי! וְכִי תֵּימָא: הוּא הַדִּין דַּאֲפִילּוּ מֵת וְאַחַר כָּךְ גֵּירֵשׁ צָרָתָהּ מוּתֶּרֶת, אֶלָּא "זוֹ הִיא" לְמַעוּטֵי מַאי – לְמַעוּטֵי כָּנַס וְאַחַר כָּךְ גֵּירֵשׁ,

The Gemara raises a question from the opposite perspective: **And according to Rav Naḥman,** who deduced from the earlier mishna that the levirate bond is not substantial, the deduction **of Rav Ashi** that the levirate bond is substantial is **difficult. And if you would** try to resolve this in a similar manner and **say:** With regard to the ruling in the present mishna, which states that the sister's **rival wife,** i.e., the unrelated woman, **is permitted, the same is true even if** Levi had **died and** then **afterward** the brother married to the other sister **divorced** his wife, there is a difficulty. If that is the case, then **what does** the phrase **this is,** cited at the end of the mishna, come **to exclude?**[N] If we follow this explanation then the same ruling would hold true in all cases. The Gemara responds: **It excludes** the case where Shimon first **married** the unrelated woman **and** only **afterward divorced** the sister, as in such circumstances the unrelated woman is most certainly a rival wife of Reuven's wife's sister and is therefore not permitted.

הָנִיחָא אִי סָבַר לָהּ כְּרַבִּי יִרְמְיָה, דְּאָמַר: תַּבְרָא, מִי שֶׁשָּׁנָה זוֹ לֹא שָׁנָה זוֹ,

The Gemara states: **This works out well if he holds in accordance with** the opinion of **Rabbi Yirmeya, who said** with regard to a seeming contradiction between this mishna and an earlier mishna (13a): The *mishnayot* are **disjointed; he who taught this** mishna **did not teach that** mishna. The earlier mishna established the principle that if a man was married to two women, one of whom was a forbidden relative, and he divorced the forbidden relative before he died, then the rival wife is no longer prohibited to the brothers.

וְהַאי תַּנָּא סָבַר מִיתָה מַפֶּלֶת, וְהַאי תַּנָּא סָבַר נִישּׂוּאִין הָרִאשׁוֹנִים מַפִּילִים.

This dispute is based upon the following: **This** *tanna* from the earlier mishna **holds that death determines** her status when **she happens** before the brothers, i.e., the crucial moment for determining whether the prohibition relating to rival wives applies is the moment at which the brother dies. In other words, whether the *yevama* is permitted to the *yavam* is determined by the status of the *yevama* at that given moment. Therefore, in the case where he had married a forbidden relative and later divorced her, the rival wife would be permitted. **And this** *tanna* of our present mishna **holds that the original marriage determines** her status when **she happens** before the brothers. If, at the time the woman was married to the deceased brother she was forbidden as a close relative, and her rival wife was likewise forbidden as the rival wife of a forbidden relative, then even though the status of the relative had changed at the time of the death of the brother, both she and her rival wife remain forbidden.

"זוֹ הִיא" לְמַעוּטֵי כָּנַס וּלְבַסּוֹף גֵּירֵשׁ. אֶלָּא אִי סָבַר לָהּ כְּרָבָא, דְּאָמַר לְעוֹלָם חַד תַּנָּא הוּא, וְ"זוֹ וְאֵין צָרִיךְ לוֹמַר זוֹ" קָתָנֵי – "זוֹ הִיא" לְמַעוּטֵי מַאי? עַל כָּרְחָךְ כְּרַבִּי יִרְמְיָה סְבִירָא לֵיהּ.

According to this opinion, it is indeed possible to state that the phrase **this is** comes **to exclude** the case where **he married** one woman **and ultimately divorced** the other. According to this mishna, in that case, the rival wives would be prohibited. **However, if he holds in accordance with** the opinion of **Rava, who said: Actually,** understand **this** to be the opinion of **a single** *tanna,* **and he teaches** the mishna employing the style: **This, and it is unnecessary to say that,** a difficulty remains. According to Rava, both *mishnayot* maintain the position that in the case where the *yavam* married one woman and ultimately divorced the other, the rival wife would be permitted. If that is the case, **what** does the phrase **this is** come **to exclude?** In what case would the rival wife be prohibited to the *yavam*? The Gemara responds: **Perforce** Rav Naḥman **holds in accordance with** the opinion of **Rabbi Yirmeya** with regard to his interpretation of the *mishnayot.*

NOTES

What does the phrase: This is, come to exclude – זוֹ הִיא לְמַעוּטֵי מַאי: The commentaries held different opinions as to the meaning of this passage and its practical implications. According to Rashi, both Rav Naḥman and Rav Ashi hold in accordance with the opinion of Rabbi Yirmeya that this mishna follows the opinion that the original marriage determines the status of the woman when she happens before the brothers for levirate marriage. Therefore, according to Rav Ashi, the phrase: This is, comes to exclude the case where one of the husbands married to a sister divorces his wife after the brother married to the unrelated woman dies. If he subsequently marries the unrelated woman and dies, this woman is forbidden upon his death to his other brother because she became the rival wife of his wife's sister by levirate bond. This is all the more true in the case where he married her prior to divorcing his wife. For Rav Naḥman, the phrase: This is, comes to exclude specifically the case where he married and then later divorced. Rava, however, holds that: This is, comes to exclude the case where he dies without divorcing his wife at all.

The Rif's opinion on this matter is complicated. He rules in accordance with Rav Ashi's opinion that if Levi, the brother married to the unrelated woman, dies before Shimon divorces the sister to whom he is married, then when Shimon also dies the unrelated woman is forbidden to his brother Reuven as the rival wife of his wife's sister through the levirate bond. He also rules that the time of death of the husband determines the woman's status with regard to levirate marriage. It is unclear why it should matter whether the divorce took place before or after Levi died. As long as Shimon had already divorced the sister before he died, the unrelated woman should not be regarded as the rival wife of a forbidden relative.

The Rif offers two explanations as to why she is nevertheless forbidden to Reuven under such circumstances. According to the first explanation, this is a special stringency that is an extension of the rabbinic decree that the levirate bond creates substantial relationships. Since at the time of Levi's death she was the rival wife of Reuven's wife's sister due to the levirate bond, she is forbidden to Reuven after Shimon's death. This is despite the fact that in the parallel case, where Shimon was actually married to her and to Reuven's wife's sister, and then Shimon divorced the sister and subsequently died, she would be permitted to Reuven, because at the time of Shimon's death she was not the rival wife of a forbidden relative.

The Rif's second, preferred explanation is that in this case, at the moment of Levi's death, the unrelated woman becomes the rival wife of Reuven's wife's sister due to the levirate bond. She is therefore rendered forbidden to Reuven as such. Even though she loses this status after Shimon divorces his wife, once she was rendered forbidden to Reuven the first time she happened before him for levirate marriage, she can no longer be rendered permitted to him.

HALAKHA

Uncertainty with regard to the rival wife of a forbidden relative – סָפֵק צָרַת עֶרְוָה: If a woman underwent a betrothal whose status is uncertain or a divorce whose status is uncertain with the deceased brother, and she was a forbidden relative to her brother-in-law, and the deceased brother had another wife, then that rival wife must perform *ḥalitza* and may not enter into levirate marriage (Rambam *Sefer Nashim, Hilkhot Yibbum* 6:22; *Shulḥan Arukh, Even HaEzer* 173:3).

Uncertainty with regard to betrothal – סָפֵק קִדּוּשִׁין: If both the man and the woman were standing in the public domain, or in a domain that did not belong to either, and he threw her the betrothal item but it was lost before it reached her hand, if it fell in a place that was possibly closer to him and possibly closer to her in such a way that both could have guarded the object, or both could equally have not guarded the object, then this is a case of betrothal whose status is uncertain (Rambam *Sefer Nashim, Hilkhot Ishut* 4:22; *Shulḥan Arukh, Even HaEzer* 30:5).

וּלְרָבָא, הָנִיחָא אִי סָבַר לַהּ כְּרַב אַשִׁי – ״זוֹ הִיא״ לְמַעוּטֵי מֵת בְּלֹא גֵּירֵשׁ, אֶלָּא אִי סָבַר לַהּ כְּרַב נַחְמָן: ״זוֹ הִיא״ לְמַעוּטֵי מַאי? עַל כָּרְחָךְ כְּרַב אַשִׁי סְבִירָא לֵיהּ.

The Gemara raises a question from a different perspective: **And according to Rava,** who maintains that in both cases the rival wife is permitted, **this works out well if he holds in accordance** with the opinion **of Rav Ashi** that the levirate bond is substantial. In that case the phrase **this is** comes **to exclude** the case where **he died without divorcing his wife.** In this case the rival wife is forbidden because the entire time she was the rival wife of a forbidden relative by levirate bond. **If, however, he holds in accordance** with the opinion of **Rav Naḥman** in this matter, **what** does the phrase **this** is come **to exclude?** The Gemara answers: **Perforce** Rava **holds in accordance with** the opinion of **Rav Ashi.** Accordingly, with regard to this *halakha* there is a connection between the various opinions as to how to interpret the *mishnayot* and the dispute.

מתני׳ וְכוּלָּן שֶׁהָיוּ בָּהֶן קִדּוּשִׁין אוֹ גֵּרוּשִׁין בְּסָפֵק – הֲרֵי אֵלּוּ הַצָּרוֹת חוֹלְצוֹת וְלֹא מִתְיַבְּמוֹת. כֵּיצַד סָפֵק קִדּוּשִׁין? זָרַק לָהּ קִדּוּשִׁין, סָפֵק קָרוֹב לוֹ סָפֵק קָרוֹב לָהּ – זֶהוּ סָפֵק קִדּוּשִׁין.

MISHNA And if **any of these** fifteen women who are prohibited as forbidden relatives **had undergone a betrothal or divorce** whose status **is uncertain**[H] with the deceased brother, **then those** women who were their **rival wives** must **perform *ḥalitza* and may not enter into levirate marriage** since they are possibly the rival wives of forbidden relatives. The mishna elaborates: **How** could there be a situation of **uncertainty** with regard to **betrothal?**[H] If in the public domain **he threw her** an item for the purpose of **betrothal** and there were eight cubits between them, and the item **was possibly closer to him**[N] and did not enter into her domain, and **possibly closer to her,** i.e., within four cubits of her, whereby she could acquire the object, **this is** a case of **uncertainty** with regard to **betrothal.**

סָפֵק גֵּרוּשִׁין – כָּתַב בִּכְתַב יָדוֹ וְאֵין עָלָיו עֵדִים, יֵשׁ עָלָיו עֵדִים וְאֵין בּוֹ זְמַן, יֵשׁ בּוֹ זְמַן וְאֵין בּוֹ אֶלָּא עֵד אֶחָד – זֶהוּ סָפֵק גֵּרוּשִׁין.

Uncertainty with regard to **divorce** occurs when, for instance, **he wrote a** bill of divorce **in his handwriting**[N] **but there are no** signatures of **witnesses on** the document, or **there are** the signatures of **witnesses** on the document **but there is no date** written **in it,** or **the date is** written **in it but there is only** the signature of **a single witness.** Since there is doubt as to whether these three kinds of bills of divorce are valid, a woman who was divorced through them is only possibly divorced, and so **this** case **is** called **uncertainty** with regard to **divorce.**[N]

גמ׳ וְאִילּוּ בְּגֵרוּשִׁין סָפֵק קָרוֹב לוֹ סָפֵק קָרוֹב לָהּ – לָא קָתָנֵי.

GEMARA The Gemara remarks: **But yet when** discussing **divorce, it does not teach** the case where it is **uncertain** if the bill of divorce **is closer to him, and uncertain if it is closer to her.** It would have been appropriate to describe this case, as it parallels the case involving the object of betrothal. He could have tossed it in such a way that it was not clear to whom the bill was closer.

NOTES

Possibly closer to him – סָפֵק קָרוֹב לוֹ: Rashi interprets this *halakha* as pertaining to the specific instance where there were exactly eight cubits between the two (see *Gittin* 78a). The Rashba, however, maintains that those conditions were stated specifically in the case of a bill of divorce, as it is required that the bill of divorce be delivered either into the woman's hand or into her domain. In contrast, with regard to betrothal, this condition is not necessary. Therefore, it is possible to establish that in this case there were more than eight cubits between them but there was doubt as to whether the item of betrothal was close enough to her that she could successfully guard it.

He wrote a bill of divorce in his handwriting – כָּתַב בִּכְתַב יָדוֹ: Rashi derives proof that a handwritten document is considered authoritative from the *halakhot* of documents where a bill of debt handwritten by the debtor is effectual even without witnesses, allowing the collection of payment of the debt from his available property. *Nimmukei Yosef* claims that these are not similar cases, since in monetary law a bill serves merely as evidence as to what had transpired, whereas a bill of divorce in fact creates the divorce itself. Accordingly, he offers an alternative reason. Since the verse states: "And he writes her a bill of divorce," if the man divorcing his wife himself writes the bill, this sufficiently fulfills the primary requirements of the *halakha*. The opinion in the Jerusalem Talmud, however, accords with that of Rashi, as a comparison is drawn between a handwritten bill of divorce and the *halakhot* of monetary documents.

This is uncertainty with regard to divorce – זֶהוּ סָפֵק גֵּרוּשִׁין: In truth, there is no actual doubt with regard to the divorce itself, since by Torah law these bills of divorce are effective. If she were to remarry subsequent to such a bill she would not require a divorce from her second husband. Rather, the Sages rendered these bills of divorce disqualified for various reasons, some of which are elucidated later. In any case, since they are not to be used *ab initio*, the Sages judged a woman who was divorced through them to be a divorcée whose status is uncertain. This is how the mishna is explained in the Jerusalem Talmud (see *Penei Moshe* there).

מַאי טַעְמָא? אָמַר רַבָּה: אִשָּׁה זוֹ בְּחֶזְקַת הֶיתֵּר לַשּׁוּק עוֹמֶדֶת, וּמִסָּפֵק אַתָּה בָּא לְאוֹסְרָהּ – אַל תַּאַסְרֶנָּה מִסָּפֵק.

The Gemara asks: **What is the reason** the mishna did not present this situation as well? **Rabba said:** When this type of uncertainty exists, the performance of *ḥalitza* is not mandatory, as **this woman,** the rival wife, **has the presumptive status of being permitted** to marry a man **from the** general **public.**[N] At the time of her marriage she was rendered a rival wife of a forbidden relative. **And due to an uncertainty** alone **would you render her forbidden** to the general public until she performs *ḥalitza*, simply because it is unclear to us whether or not the forbidden relative had indeed been divorced? **Do not render her forbidden due to an uncertainty.** This is not, however, the case with the various bills of divorce mentioned in the mishna, for they are all certainly considered effective bills of divorce, even if the circumstances involved raise some questions or doubts.

אֲמַר לֵיהּ אַבָּיֵי: אִי הָכִי בְּקִדּוּשִׁין נַמִי, נֵימָא: אִשָּׁה זוֹ בְּחֶזְקַת הֶיתֵּר לְיַבֵּם עוֹמֶדֶת, וּמִסָּפֵק אַתָּה בָּא לְאוֹסְרָהּ – אַל תַּאַסְרֶנָּה מִסָּפֵק!

Abaye said to him: If that is so, let us say in the case of **betrothal as well** that **this woman,** the rival wife, **has the presumptive status of being permitted to the *yavam***[N] before he betrothed the forbidden relative, **and due to the uncertainty** whether she is the rival wife of a forbidden relative **would you come and render her forbidden? Do not render her forbidden due to an uncertainty.** Consequently, you should permit her to enter into levirate marriage.

– הָתָם לְחוּמְרָא.

The Gemara explains: **There,** with regard to betrothal, the *halakha* follows **the stringent ruling,** because the rival wife is certainly his wife and requires levirate marriage. As there is uncertainty with regard to the betrothal with the forbidden relative, the ruling is stringent; she may not enter into levirate marriage and must only perform *ḥalitza*.

הַאי – חוּמְרָא דְּאָתֵי לִידֵי קוּלָּא הוּא; זִימְנִין דְּאָזֵיל הוּא וּמְקַדֵּשׁ לָהּ לַאֲחוֹתָהּ קִדּוּשֵׁי וַדַּאי,

The Gemara objects: Yet **this is a stringency that might bring about a leniency**[N] in another scenario. How so? **Sometimes** that same man who betrothed the forbidden relative might **go and betroth her sister** with **a betrothal** whose status is **certain.** If one says that due to a stringency the rival wife may not enter into levirate marriage due to her possible status as the rival wife of a forbidden relative, people might come to assume that the betrothal with the forbidden relative was a valid betrothal, and that the subsequent betrothal with her sister was not valid, since she is his wife's sister. This would be assumed because they would not know that the status of the first betrothal was itself uncertain and that only due to a stringent ruling is the rival wife not allowed to enter into levirate marriage. In fact, the status of the betrothal with the sister of the forbidden relative is also uncertain. As a result of this ruling, however, people might be led to think that a man's wife, i.e., the sister of the forbidden relative, is in fact permitted.

NOTES

Has the presumptive status of being permitted to a man from the general public – בְּחֶזְקַת הֶיתֵּר לַשּׁוּק עוֹמֶדֶת: *Tosafot* raise two issues with regard to this *halakha*. The first relates to the woman's presumed permitted status: If the forbidden relative was his first wife, and later he married this other woman, only after which he performed a divorce whose status is uncertain with the forbidden relative, then clearly the rival wife is presumed to be permitted to the general public. However, if he first divorced the forbidden relative with a divorce whose status is uncertain and later married the rival wife, what reason could there be for the rival wife to have the presumptive status of being permitted? *Tosafot* explain that even here it makes sense for her to have the presumptive status of being permitted, since the marriage to the forbidden relative was certain and the divorce was uncertain. Therefore, at the time of the rival wife's marriage, due to the marriage whose status was certain that had previously taken place, the rival wife was rendered a rival wife of a forbidden relative. The Ramban, on the other hand, explains that this passage was said only with regard to the case where he married the rival wife and then later divorced the forbidden relative, but in the opposite case there would be no presumption of permissibility.

The second issue is more fundamental. It says that this woman is presumed to be permitted to the general public. However, it would seem that she had not yet merited such a status, as she was formerly married and therefore should have the status of a married woman who is forbidden to the public; only when her husband dies is there doubt with regard to the obligation of levirate marriage, and the question arises as to whether she should be permitted to the general public or not. This question is strengthened in light of the point some commentaries add that in the context of other *halakhot*, such as when there is doubt as to whether an animal was slaughtered properly, we presume from prohibition to prohibition. In other words, the prohibition against eating the animal in its life was not nullified even after it was slaughtered before us. Similarly, the woman should remain prohibited to the general public as a man's wife until we are certain that this prohibition no longer applies. The Ramban resolves this by saying that it is possible for an animal to remain prohibited, for certain reasons, even after its death, and therefore the prohibition is not automatically terminated with its death. This is different from the case of a woman, whose prohibited status ceases upon the death of her husband. The Rashba explains that an animal does not lose its prohibited status until some act is done, i.e., the appropriate slaughtering rituals, in order to render it fit for consumption. For a woman, however, the death of her husband suffices without any additional action (see *Tosafot Yeshanim*).

Has the presumptive status of being permitted to the *yavam* – בְּחֶזְקַת הֶיתֵּר לְיַבֵּם עוֹמֶדֶת: Here too the commentaries ask: This *halakha* is understandable in circumstances where he was first married to the rival wife and then later performed a betrothal whose status is uncertain with the forbidden relative, as it is clear that betrothal whose status is uncertain is not strong enough to nullify the rival wife's status as being permitted to the *yavam*. If, however, the betrothal whose status is uncertain took place first, then why would one assume the rival wife was permitted to the *yavam*? They explain that because the forbidden relative was originally single, and there is a doubt whether she lost this status, she maintains her presumed status as unmarried, and her rival wife cannot be rendered forbidden due to a betrothal whose status is uncertain (*Tosafot Yeshanim*).

A stringency that might bring about a leniency – חוּמְרָא דְּאָתֵי לִידֵי קוּלָּא: Often the Sages are stringent in places of doubt in order to prevent individuals from transgressing, and this is generally the reason for the tendency toward stringency. Occasionally, however, such as here, it is possible that stringency in one place will lead to a leniency in another. In such cases, it is best to leave the matter alone.

וְאִי נַמִּי זִימְנִין דְּאָתָא אַחֵר וּמְקַדֵּשׁ לָהּ לְדִידָהּ קִדּוּשֵׁי וַדַּאי, וְכֵיוָן דְּאָסַר לָהּ מָר לְצָרָה לְיִיבּוּמֵי, אָמְרִי: דְּקַמָּא – קִדּוּשִׁין וּדְבַתְרָא – לָאו קִדּוּשִׁין.

Alternatively, sometimes another man might come and betroth the forbidden relative **herself** with **a betrothal** whose status is **certain, and since the Master** rendered it **prohibited** for **the rival wife to enter into levirate marriage,** people would **say** that the betrothal **of the first** man, i.e., the deceased brother, was a fully effective **betrothal, and** that the betrothal **of the latter** man **was not** a valid **betrothal.** If she was married to the first man, then she is forbidden to the second as the man's wife, and betrothal cannot take effect with her. However, since the status of her betrothal to the first man was uncertain, then she is also considered possibly betrothed to the second man and would require a divorce from him as well. As a result, one can find a situation that would lead people to think that a man's wife is in fact permitted.

Perek **III**
Daf **31** Amud **a**

NOTES

All will know that this is merely a stringency – וּמֵידַע יָדְעִי דְּחוּמְרָא בְּעָלְמָא הוּא: The Rosh raises an objection: How would they know that this is a stringency? With regard to the case where there is a betrothal whose status is uncertain, if the rival wife is required to perform *ḥalitza* because she is not exempt from levirate marriage, it would be known that this is a stringent measure. With regard to divorce, however, they might think that the man is performing the *ḥalitza* simply because he does not wish to marry her for some other reason, and so there is no proof from here that there is a stringency involved. He resolves this by saying that Abaye is objecting to Rabba's line of reasoning, where it was suggested that requiring *ḥalitza* would constitute a stringency that could lead to a leniency. In that context it was clear that Rabba assumed that people were aware of why *ḥalitza* was being performed (*Tosefot HaRosh*).

If she performs *ḥalitza* she might also enter into levirate marriage – אִם חוֹלֶצֶת מִתְיַיבֶּמֶת: The following objection could be raised: Since in several places the Sages declared that a woman must perform *ḥalitza* due to some doubt, why did they not fear that she might mistakenly enter into levirate marriage in those cases as well? The commentaries resolve this by saying that if the concern and the doubt are general, then there is no reason to assume that they might make this mistake. Here, however, a new decree is being introduced by requiring *ḥalitza* for this woman, and therefore it is necessary to check that in fact all of the problems are solved thereby (*Yosef Lekaḥ*).

Let her enter into levirate marriage and there is no problem with that – תִּתְיַיבֵּם וְאֵין בְּכָךְ כְּלוּם: The talmudic discussion is as follows: Initially, the Gemara assumed that the concern lest she enter into levirate marriage was that this would nullify the rabbinic decree requiring the woman to perform *ḥalitza* in this case. This response indicates that the concern is not for the rabbinic ordinance, but rather for the status of the woman, and since here she is presumed permissible, there is no reason to be concerned lest she enter into levirate marriage (Ritva; see *Melo HaRo'im*).

כֵּיוָן דְּקָא מַצְרְכַתְּ חֲלִיצָה – מֵידַע יָדְעִי דְּחוּמְרָא בְּעָלְמָא הוּא. אִי הָכִי גֵּירוּשִׁין נַמִּי לִיתְנֵי, וְלִיצְרְכָהּ חֲלִיצָה, וּמֵידַע יָדְעִי דְּחוּמְרָא בְּעָלְמָא הוּא!

Rabba answered: **Since you require *ḥalitza*** and you do not exempt her completely, all will **know that this is merely a stringency**[N] and that the Sages did not decide with certitude that the first betrothal was fully valid. Consequently, they would not come to disregard the other betrothal. Abaye raised a challenge: **If so, let** the mishna **teach** the case where it is uncertain whether the item is closer to him or closer to her with regard to **divorce, and** stipulate **that she requires *ḥalitza*. And they would know that this is merely a stringency** and not make a mistake.

אִם אַתָּה אוֹמֵר חוֹלֶצֶת – מִתְיַיבֶּמֶת. הָכָא נַמִּי: אִם אַתָּה אוֹמֵר חוֹלֶצֶת – מִתְיַיבֶּמֶת! וְתִתְיַיבֵּם, וְאֵין בְּכָךְ כְּלוּם – אַחֲזָקָה קָא קַיְימָא.

He answered him: A mistake could in fact be made here, as, **if you say that she** must **perform *ḥalitza*** then **she** may also **enter into levirate marriage.** People might mistakenly think that if she is suitable for *ḥalitza* then she is also suitable for levirate marriage, and as a result the woman might enter into levirate marriage, despite the fact that it is forbidden for her to do so. Abaye objected: **Here too,** in the case of uncertain betrothal, the concern exists that **if you say that she performs *ḥalitza*** then **she** might also **enter into levirate marriage.**[N] Rabba answered: **So let her enter into levirate marriage, and** there is **no** problem **with that.**[N] In this instance **she remains with** her **presumptive status** as permitted because she was originally assumed to be permitted and was rendered forbidden only due to our concern. However, there would be no actual transgression involved even if she were to enter into levirate marriage.

אֵיתִיבֵיהּ אַבָּיֵי: נָפַל הַבַּיִת עָלָיו וְעַל בַּת אָחִיו, וְאֵין יָדוּעַ אֵיזֶה מֵהֶם מֵת רִאשׁוֹן – צָרָתָהּ חוֹלֶצֶת וְלֹא מִתְיַיבֶּמֶת.

Abaye raised an objection to Rabba by citing a case where even in places of doubt, the woman requires *ḥalitza*. As we learned in a mishna (67b): **A house fell on him,** on a certain man, **and on his brother's daughter** to whom this man was married, and he was childless, **and it is unknown which of them died first.** If the deceased wife had a rival wife, then **her rival wife** must **perform *ḥalitza* but may not enter into levirate marriage.** If the man had died first, then at the time of his death the rival wife was forbidden to the *yavam* as the rival wife of his daughter and exempt from levirate marriage. If, however, the daughter had died first, then at the time of the husband's death the second wife was not the rival wife of a forbidden relative, and requires levirate marriage. It is due to this doubt that she must perform *ḥalitza* and may not enter into levirate marriage.

אַמַּאי? הָכָא נַמִּי נֵימָא: אִשָּׁה זוֹ בְּחֶזְקַת הֶיתֵּר לַשּׁוּק עוֹמֶדֶת, וּמִסָּפֵק אַתָּה בָּא לְאוֹסְרָהּ – אַל תַּאַסְרֶנָּה מִסָּפֵק!

And according to Rabba's opinion, **why** is that so? **Here too, let us say: This woman,** the rival wife, **has the presumptive status of** being **permitted** to marry a man **from the general public.** This is because she was exempt from levirate marriage for the entire period of her marriage as the rival wife of a forbidden relative. **And due to the uncertainty** whether her rival wife was the first to die **you come to render her forbidden** and require that she perform *ḥalitza*. **Do not render her forbidden due to an uncertainty.**

וכי תימא: הכא נמי לחומרא – חומרא דאתי לידי קולא הוא, שאם אתה אומר חולצת – מתייבמת! גירושין דשכיחי גזרו בהו רבנן, מפולת דלא שכיחי – לא גזרו בהו רבנן.

And if you would say: Here too, we rule **more stringently** due to the uncertainty. Nevertheless, **this would be a stringency that brings about a leniency, for if you say that she must perform *ḥalitza*, she** may also **enter into levirate marriage.** However, it is forbidden for her to enter into levirate marriage, because she is possibly forbidden to the *yavam* as the rival wife of his daughter and therefore forbidden just like the daughter herself. Rabba replied: In cases of **divorce, which are common, the Sages issued a rabbinic decree** preventing her from performing *ḥalitza* due to a concern that if she were required to perform *ḥalitza* then she may enter into levirate marriage as well. In cases of **collapse, which are not common,**[N] **the Sages did not issue a rabbinic decree,** because they did not introduce decrees with regard to uncommon matters.

אי נמי: גירושין דקיימא ערוה דקא מוכח, וצרתה קמצרכת לה חליצה – אמרי: קמו ביה רבנן בגיטא דגיטא מעליא הוא, ואתו לייבומי לצרה. מפולת – מי קמו בהו רבנן במפולת?

Alternatively, there is another reason to differentiate between the cases. In the case of **divorce where there is a forbidden relative who indicates** that the rival wife is forbidden due to her status as the rival wife of a forbidden relative, **and you require that her rival wife perform *ḥalitza*,** people will say: **The Sages determined that this bill of divorce is a full-fledged bill of divorce.** Consequently, they required her rival wife to perform *ḥalitza*, **and** people **may come to consummate the levirate marriage with the rival wife** based on this mistaken assumption. In cases of **collapse,** however, **could the Sages have determined** who died first **in the collapse?** As it is known to all that there was a doubt that could not be clarified, it is clear that the Sages required the rival wife to perform *ḥalitza* only due to this uncertainty. Therefore, there is no concern that she would come to enter into levirate marriage because of this *ḥalitza*.

וגבי גירושין מי לא תנן? והתנן: היתה עומדת ברשות הרבים וזרקו לה, קרוב לה – מגורשת, קרוב לו – אינה מגורשת. מחצה על מחצה – מגורשת ואינה מגורשת.

The Gemara asks: **But did we not learn** in a mishna about the case where it is uncertain whether the bill of divorce is closer to him or closer to her **with regard to** situations of **divorce** whose status is uncertain? **And didn't we learn** in a mishna: In a case where his wife **was standing in the public domain and he threw her** the bill of divorce, if the bill landed **closer to her, she is divorced.** If it was **closer to him, she is not divorced.** If it was **half and half,** i.e., if the bill of divorce landed midway between the man and the woman, there is uncertainty whether **she is divorced or** whether **she is not divorced.**[H]

ואמרינן: למאי הלכתא – דאי כהן הוא אסורה ליה, ואי ערוה היא – צרתה בעיא חליצה. ולא אמרינן שאם אתה אומר חולצת מתייבמת!

And we say: With regard to what *halakha*[N] was the ruling said that she is both divorced and not divorced? The Gemara explains that this affects two areas of *halakha*. The first is **that if** the man divorcing his wife **is a priest,** then his wife **is forbidden to him** due to the uncertainty that she may in fact be divorced through that bill of divorce. Consequently, he would then be unable to remarry her. The second ramification is that **if** the woman being divorced **was a forbidden relative** to her husband's brother, and her husband died childless, then **her rival wife would require *ḥalitza*.** The mishna indicates that in this type of divorce whose status is uncertain as well, the Sages require the rival wife to perform *ḥalitza*, and **we do not say that if you say** that she must **perform *ḥalitza*,** she may **enter into levirate marriage.** Here there is no such concern.

HALAKHA

A bill of divorce about which it is uncertain if it was closer to her – גט שספק קרוב לה: If a man and his wife were standing in the public domain, or in a domain that did not belong to either of them, and the husband threw her a bill of divorce, the *halakha* is as follows: If it was closer to her, she is divorced. If it was closer to him, she is not divorced. If it was midway between them, she is both divorced and not divorced. In such a case, if her husband was a priest she would be forbidden to him, and if she herself was a forbidden relative with regard to her brother-in-law, then her rival wife must perform *ḥalitza* and may not enter into levirate marriage (Rambam *Sefer Nashim, Hilkhot Geirushin* 5:13; *Shulḥan Arukh, Even HaEzer* 139:13).

NOTES

Cases of collapse, which are not common – מפולת דלא שכיחי: The Rashash raises an objection: If the Sages did not enact rabbinic decrees for matters that were not common, then why did they nevertheless issue a decree for the woman in this case, i.e., that she must perform *ḥalitza*? He responds that they decreed that she must perform *ḥalitza* for a different reason that is common: They were concerned that others might conclude that any time a forbidden relative dies, the rival wife does not require *ḥalitza*. In *Ḥiddushei Batra* this is resolved by the explanation that in cases where the woman's presumptive status cannot be conclusively determined, it cannot be relied upon with regard to Torah law. In this case, as there is no way to determine whether the rival wife was the rival wife of a forbidden relative at the time of death, her presumptive status cannot be relied upon and she must perform *ḥalitza*. However, the concern that others might mistakenly take her in levirate marriage is not commonplace, and therefore the Sages did not enact a decree on the basis of such a concern.

And we say: With regard to what *halakha* – ואמרינן למאי הלכתא: One could object to this interpretation of the mishna in light of the fact that it was asserted by the *amora'im*. How can the Gemara then object to Rabba, an *amora* himself, from their statement? In *Ḥiddushei Batra* the answer is given that perhaps this interpretation of the mishna was an authoritative tradition that had been passed down. *Arukh LaNer* writes that this interpretation could be deduced from the language of the mishna itself, since it does not state that she is a divorcée whose status is uncertain but rather that she is both divorced and not divorced, implying that the matter must be ruled stringently, as though she were both divorced and not divorced.

הָא אִיתְּמַר עֲלָהּ, רַבָּה וְרַב יוֹסֵף דְּאָמְרִי תַּרְוַויְיהוּ: הָכָא בִּשְׁתֵּי כִּיתֵּי עֵדִים עָסְקִינַן, אַחַת אוֹמֶרֶת: קָרוֹב לָהּ, וְאַחַת אוֹמֶרֶת: קָרוֹב לוֹ, דַּהֲוָה לֵיהּ סְפֵיקָא דְּאוֹרַיְיתָא. וּמַתְנִיתִין דְּהָכָא בְּכַת אַחַת, דַּהֲוָה לֵיהּ סְפֵיקָא דְּרַבָּנַן.

The Gemara responds: **But wasn't it stated with regard to** that mishna that this is referring to a very specific set of circumstances? It is **Rabba and Rav Yosef who both say:** The doubt here does not result from the facts of the case themselves, but from conflicting testimonies and an inability to decide between them. **Here, we are dealing with two sets of witnesses, one** of which **says** that the bill fell **closer to her, and one** of which **says** that it fell **closer to him. This,** then, **is an uncertainty** in matters **of Torah** law, for in this case there are two testimonies, each one complete by itself, yet they contradict one another. Such instances are deemed to have the status of an uncertainty with regard to Torah law, and therefore the ruling is stringent. **But the mishna here is referring to one set**[N] of witnesses who were divided in their testimony or who could not clarify exactly what had occurred. **This is** considered to be **an uncertainty** in matters **of rabbinic** law[N] alone, as there is only a single uncorroborated testimony, and in cases of uncertainty in matters of rabbinic law the ruling is lenient.

וּמִמַּאי דְּמַתְנִיתִין דְּהָכָא בְּכַת אַחַת? דּוּמְיָא דְּקִדּוּשִׁין, מַה קִּדּוּשִׁין בְּכַת אַחַת – אַף גֵּירוּשִׁין בְּכַת אַחַת. וְקִדּוּשִׁין גּוּפַיְיהוּ מִמַּאי דִּבְכַת אַחַת, דִּלְמָא בִּשְׁתֵּי כִּיתֵּי עֵדִים? אִי בִּשְׁתֵּי כִּיתֵּי עֵדִים – תִּתְיַיבֵּם, וְאֵין בְּכָךְ כְּלוּם.

The Gemara asks: **And from where** is it known **that the mishna here** is referring to a case of uncertainty **with one set** of witnesses? The Gemara responds: **It is similar to that of betrothal. Just as** with regard to **betrothal** it is referring to a case of uncertainty **with one set of witnesses, so too,** with regard to **divorce** it is referring to a case **of one set** of witnesses. The Gemara wonders: **And** with regard to **betrothal itself, from where** is it known that the mishna is referring to a case of uncertainty **that** involves **one set** of witnesses? **Perhaps** it is referring to a case **of two sets** of witnesses? The Gemara answers: **If** the mishna is referring to a case **of two sets of witnesses** who contradict one another, then **let her enter into levirate marriage, and there is no** problem **with that,** as there are two witnesses testifying that there was never a betrothal. Therefore, both the cases of betrothal and divorce must be referring to a situation where there is one set of witnesses.

קַיְימִי עֵדִים וְקָאָמְרִי "קָרוֹב לָהּ" וְאַתְּ אָמְרַתְּ תִּתְיַיבֵּם וְאֵין בְּכָךְ כְּלוּם?! וְתוּ: בִּשְׁתֵּי כִּיתֵּי עֵדִים נַמִי סְפֵיקָא דְּרַבָּנַן הִיא, דְּאָמְרִינַן: אוֹקֵי תְּרֵי לְבַהֲדֵי תְּרֵי, וְאִשָּׁה אוֹקְמָהּ אַחֲזָקָה.

The Gemara challenges: How can one say that? After all, **there are witnesses who are standing** before us **and saying** that the object of betrothal fell **closer to her.** Accordingly, she was betrothed and her rival wife is the rival wife of a forbidden relative. **And** yet **you say to let her enter into levirate marriage and** there is **no** problem **with that? And furthermore,** with regard to the fundamental difference between two pairs of witnesses and a single pair, the case **of two pairs of witnesses is also** considered an **uncertainty** in matters of **rabbinic** law. This is not considered to be uncertainty with regard to the reality of what actually happened, which would be a case of uncertainty in matters of Torah law, but rather a contradiction between two opposing testimonies. In these cases **we say: Place two** witnesses **against two**[N] witnesses, and let the two testimonies cancel each other out. Therefore, the *halakha* would be to **let the woman remain in her original presumptive status.** Accordingly, this type of uncertainty stems only from rabbinic law and not from Torah law.

מִידֵּי דַּהֲוָה אַנִּכְסֵי דְּבַר שְׁטְיָא. דְּבַר שְׁטְיָא זַבֵּין נִכְסֵי, אָתוּ בֵּי תְּרֵי וְאָמְרִי: כְּשֶׁהוּא חָלִים זַבֵּין, וַאֲתוּ בֵּי תְּרֵי וְאָמְרוּ: כְּשֶׁהוּא שׁוֹטֶה זַבֵּין. וַאֲמַר רַב אַשִׁי: אוֹקֵי תְּרֵי לַהֲדֵי תְּרֵי

The Gemara cites a proof for this: This is **just as it is in** the case **concerning the property of** a man named **Bar Shatya,**[HB] who was referred to by this name because he would occasionally go insane. The case is as follows: **Bar Shatya sold property. Two** witnesses **came** forward **and said that he sold** it **when** he was **healthy** and therefore the sale was valid. **And two** others **came** forward **and said that he sold** it **when** he was **insane,** and so the sale was void. **Rav Ashi said** with regard to this matter: **Place two** witnesses **against two** witnesses and let the testimonies cancel each other out. As there is no valid testimony to rely on,

NOTES

The mishna…is referring to one set – מַתְנִיתִין...בְּכַת אַחַת: The commentaries have differing opinions as to what is meant by uncertainty with one set of witnesses. According to Rashi and those who follow his opinion, this is a case where one witness says that the bill of divorce was closer to him and one witness says that it was closer to her. According to Rabbeinu Ḥananel and the Rashba, the witnesses themselves are uncertain with regard to the facts (see *Beit Shmuel* and the later commentaries).

Uncertainty in matters of Torah law…uncertainty in matters of rabbinic law – סְפֵיקָא דְּאוֹרַיְיתָא...סְפֵיקָא דְּרַבָּנַן: In cases of uncertainties that arise either because the exact circumstances cannot be ascertained or because no clear halakhic decision has emerged, the principle is: In cases of Torah law, one adopts the stringent practice; in cases of rabbinic law, one adopts the lenient practice.

Place two against two – אוֹקֵי תְּרֵי לְבַהֲדֵי תְּרֵי: Although it seems here that the Gemara concludes that whenever two witnesses contradict another two witnesses it is considered an uncertainty in matters of rabbinic law, there are nevertheless those who disagree with this opinion and hold that this is considered a case of uncertainty in matters of Torah law. There are also those who differentiate between cases of prohibitions and monetary cases. The basis for this debate lies primarily in the question of whether both testimonies, despite the contradiction between them, nevertheless negate fully the previously existing presumptions altogether, or perhaps, since there is no definitive testimony on the matter, the original presumption remains in place (see *Derush VeḤiddush* on marriage contracts).

HALAKHA

The property of Bar Shatya – נִכְסֵי דְּבַר שְׁטְיָא: With regard to one who is sometimes sane and sometimes insane, when he is sane he is like a fully responsible agent for all matters, and all of his actions are binding. When he is insane, all of his actions are null and void.

If two witnesses come forth and say that he made a sale while insane, and two others testify that he made the sale while sane, any real estate remains in the possession of the seller, and movable property remains in the possession of the possessor (Rema, in accordance with *Tosafot* and Rosh; Rambam *Sefer Kinyan, Hilkhot Mekhira* 29:5; *Shulḥan Arukh, Ḥoshen Mishpat* 235:21).

BACKGROUND

Bar Shatya – בַּר שְׁטְיָא: Bar Shatya was a man who suffered from a psychological ailment that caused him to suffer periodic fits, but who nevertheless had his wits about him between bouts. In other words, he was sometimes sane and sometimes insane. With some of these ailments the fits occur with relative regularity, and with some they are caused by specific circumstances, but there can most certainly be periods when the individual is sane, lacking any abnormalities in his behavior whatsoever. It is for this reason that the *halakha* concludes that at times of sanity he is considered a normal individual, both with regard to his obligation to fulfill mitzvot and the legal validity of his actions. However, since the bouts of insanity occur at various times, and not always in a manner that is immediately recognizable to all, it is important to determine his mental state at the relevant times in order to ascertain the legal validity of specific actions.

וְאַרְעָא אוֹקְמָא בְּחֶזְקַת בַּר שַׁטְיָא.

let the land remain in the possession of Bar Shatya. Since no substantiated proof was brought forth, the land remains in the hands of its current possessor. As such, the same should be true with regard to cases of betrothal and divorce whose status is uncertain; the woman should remain in her former presumptive status.

אֶלָּא אָמַר אַבַּיֵי: ״יַגִּיד עָלָיו רֵיעוֹ״; תָּנָא בְּקִידּוּשִׁין – וְהוּא הַדִּין לְגֵירוּשִׁין, תָּנָא בְּגֵירוּשִׁין – וְהוּא הַדִּין לְקִידּוּשִׁין.

Rather, Rabba's understanding of the mishna must be rejected, and **Abaye said:** The mishna should be understood according to that which is written: **"His fellow speaks of him"** (Job 36:33). This principle teaches that a related case can be inferred from the single case cited. The mishna **teaches** the case where it is uncertain whether the item is closer to him or closer to her **with regard to betrothal, and the same is true with regard to divorce** if it is uncertain whether the bill of divorce fell closer to him or closer to her. Similarly, the mishna **teaches** the case of bills that were written in a questionable manner **with regard to divorce, and the same is true with regard to betrothal.**

אֲמַר לֵיהּ רָבָא: אִי יַגִּיד עָלָיו רֵיעוֹ – מַאי ״זֶהוּ״ דְּקָתָנֵי?

Rava said to him: If you understand that the legal ruling in all of these cases is the same, and the mishna was written in the style of: **His fellow speaks of him,**[N] then **what is** the meaning of the term: **This is, that** the mishna **teaches?** The mishna in fact emphasizes that this is a betrothal whose status is uncertain and this is a divorce whose status is uncertain, which indicates this case alone and no other.

אֶלָּא אָמַר רָבָא: כׇּל שֶׁיֵּשׁ בְּקִידּוּשִׁין – יֵשׁ בְּגֵירוּשִׁין, וְיֵשׁ בְּגֵירוּשִׁין מַה שֶּׁאֵין בְּקִידּוּשִׁין. וְ״זֶהוּ״ דְּגֵירוּשִׁין לָאו דַּוְקָא, אֶלָּא מִשּׁוּם דְּתָנָא ״זֶהוּ״ בְּקִידּוּשִׁין – תָּנָא נָמֵי ״זֶהוּ״ בְּגֵירוּשִׁין. וְ״זֶהוּ״ דְּקִידּוּשִׁין לְמַעוּטֵי מַאי? לְמַעוּטֵי זְמַן, דְּלֵיכָּא בְּקִידּוּשִׁין.

Rather, Rava said: All of the cases **that exist with regard to betrothal** whose status is uncertain **exist** in cases **of divorce** as well. However, **there are** some cases of uncertainty **with regard to divorce that do not exist with regard to betrothal,** as betrothal performed with a questionable bill is not disqualified. Accordingly, the term: **This is,** utilized in the mishna **with regard to divorce, is not specific** and does not imply exclusion of the case where it is possibly closer to him and possibly closer to her. **Rather, because** the mishna **teaches** the ruling of: **This is, with regard to betrothal,** where it is specific **it teaches** the phrase: **This is, with regard to divorce as well.** The Gemara asks: **And what does** the phrase: **This is,** mentioned **with regard to betrothal,** come **to exclude?** The Gemara answers: **It** comes **to exclude** the matter of the **date, which is not** essential **with regard to betrothal,** as when one betroths a woman by means of a document the date need not be written.

וּמִפְּנֵי מָה לֹא תִּקְּנוּ זְמַן בְּקִידּוּשִׁין? הָנִיחָא לְמַאן דְּאָמַר מִשּׁוּם פֵּירֵי – אֲרוּסָה לֵית לַהּ פֵּירֵי.

The Gemara asks about this matter itself: **And for what** reason **did they not institute** that **the date** must be included **in the betrothal** document? **This** policy **works out well according to the one who says** that the reason the Sages instituted that the date must be written on a bill of divorce **is due to the profits.** As the husband receives the profits from the wife's properties during the period of their marriage, it was necessary to write a date on the bill of divorce in order to know at what point his right to receive or sell these items was terminated. However, it was not necessary to include a date on a deed of betrothal, as this document serves only to create a bond of betrothal, **and there are no profits from a betrothed woman.**[H] A husband does not have the right to receive profits from his betrothed's property until she is his full-fledged wife.

NOTES

If it was written in the style of his fellow speaks of him, etc. – **אִי יַגִּיד עָלָיו רֵיעוֹ וכו׳**: *Tosafot* suggest a different difficulty with this solution: If the Gemara was using this style, it could have listed all the examples in the context of the first betrothal, and only one in the context of divorce. Similarly, the Rivan points out that Abaye was not precise in his explanation of the mishna, because according to all opinions there is no requirement to include the date in betrothals, and therefore it is clear that not all matters stated with regard to divorce are relevant to cases of betrothal. These issues can be resolved by suggesting that the Gemara raised only a single difficulty among several possible difficulties that could have been raised.

HALAKHA

There are no profits from a betrothed woman – **אֲרוּסָה לֵית לַהּ פֵּירֵי**: The husband receives the profits from his wife's property following their marriage, but not the profits from the property of a woman to whom he was only betrothed (Rambam *Sefer Nashim*, *Hilkhot Ishut* 12:1, 3; *Shulḥan Arukh*, *Even HaEzer* 69:1, 3).

HALAKHA

Due to the daughter of his sister – **מִשּׁוּם בַּת אֲחוֹתוֹ**: The Sages instituted that one must include the date of the writing in the bill of divorce just as in other legal documents. This is in order that he not come to cover for his wife if she were licentious, giving her an undated bill so that she might claim that her misdeeds took place after she received the bill of divorce (Rambam *Sefer Nashim, Hilkhot Geirushin* 1:24; *Shulḥan Arukh, Even HaEzer* 127:1).

אֶלָּא לְמַאן דְּאָמַר מִשּׁוּם בַּת אֲחוֹתוֹ – לִיתַקֵּין זְמַן!

However, according to the one who says that the Sages instituted the requirement of including the date in the bill of divorce **due to** a case where a man is married to **the daughter of his sister,**[HN] then **they should institute** that he must include **the date** in a deed of betrothal as well. Occasionally a man might marry the daughter of his sister, whom he loves all the more because she is his close relative in addition to being his wife. If he knows that she acted licentiously while she was married to him, he might grant her a bill of divorce without a date so as to save her from the death penalty. Were witnesses to come forth and testify to her behavior, she could claim that at the time of her licentious act she was already a divorced woman. If this was indeed the reason for the Sages' instituting the requirement of including the date in a bill of divorce, then the date should be included in a deed of betrothal as well, for an undated document of betrothal could be utilized equally well to prove the innocence of the daughter of his sister. If she acted licentiously in the period prior to her betrothal, she would not be penalized. Therefore, the date should be written on this document as well.

מִשּׁוּם דְּאִיכָּא דִּמְקַדֵּשׁ בְּכַסְפָּא וְאִיכָּא דִּמְקַדֵּשׁ בִּשְׁטָרָא – לָא תְּקוּן רַבָּנַן זְמַן.

The Gemara answers: **Because there are those who betroth by means of money and those who betroth by means of a deed,**[N] **the Sages did not institute** that **the date** must be written in the document. As the date of the betrothal has no place in the act of betrothal by means of money, the Sages did not distinguish between the various modes of betrothal.

אֲמַר לֵיהּ רַב אַחָא בְּרֵיהּ דְּרַב יוֹסֵף לְרַב אָשֵׁי: וְהָא עַבְדָּא, דְּאִיכָּא דְּקָנֵי בְּכַסְפָּא וְאִיכָּא בִּשְׁטָרָא, וּתְקוּן רַבָּנַן זְמַן! הָתָם רוּבָּא בִּשְׁטָרָא, הָכָא – רוּבָּא בְּכַסְפָּא.

Rav Aḥa, son of Rav Yosef, said to Rav Ashi: But with regard to **a slave,**[N] **where there are** those **who acquire** them **with money and there are** those who acquire them **with a deed, the Sages** nevertheless **instituted** that **the date** must be written in a slave's deed of purchase. He responded: **There,** with regard to slaves, **the majority** of people purchase them **by means of a deed. Here,** with regard to betrothal, **the majority** of people perform betrothal **by means of money.**

אִיבָּעֵית אֵימָא: מִשּׁוּם דְּלָא אֶפְשָׁר. הֵיכִי לִיעֲבֵיד? לִינְחָה גַּבֵּי דִּידַהּ – מַחְקָה לֵיהּ. לִינְחָה גַּבֵּי דִּידֵיהּ – זִמְנִין דְּבַת אֲחוֹתוֹ הִיא, וּמְחַפֶּה עֲלַהּ.

If you wish, say a different reason why the Sages did not institute that the date must be included in a deed of betrothal. This is **due to** the fact that **it is not possible** to institute this in a manner that will ensure that no problems will result. **How would we do** this? If **we leave** the deed of betrothal **with her, she will erase** the date, and so it would remain impossible to prove the juncture at which her licentious behavior took place. If **we leave** the deed **with him,** then **there are times when she is his sister's daughter and he might cover for her** by erasing the date himself.

NOTES

Due to the daughter of his sister – **מִשּׁוּם בַּת אֲחוֹתוֹ**: Marriage to any relative, and not only to the daughter of one's sister, is cause for concern in this regard, because a man is apt to show additional favor to her since she is part of his family. Moreover, since she is his relative, he may wish to save his family from disgrace and would therefore tend to cover for her misbehavior (see Rivan). The daughter of his sister was mentioned specifically because the Sages recommended marrying the daughter of one's sister, and therefore this phenomenon was relatively common.

There are those who betroth by means of money and those who betroth by means of a deed – **אִיכָּא דִּמְקַדֵּשׁ בְּכַסְפָּא וְאִיכָּא דִּמְקַדֵּשׁ בִּשְׁטָרָא**: There are three ways of betrothing a woman. The first is with money or its equivalent, such as a ring, which the bridegroom gives to the bride. The second is with a document in which he attests that he is betrothing the woman. The third is by engaging in sexual intercourse for the explicit purpose of betrothal. The third method, though legally valid, was banned by the Sages to prevent licentiousness.

But with regard to a slave – **וְהָא עַבְדָּא**: Rashi and those who follow his line of reasoning comment that the issue being discussed is the deed of purchase for a slave, and the date is required in order to know at what moment ownership of all of the slave's possessions was transferred to his master. According to this opinion, the reasoning applies not only to the case of a slave but also to all deeds of purchase. This interpretation is supported by the use of the term: Who acquire.

However, *Tosafot* and most other early commentaries object to this interpretation for various reasons. They explain that the issue at hand is a slave's bill of release, which requires a date in order to determine at what point he is allowed to marry a Jewish woman, or at what point a maidservant would be allowed to marry a Jew. Indeed, the master might have an interest in covering for children born to his slave so as to render them eligible for marriage. These commentaries interpret the word: Acquisition, as referring to the slave acquiring himself, i.e., acquiring his freedom, despite the linguistic difficulties with such a reading.

לִינְחָה גַּבֵּי עֵדִים, אִי דִּזְכִירִי – לֵיתוּ לִיסְהוּד, וְאִי לָא – זִמְנִין דְּחָזוּ מִכְּתָבָא, וַאֲתוּ מְסַהֲדִי. וְרַחֲמָנָא אָמַר: ״מִפִּיהֶם״, וְלֹא מִפִּי כְּתָבָם.

If **we leave it with the witnesses** who signed the document, **if they remember** themselves the date when the deed was given to the woman, the date need not be written in the document itself, for **let them come forth and testify** from their memory. **And if** they do **not** remember by themselves, then **there are times when they see** the date **that is written and come forth to testify**[N] on that basis. **And the Merciful One states:** "By the mouth of two witnesses, or at the mouth of three witnesses, shall a matter be established" (Deuteronomy 19:15). From this verse it is derived: **From their mouths, and not from their writings,**[NH] indicating that testimony is proper only if the individual stated it of himself, and not on the basis of what is written.

– אִי הָכִי בְּגֵירוּשִׁין נַמִּי נֵימָא הָכִי! הָתָם לְהַצָּלָה דִּידָהּ קָאָתֵי, הָכָא – לְחוֹבָה דִּידָהּ קָאָתֵי.

The Gemara asks: **If that is so, let us say that with regard to divorce as well.** In cases of divorce there should also be a concern lest the woman erase the date on the bill of divorce in her possession. The Gemara responds: **There,** in the case of a bill of divorce, the date **comes to save her,**[N] since the bill of divorce removes her status as a man's wife. She therefore would fear erasing anything lest she disqualify the bill altogether, thereby possibly rendering herself a married woman again (Ramban). **Here,** however, when dealing with a deed of betrothal, the date **comes to her disadvantage,** since until now she was presumed to be a single woman, and if there is no date on the document then she clearly cannot be punished.

מתני׳ שְׁלֹשָׁה אַחִין, נְשׂוּאִין שָׁלֹשׁ נָכְרִיּוֹת, וּמֵת אֶחָד מֵהֶן, וְעָשָׂה בָּהּ הַשֵּׁנִי מַאֲמָר וָמֵת – הֲרֵי אֵלּוּ חוֹלְצוֹת וְלֹא מִתְיַיבְּמוֹת.

MISHNA In the case of **three brothers** who **were married to three unrelated women,**[N] **and one of the brothers died,** the following occurred: **The second** brother **performed levirate betrothal with** the wife of the deceased brother **and** before he was able to consummate the levirate marriage **he died** as well, leaving behind two women who happen before the third brother for levirate marriage. **Then those** two women must **perform *ḥalitza* and may not enter into levirate marriage.**

שֶׁנֶּאֱמַר ״וּמֵת אֶחָד מֵהֶן יְבָמָהּ יָבֹא עָלֶיהָ״ שֶׁעָלֶיהָ זִיקַת יָבָם אֶחָד וְלֹא שֶׁעָלֶיהָ זִיקַת שְׁנֵי יְבָמִין. רַבִּי שִׁמְעוֹן אוֹמֵר: מְיַיבֵּם לְאֵיזוֹ שֶׁיִּרְצֶה, וְחוֹלֵץ לַשְּׁנִיָּה.

As it is stated: "If brothers dwell together **and one of them dies** and he has no child, the wife of the dead man shall not be married outside of the family to one not of his kin; **her brother-in-law will have intercourse with her**" (Deuteronomy 25:5). This teaches that a woman eligible for levirate marriage is one **who has one levirate relationship and not one who has a double levirate relationship.**[NH] In this case, the wife of the first deceased brother requires levirate marriage due to both the marriage with her first husband as well as the levirate betrothal with the second brother. **Rabbi Shimon says: He** may **consummate the levirate marriage with whichever** woman **he wishes and then perform *ḥalitza* with the second.**

NOTES

They see what is written and come forth to testify – חָזוּ מִכְּתָבָא וַאֲתוּ מְסַהֲדִי: Some early commentaries ask: Why not leave the document with the witnesses who signed it and let its validity be established by the ratification of legal documents, just as would happen with any other bill? See *Tosefot HaRosh*, who explains why there is more reason for concern here than with other documents. The Rashba writes that since this document is not ratified in the usual manner and it merely serves as a form of reminder, the *halakhot* relevant to other bills do not apply to it. The Meiri explains that the ratification of a document is legally sufficient only in monetary cases; in cases involving prohibitions the Sages were reluctant to rely upon this.

From their mouths and not from their writings – מִפִּיהֶם וְלֹא מִפִּי כְּתָבָם: There are several different opinions among the early commentaries as to how to understand this ruling, as well as how to understand the principle that any document that has had the signatures of the witnesses confirmed is considered valid, regardless of whether the witnesses themselves remember the testimony.

The reason that written testimony is invalid depends on how one views its role. According to Rashi and the Razah, since a bill of debt is not written without the borrower's explicit knowledge, its validity does not rest upon what is written by the witnesses but rather upon the statement of obligation expressed by the one who wrote the document. According to the Ramban, however, testimony written as a deed falls under a legal category of its own, and is considered as though the testimony were checked and affirmed by the court. Therefore, the disqualification of written testimony expressed by the principle of: From their mouths, applies only in cases where there is no legal document.

In the opinion of Rabbeinu Tam, the disqualification of: From their mouths, applies only where the witnesses are incapable of testifying orally, but if they are capable of testifying, then their testimony is admissible in written form as well. The Rambam is of the opinion that according to Torah law there is no legal validity to written testimony, but the Sages nevertheless ordained that validity of documents could be legally established by the signatures of witnesses (see Rif and his commentaries; *Tosafot*; Ramban).

It comes to save her – לְהַצָּלָה דִּידָהּ קָאָתֵי: Most of the commentaries explain according to the opinion of *Tosafot*, who hold that since the bill of divorce renders her an unmarried woman, she is fearful that if she erases any part of it, it might be disqualified. This is not the case with a deed of betrothal, which renders her a married woman. The same explanation is mentioned by the Ramban, Rashba, and the Ritva. See also Rashi's interpretation.

Married to three unrelated women – נְשׂוּאִין שָׁלֹשׁ נָכְרִיּוֹת: The early commentaries, among them the Rivan, point out that the *tanna* could have taught here that one of the brothers was single, as the marital status of the third brother does not impact the *halakha*. The *Tiferet Yisrael* explains that because the status of the third brother has no legal implications, the *tanna* opted to teach this in the most concise fashion.

A double levirate relationship – זִיקַת שְׁנֵי יְבָמִין: The early commentaries remark that this really means that she requires two levirate marriages and not a levirate bond with two *yevamin*. The concern here is that she has two levirate obligations from two different husbands, which is referred to in other sources as: A wife of two deceased men.

HALAKHA

From their mouths and not from their writings – מִפִּיהֶם וְלֹא מִפִּי כְּתָבָם: By Torah law, in monetary cases, and all the more so in capital cases, testimony is inadmissible unless it is received orally from the witnesses. It may not be handwritten. If their testimony is sent to the court in written form it is inadmissible.

The *Sma* states that it is customary to receive written testimony when the witnesses remember and are fit for oral testimony (see *Tosafot*, Rosh, *Tur*, and Mordekhai). In the opinion of the Rambam, in cases where the witnesses are signed on a document and they come to the court and confirm their signatures but state that they do not recall the event itself, the document is ruled invalid. *Tosafot* and others disagree and hold that their signatures are efficacious in this case. Even the later commentaries were divided over this matter: The Maharshal rules in accordance with *Tosafot*, while the *Shakh* rules in accordance with the Rambam (Rambam *Sefer Shofetim, Hilkhot Edut* 3:4, 8:5; *Shulḥan Arukh, Ḥoshen Mishpat* 28:11–12, 46:10).

A double levirate relationship – זִיקַת שְׁנֵי יְבָמִים: In the case of three brothers married to women who were not related to one another, if one brother died and his brother performed levirate betrothal with the deceased's wife but died prior to entering into marriage with her, then both the wife of the brother who died first as well as the wife of the brother who died second must perform *ḥalitza* and may not enter into levirate marriage. The Sages decreed that they may not enter into levirate marriage due to a concern lest others come to consummate the levirate marriage with two women from a single household (Rambam *Sefer Nashim, Hilkhot Yibbum* 7:27; *Shulḥan Arukh, Even HaEzer* 174:4).

גמ׳ וְאִי זִיקַת שְׁנֵי יְבָמִין דְּאוֹרַיְיתָא, חֲלִיצָה נַמִּי לָא תִּיבָּעֵי! אֶלָּא מִדְּרַבָּנַן, וּגְזֵירָה שֶׁמָּא יֹאמְרוּ שְׁתֵּי יְבָמוֹת הַבָּאוֹת מִבַּיִת אֶחָד מִתְיַיבְּמוֹת.

GEMARA The Gemara asks: **If** the *halakha* that a woman who has **a double levirate relationship** is exempt from levirate marriage is **by Torah** law, as indicated by the proof offered in the mishna, **she should not require *ḥalitza* as well,** but be completely exempt. **Rather,** it is **by rabbinic** law. The restriction on levirate marriage in this case is not by Torah law, as by Torah law the brother is allowed to consummate the levirate marriage with both of these women since each was the wife of a different brother. The requirement for *ḥalitza* in this case was instituted as a rabbinic **decree lest** people **say**[N] that **two *yevamot* who come from a single household can enter into levirate marriage.** Since the second brother had performed levirate betrothal, people might come to think that both were actually married to him. If the third brother consummates the levirate marriage with both women, it would lead people to think that it is permitted to take two of a brother's wives in levirate marriage, when in fact the Torah allows the *yavam* to marry only a single wife of the deceased.

וְנִיַיבֵּם לַחֲדָא וְנִיחְלוֹץ לַחֲדָא! גְּזֵירָה שֶׁמָּא יֹאמְרוּ: בַּיִת אֶחָד, מִקְצָתוֹ בָּנוּי

The Gemara asks: **So let him consummate the levirate marriage with one** woman **and perform *ḥalitza* with** the other **one,** and this would eliminate our concern. The Gemara responds: We do not do this due to a rabbinic **decree lest they say:** When there are two women from **a single household, part of it** must **be built**

NOTES

A rabbinic decree lest people say – גְּזֵירָה שֶׁמָּא יֹאמְרוּ: This explanation of the ruling in the mishna is difficult, as the mishna explicitly states that the reason for this ruling is due to a double levirate bond and not due to a rabbinic decree. This can be resolved by explaining that the primary question of the Gemara is not about this woman, but rather about her rival wife. If the woman with a double levirate bond is not eligible for levirate marriage, then why is her rival wife not exempt from the obligation of *ḥalitza* as the rival wife of a forbidden relative?

The Gemara therefore answers that the prohibition proscribing the woman in the mishna is due to a rabbinic decree. Based on this assertion, the Gemara asks: If the woman is prohibited based on a rabbinic decree, why does the rival wife require *ḥalitza* as well, as the rival wife of a woman prohibited due to a mitzva is generally permitted to enter into levirate marriage? Consequently, they state that there is an additional decree requiring the rival wife to perform *ḥalitza*, and accordingly the suggestion: Let him enter into levirate marriage with one, in fact means that he should take the rival wife in levirate marriage and perform *ḥalitza* with the wife of the first brother (*Melo HaRo'im*).

Perek **III**
Daf **32** Amud **a**

וּמִקְצָתוֹ חָלוּץ.

and part of it must **be released by *ḥalitza*.** That is, if two women were married to a single man, one of these women must enter into levirate marriage and the other must perform *ḥalitza*.

וְיֹאמְרוּ! אִי דְּמִיַּיבֵּם וַהֲדַר – חָלֵיץ הָכִי נַמִּי,

The Gemara wonders: **So let them say** it. Why would it be problematic if people thought that? Even were they to act upon this mistaken assumption it would cause no harm, as there is no transgression involved in performing *ḥalitza*. The Gemara answers: **If he were to consummate the levirate marriage** with one and then later **proceed to perform *ḥalitza***[N] with the other, then **indeed** there would be no reason for concern.

אֶלָּא גְּזֵירָה דִּילְמָא חָלֵיץ בְּרֵישָׁא וַהֲדַר מְיַיבֵּם, וְקָם לֵיהּ בְּ״אֲשֶׁר לֹא יִבְנֶה״, וְרַחֲמָנָא אָמַר: כֵּיוָן שֶׁלֹּא בָּנָה – שׁוּב לֹא יִבְנֶה.

Rather, the requirement to perform *ḥalitza* with both women is a rabbinic **decree** that was instituted **lest he first perform *ḥalitza***[N] with one of his brother's wives **and subsequently consummate the levirate marriage** with the other. Under such circumstances, he would in fact be violating a prohibition. Once he performs *ḥalitza* with the first woman **he is subject to** the prohibition indicated by the verse "So shall it be done to the man **who does not build** his brother's house" (Deuteronomy 25:9). In this verse **the Merciful One states** that **once he did not build** his brother's house but rather opted to perform *ḥalitza* with one of his brother's wives, **he may not proceed to build** it by consummating the levirate marriage with a different wife.

NOTES

If he were to consummate the levirate marriage and proceed to perform *ḥalitza* – אִי דְּמִיַּיבֵּם וַהֲדַר חָלֵיץ: From the commentaries it seems that this statement is referring to any case where two rival wives happen before a brother for levirate marriage, as there would be no harm were he to consummate the levirate marriage with one and then perform *ḥalitza* with the other. This is because there is no prohibition against performing *ḥalitza* that does not fulfill a mitzva. Rather, the rabbinic decree was ordained due to the possibility of reversing the order and performing the *ḥalitza* prior to consummating the levirate marriage. It is clear, however, from the words of the author of the *Halakhot Gedolot*, that he holds that the Gemara is referring specifically to a case involving both a wife of two deceased men and another woman, such that it would be permitted for him to consummate the levirate marriage with the rival wife first and then perform *ḥalitza* with the wife with whom levirate betrothal was performed. It is only in this case that the Sages issued a decree lest he first perform *ḥalitza* with the woman with whom levirate betrothal had been performed. It would seem that these two opinions are based on different textual versions of the Gemara.

A rabbinic decree lest he…perform *ḥalitza* – גְּזֵירָה דִּילְמָא חָלֵיץ: In the Jerusalem Talmud as well the question of why the rival wife should not enter into levirate marriage is raised, and there it states that the mishna follows Rabbi Meir's opinion, which establishes the principle: So long as you cannot take me in levirate marriage, you cannot take my rival wife in levirate marriage. Accordingly, in every case where one of the wives is forbidden to enter into levirate marriage, her rival wife is likewise forbidden.

אֲמַר רָבָא: נָתַן גֵּט לְמַאֲמָרוֹ – הוּתְּרָה צָרָתָהּ, אֲבָל הִיא אֲסוּרָה, דְּמִחַלְּפָה בְּבַעֲלַת גֵּט.

Rava said: If the brother who performed levirate betrothal in the case described in the mishna subsequently **gave a bill of divorce** to that wife in order to nullify **his levirate betrothal**[H] before he died, **her rival wife is rendered permitted**[N] to the third brother. The third brother is allowed to consummate the levirate marriage with the wife of the second brother because this wife is no longer considered to be the rival wife of a woman with a double levirate relationship. The bill of divorce serves to nullify the act of levirate betrothal completely. **However,** the woman with whom the brother performed levirate betrothal and then received the bill of divorce **is forbidden** to the third brother. Why is this? **She might be confused with** a woman **who receives a bill of divorce.** In general cases where levirate betrothal was not performed, if a man gives a *yevama* a bill of divorce, he is no longer allowed to consummate the levirate marriage with her. If it were permitted to consummate the levirate marriage in this case, people might mistakenly do so in other cases of divorce as well.

אִיכָּא דְּאָמְרִי, אֲמַר רָבָא: נָתַן גֵּט לְמַאֲמָרוֹ – הוּתְּרָה אֲפִילּוּ הִיא, מַאי טַעֲמָא? מַאי דַּעֲבַד בָּהּ – שְׁקַלֵיהּ.

There are those **who say** an alternative formulation of Rava's statement. **Rava said:** If the second brother **gave a bill of divorce** to the wife of the first deceased brother in order to nullify **his levirate betrothal** to her, then **even she** herself **is permitted**[N] to enter into levirate marriage with the third brother. **What is the reason** for this? **That which he performed with her, he removed.** The levirate betrothal was completely nullified by the bill of divorce, and it is as though he had done nothing at all. Therefore, as far as the third brother is concerned, she remains with her original, single levirate bond, as though her status had never been changed by the second brother.

מתני׳ שְׁנֵי אַחִין נְשׂוּאִין שְׁתֵּי אֲחָיוֹת, וּמֵת אֶחָד מֵהֶן, וְאַחַר כָּךְ מֵתָה אִשְׁתּוֹ שֶׁל שֵׁנִי – הֲרֵי זוֹ אֲסוּרָה עָלָיו עוֹלָמִית, הוֹאִיל וְנֶאֶסְרָה עָלָיו שָׁעָה אַחַת.

MISHNA In the case where **two brothers were married to two sisters,**[HB] and one of the brothers **died,** the widow at this point would be exempt from levirate marriage as the sister of his wife. **And afterward the wife of the second** brother **died.** Although the *yevama* is no longer the sister of his wife, **this woman is nevertheless forbidden to him forever, since she had** already **been forbidden to him at one time.**

HALAKHA

Gave a bill of divorce in order to nullify his levirate betrothal – נָתַן גֵּט לְמַאֲמָרוֹ: In the case where a woman whose husband died childless happened before the *yavam* for levirate marriage and he performed levirate betrothal but later gave her a bill of divorce explicitly nullifying that levirate betrothal, the levirate betrothal is null and void, and it is permitted for her to enter into levirate marriage with his brothers. However, as per Rashi and Rambam, it is not permitted for her to enter into levirate marriage with him. If this *yavam* died and she happened before a different brother, she is allowed to enter into levirate marriage and is not considered a wife of two deceased men, in accordance with the latter formulation of Rava, which generally signifies the definitive legal ruling (Rambam *Sefer Nashim, Hilkhot Yibbum* 6:29; *Shulḥan Arukh, Even HaEzer* 174:5).

Two brothers were married to two sisters – שְׁנֵי אַחִין נְשׂוּאִין שְׁתֵּי אֲחָיוֹת: If two brothers were married to two sisters and one of the brothers died, even if the surviving brother's wife later died, the first wife remains exempt from levirate marriage, because she was forbidden to him at one time, i.e., during her sister's life (Rambam *Sefer Nashim, Hilkhot Yibbum* 7:12; *Shulḥan Arukh, Even HaEzer* 175:1).

NOTES

Her rival wife is rendered permitted – הוּתְּרָה צָרָתָהּ: Most of the commentaries follow Rashi in understanding the term rival wife to refer to the full wife of the second brother, who by virtue of levirate betrothal became a rival wife of sorts to the wife of two deceased men. However, the Rashba, along with *Nimmukei Yosef*, holds that the term rival wife refers to her actual rival wife. The case would therefore be one where the first brother had two wives, one of whom received levirate betrothal and later a bill of divorce from the second brother, and the other was her rival wife. Rava's statement permitting the rival wife is referring to her actual rival wife.

Even she is permitted – הוּתְּרָה אֲפִילּוּ הִיא: The commentaries and legal authorities were in dispute over to whom, in fact, such a woman would be permitted. Some said that in cases where a *yavam* both performed levirate betrothal and gave a bill of divorce to a woman, she is even permitted to marry that *yavam*. As the levirate betrothal was completely canceled by the bill of divorce, she reverts to her status as a woman with whom he has a levirate bond (Rivan). Others say that she is never again permitted to the man who gave her the bill of divorce but she is permitted to the other brothers (Ramban).

The Ritva explains the difference between the two formulations of Rava's statement. According to the latter version, the prohibition against consummating the levirate marriage with the woman who received the bill of divorce is by rabbinic law. Consequently, the Sages did not institute a decree in the case where the bill of divorce was issued in order to rescind the levirate marriage, which would prevent the violation of another decree due to the possibility of confusion with a woman who only received a bill of divorce. According to the first formulation, however, no special distinction was made for the woman who received a bill of divorce after levirate betrothal, so that there is in fact only one single decree for all *yevamot* who received bills of divorce under any circumstances.

BACKGROUND

Two brothers and two sisters – שְׁנֵי אַחִין וּשְׁתֵּי אֲחָיוֹת: The brothers Reuven and Shimon married two sisters, Milka and Ḥogla, respectively. When Shimon died childless, his wife Ḥogla happened before Reuven for levirate marriage, but was rendered exempt from both levirate marriage and *ḥalitza*, as she was the sister of his wife Milka. Even were Milka to later die, Ḥogla would never again be permitted to Reuven.

NOTES

Where she is disassociated from this household, etc. – דְּקָא מִידַּחְיָא מֵהַאי בֵּיתָא וכו׳: It would seem that the opposite conclusion could have been drawn as well. The Gemara could have suggested that in the case at hand, the sister reverted to being eligible for levirate marriage during the original period in which she happened before this brother for levirate marriage, whereas in the case of two *yevamin*, she was forbidden to the *yavam* for the entire period following the death of her first husband. Accordingly, it would be more likely to render her permitted in this case. One must conclude that once she was rendered disqualified to enter into levirate marriage with the brother at one time during the period when she happened before the brothers as a forbidden relative, she can never again revert to a permitted status (Ritva).

For violating the prohibition against marrying a brother's wife and…a wife's sister – מִשּׁוּם אֵשֶׁת אָח וּמִשּׁוּם אֲחוֹת אִשָּׁה: Rashi explains that this refers to a case where the relations took place during his wife's lifetime, for then he would be liable to receive punishment for marrying a wife's sister. Rabbeinu Ḥananel, however, holds that the case here is the same as that of the mishna, i.e., a situation where the wife died. The early commentaries (Rashba) were perplexed by this opinion, for even though the language in the *Tosefta* seems to support Rabbeinu Ḥananel's interpretation, it is difficult to understand how he might be held liable to receive punishment for marrying his wife's sister after his wife's death (see Meiri).

גמ׳ פְּשִׁיטָא! הַשְׁתָּא, וּמַה הָתָם דְּלָא מִידַּחְיָא מֵהַאי בֵּיתָא לְגַמְרֵי – אָמְרַתְּ לָא, הָכָא דְּקָא מִידַּחְיָא מֵהַאי בֵּיתָא לְגַמְרֵי – לֹא כׇּל שֶׁכֵּן?! תָּנָא הָא תָּנָא בְּרֵישָׁא, וְהַדַר חֲזָיָא לְהֶיתֵּירָא וְשַׁרְיָא, וַהֲדַר חֲזָיָא לְאִיסּוּרָא. וְאַיְּידֵי דַּחֲבִיבָה לֵיהּ – אַקְדְּמַהּ, וּמִשְׁנָה לֹא זָזָה מִמְּקוֹמָהּ.

GEMARA The Gemara asks: **Isn't this obvious? Now, just as there,** in the earlier *mishnayot*, where there was a third brother and so the woman **was not disassociated from this household completely,** as the levirate obligation existed between her and the third brother to whom she was permitted, **you said** that **she may not** enter into levirate marriage because she was forbidden at one time, **here,** in the case of only two brothers, **where she is disassociated from this household**[N] **completely, is it not all the more so** clear that it should be prohibited for her to enter into levirate marriage? The Gemara answers: **The *tanna* taught this** mishna **at first,** at which time **he saw it** fitting to rule that **those** other cases are **permitted, and** therefore he **permitted them. And then he** subsequently **saw it** fitting to rule that **they are forbidden. And since** that case was novel, **it was beloved to him, he taught it earlier.** But despite the fact that this mishna was no longer necessary, **the mishna does not move from its place.**

תָּנוּ רַבָּנַן: בָּא עָלֶיהָ – חַיָּיב עָלֶיהָ מִשּׁוּם אֵשֶׁת אָח, וּמִשּׁוּם אֲחוֹת אִשָּׁה, דִּבְרֵי רַבִּי יוֹסֵי. רַבִּי שִׁמְעוֹן אוֹמֵר: אֵינוֹ חַיָּיב אֶלָּא מִשּׁוּם אֵשֶׁת אָח בִּלְבַד. וְהָא תַּנְיָא, רַבִּי שִׁמְעוֹן אוֹמֵר: אֵינוֹ חַיָּיב אֶלָּא מִשּׁוּם אֲחוֹת אִשָּׁה בִּלְבַד!

§ **The Sages taught:** If **he engaged in sexual intercourse** with this woman who was forbidden to him, **he is liable** to receive punishment **for** violating the prohibition against marrying **a brother's wife,** because she was never rendered permitted by the levirate mitzva, **and** he is liable to receive punishment **for** violating the prohibition against marrying **a wife's sister;**[N] this is **the statement of Rabbi Yosei. Rabbi Shimon says: He is liable** to receive punishment **only for** violating the prohibition proscribing **a brother's wife.** Rabbi Shimon holds that one prohibition does not take effect where another prohibition is already in place, and since she was already forbidden as his brother's wife, the additional prohibition cannot take effect. The Gemara asks: **But isn't it taught** in a *baraita*, **Rabbi Shimon says: He is liable only due to** the prohibition against marrying **a wife's sister?**

לָא קַשְׁיָא: כָּאן – שֶׁנָּשָׂא חַי וְאַחַר כָּךְ נָשָׂא מֵת, כָּאן – שֶׁנָּשָׂא מֵת וְאַחַר כָּךְ נָשָׂא חַי.

The Gemara answers: This is **not difficult. Here,** in the second *baraita*, it is referring to a case **where the living** brother **married** his wife first **and afterward the** brother who is now **deceased** married her sister. In that case, the first prohibition to take effect on the *yevama* was that of a wife's sister, and only later, when she was married to his now-deceased brother, did the additional prohibition proscribing a brother's wife take effect. **There,** in the first *baraita*, it is referring to a case **where the** brother who is now **deceased married** his wife first, whereby she became forbidden to the brother as a brother's wife, **and afterward the living** brother **married** her sister, rendering her forbidden as his wife's sister as well.

וְרַבִּי שִׁמְעוֹן, הֵיכָא דְּנָשָׂא מֵת וְאַחַר כָּךְ נָשָׂא חַי, כֵּיוָן דְּאִיסּוּר אֲחוֹת אִשָּׁה לָא חָיֵיל – תִּתְיַיבֵּם יַבּוּמֵי!

The Gemara asks: **And** according to the opinion of **Rabbi Shimon,** in a case **where the deceased** brother **married** one of the sisters first, in which case she was forbidden to his brother as a brother's wife, **and afterward the living** brother **married** her sister, the only prohibition in place is that of a brother's wife. Therefore, **since the prohibition** with regard to **a wife's sister never took effect,** then after her husband died **she should** now **enter into levirate marriage.** As the prohibition proscribing a brother's wife is canceled in the face of the levirate mitzva, she should indeed enter into levirate marriage.

אֲמַר רַב אַשִׁי: אִיסּוּר אֲחוֹת אִשָּׁה מִיתְלָא תָּלֵי וְקָאֵי, אִי פָּקַע אִיסּוּר אֵשֶׁת אָח – אָתֵי אִיסּוּר אֲחוֹת אִשָּׁה וְחָיֵיל, וְהִילְכָּךְ לָא פָּקַע.

Rav Ashi said: The prohibition with regard to **a wife's sister remains suspended. If the prohibition** proscribing **a brother's wife is terminated, the prohibition** proscribing **a wife's sister comes and takes effect. Therefore,** it is clear that the prohibition proscribing a wife's sister **is not** completely **terminated.** Accordingly, when a man dies and the prohibition proscribing a brother's wife is overridden by the levirate mitzva, the prohibition proscribing a wife's sister takes effect and she is forbidden to him due to that. The moment the first prohibition ceases to exist, the second immediately takes effect.

וְסָבַר רַבִּי יוֹסֵי אִיסּוּר חָל עַל אִיסּוּר? וְהָא תַּנְיָא: עָבַר עֲבֵירָה שֶׁיֵּשׁ בָּהּ שְׁתֵּי מִיתוֹת – נִידּוֹן בַּחֲמוּרָה, רַבִּי יוֹסֵי אוֹמֵר: נִידּוֹן בְּזִיקָה הָרִאשׁוֹנָה הַבָּאָה עָלָיו.

The *baraita* indicates that Rabbi Yosei holds that if the brother consummated the levirate marriage with this woman he violated two prohibitions. The Gemara asks: **And does Rabbi Yosei hold** that **a prohibition takes effect** where another **prohibition** already exists?[N] **But isn't it taught** in a *baraita*: **One who committed a transgression deserving of two death penalties**[H] **is sentenced to the harsher** of the two deaths?[N] One would be guilty of such a transgression if he engaged in intercourse with a forbidden relative who was also a married woman, as he would incur one death penalty due to her being a forbidden relative and one death penalty due to her being a married woman. **Rabbi Yosei says: He is sentenced according to the first relationship that applied to him** with regard to this woman.

וְתַנְיָא: כֵּיצַד אָמַר רַבִּי יוֹסֵי נִידּוֹן בְּזִיקָה הָרִאשׁוֹנָה הַבָּאָה עָלָיו? חֲמוֹתוֹ וְנַעֲשֵׂית אֵשֶׁת אִישׁ – נִידּוֹן בַּחֲמוֹתוֹ, אֵשֶׁת אִישׁ וְנַעֲשֵׂית חֲמוֹתוֹ – נִידּוֹן בְּאֵשֶׁת אִישׁ.

And it is taught in a *baraita*: **In what case did Rabbi Yosei say that he is sentenced according to the first relationship that applied to him?** If this woman was **his mother-in-law** who was widowed or divorced, and therefore forbidden to him only due to her status as his mother-in-law, and later she married **and became** forbidden as **a married woman** and he engaged in sexual relations with her, then **he is sentenced for** violating the prohibition proscribing **his mother-in-law,** since this was the first prohibition to apply. Alternatively, if she was **a married woman** and then he married her daughter so that she then **became his mother-in-law,** and then had sexual relations with her, **he is sentenced for** violating the prohibition proscribing **a married woman.**

NOTES

A prohibition takes effect where another prohibition already exists – **אִיסּוּר חָל עַל אִיסּוּר**: The Meiri comments that the question whether a prohibition takes effect where another prohibition exists is not a matter that relates to the essence of the prohibitions themselves but rather to the penalties that are incurred by them. Therefore, the principle that a prohibition does not take effect where another prohibition already exists expresses the idea that a transgressor is not doubly penalized for two violations, so that if he committed two transgressions requiring sin-offerings, he need bring only one sin-offering.

The later commentaries deliberated over how to understand the Gemara's question both with regard to the opinion of Rabbi Shimon and in light of Rav Ashi's novel idea. It would seem that the discussion revolves around the question of how to view the additional prohibition: Does it actually not take effect, or is there simply no practical possibility of applying it when another prohibition already exists?

Sentenced to the harsher of the two deaths – **נִידּוֹן בַּחֲמוּרָה**: There are four forms of capital punishment prescribed by the Torah and administered by a court of twenty-three members. They are, in diminishing order of harshness: Stoning, burning, decapitation by sword, and strangulation. The punishment for engaging in intercourse with one's mother-in-law is burning, whereas the punishment for engaging in intercourse with a married woman is strangulation. Therefore, according to this opinion in the *baraita*, one who engaged in intercourse with his mother-in-law who is also a married woman is sentenced to death by burning (Rashi).

HALAKHA

One who committed a transgression deserving of two death penalties – **עָבַר עֲבֵירָה שֶׁיֵּשׁ בָּהּ שְׁתֵּי מִיתוֹת**: One who committed a single transgression deserving of two death penalties, such as engaging in relations with his mother-in-law while she was a married woman, is sentenced to the harsher penalty (Rambam *Sefer Shofetim*, *Hilkhot Sanhedrin* 14:4).

Perek **III**
Daf **32** Amud **b**

אָמַר רַבִּי אַבָּהוּ: מוֹדֶה רַבִּי יוֹסֵי בְּאִיסּוּר מוֹסִיף.

Rabbi Abbahu said: Rabbi Yosei concedes that a prohibition takes effect where another prohibition already exists **when it is an expanded prohibition.**[N] An expanded prohibition is a prohibition that has a greater scope than the original prohibition, either because it applies with greater severity or because it applies to additional individuals. Rabbi Yosei holds that if the second prohibition incorporates additional individuals into the list of those for whom the original item is prohibited, then it takes effect in addition to the previous prohibition that had a more limited range.

NOTES

An expanded prohibition and a more inclusive prohibition – **אִיסּוּר מוֹסִיף וְאִיסּוּר כּוֹלֵל**: Even though both an expanded prohibition and a more inclusive prohibition are similar in that for both, the scope of the original prohibition is enlarged in some way, they nevertheless differ both in their fundamental natures as well as in their details. An expanded prohibition is defined as a prohibition that adds an additional element of prohibition to the item that is already prohibited. A more inclusive prohibition, on the other hand, occurs when the prohibition now includes other items, even if for the original item there is no actual addition to the prohibition itself.

An expanded prohibition comes about in two ways, either because it applies with greater severity or because it applies to additional individuals. The first might come about, for instance, when a prohibition against deriving benefit takes effect where a prohibition against consumption already exists, since here the second prohibition, against deriving benefit, is of greater severity. The second occurs when, as in the present talmudic discussion, the prohibition applies to a greater number of individuals, when it is not only prohibited for the original subject to perform an activity with a specific item, but it comes to be prohibited for others to perform that activity as well (Ritva), e.g., this woman was forbidden to one brother, and she is subsequently forbidden to all the brothers. A more inclusive prohibition occurs when the same prohibition applies to the same individual but with more items, e.g., it becomes prohibited for one brother to marry all the sisters of a woman instead of just the woman herself. The later commentaries examined these distinctions, since, e.g., with regard to the *halakhot* of forbidden relatives, the difference between a more inclusive prohibition and an expanded prohibition depends on the individual in question. That which is an expanded prohibition for a man is at the same time a more inclusive prohibition from the woman's perspective, and the opposite holds true as well (see *Yosef Lekah*). According to the *Ḥazon Ish* it is clear that the ruling goes according to the perspective of the man and not according to the woman.

In addition to these fundamental differences, the details of these two categories differ as well. It would seem from *Tosafot* that a more inclusive prohibition does not take effect where another prohibition exists unless it is more severe, but never where it is more lenient (*Keren Ora*). Moreover, according to *Tosafot*, a more inclusive prohibition takes effect only where the prohibition is for a single category. In other words, those to whom the prohibition applies must all be included within a single category of the prohibition. This is not the case, for example, when a man marries a woman, for even though all of her relatives are rendered forbidden to him it is nevertheless for different reasons: One is her mother, the other her sister, etc. The Rashba, however, disagrees on this point.

The *Ḥazon Ish* writes that an expanded prohibition takes effect only when it actually causes additional prohibitions, i.e., there must in fact be additional people in the world who become subject to this prohibition. So, for example, where a man engages in relations with his wife's sister who became his brother's wife, the second prohibition would take effect only if there were in fact additional brothers who were incorporated into the prohibition by the marriage. Therefore, if there were only two brothers in the family, the prohibition of a brother's wife would not apply.

תינח – היכא דנשא חי ואחר כך נשא מת, מגו דאתוסף איסור לגבי אחים – אתוסף איסור לגבי דידיה.

The Gemara asks: This **works out well** in cases **where the living** brother **married** his wife first, and her sister became forbidden to him as a wife's sister, **and then afterward the** brother who was subsequently **deceased married** his wife's sister. In that case it is possible to say: **Since a prohibition was added for** all **the brothers,**[N] **a prohibition was added for** the living brother as well, and he is liable due to both prohibitions, as this prohibition is more wide-ranging than the previous one. In other words, at first this sister was permitted to the other brothers, and when the second brother married her she was rendered a brother's wife and so she was additionally forbidden to the other brothers.

אלא, היכא דנשא מת ואחר כך נשא חי, מאי איסור מוסיף איכא?

However, where the **deceased** brother **married** first and **afterward** the **living** brother **married** her sister, **in what way is there a prohibition that adds?** No additional individuals were incorporated into the prohibition as a result of the marriage of the living brother with the sister, since the prohibition here proscribing a wife's sister applies to him alone.

וכי תימא: מגו דאיתסר בכולהו אחוותא – האי איסור כולל הוא!

And if you would say: Since he himself now married a sister **he became prohibited to all of the other sisters,** as opposed to the prior state of affairs where only his brother was married to one of the sisters and all of the other sisters were permitted to him, and therefore an additional prohibition now applies to him, this is difficult. In this case the new prohibition is not considered an expanded prohibition, but rather **it is** considered **a more inclusive prohibition.**[N] It is more inclusive and more comprehensive in that it adds additional aspects to the prohibition for the same individual. This is not called an expanded prohibition, as it does not add prohibitions to additional individuals.

אלא אמר רבא: מעלה אני עליו כאילו עשה שתים, ואינו חייב אלא אחת. וכן כי אתא רבין אמר רבי יוחנן: מעלה אני עליו כאילו עשה שתים, ואינו חייב אלא אחת. מאי נפקא מינה? לקברו בין רשעים גמורים.

Rather, Rava said[N] that when Rabbi Yosei stated in the *baraita* that the man is liable due to both prohibitions, for a brother's wife and for a wife's sister, he meant to say: **I ascribe to him** liability **as though he transgressed twice,** since indeed he violated two prohibitions, **yet he is liable** to receive punishment in human courts **on only one** count. **And likewise, when Ravin came** from Eretz Yisrael to Babylonia, he said that **Rabbi Yoḥanan said: I ascribe to him** liability **as though he transgressed twice, yet he is liable** to receive punishment **on only one** count. The Gemara asks: **What difference does it make** if we consider it as though he transgressed twice? The Gemara answers: It affects the decision whether or not **to bury him among the completely wicked.**[N] Just as a righteous individual is not buried among the wicked, so too, a wicked individual is not buried among those more wicked than himself. He who violated this prohibition is considered as though he committed two transgressions and not one, and so he would be buried accordingly.

NOTES

Since a prohibition was added for the brothers – **מגו דאתוסף איסור לגבי אחים**: The Gemara could have suggested that there is a different expanded prohibition; a prohibition was added to the entire populace since previously this woman was available for marriage but now she is a married woman. Nevertheless, the Gemara preferred to mention the prohibition proscribing a brother's wife, since it is not always nullified following the death of the husband (Ritva).

This is considered a more inclusive prohibition – **האי איסור כולל הוא**: The Rivan asks: Could not Rabbi Abbahu have said that Rabbi Yosei also concedes in cases of more inclusive prohibitions? He answers that since an expanded prohibition is more severe, it stands to reason that Rabbi Yosei concedes in that case specifically. Other commentaries point out that since Rabbi Yosei disagrees in the case of a married woman who became his mother-in-law, which is a more inclusive prohibition because he became forbidden to her and to her relatives, we can conclude that Rabbi Yosei does not in fact agree in these cases (see Ritva).

Rather Rava said – **אלא אמר רבא**: Some commentaries maintain that Rava's statement serves only to resolve Rabbi Yosei's opinion with regard to a wife's sister. However, most of the commentaries agree with the opinion of Rashi and assert that the word rather here indicates a fundamental dispute with Rabbi Abbahu, in that Rava holds that Rabbi Yosei does not concede that an additional prohibition can take effect where a prohibition already exists.

Among the completely wicked – **בין רשעים גמורים**: Many early commentaries had a version of the text that read: Among the severely wicked, and therefore did not interpret this like Rashi, who explains this as meaning that he should be buried with those who had been stoned to death. They point out that he did not commit a crime so heinous as to deserve such a burial place. Rather, they state, he should be buried among those who were wicked like himself. *Tosefot HaRosh* explains that Rabbi Yosei holds that this man should be buried together with someone who committed sins with two different women, such as a brother's wife and a wife's sister, since he committed both of these transgressions as well. On the other hand, Rabbi Shimon holds that another prohibition cannot take effect where a prohibition already exists, so it is considered as though he committed a single transgression.

וּבִפְלוּגְתָּא, דְּאִיתְּמַר: זָר שֶׁשִּׁימֵּשׁ בְּשַׁבָּת, רַבִּי חִיָּיא אוֹמֵר: חַיָּיב שְׁתַּיִם, בַּר קַפָּרָא אוֹמֵר: אֵין חַיָּיב אֶלָּא אַחַת. קָפַץ רַבִּי חִיָּיא וְנִשְׁבַּע: הָעֲבוֹדָה! כָּךְ שָׁמַעְתִּי מֵרַבִּי: שְׁתַּיִם. קָפַץ בַּר קַפָּרָא וְנִשְׁבַּע: הָעֲבוֹדָה! כָּךְ שָׁמַעְתִּי מֵרַבִּי: אַחַת.

§ The Gemara comments that the issue of a prohibition taking effect where another prohibition already exists is taught **in the dispute** found in a *baraita*, **where it was stated:** With regard to **a non-priest who served** in some capacity in one of the Temple services, such as the burning of a burnt-offering on the altar **on Shabbat,**[H] **Rabbi Ḥiyya says: He is liable** to receive punishment on **two** counts,[N] both because he was a non-priest serving in the Temple and because he desecrated Shabbat. **Bar Kappara**[P] **says: He is liable** on **only one** count. **Rabbi Ḥiyya jumped up and swore:**[N] I swear **by the Temple service**[N] that **this I heard from Rabbi** Yehuda HaNasi: He is liable on **two** counts. **Bar Kappara jumped up and swore:** I swear **by the Temple service** that **this I heard from Rabbi** Yehuda HaNasi: He is liable on **one** count.

הִתְחִיל רַבִּי חִיָּיא לָדוּן: שַׁבָּת לַכֹּל נֶאֶסְרָה, כְּשֶׁהוּתְּרָה בַּמִּקְדָּשׁ – אֵצֶל כֹּהֲנִים הוּתְּרָה, לְכֹהֲנִים הוּתְּרָה וְלֹא לְזָרִים, יֵשׁ כָּאן מִשּׁוּם זָרוּת, וְיֵשׁ כָּאן מִשּׁוּם שַׁבָּת. הִתְחִיל בַּר קַפָּרָא לָדוּן: שַׁבָּת לַכֹּל נֶאֶסְרָה, כְּשֶׁהוּתְּרָה – בַּמִּקְדָּשׁ הוּתְּרָה, אֵין כָּאן אֶלָּא זָרוּת.

Since the matter could not be decided by tradition, **Rabbi Ḥiyya began to deliberate** and analyze the question logically. Prohibited labor on **Shabbat was prohibited to all. When** prohibited labor **was permitted in the Temple** for the purposes of the Temple service, **it was permitted** only **for priests.** This indicates that **it was permitted for priests and not for non-priests.** Therefore, when a non-priest serves in the Temple on Shabbat, **there is** a transgression **here due to** his serving as **a non-priest and there is** a transgression **here due to** his desecrating **Shabbat. Bar Kappara began to deliberate** in a different manner: **Shabbat was prohibited to all. When it was permitted it was permitted in the Temple,** so that if it was permitted for one to serve in the Temple, it was permitted for him to serve on Shabbat. Therefore, **there is** a transgression **here only** for his serving as **a non-priest,** since if this man were a priest his service would have been permitted. Therefore, he is not liable to receive punishment for desecrating Shabbat.

בַּעַל מוּם שֶׁשִּׁימֵּשׁ בְּטוּמְאָה, רַבִּי חִיָּיא אוֹמֵר: חַיָּיב שְׁתַּיִם, בַּר קַפָּרָא אוֹמֵר: אֵין חַיָּיב אֶלָּא אַחַת. קָפַץ רַבִּי חִיָּיא וְנִשְׁבַּע: הָעֲבוֹדָה! כָּךְ שָׁמַעְתִּי מֵרַבִּי: שְׁתַּיִם, קָפַץ בַּר קַפָּרָא וְנִשְׁבַּע: הָעֲבוֹדָה! כָּךְ שָׁמַעְתִּי מֵרַבִּי: אַחַת.

They disagreed over a similar issue as well, the case of a priest **with a blemish who served** in the Temple by sacrificing a public offering, which overrides ritual impurity, **while** he was **ritually impure.**[N] **Rabbi Ḥiyya says: He is liable on two** counts, both for serving with a blemish and for being ritually impure. **Bar Kappara says: He is liable on only one** count, for serving with a blemish. **Rabbi Ḥiyya jumped up and swore:** I swear **by the Temple service** that **this I heard from Rabbi** Yehuda HaNasi: **He** is liable on **two** counts. **Bar Kappara jumped up and swore:** I swear **by the Temple service** that **this I heard from** Rabbi Yehuda HaNasi: He is liable on **one** count.

הִתְחִיל רַבִּי חִיָּיא לָדוּן: טוּמְאָה לַכֹּל נֶאֶסְרָה, כְּשֶׁהוּתְּרָה בַּמִּקְדָּשׁ – אֵצֶל כֹּהֲנִים תְּמִימִים הוּתְּרָה, לְכֹהֲנִים תְּמִימִים הוּתְּרָה וְלֹא לְבַעֲלֵי מוּמִין, יֵשׁ כָּאן מִשּׁוּם בַּעֲלֵי מוּמִין, וְיֵשׁ כָּאן מִשּׁוּם טוּמְאָה. הִתְחִיל בַּר קַפָּרָא לָדוּן: טוּמְאָה לַכֹּל נֶאֶסְרָה, כְּשֶׁהוּתְּרָה בַּמִּקְדָּשׁ – הוּתְּרָה, אֵין כָּאן אֶלָּא מִשּׁוּם בַּעַל מוּם,

Rabbi Ḥiyya began to deliberate.[N] **Ritual impurity was prohibited to all,** as it was prohibited for all individuals who are ritually impure to enter into the Temple. **When it was permitted in the Temple** in circumstances where the entire public was impure, **it was permitted for unblemished priests.** Therefore, **it was permitted** only **for unblemished priests and not for** priests **with blemishes.** Consequently, if that priest with a blemish served while impure, **there is** a transgression **here due to** his status as **a blemished** priest **and there is** a transgression **here due to ritual impurity. Bar Kappara began to deliberate** in a different manner: **Ritual impurity was prohibited to all. When it was permitted in the Temple, it was permitted** for all. Therefore, the only problem was that this priest was blemished, and so **there is** a transgression **here only due to** his status as **a blemished** priest.

HALAKHA

A non-priest who served on Shabbat, etc. – זָר שֶׁשִּׁימֵּשׁ בְּשַׁבָּת וכו׳: A non-priest who served in the Temple on Shabbat was liable to receive punishment both for violating Shabbat and for serving as a non-priest. Similarly, a blemished priest who served in the Temple service while ritually impure was liable both for serving while ritually impure as well as for serving as a blemished priest (Rambam *Sefer Avoda, Hilkhot Biat HaMikdash* 9:12).

NOTES

He is liable on two counts – חַיָּיב שְׁתַּיִם: According to Rashi and other commentaries, this means that he transgressed two prohibitions, the repercussions being that he is considered completely wicked. Ramban explains that this refers to the sets of lashes he would receive, according to the opinion that one receives lashes even for a prohibition for which one is punished with execution by the courts. One who violates such a prohibition is punished with lashes if certain factors prevent the court from administering the death penalty. One commentary explains that with regard to the three questions over which Rabbi Ḥiyya and Bar Kappara disagree, they differ from one another on precisely this point; the first is referring to a negative mitzva and court-administered capital punishment, the second to a negative mitzva and *karet*, and the third is referring to two negative mitzvot (Re'em Horowitz).

Rabbi Ḥiyya jumped up and swore, etc. – קָפַץ רַבִּי חִיָּיא וְנִשְׁבַּע וכו׳: It is possible that Rabbi Yehuda HaNasi changed his mind, and so both of them could indeed hear the words of Rabbi accurately, but at different times (*Ramat Shmuel*).

The Temple service – הָעֲבוֹדָה: According to the Maharsha, this form of oath, which is used on numerous occasions in the Babylonian Talmud, is not in fact referring to the Temple service, since at that time there was no Temple. The word service refers to divine service in accordance with the statement by the Rambam that an oath taken with the divine name is a form of service. The vowels of the word *avoda* are identical to the vowels of the four-letter divine name.

A non-priest on Shabbat, a blemished priest while ritually impure – זָר בְּשַׁבָּת, בַּעַל מוּם בְּטוּמְאָה: The Ramban writes that the Gemara could have asked many different questions, one of which was with regard to a blemished priest who served on Shabbat, yet it chose to use one example of many. However, it did not ask about a non-priest who served while ritually impure, because non-priests were never warned against performing the Temple service while ritually impure (Rivan; *Tosafot*). The Meiri contends that this question could have been asked as well.

Rabbi Ḥiyya began to deliberate – הִתְחִיל רַבִּי חִיָּיא לָדוּן: As later becomes clear, the essence of the dispute between these two Sages revolves around the question of whether a prohibition takes effect where another prohibition already exists. Nevertheless, it was important to clarify the opinion of Rabbi Yehuda HaNasi in these cases. Accordingly, the choice of the words: Began to deliberate, is precise, since this served only as a preliminary clarification of the opinions but did not constitute the heart of the discussion (Rashba).

PERSONALITIES

Bar Kappara – בַּר קַפָּרָא: This Sage was among the last of the *tanna'im*, a leading pupil of Rabbi Yehuda HaNasi, and a colleague of Rabbi Shimon ben Rabbi Yehuda HaNasi and Rabbi Ḥiyya. His first name is unknown, although some say that he was the son of Rabbi Elazar HaKappar, and, being born after his father's death, was named Elazar as well.

Bar Kappara was among the greatest halakhic authorities of his generation, who even compiled a collection of *baraitot* called *Mishnat bar Kappara*. Excerpts from this compilation are cited several times throughout the Talmud. Bar Kappara was also famous for his sermons, and he was a master of language as well. Several proverbs, poetic phrases, and words of prayer are recorded in his name.

As he had a sense of humor and a sharp wit, he would often aim amusing criticism at the Sages, including the members of Rabbi Yehuda HaNasi's household. For this reason, and despite his closeness to his teacher, bar Kappara was never ordained. Bar Kappara was well versed in general wisdom and was therefore often sent to represent the Jewish community before the Roman authorities.

The majority of prominent *amora'im* of the first generation were among his students. The prominent *amora* Rabbi Yehuda ben Pedaya (bar Padda) was his nephew. He was among the Sages in the southern part of Eretz Yisrael, and active in the city of Parod, where he is buried.

HALAKHA

A non-priest who ate a bird killed by pinching – זָר שֶׁאָכַל מְלִיקָה: A non-priest who ate from a bird sin-offering is liable to receive punishment on two counts, one as a non-priest who ate consecrated animals, and one for eating an unslaughtered animal carcass (Rambam *Sefer Avoda, Hilkhot Ma'aseh HaKorbanot* 11:9).

NOTES

Pinching – מְלִיקָה: Turtledoves and young pigeons sacrificed as offerings in the Temple were killed not by ritually slaughtering them with a knife like other offerings, but rather by pinching their necks. This was considered an especially difficult activity to perform. The priest would hold the bird in his left hand with its legs and wings between his fingers, and the back of its neck stretched out and facing upward. With his right fingernail, which he grew especially long for this purpose, the priest would cut the bird's neck and spine from the back until he reached and severed its windpipe and gullet. If the bird was to be sacrificed as a burnt-offering, the priest would completely sever its head. If it was to be sacrificed as a sin-offering, he would leave the head partially attached. A bird killed by pinching and sacrificed as a sin-offering was permitted to be eaten by the priests, while a bird that was killed by pinching but not intended for sacrificial use was considered an unslaughtered carcass, and it was not permitted to eat it. The pinching could be performed only by a priest, whereas the slaughtering of animal offerings in the Temple could be performed by a non-priest.

זָר שֶׁאָכַל מְלִיקָה, רַבִּי חִיָּיא אוֹמֵר: חַיָּיב שְׁתַּיִם, בַּר קַפָּרָא אוֹמֵר: אֵין חַיָּיב אֶלָּא אַחַת. קָפַץ רַבִּי חִיָּיא וְנִשְׁבַּע: הָעֲבוֹדָה! כָּךְ שָׁמַעְתִּי מֵרַבִּי: שְׁתַּיִם. קָפַץ בַּר קַפָּרָא וְנִשְׁבַּע: הָעֲבוֹדָה! כָּךְ שָׁמַעְתִּי מֵרַבִּי: אַחַת.

They disagreed over a similar issue as well. This dispute is with regard to **a non-priest who ate a** bird sin-offering that was killed by **pinching**[H] the back of its neck. It is permitted for priests to consume such an offering, but it is prohibited to consume any other bird killed in such a manner, since it was not ritually slaughtered. **Rabbi Ḥiyya says: He is liable** to receive punishment **on two** counts, both for being a non-priest who ate a priestly offering and for eating something that was not properly slaughtered. **Bar Kappara says: He is liable on only one** count. **Rabbi Ḥiyya jumped up and swore:** I swear **by the Temple service** that **this I heard from Rabbi** Yehuda HaNasi: He is liable on **two** counts. **Bar Kappara jumped up and swore:** I swear **by the Temple service** that **this I heard from Rabbi** Yehuda HaNasi: He is liable on **one** count.

הִתְחִיל רַבִּי חִיָּיא לָדוּן: נְבֵלָה לַכֹּל נֶאֶסְרָה, כְּשֶׁהוּתְּרָה בַּמִּקְדָּשׁ – אֵצֶל כֹּהֲנִים הוּתְּרָה, לְכֹהֲנִים הוּתְּרָה וְלֹא לְזָרִים. יֵשׁ כָּאן מִשּׁוּם זָרוּת, וְיֵשׁ כָּאן מִשּׁוּם מְלִיקָה. הִתְחִיל בַּר קַפָּרָא לָדוּן: נְבֵלָה לַכֹּל נֶאֶסְרָה, כְּשֶׁהוּתְּרָה בַּמִּקְדָּשׁ – הוּתְּרָה, אֵין כָּאן אֶלָּא מִשּׁוּם זָרוּת.

Rabbi Ḥiyya began to deliberate. An unslaughtered animal carcass was prohibited to all. When it was permitted in the Temple, it was permitted to priests alone. Since **it was permitted to priests and not to non-priests, there is** a transgression **here due to** his **status as a non-priest** who ate of the sin-offering **and there is** a transgression **here due to** eating an animal killed by **pinching.**[N] **Bar Kappara began to deliberate: An unslaughtered animal carcass was prohibited to all. When it was permitted in the Temple, it was permitted** to all. Therefore **there is** a transgression **here only for being a non-priest,** since if he were a priest there would be no prohibition at all.

Perek **III**
Daf **33** Amud **a**

בְּמַאי קָמִיפַּלְגִי? בְּאִיסּוּר כּוֹלֵל, וְאַלִּיבָּא דְּרַבִּי יוֹסֵי: רַבִּי חִיָּיא סָבַר, רַבִּי יוֹסֵי בְּאִיסּוּר כּוֹלֵל מִיחַיֵּיב תַּרְתֵּי; בַּר קַפָּרָא סָבַר, לָא מִיחַיֵּיב אֶלָּא חֲדָא.

The Gemara asks: **With regard to what** principle **do they disagree?**[N] The Gemara suggests that they disagree with regard to the issue of **a more inclusive prohibition, and** this dispute pertains to the status of a more inclusive prohibition specifically **according to** the opinion of **Rabbi Yosei. Rabbi Ḥiyya holds that Rabbi Yosei** is of the opinion that **in the case of a more inclusive prohibition, one is liable on two counts. Bar Kappara holds** that Rabbi Yosei is of the opinion that **one is liable only on one** count.

וּמַאי אִיסּוּר כּוֹלֵל אִיכָּא הָכָא? בִּשְׁלָמָא זָר, מֵעִיקָּרָא שָׁרֵי בִּמְלָאכָה וְאָסוּר בַּעֲבוֹדָה, אָתְיָא לַהּ שַׁבָּת – מִגּוֹ דְּקָא מִיתְּסַר בִּמְלָאכָה מִיתְּסַר נָמֵי בַּעֲבוֹדָה.

The Gemara asks: **And what more inclusive prohibition is there here** in these cases? **Granted,** in the case of **a non-priest** who served in the Temple on Shabbat, **initially he was permitted to perform labor** every day **and was prohibited from** engaging in **the Temple service.** When **Shabbat came, since he is** now **prohibited from** engaging in **prohibited labor** in all contexts due to Shabbat, **he is also prohibited from** engaging in labors related to the Temple **service** due to Shabbat. Indeed, the additional prohibition of Shabbat was added to the previously existing prohibition against performing service in the Temple. This is a more inclusive prohibition since it also includes prohibited labor outside of the Temple.

NOTES

With regard to what do they disagree – בְּמַאי קָמִיפַּלְגִי: Both the early and later commentaries ask: Why did the Gemara see fit to repeat this question when Rabbi Ḥiyya and bar Kappara explicitly stated the reasoning behind their positions? *Tosefot HaRosh* states that the Sages of the Talmud held a tradition that the root of the dispute was not based upon the previously suggested interpretation. The Rivan, however, states that this question is directed specifically toward bar Kappara, since his reasoning does not seem sufficient. Others say that because the two Sages demonstrated that each of these issues could be viewed from two different angles, they would not have depended solely upon their explicit explanations (*Tosafot Yeshanim*). The Rashba writes that there must be an alternate rationale behind this dispute, as otherwise one of the Sages would be telling a falsehood. Moreover, the words: Began to deliberate, indicate that this was not their primary reasoning, but that they intended to present further proofs of their statements (see *Tosafot*).

בַּעַל מוּם, מֵעִיקָּרָא שָׁרֵי בַּאֲכִילָה וְאָסוּר בַּעֲבוֹדָה, אִיטַּמֵּי לֵיהּ, מִגּוֹ דְּקָא מִיתְּסַר בַּאֲכִילָה מִיתְּסַר נַמִי בַּעֲבוֹדָה, אֶלָּא מְלִיקָה – בְּבַת אַחַת הִיא דְּמַשְׁכַּחַתְּ לַהּ, בְּאִיסּוּר כּוֹלֵל לָא מַשְׁכַּחַתְּ לַהּ!

The same is true with regard to **a blemished priest** who served in the Temple while ritually impure: **Initially,** prior to his becoming ritually impure, **he was allowed to eat** from the consecrated animals **but was prohibited from** performing **the** Temple **service,** like all blemished priests. When **he was rendered ritually impure, since he is** now **prohibited from eating** of the consecrated items, **he is also prohibited from** performing the Temple **service** due to that same ritual impurity. There is, then, a more inclusive prohibition here. **However,** with regard to the case of a bird that was killed by **pinching, you find** that the prohibition against the eating of consecrated items by a non-priest and the prohibition against eating an unslaughtered animal carcass take effect **simultaneously.**[N] **You do not,** however, **find a more inclusive prohibition** here as there was no original prohibition that took effect beforehand. Instead, this is a case of two prohibitions that take effect simultaneously.

אֶלָּא קָמִיפַּלְגִי בְּאִיסּוּר בְּבַת אַחַת וְאַלִּיבָּא דְּרַבִּי יוֹסֵי: רַבִּי חִיָּיא סָבַר, רַבִּי יוֹסֵי בְּאִיסּוּר בַּת אַחַת מִיחַיֵּיב תַּרְתֵּי, וּבַר קַפָּרָא סָבַר, לָא מִיחַיֵּיב אֶלָּא חֲדָא.

Rather, the previous explanation is rejected and the Gemara suggests instead that **they disagree with regard to** an additional **prohibition** that takes effect **simultaneously, and** this dispute pertains to the status of these prohibitions specifically **according to** the opinion of **Rabbi Yosei.**[N] **Rabbi Ḥiyya holds that Rabbi Yosei** is of the opinion that **one is liable on two** counts in cases of **prohibitions** that take effect **simultaneously. And bar Kappara holds** that Rabbi Yosei is of the opinion that **one is liable only on a single** count.

וְהָכָא – מַאי אִיסּוּר בַּת אַחַת אִיכָּא הָכָא? זָר שֶׁשִּׁימֵּשׁ בְּשַׁבָּת, כְּגוֹן דְּאַיְיתֵי שְׁתֵּי שְׂעָרוֹת בְּשַׁבָּת, דְּהָוְיָא לְהוּ זָרוּת וְשַׁבָּת בַּהֲדֵי הֲדָדֵי.

The Gemara challenges this explanation: **But here,** in the first two instances, **what** case of **simultaneous prohibitions is there here?** In the two previous cases the prohibitions took effect one after the other, and not simultaneously. The Gemara answers that these cases can also be interpreted as occurring simultaneously as follows: With regard to **the non-priest who served on Shabbat, this would be in a case where** a minor **grew two** pubic **hairs,**[N] signaling adulthood **on Shabbat.** Before that point he was considered a minor and therefore not liable for his actions. Therefore, **this is** a case where the prohibition against serving as **a non-priest and** the prohibition against violating **Shabbat** took effect **together.**

בַּעַל מוּם נַמִי – כְּגוֹן דְּאַיְיתֵי שְׁתֵּי שְׂעָרוֹת וְאִיטַּמֵּי לֵיהּ, דְּהָוְיָא לֵיהּ בַּעַל מוּם וְטוּמְאָה בַּהֲדֵי הֲדָדֵי. אִי נַמִי: שֶׁחָתַךְ אֶצְבָּעוֹ בְּסַכִּין טְמֵאָה.

With regard to the case of **one who was blemished,** this can be explained **as well:** This is referring to a case **where** a minor **grew two** pubic **hairs and** was immediately **rendered ritually impure. This is** a case where the prohibition with regard to **a blemished** priest **and** the prohibition with regard to **ritual impurity** took effect **together. Alternatively,** it could be a case **where he cut off his finger with a ritually impure knife.**[HN] Here, the cut and removal of his finger rendered him simultaneously blemished and ritually impure.

בִּשְׁלָמָא לְרַבִּי חִיָּיא, כִּי אַתְנְיֵיהּ לְדִידֵיהּ – אַלִּיבָּא דְּרַבִּי יוֹסֵי, כִּי אַתְנְיֵיהּ לְבַר קַפָּרָא – אַלִּיבָּא דְּרַבִּי שִׁמְעוֹן, אֶלָּא לְבַר קַפָּרָא – רַבִּי חִיָּיא שַׁקּוֹרֵי קָא מְשַׁקֵּר?!

Following this clarification of the dispute, the matter is now considered from a different angle: **Granted, according to** the opinion of **Rabbi Ḥiyya,** the dispute between his version of Rabbi Yehuda HaNasi's ruling and that of bar Kappara can be explained as follows: **When Rabbi** Yehuda HaNasi **taught** Rabbi Ḥiyya, he taught him **according to** the opinion of **Rabbi Yosei,** and Rabbi Yosei holds that there are cases where two prohibitions can both take effect. And **when** Rabbi Yehuda HaNasi **taught bar Kappara,** he did so **according to** the opinion of **Rabbi Shimon** who holds that a new prohibition can never take effect where another prohibition already exists. Therefore, Rabbi Ḥiyya could understand why bar Kappara insisted on his opinion. Rabbi Ḥiyya thought that bar Kappara was in fact relating an accurate statement of Rabbi Yehuda HaNasi, as Rabbi Yehuda HaNasi was relating to the opinion of Rabbi Shimon. Rabbi Ḥiyya assumed that bar Kappara did not understand that Rabbi Yehuda HaNasi's statement was not in accordance with Rabbi Yosei's opinion. **According to bar Kappara, however, was Rabbi Ḥiyya then telling a falsehood?** How would bar Kappara relate to Rabbi Ḥiyya's oath? Did he think that Rabbi Ḥiyya would swear that he heard words from Rabbi Yehuda HaNasi that were never said?

NOTES

Pinching…takes effect simultaneously – מְלִיקָה בְּבַת אַחַת: *Tosafot* ask: Why is this case considered a case of prohibitions that take effect simultaneously, when the prohibition with regard to an unslaughtered animal carcass takes effect before the prohibition for a non-priest to eat consecrated food? Rabbi Avraham *Av Beit Din* explains that the case of eating a bird killed by pinching is also a case of a minor who grew two pubic hairs. He maintains that from that moment of maturity both prohibitions take effect at once. Indeed, the person in this case is both a non-priest and he is prohibited from eating from the pinched bird. This cannot, however, be said with regard to the case of ritual impurity, since the prohibition cannot apply unless one was actually rendered impure. The early commentaries discussed this opinion. Some rejected it (Rashba), while others showed how it could be supported (Ramban; Ritva).

A prohibition that takes effect simultaneously and according to Rabbi Yosei – אִיסּוּר בְּבַת אַחַת וְאַלִּיבָּא דְּרַבִּי יוֹסֵי: All agree that it is more reasonable for two prohibitions to take effect in cases where the prohibitions take effect simultaneously, as opposed to cases where an additional prohibition takes effect after the first has already taken effect. *Tosefot HaRosh* adds, however, that there is still a certain deficiency in cases where two prohibitions take effect at once. He maintains that in these cases the less severe prohibition would not take effect together with a more severe prohibition. However, in cases of additional prohibitions that take effect one after another, one could maintain that any additional prohibition would take effect, no matter how minor.

Where he grew two pubic hairs, etc. – דְּאַיְיתֵי שְׁתֵּי שְׂעָרוֹת וכו׳: The *Ḥazon Ish* says that one cannot explain the case of a brother's wife and a wife's sister as prohibitions that take effect simultaneously when one grows two pubic hairs. This is because there is a distinction between prohibitions that apply to a person himself, which apply immediately upon reaching adulthood, and prohibitions that apply to an object (see Ramban and Rashba).

Where he cut off his finger with a ritually impure knife – שֶׁחָתַךְ אֶצְבָּעוֹ בְּסַכִּין טְמֵאָה: *Tosafot* point out a difficulty with this explanation: While impurity is contracted immediately upon contact, the blemish appeared only afterward, and therefore this is not a case of simultaneous prohibitions. They resolve this by explaining that the situation is one where the finger was only loosely attached, so that by a single cut both the impurity was transferred and the blemish appeared at once. The Meiri adds that it must be that another individual cut one's finger off, for if one had himself wielded the knife, he would have been rendered impure already at the moment of contact with the knife. In contrast, *Tosafot Yeshanim* hold that since these two occurrences were so close in time, they are in fact considered a single act, and therefore both prohibitions took effect simultaneously.

HALAKHA

A prohibition that takes effect where another prohibition exists – אִיסּוּר חָל עַל אִיסּוּר: There is a general principle of prohibitions in the Torah that states that a prohibition cannot take effect where another prohibition exists unless both of the prohibitions take effect simultaneously or one prohibition makes additions to the previous prohibition or if it comes to include other matters that were not in the original prohibition (Rambam *Sefer Kedusha, Hilkhot Issurei Bia* 17:8, *Hilkhot Ma'akhalot Assurot* 8:6, and *Sefer Korbanot*, *Hilkhot Shegagot* 4:1).

אֶלָּא: קָמִיפַּלְגִי בְּאִיסּוּר בַּת אַחַת, וְאַלִּיבָּא דְּרַבִּי שִׁמְעוֹן. בִּשְׁלָמָא לְרַבִּי חִיָּיא, קָא מִישְׁתַּבַּע לְאַפּוּקֵי לְרַבִּי שִׁמְעוֹן מֵחֶזְקֵיהּ, אֶלָּא לְבַר קַפָּרָא – לָמָּה לֵיהּ לְאִשְׁתַּבּוּעֵי? קַשְׁיָא.

Rather, this must be explained differently: Rabbi Ḥiyya and bar Kappara **disagree** with regard to cases where two **prohibitions** take effect **simultaneously, and** this dispute pertains to the status of these prohibition specifically **according to** the opinion of **Rabbi Shimon.** It could be suggested that when the two prohibitions take effect simultaneously, Rabbi Shimon would concede that they both take effect. However, this explanation raises a difficulty as well: **Granted, according to Rabbi Ḥiyya** it is clear why **he was swearing.** He did so in order **to exclude** the understanding of **Rabbi Shimon's** opinion that was based on **his presumed** opinion. As it was known that Rabbi Shimon holds that a new prohibition cannot take effect where another prohibition exists; this is the default understanding of his opinion. Therefore, it was incumbent upon Rabbi Ḥiyya to take an oath in order to emphasize that despite Rabbi Shimon's general opinion, in cases where the prohibitions take effect simultaneously, he would concede that both prohibitions can take effect. **However, according to bar Kappara, why was it necessary to swear?** It would have sufficed for him simply to make his statement, as it concurs with the default understanding of Rabbi Shimon's opinion. The Gemara comments: Indeed, this is **difficult.**

בִּשְׁלָמָא לְבַר קַפָּרָא, כִּי אַתְנְיֵיהּ רַבִּי לְדִידֵיהּ – אַלִּיבָּא דְּרַבִּי שִׁמְעוֹן, כִּי אַתְנְיֵיהּ לְרַבִּי חִיָּיא – אַלִּיבָּא דְּרַבִּי יוֹסֵי. אֶלָּא לְרַבִּי חִיָּיא, בַּר קַפָּרָא שַׁקּוּרֵי קָא מְשַׁקֵּר?

One can raise a difficulty with this explanation from a different angle as well: **Granted, according to bar Kappara, when Rabbi** Yehuda HaNasi **taught him,** he taught him **according to** the opinion of **Rabbi Shimon,** who holds that two prohibitions cannot take effect even in cases when they occur simultaneously, and **when he taught** the ruling **to Rabbi Ḥiyya** it was **according to** the opinion of **Rabbi Yosei.** Accordingly, Rabbi Ḥiyya did in fact swear that he heard that one is liable only on one count, but he wrongly understood that this was Rabbi Shimon's opinion. **However, according to Rabbi Ḥiyya,** who holds that Rabbi Shimon concedes that in cases where the prohibitions take effect simultaneously one is liable for both, was **bar Kappara lying?** His statement would accord neither with Rabbi Shimon nor with Rabbi Yosei.

אָמַר לָךְ רַבִּי חִיָּיא: כִּי אַתְנְיֵיהּ רַבִּי לְדִידֵיהּ – תַּרְתֵּי לִפְטוֹר אַתְנְיֵיהּ,

The Gemara answers: **Rabbi Ḥiyya** could have **said to you** that this is what transpired: **When Rabbi** Yehuda HaNasi **taught him,** bar Kappara, **he taught him two** cases involving **exemptions,** i.e., the cases of a non-priest who served in the Temple on Shabbat and that of the blemished priest who served while ritually impure. Both of these are cases of more inclusive prohibitions, and he was informing bar Kappara that Rabbi Shimon holds them liable on only one count, because Rabbi Shimon holds that a prohibition takes effect where another prohibition already exists only if the prohibitions take effect simultaneously, but not in cases of more inclusive prohibitions.

Perek **III**
Daf **33** Amud **b**

וְאִיסּוּר כּוֹלֵל אַתְנְיֵיהּ, וְאַלִּיבָּא דְּרַבִּי שִׁמְעוֹן, וַחֲזָיָא לְבַר קַפָּרָא לְזָר שֶׁאָכַל מְלִיקָה, וְאַיְּידֵי דְּדָמְיָא לָהּ – עַרְבֵּהּ בַּהֲדַיְיהוּ, וְעַיֵּין בָּהּ, וְלָא אַשְׁכַּח אֶלָּא בְּבַת אַחַת.

And he taught him the ruling with regard to **a more inclusive prohibition,** that in such cases there is an exemption, **and** this ruling is **in accordance with** the opinion of **Rabbi Shimon. And bar Kappara** then saw the case of **a non-priest who ate** a bird killed by **pinching, and since it was similar** to the previous cases, **he mixed them together.** Then, sometime later, it seemed to him as though he had in truth heard all of these cases together from Rabbi Yehuda HaNasi, **but** when **he examined this** last case, **he found** that it could exist **only** if the events occurred **simultaneously.**

וְסָבַר: מִדְּהָא בְּבַת אַחַת – הָא נַמִי בְּבַת אַחַת, וּמִדְּהָנָךְ לִפְטוֹר – הָנָךְ נַמִי לִפְטוֹר.

And he concluded that **since** the case of a non-priest eating a bird killed by pinching can occur only in a scenario where the prohibitions take effect **simultaneously,** the other cases are instances of **simultaneous** prohibitions **as well. And** similarly, **since** he was taught **to exempt** one individual from a second prohibition in **those cases, these cases** were taught **to exempt** one individual from a second prohibition **as well.** Therefore, according to Rabbi Ḥiyya, bar Kappara did not knowingly speak falsely. Rather, he heard certain matters from Rabbi Yehuda HaNasi and then mistakenly merged with them other matters. As a result, he confused the issue.

מֵיתִיבִי: זָר שֶׁשִּׁימֵּשׁ בְּשַׁבָּת, וּבַעַל מוּם שֶׁשִּׁימֵּשׁ בְּטוּמְאָה – יֵשׁ כָּאן מִשּׁוּם זָרוּת, וּמִשּׁוּם שַׁבָּת, וּמִשּׁוּם בַּעַל מוּם, וּמִשּׁוּם טוּמְאָה, דִּבְרֵי רַבִּי יוֹסֵי. רַבִּי שִׁמְעוֹן אוֹמֵר: אֵין כָּאן אֶלָּא מִשּׁוּם זָרוּת וּבַעַל מוּם בִּלְבַד. וְאִילּוּ מְלִיקָה שַׁיְּירָה.

The Gemara **raises an objection** to the statement of bar Kappara from a *baraita*: In the case of **a non-priest who served on Shabbat and** the case of **a blemished priest who served while ritually impure, there is** liability **here, due to** the prohibition against serving as **a non-priest; and due to** the prohibition against desecrating **Shabbat; and due to** the prohibition against serving as **a blemished priest; and due to** the prohibition against serving after contracting **ritual impurity.** This is **the statement of Rabbi Yosei. Rabbi Shimon says: There is** liability **here only due to** the prohibition against serving as **a non-priest and due to** the prohibition against serving as **a blemished priest.** The Gemara notes: **And yet** the case of a non-priest who ate a bird killed by **pinching was left out**[N] and not mentioned among the cases subject to this dispute.

לְמַאן שַׁיְּירָה? אִילֵימָא לְרַבִּי יוֹסֵי – הַשְׁתָּא רַבִּי יוֹסֵי בְּאִיסּוּר כּוֹלֵל מִיחַיֵּיב שְׁתַּיִם, בְּאִיסּוּר בַּת אַחַת מִיבַּעְיָא? אֶלָּא לָאו – לְרַבִּי שִׁמְעוֹן וּבְאִיסּוּר כּוֹלֵל הוּא דְּפָטַר – אֲבָל בְּאִיסּוּר בְּבַת אַחַת מִיחַיֵּיב, תְּיוּבְתָּא דְּבַר קַפָּרָא! תְּיוּבְתָּא.

The Gemara asks: **According to whom was this left out?** That is, according to the opinion of which *tanna* would this question arise? **If we say** that this was left out **according to** the opinion of **Rabbi Yosei,** it is difficult. **Now** that **Rabbi Yosei** holds, even **in** cases of a **more inclusive prohibition, that one is liable on two** counts,[N] as was stated with regard to a non-priest who served on Shabbat, **is** it **necessary** to state that in the case **where the** additional **prohibition** takes effect **simultaneously** one would be liable on two counts? **Rather, is it not according to** the opinion of **Rabbi Shimon** that this case was left out, as Rabbi Shimon would concede that in this case one is liable on two counts? Therefore, Rabbi Shimon **exempts** one from liability for the second prohibition in cases of **more inclusive prohibitions, but in** cases of **simultaneous prohibitions** he would **deem** one **liable** on two counts. The Gemara summarizes: **The refutation** of the opinion **of bar Kappara is** indeed **a conclusive refutation,** and his statements are rejected.

״זָר שֶׁשִּׁימֵּשׁ בְּשַׁבָּת״, בְּמַאי? אִי בִּשְׁחִיטָה – שְׁחִיטָה בְּזָר כְּשֵׁרָה, וְאִי בְּקַבָּלָה וְהוֹלָכָה – טִלְטוּל בְּעָלְמָא הוּא.

The Gemara raises a question with regard to one of the laws mentioned above. The *baraita* mentioned the case of **a non-priest who served on Shabbat.** The Gemara wonders: **In what** form of service did he perform in the Temple? **If** this is referring to a case where a non-priest performed **the slaughtering** of the sacrificial animal, there would be no prohibition, as the **slaughtering by a non-priest is valid. And if** it is referring to **receiving** the blood **and carrying** the blood to the altar, while this is a case where he would be liable as a non-priest performing the service of a priest, insofar as Shabbat is concerned **this is a case only of moving,** and it does not entail a violation of any prohibited labor.

NOTES

And yet the case of a non-priest who ate a bird killed by pinching was left out – וְאִילּוּ מְלִיקָה שַׁיְּירָה: The question arises: How can evidence be derived from the fact that this *halakha* is absent? Must the *tanna* teach all of the cases? The commentaries answer that were the case of eating of a bird killed by pinching indeed included in this dispute, it would have been appropriate to state it here because it would teach the novel ruling that Rabbi Shimon dissents even in cases of simultaneous prohibitions. Moreover, if the dispute was indeed about simultaneous prohibitions, then in the case of a non-priest who served on Shabbat, Rabbi Shimon would hold that the more severe prohibition of Shabbat would apply, not the prohibition against being a non-priest. The fact that Rabbi Shimon states that one would be liable only for serving as a non-priest indicates that the case is one of two prohibitions that take effect one after another, where one is liable only for the first prohibition (*Arukh LaNer*).

One is liable on two counts – מִיחַיֵּיב שְׁתַּיִם: According to all opinions, this does not refer to two sin-offerings but rather the transgression of two prohibitions, each according to its own ruling (Ramban; Rashba).

אִי בְּהַקְטָרָה – וְהָאָמַר רַבִּי יוֹסֵי: הַבְעָרָה לְלָאו יָצָאתָה!

If he served **by burning**[N] the sacrificial portions on the altar, then this discussion follows the opinion of Rabbi Yosei, **but didn't Rabbi Yosei say** that the prohibition against **kindling on Shabbat was** singled **out** to teach that one who lights a fire on Shabbat merely violates **a prohibition?** This is as opposed to the other prohibited labors, which incur death penalties when violated willfully and entail the bringing of a sin-offering when violated unintentionally. Why, then, would Rabbi Yosei deem one liable for two sin-offerings?

אָמַר רַב אַחָא בַּר יַעֲקֹב: בִּשְׁחִיטַת פָּרוֹ שֶׁל כֹּהֵן גָּדוֹל, וּכְדִבְרֵי הָאוֹמֵר: שְׁחִיטַת פָּרוֹ שֶׁל כֹּהֵן גָּדוֹל בְּזָר – פְּסוּלָה. אִי הָכִי מַאי אִירְיָא זָר, אֲפִילּוּ כֹּהֵן הֶדְיוֹט נַמִי! שֶׁזָּר אֶצְלוֹ קָאָמַר.

Rav Aḥa bar Yaakov said: The service referred to **in** this case is **the slaughtering of the High Priest's bull**[N] on Yom Kippur, **and this is in accordance with the statement of the one who says** that **the slaughtering of the High Priest's bull**[N] **is disqualified** if performed **by a non-priest,** for this service is designated specifically for the High Priest alone. The Gemara asks: **If so,** that this is referring to the slaughtering of the High Priest's bull, then **why specifically** state **a non-priest? The same would hold true even** for **a common priest as well.** The Gemara answers: **This is referring to one who is as a non-priest in relation to** the High Priest and not to an actual non-priest. The Hebrew word *zar* literally means foreigner, and this type of service is considered foreign to a common priest as well as a non-priest.

מַתְקִיף לָהּ רַב אַשִׁי: מִידֵּי חַטָּאוֹת קָתָנֵי, אוֹ לָאוֵי קָתָנֵי? אֶלָּא: אִיסּוּרֵי בְּעָלְמָא קָא חָשֵׁיב. לְמַאי נָפְקָא מִינָּהּ – לְקוֹבְרוֹ בֵּין רְשָׁעִים גְּמוּרִים.

Rav Ashi strongly objects to this: The previous rejection that was based on the idea that the act of burning was not a full-fledged prohibited labor is in fact groundless. **Is the** *tanna* **teaching** how many **sin-offerings** would be incurred, **or is he teaching** how many **negative mitzvot** are being violated? **Rather, he merely** enumerates **the prohibitions**[N] violated by a certain action, without detailing their severities, and therefore the desecration of Shabbat involved in the Temple service can be any Shabbat violation. The Gemara asks: **What practical difference does it make** how many prohibitions are involved? The Gemara answers: It affects the decision whether or not **to bury him among the completely wicked.** If he violated two prohibitions, he is considered wicked on two counts and consequently must be buried accordingly.

מתני׳ שְׁנַיִם שֶׁקִּידְּשׁוּ שְׁתֵּי נָשִׁים, וּבִשְׁעַת כְּנִיסָתָן לְחוּפָּה הֶחְלִיפוּ אֶת שֶׁל זֶה לָזֶה וְאֶת שֶׁל זֶה לָזֶה – הֲרֵי אֵלּוּ חַיָּיבִין מִשּׁוּם אֵשֶׁת אִישׁ. וְאִם הָיוּ אַחִין – מִשּׁוּם אֵשֶׁת אָח, וְאִם הָיוּ אֲחָיוֹת – מִשּׁוּם אִשָּׁה אֶל אֲחוֹתָהּ, וְאִם הָיוּ נִדּוֹת – מִשּׁוּם נִדָּה.

MISHNA In the case of **two men who betrothed two women, and at the time that they entered the wedding canopy,** after the betrothal, the men **switched**[H] **this** wife **with that** wife **and that** one **with this** one, **then these** two men **are liable for** engaging in forbidden sexual relations with **a married woman,** since each of them had intercourse with his fellow's wife. The act of betrothal is sufficient to prohibit a woman to all other men as a married woman. Therefore, when the women were switched, both men transgressed this violation. **And if they were brothers,**[N] then they are also liable **for** forbidden sexual relations with **a brother's wife. And if** these women **were sisters,** then they are liable **for** taking **a wife and her sister** as well. **And if they were menstruating women,** they would be liable **for** intercourse with **a menstruating woman** as well.

NOTES

If by burning – אִי בְּהַקְטָרָה: Rashi and others explain that this refers to the burning of the sacrificial portions on the altar. However, the Ritva seems to hold that this refers to the burning of incense. It is stated in the Jerusalem Talmud, in tractate *Shabbat*, that Rabbi Yosei does not deem one liable for kindling but rather for cooking. Although this seems to support Rashi's understanding, it can also be interpreted according to the Ritva's opinion.

The slaughtering of the High Priest's bull – שְׁחִיטַת פָּרוֹ שֶׁל כֹּהֵן גָּדוֹל: *Arukh LaNer* notes that this phrase in the Gemara indicates that the term Shabbat here is not referring to actual Shabbat but rather Yom Kippur, which is also called Shabbat. This is not a certain proof, however, since it could also be referring to a Yom Kippur that occurred on Shabbat. The Rivan writes that this suggested resolution of the Gemara is inexact, for even if the slaughtering of the High Priest's bull by a non-priest is prohibited, it is still not a prohibition that incurs *karet*, nor is it a negative mitzva. It would seem that the Gemara itself did not raise this objection because the suggestion is not sustained in the end.

The High Priest's bull – פָּרוֹ שֶׁל כֹּהֵן גָּדוֹל: On Yom Kippur, the High Priest sacrifices a bull as a sin-offering for himself, his family, and all the members of the priesthood (see Leviticus, chapter 16).

Rather he merely enumerates the prohibitions – אֶלָּא אִיסּוּרֵי בְּעָלְמָא קָא חָשֵׁיב: Rashi explains that according to this conclusion, Rabbi Yosei must be referring to receiving and carrying the blood. However, *Tosafot Yeshanim* explains that it is possible that he is even referring to burning. Although this does not entail the bringing of a sin-offering according to Rabbi Yosei, it is nevertheless prohibited by Torah law.

And if they were brothers, etc. – וְאִם הָיוּ אַחִין וכו׳: The commentaries note: If the mishna wanted to demonstrate cases where several prohibitions are violated by a single act, it could have enumerated more prohibitions. For example, it could have taught that these men were already married, and that the women that they inadvertently married were the daughters of their wives from a previous marriage. They therefore conclude that the mishna served to teach us only the different types of prohibitions that might be mutually applicable, each on the basis of the other's actions. Although according to this understanding it would have been unnecessary to mention the prohibition with regard to a menstruating woman, this case teaches a novelty in that it pertains to something that is presently prohibited but will eventually become permitted (*Tosefot HaRosh*).

HALAKHA

Switched women – נָשִׁים שֶׁהוּחְלְפוּ: If two men betrothed two women, who were then switched when they entered the wedding canopy, they are liable for having intercourse with a married woman. If they are brothers, they are also liable for intercourse with a brother's wife. If the women are sisters, they are also liable for intercourse with a wife's sister. If the women were menstruating, they are also liable for intercourse with a menstruating woman (Rambam *Sefer Korbanot*, *Hilkhot Shegagot* 4:1).

וּמַפְרִישִׁין אוֹתָן שְׁלֹשָׁה חֳדָשִׁים, שֶׁמָּא מְעוּבָּרוֹת הֵן, וְאִם הָיוּ קְטַנּוֹת שֶׁאֵינָן רְאוּיוֹת לֵילֵד – מַחֲזִירִים אוֹתָן מִיָּד, וְאִם הָיוּ כֹּהֲנוֹת – נִפְסְלוּ מִן הַתְּרוּמָה.

And following these forbidden sexual relations, **we separate** these women from their husbands **for three months,**[H] **lest they were impregnated** by that forbidden act of intercourse. Doing so makes it possible to distinguish a child born of these relations, so that he could be rendered a *mamzer*. **And if they were female minors and unable to bear children, then we immediately return them** to their original husbands. **And if they were daughters of priests, they are** thereby **disqualified from eating of *teruma*.** By engaging in illicit sexual acts, they were rendered forbidden to priests and disqualified from eating *teruma*.

גמ׳ ״הֶחֱלִיפוּ״, מִידֵי בִּרְשִׁיעֵי עָסְקִינַן?! וְתוּ: הָא דְּתָנֵי רַבִּי חִיָּיא: הֲרֵי כָּאן שֵׁשׁ עֶשְׂרֵה חַטָּאוֹת. אִי בְּמֵזִיד – מִי אִיכָּא קׇרְבָּן? אָמַר רַב יְהוּדָה, תְּנֵי: הוּחְלְפוּ.

GEMARA In the mishna it states: **They switched** this one with that one. **Are we dealing with** such **wicked individuals**[N] that they would intentionally switch their wives? **And furthermore,** consider **that which Rabbi Ḥiyya taught** on this subject: **There are sixteen sin-offerings here,** four sin-offerings for each of the men and four for each of the women. Yet, **if** they had acted **intentionally would there be an offering?**[N] Sacrifices are brought only for unintentional acts. **Rav Yehuda said: Teach** instead **they were switched,** which indicates that the switching was not done intentionally; rather, the women were accidentally mixed up.

הָכִי נַמִי מִסְתַּבְּרָא, דְּקָתָנֵי סֵיפָא: אִם הָיוּ קְטַנּוֹת שֶׁאֵינָן רְאוּיוֹת לֵילֵד – מַחֲזִירִין אוֹתָן מִיָּד. וְאִי בְּמֵזִיד – מִי שַׁרְיָא? הָא לָא קַשְׁיָא: פִּיתּוּי קְטַנָּה – אוֹנֶס הוּא, וְאוֹנֶס בְּיִשְׂרָאֵל מִישְׁרָא שָׁרֵי.

The Gemara comments: **This, too, stands to reason from the fact that the latter clause teaches: If they were female minors and unable to bear children, then we immediately return them. And if** this had been done **intentionally, would it be permitted** to return a woman who had engaged in illicit sexual acts to her husband? The Gemara comments: **This is not difficult** and does not disprove the notion that the act was intentional. Even if the act was intentional, these women would be permitted to return to their husbands. This is because the **seduction of a minor girl is** considered **rape, and** after **rape** a woman **is permitted** to return **to an Israelite**[H] husband.

אֶלָּא דְּקָתָנֵי: מַפְרִישִׁין אוֹתָן שְׁלֹשָׁה חֳדָשִׁים שֶׁמָּא מְעוּבָּרוֹת הֵן. הָא לָאו מְעוּבָּרוֹת – שַׁרְיָין, וְאִי בְּמֵזִיד – מִי שָׁרֵי? אֶלָּא לָאו שְׁמַע מִינַּהּ: הוּחְלְפוּ, שְׁמַע מִינַּהּ.

However, this can be derived from a different point **that** the mishna **teaches: We separate** these women from their husbands **for three months,** as **perhaps they became pregnant.** From here it can be deduced: **Were** it to become clear after three months that **they are not pregnant, they are permitted** to return to their husbands. **And if** they had acted **intentionally, would this be permitted? Rather,** must **one not conclude from here** that the mishna is referring to a case where **they were switched** inadvertently? The Gemara summarizes: Indeed, **conclude from here** that this is the case.

HALAKHA

We separate them for three months – מַפְרִישִׁין אוֹתָן שְׁלֹשָׁה חֳדָשִׁים: In cases where a woman was mistakenly married in a forbidden manner, if she engaged in sexual intercourse, she is then separated for three months to check if she became pregnant. This is in order to distinguish between an illegitimate child and one who was conceived lawfully. If she was a minor, she is not separated, since the Sages did not make decrees for impossible eventualities (Rambam *Sefer Nashim, Hilkhot Geirushin* 11:18; *Shulḥan Arukh, Even HaEzer* 13:8).

After rape a woman is permitted to return to an Israelite – אוֹנֶס בְּיִשְׂרָאֵל מִישְׁרָא שָׁרֵי: If the wife of an Israelite was raped, she is permitted to her husband but forbidden to priests, such that if she is widowed, she is prohibited from marrying a priest (Rambam *Sefer Kedusha, Hilkhot Issurei Bia* 18:7–8; *Shulḥan Arukh, Even HaEzer* 6:11).

NOTES

Are we dealing with wicked individuals, etc. – מִידֵי בִּרְשִׁיעֵי וכו׳: Although there are several *halakhot* in the Mishna that deal with cases of wicked individuals such as these, were the reference here to an intentional act, this particular mishna would not have taught anything especially novel. The only novel teaching would be the need to bury them among the completely wicked. If, however, the mishna is referring to a case where the men acted unintentionally, the novel element is the number of sin-offerings that they are obligated to bring (Rashash).

If intentionally, would there be an offering – אִי בְּמֵזִיד מִי אִיכָּא קׇרְבָּן: Although it could be suggested that the husbands acted intentionally while the women were unaware and therefore acted unwittingly, such an explanation is not reasonable as the Mishna does not generally refer to two different types of behavior within a single case (Ramban).

Perek **III**
Daf **34** Amud **a**

וּמַאן הַאי תַּנָּא דְּאִית לֵיהּ אִיסּוּר כּוֹלֵל וְאִיסּוּר מוֹסִיף וְאִיסּוּר בַּת אַחַת?

The Gemara asks: According to Rabbi Ḥiyya, who teaches that this case incurs sixteen sin-offerings, **who is this *tanna* who holds** that a prohibition takes effect where another prohibition already exists[H] for **a more inclusive prohibition, an expanded prohibition, and a simultaneous prohibition?** If these men are brothers, the moment that one betrothed a woman, that woman was immediately rendered forbidden to the second brother both as a married woman and as his brother's wife. When the second brother betrothed her sister, this added the prohibition pertaining to his wife's sister. This is a more inclusive prohibition because, as a result of this betrothal, the second brother is prohibited from engaging in sexual intercourse not only with his wife's sister, who is his brother's wife, but also with all of her other sisters. When this woman becomes a menstruating woman, she is forbidden to her husband as well, which is an expanded prohibition. Consequently, the mishna includes examples of all three types of prohibitions and asserts that they all take effect in this case. Therefore, the Gemara wonders which *tanna* holds that in each of these cases the prohibition takes effect even where another prohibition exists.

HALAKHA

A prohibition takes effect where another prohibition already exists – אִיסּוּר חָל עַל אִיסּוּר: A prohibition takes effect where another prohibition already exists only if both prohibitions take effect simultaneously, or if the second prohibition is a more inclusive prohibition or an expanded prohibition (Rambam *Sefer Korbanot, Hilkhot Shegagot* 4:1).

HALAKHA

Obligation to bring four sin-offerings and one guilt-offering for a single eating – חִיּוּב אַרְבַּע חַטָּאוֹת וְאָשָׁם אֶחָד בַּאֲכִילָה אַחַת: One who was ritually impure and ate an olive-bulk of prohibited fats that were leftover from a consecrated animal on Yom Kippur is obligated to bring four sin-offerings: One for eating prohibited fat, one for eating *notar*, one for eating consecrated food while ritually impure, and one for eating on Yom Kippur. This ruling applies in a case where one had previously eaten other food, so that altogether he ate a total of a date-bulk. In addition, he is obligated to bring a guilt-offering for deriving benefit from consecrated property (Rambam *Sefer Korbanot, Hilkhot Shegagot* 6:4).

אָמַר רַב יְהוּדָה אָמַר רַב: רַבִּי מֵאִיר הִיא. דְּתַנְיָא: יֵשׁ אוֹכֵל אֲכִילָה אַחַת וְחַיָּיב עָלֶיהָ אַרְבַּע חַטָּאוֹת וְאָשָׁם אֶחָד.

Rav Yehuda said that Rav said: This is the opinion of **Rabbi Meir,**[N] **as it is taught** in a *baraita*: **There is** one who performs a single act of **eating**[N] an olive-bulk of food, **and he is liable to bring four sin-offerings and one guilt-offering.**[H]

טָמֵא שֶׁאָכַל חֵלֶב וְהוּא נוֹתָר מִן מוּקְדָּשִׁין בְּיוֹם הַכִּפּוּרִים.

How so? This *halakha* applies to one who is **ritually impure who ate** forbidden **fat**[N] that was ***notar* from a consecrated offering,** i.e., it remained after the time when it was permitted to eat it, and this occurred **on Yom Kippur.** One who did this is liable to bring one sin offering for eating consecrated food while impure, one for eating forbidden fat, one for eating *notar*,[N] and one for eating on Yom Kippur. He is also liable to bring a guilt-offering for misuse of consecrated items. In this case, it was prohibited to eat the fat from the moment the animal was born. When the animal was consecrated, the prohibition against deriving benefit from it took effect on the entire animal, rendering this an expanded prohibition. When the priest became ritually impure and thereby prohibited from partaking of all sanctified foods, a more inclusive prohibition took effect. The moment the fat was rendered *notar*, it became prohibited to offer it on the altar as well, so that that is another instance of an expanded prohibition. Lastly, on Yom Kippur, an additional, more inclusive prohibition took effect because on Yom Kippur it is prohibited to eat all food, even that which is not consecrated.

רַבִּי מֵאִיר אוֹמֵר: אִם הָיְתָה שַׁבָּת וְהוֹצִיאוֹ בְּפִיו – חַיָּיב. אָמְרוּ לוֹ: אֵינוֹ מִן הַשֵּׁם.

Rabbi Meir says: There is one more sin-offering for which he may be liable. **If it was Shabbat and he carried** this olive-bulk of food from one domain to another **in his mouth,**[N] **he is liable** for carrying out on Shabbat. The Rabbis **said to** Rabbi Meir: Liability for the sin-offering that you added **is not** incurred **from** violation **of the** same **type** of prohibition. He is liable for carrying out the food, not for eating it. In this example, the prohibitions of Shabbat and Yom Kippur take effect at the same moment, and therefore this last case would be an instance of simultaneous prohibitions, and Rabbi Meir holds that they take effect as well. Therefore, this *baraita* demonstrates that Rabbi Meir holds that prohibitions take effect where other prohibitions already exist in all of these instances: More inclusive prohibitions, expanded prohibitions, and simultaneous prohibitions.

NOTES

This is the opinion of Rabbi Meir – רַבִּי מֵאִיר הִיא: From the fact that the Gemara ascribes this opinion to Rabbi Meir, some infer that Rabbi Yosei does not hold that more inclusive prohibitions take effect where another prohibition already exists (see *Keren Or*). Many early commentaries, however, suggest that Rabbi Yosei maintains that more inclusive prohibitions take effect as well, and here the Gemara simply sought out a source where a *tanna* explicitly states that all three types of prohibitions do, in fact, take effect (*Tosafot Yeshanim*; Ritva; Meiri).

There is one who performs a single act of eating, etc. – יֵשׁ אוֹכֵל אֲכִילָה אַחַת וכו׳: Rabbeinu Ḥananel explains that the simultaneous prohibitions here involve one who was rendered ritually impure and then grew two pubic hairs, indicating that he reached maturity. Under such circumstances, both the prohibition against eating consecrated food while ritually impure and the prohibition against eating forbidden fats take effect at once. Accordingly, the first *tanna* also holds that these three types of prohibitions, i.e., expanded prohibitions, more inclusive prohibitions, and simultaneous prohibitions, all take effect where another prohibition already exists. The Gemara, however, preferred to attribute this opinion to Rabbi Meir because unattributed *mishnayot* are generally considered to follow Rabbi Meir's opinion (see Rivan).

The Rif quotes this opinion and disagrees on several counts. He explains that the instance of simultaneous prohibitions referred to here is specifically in the addition cited in the name of Rabbi Meir: Carrying on Yom Kippur and carrying on Shabbat. Because Yom Kippur occurred on Shabbat, these prohibitions took effect simultaneously. According to this opinion, it is clear why the mishna was attributed to Rabbi Meir and not to the first *tanna*, for even if the first *tanna* agrees in principle with the ruling of simultaneous prohibitions, the ruling was stated explicitly only by Rabbi Meir. Rashi also explains that the ruling with regard to simultaneous prohibitions is derived from Rabbi Meir's statement. However, according to Rashi's opinion, there is no prohibition against carrying from domain to domain on Yom Kippur. Therefore, he explains that the two simultaneous prohibitions are the prohibition against eating on Yom Kippur and the prohibition against carrying on Shabbat (see Ramban and Rashba).

Fat – חֵלֶב: This refers to the animal fats that are prohibited by Torah law. Intentionally eating these fats from kosher domesticated animals is incurs *karet* (see Leviticus 7:22–25), while one who does so unwittingly is liable to bring a sin-offering. The fats of non-domesticated kosher animals and of kosher birds may be eaten. Among the signs differentiating forbidden fats from permitted fats is that the forbidden fats lie above the meat and are not entwined with it. They are enclosed by a thin membrane and are easily peeled away from the meat. Most of the forbidden fats of a sacrificial animal were sacrificed on the altar.

***Notar* – נוֹתָר:** This refers to parts of an offering left over after the time permitted for it to be eaten. One who eats the leftover portion of an offering is liable for punishment by *karet*. The Sages decreed that the leftover portion should be considered ritually impure, so that the priests would be prompt and meticulous in its removal.

And he carried it in his mouth – וְהוֹצִיאוֹ בְּפִיו: Some early commentaries had a variant text that read only: And carried it out. This version raises a question: If there is no connection between this last activity and the eating previously mentioned, why did Rabbi Meir add this prohibited labor in particular when he could have cited any other prohibited labor performed at the same moment? His choice is understandable according to the version that reads: He took it out in his mouth, because eating can be considered a form of placing an item, which is a requisite element of the prohibition against carrying. Without it, there is no liability.

According to a different version, however, this choice would seem arbitrary. In truth, even according to the current version, there is difficulty, as the Sages debated the question of whether carrying in one's mouth would indeed be considered carrying, as this is not the normal way to carry food. Nonetheless, in this case, since one is doing so as part of the act of eating, it is considered normal to carry in one's mouth and he would be liable.

וְרַבִּי מֵאִיר אַלִּיבָּא דְּמַאן? אִי אַלִּיבָּא דְּרַבִּי יְהוֹשֻׁעַ – הָאָמַר: טָעָה בִּדְבַר מִצְוָה פָּטוּר. אֶלָּא אַלִּיבָּא דְּרַבִּי אֱלִיעֶזֶר.

The Gemara continues to clarify the opinion of Rabbi Meir: **And in accordance with whose opinion is** the statement of **Rabbi Meir?**[N] If you say that **it is in accordance** with the opinion of **Rabbi Yehoshua,** this is difficult. **Didn't** Rabbi Yehoshua **say that one who erred with** regard to **a mitzva is exempt** from bringing a sin-offering, i.e., one who unwittingly performed a transgression while intending to perform a mitzva is exempt from punishment?[H] In the case in the mishna as well, the men intended to perform the mitzva of marriage but unwittingly violated a transgression because the wives were switched. Therefore, according to the opinion of Rabbi Yehoshua, they should be exempt from a sin-offering. **Rather,** this must be **in accordance with** the opinion of **Rabbi Eliezer,** who holds that even if one mistakenly transgressed while attempting to perform a mitzva, he is still obligated to bring a sin-offering.

אִיבָּעֵית אֵימָא: לְעוֹלָם אַלִּיבָּא דְּרַבִּי יְהוֹשֻׁעַ, כִּי קָאָמַר רַבִּי יְהוֹשֻׁעַ: טָעָה בִּדְבַר מִצְוָה פָּטוּר – הָנֵי מִילֵּי גַּבֵּי תִּינוֹקוֹת, דִּזְמַנּוֹ בָּהוּל. אֲבָל הַאי, כֵּיוָן דְּאֵין זְמַנּוֹ בָּהוּל – לָא.

If you wish, resolve this differently and **say: Actually,** this can be explained even **according to** the opinion of **Rabbi Yehoshua. When Rabbi Yehoshua says that one who erred with regard to a mitzva is exempt, this applies** only **to** the case of **babies** who were mixed up in such a way that on Shabbat the *mohel* mistakenly circumcised a baby whose time had not yet come for circumcision. Since the *mohel* did not fulfill the mitzva of circumcision, he should be liable for performing prohibited labor on Shabbat. However, Rabbi Yehoshua exempts him from a sin-offering **since** he is **pressed for time.** Because circumcision must be performed only on the day specified, he was rushed and anxious to perform the circumcision, and due to this sense of urgency he erred and thought that the proper time was on Shabbat. **In this** case in the mishna, **however,** where the mistake involved marriage, **since** the brothers were **not pressed for time** Rabbi Yehoshua does **not** deem the brothers exempt.

וַהֲרֵי תְּרוּמָה דְּאֵין זְמַנּוֹ בָּהוּל, וְקָפָטַר! דִּתְנַן: הָיָה אוֹכֵל בִּתְרוּמָה, וְנוֹדַע שֶׁהוּא בֶּן גְּרוּשָׁה אוֹ בֶּן חֲלוּצָה – רַבִּי אֱלִיעֶזֶר מְחַיֵּיב קֶרֶן וָחוֹמֶשׁ, וְרַבִּי יְהוֹשֻׁעַ פּוֹטֵר.

The Gemara objects: **And yet** in the case of eating ***teruma*****, where one is not pressed for time and** nevertheless Rabbi Yehoshua **exempts** him if the act involved a mitzva, **as we learned** in a mishna (*Pesaḥim* 72b): If a priest **was partaking of *teruma* and it became known that he was the son of a divorced woman**[N] **or the son of a *ḥalutza*** and thereby disqualified from the priesthood and prohibited from eating *teruma*,[H] **Rabbi Eliezer deems** him **liable** to pay **the** value of the **principal and** an additional **fifth,** like any non-priest who unwittingly ate *teruma*. However, **Rabbi Yehoshua exempts** him because at the time of consumption he intended to perform a mitzva, for he thought that he was a priest eating of the *teruma*.

הָא אִיתְּמַר עֲלַהּ, אָמַר רַב בֵּיבָי בַּר אַבַּיֵי: הָכָא בִּתְרוּמָה בְּעֶרֶב הַפֶּסַח עָסְקִינַן, דִּזְמַנָּהּ בָּהוּל.

The Gemara responds: **But wasn't it stated with regard to** that mishna: **Rav Beivai bar Abaye said: Here we are dealing with** leavened ***teruma*** that was being eaten by the priest **on the eve of Passover, for he is pressed for time.** In this case, he would rush to eat it so that it would not have to be burned.

וְאִי בָּעֵית אֵימָא: בְּאִיסּוּר בַּת אַחַת, וְאַלִּיבָּא דְּרַבִּי שִׁמְעוֹן.

The Gemara offers a different attribution of the mishna: **And if you wish, say** a different explanation: The mishna is not according to the opinion of Rabbi Meir, who deems one liable in cases of more inclusive prohibitions and expanded prohibitions. Rather, the mishna is referring only to cases **of simultaneous prohibitions, and in accordance with** the opinion of **Rabbi Shimon.**

בִּשְׁלָמָא כּוּלְּהוּ – מַשְׁכַּחַתְּ לְהוּ, דְּשַׁוְּינְהוּ שָׁלִיחַ, וְשַׁוּוֹ אִינְהוּ שָׁלִיחַ, וּפָגַע שָׁלִיחַ בְּשָׁלִיחַ. אֶלָּא נִדּוֹת – הֵיכִי מַשְׁכַּחַתְּ לַהּ?

The Gemara asks: **Granted,** with regard to **all of** the prohibitions in the mishna, **you can find that they** take effect simultaneously in the case **where** the men **appointed** a single **agent** to betroth the women for them, **and** the women **appointed an agent** to accept the betrothals for them, **and** one **agent encounters** the other **agent.** In this scenario, all the men become betrothed to all the women the moment that the agents meet, and the prohibitions all take effect simultaneously. **However,** with regard to the prohibition pertaining to **menstruating women, how can you find** the case where both women become menstruating women at the exact time of betrothal?

NOTES

And in accordance with whose opinion is the statement of Rabbi Meir – וְרַבִּי מֵאִיר אַלִּיבָּא דְּמַאן: Most commentaries explain, like Rashi, that this question relates to the present mishna, which was attributed to Rabbi Meir. However, Rabbeinu Ḥananel explains that this question relates to the mishna pertaining to the eating of prohibited fats. Because the latter mishna is dealing the prohibition of *notar*, it could be said that one was attempting to perform a mitzva, for he intended to remove the leftover foods to be burnt. The Rif and early commentaries disagree with this ruling.

And it became known that he was the son of a divorced woman – וְנוֹדַע שֶׁהוּא בֶּן גְּרוּשָׁה: Some later commentaries wonder: Why should this priest be held liable? Since it was impossible for him to know beforehand that he would be disqualified, this should be considered a circumstance beyond his control, and he should therefore be exempt. The Ritva explains that the mishna is referring to a situation where a public rumor had been spread that this priest was disqualified, and so he should have acted with more caution.

HALAKHA

An unwitting violation in a matter that involved a mitzva – שָׁגַג בִּדְבַר מִצְוָה: One who performs a transgression that requires the bringing of a sin-offering in the course of performing a mitzva is exempt from the obligation to bring an offering. This ruling applies only when one was both obligated to perform the mitzva and pressed for time (Rambam *Sefer Korbanot*, *Hilkhot Shegagot* 2:8).

A priest who was partaking of *teruma* and it became known that he was disqualified – כֹּהֵן אוֹכֵל תְּרוּמָה וְנוֹדַע שֶׁהוּא פָּסוּל: If a priest was eating *teruma* and was informed that he was the son of a divorced woman or the son of a *ḥalutza*, he must pay the principal alone but does not need to add a fifth of the sum that is the usually a penalty for unintentionally eating *teruma*. If at the time of eating he was pressed for time, such as is the case of eating leavened *teruma* on the eve of Passover, then he is exempt from payment, in accordance with the opinion of Rabbi Yehoshua and the conclusion in the Gemara (Rambam *Sefer Zera'im*, *Hilkhot Terumot* 10:12).

BACKGROUND

Continually discharge blood – שׁוֹפְעוֹת: Generally, the flow of blood during a menstrual cycle continues several days. Although there are differences between the days insofar as the amount of blood is concerned, a woman is considered to be continually discharging blood during the entirety of her menstruation, generally five to seven days.

אָמַר רַב עַמְרָם אָמַר רַב: בְּשׁוֹפְעוֹת מִתּוֹךְ שְׁלֹשָׁה עָשָׂר לְאַחַר שְׁלֹשָׁה עָשָׂר לְאִחַיּוּבֵי אִינְהוּ, מִתּוֹךְ שְׁנֵים עָשָׂר לְאַחַר שְׁנֵים עָשָׂר – לְחַיּוּבֵי אִינְהִי.

Rav Amram said that Rav said: This is referring to a situation **where** the women **continuously discharge** menstrual blood[B] **from within the thirteenth**[N] year of the brothers **until after** they reached the age of **thirteen,** in order **to deem** the men **liable** for the prohibition pertaining to a menstruating woman. At the moment that the boys reached maturity and the betrothals went into effect, the sisters were forbidden as menstruating women. And the women were continuously discharging blood **from within the twelfth** year of the women **until after** the age of **twelve, in order to deem** the women **liable** for engaging in relations as a menstruating woman. Therefore, if this took place in such a way that on the exact day when the men reached maturity, i.e., their thirteenth birthday, the women reached maturity, i.e., their twelfth birthday, and at that moment they were menstruating, then all of the prohibitions would take effect simultaneously and they would be liable on all counts, according to Rabbi Shimon as well.

״מַפְרִישִׁים אוֹתָן״. וְהָא אֵין אִשָּׁה מִתְעַבֶּרֶת בְּבִיאָה רִאשׁוֹנָה! אָמַר רַב נַחְמָן אָמַר רַבָּה בַּר אֲבוּהּ: שֶׁבְּעָלוּ וְשָׁנוּ. וְאֶלָּא הָא דְּתָנָא רַבִּי חִיָּיא: הֲרֵי כָּאן שֵׁשׁ עֶשְׂרֵה חַטָּאוֹת, תְּלָתִין וְתַרְתֵּין הָוְיָין!

§ The mishna taught that **we separate** these women from their husbands for three months, as perhaps they became pregnant. The Gemara asks: **But isn't** it known that a virgin **woman does not become pregnant**[N] **from her first sexual act? Rav Naḥman said that Rabba bar Avuh said:** This is referring to a situation **where they engaged in intercourse and then repeated** the act, so that it is possible that the women were impregnated during the second act of intercourse. The Gemara asks: **But** if this is so, how can one explain **that which Rabbi Ḥiyya teaches:**[N] **Here, then, are sixteen sin-offerings?** If there were indeed two acts of intercourse, then **there** should **be thirty-two** sin-offerings, since each prohibition was violated twice.

וְלִיטַעֲמִיךְ, לְרַבִּי אֱלִיעֶזֶר, דִּמְחַיֵּיב עַל כָּל כֹּחַ וְכֹחַ, טוּבָא הָוְיָין! אֶלָּא, דִּבְכֹחַ רִאשׁוֹן קָחָשֵׁיב – הָכִי נַמִּי דְּבִיאָה רִאשׁוֹנָה קָחָשֵׁיב.

The Gemara answers: **And according to your reasoning, that** Rabbi Ḥiyya's enumeration of sin-offerings applies to all acts of intercourse, then **according to** the opinion of **Rabbi Eliezer, who deems one liable** to bring a sin-offering **for each and every thrusting** movement during a single act of intercourse, there would **be many** prohibitions that were violated. This would greatly multiply the number of sin-offerings required. **Rather,** it must be that Rabbi Ḥiyya, with regard to Rabbi Eliezer's opinion, **is enumerating** only **the first thrusting** movement **in the intercourse. And so too,** with regard to the Rabbis' opinion, **he is enumerating** only **the first act of intercourse.** If there were two acts of intercourse, however, the number of sin-offerings would be doubled.

אָמַר לֵיהּ רָבָא לְרַב נַחְמָן:

Rava said to Rav Naḥman:

NOTES

Where they continuously discharge blood from within the thirteenth, etc. – בְּשׁוֹפְעוֹת מִתּוֹךְ שְׁלֹשָׁה עָשָׂר וכו׳: Rashi posits that this is a case where male minors betrothed female minors prior to maturity, so that the betrothals and the prohibition with regard to a menstruating woman took effect simultaneously. *Tosafot*, the Ramban, and the Rashba question this explanation: Since there is no legal efficacy to an act performed by minors, how could these betrothals later take effect? Even if one were to suggest that this explanation follows Rabbi Meir's opinion, that it is possible to perform betrothal to effect acquisition with an item that has not yet come into being, it is still unclear whether this principle would apply to this a case, where the one performing the betrothal is in fact a minor himself. Rivan and *Tosefot HaRosh* explain that if the betrothal was conditional and previously agreed upon, it could take effect upon their arrival at maturity (see *Mishne LaMelekh*).

Due to this difficulty, many early commentaries preferred Rabbeinu Ḥananel's version of the text which reads: They were continuously discharging blood from within three until after three. This indicates that the situation is one of female minors betrothed by their fathers to adult males. Before the age of three, any intercourse that takes place has no legal status, so that none of the prohibitions mentioned could apply. When they reached the age of three all of the prohibitions took effect simultaneously. This would create a situation where the males would be liable for all of the prohibitions. However, when the Gemara states: Continuously discharging blood from within twelve, this is a separate scenario. It is a case where the women reached maturity and would therefore be liable for these prohibitions. According to this opinion, all of the prohibitions did not affect both the men and women at the same time. Rather there are two different scenarios: One in which all the prohibitions affected the men at the same time, and one where all the prohibitions affected the women at the same time. As a result, there is no need to adopt Rashi's unlikely description that this refers to two twin brothers who betrothed two twin sisters who were exactly one year younger than them.

But isn't it known that a virgin woman does not become pregnant, etc. – וְהָא אֵין אִשָּׁה מִתְעַבֶּרֶת וכו׳: The early commentaries ask: Why does the Gemara assume that this case refers to virgins? Perhaps it refers to women who had previously engaged in permissible intercourse, such as widows, or even women who had engaged in illicit intercourse. According to Rabbeinu Ḥananel's reading, which states that this is a case of three-year-old girls, this question is irrelevant. However, according to Rashi's version of the text, this is difficult. *Tosefot HaRosh*, citing the name Maharam MiRotenburg, states that these women were necessarily virgins because the mishna was particular in stating that these prohibitions took effect only following entrance into the wedding canopy. Had these women been previously married, they would have already been subject to the prohibition pertaining to a married woman. Additionally, the Ritva explains the following: Given that neither the men nor the women were aware that the mix-up took place, it stands to reason that the women were modest virgins who would not be suspected of illicit sexual acts.

But if this is so, how can one explain that which Rabbi Ḥiyya teaches, etc. – וְאֶלָּא הָא דְּתָנָא רַבִּי חִיָּיא וכו׳: Rashi explains that since the Gemara, in its previous discussion of Rabbi Meir's opinion, already established that the mishna is in accordance with Rabbi Eliezer's opinion, it was necessary to explain the *baraita* about the number of potential sin-offerings in the mishna in accordance with Rabbi Eliezer's opinion as well. Moreover, only according to Rabbi Eliezer is one obligated to bring more than one sin-offering for acts of intercourse performed in one lapse of awareness (see 92a and *Karetot* 15a). Rashi argues that the notion that each thrusting movement obligates one in a separate sin-offering is an extension of this idea.

According to the Vilna Gaon, the attempt to resolve Rabbi Ḥiyya's *baraita* in this context is a textual corruption, and both the question and the answer should be omitted (*Haggahot HaGra*). Once the Gemara explained that the mishna could be understood in accordance with Rabbi Shimon's opinion, in a case where all the prohibitions took effect simultaneously, it was unnecessary to further posit that it follows Rabbi Eliezer.

וְהָא תָּמָר בְּבִיאָה רִאשׁוֹנָה אִיעַבְּרָא! אָמַר לֵיהּ: תָּמָר בְּאֶצְבַּע מָעֲכָה. דְּאָמַר רַבִּי יִצְחָק: כׇּל מוֹעֲכוֹת שֶׁל בֵּית רַבִּי תָּמָר שְׁמָן, וְלָמָּה נִקְרָא שְׁמָן תָּמָר? עַל שֵׁם תָּמָר שֶׁמָּעֲכָה בְּאֶצְבְּעָהּ. וְהָא הָווּ עֵר וְאוֹנָן! עֵר וְאוֹנָן שִׁמְּשׁוּ שֶׁלֹּא כְּדַרְכָּן.

But didn't Tamar become pregnant from the first act of intercourse,[NB] despite the fact that she was a virgin at the time of her sexual act with Judah? Rav Naḥman **said: Tamar broke** her hymen **with her finger** prior to intercourse, and it is due to this that she became pregnant from the first act of intercourse, **as Rabbi Yitzḥak said: All of those** women **from the household of Rabbi** Yehuda HaNasi **who break** their hymens[N] **are named Tamar** by nickname. **And why are they named Tamar?** They are called this **on account of Tamar, who broke** her hymen **with her finger.** The Gemara wonders about the proof from Tamar itself: **But weren't there Er and Onan,** her previous husbands, who presumably engaged in sexual intercourse with her? The Gemara responds: **Er and Onan engaged in sexual intercourse in an atypical manner,** i.e., anal intercourse, and therefore she was still a virgin.

מֵיתִיבֵי: כׇּל עֶשְׂרִים וְאַרְבָּעָה חֹדֶשׁ דָּשׁ מִבִּפְנִים וְזוֹרֶה מִבַּחוּץ, דִּבְרֵי רַבִּי אֱלִיעֶזֶר. אָמְרוּ לוֹ: הַלָּלוּ אֵינוֹ אֶלָּא כְּמַעֲשֵׂה עֵר וְאוֹנָן!

The Gemara **raises an objection** from the *Tosefta* (*Nidda* 5:6): After a woman gives birth, her husband **penetrates inside and spills** his semen **outside**[H] for **the entire twenty-four months** during which the baby is breastfeeding, so that his wife not become pregnant, as that would terminate her milk production and the child might die. This is **the statement of Rabbi Eliezer. They said to him: These** acts **are nothing other** than acts **similar to those of Er and Onan,** which are prohibited. Regardless, it can be deduced from here that Er and Onan engaged in normative sexual intercourse with Tamar, only they did not fully complete the sexual act.

כְּמַעֲשֵׂה עֵר וְאוֹנָן, וְלֹא כְּמַעֲשֵׂה עֵר וְאוֹנָן. כְּמַעֲשֵׂה עֵר וְאוֹנָן – דִּכְתִיב ״וְהָיָה אִם בָּא אֶל אֵשֶׁת אָחִיו וְשִׁחֵת אַרְצָה״, וְלֹא כְּמַעֲשֵׂה עֵר וְאוֹנָן, דְּאִילּוּ הָתָם – שֶׁלֹּא כְּדַרְכָּהּ, וְהָכָא – כְּדַרְכָּהּ.

The Gemara answers: The *Tosefta* actually means that what they did was **similar to the act of Er and Onan** in some ways, but **not similar to the act of Er and Onan** in other ways. The Gemara elaborates: **It was similar to the act of Er and Onan** in that there was a spilling of semen, **as it is written: "And it came to pass when he had intercourse with his brother's wife, that he spilled it on the ground"** (Genesis 38:9). Yet it was **not similar to the act of Er and Onan, as there** Er and Onan engaged in sexual intercourse **in an atypical manner,** i.e., anal intercourse, **while here** the *Tosefta* is referring to sexual intercourse **in a typical manner.**

בִּשְׁלָמָא אוֹנָן – דִּכְתִיב בֵּיהּ ״וְשִׁחֵת אַרְצָה״, אֶלָּא עֵר מְנָלַן? אֲמַר רַב נַחְמָן בַּר יִצְחָק: דִּכְתִיב ״וַיָּמֶת גַּם אוֹתוֹ״, אַף הוּא בְּאוֹתוֹ מִיתָה מֵת. בִּשְׁלָמָא אוֹנָן – מִשּׁוּם ״לֹא לוֹ יִהְיֶה הַזָּרַע״, אֶלָּא עֵר מַאי טַעֲמָא עֲבַד הָכִי? כְּדֵי שֶׁלֹּא תִּתְעַבֵּר וְיִכְחִישׁ יׇפְיָהּ.

The Gemara continues to clarify what took place: **Granted, Onan** engaged in unnatural sexual intercourse with her, **as it is written with regard to his act: "That he spilled it on the ground"** (Genesis 38:9). **However, from where do we** derive that Er engaged in unnatural sexual intercourse with her? **Rav Naḥman bar Yitzḥak said: As it is written** with regard to Onan: **"And He slew him also"** (Genesis 38:10). This indicates that **he, too, died the same death** for performing the same transgression as his brother. The Gemara asks: **Granted, Onan** engaged in anal intercourse because he did not want Tamar to give birth as "he knew that **the seed would not be his"** (Genesis 38:9). **However,** with regard to **Er, what is the reason he acted** in **this** way? The Gemara responds: He did so in order **that she not become pregnant and become less beautiful** as a result of her pregnancy.

NOTES

But didn't Tamar become pregnant from the first act of intercourse – וְהָא תָּמָר בְּבִיאָה רִאשׁוֹנָה אִיעַבְּרָא: The Maharsha raises a challenge: Why did the Gemara assume that Tamar was impregnated by her first act of intercourse, so that it was necessary to entertain far-fetched ideas in order to explain how she became pregnant? Indeed, according to the simple understanding of the biblical narrative, Tamar's first husbands had typical sexual intercourse with her (see Genesis, chapter 38, and Rashi's commentary there; see *Midrash Rabba*).

The Maharsha suggests that perhaps support for the idea that Er and Onan did not engage in typical intercourse can be found in an interpretation of the verses in the Torah. Indeed, the Rashash presents evidence from Ibn Ezra's commentary, which cites the interpretation that the phrase "and he spilled it on the ground" is referring to unnatural intercourse. Ibn Ezra ultimately rejects this interpretation.

The various commentaries challenge this suggestion based on the fact that this verse is stated only with regard to Onan, not Er. *Ramat Shmuel* tries to resolve this problem by invoking the opinion that Judah, after the entire ordeal became known to him, did not cease his relations with her. It interprets the verse that reads: "And he knew her again no more" (Genesis 38:26) to mean: He did not cease to know her, i.e., to engage with her sexually. This was permitted because Tamar had engaged only in unnatural intercourse with her previous husbands, and according to the Noahide laws she was never considered to be married to his sons. Accordingly, this opinion serves as a support for the idea that Er and Onan did not engage in natural intercourse.

All of those from the household of Rabbi Yehuda HaNasi who break their hymens – כׇּל מוֹעֲכוֹת שֶׁל בֵּית רַבִּי: Some early commentaries cite a version of the text that reads: The household of David. The commentaries explain the rationale behind the women's behavior according to both readings. The Ritva states these women were so upright that they did not want any act of intercourse to be in vain, and therefore they wished to become pregnant even from the first act. The Meiri points out that the disciples of the household of Rabbi Yehuda HaNasi were exceedingly pious in their separation from women and the soldiers of David's household were often off in battle. Therefore, their wives wanted to ensure that they would become pregnant from the first act of intercourse.

HALAKHA

Penetrates inside and spills outside – דָּשׁ מִבִּפְנִים וְזוֹרֶה מִבַּחוּץ: A man is prohibited from engaging in intercourse with his wife in a way that entails the spilling of his seed outside her body. One who does so has emitted semen in vain, which is a great sin (Rambam *Sefer Kedusha*, *Hilkhot Issurei Bia* 21:18; *Shulḥan Arukh*, *Even HaEzer* 23:1).

BACKGROUND

Become pregnant from the first act of intercourse – בְּבִיאָה רִאשׁוֹנָה אִיעַבְּרָא: According to contemporary medical knowledge, the fact that a woman is a virgin does not prevent her, in purely physiological terms, from becoming pregnant. However, it may be presumed that the pain that accompanies her first act of intercourse along with the accompanying psychological factors can cause tension and other effects. These could render the possibility of impregnation minimal. The women of Rabbi Yehuda HaNasi's house prepared themselves both physically and emotionally for intercourse and were therefore able to become pregnant.

תָּנוּ רַבָּנַן: ״אוֹתָהּ״ פְּרָט לְכַלָּה, דִּבְרֵי רַבִּי יְהוּדָה. וַחֲכָמִים אוֹמְרִים: פְּרָט לְשֶׁלֹּא כְּדַרְכָּהּ. אֲמַר לֵיהּ הוֹן בְּרֵיהּ דְּרַב נַחְמָן לְרַב נַחְמָן: לֵימָא קָא סָבַר רַבִּי יְהוּדָה הַתּוֹרָה חָסָה עַל תַּכְשִׁיטֵי כַלָּה? אֲמַר לֵיהּ: לְפִי שֶׁאֵין אִשָּׁה מִתְעַבֶּרֶת מִבִּיאָה רִאשׁוֹנָה.

The Sages taught: The verse states: "And the woman, **with whom** a man shall lie giving seed, they shall both bathe themselves in water, and be unclean until the evening" (Leviticus 15:18). The extra term **"with whom"** comes **to exclude a bride** who does not become ritually impure; this is **the statement of Rabbi Yehuda. And the Rabbis say: It excludes** the case of sexual intercourse performed **in an atypical manner.**[H] **Hon,**[P] **son of Rav Naḥman, said to Rav Naḥman: Shall we say that Rabbi Yehuda holds: The Torah spared a bride's adornments,** including her make-up, and therefore exempted her from submersion in water, as that might cause them ruin? Rav Naḥman **said to him:** That is not the reason. Rather, **it is because a woman does not become pregnant from the first act of intercourse.** Therefore, that act of intercourse would not cause ritual impurity, as it is not considered intercourse that can result in the implanting of seed.

בְּמַאי קָמִיפַּלְגִי? רַבָּנַן סָבְרִי ״שִׁכְבַת זֶרַע״ פְּרָט לְהַעֲרָאָה: ״אוֹתָהּ״ פְּרָט לְשֶׁלֹּא כְּדַרְכָּהּ. וְרַבִּי יְהוּדָה סָבַר: שֶׁלֹּא כְּדַרְכָּהּ וְהַעֲרָאָה – מִ״שִּׁכְבַת זֶרַע״ נָפְקָא: ״אוֹתָהּ״ פְּרָט לְכַלָּה.

The Gemara asks: **With regard to what do** Rabbi Yehuda and the Rabbis **disagree? The Rabbis hold** that the phrase **"giving seed" excludes the initial stage of intercourse,**[N] during which there is no emission of semen.[H] And the extra phrase **"with whom" excludes intercourse that is performed in an atypical way. Rabbi Yehuda,** on the other hand, **holds that** the exclusion of both **atypical** sexual intercourse **and the initial stage of intercourse were derived from** the phrase **"giving seed,"** as neither of these are sexual acts that might bring about the birth of a seed, i.e., a child. The phrase **"with whom"** then **excludes a bride.**[N]

כִּי אֲתָא רָבִין אָמַר רַבִּי יוֹחָנָן: כָּל שֶׁשָּׁהֲתָה אַחַר בַּעְלָהּ עֶשֶׂר שָׁנִים וְנִשֵּׂאת – שׁוּב אֵינָהּ יוֹלֶדֶת. אָמַר רַב נַחְמָן: לֹא שָׁנוּ אֶלָּא שֶׁאֵין דַּעְתָּהּ לְהִנָּשֵׂא, אֲבָל דַּעְתָּהּ לְהִנָּשֵׂא – מִתְעַבֶּרֶת. אֲמַר לֵיהּ רָבָא לְבַת רַב חִסְדָּא: קָא מְרַנְּנֵי רַבָּנַן אַבַּתְרִיךְ. אֲמָרָה לֵיהּ: אֲנָא דַּעְתַּאי עֲלָךְ הֲוַאי.

On the topic of intercourse that cannot result in conception, the Gemara relates the following: **When Ravin came** from Eretz Yisrael to Babylonia, he said that **Rabbi Yoḥanan said:** Any woman who **waits after her husband** has died or divorced her for **ten years** without intercourse **and is then married can no longer bear children. Rav Naḥman said: They taught** this principle **only** with regard to cases **where she did not intend to get married** at a later time, **but if she intended to get married** at some point, **she can become pregnant** later on. **Rava said to** his wife, the **daughter of Rav Ḥisda:**[N] **The Sages are gossiping about you.** From the time she was widowed from her first husband until the time that she was married to Rava, more than ten years passed, yet she bore him children. It seemed as though she had engaged in intercourse in the meantime. **She said to him: My mind was on you.** Indeed, it is told that already as a young girl she prophesized that she would marry Rava.

הַהִיא דַּאֲתְיָא לְקַמֵּיהּ דְּרַב יוֹסֵף, אָמְרָה לוֹ: רַבִּי, אֲנָא שֶׁהִיתִי אַחַר בַּעְלִי עֶשֶׂר שָׁנִים וְיָלַדְתִּי. אָמַר לָהּ: בִּתִּי, אַל תּוֹצִיאִי לַעַז עַל דִּבְרֵי חֲכָמִים. אָמְרָה לֵיהּ: לְגוֹי נִבְעַלְתִּי.

The Gemara relates: **A certain** woman **who came before Rav Yosef said to him: My teacher, I waited after my husband's** death **for ten years,** and nevertheless **I gave birth. He said to her: My daughter, do not cast aspersions on the statement of the Sages. She said to him** in confession: **I had sexual intercourse with a gentile** during those ten years.

HALAKHA

Ritual impurity from atypical intercourse – טוּמְאַת בִּיאָה שֶׁלֹּא כְּדַרְכָּהּ: If one engages in anal intercourse with his wife, she remains ritually pure because the Torah ruled there to be ritual impurity in the concealed parts of the body only from typical intercourse (Rambam *Sefer Tahara, Hilkhot Avot HaTumot* 5:9).

Ritual impurity in the initial stage of sexual intercourse – טוּמְאַת הַעֲרָאָה: If one engages in the initial stage of sexual intercourse with a woman, or even full intercourse but did not emit semen, then both the man and woman are ritually pure (Rambam *Sefer Tahara, Hilkhot Avot HaTumot* 5:10).

PERSONALITIES

Hon – הוֹן: This Sage, one of Rav Naḥman's sons, is rarely mentioned. It may be assumed that he is identical with Huna, son of Rav Naḥman, and that Hon is a nickname or a Hebrew form of the same name.

NOTES

Initial stage of intercourse – הַעֲרָאָה: The Gemara presents a dispute as to the definition of the initial stage of intercourse (55b). One opinion maintains that the initial stage of intercourse occurs at the moment of external contact of the sexual organs. The other holds that the initial stage of intercourse is defined by the penetration of the corona. With regard to forbidden relations, one is liable for violating a prohibition if one engaged in this initial stage of intercourse, even if one did not complete the act of intercourse.

With whom excludes a bride – אוֹתָהּ פְּרָט לְכַלָּה: This Torah law, which requires both the man and the woman to immerse following intercourse, is understood to be a special decree stated by the verses, as it does not follow the usual laws of ritual impurity. It overrides the principle that an emission of semen causes ritual impurity only upon touch, which does not include contact with concealed parts of the body. This decree of ritual impurity is imparted even though intercourse applies only to acts of full-fledged intercourse that can lead to childbirth.

The daughter of Rav Ḥisda – בַּת רַב חִסְדָּא: The daughter of Rav Ḥisda was married to Rami bar Ḥama. Over ten years after he died, she married Rava. The Gemara relates an incident that took place when she was a young girl (*Bava Batra* 12b). She was sitting in her father's lap when Rava and Rami bar Ḥama, both students of Rav Ḥisda, were sitting before him. Rav Ḥisda asked his daughter which of the two she desired, and she answered: Both. Rava responded: I will be the last.

אָמַר שְׁמוּאֵל: וְכוּלָּן צְרִיכוֹת לְהַמְתִּין שְׁלֹשָׁה חֳדָשִׁים, חוּץ מִגִּיּוֹרֶת וּמְשׁוּחְרֶרֶת קְטַנָּה. אֲבָל קְטַנָּה בַּת יִשְׂרָאֵל – צְרִיכָה לְהַמְתִּין שְׁלֹשָׁה חֳדָשִׁים.

§ **Shmuel said: And all of those** women who had sexual intercourse, and there is therefore a concern that they might be pregnant, **must wait three months** before marrying so as to differentiate between a child born from the previous intercourse and a child born from this marriage, **except for a female convert** who is a minor **and a female released slave who is a minor.** Although it is possible that they had sexual intercourse, they cannot become pregnant in any case. **However, a female Israelite who was a minor** and had intercourse **must wait three months** like all other women.

וּבְמַאי? אִי בְּמֵיאוּן – וְהָאָמַר שְׁמוּאֵל דְּלָא בָּעְיָא. וְאִי בְּגֵט – הָאָמְרָה שְׁמוּאֵל חֲדָא זִימְנָא. דְּאָמַר שְׁמוּאֵל: מֵיאֲנָה בּוֹ – אֵינָהּ צְרִיכָה לְהַמְתִּין שְׁלֹשָׁה חֳדָשִׁים, נָתַן לָהּ גֵּט – צְרִיכָה לְהַמְתִּין שְׁלֹשָׁה חֳדָשִׁים! אֶלָּא בִּזְנוּת.

The Gemara asks: **And with regard to what** situation is this statement referring? **If it is** referring to a minor who was released from her marriage **by refusal,** as a minor girl who was married to a man by her mother or brothers may refuse to remain married to her husband until reaching majority, **but didn't Shmuel say that she is not required** to wait three months? **And if** it is referring to a woman who received **a bill of divorce** as a minor, **didn't Shmuel** already **state** this *halakha* **one time?** Why would he repeat this ruling, **as Shmuel said: A female minor who refused** her husband **need not wait three months** before her second marriage,[H] but if **he gave her a bill of divorce, she must wait three months,**[H] so as not to make a distinction between an adult divorcée and a minor divorcée. **Rather,** it must be that this is referring to a female minor who was involved in **licentious sexual intercourse.**

HALAKHA

Waiting period for a female minor who performed refusal – הַמְתָּנָה בִּמְמָאֶנֶת: A female minor who refused her husband is not required to wait three months before marrying another man, as the rabbinic decree did not include her (Rambam *Sefer Nashim, Hilkhot Geirushin* 11:22; *Shulḥan Arukh, Even HaEzer* 13:6).

Waiting period for a divorced woman – הַמְתָּנָה בִּגְרוּשָׁה: Every woman who was divorced must wait three months before marrying another man. The Sages did not distinguish between divorced women, so that even a minor divorced woman who cannot bear children must still wait three months (Rambam *Sefer Nashim, Hilkhot Geirushin* 11:20; *Shulḥan Arukh, Even HaEzer* 23:1).

Perek **III**
Daf **35** Amud **a**

וְגָזְרוּ רַבָּנַן קְטַנָּה מִשּׁוּם גְּדוֹלָה.

And, although there is no possibility for her to become pregnant, **the Sages issued** a rabbinic **decree** requiring the three month waiting period **for a female minor due to** this requirement for **a female adult** who engaged in promiscuous sexual acts.

וּמִי גָּזְרִינַן קְטַנָּה מִשּׁוּם גְּדוֹלָה? וְהָתְנַן: אִם הָיוּ קְטַנּוֹת שֶׁאֵינָן רְאוּיוֹת לֵילֵד – מַחֲזִירִין אוֹתָן מִיָּד! אָמַר רַב גִּידֵּל אָמַר רַב: הוֹרָאַת שָׁעָה הָיְתָה. מִכְּלָל דַּהֲוַאי?! אֶלָּא כְּהוֹרָאַת שָׁעָה הָיְתָה, וְחִילּוּף לָא שְׁכִיחַ.

The Gemara asks: **And do we issue a decree** with regard to **a female minor due to** the ruling for **a female adult? But didn't we learn** in the mishna: **If they were female minors who could not bear children, we return them**[H] **immediately** to their husbands? This indicates that there is no concern for pregnancy, and the Sages did not issue a decree in this case. **Rav Giddel said** that **Rav said: This was a provisional edict** issued in exigent circumstances, and therefore one cannot extrapolate from the case in the mishna to other situations. The Gemara wonders: Can one assume **by inference that there was** such an occurrence? It would seem from the mishna that this was merely a possibility and not an actual occurrence, for if it actually happened it would have been appropriate for the mishna to relate the actual case. **Rather,** the ruling in the mishna is **like a provisional edict in that switching** of wives, such as described in the mishna, **is uncommon,** and in cases that are not common, the Sages do not issue a decree. Therefore, in the case of the mishna, the female minors were not required to wait.

HALAKHA

If they were female minors…we return them – אִם הָיוּ קְטַנּוֹת...מַחֲזִירִין אוֹתָן: In situations where a woman was mistakenly married and then removed from her husband by a court, if she was a minor at the time, she is allowed to marry another man. She need not wait because this is an uncommon occurrence and was not included in the rabbinic decree (Rambam *Sefer Nashim, Hilkhot Geirushin* 11:23; *Shulḥan Arukh, Even HaEzer* 13:8).

לִישָּׁנָא אַחֲרִינָא אָמְרִי לָהּ, אָמַר שְׁמוּאֵל: כּוּלָּן צְרִיכוֹת לְהַמְתִּין שְׁלֹשָׁה חֳדָשִׁים, חוּץ מִגִּיּוֹרֶת וּמְשׁוּחְרֶרֶת גְּדוֹלָה. [אֲבָל] קְטַנָּה בַּת יִשְׂרָאֵל – אֵינָהּ צְרִיכָה לְהַמְתִּין שְׁלֹשָׁה חֳדָשִׁים. בְּמַאי? אִי בְּמֵיאוּן – הָאֲמָרָהּ שְׁמוּאֵל חֲדָא זִימְנָא, אִי בְּגֵט – הָא קָאָמַר שְׁמוּאֵל דִּבְעֲיָא, דְּאָמַר שְׁמוּאֵל: מֵיאֲנָה בּוֹ – אֵינָהּ צְרִיכָה לְהַמְתִּין שְׁלֹשָׁה חֳדָשִׁים, נָתַן לָהּ גֵּט – צְרִיכָה לְהַמְתִּין שְׁלֹשָׁה חֳדָשִׁים! אֶלָּא בִּזְנוּת, וּזְנוּת בִּקְטַנָּה לָא שְׁכִיחַ.

Some say another version of what was taught: **Shmuel said:**[N] **All** women **must wait three months, except for a female convert** who is an adult **and a freed maidservant**[H] who is an adult; these women need not wait. **However, an Israelite female minor need not wait three months** in any case. The Gemara clarifies: **With regard to what** situation is this statement referring? **If** it is referring to a female minor released from her marriage **by refusal,** it would be superfluous, **as didn't Shmuel** already **state this** *halakha* **one time? If** it is referring to a woman released **by a bill of divorce,** but **didn't Shmuel say that** in that case **she is required** to wait, **as Shmuel said:** If **she refused him she need not wait three months,** but **if he gave her a bill of divorce, she must wait three months? Rather,** this is referring to cases of **promiscuous sexual intercourse,** and an occurrence of **promiscuous sexual intercourse with female minors is uncommon,** and the Sages did not issue rabbinic decrees in uncommon instances.

גִּיּוֹרֶת וּמְשׁוּחְרֶרֶת, דִּשְׁכִיחַ בְּהוּ זְנוּת, לִיגְזוֹר! הוּא דְּאָמַר כְּרַבִּי יוֹסֵי. דְּתַנְיָא: הַגִּיּוֹרֶת וְהַשְּׁבוּיָה וְהַשִּׁפְחָה שֶׁנִּפְדּוּ וְשֶׁנִּתְגַּיְּירוּ וְשֶׁנִּשְׁתַּחְרְרוּ – צְרִיכוֹת לְהַמְתִּין שְׁלֹשָׁה חֳדָשִׁים, דִּבְרֵי רַבִּי יְהוּדָה. רַבִּי יוֹסֵי מַתִּיר לֵיאָרֵס וְלִינָּשֵׂא מִיָּד. אָמַר רַבָּה: מַאי טַעֲמָא דְּרַבִּי יוֹסֵי – קָסָבַר: אִשָּׁה מְזַנָּה מְשַׁמֶּשֶׁת בְּמוֹךְ כְּדֵי שֶׁלֹּא תִּתְעַבֵּר.

The Gemara suggests: **Let** the Sages **issue a decree** requiring **a female convert and a released maidservant** to wait three months, as at the time that one was a gentile and the other a maidservant, **promiscuous sexual intercourse was common for them.** The Gemara responds: Shmuel **stated** his *halakhic* ruling **in accordance with the** opinion of **Rabbi Yosei, as it is taught** in a *baraita*: In the case of **the female convert; and the captured woman,** who is suspected of having been raped during her imprisonment; **and the maidservant, who were redeemed or who were converted or who were released, must wait three months** prior to marriage. This is **the statement of Rabbi Yehuda. Rabbi Yosei allows** them **to be betrothed and married immediately. Rabba said: What is the reasoning of Rabbi Yosei? He holds that a woman who engages in promiscuous sexual intercourse uses** a contraceptive **resorbent** that she places at the opening of her womb **so as not to become impregnated.** Therefore, there is no concern that she might be pregnant.

אָמַר לֵיהּ אַבַּיֵי: בִּשְׁלָמָא גִּיּוֹרֶת, כֵּיוָן דְּדַעְתָּהּ לְאִיגַּיּוֹרֵי – מְנַטְּרָה נַפְשָׁהּ. כְּדֵי לְהַבְחִין בֵּין זֶרַע שֶׁנִּזְרַע בִּקְדוּשָּׁה וּבֵין זֶרַע שֶׁנִּזְרַע שֶׁלֹּא בִּקְדוּשָּׁה. שְׁבוּיָה וְשִׁפְחָה נַמִי, דְּשָׁמְעִי מִמָּרַיְיהוּ וּמְנַטְּרֵי נַפְשַׁיְיהוּ. אֶלָּא יוֹצֵאת בְּשֵׁן וָעַיִן – הֵיכִי מַשְׁכַּחַתְּ לָהּ?

Abaye said to him: Granted, a female convert does this. **Since she is determined to convert, she guards herself** so as not to be impregnated while still a gentile **in order to distinguish between children conceived in sanctity,** i.e., after her conversion, **and children conceived out of sanctity.**[N] **A captured woman and a maidservant** would **also** be cautious because **they hear from their masters** that they are about to be redeemed or that they are about to be released, **and they guard themselves** so as not to be impregnated. **However,** with regard to a maidservant who **is released due to** damage caused her by her masters, i.e., loss of one of her extremities such as **a tooth or an eye, how can you find** a case where there is no concern for her becoming impregnated? Since she could not have known in advance that she would be released, she would have had no reason to be careful not to become pregnant.

וְכִי תֵּימָא: כָּל דְּמִמֵּילָא מוֹדֶה רַבִּי יוֹסֵי – וְהָתְנַן: אֲנוּסָה וּמְפוּתָּה צְרִיכָה לְהַמְתִּין שְׁלֹשָׁה חֳדָשִׁים, דִּבְרֵי רַבִּי יְהוּדָה. רַבִּי יוֹסֵי מַתִּיר לֵיאָרֵס וְלִינָּשֵׂא מִיָּד!

And if you would say that in **any** case **where** the situation occurs **by itself,** as in the case where a woman was unaware of her pending release, **Rabbi Yosei concedes** that she must indeed wait, this is difficult. **But didn't we learn** in a mishna: **A woman who was raped and a woman who was seduced**[NH] **must wait three months** as perhaps she became pregnant; this is **the statement of Rabbi Yehuda. Rabbi Yosei permits her to be betrothed and to be married immediately.** Clearly, a woman who was raped could not have prepared herself ahead of time so as not to become pregnant.

NOTES

Shmuel's opinion – שִׁיטַת שְׁמוּאֵל: Clarification of Shmuel's opinion, according to both formulations, and the relationship between his statement and the various tannaitic opinions on this issue is crucial to the understanding of the progression of the discussion here as well as the final halakhic conclusions (see 40a and onward).

According to Rabbeinu Ḥananel, Rashi, and other commentaries, Shmuel does not rule in accordance with Rabbi Yosei's opinion in all cases. Rather, in some situations he rules in accordance with the opinion of Rabbi Yehuda and holds that a woman who was raped or seduced requires a waiting period. Because Shmuel maintains that the primary reason for allowing a woman to marry immediately is the use of a contraceptive resorbent, in cases of rape and seduction he is concerned that the post-intercourse contraceptive will not be sufficient. Converts and released maidservants, however, would certainly protect themselves prior to intercourse (*Tosefot Rid*; see Responsa of the Radbaz 1:196).

Alternatively, Shmuel ruled that it is appropriate to issue a rabbinic decree in cases of rape and seduction, but not for converts, since occurrences of conversion are uncommon (Ramban; Rashba; see Razah).

However, according to the Rif, the Rambam, and other commentaries, Shmuel rules in accordance with the opinion of Rabbi Yosei on all issues. When he said: Except for female converts and released maidservants who were adults, he did not intend to imply that raped and seduced women require a waiting period for the purpose of distinction. On the contrary, he meant to say that even those who were not so cautious, since they nevertheless intended to convert, take steps to prevent pregnancy. If so, this is all the more true for women who were raped or seduced (Ramban).

The Ra'avad explains a different rationale for Shmuel's distinction with regard to converts and released maidservants. In these cases, there are two uncertainties: First, there is uncertainty as to whether the woman engaged in intercourse at all. Second, even if you say that she did engage in sexual intercourse, she might not have become pregnant. This is not the case for a raped or seduced woman. Since she certainly had intercourse, the only uncertainty that remains is whether or not she became pregnant. Therefore, she should be required to observe the waiting period.

In order to distinguish between children conceived in sanctity and children conceived out of sanctity – לְהַבְחִין בֵּין זֶרַע שֶׁנִּזְרַע בִּקְדוּשָּׁה וּבֵין זֶרַע שֶׁנִּזְרַע שֶׁלֹּא בִּקְדוּשָּׁה: Although when a pregnant woman converts, her fetus is converted along with her and does not need to immerse after birth, it is necessary to know the child's status at the time of his conception. As a child who converts no longer maintains the familial connections that he had before his conversion, it is important to know at what point he converted in order to establish his family status vis-à-vis children in that family who are conceived later.

A woman who was raped and a woman who was seduced – אֲנוּסָה וּמְפוּתָּה: With regard to this issue, in the Jerusalem Talmud there is also a ruling that women who were raped or seduced need not wait. There the question is raised as to why the mishna requires the women who were mistakenly switched, which is a type of rape, to nevertheless have a waiting period. This question is sharpened by the assertion that it is inappropriate to issue a rabbinic decree in cases of switched wives since this is an uncommon occurrence. The Gemara there answers that the ruling in the mishna comes to rectify the child's status. The Vilna Gaon explains that there is a distinction between the purposes of the separation period in different cases. In cases of rape and the like, the decree was made in order to know with certainty who was the father of the child. In this case, the rabbinic decree was not applied. However, in the case of the mishna, the separation is necessary in order to determine whether or not the child is a *mamzer*, and therefore the rabbinic decree was issued.

HALAKHA

A female convert and a freed maidservant – גִּיּוֹרֶת וּמְשׁוּחְרֶרֶת: Female converts and maidservants who were married before they became Jewish are required to wait three months before marrying. If the husbands converted they must separate from them for three months in order to distinguish between children conceived before and after the conversion. This ruling is in accordance with the opinion of Rabbi Yehuda, as explained by Abaye (*Maggid Mishne*; Rambam *Sefer Nashim*, *Hilkhot Geirushin* 11:21; *Shulḥan Arukh*, *Even HaEzer* 13:5).

A woman who was raped and a woman who was seduced, etc. – אֲנוּסָה וּמְפוּתָּה וכו׳: Women who were raped or seduced, and indeed any woman who engaged in promiscuous sexual acts, as well as a woman who was captured, need not wait three months. This ruling is in accordance with the opinion of Rabbi Yosei (Rambam). Some say that if the females are adult women and fit to become pregnant they must wait, in accordance with the opinions of Rabbi Yehuda and Shmuel (Rema; Rambam *Hilkhot Geirushin* 11:22; *Shulḥan Arukh*, *Even HaEzer* 13:6).

אֶלָּא אֲמַר אַבַּיֵי: אִשָּׁה מְזַנָּה מִתְהַפֶּכֶת, שֶׁלֹּא תִּתְעַבֵּר. וְאִידָךְ: חָיְישִׁינַן שֶׁמָּא לֹא נִתְהַפְּכָה יָפֶה יָפֶה.

Rather, Abaye said: A woman who engages in promiscuous sexual intercourse turns over[NB] following intercourse, trying to prevent the absorption of the semen, so as not to become pregnant. Maidservants act in a similar manner. The Gemara asks: If indeed she tries not to become pregnant, how then would the other opinion, that of Rabbi Yehuda, explain why she must wait three months? The Gemara responds: We are concerned that perhaps she did not turn over well enough and therefore became pregnant.

"וְאִם הָיוּ כֹּהֲנוֹת" כו׳. כֹּהֲנוֹת – אִין, יִשְׂרְאֵלִית – לָא?! אֵימָא: אִם הָיוּ נְשֵׁי כֹּהֲנִים. נְשֵׁי כֹּהֲנִים – אִין, נְשֵׁי יִשְׂרְאֵלִים – לָא?

§ With regard to the case of two betrothed women who were switched at the time they entered the wedding canopy, the mishna states: **And if they were daughters of priests,** they are disqualified from partaking in *teruma*. The Gemara asks: Does this indicate that with regard to the **daughters of priests, yes,** they are disqualified from partaking in *teruma*, but with regard to **the daughter of an Israelite, no,** she would not be disqualified? It would seem that an Israelite woman married to a priest should most certainly be disqualified from eating of her husband's *teruma*. The Gemara answers: Rather, **say: If they were the wives of priests** then they are disqualified. The Gemara questions this formulation: Does this indicate that with regard to the **wives of priests, yes,** they are disqualified, but with regard to the **wives of Israelites, no,** they are not disqualified, and if their husbands died, they would be suitable for marriage to the priests?

וְהָאֲמַר רַב עַמְרָם: הָא מִילְּתָא אֲמַר לָן רַב שֵׁשֶׁת, וְאַנְהֲרִינְהוּ לְעַיְינִין מִמַּתְנִיתִין: אֵשֶׁת יִשְׂרָאֵל שֶׁנֶּאֶנְסָה, אַף עַל פִּי שֶׁמּוּתֶּרֶת לְבַעְלָהּ – פְּסוּלָה לִכְהוּנָּה!

The Gemara objects to this: **But didn't Rav Amram say: Rav Sheshet said this matter to us, and he lit our eyes** by showing us that this ruling is indicated **from what was stated in the mishna** (*Yevamot* 53b). He said: **The wife of an Israelite who was raped, even though she is permitted to** return to **her husband, she is** nevertheless **disqualified from the priesthood.**[NH] If her husband later dies, she may not marry a priest, for although she is permitted to her husband the rape disqualified her for matters of priesthood.

אֲמַר רָבָא, הָכִי קָאָמַר: אִם הָיוּ כֹּהֲנוֹת נְשׂוּאוֹת לְיִשְׂרָאֵל – נִפְסְלוּ מִן הַתְּרוּמָה דְּבֵי נָשַׁיְיהוּ.

Rava resolved this and said: This is what the *tanna* is saying in the mishna: **If they were daughters of priests** who **were married to an Israelite, they are disqualified from the *teruma*[H] that is from the household of their fathers,** so that if their husbands die while they are childless, they may not go back to eat of the *teruma* in the house of their fathers. While other childless daughters of priests are again qualified to eat of the *teruma* the moment they leave their Israelite husbands, these women were disqualified by their act of forbidden sexual intercourse.

הדרן עלך ארבעה אחין

NOTES

Turns over – מִתְהַפֶּכֶת: According to *Tosafot Yeshanim*, there is room to differentiate between a maidservant who is released due to the loss of a tooth or an eye and a woman who was raped or seduced because an ordinary maidservant is not concerned with becoming pregnant. In fact, she might even desire it. According to this explanation, even Rabbi Yosei would agree that she requires a waiting period. On the other hand, the *Hazon Ish* holds that the primary dispute between Rabba and Abaye is not over the type of preventive measure chosen, i.e., the resorbent and turning over, respectively, as it might seem, but rather over the following question: Does a woman who is not married desire to become pregnant? In Abaye's opinion, she never desires this.

Disqualified from the priesthood – פְּסוּלָה לִכְהוּנָּה: The primary reason for this ruling is that any woman who engaged in intercourse, willingly or unwillingly, with a man for whom she incurs *karet* is considered a *zona*. Although a *zona* is not forbidden to an Israelite, except for in some special cases, she is nevertheless disqualified from marrying into the priesthood or partaking of *teruma* (see Rashi and *Tosafot*).

BACKGROUND

Turns over – מִתְהַפֶּכֶת: Medically speaking, turning over after intercourse is not an effective method of pregnancy prevention. However, it would seem that the Gemara is not referring specifically to the act of turning over, but rather to the fact that a woman who does not desire to become pregnant will take any measures necessary in addition to turning over, including taking drugs and the like. The Gemara's concern that she might not have turned over sufficiently therefore seems justified, since no measure taken following intercourse can fully ensure that a woman will not conceive.

HALAKHA

A married woman who was raped – אֵשֶׁת אִישׁ שֶׁנֶּאֶנְסָה: While a woman who was married to an Israelite and raped is permitted to her husband, she nevertheless may not marry a priest if her husband dies, as the act of prohibited intercourse disqualified her from marrying into the priesthood. This ruling is in accordance with the statement of Rav Sheshet (Rambam *Sefer Kedusha, Hilkhot Issurei Bia* 18:7; *Shulḥan Arukh, Even HaEzer* 13:6, 11).

Daughters of priests disqualified from partaking of *teruma* – כֹּהֲנוֹת נִפְסָלוֹת לִתְרוּמָה: If the daughter of a priest was married to an Israelite and was raped by another man, she is permitted to her husband. If she is divorced or widowed, she is prohibited from partaking of the *teruma* from her father's household, even if she has no children from her Israelite husband. This ruling is in accordance with the statement of Rava (Rambam *Sefer Zera'im, Hilkhot Teruma* 6:10).

Summary of **Perek III**

The nature of the levirate bond is not conclusively defined in this chapter. It is clear that the issue, which is disputed among the *amora'im*, is in fact a matter of dispute among the *tanna'im* as well. The various opinions and their conclusions on this matter are found within the many *mishnayot* of this chapter and in disputes pertaining to related fields that touch upon the status of women requiring levirate marriage.

The general halakhic conclusion is that the levirate bond is substantial, and it begins at the moment of the husband's death. The bond created is of a unique nature, at once similar in effect to the bond of betrothal yet with clear differences. Due to its unique status, the levirate bond can exist between a single woman and several *yevamin* at once, and need not be limited to a single *yavam*.

The problems that arise from combinations of possible situations involving different relatives led to discussion of a wider question in this chapter: To what extent might a prohibition take effect where another prohibition already exists? All of the different opinions were clarified, from those that maintain that prohibitions do take effect where others already exist to those that propose that they can take effect only under special circumstances, e.g., when there are more inclusive prohibitions, expanded prohibitions, or simultaneous prohibitions.

This chapter also discussed halakhic rulings in cases involving uncertainties. For example, the status of a woman who happens before a *yavam* is unclear because her betrothal or divorce is in doubt. In such cases, it was determined that the woman, and sometimes it is two women, require the act of *ḥalitza* in order to resolve the situation.

Image **Credits**

My Notes

My Notes

My Notes

My Notes

My Notes

זו חֲדַיָּיב, נְהַר גּוֹזָן — זו גִּינְזַק, וְעָרֵי מָדַי — זו חַמְדָן וְחַבְרוֹתֶיהָ, וְאָמְרִי לָהּ: זו נִיהָר וְחַבְרוֹתֶיהָ. חַבְרוֹתֶיהָ מַאן? אָמַר שְׁמוּאֵל: כַּרְךְ, מוּשְׁכֵי, חִידְקֵי וְדוֹמַקְיָא. א"ר יוֹחָנָן: וְכוּלָּן לִפְסוּל, כִּי אַמְרִיתָהּ קַמֵּיהּ דִּשְׁמוּאֵל: א"ל: בְּנָךְ (א) הַבָּא מִן יִשְׂרְאֵלִית קָרוּי בִּנְךָ, וְאֵין בִּנְךָ הַבָּא מִן הַגּוֹיָה קָרוּי בִּנְךָ — אֶלָּא בְּנָהּ. וְהָאִיכָּא בָּנוֹת, וְאָמַר רָבִינָא: ש"מ בֶּן בִּתְּךָ הַבָּא מִן הַגּוֹי קָרוּי בִּנְךָ! גְּמִירִי דְּבָנָתָא דְּהַהוּא דָּרָא אִיצְטְרוּיֵי אִצְטְרוּ. אִיכָּא דְּאָמְרִי: כִּי אַמְרִיתָהּ קַמֵּיהּ דִּשְׁמוּאֵל א"ל: לֹא זָזוּ מִשָּׁם עַד שֶׁעֲשָׂאוּם גּוֹיִם גְּמוּרִים, שֶׁנֶּאֱמַר "בַּה' בָּגָדוּ כִּי בָנִים זָרִים יָלָדוּ". יְתֵיב רַב יוֹסֵף אֲחוֹרֵיהּ דְּרַב כָּהֲנָא, וִיתֵיב רַב כָּהֲנָא קַמֵּיהּ דְּרַב יְהוּדָה, וִיתֵיב וְקָאָמַר: עֲתִידִין יִשְׂרָאֵל דְּעָבְדֵי יוֹמָא טָבָא כִּי חָרְבֵי תַּרְמוֹד. וְהָא חָרֵיב! הַהִיא תַּמּוֹד הֲוַאי. רַב אַשִׁי אָמַר: הַיְינוּ תַּרְמוֹד הַיְינוּ תַּמּוֹד, אַבְפּוּלֵי הוּא דִּמְבַלְּבַל. חָרֵיב מֵהַאי גִּיסָא — אוֹתֵיב מֵהַאי גִּיסָא, וְאִי חָרֵיב מֵהַאי גִּיסָא — אוֹתֵיב מֵהַאי גִּיסָא. יְתֵיב רַב הַמְנוּנָא קַמֵּיהּ דְּעוּלָּא וְקָא הָוֵי בִּשְׁמַעְתָּא. אָמַר: מַה גַּבְרָא וּמַה (ב) גַּבְרָא, אִי לָאו דְּהַרְפַּנְיָא מָאתֵיהּ! אִכְסִיף. א"ל: כְּסַף גּוּלְגַּלְתָּא דִּיהִיבְנָא יָהֲבַת? א"ל: לְפוּם נַהְרָא. א"ל: א"כ — מִפּוּם נַהְרָא אַתְּ. מַאי הַרְפַּנְיָא? אָמַר ר' זֵירָא: הַר שֶׁהַכֹּל פּוֹנִין בּוֹ. בְּמַתְנִיתָא תָּנָא: כֹּל שֶׁאֵין מַכִּיר מִשְׁפַּחְתּוֹ וְשִׁבְטוֹ נִפְנֶה לְשָׁם. אָמַר רָבָא: וְהִיא עֲמוּקָּה מִשְּׁאוֹל, שֶׁנֶּאֱמַר "מִיַּד שְׁאוֹל אֶפְדֵּם מִמָּוֶת אֶגְאָלֵם", וְאִילּוּ פְּסוּל דִּידְהוּ — לֵית לְהוּ תַּקַּנְתָּא. פְּסוּלֵי דְהַרְפַּנְיָא מִשּׁוּם פְּסוּלֵי דְּמֵישָׁן וּפְסוּלֵי דְּמֵישָׁן מִשּׁוּם פְּסוּלֵי דְתַרְמוֹד, פְּסוּלֵי דְתַרְמוֹד מִשּׁוּם עַבְדֵי שְׁלֹמֹה, וְהַיְינוּ דְּאָמְרִי אִינָשֵׁי: קַבָּא רַבָּא וְקַבָּא זוּטָא, מִיגַּנְדַּר וְאָזֵיל לִשְׁאוֹל, וּמִשְּׁאוֹל לְתַרְמוֹד, וּמִתַּרְמוֹד לְמֵישָׁן, וּמִמֵּישָׁן לְהַרְפַּנְיָא.

הדרן עלך חמש עשרה נשים

כֵּיצַד [ב]אֵשֶׁת אָחִיו שֶׁלֹּא הָיָה בְּעוֹלָמוֹ? שְׁנֵי אַחִים, וּמֵת אֶחָד מֵהֶן; וְנוֹלַד לָהֶן אָח, וְאח"כ יִיבֵּם הַשֵּׁנִי אֶת אֵשֶׁת אָחִיו וָמֵת. הָרִאשׁוֹנָה יוֹצְאָה מִשּׁוּם אֵשֶׁת אָחִיו שֶׁלֹּא הָיָה בְּעוֹלָמוֹ, וְהַשְּׁנִיָּה מִשּׁוּם צָרָתָהּ. עָשָׂה בָּהּ מַאֲמָר וָמֵת — שְׁנִיָּה חוֹלֶצֶת וְלֹא מִתְיַיבֶּמֶת.§ **גמ'** אָמַר רַב נַחְמָן: מַאן דְּתָנֵי רִאשׁוֹנָה לָא מִשְׁתַּבֵּשׁ, מַאן דְּתָנֵי שְׁנִיָּה לָא מִשְׁתַּבֵּשׁ. מַאן דְּתָנֵי רִאשׁוֹנָה

זו חדייב נהר גוזן וכו' מגשכי חידקי ודומקיא. לפסול. רובן ממזרים, שנטמעו *עשרת השבטים בגוים, ובניהן הרי הן כישראלים, ונוהג בהן איסור ממזרות. והן לא נזהרו ונשאו זה אחותו או בתו, ובני הן ממזרים. כי אמריתה קמיה דשמואל. על סמכא מילתיה דרב יהודה *(משמיה דרב) שלא (ג) קאמר, *ואסר סעודתו של רב אסי בה לפני שמואל) וקאמר: כי הדר אמריתה לקמה דרב אסי קמיה דשמואל, דחושין לקדושין. אמר בנך הבא מישראלית קרוי בנך ואין בנך הבא מן הגויה קרוי בנך אלא בנה. דנפקא לן מ"כי יסיר את בנך מאחרי" (דברים ז) ולא כתיב כי תסיר את בנך — אלמא: לאו אבתו לא תקח לבנך מדבר, דאל"כ הוה לו לומר כי הגויה תסיר, ש"מ דאי נמי יולדת בן לעבודה זרה — לא בנך מיקרי, ולא קרינן ביה "כי תסיר את בנך". הילכך, גוים גמורים הם. והאיכא בנות, שנשאו, ונשאום גוים והולידו מהם. ואמר רבינא. לקמן בפ"ב (דף כג.) בן בתך הבא מן הגוי קרוי בנך, דכתיב "בתך לא תתן לבנו כי יסיר את בנך מאחרי". מדלא כתיב כי תסיר, ש"מ דאבתך לא תתן לבנו קאי, וה"ק: שמא תלד לו בן ויסירנו הלה מאחרי, וקא קרי ליה בנך, וליהוו לקידושין. דההוא דרא. דעשרת השבטים. איצטרויי איצטרו. (ד) נעקר רחמן מלקלוט זרע, ונעשו עקרות. איצטרו. לשון פיקוע, כמו *טילא חריפי דמלגי זיקי (ע"ז ד' ג.), וכמו לירית דסיפי (פסחים דף מג:). יומא טבא. משום דממזרים הם, ומשמעים במקהל ופוסלים אותן. הייני תרמוד הייני תמוד, ודקאמר הא חריב — לא חריב כולה. דאבפולי אבפול. שמתגרה מישן דחתלה וניגנים מכאן. וקא הוי. מקשה. אמר. עולא עליה דרב המנונא: מה גברא ומה גברא! כמה הוא גדול. אי לאו דהרפניא מאתיה. שאינם מיוחסים. שהכל פונים שם. כל פסולין שאין מוצאין אשה פונין והולכין שם. והיא עמוקה. וקשה לדבר זה יותר מגיהנם. דאילו ליורדי גיהנם איכא תקנתא, דכתיב "מיד שאול אפדם ממות אגאלם", ואילו פסולי דידהו לית להו תקנתא. משום פסולי דמישן. שקרובה לה, ומתערבין בהן. ואמר בפרק "עשרה יוחסין" (קידושין עא:) מישון מתה. וקחשיב מפרש פסולייהו. קבא רבא וקבא זוטא. איפה גדולה ואיפה קטנה, שניהם מעוותים. כלומר: כל הפסולין מתגלגלים ויורדים לשאול, ומשאול לתרמוד. כלומר: שמשאול גרוע מתרמוד, ומתגלגל משאול לתרמוד. ושמעתא כדלעיל: דאילו ליורדי גיהנם איכא תקנתא, ולפסול דידהו אין טהרה. מיגנדר. מתגלגל.

הדרן עלך חמש עשרה נשים

כֵּיצַד אֵשֶׁת אָחִיו שֶׁלֹּא הָיָה בְּעוֹלָמוֹ. פּוֹטֶרֶת צָרָתָהּ. וְנוֹלַד לָהֶם אָח. וּמְלָאָהּ זְקוּקָה לְיַבֵּם, וְעָלָיו אֲסוּרָה מִשּׁוּם אֵשֶׁת אָחִיו שֶׁלֹּא הָיָה בְּעוֹלָמוֹ. וְאח"כ יִיבֵּם הַשֵּׁנִי אֶת אֵשֶׁת אָחִיו. וְלוֹ אִשָּׁה אַחֶרֶת, וּמֵת. הָרִאשׁוֹנָה. זוֹ הִיא אֵשֶׁת (ה) רְאוּבֵן שֶׁנָּפְלָה לְפָנָיו כְּבָר פַּעַם אַחַת. יוֹצְאָה. וְנִפְטֶרֶת מִזֶּה מִשּׁוּם אֵשֶׁת אָחִיו שֶׁלֹּא הָיָה בְּעוֹלָמוֹ כו'. עָשָׂה בָּהּ. זֶה שֶׁמֵּת מַאֲמָר, וְלֹא הִסְפִּיק לְכוֹנְסָהּ עַד שֶׁמֵּת. שְׁנִיָּה חוֹלֶצֶת. וְלֹא מִיפַּטְרָא מִשּׁוּם צָרַת עֶרְוָה, דְּלָאו צָרָתָהּ מַמָּשׁ הִיא. וְלֹא מִתְיַיבֶּמֶת. דְּמַאֲמָר קוֹנֶה מִקְצָת, וַהֲוַאי צָרַת עֶרְוָה בְּמִקְצָת מִדְּרַבָּנַן. **גמ'** מַאן דְּתָנֵי רִאשׁוֹנָה. מַאן דְּקָרֵי לָהּ רִאשׁוֹנָה לְהָךְ שֶׁנָּפְלָה לְפָנָיו שְׁנֵי פְּעָמִים — לָא מִשְׁתַּבֵּשׁ, וּמַאן דְּקָרֵי לָהּ שְׁנִיָּה — לָא מִשְׁתַּבֵּשׁ. רִאשׁוֹנָה

ואין בנך הבא מן הגויה קרוי בנך אלא בנה. פירש בקונטרס: דמדכתב "כי יסיר" ולא כתב "כי תסיר" משמע דלא קאי א"בתו לא תקח לבנך", דאי (ו) יולדת בן לעבודה זרה — לאו בנך מיקרי ולא קרינן ביה "כי תסיר את בנך". אלא אבתך לא תתן לבנו קאי, וה"ק: שמא תלד בן, ויסירנו האב מאחרי, שאותו קרוי בנך. וקשה לר"ת: לפירושו דפי' בנך קרוי בנך — היינו בנך הבא מן הישראלית, שאביו גוי, דעליה קאי "כי יסיר", וא"כ אמאי מייתי ואמר רבינא בן בתך כו' הרי הן מנהם דברי שמואל! ורבינא נמי, מאי קאמר (ז) ש"מ מדר' יוחנן? מה שייך לומר ש"מ — דהן מנהם דברי רבי יוחנן! ואומר ר"ת: ד"כי יסיר" אבתו לא תקח לבנך קאי, והכי קאמר: כי יסיר החותן את בנך מאחרי, והיינו הסרה — שאין הזרע מתייחס אחר בנך אלא אחר הגויה, דאין קרוי בנך אלא בנה. ושמואל ורבי יוחנן לא פירשו כלום בגוי הבא על בת ישראל, אלא רבינא מדקדק דבן בתך הבא מן הגוי קרוי בנך, מדלא כתב "כי יסיר את בתך" — ש"מ דלית בה הסרה, משום דמתייחס אחריה. ואין נראה לר"י, ד"כי יסיר" משמע כמו הסרה מאת הקב"ה, כדמתרגמי' "מבתר פולחני" ודרשי' נמי מכי יסיר לרבות כל המסירים. ועוד פירש ר"ת בע"א: דשמואל ורבי יוחנן דייקי מ"כי יסיר את בנך" — דמשמע דוקא על הסרתו הקפיד הכתוב, שלא יעשהו. ולא על הסרת בן בנו, דכיון דבא מן הגויה אין קרוי בנך אלא בנה מדלא כתיב כי יסירם, או כי יסיר בנך ורעו מאחרי. ורבינא דייק: ש"מ בן בתך הבא מן הגוי קרוי בנך, דדוקא בבנך (ח) "כי יסיר את בנך" למעוטי זרעו, אבל בבתך — אפי' מזרעו יש לחוש להסרה.

פסולי דמישן משום פסולי דתרמוד. והא דאמר בפרק בני דקדושין (דף מט:): עשרה קבין עזות ירדו לעולם, תשעה נטלה מישן ואחת כל העולם. פי': לפי שהן ממזרים. הא דלא נקט תרמוד שפסולין יותר — שמא אתגרבו למישן עד שגדלו יותר מתרמוד, ושמא בתרמוד היו רוב גוים, ובמישן רוב ישראל.

משאול לתרמוד. שאול קורא *בבל, לפי שתחילה גלו כולם לבבל כשרים ופסולים, ומבבל הלכו כל הפסולים לתרמוד. כדאמר ב"עשרה יוחסין" (קידושין סט:) דלא עלה עזרא מבבל עד שעשאה כסולת נקיה. ומונה כסדר שהלכו הפסולים מזו לזו, כמו שהקב הולך ומתגלגל מכאן לכאן.

הדרן עלך חמש עשרה נשים

כיצד. עשה בה מאמר. דסיפא (דף יח:) לא אצטריך, דמרישא שמעי' לה, אלא איידי דמתני ליה ברישא תנא להו נמי בסיפא.

מאן דתני ראשונה לא משתבש. הכא לא בעי: מאן דתני ראשונה אמאי לא תני שניה, כדדייק בריש מס' ע"ז (דף ב. ושם): מאן דתני אידיהן מ"ט לא תני עידיהן. דהתם בעי משום דה"ל למיתני לשון עדות, כדכתיב "יתנו עדיהן ויצדקו", ובתר דמשני דתברא עדיף — הדר פריך: מאן דתני עידיהן — מאי טעמא לא תני אידיהן? אשת

סח א מיי' פ"ב מהל' [illegible]

א ב מיי' פ"ו מהל' יבום הלכה יז סמג עשין נא נב טוש"ע אה"ע סימן קעג סעיף יב:

תוספות ישנים

ואמר [illegible]

כיצד. ר' שמעון אומר מייבם לאיזו שירצה וחולץ לשניה. נראה דמייבם לאיזו שירצה לא קאי אעשה בה מאמר דהא ר' שמעון סבר לקמן חלץ לבעלת מאמר לא נפטרה צרתה:

הגהות הב"ח

[illegible]

תוספות חד מקמאי

פרק כיצד. הא דתנן עשה בה מאמר ומת חולצת ולא מתיבמת ה"ה אע"ג דלא עבד בה מאמר שניה מחלין חלצה יבומי לא מיבמה דקי"ל כשמואל דאמר יש זיקה אפי' בתרי אחי וה"ל צרת א)אחות אשה בזיקה. והא דקתני עשה בה מאמר לאפוקי מב"ש דאמרי מאמר קונה קנין גמור קמ"ל:

א) נ"ל אשת אחיו שלא היה בעולמו בזיקה

תורה אור

ראשונה לא משתבש. מאי ראשונה — ראשונה לנפילה, ומאן דתני שניה לא משתבש: מאי שניה — שניה לנשואין. מי לא עסקינן דיבם ואח"כ כנס? אלא: מאי שניה — שניה בנשואין. אשת אחיו שלא היה בעולמו היכא כתיבא? אמר רב יהודה אמר רב: אמר קרא (דברים כה) °"כי ישבו אחים יחדו" — שהיתה להם ישיבה אחת בעולם, פרט לאשת אחיו שלא היה בעולמו. "יחדו" — מיוחדים בנחלה, [א]פרט לאחיו מן האם. רבה אמר: אחין מן האב — יליף *"אחוה" "אחוה" מבני יעקב, מה להלן מן האב ולא מן האם, אף כאן מן האב ולא מן האם. ולילף "אחוה" "אחוה" מעריות! דנין "אחים" מ"אחים", ואין דנין אחים מ"אחיך". מאי נפקא מינה? הא *תנא דבי רבי ישמעאל: (ויקרא יד) °"ושב הכהן" °"ובא הכהן" זו היא שיבה זו היא ביאה! *ה"מ היכא דליכא מידי דדמי ליה, אבל היכא דאיכא מידי דדמי ליה — מדדמי ליה ילפינן. ולילף "אחוה" "אחוה" מלוט, דכתיב (בראשית יג) °"כי אנשים אחים אנחנו"! מסתברא, מבני יעקב הוה ליה למילף, משום דמפני. מדהוה ליה למכתב "שנים עשר עבדיך בני אבינו" וכתיב "אחים" — ש"מ לאפנויי. ואיצטריך למכתב "אחים", ואיצטריך למכתב "יחדו". דאי כתב רחמנא "אחים" ה"א: לילף "אחוה" "אחוה" מלוט. וכי תימא לא מפני — לאיי, אפנויי מפני, מדהוה ליה למכתב "רעים" וכתיב "אחים", שמע מינה לאפנויי — כתב רחמנא "יחדו", המיוחדים בנחלה. ואי כתב רחמנא "יחדו", הוה אמינא: דמייחדי באבא ובאמא, צריכא. והא מהיכא תיתי? *יבום בנחלה תלא רחמנא, ונחלה מן האב ולא מן האם היא! איצטריך, סד"א: הואיל וחידוש הוא, דקמשתרי ערוה גביה — אימא עד דמייחדי באבא ובאמא, צריכא. אמר רב הונא אמר רב: שומרת יבם שמתה — מותר באמה. אלמא קסבר: *אין זיקה. ולימא: הלכה כדברי האומר אין זיקה! אי הוה אמר הכי ה"א: הנ"מ בתרי, אבל בחד יש זיקה. ולימא: הלכה כדברי האומר אין זיקה אפי' בחד?! אי אמר הכי הוה אמינא אפילו מחיים, קמשמע לן: לאחר מיתה — אין, מחיים — לא, משום *דאסור לבטל מצות יבמין. תנן: *יבמתו שמתה — מותר באחותה. באחותה אין, באמה לא! הוא הדין דאפילו באמה, ואיידי דתנא רישא אשתו שמתה מותר באחותה, באחותה — אין, אבל באמה — לא, דהויא לה איסורא דאורייתא, תנא נמי סיפא מותר באחותה. ורב יהודה אמר: [ב]שומרת יבם שמתה — אסור באמה. אלמא קסבר: *יש זיקה. ולימא: הלכה כדברי האומר יש זיקה! אי הוה אמר הכי הוה אמינא: הנ"מ בחד, אבל בתרי אין זיקה. והא כי פליגי — בתרי פליגי! אלא, אי אמר הכי הוה

רש"י

ראשונה לנפילה. שנפלה ראשונה לייבום, קודמת לזו בפעם ראשונה. שניה לנישואין. לנישואין של שני, שהוא היה נשוי כבר האחרת כשנפלה זאת לפניו: ופרכינן. מי לא עסקינן. כלומר, מי לא מיתוקמא נמי מתני' דייבם אשת אחיו תחילה, ואח"כ כנס את האחרת, דלא הויא הך יבמה שניה לנישואין. אלא שניה בנישואין. שנישאת שני פעמים, אחת לבעל ואחת ליבם. היכא כתיבא. לאיסורא. המיוחדים בנחלה. הראויין לירש זה את זה. אחוה אחוה. "כי ישבו אחים", "שנים עשר אחים בני אבינו" (בראשית מב). מעריות. "ערות אשת אחיך", וקי"ל לקמן בפרק "הבא על יבמתו" (דף נה.), דאפילו אחיך מן האם ולא מן האב. זו היא שיבה כו'. דאע"ג דלא דמו קראי להדדי, כיון דתרוייהו בביאת כהן משתעי — דיינינן בהו ג"ש: מה להלן חולץ וקוצה וטח כו'. מלוט כי אנשים אחים אנחנו. ותתייבם אשת אחי אביו, שהרי בן אחיו היה (א). המיוחדים בנחלה. שחולקין נחלה אחת, לאפוקי לוט שאין חולקין נחלה אחת. והא מהיכא תיתי. דלימא עד דמייחדי באבא ובאמא? והא ייבום בנחלה תליא, דכתיב (דברים כה) "יקום על שם אחיו המת", ואוקמינן לקמן (דף כד.) "על שם אחיו" — לנחלה, שיירש המייבם כל נכסי המת, ואין אחין חולקין עמו. אין זיקה. זיקת יבמתו שמתה לא חשיבא למיהוי כארוסה, להאסר (ב) אמו עליו משום חמותו. ולימא הלכה כדברי האומר אין זיקה. דתנן בפ' "החולץ" (לקמן מא.): שומרת יבם שקדש אחיו את אחותה של יבמה, ותלה הייבום באחיו — משום רבי יהודה בן בתירא אמרו, אומרים לזה שקדש אחות יבמתו: המתן מלכנוס. לפי שאחות זקוקתו היא, הואיל ולאחר שנזקקה אחותה לו קדש את זו — צריך להמתין עד שתתייבם היבמה לאחיו, דפקעה זיקה. ואמר שמואל: הלכה כרבי יהודה. ומדקאמר הלכה — מכלל דפליגי עליה ואמרי: אין זיקה לאחין חשיבא לאסור עליהן קרובותיה. ה"מ. דלא חשיבא זיקה להיות אסורות קרובות בתרי אחין — כשנפלה לפני שני יבמין, כגון ההיא פלוגתא דר"י ורבנן, דכיון דלא ידיע קמי מאן מינייהו רמיא, לא חשיבא למיסר קרובות. אבל בחד. שאין שם אלא יבם אחד, דודאי עליה רמיא, אימא דמיא ככנוסה, ויאסר באמה. ולימא הלכה כדברי האומר אין זיקה אפילו בחד. ר"ע קא"ל בפ' "ד' אחין" (לקמן כט:): שומרת יבם אין יבמה מיפר נדריה לא לאחד ולא לשנים. כלומר: בין שנפלה לפני יבם אחד, בין שנפלה לפני שנים, דלא קרינן ביה "אישה"*. ה"א אפי' מחיים. (ג) יבמה מותר באמה קודם חליצה, ותצא היבמה לשוק משום בת אשתו. דאסור לבטל כו'. ואי נסיב אמה מחיים — מבטל למצוה לגמרי מיבום ומחליצה. יבמתו שמתה מותר באחותה. דאפי' אשתו מתה מותר באחותה. אבל אמו, דלגבי אשתו אסורה אף לאחר מיתת אשתו — ביבמתו נמי אסורה. איסורא דאורייתא. חמות' אסר רחמנא, ולא פליג בין מחיים בין לאחר מיתה, כדפליג באחות אשה, כדכתיב "עליה בחייה". יש זיקה. זיקת ייבום הויא ככנוסה, ואוסרת אמה על היבם משום חמותו. והא כי פליגי. ר"י ורבנן בתרי [הוא] דפליגי, כדקתני (לקמן דף מא.): המתן עד שיעשה אחיך מעשה.

באחותה

תוספות

אשת אחיו שלא היה בעולמו היכא כתיבא. וא"ת: תיפוק ליה מדכתיב (משלי ג) "דרכיה דרכי נועם" ומהאי טעמא עבדינן מתים כחיים לענין יבום, בפ' "יש מותרות" (לקמן פז:), אע"ג דאיצטריך למילי אחריני, כדאמר בפרקין* גבי מלוה בגדול לייבם, א"כ, אשת אחיו שלא היה בעולם דכתב רחמנא — ל"ל? ובפרק "ב"ש" (לקמן קיא:) נמי דייקינן מיני' דקטן זוקק ליבום. מ"מ, משמע דעיקריה לגופיה איצטריך. ואר"י: דאיצטריך להיכא דחמותה של יבמה מעוברת, דהוי שפיר "דרכי נועם" ותמתין, שמא תלד זכר ותהא זקוקה לו:

אחוה אחוה מבני יעקב. לענין אשת אחיו שלא היה בעולמו אין סברא למילף מבני יעקב, דלא מיקרי אחים אא"כ הם בעולם אחד כבני יעקב, דפשיטא דמיקרי אחין, ואי לאו דמיעט קרא בהדיא — לא הוה שייך למילף מבני יעקב לענין הך מילתא.

ולימא הלכה כדברי האומר אין זיקה. פי' בקונט': דרבנן דרבי יהודה בן בתירא דמייתי לקמן, מדפסיק שמואל כר' יהוד' בן בתירא דאמר יש זיקה — מכלל דפליגי רבנן. וקש': דדלמא בעלמא סברי רבנן דיש זיקה, והתם שרו ולא מצרכי להמתין שיעשה אחיו מעשה — משום דקידושין מפקעי זיקה, דהא חשיב בסוף "הערל" (לקמן דף פג.) ובפ"ב דמגילה (דף יח:) ההיא דרבי יהודה בן בתירא יחידאה, דדייקינן דשמואל חייש ליחידאה מדפסיק כר' יהודה. ואמאי חשיב ליה יחידאה? והא כמה תנאים סברי דיש זיקה. ורב אשי דייק מסתם מתניתין דפ' "ד' אחין" (לקמן ל. ושם): זאת אומרת יש זיקה, ואפי' בתרי אחין! אלא ודאי בההוא דר"י מודו כולהו דע"י קדושין פקעה זיקה. ובסוף שמעתין (דף יט.) דמצריך תרי מילי דשמואל היה יכול לומר אי אשמועינן יש זיקה ה"א בההיא דר"י דקידושין מפקעי זיקה, אלא טעמא אחרינא אשכח. ואין לפרש דכדברי האומר אין זיקה היינו ר"מ, דא"כ מאי קאמר ה"א ה"מ בתרי, הא ר"מ בחד נמי קאמר דאין זיקה! וליכא למימר נמי דהיינו ר' יהושע דאמר יפר לאחד ולא לשנים — דהא בפ' "ד' אחין" מוקי פלוגתייהו בעבד בה מאמר, ופליגי אי מאמר קונה אי לאו! וי"ל: דאין נ"ל לחלק משום קידושין. ורב יוסף דקרי ליה יחידאה קסבר דכולהו תנאי סברי אין זיקה, ולית ליה דרב אשי דדייק ממתני' דפ' "ד' אחין" דיש זיקה. דה"נ פליגי עליה התם. וכן משמע ב"החולץ" (לקמן מ.) דקרי רב יוסף משנה שאינה צריכה להא דתנן: יבמתו שמתה מותר באחותה, ואע"ג דבעי למידק מינה בשמעתין דיש זיקה. אלא דרב יוסף לא בעי למימר דאתא לאשמועינן דיש זיקה, משום דסבר דאין זיקה לכולי עלמא.

אבל מחיים לא דאסור לבטל מצות יבמין. ואפילו ר"ג דאמר: אם מיאנה — מיאנה, מודה הכא. דשאני התם שכבר נשואה לו. וא"ת: ומנלן דסבר אין זיקה? דלמא לעולם יש זיקה, ולאחר מיתה שרי משום דפקעה זיקה, כדאמר בסמוך! וי"ל: דאע"פ שהש"ס עושה בסמוך צריכות', האמת הוא דאי יש זיקה — לאחר מיתה נמי אסור, דזיקה בכדי לא פקעה.

והאי

עין משפט נר מצוה

ב א מיי' פ"א מהל' יבום הלכה א סמג עשין כח טוש"ע אה"ע סימן קנז סעיף א:

ג ב מיי' שם הלכה יג סמג עשין שם ולאוין קי טוש"ע שם סימן קנט סעיף ה.

מסורת הש"ס

לקמן כד.

[ע' תוס' יומא ב: ד"ה הנ"מ ותו' מנחות ד. ד"ה מאי נ"מ מה שהגיהו בקושיא]

ב"ב קי: [לקמן כב.]

עירובין נא. יומא ב: נזיר ה. מכות יג: הוריות ח: חולין פה. מנחות ד. מה: בכורות לב. נדה כב:

[לקמן כ: כז. ועי' לקמן מ.]

[לקמן כו: ל. נא. נג.]

[לקמן יח. וש"נ]

*לקמן מט

[עמ"ש תוס' לקמן כט סד"ה כגון]

[לקמן ל. נא. נג.]

הגהות הב"ח

(א) רש"י ד"ה מלוט וכו' היה הס"ד ואח"כ מ"ה כתב רחמנא יחדו המיוחדין בנחלה וכו' לאפוקי אחוה דלוט שאין: (ב) ד"ה אין זיקה וכו' להאסר אמה עליו: (ג) ד"ה ה"א אפילו מחיים מחיי היבמה מותר באמה:

תוספות ישנים

ואי כתב רחמנא יחדו. ל"ע אמאי אצטריך למכתב אחים דלוט ויחדו לאפוק מתרווייהו דמשום דכתוב חד אצטריך אידך. וי"ל דמסברא ידעי' דמייחד באבא ואמא משום חומר דאשת אח דמישתריא גביה. וא"כ אצטריך אחים לומר דלא דווי' אחוה מיוחדת גמורה דהא אף מאחין דלוט אית לן למילף וכיון דאצטריך אחים בלוט אצטריך נמי יחדו כדמפרש תלמודא: באחותה אין באמה לא. וא"ת מאי קא פריך דלמא חסיא כמאן דאמר יש זיקה דהא איכא כמה תנאי דקא סברי יש זיקה וי"ל דפריך שפיר דמסתבר דהלכתא כאותה מתניתא דמייתי דהויא מחלוקת ואח"כ סתם. שהמחלוקת הוא בהחולץ גבי שומרת יבם שקדש אחיו אחותה דהיינו ר"י בן בתירה ורבנן דפליגי עליה כדקאמר שמואל הלכה מכלל דפליגי רבנן עליה וסתם ישנו בהחולץ בסוף המשנה והלכה כסתם כ"ע להר"ס: ולימא הלכה כדברי האומר יש זיקה. מצינן לפרש דהיינו ר"י בן בתירה דאפי' בקידש סבר יש זיקה: והא כי פליגי בתרי פליגי פי' אף בתרי וא"כ היה לו לאתויה לפרש דבריו כדי שלא יבא לטעות בהם.

תוספות חד מקמאי

אסיקנא דאחין מן האב מיבמין אע"פ שאין אחים מן האם. מן האם ולא מן האב אין מיבמין:

גליון הש"ס

תוס' ד"ה אבל מחיים וכו'. שכבר נשואה לו. עיין לקמן קד ע"א תד"ה אי כר"ג:

הֲוָה אָמִינָא: מֵחַיִּים, אֲבָל לְאַחַר מִיתָה פָּקְעָה לָהּ זִיקָה, קמ"ל דְּזִיקָה בִּכְדִי לָא פָּקְעָה. לֵימָא מְסַיֵּיע לֵיהּ: יְבִמְתּוֹ שֶׁמֵּתָה מוּתָּר בַּאֲחוֹתָהּ, בַּאֲחוֹתָהּ – אִין, בְּאִמָּהּ – לָא. ה"ה דַּאֲפִי' בְּאִמָּהּ, וְאַיְּידֵי דִּתְנָא רֵישָׁא אִשְׁתּוֹ שֶׁמֵּתָה מוּתָּר בַּאֲחוֹתָהּ, דַּוְקָא בַּאֲחוֹתָהּ אֲבָל בְּאִמָּהּ לָא, דַּהֲוְיָא לָהּ אִיסּוּרָא דְּאוֹרַיְיתָא – תְּנָא נַמִי סֵיפָא מוּתָּר בַּאֲחוֹתָהּ. מְתִיב רַב הוּנָא בַּר חִיָּיא: עָשָׂה בָּהּ מַאֲמָר וּמֵת – שְׁנִיָּה חוֹלֶצֶת וְלֹא מִתְיַיבֶּמֶת. טַעְמָא – דַּעֲבַד בָּהּ מַאֲמָר, הָא לָא עֲבַד בָּהּ מַאֲמָר – שְׁנִיָּה נַמִי יַבּוּמֵי מְיַיבְּמָה. וְאִי אָמְרַתְּ יֵשׁ זִיקָה, הָוְיָא לָהּ [א]צָרַת אֵשֶׁת אָחִיו שֶׁלֹּא הָיָה בְּעוֹלָמוֹ בְּזִיקָה! אֲמַר רַבָּה: הוּא הַדִּין דְּאע"ג דְּלָא עֲבַד בָּהּ מַאֲמָר – שְׁנִיָּה מְחַלַּץ חָלְצָה, יַבּוּמֵי לָא מְיַיבְּמָה, וְהָא דְּקָתָנֵי מַאֲמָר – *לְאַפּוּקֵי מִבּ"ש, דְּאָמְרִי: מַאֲמָר קוֹנֶה קִנְיָן גָּמוּר, קמ"ל. אֵיתִיבֵיהּ אַבָּיֵי: *שְׁנֵי אַחִין בָּעוֹלָם אֶחָד, וּמֵת אֶחָד מֵהֶן בְּלֹא וָלָד, וְעָמַד הַשֵּׁנִי הַזֶּה לַעֲשׂוֹת מַאֲמָר בִּיבִמְתּוֹ, וְלֹא הִסְפִּיק לַעֲשׂוֹת בָּהּ מַאֲמָר עַד שֶׁנּוֹלַד לוֹ אָח, וּמֵת, הָרִאשׁוֹנָה יוֹצְאָה מִשּׁוּם אֵשֶׁת אָחִיו שֶׁלֹּא הָיָה בְּעוֹלָמוֹ, וּשְׁנִיָּה – אוֹ חוֹלֶצֶת אוֹ מִתְיַיבֶּמֶת. וְאִי אָמְרַתְּ יֵשׁ זִיקָה – הָוְיָא לָהּ צָרַת אֵשֶׁת אָחִיו שֶׁלֹּא הָיָה בְּעוֹלָמוֹ בְּזִיקָה! הָא מַנִּי – ר"מ הִיא, דְּאָמַר: אֵין זִיקָה. וּמִי סְבִירָא לֵיהּ לְרַבִּי מֵאִיר אֵין זִיקָה? וְהָתְנַן: *אַרְבָּעָה אַחִים, שְׁנַיִם מֵהֶן נְשׂוּאִים שְׁתֵּי אֲחָיוֹת, וּמֵתוּ הַנְּשׂוּאִין הָאֲחָיוֹת – הֲרֵי אֵלּוּ חוֹלְצוֹת וְלֹא מִתְיַיבְּמוֹת. וְאִי ס"ד סָבַר ר"מ אֵין זִיקָה – *הָנֵי מִתְּרֵי בָּתֵּי קָאָתְיָין, הַאי לְיַיבֵּם חֲדָא וְהַאי לְיַיבֵּם חֲדָא! לְעוֹלָם אֵין זִיקָה, מִשּׁוּם דְּקָסָבַר: *אָסוּר לְבַטֵּל מִצְוַת יְבָמִין, דְּדִלְמָא אַדְּמְיַיבֵּם חַד מָיֵית אִידָךְ, וְקָא בָּטְלַתְּ מִצְוַת יְבָמִין. וְאִי אֵין זִיקָה – תִּיבָּטֵל, דְּהָא ר"ג אֲמַר אֵין זִיקָה, וּמוּתָּר לְבַטֵּל מִצְוַת יְבָמִין. דִּתְנַן: *ר"ג אוֹמֵר: אִם מֵאֲנָה – מֵאֲנָה, וְאִם לֹא מֵאֲנָה – תַּמְתִּין עַד שֶׁתַּגְדִּיל וְתֵצֵא הַלֵּזוּ מִשּׁוּם אֲחוֹת אִשָּׁה! אֲמַר לֵיהּ: דְּרַבָּן גַּמְלִיאֵל אַדְּרַבִּי מֵאִיר קָרָמֵית? לָא, הָכִי (א) קָאָמְרִינַן: ר"מ חָיֵישׁ אֲפִי' לִסְפֵיקָא, ר"ג – אֲפִילּוּ לְוַדַּאי לָא חָיֵישׁ?! דִּלְמָא, מַאן דְּלָא חָיֵישׁ אֲפִי' לְוַדַּאי לָא חָיֵישׁ, וּמַאן דְּחָיֵישׁ – אֲפִי' לִסְפֵיקָא חָיֵישׁ. •א"ל אַבָּיֵי לְרַב יוֹסֵף: הָא דְּרַב יְהוּדָה – דִּשְׁמוּאֵל הִיא, דִּתְנַן:

שׁוֹמֶרֶת

בַּאֲחוֹתָהּ אִין. דַּאֲפִי' כְּנוּסָה שֶׁמֵּתָה מוּתָּר בַּאֲחוֹתָהּ. עָשָׂה בָּהּ מַאֲמָר. מַתְנִי' הִיא (ג). מְחַלַּץ חָלְצָה. נָכְרִית. יַבּוּמֵי לָא מְיַיבְּמָה. דְּהָוְיָא צָרַת עֶרְוָה בְּזִיקָה. שֶׁכְּשֶׁנָּפְלָה לִפְנֵי אָחִיו קוֹדֶם מוֹתוֹ וְנִזְקְקָה לוֹ, נַעֲשֵׂית צָרָה לְאִשְׁתּוֹ בְּזִיקָה, וְהָוְיָא הַשְׁתָּא הָךְ נָכְרִית לְגַבֵּיהּ צָרַת עֶרְוָה בִּשְׁבִיל זִיקָה שֶׁזִּיקָתָהּ כָּאַחִין בָּהּ. מִדְּב"ש. בְּפֶ' "ד' אַחִין" (לקמן ד' כט.), ב"ש אוֹמְרִים אִשְׁתּוֹ עִמּוֹ וְהַלֵּזוּ תֵּצֵא מִשּׁוּם אֲחוֹת אִשָּׁה כו'. קִנְיָן גָּמוּר. וְתֶיהֱוֵי צָרַת עֶרְוָה, וְתִיפָּטֵר אַף מִן הַחֲלִיצָה, קמ"ל. עַד שֶׁנּוֹלַד לוֹ אָח וּמֵת אוֹתוֹ שֵׁנִי. וְלוֹ אִשָּׁה אַחֶרֶת, וְנָפְלוּ שְׁתֵּיהֶן לִפְנֵי הַנּוֹלָד. בְּזִיקָה. שֶׁנִּזְקְקָה לַשֵּׁנִי לִפְנֵי מוֹתוֹ, וְנַעֲשֵׂית צָרָה לְאִשְׁתּוֹ. ר"מ הִיא. ר"מ קָאָמַר לָהּ לְהָךְ בָּרַיְיתָא בְּפִירְקִין, (ג) דְּאָמַר תַּנְיָא כְּווֹתֵיהּ דְּרַב פַּפָּא, וּמַיְיתֵי לָהּ לְהָךְ מַתְנִיתָא, וְקָתָנֵי סֵיפָא דִּבְרֵי ר"מ. וּמֵתוּ הַנְּשׂוּאִין שְׁתֵּי הָאֲחָיוֹת. וְנָפְלוּ שְׁתֵּיהֶן יַחַד לִפְנֵי הָאַחִין. וְלֹא מִתְיַיבְּמוֹת. מִשּׁוּם דְּתַרְוַיְיהוּ זְקִיקֵי לֵיהּ לְהַאי, וְתַרְוַיְיהוּ זְקִיקֵי לֵיהּ לְהַאי, וְאִי נָסֵיב חַד חֲדָא – [קָא] פָּגַע בַּאֲחוֹת זְקוּקָתוֹ. מִתְּרֵי בָּתֵּי. מִשְּׁנֵי אַחִין נָפְלוּ. לְעוֹלָם אֵין זִיקָה. וְהָא דְּקָאָמַר לֹא מִתְיַיבְּמוֹת – מִשּׁוּם דְּאָסוּר לְבַטֵּל מִצְוַת יְבָמִין, וְאִי אָמְרַתְּ לְיַיבֵּם הַאי חֲדָא – דִּלְמָא מָיֵית אִידָךְ אָח, וְלָא מְיַיבֵּם לְאִידָךְ, וְנָפְקָא מֵהַאי מִשּׁוּם אֲחוֹת אִשָּׁה מֵחֲלִיצָה וּמִיִּבּוּם, הִלְכָּךְ אָמְרִינַן לֵיהּ לְקַמָּא חֲלוֹץ, דְּאִי נַמִי מָיֵית אִידָךְ – הָדַר הַאי חוֹלֵץ וְחָלֵין לָהּ. וּמִדִּינָא לְבָתַר חֲלִיצָה דְּקַמָּא מָצֵי אִידָךְ לְיַיבּוּמֵי, דְּהַשְׁתָּא מִיקַּיְימָא מִצְוַת יְבָמִין בְּתַרְוַיְיהוּ, אֶלָּא גְּזֵירָה דִּלְמָא אָתֵי לְיַיבּוּמֵי בְּרֵישָׁא. וְאִי אֵין זִיקָה. דְּלֵית לֵיהּ אִיסּוּר זִיקָה – תִּיבָּטֵל מִצְוַת יְבָמִין וְלָא אִיכְפַּת לָן. דְּמַאן דְּלֵית לֵיהּ אִיסּוּר זִיקָה, לָא חָיֵישׁ נַמִי לְבִטּוּל מִצְוַת יְבָמִין. דְּהָא לר"ג דְּשָׁמְעִינַן לֵיהּ אֵין זִיקָה. בְּפֶ' ר"ג (לקמן דף נא.) שָׁמְעִינַן לֵיהּ נַמִי דְּאָמַר מוּתָּר לְבַטֵּל מִצְוַת יְבָמִין בְּפֶרֶק ב"ש (לקמן קט.). דִּתְנַן ר"ג אוֹמֵר כו'. שְׁנֵי אַחִין נְשׂוּאִין שְׁתֵּי אֲחָיוֹת, אַחַת גְּדוֹלָה וְאַחַת קְטַנָּה, וּמֵת בַּעְלָהּ שֶׁל גְּדוֹלָה וְנָפְלָה לִפְנֵי בַּעַל הַקְּטַנָּה, מְלַמְּדִים אֶת הַקְּטַנָּה לְמָאֵן בְּבַעְלָהּ וְלַעֲקוֹר נִשּׂוּאֶיהָ כְּדֵי לְיַיבֵּם אֶת זוֹ, שֶׁזִּיקָתָהּ שֶׁל זוֹ חֲמוּרָה לֶאֱסוֹר הַקְּטַנָּה עָלָיו, שֶׁלֹּא הָיוּ נִשּׂוּאֶיהָ גְּמוּרִים, שֶׁמָּא תְּמָאֵן – וּלְכָךְ לֹא תּוֹצִיא אֶת זוֹ מִשּׁוּם אֲחוֹת אִשָּׁה. ר"ג אוֹמֵר אִם מֵיאֲנָה מֵיאֲנָה. וְתִתְיַיבֵּם הַגְּדוֹלָה. וְאִם לָאו – תַּמְתִּין גְּדוֹלָה עַד שֶׁתַּגְדִּיל קְטַנָּה, וְיִבְעוֹל, וְיִהְיוּ קִידּוּשִׁין גְּמוּרִין, וְתֵצֵא גְּדוֹלָה מִשּׁוּם אֲחוֹת אִשָּׁה. אַלְמָא: אֵין זִיקָה, מִדְּשָׁרֵי קְטַנָּה עֲלֵיהּ, וּמוּתָּר לְבַטֵּל מִצְוַת יְבָמִין. וּלְר"מ נַמִי, אִי סָבַר אֵין זִיקָה – לֵימָא נַמִי מוּתָּר לְבַטֵּל מִצְוַת יְבָמִין. רַבָּן גַּמְלִיאֵל אַדְּר"מ קָרָמֵית. נְהִי נַמִי דִּבְזִיקָה סְבִירָא לְהוּ כִּי הֲדָדֵי, בְּבִיטּוּל יְבָמִין פְּלִיגֵי. אֲפִילּוּ לִסְפֵיקָא. כִּי הַהִיא דִּלְעֵיל, אַדְּמְיַיבֵּם חַד – מָיֵית אִידָךְ. וְרַבָּן גַּמְלִיאֵל, אֲפִי' הֵיכָא דְּוַדַּאי בָּטְלָה, כְּגוֹן הָכָא דְּתַמְתִּין עַד שֶׁתַּגְדִּיל – לָא חָיֵישׁ. הָא דְּרַב יְהוּדָה. דְּאָמַר לְעֵיל אָסוּר בְּאִמָּהּ, דְּיֵשׁ זִיקָה. דִּשְׁמוּאֵל הִיא. מִשְּׁמֵיהּ דִּשְׁמוּאֵל רַבֵּיהּ שְׁמִיעַ לֵיהּ, וְלָא מֵרַב, דַּהֲוָה נַמִי רַבֵּיהּ.

שׁוֹמֶרֶת

והאי דקתני מאמר לאפוקי מב"ש. תימה: דמה צריך למיתני בשני מקומות לאפוקי מב"ש? דלקמן בפ' "ד' אחין" (דף ל.) גבי ג' אחים, שנים מהם נשואים שתי אחיות כו', קתני נמי: עשה בה מאמר ומת (ד) חולצת ולא מתייבמת, וקאמר רב אשי בגמ': דה"ה אע"ג דלא עשה בה מאמר, דיש זיקה. והא דקתני מאמר – לאפוקי מב"ש! וי"ל: דאי לאו משנה יתירה הוה דייקינן מתני' כפשטה, דמשמע דוקא עשה בה מאמר. ורב דאמר אין זיקה – סבר דמסברא ה"א דיש זיקה, ואי לאו משנה יתירה הוה אמרי' דנקט עשה בה מאמר לאפוקי מב"ש.

הא מני ר"מ. דקתני בסיפא דברי ר"מ. לעיל דפריך ממתני' ה"מ לשנויי נמי הא מני רבי מאיר, אלא דניחא ליה לתרוצי סתמא דמתני' כוותיה.

הני מתרי בתי קאתיין. הלשון מגומגם, דמשמע דאפשר להם להיות מבית אחד, ולא ה"ל למימר טפי אלא: ואי אין זיקה האי לייבם חדא כו'.

משום דקסבר אסור לבטל מצות יבמין. הא דלא כר"ע, דלרבי עקיבא כי חלין נמי בטיל מצות יבמין, (ה) (*מדאידך) דדריש בפרק "החולץ" (לקמן מד. ושם) "בית חלוץ" – הכתוב קראו ביתו, ומדאורייתא אחות חלוצה הויא כאחות אשה.

דלמא אדמייבם חד מיית אידך כו'. וא"ת: הא רבנן למיתה לא חשו, דלית להו שמתקנין לו אשה אחרת שמא תמות אשתו (יומא ב). ור"מ גופיה לא חייש לשמא יבקע הנוד, ולא לשמא ימות, בפרק "כל הגט" (גיטין דף כח. ושם)! וי"ל: דלאלתר דוקא לא חייש, אבל הכא – פעמים שמאחר זמן גדול מלחלוץ ומלייבם אחר חברו, ובזמן מרובה חיישינן שמא ימות לכ"ע. ואע"ג דאביי מדמה שמא מת לשמא ימות, ולשמא מת לא חייש ר"מ אפי' לזמן מרובה, דתנן (שם): בת ישראל הנשואה לכהן, והלך בעלה למדינת הים – אוכלת בתרומה בחזקת שהוא קיים. ושמעתין אתיא כאביי, דמשמע דקבלה מיניה אביי – לא מדמי להו לגמרי, אלא שמא ימות לאלתר לשמא מת לזמן מרובה. תדע דלא לגמרי מדמי, דהא לר' יהודה דחייש לשמא ימות לאלתר, אי הוה חייש נמי לשמא מת לאלתר – א"כ אשת כהן שיצא בעלה מפתח ביתו לא תאכל בתרומה אלא כשרואה בעלה בפניה חי! וא"ת: וליחלוץ חד והדר לייבם אידך, דתו ליכא למיחש לביטול יבמין! וי"ל: דגזרינן דלמא אתי לייבם ברישא. וריב"ן פי': משום דבשעת נפילה לא חזו תרווייהו, כל זמן שלא חלץ לאחת. וקשיא לפירושו: דאותה שנפלה תחילה תשתרי כי חלץ לשניה, דהוה לה יבמה שהותרה ונאסרה – דתחזור להתירה הראשון!

מיאנה מיאנה ואם לאו תמתין עד שתגדיל. ופי' בקונטרס: תמתין גדולה עד שתגדיל הקטנה. ואין הלשון משמע כן, דלא הוה ליה למימר "הלזו" אלא: ותצא משום אחות אשה, הואיל דתמתין נמי אגדולה קאי! אלא נראה דתמתין הקטנה מלבעול עד שתגדיל. אבל בקטנות אסור לבעול, אע"ג דסבר אין זיקה, דמכוער הדבר, כיון דבהאי ביאה לא מיפטרה גדולה.

שומרת

כ"ה בדפו"

[לקמן כט: ל. נח:]

[לקמן יט.]

זמן כג: ס. כז: עדיות פ"ה מ"ה

[לקמן כו.]

עיל יז: לקמן כז. כו. כח.]

לקמן עט: קט.

ד א טוש"ע אה"ע סימן קעג סעיף יב:

תוספות ישנים

לימא מסייע ליה יבמתו שמתה כו' אע"ג דפליגי תנאי בה מ"מ מייתי שפיר דהלכה כן משום דהוי מחלוקת ואח"כ סתם א"נ מייתי מהכא דאפילו לאחר מיתה לא פקעה ליה זיקה ובהא לא איירו תנאי כלל: **ואי** אמרת יש זיקה הוה צרת אשת אחיו שלא היה בעולמו בזיקה. וא"ת ומאי קא מייתי הלא ידעי' דאיכא תנאי דסברי אין זיקה. וי"ל דהכי פריך אא"ב דאפי' למ"ד יש זיקה לאחר מיתה פקעה לה זיקה שפיר דאתיא הך אפי' למ"ד יש זיקה. אלא כיון דאמרת דמיתה לא פקעה לה זיקה תקשי מהך אי סברת יש זיקה דא"כ זיקה חזקה היא כיון דמיתה לא פקעה לה ואין לנו לחלק בין מתה היא למת הוא כיון שהזיקה חזקה כ"כ דמיתה לא פקעה לה: **לאפוקי** מב"ש. וא"ת למה לי הא ידעינן דב"ש במקום ב"ה אינה משנה וי"ל דאצטריך לאפוקי משום דאיכא דסבר כאותה ברייתא וא"ת לקמן נמי אמרינן לאפוקי מב"ש וי"ל דאי לאו יתירא דב' משניות ה"א הכא מסברא טעמא דעבד בה מאמר ולא הוה אמינא ה"ה לאע"ג דלא עבד בה מאמר: **אדמייבם** חד מיית אידך וקא מבטלא מצות יבמין. וא"ת ולחלוץ ברישא והדר לייבם דאי לא מיית אידך לייבם ואי מיית לחלוץ האי וי"ל דגזרינן דלמא מייבם ברישא:

הגהות הב"ח

(א) גמ' אדר' מאיר קרמית לא הכי קאמינא ר' מאיר וכו' ורבן גמליאל: (ב) רש"י ד"ה עשה וכו' מתני' היא כ"ב בדף יז ע"א: (ג) ד"ה ר' מאיר וכו' בפירקין דף י"ט ע"א דאמר תניא כותיה דרב פפא ומייתי: (ד) תום' ד"ה והאי וכו' ומת נכרית חולצת: (ה) ד"ה משום וכו' בטיל מצות יבמין אי מת אידך דדריש כנ"ל להגיה:

גליון הש"ס

גמ' א"ל אביי לרב יוסף הא דר"י דשמואל היא. עירובין דף ז ע"א ד' פה ע"א כתובות ד' יב ע"ב:

ה א טוש"ע אה"ע סימן קנט סעיף ה:
ו ב מיי' פ"ו מהלכות יבום הלכה יז סמג עשין נח טוש"ע אה"ע סימן קעג סעיף יב:

*שומרת יבם שקידש אחיו את אחותה, משום ר' יהודה בן בתירה אמרו: אומרים לו, המתן עד שיעשה אחיך מעשה. *ואמר שמואל: הלכה כר' יהודה בן בתירה. א"ל: דאי דרב מאי? (*א"ל): קשיא דרב אדרב! דלמא אמוראי נינהו, ואליבא דרב? כיון דאיתמר משמיה דשמואל בהדיא, ומשמיה דרב כאמוראי – לא שבקינן משמיה דשמואל בהדיא ומוקמינן כאמוראי ואליבא דרב. אמר רב כהנא, אמריתה לשמעתא קמיה דרב זביד מנהרדעא, אמר: אתון הכי מתניתו לה, אנן בהדיא מתנינן: (א) אמר רב יהודה אמר שמואל: שומרת יבם שמתה – אסור באמה. אלמא *קסבר: יש זיקה. ואזדא שמואל לטעמיה, דאמר שמואל: הלכה כרבי יהודה בן בתירה. וצריכי, דאי אשמעינן יש זיקה – ה"א: ה"מ – בחד, אבל בתרי – לא, [א]קמ"ל. ואי אשמעינן הלכה כר' יהודה בן בתירה – ה"א ה"מ מחיים, אבל לאחר מיתה – פקעה לה זיקה, קמ"ל: דזיקה בכדי לא פקעה.§

מתני' [ב]שני אחים ומת אחד מהן, ויבם השני את אשת אחיו, ואח"כ נולד להן אח ומת – הראשונה יוצאה משום אשת אחיו שלא היה בעולמו, והשניה משום צרתה, *עשה בה מאמר, ומת – השניה חולצת ולא מתייבמת. *ר"ש אומר: מייבם לאיזו מהן שירצה, או חולץ לאיזו מהן שירצה.§

גמ' *אמר רב אושעיא: חלוק היה ר"ש אף בראשונה. ממאי מדקתני משנה יתירה – בבא דרישא למאן קתני לה? אילימא לרבנן – השתא יבם ולבסוף נולד, דכי אשכחה בהתירא אשכחה, אסרי רבנן – נולד ואח"כ יבם מיבעיא? אלא לאו לר"ש איצטריך, ותנא רישא להודיעך כחו דר"ש, ותנא סיפא להודיעך כחן דרבנן. ובדין הוא דנפלוג ר"ש ברישא, אלא נטר להו לרבנן עד דמסיימי למילתייהו, והדר פליג עלייהו. אלא, אשת אחיו שלא היה בעולמו, לר"ש היכי משכחת לה? בחד אחא, ומית, ונולד לו אח. אי נמי: בתרי, ולא יבם ולא מית. בשלמא יבם ואח"כ נולד – כי אשכחה בהתירא אשכחה, אלא נולד ואח"כ יבם – מאי טעמא? קסבר: יש זיקה, וזיקה כבנוסה דמיא. מתקיף לה רב יוסף: השתא זיקה ומאמר מספקא ליה לר"ש אי כבנוסה דמיא אי לאו כבנוסה דמיא, זיקה לחודה מיבעיא? מאי היא? דתנן: *שלשה אחין נשואין שלש נשים נכריות, ומת אחד מהם ועשה בה שני מאמר, ומת – הרי אלו חולצות ולא מתייבמות, שנאמר °"ומת אחד מהם (דברים כה) יבמה יבא עליה" – מי שעליה זיקת יבם אחד, ולא שעליה זיקת שני יבמין. רבי שמעון אומר: מייבם לאיזהו מהן שירצה, וחולץ לשניה. יבומי תרווייהו לא – דדלמא יש זיקה, והוו שני יבמות הבאות
מבית

תורה אור

שומרת יבם. ממתנת לייבום יבמה. שקידש אחיו. של יבם את אחותה אחר שנפלה זו לפניו. אומרים לו. למארס: המתן מלכנוס, לפי שאחות זקוקתך היא. עד שיעשה אחיך מעשה. עד שייבם אחיך את היבמה, ותפקע זיקתה ממך. אלמא: זיקה אסרה לאחותה. א"ל. רב יוסף לאביי: ואי משמיה דרב אמרה מאי קשיא לך? דרב אדרב. דא"ר הונא אמר רב לעיל מותר באמה. אמוראי נינהו. רב הונא ורב יהודה תלמידי דרב הוו, ופליגי אליביה. כיון דאיתמר משמיה דשמואל בהדיא. דיש זיקה, דשמואל עצמו אמרה ולא תלמידו משמו, ומלינו למימר דרב יהודה תלמידו מכלל אותה שמועה אמר להאי דידיה. ומשמיה דרב איתמר כאמוראי. בפלוגתא, דהא פליג רב הונא – לא שבקינן כו'. הכי קמתניתו לה. לרב יהודה דלעיל, בסתמא, שלא הזכיר שם רבו. ולריכיתו למידק, הא דרב יהודה – דשמואל היא: ה"ג: אנן בהדיא מתנינן לה. ואזדא שמואל לטעמיה. כולה רב כהנא אמרה. ה"מ מחיים. כל זמן שיבמתו קיימת. **מתני'** ומת. המייבם. מייבם לאיזו שירצה. ופטורה חברתה. ולאו אעשה בה מאמר קאי, אלא ארישא, דקתני: הראשונה יוצאה כו'. דקאמר ר"ש, דכיון דכשנולד כבר נתייבמה, ולא היתה על זה בזיקת נישואי אחיו הראשון מעולם – מותרת לו. **גמ'** אף בראשונה. וקא שרי נולד ואח"כ ייבם. מדקתני משנה יתירה. לכולה ההיא בבא דרישא. דלמאן קתני לה, אי לאו דפלוגתא דר"ש עלה קיימא, ולהכי תנייה, לאשמועינן דאפי' בההיא שרי. למאן קתני לה. לאשמועינן מילתיה דמאן איצטריכא? אילימא לרבנן. לאשמועינן איסורא לרבנן, דהא לא איסור ולא היתר לר"ש שמעת מינה ברישא, דהא לא איירי בה. ונטר להו. המתין להם. והדר פליג עלייהו. דכולה חילתא. בחד אחא. דודאי מכח זיקת זה שלא היה בעולמו אסורה לזה להתייבם. אי נמי בתרי. אחים, ומת האחד, ונולד להם את השלישי. ולא ייבם. זה השני את יבמתו. ולא מת. אסורה לזה שנולד לאחר מיתה ליבמה מזיקת את שלא היה בעולמו. אבל היכא דייבמה השני – פקעה זיקת את הראשון, ונעשית אשתו של זה השני. אי נמי: לא יבמה האי שני, הואיל והוזקקה לו – הרי היא כבנוסה כדלקמן, וכשמת – מותרת לשלישי. בהתירא אשכחה. שלא נאסרה עליו שעה אחת, שלא נזקקה לו מכח הראשון כלום. יש זיקה. כשנפלה לפני השני קודם לידתו של זה, ונזקקה לו לשני – אלימא ההיא זיקה לשוויא כבנוסה, והוי ליה כייבם ולבסוף נולד. זיקת יבם אחד. כגון שלא נפלה אלא פעם אחת, או שכנסה שני ופקעה זיקה ראשונה. וכשמת אין כאן אלא זיקת ייבום של שני, או לא עשה בה מאמר ומת – אין כאן אלא זיקת ייבום ראשון, ועכשיו יש כאן זיקת ייבום של שני יבמין, שיש עליה קצת זיקה מן הראשון, דכל זמן שלא נתייבמה – לא פקע זיקתה מן השני, וצרתה, אשת השני, אסורה משום דידה. מייבם לאיזו שירצה. דלית ליה הך דרשה דזיקת שני יבמים, דאי מאמר קונה – הרי היא אשת שני, ואין כאן אלא זיקתו. ואם אין קונה – הרי הוא כמו שאינו, ואין כאן אלא זיקת ראשון. וחולץ לשניה. משום ספיקא, כדמפרש ואזיל:
מבית

שומרת יבם שקידש אחיו את אחותה כו'. אר"י: דדוקא קידש אומרים לו המתן מלישא, משום דבשעת נישואין נראה כנושא אחות זקוקתו. אבל אם נשא כבר, שהיא אשתו גמורה – פקע לה זיקה לגמרי ואין צריך להמתין מלבעול. ודוקא קידש אחר נפילה, כדמוכח ב"החולץ" (לקמן מא. ושם) דבקידש באיסור איירי, דמסיק עלה: מתה אשתו מותר ביבמתו, משום דהואי יבמה שהותרה ונאסרה וחזרה והותרה. אבל אם קידש בהיתר קודם נפילה, שלא היתה אחות זקוקתו בשעת קידושין – א"צ להמתין כלל. **אומרים** לו המתן. וא"ת: למה צריך להמתין? דכיון דקדשה פקעה לה זיקה לגמרי, כדמוכח בפ' "ד' אחים" (לקמן כט. ושם) גבי הא דא"ר אלעזר: מאמר לב"ש אינו קונה קנין גמור אלא לדחות צרה בלבד, א"ר אבין אף אנן נמי תנינא: ב"ש אומר יקיימו, דיעבד אין, לכתחלה – לא. ואי ס"ד דמאמר קונה קנין גמור – זה יעשה מאמר ויקנה, וזה יעשה מאמר ויקנה! ומאי קושיא? אפי' קני קנין גמור, הא אמרי' הכא דצריך להמתין בקידושין דאורייתא! ולפי מאי דפרישית לעיל(ג), דמש"ה חשיב לר"י בן בתירה יחידאה – א"ש. וי"ל: דלר"י בן בתירה, דסבר יש זיקה, אין הקידושין מפקיעים הזיקה. אבל ר' אבין סבר אין זיקה, ולא אסור לייבם אלא משום ביטול מצות יבמין. ולהכי פריך אי מאמר קונה לב"ש קנין גמור זה יעשה קנין גמור – ויקנה וזה יעשה מאמר ויקנה, ויכולים לעשות ע"י שליח בבת אחת, דליכא ביטול מצות יבמין. והא דשרי הכא לקיימה, אפי' לרבי יהודה בן בתירה, ובפ' "ד' אחין"(ג) ששניהם נשואים ב' אחיות דאייתי לעיל, קתני סיפא קדמו וכנסו יוציאו! אר"י: דשאני גבי ד' אחים, שהאחיות לא היו באות לעולם לכלל היתר, שכל אחת אחות זקוקתו. אבל היכא דאחות יבמה אתיא לכלל היתר, לאחר שיעשה אחיו מעשה – לא התירו להוציא. **דאי** דרב מאי. וא"ת: דבסוף פ"ק דכתובות (דף יב:) נמי אמרינן הא דרב יהודה – דשמואל היא, ולא פריך דאי דרב מאי! וי"ל: דהכא משמע דרב יהודה משמיה דרב קאמר לה, דקאי ארב הונא דקאמר משמיה דרב שומרת יבם שמתה מותר באמה.

משכחת לה בחד אחא. וא"ת: לעיל בפ"ק (דף ט: ושם) בשמעתיה דלוי קאמר: בפלוגתא לא קמיירי, ופריך: והא א"ר אושעיא חלוק היה ר"ש אף בראשונה, הא לרבי אושעיא נמי משכחת לה בחד אחא, ולפטור צרתה וצרת צרתה נמי משכחת לה למאי דאמר לקמן דמודי ר"ש בזיקת שני יבמין דלאו ככנוסה דמיא! וי"ל: דמתני' דפרקין אתא לפרושי פרקין קמא, דקתני: כיצד אשת אחיו שלא הי' בעולמו. ולר' אושעיא דחלוק ר"ש אף בראשונה – ע"כ מתני' דפרק קמא איירי בפלוגתא.
שמא

הגהות הב"ח

(א) גמ' בהדיא מתנינן לה אמר: (ב) תום' ד"ה אומרים וכו' דפרישית לעיל כ"ב דף יז בד"ה ולימא: (ג) בא"ד ובפ' ד' אחין שׁשניס מהן נישואין ב':

תוספות ישנים

מאי טעמא דקסבר יש זיקה וזיקה ככנוסה. והאי דקאמר בתרי ולא ייבם ולא מית משמע דאין זיקה דאי זיקה ככנוסה אפי' לא יבם הוי כמו יבם. היינו משום דלא מית אבל במית זיקה הוי ככנוסה. וא"ת כיון דזיקה הוי ככנוסה אמאי נקט במתני' יבם בלא יבם נמי שריא ליה לר' שמעון דהוי כמו יבם ואח"כ נולד וי"ל דנקט יבם משום דמפרש הכא אשת אחיו שלא היה בעולמו דפרקין קמא וקאמר דכלהו פוטרות צרותיהן וצרות צרותיהן ואי לא ייבם לא משכחת בגוה צרה:

מגילה יח: לקמן מא.
שם
רש"ל מ"ז
[לקמן כז.]
עי' תוס' ריש פרקין
[לעיל ט:]
[לעיל ט: וצ"ל אמר רבי אושעיא וע' תוס' עירובין סח. ד"ה אמר ותוס' לקמן יט. ד"ה ועוד וכן איתא לעיל ט: רבי אושעיא]

תורה אור

מִבַּיִת אֶחָד, יַבּוּמֵי חֲדָא וְאִיפְּטוֹר אִידָךְ — לָא, דִּדְלְמָא אֵין זִיקָה כִּכְנוּסָה וְהָווּ לְהוּ שְׁתֵּי יְבָמוֹת הַבָּאוֹת מִשְּׁנֵי בָתִּים. אַלְמָא: מְסַפְּקָא לֵיהּ. וְכִי תֵּימָא: מִדְּאוֹרַיְיתָא ה"נ דְּמִיַּיבְּמָא חֲדָא, וּמִפַּטְרָא חֲדָא, וּמִדְּרַבָּנַן הוּא דְּאָסוּר, גְּזֵירָה מִשּׁוּם שֶׁמָּא יֹאמְרוּ: ב' יְבָמוֹת הַבָּאוֹת מִשְּׁנֵי בָתִּים, חֲדָא מִיַּיבְּמָא וְאִידָךְ מִיפַּטְרָא בְּוּלָא כְלוּם, וְהָא טַעֲמָא דְּר"ש מִשּׁוּם מַאֲמָר וְלָאו מַאֲמָר הוּא! דְּתַנְיָא, אָמַר לָהֶם רַבִּי שִׁמְעוֹן לַחֲכָמִים: אִם מַאֲמָרוֹ שֶׁל שֵׁנִי מַאֲמָר — אֵשֶׁת שֵׁנִי הוּא בּוֹעֵל, וְאִם מַאֲמָרוֹ שֶׁל שֵׁנִי אֵינוֹ מַאֲמָר — אֵשֶׁת רִאשׁוֹן הוּא בּוֹעֵל. אֲמַר לֵיהּ אַבַּיֵי: וְלָא שָׁנֵי לָךְ בֵּין זִיקַת יָבָם אֶחָד לְזִיקַת שְׁנֵי יְבָמִים? דִּלְמָא, כִּי אר"ש זִיקָה כִּכְנוּסָה דָּמְיָא — בְּיָבָם אֶחָד, אֲבָל בִּשְׁנֵי יְבָמִין — לָא. וּמִי שָׁנֵי לֵיהּ לְר"ש? וְהָתַנְיָא, כְּלָל אר"ש: כָּל שֶׁהַלֵּידָה קוֹדֶמֶת לַנִּשּׂוּאִין — לֹא חוֹלֶצֶת וְלֹא מִתְיַיבֶּמֶת, נִשּׂוּאִין קוֹדֶם לַלֵּידָה — אוֹ חוֹלֶצֶת אוֹ מִתְיַיבֶּמֶת. מַאי לָאו בְּיָבָם אֶחָד, וְקָתָנֵי: לֹא חוֹלֶצֶת וְלֹא מִתְיַיבֶּמֶת! לֹא, בִּשְׁנֵי יְבָמִים. אֲבָל בְּיָבָם אֶחָד מַאי, הָכִי נַמִי אוֹ חוֹלֶצֶת אוֹ מִתְיַיבֶּמֶת? אִי הָכִי, אַדְּתָנֵי נִשּׂוּאִין קוֹדְמִין לַלֵּידָה אוֹ חוֹלֶצֶת אוֹ מִתְיַיבֶּמֶת — לִיפְלוֹג וְלִיתְנֵי בְּדִידָהּ: בד"א — בִּשְׁנֵי יְבָמִים, אֲבָל בְּיָבָם אֶחָד — אוֹ חוֹלֶצֶת אוֹ מִתְיַיבֶּמֶת! כּוּלָּהּ בִּשְׁנֵי יְבָמִין קָמַיְירֵי. וְאֶלָּא מַאי כְּלָלָא? וְעוֹד, מְתִיב רַב אוֹשַׁעְיָא: *ג' אַחִין, שְׁנַיִם מֵהֶן נְשׂוּאִין שְׁתֵּי אֲחָיוֹת, אוֹ אִשָּׁה וּבִתָּהּ, אוֹ אִשָּׁה וּבַת בִּתָּהּ, אוֹ אִשָּׁה וּבַת בְּנָהּ — הֲרֵי אֵלּוּ חוֹלְצוֹת וְלֹא מִתְיַיבְּמוֹת, וְר"ש פּוֹטֵר. וְאִי ס"ד קָסָבַר ר"ש זִיקָה כִּכְנוּסָה דָּמְיָא — לְיַיבֵּם לְקַמַּיְיתָא וְתִיפָּטֵר אִידָךְ! אָמַר רַב עַמְרָם: מַאי פּוֹטֵר נַמִי — פּוֹטֵר בַּשְּׁנִיָּה. וְהָתַנְיָא: *ר"ש פּוֹטֵר בִּשְׁתֵּיהֶן! אָמַר רָבָא: שְׁנִיָּה שֶׁבְּזוּג זֶה וְהַשְּׁנִיָּה שֶׁבְּזוּג זֶה. קָא טָעֵי רָבָא בְּאַרְבָּעָה זוּגֵי, חֲדָא: דְּ"אוֹ" "אוֹ" קָתָנֵי. וְעוֹד: "רַ' שִׁמְעוֹן פּוֹטֵר בְּאַרְבַּעְתָּן" מִיבָּעֵי לֵיהּ. וְעוֹד: תַּנְיָא, ר"ש פּוֹטֵר בִּשְׁתֵּיהֶן מִן הַחֲלִיצָה וּמִן הַיִּיבּוּם, שֶׁנֶּאֱ' °"וְאִשָּׁה אֶל אֲחוֹתָהּ לֹא תִקָּח לִצְרוֹר" •בְּשָׁעָה שֶׁנַּעֲשׂוּ צָרוֹת זוֹ לָזוֹ לֹא יְהֵא לָךְ לִיקּוּחִין אֲפִי' בְּאַחַת מֵהֶן. אֶלָּא אָמַר רַב אַשִׁי: אִי דְּנְפוּל בְּזֶה אַחַר זֶה — הָכִי נַמִי. הָכָא בְּמַאי עָסְקִינַן — דִּנְפוּל בְּבַת אַחַת, וְרַבִּי שִׁמְעוֹן סָבַר לָהּ *כְּרַבִּי יוֹסֵי הַגְּלִילִי, דְּאָמַר: אֶפְשָׁר לְצַמְצֵם. רַב פַּפָּא אָמַר: בְּיִיבֵּם וְאח"כ נוֹלַד — פְּלִיג ר"ש, בְּנוֹלַד וְאח"כ יִיבֵּם — לָא פְּלִיג, וְתַרְוַויְיהוּ לְרַבָּנַן אִיצְטְרִיךְ, *וְ"לֹא זוֹ אַף זוֹ" קָתָנֵי. תַּנְיָא כְּוָותֵיהּ דְּרַב פַּפָּא, וּתְיוּבְתָּא דְּרַ' אוֹשַׁעְיָא: שְׁנֵי אַחִים בָּעוֹלָם אֶחָד, וּמֵת אֶחָד מֵהֶם בְּלֹא וָלָד, וְעָמַד הַשֵּׁנִי הַזֶּה לַעֲשׂוֹת מַאֲמָר בִּיבִמְתּוֹ, וְלֹא הִסְפִּיק לַעֲשׂוֹת בָּהּ מַאֲמָר עַד שֶׁנּוֹלַד לוֹ אָח, וּמֵת. הָרִאשׁוֹנָה יוֹצְאָה מִשּׁוּם אֵשֶׁת אָחִיו שֶׁלֹּא הָיָה בְּעוֹלָמוֹ, וּשְׁנִיָּה אוֹ חוֹלֶצֶת אוֹ מִתְיַיבֶּמֶת. עָשָׂה בָּהּ מַאֲמָר, וְאח"כ נוֹלַד אָח, אוֹ שֶׁנּוֹלַד לוֹ אָח וְאח"כ עָשָׂה בָּהּ מַאֲמָר, וּמֵת — הָרִאשׁוֹנָה יוֹצְאָה מִשּׁוּם אֵשֶׁת אָחִיו שֶׁלֹּא הָיָה בְּעוֹלָמוֹ, וּשְׁנִיָּה חוֹלֶצֶת וְלֹא מִתְיַיבֶּמֶת. רַ'

רש"י

מִבַּיִת אֶחָד. וְרַחֲמָנָא אָמַר "אֶת בֵּית אָחִיו" (דברים כה) — בַּיִת אֶחָד הוּא בּוֹנֶה, וְאֵינוֹ בּוֹנֶה שְׁנֵי בָתִּים. וּלְמִיפְטְרָה אִידָךְ. דְּזִיקָה כִּכְנוּסָה דָּמְיָא, וְכ"ש זִיקָה וּמַאֲמָר. גְּזֵירָה שֶׁמָּא יֹאמְרוּ שְׁתֵּי יְבָמוֹת הַבָּאוֹת מִשְּׁנֵי בָתִּים. וְנָפְלוּ כְּבַת אַחַת כְּגַמְלוּס, דְּלֵיכָּא לְמֵימַר שֶׁהָרִאשׁוֹנָה הוּזְקְקָה לְבַעַל הַשְּׁנִיָּה, וְאָתֵי לְמֵימַר נַמִי תִּתְיַיבֵּם חֲדָא וְתִיפָּטֵר אִידָךְ. מִשּׁוּם מַאֲמָר וְלֹא מַאֲמָר. סָפֵק מַאֲמָר קוֹנֶה סָפֵק אֵינוֹ קוֹנֶה. בְּיָבָם אֶחָד. כְּגוֹן מַתְנִי' דַּהֲווּ שְׁנֵי אַחִין, וְכִי מָיֵית חַד — זְקוּקָה לְהַאי לְחוּדֵיהּ, וְרַמְיָא עֲלֵיהּ. הִלְכָּךְ, אע"פ שֶׁלֹּא כְּנָסָהּ עַד שֶׁנּוֹלַד הַשְּׁלִישִׁי — הָוֵה לֵיהּ כְּיִיבֵּם וּלְבַסּוֹף נוֹלַד. אֲבָל בִּשְׁנֵי יְבָמִים. כְּגוֹן הָךְ דִּשְׁלֹשָׁה אַחִין, דְּפָשׁוּ לְהוּ תְּרֵי — לָא. וּמִי שָׁנֵי לֵיהּ. וְשָׁרֵי לֵיהּ בְּנוֹלַד וּלְבַסּוֹף יִיבֵּם? וְהָתַנְיָא. כָּל שֶׁהַלֵּידָה שֶׁל שְׁלִישִׁי קוֹדֶמֶת לַנִּשּׂוּאִין שֶׁל שֵׁנִי — לֹא חוֹלֶצֶת, אַלְמָא מוֹדֶה ר"ש בְּהָא! מַאי לָאו בְּיָבָם אֶחָד. שֶׁכְּשֶׁמֵּת רִאשׁוֹן לֹא נִשְׁאַר אֶלָּא אָח אֶחָד, וְאח"כ נוֹלַד זֶה. לֹא בִּשְׁנֵי יְבָמִין. שֶׁהָיוּ שְׁלֹשָׁה אַחִים, וּמֵת אֶחָד מֵהֶן, וְנָפְלָה לִפְנֵי הַשְּׁנַיִם, וְנוֹלַד לָהֶם אָח — הַהִיא וַדַּאי אֲסִירָא עָלָיו דְּהַאי בַּתְרָא, אֲפִילּוּ לְאַחַר שֶׁיִּיבְּמוּהָ שְׁנַיִם הָרִאשׁוֹנִים וּמֵתוּ. דְּהָא וַדַּאי נוֹלַד וּלְבַסּוֹף יִיבֵּם הוּא, דְּהַהִיא זִיקָה דַּהֲוְיָא לָהּ גַּבֵּי הָנֵי קוֹדֶם לֵידָתוֹ שֶׁל זֶה לָא אַלִּימָא לְשַׁוְויָהּ כִּכְנוּסָה לְמֶהֱוֵי כְּיִיבֵּם וּלְבַסּוֹף נוֹלַד. כּוּלָּהּ בִּשְׁנֵי יְבָמִין קָמַיְירֵי. בִּשְׁנֵי יְבָמִין בָּעֵי לְאַשְׁמוּעִינַן אִיסּוּרָא וְהֶיתֵּרָא. אֶלָּא מַאי כְּלָלָא. הוֹאִיל וּבְיָבָם אֶחָד אֲפִילּוּ לֵידָה קוֹדֶמֶת לַנִּשּׂוּאִין שָׁרֵי, הֵיכִי מָצֵי לְמִיתְנֵי כָּל שֶׁהַלֵּידָה קוֹדֶמֶת לַנִּשּׂוּאִין לֹא חוֹלֶצֶת וְלֹא מִתְיַיבֶּמֶת, וְקָתָנֵי: כְּלָל א"ר שִׁמְעוֹן, הָא זִמְנִין דְּלָא הָוֵי הָכִי! חוֹלְצוֹת. אִם מֵתוּ הַנְּשׂוּאִין אֶת הַקְּרוֹבוֹת, וְנָפְלוּ לִפְנֵי הַשְּׁלִישִׁי — הֲרֵי אֵלּוּ חוֹלְצוֹת. וְלֹא מִתְיַיבְּמוֹת. הוֹאִיל וְתַרְוַויְיהוּ זְקִיקָן לֵיהּ — קָא פָּגַע בִּקְרוֹבַת זְקוּקָתוֹ. רַבִּי שִׁמְעוֹן פּוֹטֵר. אַף מִן הַחֲלִיצָה, כִּדְקָתָנֵי לְקַמָּן בִּשְׁמַעְתִּין, מִ"לִּצְרוֹר". לְיַיבְּמָהּ לְקַמַּיְיתָא. הַהִיא דְּנָפְלָה בְּרֵישָׁא, וַאֲפִי' לֹא הִסְפִּיק לְכוֹנְסָהּ עַד שֶׁנָּפְלָה אֲחוֹתָהּ — מַאי אִיכְפַּת לָן דַּהֲוֵי זִיקָה קַמַּיְיתָא כִּכְנוּסָה, וְתִיפָּטֵר בַּתְרַיְיתָא מִשּׁוּם אֲחוֹת אִשָּׁה, וְקַמַּיְיתָא תִּתְיַיבֵּם, דִּכְיָבָם אֶחָד דּוֹמֶה! *(דְּהָא כִּי נָפְלָה מֵעִיקָּרָא לָא נָפְלָה אֶלָּא קַמֵּי חַד, דִּלְגַבֵּי אִידָךְ — עֶרְוָה הִיא מִשּׁוּם אֲחוֹת אִשָּׁה, וְלָא רָמְיָא קַמֵּיהּ כְּלָל). בַּשְּׁנִיָּה. שֶׁנָּפְלָה אַחֲרוֹנָה. שְׁנִיָּה שֶׁבְּזוּג זֶה. אִם הָיוּ שְׁלֹשָׁה אַחִין, שְׁנַיִם מֵהֶן נְשׂוּאִין שְׁתֵּי אֲחָיוֹת וְאִשָּׁה וּבִתָּהּ, וּמֵתוּ שְׁנֵיהֶם וְנָפְלוּ לִפְנֵי הַשְּׁלִישִׁי, אַחַת מִן הָרִאשׁוֹנוֹת מִתְיַיבֶּמֶת, וּשְׁתַּיִם הָאַחֲרוֹנוֹת פְּטוּרוֹת. דְּחֲדָא מִן הָרִאשׁוֹנוֹת חֲשׁוּבָה כִּכְנוּסָה וּמִתְיַיבֶּמֶת, וְהַשְּׁנִיּוֹת פְּטוּרוֹת, אַחַת — מִשּׁוּם עֶרְוָה, דְּהָא מִינַּיְיהוּ מִן הָרִאשׁוֹנוֹת דַּחֲשִׁיבָא כִּכְנוּסָה אִית לָהּ חֲדָא קְרוֹבָה בִּשְׁתַּיִם הַשְּׁנִיּוֹת. נִמְצֵאת הָאַחַת יוֹצֵאת מִשּׁוּם עֶרְוָה, וּשְׁנִיָּה מִשּׁוּם צָרָתָהּ. וְקָטָעֵי רָבָא בְּהָנָךְ אַרְבָּעָה זוּגֵי. דְּמַתְנִי', דִּס"ד דְּרָבָא דְּמַיְירֵי כְּשֶׁנָּפְלוּ כּוּלָּן לִפְנֵי יָבָם אֶחָד, מִדְּמְתָרֵץ שְׁנִיָּה שֶׁבְּזוּג זֶה וּשְׁנִיָּה שֶׁבְּזוּג זֶה. וְטָעוּת הוּא בִּידֵיהּ, חֲדָא: דְּ"אוֹ" "אוֹ" קָתָנֵי, אוֹ אִשָּׁה וּבִתָּהּ כו', אַלְמָא: לָאו כּוּלְּהוּ בְּחַד בֵּיתָא עָסְקִינַן. וְעוֹד. א"כ, דְּכוּלְּהוּ בְּחַד בֵּיתָא עָסְקִינַן, שֶׁהָיוּ ג' אַחִים, שְׁנַיִם מֵהֶם נְשׂוּאִין שְׁתֵּי אֲחָיוֹת, וְאִשָּׁה וּבִתָּהּ וְאִשָּׁה וּבַת בִּתָּהּ וְאִשָּׁה וּבַת בְּנָהּ — כָּל אֶחָד נָשׂוּי אַרְבַּע נָשִׁים, וּמֵתוּ וְנָפְלוּ לִפְנֵי הַשְּׁלִישִׁי, וְקָא"ר שִׁמְעוֹן דְּאַחַת מִן הָרִאשׁוֹנוֹת מִתְיַיבֶּמֶת וְהַשְּׁנִיּוֹת פְּטוּרוֹת — אַרְבַּעְתָּן מִיבָּעֵי לֵיהּ, דְּהָא ד' שְׁנִיּוֹת אִיכָּא! בְּשָׁעָה שֶׁנַּעֲשׂוּ אֲחָיוֹת צָרוֹת זוֹ לָזוֹ. כְּגוֹן הָכָא, שֶׁנָּפְלוּ לִפְנֵי יָבָם אֶחָד. אֲפִי' בְּאַחַת מֵהֶן. אַלְמָא: תַּרְוַויְיהוּ פְּטוּרֵי. אִי דִּנְפוּל בְּזוֹ אַחַר זוֹ ה"נ. דְּזִיקָה כִּכְנוּסָה דָּמְיָא, וְקַמַּיְיתָא מִתְיַיבֶּמֶת דְּנָפְלָה אֲפִילּוּ לְאַחַר נְפִילַת שְׁנִיָּה. כְּרַבִּי יוֹסֵי הַגְּלִילִי. בִּבְכוֹרוֹת (יז.): רָחֵל שֶׁלֹּא בִּכְּרָה וְיָלְדָה שְׁנֵי זְכָרִים, וְיָצְאוּ שְׁנֵי רָאשֵׁיהֶם כְּאֶחָד, ר' יוֹסֵי אוֹמֵר: שְׁנֵיהֶן לַכֹּהֵן, וַחכ"א: אֶחָד לוֹ וְאֶחָד לַכֹּהֵן, דְּאִי אֶפְשָׁר לְצַמְצֵם וְלָצֵאת שְׁנֵיהֶם כְּאֶחָד, אֶלָּא אֶחָד יוֹצֵא רִאשׁוֹן וּפוֹטֵר אֶת הָרֶחֶם, וְהַשֵּׁנִי חוּלִּין. וּמִשּׁוּם דְּלָא יָדַע הֵי מִינַּיְיהוּ — הָווּ תַּרְוַויְיהוּ סְפֵק בְּכוֹרוֹת, וְנוֹתֵן אֶחָד לַכֹּהֵן וְהַשֵּׁנִי יִרְעֶה עַד שֶׁיִּסְתָּאֵב, וְיֵאָכֵל בְּמוּמוֹ לְבַעַל הַבַּיִת. וְהָכָא נַמִי סָבַר ר"ש אֶפְשָׁר לְצַמְצֵם מִיתַת שְׁנֵי אַחִים כְּאֶחָד, וְלֵיכָּא חֲדָא דְּתֶיהֱוֵי רִאשׁוֹנָה, וּשְׁתֵּיהֶן פְּטוּרוֹת, כִּדְיָלֵיף טַעַם מִ"לִּצְרוֹר". דְּאִי לָאו כְּר' יוֹסֵי הַגְּלִילִי — הָוְיָא לָהּ חֲדָא רִאשׁוֹנָה, וְלָא יָדַע הֵי מִינַּיְיהוּ, וְתַרְוַויְיהוּ לִיבְּעוּ חֲלִיצָה. רַב פַּפָּא. לְעֵיל מְהַדַּר, וּפְלִיג אַדְּרַבִּי אוֹשַׁעְיָא. וְתַרְוַויְיהוּ בָּבֵי דְּמַתְנִי' לְרַבָּנַן אִיצְטְרִיכוּ, לְאַשְׁמוּעִי' דְּרַבָּנַן בְּתַרְוַויְיהוּ פָּטְרֵי. וּדְקָא קַשְׁיָא לָךְ, בָּבָא דְּרֵישָׁא לָמָּה לִי? פְּשִׁיטָא דְּבְנוֹלַד וּלְבַסּוֹף יִיבֵּם פָּטְרֵי! לֹא זוֹ אַף זוֹ קָתָנֵי. כְּלוֹמַר, אַשְׁמוּעִינַן בְּרֵישָׁא נוֹלַד וּלְבַסּוֹף יִיבֵּם, וַהֲדַר תָּנָא יִיבֵּם וּלְבַסּוֹף נוֹלַד. לוֹמַר לָךְ: דְּלָא זוֹ בִּלְבַד דְּנוֹלַד וּלְבַסּוֹף יִיבֵּם פְּטוּרָה — אֶלָּא אַף דְּיִיבֵּם וּלְבַסּוֹף נוֹלַד נַמִי פְּטוּרָה. כְּוָותֵיהּ דְּרַב פַּפָּא. דְּמוֹדֵי ר"ש בְּנוֹלַד וּלְבַסּוֹף יִיבֵּם. וְעָמַד הַשֵּׁנִי כו'. לְקַמָּן פָּרֵיךְ: לָמָּה לִי לְמִיתְנֵי עָמַד וְלֹא הִסְפִּיק? וּשְׁנִיָּה. אִשְׁתּוֹ שֶׁל שֵׁנִי. עָשָׂה בָּהּ מַאֲמָר כו'. חוֹלֶצֶת, דְּלָא אַלִּים מַאֲמָר לְשַׁוְויָהּ צָרַת עֶרְוָה לְמֵיפַק בְּוּלָא כְלוּם.

ר"ש

תוספות

שמא יאמרו שתי יבמות כו'. פירש בקונט' שנפלו בבת אחת, כר' יוסי הגלילי, דאמר אפשר לצמצם. ועי"ל: כגון שהראשונה היא ערוה לאחיו השני שמת, שלא היתה זקוקה לו כלל.

והא טעמא דר"ש משום מאמר ולאו מאמר הוא דתניא וכו'. הו"מ לשנויי דלדבריהם דרבנן קא"ל.

דתניא אמר להם ר"ש כו'. והא דאמר בפ' "ר"ג" (לקמן נא:) דר"ש סבר דמאמר קונה קנין גמור — היינו לענין שאין ביאה ומאמר אחריו, אבל לא עביד לה ככנוסה.

ועוד מתיב רב אושעיא. כאן מוכיח כפר"ת דרבי אושעיא לאו היינו רב אושעיא *דההיא דפ' "הדר" בעירובין (ד' סח. ושם) דקסבר התם ר' אושעיא דאין ברירה, ובפרק בתרא דבילה (ד' לז: ושם) אית ליה לר' אושעיא ברירה.

רבי

תוספות ישנים

פוטר בארבעתן. תימה אמאי לא קאמר בשבעתן דהא כי לקח אחת מן נשי ראובן לא יקח מנשי שמעון כלום ולא מנשי ראובן. מנשי ראובן לא יקח לפי שמבית אחד אין לו לייבם אלא אחת והאחרות פטורות. וגם מנשי שמעון לא יקח כי האחת הערוה לאותה שלקח א"כ כל נשי שמעון הם צרת ערוה. ומזה נוכל לתרץ דלא חשש למתני פוטר בשלש הצרות שנפלו עם אותה שמייבם דפשיטא הוא שאין לו לייבם מארבעתן אלא אחת ואותה שירצה יקח לו דכלהו חזיא ליה. אבל הד' האחרונות כלהו אסורות לו ובהגי הו"ל למכתב פוטר בארבעתן כ"כ לראב"י אבל מ"מ קשה דהיכי קאמר אי דנפול בזה אחר זה הכי נמי דר' שמעון סבר הכא יש זיקה וזיקה ככנוסה דמיא הא אמרינן דבשני יבמין לא אמרינן זיקה ככנוסה וה"נ כיון דאיכא הרבה יבמות אין לנו לומר לר' שמעון דזיקה ככנוסה דמיא משום דלא ידעינן איזה מהם יקח ואין הזיקה מיוחדת וע"ק אמאי נקט דנשואין ד' זוגי (איסור) כי נמי אינם נשואין רק ב' אחיות ושאר נשותיהן נכריות אמת הדבר דכשייבם א' מהן כולן פטורות. ונראה אל הקדוש דכי קאמר שניה שבזוג זו ושניה שבזוג זו מיירי שיש שמונה אחין נשואים אותם שמנה נשים שתי אחיות ואשה ובתה ואשה ובת בתה ואשה ובת בנה כל א' וא' אחת מהן. והשתא הראשון שמת אשתו מתייבמת והשניה יוצאה משום אחות ערוה אשת מי שמת שני ערוה לאשת הראשון וכן כולן אשת מי שמת ראשון מתייבמת ואשת מי שמת אחריו ערוה. והשתא איכא ד' מהם ראויות לייבם לזה האח שנפלו כלם לפניו וד' מהן יש שאינן ראויות להתייבם וניחא דקאמר פוטר בארבעתן וכן כלהו קושיות מתורץ (ממני) [בזה]:

[לקמן כח:]

[לקמן כח: קדושין נ:]

ויקרא יח

*כל זה בס"א ליתא

[לקמן כח. שבועות לב. בכורות ט. יז. יח.]

[גיטין טו: ב"מ לח. הוריות ב.]

גליון הש"ס

גמ' בשעה שנעשו צרות. ע' קידושין דף נ ע"ב תד"ה אי הכי:

תורה אור

רַ' שִׁמְעוֹן אוֹמֵר: בִּיאָתָהּ אוֹ חֲלִיצָתָהּ שֶׁל אַחַת מֵהֶם פּוֹטֶרֶת צָרָתָהּ, חָלַץ לְבַעֲלַת מַאֲמָר לֹא נִפְטְרָה צָרָה. כְּנָסָהּ וָמֵת, וְאח"כ נוֹלַד לוֹ אָח, אוֹ שֶׁנּוֹלַד לוֹ אָח וְאח"כ כְּנָסָהּ וָמֵת — שְׁתֵּיהֶן פְּטוּרוֹת מִן הַחֲלִיצָה וּמִן הַיִּיבּוּם. כְּנָסָהּ וְנוֹלַד לוֹ אָח, וְאח"כ מֵת — שְׁתֵּיהֶן פְּטוּרוֹת מִן הַחֲלִיצָה וּמִן הַיִּיבּוּם, דִּבְרֵי ר"מ. וְרַ' שִׁמְעוֹן אוֹמֵר: הוֹאִיל וּבָא וּמְצָאָהּ בְּהֶיתֵּר, וְלֹא עָמְדָה עָלָיו שָׁעָה אַחַת בְּאִיסּוּר — מְיַיבֵּם לְאֵיזוֹ מֵהֶן שֶׁיִּרְצֶה, אוֹ חוֹלֵץ לְאֵיזוֹ מֵהֶן שֶׁיִּרְצֶה. הָא בָּבָא דְּסֵיפָא לְמַאן קָתָנֵי לָהּ? אִילֵימָא לְרַ' מֵאִיר קָתָנֵי לָהּ — מִכְּדִי, לָא שָׁנֵי לֵיהּ לְרַבִּי מֵאִיר בֵּין יִיבֵּם וְאח"כ נוֹלַד, בֵּין נוֹלַד וְאח"כ יִיבֵּם — לְעַרְבִינְהוּ וְלִתְנִינְהוּ! אֶלָּא, לָאו רַבִּי שִׁמְעוֹן, וּבְיִיבֵּם וְאח"כ נוֹלַד — פָּלֵיג, בְּנוֹלַד וְאַחַר כָּךְ יִיבֵּם — לָא פָּלֵיג, ש"מ. אֲמַר מָר: עָמַד הַשֵּׁנִי לַעֲשׂוֹת מַאֲמָר בִּיבִמְתּוֹ, וְלֹא הִסְפִּיק לַעֲשׂוֹת מַאֲמָר בִּיבִמְתּוֹ עַד שֶׁנּוֹלַד לוֹ אָח, וָמֵת — רִאשׁוֹנָה יוֹצְאָה מִשּׁוּם אֵשֶׁת אָחִיו שֶׁלֹּא הָיָה בְּעוֹלָמוֹ, וּשְׁנִיָּה — אוֹ חוֹלֶצֶת אוֹ מִתְיַיבֶּמֶת. מַאי עָמַד וּמַאי לֹא הִסְפִּיק? אִי עֲבַד — עֲבַד, וְאִי לֹא עֲבַד — לָא עֲבַד! אֶלָּא: עָמַד — מִדַּעְתָּהּ, וְלֹא הִסְפִּיק מִדַּעְתָּהּ, אֶלָּא בְּעַל כָּרְחָהּ. וּדְלָא כְּרַבִּי דְּתַנְיָא: *הָעוֹשֶׂה מַאֲמָר בִּיבִמְתּוֹ שֶׁלֹּא מִדַּעְתָּהּ, רַ' אוֹמֵר: קָנָה, וחכ"א: לֹא קָנָה. מ"ט דְּרַ'? גָּמַר מִבִּיאָה דִּיבָמָה, מַה בִּיאָה דִּיבָמָה בְּעַל כָּרְחָהּ, אַף קִדּוּשִׁין דִּיבָמָה בְּעַל כָּרְחָהּ. וְרַבָּנַן גָּמְרֵי מִקִּדּוּשִׁין דְּעָלְמָא, מַה קִּדּוּשִׁין דְּעָלְמָא — מִדַּעְתָּהּ, אַף קִדּוּשִׁין דִּיבָמָה — מִדַּעְתָּהּ. בְּמַאי קָמִיפַּלְגִי? מָר סָבַר: מִילֵּי דִּיבָמָה מִמִּילֵּי דִּיבָמָה הֲוָה לֵיהּ לְמֵילַף, וּמָר סָבַר: מִילֵּי דְּקִדּוּשִׁין מִמִּילֵּי דְּקִדּוּשִׁין הֲוָה לֵיהּ לְמֵילַף. עָשָׂה בָּהּ מַאֲמָר וְאח"כ נוֹלַד לוֹ אָח, אוֹ שֶׁנּוֹלַד לוֹ אָח וְאח"כ עָשָׂה בָּהּ מַאֲמָר, וּמֵת, רִאשׁוֹנָה יוֹצְאָה מִשּׁוּם אֵשֶׁת אָחִיו שֶׁלֹּא הָיָה בְּעוֹלָמוֹ, וּשְׁנִיָּה חוֹלֶצֶת וְלֹא מִתְיַיבֶּמֶת. ר"ש אוֹמֵר: בִּיאָתָהּ אוֹ חֲלִיצָתָהּ שֶׁל אַחַת מֵהֶן פּוֹטֶרֶת צָרָתָהּ. ר"ש אַהַיָּיא קָאֵי? אִילֵימָא אַנּוֹלַד לוֹ אָח וְאח"כ עָשָׂה בָּהּ מַאֲמָר — הָא אָמְרַתְּ בְּנוֹלַד וּלְבַסּוֹף יִיבֵּם לָא פָּלֵיג ר"ש! אֶלָּא — אַעָשָׂה בָּהּ מַאֲמָר וְאח"כ נוֹלַד לוֹ אָח. חָלַץ לְבַעֲלַת מַאֲמָר לֹא נִפְטְרָה צָרָה, מ"ט? מִשּׁוּם דַּהֲוַאי צָרָה וַדַּאי וּבַעֲלַת מַאֲמָר סָפֵק, *וְאֵין סָפֵק מוֹצִיא מִידֵי וַדַּאי. יָתֵיב רַב מְנַשֶּׁה בַּר זְבִיד קַמֵּיהּ דְּרַב הוּנָא, וִיתֵיב וְקָאָמַר: מַאי טַעְמָא דר"ש? מ"ט דר"ש?! כִּדְאָמַר טַעֲמָא: הוֹאִיל וּבָא וּמְצָאָהּ בְּהֶיתֵּר, וְלֹא עָמְדָה עָלָיו שָׁעָה אַחַת בְּאִיסּוּר! אֶלָּא: מַאי טַעְמָא דְּרַבָּנַן? אֲמַר קְרָא "וּלְקָחָהּ לוֹ לְאִשָּׁה *וְיִבְּמָהּ" — עֲדַיִין יִבּוּמִים הָרִאשׁוֹנִים עָלֶיהָ. אֶלָּא, הָא דִּתְנַן: *כְּנָסָהּ — הֲרֵי הִיא כְּאִשְׁתּוֹ לְכָל דָּבָר, *וְאָמַר רַבִּי יוֹסֵי בַּר חֲנִינָא: מְלַמֵּד שֶׁמְּגָרְשָׁהּ

רש"י

ר"ש אומר ביאתה כו'. מפרש לקמיה דאעשה בה מאמר ואח"כ נולד לו אח קאי, ומשום דקסבר מאמר ספק קונה ספק אינו קונה כדאמר לעיל, ומפרש ר"ש ואזיל. **חלץ לבעלת מאמר לא נפטרה צרה.** כלומר, הא דקאמינא ביאתה או חליצתה של אחת מהן פוטרת צרתה — כגון שיהא חולץ או מייבם לשניה, והראשונה פטורה ממ"נ: אי מאמר קני — הוי ליה ייבם ולבסוף נולד, ואפי' ראשונה מותרת לר' שמעון, ובחליצה דאידך מיפטרה, דהא מאמר כנוסה, והוו להו מבית אחד. ואי מאמר לא קני — הרי שפיר ייבם לשניה, דאשת אחיו שהיה בעולמו היא, ואינה צרת ערוה. וראשונה אלא משום אשת אחיו שלא היה בעולמו. אבל חלץ לבעלת מאמר, שהיא ראשונה — לא נפטרה צרה, דדלמא מאמר לא קני, ומילא פטורה משום אשת אחיו שלא היה בעולם, וחליצתה אינה חליצה. והכי מפרש לקמן. **או שנולד לו אח.** דה"ל נולד ולבסוף ייבם. **שתיהן פטורות.** בהא לא פליג ר"ש, וכרב פפא. **הך בבא דסיפא.** ייבם ולבסוף נולד. **למאן קתני לה.** כלומר, להודיע כחו של מי קתני לה בפני עצמה, ולא עירבה עם נולד ולבסוף ייבם? **אילימא לר"מ.** לאשמועינן דבהא נמי אסר, ולאו למימר דר"ש אהך לחודה הוא דפליג. **לערבינהו.** לבבי, וליתני ברישא הכי: כנסה ומת ואח"כ נולד לו אח, או שנולד לו אח ואח"כ כנסה ומת, או שכנסה ונולד לו אח ואח"כ מת — שתיהן פטורות. אלא מדפלגינהו — ש"מ משום דאיירי בה ר"ש היא דאשמועינן דבהא לחודה פליג, משום דבא ומצאה בהיתר, אבל ברישא — מודה. **אלא בעל כרחה.** וקמ"ל דמאמר בע"כ ואפילו למקצת לא קני, ושניה יבומי נמי מייבמה. **ביאה דיבמה.** אמרי' בפ"ק (דף ח:): "ויבמה" — בעל כרחה; דאם בא עליה, אפי' באונס — קנאה. **קדושין דעלמא.** "והלכה והיתה לאיש אחר" (דברים כד) — מדעתה משמע. **אי נימא אנולד לו אח.** קודם מאמר, בהא לימא ר"ש ביאת השניה כשרה? והא דייקת מסיפא דבנולד ולבסוף ייבם לא פליג, והוה ליה אשת אחיו שלא היה בעולמו, ודלמא מאמר קני וה"ל שניה צרת ערוה! ועוד: מאי פוטרת צרתה איכא? הא מיפטרה וקיימא, דאשת אחיו שלא היה בעולמו היא. **אלא אעשה בה מאמר ואח"כ נולד אח.** ואשמועינן ברישא דמאמר ספק קונה לגמרי ספק לא קונה, *אפי' מקצת לא מהני, הלכך מייבם או חולץ לשניה ממ"נ: אי מאמר המת קנין גמור הוא — הוה ליה ייבם ולבסוף נולד, ואפילו קמייתא חזיא לייבומי, ואי לאו קנין גמור הוא — בתרייתא שריא, דלאו צרת ערוה היא, דקנין מקצת במאמר לית ליה לר"ש. ובסיפא אשמועינן דייבם ולבסוף נולד הוא דשריא, אבל נולד ולבסוף ייבם — אסורה. דלא תימא ביאתה או חליצתה דקאמר ר"ש ברישא אנולד ואח"כ עשה בה מאמר נמי קאי. **הויא צרה ודאי.** זקוקה לייבם, דאי מאמר קני — תרווייהו חזו, דהוי ליה ייבם ולבסוף נולד. ואי מאמר לא קני — שניה חזיא, דלאו צרת ערוה היא, ובעלת מאמר ספק זקוקה ספק אין זקוקה, דדלמא לא קני והוי אשת אחיו שלא היה בעולמו, וחליצתה לאו חליצה לפטור את הודאית. מ"ט דרבנן. דאסרי בייבם ולבסוף נולד? הרי לא עמדה על זה בזיקת אחיו שלא היה בעולמו מימיו. ולקחה לו לאשה ויבמה. אע"ג שכנסה — עדיין קרויה יבמה. אית דגרס: אי הכי תיבעי חליצה, אלמה תנן כנסה הרי היא כאשתו כו' — כלומר, אי הכי דאשה שנתייבמה עדיין זיקה ראשונה עליה — תיבעי חליצה, כל אשה שנתייבמה ובא שני זה לגרשה — לא תסגי לה בגט. שמגרשה

תוספות

רבי שמעון אומר ביאתה או חליצתה כו'. פי' בקונטרס: דקסבר ר' שמעון מאמר ספק קונה ספק אינו קונה, וכשייבם או חלץ לשניה — נפטרת בעלת מאמר ממ"נ. ונראה שפי' כן, דאין ר"ל שיקנה לר"ש מדרבנן — דא"כ לא היה יכול לייבם השניה, דהויא לה צרת אשת אחיו שלא היה בעולמו במאמר. אלא ודאי קסבר דקני לגמרי, או לא קני כלל. וא"ת: אכתי צרתה היא בזיקה! וי"ל: דר"ש סבר אין זיקה. ולר"י נראה: דאפילו ס"ל דיש זיקה, ומאמר קונה קנת מדרבנן — ניחא, *דאין זיקה אוסרת, ולא המאמר, אלא היכא דאם היתה נשואה היתה אוסרת. וכאן, אם היתה נשואה היא עצמה — היתה מותרת לר"ש, דשרי ייבם ואח"כ נולד. ומ"מ אמת הוא דלר"ש אי לא קני מאמר — לא קני אפילו מדרבנן, מדקאמר לעיל: אם מאמרו של שני אינו מאמר — אשת ראשון בועל. משמע דלא קני כלל.

חליץ לבעלת מאמר לא נפטרה צרתה. וא"ת: ואמאי לא דייק מהכא תיובתא לר' אושעיא, דלדידיה כיון דהוי זיקה ככנוסה, אמאי לא נפטרה הצרה? וי"ל: מדרבנן, כדאמר לעיל: גזירה משום שתי יבמות הבאות משני בתים, חדא מיחלצה וחדא מיפטרה (א) בלא כלום.

כנסה ומת ואח"כ נולד לו אח וכו'. הא מילתא דפשיטא היא, ולא הוה צריך כלל למתנייה! ואר"י: דלא שנאה אלא לאשמועי' דהאי תנא עירובי מערב ותני מילי בהדי הדדי, ולהכי דייק מינה דבנולד ולבסוף ייבם לא פליג ר"ש, מדעריב ותני להו בהדי כנסה ומת ואח"כ נולד לו אח, דמודה בה ר"ש דאי בנולד ולבסוף ייבם פליג נמי ר"ש — א"כ בהדי סיפא הוה ליה למיערבה, ולא בהדי רישא. והשתא א"ש דלא מותיב לר' אושעיא ממתני' דלא עריב ותני להו, דאברייתא שייך למידק, כדפרישית.

לערבינהו ולתנינהו. לא כמו שפירש בקונטרס דאכולהו קאי — דאכנסה ומת ואח"כ נולד ודאי ל"פ ר"ש. אלא אתרי בתראי קאי (ב).

גמרינן מביאה דיבמה. דאע"ג דמאמר אינו אלא מדרבנן, מ"מ, מר מסתבר ליה דעשאוהו חכמים כביאה ולמר מסתבר דעשאוהו כקדושין. וכה"ג איכא בפ"ק דב"מ (ד' יא. ושם) דקאמר מר יליף מציאה מגט אע"ג דלקטן לית ליה זכיה אלא מדרבנן, כדאמרי' בסוף "הניזקין" (גיטין סה. ושם). האי

עין משפט נר מצוה

ז א מיי' פ"ב מהלכות יבום הלכה א סמג עשין נא טוש"ע אה"ע סימן קסו סעיף ג:

(נ"ל דאי זיקה רש"ל)

תוספות ישנים

ביאתה או חליצתה של אחת מהן פוטרת צרתה. ומפרש לה ואזיל חלץ לבעלת מאמר לא נפטרה צרתה וא"כ הא דקאמר ביאתה או חליצתה של אחת מהן פוטרת צרתה ר"ל מאותה שאינה בעלת מאמר דהויא אשת השני וטעמא דביאתה או חליצתה פוטרת צרתה היינו מ"נ דאי מאמר קונה תרווייהו חזיין דהוי יבם ואח"כ נולד וא"כ כי מייבם לחדא מפטרה צרתה. ואי מאמר אינו קונה מאי לייבומי אשת השני דהא לא הוי צרת אשת אחיו בעולמו [כלל] (אבל) דר' שמעון לא סבר מאמר קונה קצת ואינו קונה מכל וכל אלא אומר [או] קונה מכל וכל או אינו קונה כלל. אבל חלץ לבעלת מאמר לא נפטרה צרתה דשמא מאמר אינו קונה כלל ונמצא שהחליצה בחנם היתה ואינה כלום שהיא אשת אחיו שלא היה בעולמו וא"כ לא נפטרה צרתה וצריכה לייבם לזה. וא"ת היכי קאמר דמצי לייבם אותה שאינה בעלת מאמר הא מ"מ היתה זקוקה לאחיו השני והויא ליה אשת אח השני צרת אשת אחיו שלא היה בעולמו בזיקה וא"כ היכי מצי לייבמה. וי"ל דלרב פפא איירינן דסבר ר' שמעון אין זיקה וא"כ לא הוי צרת אשת אחיו שלא היה בעולמו. ואף לר' הושעיא דאמר לר' שמעון יש זיקה וזיקה ככנוסה לא קשה מידי דא"כ היא עצמה יכולה לייבם כיון דזיקה ככנוסה דהוי כמו יבם ואח"כ נולד:

הגהות הב"ח

(א) תוס' ד"ה חלץ וכו' בלא כלום. נ"ב ס"א שלא יבא להתיר אשת אחיו שלא היה בעולמו: (ב) ד"ה לערבינהו וכו' בתראי קאי כדפי' הס"ל:

מסורת הש"ס

קדושין מד.

[לקמן לח. פסחים ט. מח: חולין י.]

לעיל ח: לקמן לט. כתובות פב:

[עיין תוספות לעיל ח: סד"ה ויבמה]

[לקמן לח. כתובות פ:]

נ"ל ואפילו

שֶׁמְּגָרְשָׁהּ בְּגֵט וּמַחֲזִירָהּ, הָתָם נַמִי לֵימָא: "וְיִבְּמָהּ" עֲדַיִין יְבוּמִין הָרִאשׁוֹנִים עָלֶיהָ, וְתִיבָּעֵי חֲלִיצָה! שָׁאנֵי הָתָם, דְּאָמַר קְרָא "וּלְקָחָהּ לוֹ לְאִשָּׁה", כֵּיוָן שֶׁלְּקָחָהּ נַעֲשֵׂית כְּאִשְׁתּוֹ לְכָל דָּבָר. אִי הָכִי, הָכָא נַמִי! הָא כָּתַב רַחֲמָנָא "וְיִבְּמָהּ". וּמָה רָאִיתָ? מִסְתַּבְּרָא: שְׁדִי הֶיתֵּירָא אַהֶיתֵּירָא וּשְׁדִי אִיסּוּרָא אַאִיסּוּרָא. וּלְרַ' שִׁמְעוֹן, דְּאָמַר: הוֹאִיל וּבָא וּמְצָאָהּ בְּהֶיתֵּר וְלֹא עָמְדָה עָלָיו שָׁעָה אַחַת בְּאִיסּוּר, אֶלָּא מֵעַתָּה, אֲחוֹתוֹ מֵאִמּוֹ שֶׁנְּשָׂאָהּ אָחִיו מֵאָבִיו, וְאַחַר כָּךְ נוֹלַד אָח, וּמֵת — תִּתְיַיבֵּם, הוֹאִיל וּבָא וּמְצָאָהּ בְּהֶיתֵּר! אִיסּוּר אֲחוֹתוֹ לְהֵיכָן אֲזַל?! הָכָא נַמִי, אִיסּוּר אָחִיו שֶׁלֹּא הָיָה בָּעוֹלָם לְהֵיכָן אֲזַל! הַאי, אִיסּוּרָא דְּלֵית לֵיהּ הֶיתֵּירָא, הַאי — אִיסּוּרָא דְּאִית לֵיהּ הֶיתֵּירָא.

§ **מתני'** כְּלָל אָמְרוּ בַּיְּבָמָה: כָּל (א) שֶׁהִיא אִיסּוּר עֶרְוָה, לֹא חוֹלֶצֶת וְלֹא מִתְיַיבֶּמֶת. *[א]אִיסּוּר מִצְוָה וְאִיסּוּר קְדוּשָּׁה — חוֹלֶצֶת וְלֹא מִתְיַיבֶּמֶת. *[ב]אֲחוֹתָהּ שֶׁהִיא יְבִמְתָּהּ — חוֹלֶצֶת אוֹ מִתְיַיבֶּמֶת. [ג]אִיסּוּר מִצְוָה: שְׁנִיּוֹת מִדִּבְרֵי סוֹפְרִים. אִיסּוּר קְדוּשָּׁה: אַלְמָנָה לְכ"ג, גְּרוּשָׁה וַחֲלוּצָה לְכֹהֵן הֶדְיוֹט, מַמְזֶרֶת וּנְתִינָה לְיִשְׂרָאֵל, וּבַת יִשְׂרָאֵל לְנָתִין וּמַמְזֵר.

§ **גמ'** כְּלָל לְאַתּוּיֵי מַאי? אָמַר רַפְרָם בַּר פַּפָּא: לְאַתּוּיֵי צָרַת אַיְלוֹנִית, *וּכְדְרַב אַסִי. וְאִיכָּא דְּאָמְרִי: "כָּל שֶׁאִיסּוּרָהּ אִיסּוּר עֶרְוָה" הוּא דַּאֲסִירָא צָרָתָהּ, הָא לֹא אִיסּוּרָהּ אִיסּוּר עֶרְוָה — צָרָתָהּ לֹא אֲסִירָא. לְמַעוּטֵי מַאי? אָמַר רַפְרָם: לְמַעוּטֵי צָרַת אַיְלוֹנִית, וּדְלָא כְּרַב אַסִי. § "אֲחוֹתָהּ שֶׁהִיא יְבִמְתָּהּ". § אֲחוֹתָהּ דְּמַאן? אִילֵימָא דְּאִיסּוּר מִצְוָה, כֵּיוָן דְּמִדְּאוֹרָיְיתָא רַמְיָא קַמֵּיהּ פָּגַע בַּאֲחוֹת זְקוּקָתוֹ! אֶלָּא: אֲחוֹתָהּ דְּאִיסּוּר עֶרְוָה. § "אִיסּוּר מִצְוָה שְׁנִיּוֹת". § *אַמַּאי קָרֵי לֵיהּ אִיסּוּר מִצְוָה? אָמַר אַבַּיֵי: *מִצְוָה לִשְׁמוֹעַ דִּבְרֵי חֲכָמִים. § "אִיסּוּר קְדוּשָּׁה אַלְמָנָה לְכֹהֵן גָּדוֹל גְּרוּשָׁה וַחֲלוּצָה לְכֹהֵן הֶדְיוֹט", § וְאַמַּאי קָרֵי לְהוּ אִיסּוּר קְדוּשָּׁה? דִּכְתִיב "קְדוֹשִׁים יִהְיוּ לֵאלֹהֵיהֶם". תַּנְיָא, רַבִּי יְהוּדָה מַחֲלִיף: *אִיסּוּר מִצְוָה — אַלְמָנָה לְכֹהֵן גָּדוֹל, גְּרוּשָׁה וַחֲלוּצָה לְכֹהֵן הֶדְיוֹט. וְאַמַּאי קָרֵי לֵיהּ אִיסּוּר מִצְוָה? דִּכְתִי' "אֵלֶּה הַמִּצְוֹת" אִיסּוּר קְדוּשָּׁה — "שְׁנִיּוֹת מִדִּבְרֵי סוֹפְרִים", וְאַמַּאי קָרֵי לֵיהּ אִיסּוּר קְדוּשָׁ'? אָמַר אַבַּיֵי: כָּל הַמְקַיֵּים דִּבְרֵי חֲכָמִים נִקְרָא קָדוֹשׁ. א"ל רָבָא: וְכָל שֶׁאֵינוֹ מְקַיֵּים דִּבְרֵי חֲכָמִים, קָדוֹשׁ הוּא דְּלָא מִיקְרֵי, רָשָׁע נַמִי לָא מִיקְרֵי?! אֶלָּא אָמַר רָבָא: קַדֵּשׁ עַצְמְךָ בַּמּוּתָּר לָךְ. § "אַלְמָנָה לְכֹהֵן גָּדוֹל". § *קָפָסֵיק וְתָנֵי, לֹא שְׁנָא מִן הַנִּשּׂוּאִין וְלֹא שְׁנָא מִן הָאֵירוּסִין. *) בִּשְׁלָמָא מִן הַנִּשּׂוּאִין — עֲשֵׂה וְלֹא תַעֲשֶׂה, [ד]וְאֵין עֲשֵׂה דּוֹחֶה לֹא תַעֲשֶׂה וַעֲשֵׂה. אֶלָּא מִן הָאֵירוּסִין, לֹא תַעֲשֶׂה גְּרֵידָא הוּא, יָבֹא עֲשֵׂה וְיִדְחֶה לֹא תַעֲשֶׂה! אָמַר רַב גִּידֵּל אָמַר רַב: אָמַר קְרָא "וְעָלְתָה יְבִמְתּוֹ הַשַּׁעְרָה" שֶׁאֵין ת"ל "יְבִמְתּוֹ", מַה תַּלְמוּד לוֹמַר יְבִמְתּוֹ — יֵשׁ לְךָ יְבָמָה (ב) אַחַת שֶׁעוֹלָה לַחֲלִיצָה וְאֵינָהּ עוֹלָה לְיִיבּוּם. וְאֵיזוֹ — זוֹ חַיָּיבֵי לָאוִין. וְאֵימָא חַיָּיבֵי כְּרֵיתוֹת! אָמַר קְרָא "וְאִם לֹא יַחְפּוֹץ הָאִישׁ לָקַחַת" הָא חָפֵץ — מְיַיבֵּם, *[ה]כָּל הָעוֹלָה לְיִיבּוּם עוֹלָה לַחֲלִיצָה וְכָל שֶׁאֵין עוֹלָה לְיִיבּוּם — אֵינוֹ עוֹלָה לַחֲלִיצָה. א"ה, חַיָּיבֵי לָאוִין נַמִי! הָא רַבֵּי רַחֲמָנָא "יְבִמְתּוֹ". וּמָה רָאִיתָ? מִסְתַּבְּרָא

*) [ע' תוספות לעיל ה. ד"ה ואכתי]

רש"י

שֶׁמְּגָרְשָׁהּ בְּגֵט. וְאֵינָהּ צְרִיכָה חֲלִיצָה, וְאִם רָצָה לְהַחֲזִיר — מַחֲזִירָהּ, וְלָא אָמְרִינַן: מִצְוָה רַמְיָא רַחֲמָנָא עֲלֵיהּ וַעֲבַדָהּ, וּמֵהַשְׁתָּא תֵּיקוּ עֲלֵיהּ בְּאִיסּוּר אֵשֶׁת אָח. לֵימָא. עֲדַיִין יְבוּמִין הָרִאשׁוֹנִים עָלֶיהָ, וְתִיבָּעֵי חֲלִיצָה. שְׁדִי הֶיתֵּרָא. לְמִדְרַשׁ "וּלְקָחָהּ" דְּלָא תִּיבָּעֵי חֲלִיצָה. אַהֶיתֵּרָא. הֵיכָא דְּכוּלָּהּ מִילְּתָא הֶיתֵּר, כְּגוֹן בִּמְיַיבֵּם אֵשֶׁת אָח. וּשְׁדִי אִיסּוּרָא. לְמִדְרַשׁ "וְיִבְּמָהּ" — עֲדַיִין יְבוּמִין עָלֶיהָ. אַאִיסּוּרָא. הֵיכָא דְּאִיכָּא צַד אִיסּוּר, כְּמוֹ בְּאֵשֶׁת אָחִיו שֶׁלֹּא הָיָה בְּעוֹלָמוֹ. אֲחוֹתוֹ מֵאִמּוֹ שֶׁנְּשָׂאָהּ אָחִיו מֵאָבִיו. קוֹדֶם לֵידָתוֹ שֶׁל זֶה, וּכְשֶׁנּוֹלַד זֶה מְצָאָהּ נְשׂוּאָה לְאָחִיו — תִּתְיַיבֵּם לוֹ כְּשֶׁיָּמוּת זֶה, דְּהָא מְצָאָהּ בְּהֶיתֵּר יִיבּוּם. אִיסּוּר אֲחוֹתוֹ לֵית לֵיהּ הֶיתֵּר. אֲבָל אִיסּוּר אֵשֶׁת אָח אִית לֵיהּ הֶיתֵּר כְּשֶׁאֵין לוֹ בָּנִים, הִילְכָּךְ, כְּשֶׁמֵּת רִאשׁוֹן בְּלֹא בָּנִים — פָּקַע אִיסּוּרוֹ לְגַבֵּי שֵׁנִי וּנְשָׂאָהּ, וְהַשְּׁלִישִׁי מִכֹּחַ שֵׁנִי בָּא. **מתני'** לֹא חוֹלֶצֶת וְלֹא מִתְיַיבֶּמֶת. צָרָתָהּ וְכ"ש הִיא. אִיסּוּר מִצְוָה. מְפָרֵשׁ לְהוּ וְאָזֵיל. אֲחוֹתָהּ. שֶׁל עֶרְוָה כְּשֶׁהִיא יְבִמְתָּהּ. כְּגוֹן שֶׁנָּפְלוּ שְׁתֵּי אֲחָיוֹת מִשְּׁנֵי אַחִין, הָאַחַת אֲסוּרָה מִשּׁוּם עֶרְוָה, כְּגוֹן שֶׁהִיא כַּלָּתוֹ אוֹ חֲמוֹתוֹ. אוֹ חוֹלֶצֶת אוֹ מִתְיַיבֶּמֶת. אֲחוֹת הָעֶרְוָה. דְּלָא פָּגַע בַּאֲחוֹת זְקוּקָתוֹ, מִשּׁוּם דְּעֶרְוָה לָאו זְקוּקָתוֹ הִיא. שְׁנִיּוֹת. שְׁנִיּוֹת לַעֲרָיוֹת שֶׁגָּזְרוּ סוֹפְרִים עֲלֵיהֶם, וּבַגְּמָ' מְפָרֵשׁ לָהּ: לְשׁוֹן מִצְוָה וּקְדוּשָּׁה מְפָרֵשׁ בַּגְּמָרָא. אַלְמָנָה לְכ"ג. שֶׁמֵּת אָחִיו הַהֶדְיוֹט, וְנָפְלָה אַלְמְנָתוֹ לְפָנָיו. גְּרוּשָׁה וַחֲלוּצָה לְכֹהֵן הֶדְיוֹט. שֶׁעָבַר אָחִיו הַמֵּת וְנָשָׂא חֲלוּצָה וּגְרוּשָׁה, וּכְשֶׁמֵּת צְרִיכָה חֲלִיצָה, שֶׁהֲרֵי תּוֹפְסִין לוֹ בָּהּ קִידּוּשִׁין. דְּקִידּוּשִׁין תּוֹפְסִים בְּחַיָּיבֵי לָאוִין. אֲבָל יַבּוּמֵי לָא, שֶׁהֲרֵי אֲסוּרָה לוֹ לָזֶה שֶׁהוּא כֹּהֵן. וְאַפְטוּרֵי בְּלֹא כְּלוּם — לָא, דְּלָא אַלִּים לָאו לְמִיפְטְרָהּ, דְּיָלְפִי' מֵאֲחוֹת אִשָּׁה בְּפ"ק (דף ג:). **גמ'** לְאִיתּוּיֵי צָרַת אַיְלוֹנִית כְּרַב אַסִי. בְּפ"ק (דף יב.), דְּלָא חוֹלֶצֶת וְלָא מִתְיַיבֶּמֶת, דְּעֶרְוָה קָרֵינַן בָּהּ בְּאַיְלוֹנִית, דְּמִיעֲטָהּ קְרָא מֵ"אֲשֶׁר תֵּלֵד", וְקָיְימָא עֲלֵיהּ בְּאִיסּוּר אֵשֶׁת אָח, הִילְכָּךְ צָרָתָהּ צָרַת עֶרְוָה. אֵלֶּה הַמִּצְוֹת. בְּסוֹף סֵפֶר תּוֹרַת כֹּהֲנִים, וּמַשְׁמַע דְּאַכּוּלָּ' סִפְרָא קָאֵי, וְכָל אַזְהָרַת כֹּהֲנִים הָתָם כְּתִיבָא. קַדֵּשׁ עַצְמְךָ. לַעֲמוֹד וּלְהִזָּהֵר. אַף בַּמּוּתָּר לָךְ. לְהוֹסִיף עֲלֵיהֶם שְׁנִיּוֹת הַמּוּתָּר לְךָ עַל הָעֲרָיוֹת, כְּדֵי שֶׁלֹּא תָּבֹא לִידֵי עֲרָיוֹת הָאֲסוּרוֹת מִן הַתּוֹרָה. קָפָסֵיק וְתָנֵי. אַלְמָנָה לְכ"ג, לָא שְׁנָא נָפְלָה לְפָנָיו מִן הַנִּשּׂוּאִין — דְּהַיְינוּ תַּרְתֵּי לִגְרִיעוּתָא, חֲדָא — דְּאַלְמָנָה הִיא, וְאִיכָּא לָאו דְּ"אַלְמָנָה לֹא יִקָּח". וְעוֹד, דִּבְעוּלָה הִיא, וְאִיכָּא אִיסּוּר עֲשֵׂה לְגַבֵּיהּ, דִּכְתִיב "אִשָּׁה בִבְתוּלֶיהָ יִקָּח" וְלֹא בְּעוּלָה, וְלָאו הַבָּא מִכְּלַל עֲשֵׂה — עֲשֵׂה. וְלֹא שְׁנָא. נָפְלָה לְפָנָיו מִן הָאֵירוּסִין וְעוֹדָהּ בְּתוּלָה, דְּלֵיכָּא אֶלָּא לָאו דְּאַלְמָנָה. יָבֹא עֲשֵׂה. דְּ"יְבָמָהּ יָבֹא עָלֶיהָ". וְעָלְתָה הַשַּׁעְרָה מָצֵי לְמִכְתַּב. דְּהָא כְּתִיב בְּרֵישָׁא דִּקְרָא "לָקַחַת אֶת יְבִמְתּוֹ", מַה ת"ל יְבִמְתּוֹ? יֵשׁ לְךָ יְבָמָה כו'. דְּאִם כָּתַב "וְלֹא יַחְפּוֹץ הָאִישׁ לָקַחַת אֶת יְבִמְתּוֹ וְעָלְתָה הַשַּׁעְרָה" — הֲוָה מַשְׁמַע דְּהַהִיא דְּקָרֵינָא בֵּיהּ לָקַחַת — הוּא דְּקָא מַצְרְכָהּ רַחֲמָנָא וְעָלְתָה הַשַּׁעְרָה לַחֲלוֹץ. אֲבָל חַיָּיבֵי לָאוִין, דְּלָא קָרֵינַן בְּהוּ "לָקַחַת" — לָא קָרֵינַן בָּהּ "וְעָלְתָה". לְהָכִי הֲדַר כָּתַב "יְבִמְתּוֹ", לְמֵימַר דְּיֵשׁ לְךָ יְבָמָה אַחֶרֶת שֶׁעוֹלָה הַשַּׁעְרָה לַחֲלוֹץ, וְאַף עַל גַּב דְּלָא כְּתִיב בָּהּ לָקַחַת, שֶׁאֵין עוֹלָה לְיִיבּוּם. אֵימָא חַיָּיבֵי כְּרֵיתוֹת. נַמִי לֵילַף מֵהָכָא דְּלִיבָּעֵי חֲלִיצָה, וְאַמַּאי פָּטְרִינַן לְגַמְרֵי? [שייך לע"ב] *תָּפְסֵי בָהּ קִידּוּשִׁין. הִילְכָּךְ קָרֵינַן בֵּיהּ "לָקַחַת", בְּדִיעֲבַד, אֲבָל חַיָּיבֵי כְּרֵיתוֹת לָא תָּפְסֵי בְּהוּ קִידּוּשִׁין, וַאֲפִי' עָבַר הַאי יָבָם וּנְסָבָהּ — לָאו קִיחָה הִיא. לְדִדִין

תוספות

האי איסורא דאית ליה התירא. דפקע איסור אשת אח, דיכול להחזירה לאחר שגרשה. וכי היכי דפקע ליה לגבי דידיה איסור אשת אח — פקע נמי לגבי אחיו הנולד, וה"ל אשת אחיו שהיה בעולמו.

לאתויי צרת אילונית. אע"ג דמתני' לא קתני צרה, מ"מ הוי בכלל דכל שאיסורה איסור ערוה דמשמע שאיסורה בא מחמת ערוה, דהיינו הצרה. ולא הוצרך להזכיר הצרה בהדיא, משום דאפירקין דלעיל קאי. והא דלא קאמר לאיתויי צרת סוטה וצרת מחזיר גרושה, משום דאילונית דמיא טפי לעריות, שמותרות למת ואסורות לייבם.

בשלמא מן הנשואין כו'. תימה: דמן הנשואין נמי תיקשי ליה, דאמאי חולצת? כיון דאין עולה לייבום, דלא אתי עשה ודחי לא תעשה ועשה, ותיהוי כי חייבי כריתות! וי"ל דלא קאמר בשלמא אלא ממאי דאין מתייבמת.

יבא עשה וידחה לא תעשה. הקשה ריב"א: בפ"ב דסנהדרין (דף יט. ושם): דכיון דאין אשה מתעברת מביאה ראשונה, כדאמר בסוף פ' "ד' אחין" (לקמן ד' לד. ושם), היאך תתייבם? דביא' ראשונה ליכא הקמת שם, וביאה שניה אסירא ליה, כדאמר לקמן: גזירה ביאה ראשונה אטו ביאה שניה! ואר"י: דלא קשה מידי: דלא בעינן (ג) שתהא ראויה להקמת שם אלא שהיבמה והיבם יהו ראוין להקמת שם, ולא ממעטינן אלא אילונית וסרים שאינן ראוין לילד לעולם. אבל ביאה שאין יכולה להתעבר בה — לא ממעטי, כיון שהאשה או היבם ראוין לבסוף להוליד. דאל"כ תיקשה: היאך קטנה מתייבמת לרבנן? וגם לרבי מאיר היתה מתייבמת, אי לאו חששא דשמא תמצא אילונית. ובפרק "ב"ש" (לקמן דף קיא:) תנן: קטן הבא על הגדולה תגדלנו. ובפ' "הבא על יבמתו" (לקמן נה:) נמי מרבינן דנקנית בביאה שלא כדרכה והערא׳ה, אע"פ שאין מתעברת בה א).

אי הכי חייבי לאוין נמי. פי': כיון דאין עולים לייבום — לא יעלו לחליצה! ותימה לר"י: היכי מצי למימר דלא יעלו לחליצה? הא מ"יבמתו" דשמעינן דאין

עין משפט נר מצוה

ח א מיי' פ"ו מהלכות יבום הלכה ז טוש"ע אה"ע סימן קעד סעיף א:
ט ב מיי' שם פ"ז הלכה א טוש"ע שם סימן קעה סעיף ב וסעיף ד:
י ג מיי' פ"א מהלכות אישות הלכה ו סמג לאוין קי טוש"ע שם סימן טו:
יא ד מיי' פ"ו מהלכות יבום הלכה יא:
יב ה מיי' שם פ"א הלכה יט:

תוספות ישנים

א) ואע"ג דלקמן אצטריך קרא לקטן למימר שתגדלנו שמא מיניה ילפינן בעלמא א"נ שאני קטן דאינו בר הקמת שם כלל בשעתו קטן אבל אותה הבתולה לאחר ביאה ראשונה איכא בה הקמת שם. וא"ת היכי קאמר בשלמא מן הנשואין לא אתי עשה ודחי ל"ת ועשה. הא ודאי יש לנו לומר דהכא דחי ל"ת ועשה אע"ג דבעלמא לא דחי משום דהוי לאו שאינו שוה בכל. וי"ל דפריך הכי אפי' אי אמרינן דאין חלוק בין לאו השוה בכל ללאו שאינו שוה בכל (מ"מ) ולא תקשי לך מידי מן הנשואין מ"מ תקשי לך מן האירוסין דיבא עשה וידחה ל"ת: **ומשני** רבי רחמנא יבמתו. וא"ת א"כ מנלן דחייבי לאוין גרידי דלא מייבמה נוקי יבמתו בלאו ועשה וחייבי לאוין גרידי עדיין לא שמעינן וי"ל דמסתבר דאתא יבמתו לחדש ולאסור ליבם ואי לחייבי לאוין ועשה לא אצטריך דאין עשה דוחה ל"ת ועשה א) וא"כ אתא לאסור חייבי לאוין גרידי מיבום. וא"ת ונימא לחייבי לאוין ועשה אפי' חליצה לא צריכי ותפטר ונוקי יבמתו דמשמע דחליצה [מיהו צריך] בחייבי לאוין גרידי די"ל דסברא הוא לאוקמי יבמתו בכל הנך דתפסי בהו קדושי:

א) קצ"ע דלפי מש"כ בתחלה ספיר אצטריך דאף דהוי לאו ועשה שאינו שוה בכל ואפ"ה לא דחי.

הגהות הב"ח

(א) במשנה כל שאיסורה איסור ערוה לא: (ב) גמ' יש לך יבמה אחרת שעולה לחליצה: (ג) תום' ד"ה יבא וכו' דלא קשה מידי דלא בעינן ביאה שתהא:

גליון הש"ס

מתני' חולצת ולא מתייבמת. עיין בר"ש פ"ב דחלה:

עין משפט
נר מצוה

יג א מיי' פ"ו מהל' יבום הלכה י סמג עשין נא טוש"ע אה"ע סימן קעד סעי' א:
יד ב מיי' שם:
טו ג מיי' שם טוש"ע שם:
טז ד מיי' פ"ג מהל' נזירות הלכה ו:
יז ה מיי' שם ופ"י מהלכות טומאת צרעת הלכה ה ופ"ו מהלכות יבום הלכה י:

מִסְתַּבְּרָא, חַיָּיבֵי לָאוִין תָּפְסֵי בְּהוּ קִדּוּשִׁין, חַיָּיבֵי כְּרֵיתוֹת לָא תָּפְסֵי בְּהוּ קִדּוּשִׁין. מְתִיב רָבָא: אאִיסּוּר מִצְוָה וְאִיסּוּר קְדוּשָּׁה, בָּא עָלֶיהָ אוֹ חָלַץ לָהּ — נִפְטְרָה צָרָתָהּ. וְאִי ס"ד חַיָּיבֵי לָאוִין מִדְּאוֹרַיְיתָא לַחֲלִיצָה רַמְיָא, לְיִיבּוּם לָא רַמְיָא — כִּי בָּא עָלֶיהָ אַמַּאי נִפְטְרָה צָרָתָהּ? הוּא מוֹתִיב לָהּ וְהוּא מְפָרֵק לָהּ: לִצְדָדִין קָתָנֵי, בָּא עָלֶיהָ — אַאִיסּוּר מִצְוָה, חָלַץ לָהּ — אַאִיסּוּר קְדוּשָּׁה. מְתִיב רָבָא: *פְּצוּעַ דַּכָּא וּכְרוּת שָׁפְכָה, *סְרִיס אָדָם וְהַזָּקֵן [א] — אוֹ חוֹלְצִין אוֹ מְיַיבְּמִין. כֵּיצַד? מֵתוּ, וְלָהֶם (א) אַחִים וְלָהֶם נָשִׁים, וְעָמְדוּ אַחִין וְעָשׂוּ מַאֲמָר בִּנְשׁוֹתֵיהֶן, וְנָתְנוּ גֵּט, וְחָלְצוּ, מַה שֶּׁעָשׂוּ עָשׂוּ, וְאִם בְּעָלוּ קָנוּ. מֵתוּ אַחִים, וְעָמְדוּ הֵם וְעָשׂוּ מַאֲמָר בִּנְשׁוֹתֵיהֶן, וְנָתְנוּ גֵּט, אוֹ שֶׁחָלְצוּ — מַה שֶּׁעָשׂוּ עָשׂוּ. וְאִם בְּעָלוּ — קָנוּ וְאָסוּר לְקַיְּימָן, מִשּׁוּם שֶׁנֶּאֱמַר °"לֹא יָבֹא פְצוּעַ דַּכָּא". (דברים כג) וְאִי סָלְקָא דַּעְתָּךְ חַיָּיבֵי לָאוִין מִדְּאוֹרַיְיתָא לַחֲלִיצָה רַמְיָא, לְיִיבּוּם לָא רַמְיָא, אִם בְּעָלוּ — אַמַּאי קָנוּ? אֶלָּא אֲמַר רָבָא: אַלְמָנָה (ב) מִן הָאֵירוּסִין נַמִי עֲשֵׂה וְלֹא תַעֲשֶׂה הוּא, דִּכְתִיב °"קְדֹשִׁים יִהְיוּ לֵאלֹהֵיהֶם". (ויקרא כא) מַמְזֶרֶת וּנְתִינָה מַאי אִיכָּא לְמֵימַר? כְּתִיב °"וְהִתְקַדִּשְׁתֶּם" (שם יא) אִי הָכִי, כָּל הַתּוֹרָה כּוּלָּהּ נַמִי עֲשֵׂה וְלֹא תַעֲשֶׂה הוּא, דִּכְתִיב "וְהִתְקַדִּשְׁתֶּם"! אֶלָּא אֲמַר רָבָא: גְּזֵירָה אַלְמָנָה מִן הָאֵירוּסִין אַטּוּ אַלְמָנָה מִן הַנְּשׂוּאִין. מַמְזֶרֶת וּנְתִינָה מַאי אִיכָּא לְמֵימַר? גְּזֵירָה בִּמְקוֹם מִצְוָה אַטּוּ שֶׁלֹּא בִּמְקוֹם מִצְוָה. אֶלָּא מֵעַתָּה, אֵשֶׁת אָחִיו מֵאָבִיו לֹא תִתְיַבֵּם, גְּזֵירָה מִשּׁוּם אֵשֶׁת אָחִיו מֵאִמּוֹ! *יִיבּוּם בְּנַחֲלָה תְּלָא רַחֲמָנָא, מֵידַע יְדִיעַ. אִשָּׁה שֶׁאֵין לָהּ בָּנִים לֹא תִתְיַבֵּם, גְּזֵירָה מִשּׁוּם אִשָּׁה שֶׁיֵּשׁ לָהּ בָּנִים! בְּבָנִים תְּלָא רַחֲמָנָא, מֵידַע יְדִיעַ. אֵשֶׁת אָחִיו שֶׁהָיָה בְּעוֹלָמוֹ לֹא תִתְיַבֵּם, גְּזֵירָה מִשּׁוּם אֵשֶׁת אָחִיו שֶׁלֹּא הָיָה בְּעוֹלָמוֹ! בִּישִׁיבָה תְּלָא רַחֲמָנָא, מֵידַע יְדִיעַ. כָּל הַנָּשִׁים לֹא תִתְיַיבְּמָנָה, גְּזֵירָה מִשּׁוּם אַיְלוֹנִית! לָא שְׁכִיחָא. מַמְזֶרֶת וּנְתִינָה נַמִי לָא שְׁכִיחָא! אֶלָּא אֲמַר רָבָא: *בגְּזֵירָה בִּיאָה רִאשׁוֹנָה אַטּוּ בִּיאָה שְׁנִיָּה. תַּנְיָא נַמִי הָכִי: *גאִם בְּעָלוּ — קָנוּ בְּבִיאָה רִאשׁוֹנָה, וְאָסוּר לְקַיְּימָן בְּבִיאָה שְׁנִיָּה. הֲדַר אֲמַר רָבָא, וְאִיתֵּימָא רַב אַשִׁי: לָאו מִילְּתָא הִיא דַּאֲמָרִי, דְּאָמַר *רֵישׁ לָקִישׁ: דכָּל מָקוֹם שֶׁאַתָּה מוֹצֵא עֲשֵׂה וְלֹא תַעֲשֶׂה, אִם אַתָּה יָכוֹל לְקַיֵּים שְׁנֵיהֶם מוּטָב, וְאִם לָאו היָבֹא עֲשֵׂה וְיִדְחֶה אֶת לֹא תַעֲשֶׂה, הָכָא נַמִי אֶפְשָׁר בַּחֲלִיצָה דִּמְקַיֵּים עֲשֵׂה וְלֹא תַעֲשֶׂה. מֵיתִיבִי: וְאִם בְּעָלוּ קָנוּ! תְּיוּבְתָּא. § אִיתְּמַר: בִּיאַת כֹּהֵן גָּדוֹל בְּאַלְמָנָה, רַבִּי *יוֹחָנָן וְרַ' אֶלְעָזָר: חַד אָמַר: אֵינָהּ פּוֹטֶרֶת צָרָתָהּ, וְחַד אָמַר[א] פּוֹטֶרֶת צָרָתָהּ. בְּאַלְמָנָה

לִצְדָדִין קָתָנֵי. בָּא עָלֶיהָ קָאֵי אַאִיסּוּר מִצְוָה, דְּהַיְינוּ שְׁנִיּוֹת מִדִּבְרֵי סוֹפְרִים. דְּמִדְּאוֹרַיְיתָא חֲזָיָא לֵיהּ וְקַמֵּיהּ רַמְיָא, לְפִיכָךְ נִפְטְרָה צָרָתָהּ בְּבִיאָתָהּ, חָלַץ קָאֵי אַאִיסּוּר קְדוּשָּׁה דְּרַמְיָא לַחֲלִיצָה, הִילְכָּךְ חֲלִיצָתָהּ פּוֹטֶרֶת צָרָתָהּ. פְּצוּעַ דַּכָּא וּכְרוּת שָׁפְכָה. לְקַמָּן מְפָרֵשׁ לְהוּ בְּפֶרֶק "הֶעָרֵל"*. סְרִיס אָדָם. שֶׁסֵּירְסוֹ אָדָם, וְלֹא מֵחֲמַת חוֹלִי נִסְתָּרֵס מֵאֵלָיו, וַהֲוֵי כְּלָאו, דְּבִכְלַל פְּצוּעַ דַּכָּא וּכְרוּת שָׁפְכָה הוּא, וְאָסוּר לְאִשָּׁה יִשְׂרְאֵלִית, דִּכְתִיב "לֹא יָבֹא פְצוּעַ דַּכָּא". אוֹ מְיַיבְּמִין. לָאו לְכַתְּחִלָּה קָאָמַר, אֶלָּא יִיבּוּמָן יִבּוּם, שֶׁאִם בְּעָלוּ קָנוּ, כִּדְקָתָנֵי וְאָזֵיל. וְהַזָּקֵן. שֶׁפָּסַק מִלֵּידָה. וְהַאי לָאו מֵחַיְּיבֵי לָאוִין הוּא, אֶלָּא קמ"ל, דְּאַע"ג דְּלָאו בַּר אוֹלוּדֵי הוּא — בִּיאָתוֹ בִּיאָה לִקְנוֹת יְבִמְתּוֹ, וְיוֹצְאָה מִמֶּנּוּ בְּגֵט. וְנָתְנוּ גֵּט. כְּלוֹמַר, אוֹ נָתְנוּ גֵּט אוֹ חָלְצוּ. וְגֵט בִּיבָמָה מְהַנֵּי לְמִיפְסַל עָלָיו וְעַל כָּל הָאַחִין, דְּאִי בָּעֵי לְיַיבּוּמֵי — תּוּ לָא מָצֵי, דְּקָם לֵיהּ בְּשׁוּב לֹא יִבְנֶה. וְאִם בְּעָלוּ קָנוּ. וְיוֹצְאוֹת בְּגֵט בְּלֹא חֲלִיצָה. וְאָסוּר לְקַיְּימָן. אַסֵּיפָא קָאֵי, מֵתוּ אַחִין וּבָעֲלוּ הֵן אֶת יְבִמְתָּן, וְאַפְּצוּעַ דַּכָּא וְכַיּוֹצֵא בּוֹ, וְלֹא אַזָּקֵן. אֶלָּא אֲמַר רָבָא. חַיָּיבֵי לָאוִין נַמִי לְיִיבּוּם רַמְיָא. הִלְכָּךְ, אִם בְּעָלוּ — קָנוּ. וּדְקַשְׁיָא לָךְ בְּאַלְמָנָה אֲרוּסָה שֶׁנָּפְלָה לְכֹהֵן גָּדוֹל תִּתְיַיבֵּם, וְיָבֹא עֲשֵׂה וְיִדְחֶה אֶת ל"ת — אַלְמָנָה (ג) מִן הָאֵירוּסִין נַמִי כו'. גְּזֵירָה בִּיאָה רִאשׁוֹנָה. דִּמְקַיֵּים בָּהּ עֲשֵׂה, וּמָצֵי לְמִידְחֵי. אַטּוּ בִּיאָה שְׁנִיָּה. דְּלָא מָצֵי לְמִידְחֵי, דְּהָא אִיקַּיֵּים בָּהּ עֲשֵׂה. לָאו מִילְּתָא הִיא דַּאֲמְרִי. דְּבִיאָה רִאשׁוֹנָה הֲוָיָא שָׁרֵי לְכַתְּחִלָּה, אִי לָאו מִשּׁוּם גְּזֵירַת בִּיאָה שְׁנִיָּה, דְּוַדַּאי אֲפִילּוּ בִּיאָה רִאשׁוֹנָה אֲסוּרָה וְלָא אָמְרִי' תִּדְחֶה עֲשֵׂה אֶת לֹא תַעֲשֶׂה, דְּהָא אֶפְשָׁר לְהִתְקַיֵּים בַּחֲלִיצָה בְּלֹא עֲקִירַת לֹא תַעֲשֶׂה. אִם בְּעָלוּ קָנוּ. אַלְמָא מִדְּאוֹרַיְיתָא רַמְיָא קַמֵּיהּ לְמִידְחֵי לֹא תַעֲשֶׂה. תְּיוּבְתָּא. דְּרָבָא וּתְיוּבְתָּא *דְּרֵישׁ לָקִישׁ ב] דְּאָמְרִי' לְעֵיל אִם אַתָּה יָכוֹל לְקַיֵּים אֶת שְׁנֵיהֶם לֹא עָקְרִינָא לֵיהּ לְלָאו. בְּאַלְמָנָה. יְבִמְתּוֹ. פּוֹטֶרֶת. אוֹתָהּ וְאֶת צָרָתָהּ מִן הַחֲלִיצָה וְסַגֵּי לָהּ בְּגֵט.

כִּי

דלאו עולין לייבום – מהתם שמעינן דעולין לחליצה, כדדרשינן: יש לך יבמה אחרת שעולה לחליצה. ועוד: דפריך, מה ראית? פי': דלימא איפכא, ונוקי "יבמתו" לחייבי כרת, "ואם לא יחפוץ" לחייבי לאוין – היכי מצי למעוטי מאם לא יחפוץ חייבי לאוין מחליצה? הא קרינן בהו אם חפץ – יבם, דאתי עשה ודחי ל"ת, כיון דמוקמינן "יבמתו" לחייבי כריתות! וקלת היה נראה לפרש, דה"פ: א"ה, חייבי לאוין נמי נשוה חליצה וייבום מהאי קרא. ותו פריך: מה ראית, פירוש: דמהאי קרא "ולא יחפוץ" נשוה חייבי לאוין לחליצה וייבום, וליהוו בני חליצה וייבום! ואין להקשות דלמה לן קרא להכי? דלישתוק קרא מיני'. דטובא איצטריך, (ד) כדפרישית לקמן בפ' "החולץ" (דף מד.): וייבם לחדא ונחלוץ לחדא. אבל קשה: דאם כן מאי קא משני: מיסתברא חייבי לאוין תפסי בהו קדושין, דמשמע מתוך התירוץ דהוא פריך שלא יעלו חייבי לאוין לחליצה? וי"ל בדוחק דמחייבי לאוין וחייבי עשה פריך, והכי פריך: א"ה, חייבי לאוין וחייבי עשה נשוה לחליצה וייבום מהאי קרא, וחייבי לאוין יעלו גם לייבום, וחייבי עשה לא יעלו גם לחליצה. ועיקר פירכא מחייבי עשה. **מסתברא** חייבי לאוין תפסי בהו קדושין. ותימה: מנלן לאוקמי קרא בחייבי לאוין? נוקי קרא בחייבי עשה גרידא, דאע"ג דאין מייבמין – מ"מ עולים לחליצה, כיון דתפסי בהו קידושין. אבל חייבי לאוין נימא דאתי עשה ודחי לא תעשה, ויעלו גם לייבום! וי"ל: דמשמע ליה השתא לדרוש מקרא ד"יבמתו" לאסור יבום ולהצריך חליצה. אבל קשה: א"כ, היכי הוה בעי לאוקמי קרא בחייבי כריתות? והא ל"ל דהכי פריך: ולימא חייבי כריתות נמי ליבעי חליצה מהאי קרא – דהא קאמר בתר הכי ומה ראית, דמשמע: ולימא איפכא. **פצוע** דכא וכרות שפכה וסריס אדם. פירוש: סריס אדם – לאפוקי בידי שמים, שלא היה להם שעת הכושר. **אם** בעלו קנו. ה"ה דלכתחילה נמי שרי, *כדמוכח לקמן. אלא, איידי דנקט בסיפא לשון דיעבד נקט נמי ברישא לשון דיעבד. **אמר** קרא והתקדשתם. אע"ג דהאי עשה נמי הוה במלות יבום, ואיכא תרי עשה – מ"מ אין תרי עשה דוחה ל"ת ועשה. **אי** הכי, כל הנשים לא יתייבמו. כל הני פירכי לא פריך שיעקרו חכמים לגמרי מלות ייבום, והכי פי': אשת אחיו מאביו לא תתייבם, כשאינו אחיו אלא מאביו – לא תתייבם עד דמיהדי באבא ובאמא, גזיר' משום אשת אחיו מאמו. א) אשה שאין לה בנים לא תתייבם, פירוש: שאין לה עכשיו, אבל היו לה בחיי הבעל ומתו – גזירה משום אשה שיש לה בנים. אשת אחיו שהיה בעולמו כגון שבא ממדינת הים והיה מוחזק לן דלית ליה אחים, דדמי כמי שלא היה בעולמו, כל הנשים לא יתייבמו, פירוש: אשה שלא היה לה בנים מעולם לא מזה ולא מאחר, דדמיא לאילונית. **גזירה** ביאה ראשונה אטו כו'. אלמנה מן הנשואין וחייבי עשה נפקא לן מיבמתו, דאע"ג דאין עולין ליבום – עולין לחליצה. **אטו** ביאה שניה. לאו דוקא נקט ביאה שניה, דהא אפילו גמר ביאה ראשונה אסור, דיבמה נקנית בהערלה. והו"מ למימר גזירה אטו גמר ביאה. ואין להתיר ביאה שניה מטעם דנעשית אשתו לכל דבר – דאינה נעשית כאשתו *אלא היכא דשרי ליה בלא דחייה, אבל חייבי לאוין, אפילו ביאה ראשונה לא שריא אלא משום דאתי עשה ודחי לא תעשה, וביאה שניה דלית בה עשה – לא דחיא, אע"ג דבפרק "הבא על יבמתו" (לקמן נה.) לא מצריך קרא אלא לאירס ואח"כ נתמנה להיות כהן גדול, אבל נשאה קודם שנתמנה משמע דלא צריך קרא שיכול לקיימה, משום דנשאה בהיתר – התם נמי, משום דבהיתר בלא שום דחיית איסור נשאה, אבל הכא – ביאה ראשונה לא שריא אלא משום דאתי עשה ודחי לא תעשה, ביאה דמלוה – דחיא, דלאו מלוה – לא דחיא. **מיתיבי** ואם בעלו קנו. תימה: דרבא גופי' מותיב מהך ברייתא, והשתא איתותב מינה!

רנ

[ע' תוספות סוטה כו. ד"ה אשת]

[לקמן סא.]

תוספות ישנים

ואסור לקיימן לא קאי אזקן: **אי** הכי כל התורה נמי כתיב והתקדשתם. אע"ג דבפ' אלו מגלחות משמע דחשבינן ליה עשה גבי טומאה י"ל דהיינו דווקא לגבי מלתא דכתיבא בהאי פרשתא דכתיב והתקדשתם אבל לגבי כל התורה לא חשבינן ליה לעשה: **א)** א"נ פריך הכא אפכא דקא פריך אשת אח כשהוא אחיו מאביו וגם מאמו לא תתייבם גזרה משום אשת אחיו מאמו ומלות יבום תתקיים באשת אחיו מאביו בלבד דליכא בה לד אמהות ולא שייך למגזר משום אשת אחיו מאמו: **ב)** א"נ יש לפרש דקא הוי תלמודא הכא היכא שיש אח אחד שהיה בעולמו ואח אחר שלא היה בעולמו לא תתייבם אותו שבעולמו משום גזרה (לא"א) [לאח] שלא היה בעולמו ומלות יבום תתקיים היכא שאין כאן אח שלא היה בעולמו:

תוספות חד מקמאי

תניא אסור מצוה או אסור קדושה בא עליה או חלץ לה נפטרה צרתה. פצוע דכא וכרות שפכה סרים וזקן או חולצין או מייבמין כיצד מתו ולהן נשים ועמדו אחים ועשו מאמר בנשותיהם נתנו גט או שחלצו מה שעשו עשו אם בעלו קנו ואסור לקיימן משום שנאמר לא יבוא פצוע דכא אלמא מדאורייתא חייבי לאוין רמיין לייבום דאתי עשה ודחי לא תעשה. והא דקתני במתני' אלמנה לכהן גדול גרושה וחלוצה לכהן הדיוט ממזרת ונתינה לישראל חולצת ולא מתייבמת מדרבנן דגזרינן ביאה ראשונה אטו ביאה שניה ותניא נמי [הכי] אם בעלו קנו בביאה ראשונה ואסור לקיימן בביאה שנייה וביאת כ"ג באלמנה מן הנשואין אינה פוטרת צרתה דאין עשה דוחה לא תעשה ועשה אבל ביאה באלמנה מן האירוסין ובכל חייבי לאוין פוטרת צרתה כדתנינן אם בעלו ק

מסורת הש"ס

[דף ע. עה.]

[תוס' פי"א] לקמן עט ע"ש

נ"א דרב אשי

סנהדרין יט.

שבת קלג. נזיר מא. נ(דרים) מנחות מ.

[עי' תוס' לעיל ה. ד"ה ולהכי שגרסו ר' אחא]

הגהות הב"ח

(א) גמרא כיצד מתו ולהם נשים ולהם אחין ועמד אחין: (ב) שם אלמנה לכה"ג מן האירוסין נמי: (ג) רש"י ד"ה אלא וכו' אלמנה לכה"ג מן האירוסין נמי: (ד) תום' ד"ה (בע"א) אי הכי וכו' איצטריך כדפריך לקמן בפ' החולץ

גליון הש"ס

גמ' סרים אדם. ע' סוטה דף כו ע"א תד"ה אשת סרים: **שם** גזירה ביאה ראשונה. ע' לקמן פד ע"ב רש"י ד"ה והא כולה פירקין וצ"ע: **תום'** ד"ה אם בעלו וכו' כדמוכח לקמן. ע' לקמן דף פד ע"ב תד"ה שייר פצוע דכא: **ד"ה** אטו ביאה שניה וכו' אלא היכא דשרי לי' בלא דחיי'. עיין לעיל דף ח ע"ב תד"ה מלמד:

הגהות מהר"ב רנשבורג

א] גמ' איתמר וכו' וחד אמר פוטרת וכו'. נ"ב מי פ"ו מהל' יבום הלכה י ועי"ש: ב] רש"י ד"ה תיובתא דרבא ותיובתא דר"ל ונדפס בגליון נ"א לר אשי. נ"ב דר"ל לא איתותב כדלקמן בסמוך ועי' יבמות שמועה דף פ"ב ע"א:

הגהות הגר"א

[א] גמ' והזקן או חולצין או מייבמין. נ"ב בתוספתא (ספ"ב) גרים חולצין או מייבמין וכ"ה ברי"ף ורא"ש ספ"ק (א) בתוספתא פי"א שהיה כ ממש הברייתא דכאן אין או חולצין או מייבמין ועיי"ש. אלא דקמ"ל רב לדינא דגם זקן ביותר שכחו אינו מייבם לכתחלה וכמ"ש הרמב"ם וש"פ

באלמנה מן הנשואין כולי עלמא לא פליגי דלא פטרה, דאין עשה דוחה לא תעשה ועשה. כי פליגי – באלמנה מן הארוסין. מ"ד פוטרת, אתי עשה ודחי את לא תעשה, ומאן דאמר אינה פוטרת – לא אתי עשה ודחי את לא תעשה, כיון דאפשר בחליצה. מיתיבי: ואם בעלו – קנו! תיובתא. לימא תיהוי נמי תיובתא דר"ל! אמר לך ר"ל: כי אמינא אנא – היכא דמקיימי מצוה, אבל הכא, חליצה במקום ייבום לאו מצוה היא. א אמר *רבא: רמז לשניות מן התורה מנין? שנאמר °"כי את כל התועבות האל עשו אנשי הארץ". "האל" קשות, מכלל דאיכא רכות, ומאי נינהו – שניות. •ומאי משמע ד"האל" לישנא דקשה הוא? דכתיב °"ואת אילי הארץ לקח". לימא פליגא דר' לוי, *דא"ר לוי: ב קשה עונשין של מדות יותר מעונשין של עריות, שזה נאמר בהן "אל" וזה נאמר בהן "אלה". "אל" – קשה, "ואלה" – קשה מ"אל". גבי עריות נמי, הא כתיב "אלה". ההוא למעוטי מדות מכרת. אלא, מאי חומרייהו? הני אפשר בתשובה, הני – לא אפשר בתשובה. רב יהודה אמר מהכא: °"ואזן וחקר תקן משלים הרבה" ואמר עולא *א"ר אלעזר: קודם שבא שלמה היתה תורה דומה לכפיפה שאין לה אזנים, עד שבא שלמה ועשה לה אזנים. ר' אושעיא אמר מהכא: °"פרעהו אל תעבר בו שטה מעליו ועבור". אמר רב אשי: משל דר' אושעיא למה הדבר דומה – לאדם משמר פרדס, משמרו מבחוץ – כולו משתמר, משמרו מבפנים – שלפניו משתמר, שלאחריו – אינו משתמר. והא דרב אשי *בדותא היא: התם, שלפניו מיהא משתמר, הכא, אי לאו שניות – פגע בערוה גופה. רב כהנא אמר מהכא: °"ושמרתם את משמרתי" – *עשו משמרת למשמרתי. א"ל אביי לרב יוסף: הא – דאורייתא, היא דאורייתא ופירשו רבנן. כל התורה נמי פירשו רבנן! אלא: מדרבנן, וקרא – אסמכתא בעלמא.§ ת"ר: *מה הם שניות? ג אם אמו, ד ואם אביו, ה ואשת אבי אביו, ו ואשת אבי אמו, ז ואשת אחי האב מן האם, ח ואשת אחי האם מן האב, ט וכלת בנו, י וכלת בתו. כ ומותר אדם באשת חמיו ובאשת חורגו, ואסור בבת חורגו. ל וחורגו מותר באשתו ובתו. ואשת חורגו אומרת לו: אני מותרת לך, ובתי אסורה לך. בת חורגו – דאורייתא היא, דכתיב °"את בת בנה ואת בת בתה"! משום דקבעי למיתני סיפא: אשת חורגו אומרת לו: אני מותרת לך ובתי אסורה לך, ואע"ג דבתי אסורה לך מדאורייתא – בדידי לא גזור ביה רבנן, תנא רישא נמי בת חורגו. אי הכי, אשת חמיו נמי תימא: אני מותרת לך ובתי אסורה לך, דהויא אחות אשתו! הא – פסיקא ליה, הא – לא פסיקא ליה.§ אמר רב: מ ארבע נשים יש להן הפסק. נקיט רב בידיה תלת: אשת אחי האם מן האב, ואשת אחי האב מן האם, וכלתו. וזעירי מוסיף אף אשת אבי אמו. אמר רב נחמן בר יצחק, וסימניך: דעילאי דרב. ורב, מאי טעמא לא חשיב ליה? מיחלפא ליה באשת אבי אביו. וזעירי: להתם שכיח ואזיל, להכא – לא שכיח ואזיל. כלתו – דאורייתא

(ויקרא יח; יחזקאל יז; קהלת יב; משלי ד; ויקרא יח; שם)

רש"י

כי את כל התועבות האל. גבי עריות כתיב, ומשמע התועבות הקשות. מכלל דיש רכות. וקלות מהן, ואסורות. אלה. במדות כתיב "כי תועבת ה' כל עושה אלה כל עושה עול", ומדקאמר יותר משל עריות – מכלל דהא לאו קשה הוא. הכתיב אלה. "מכל התועבות האלה ונכרתו". עריות אפשר בתקנה. כל זמן שלא הוליד ממזר – יפרוש הימנה ויתכפר. אבל מדות – גזל את הרבים הוא, ואינו יודע למי יחזיר. ואע"ג דקיימא לן* יתקן בהם צרכי רבים – לאו תשובה מעלייתא הוא. ואזן. לשון אזנים, בית אחיזה, כדאמר בעירובין*: לימד דעת את העם – דאגמריה בסימני טעמא ואסברה בדדמי, גמר מילתא ממילתא, והזהיר על דברי סופרים, כדכתיב "ויותר מהמה בני הזהר" – הזהר בדברי סופרים יותר מדברי תורה, וגזר על השניות. אזנים. של קופה לאחוז בהן הקופה, ומשתמרת שלא תפול. ה"נ, ע"י שניות מתרחקין מן העריות. פרעהו. *הגילהו לאיסור, והוסיף עליו, כדי שלא תעבור בו, כמו "גדל פרע". ושמרתם את משמרתי. גבי עריות כתיב. אם אמו. אמו כתיבה, וגזרו רבנן על אם אמו כדי שלא יפגע באמו. וגזרו נמי באם אביו משום אם אמו. ואע"ג דגזירה לגזירה הוא, כדאמר לקמן: משום דתרווייהו אימא רבתא קרו להו. ואשת אבי אביו. משום אשת אביו הכתובה. ואשת אבי אמו. ואע"ג דאשת אבי (אם) אמו גזירה משום אשת אבי אביו – דתרווייהו אבא רבא קרו להו, והילכך חדא הוא. ואשת אחי האב מן האם. דמן התורה ערות אחי אביך כתיב, ואמרינן לקמן ב"הבא על יבמתו" דבאחי אביו מן האב קמשתעי. אבל אם היה אחיו של אביו מן האם שריא, וגזרו רבנן עלה משום אשת אחי אביו מן האב. ואשת אחי האם מן האב. כגון נפתלי אחי יוכבד מאביה, ונשא אשה – אסורה לאהרן משום שנייה. דאע"ג דאשת אחי אמו לא כתיבא – גזרו בה רבנן היכא דהוא אחי אמו מן האב, גזירה משום אחי אביו מן האם דהויא נמי שנייה (א) ואיכא לד אב. אבל אם היה נפתלי אחי יוכבד מן האם ולא מן האב – מיבעי לקמן בגמרא אי גזור רבנן עלה אי לאו. וכלת בנו. גזור משום כלתו. וכלת בתו. מפרש טעמא לקמן: גזירה משום כלת בנו. חורגו. בן אשתו. ואסור בבת חורגו. לקמן פריך: הא דאורייתא היא "את בת בנה", ואמאי תני לה בהדי שניות? הא פסיקא ליה. בת חורגו לעולם אסורה לו. הא לא פסיקא ליה. בת אשת חמיו האסורה לו משום אחות אשה. הואיל ולאחר מיתת אשתו מותרת לו – לא פסיקא ליה. ד' נשים שניות יש להן הפסק. שלמעלה מהן ולמטה מהן מותר. אבל האחרות, כגון אם אמו – אין (ב) להם הפסק, שלמעלה הימנה עד סוף כל הדורות הויא נמי שנייה. וכן אשת אבי אביו ואם אבי אביו למעלה מהן עד לעולם אסור. כגון אשת אבי אבי אביו ואם אבי אבי אביו. ונקיט רב בידיה תלת. לפרושי תלת מהנך ארבעה, אבל רביעית לא הוה ידע מה היא, אבל גמרא הוה גמיר דארבע נינהו. אשת אחי האם מן האב. היא לבדה שנייה, אבל אשת אחי אם אמו – מותרת. ואשת אחי האב מן האם. לבדה שנייה. אבל אשת אחי אבי אביו מן האם – מותרת וטעמא, משום דלא שייכא בהו ערוה דאורייתא. אבל אם אמו, דשייכא בדורותיה ערוה דאורייתא, כגון אמו ואשת אבי אביו, יש בדורותיה אשת אב דאורייתא. ואם אביו נמי, אע"ג דלא שייכא בדורה ערוה דאורייתא – אין לה הפסק, ואסורה אף אם אבי אביו, דמיחלפא באם אם אמו. וכלתו. יש לה הפסק. ולקמן פריך: היכי חשיב כלתו בהדי שניות? הא דאורייתא היא! ומתרץ: אימא כלת בתו, דחשבינן לה לעיל בשניות. וקאמר רב דיש לה הפסק, הואיל ולא שייכא בה איסור כלה דאורייתא. הילכך, כלת בת בתו – אין לה הפסק, וכלת בן בנו נמי אסירא, הואיל ושייכא בדורות הללו איסור כלה דאורייתא. אשת אבי אמו. יש לה הפסק, ושרינן אשת אבי אבי אמו, הואיל ולא שייכא בדורות הללו אישות אב דאורייתא. וסימן. הא דאוסיף זעירי דעילאי דרב, הוא דור אחד למעלה משניות דרב דחשיב אשת אחי האם, וזו של זעירי דור אחד למעלה (ג). אשת אבי אמו מחלפא באשת אבי אביו. דאי אמרת יש לה הפסק – אתי למימר באשת אבי אביו יש לה הפסק. והתם איכא באותם דורות אישות דאורייתא. התם שכיח דאזיל. למשפחת אביו אדם רגיל לילך, ויודע שיש שם קורבה יותר מאמו, הילכך לא מיחלפי. דאורייתא

תוספות

רב יהודה אמר (ד) ואזן וחקר. והא דאמר פרק שני דעירובין (דף כא:): בשעה שתיקן שלמה נטילת ידים ועירובין יצאת בת קול ואמרה כו' ולא חשיב שניות – שמא אחר בת קול תקנה.

ומותר באשת חמיו. ירושלמי: אשת חמיו אסורה משום* מראית העין. וא"ת: תורה היא לאסור' – הא דוד נשא רצפה בת איה! וקאמר נמי: שני חורגין שגדלו בבית – אסורה מפני מראית העין. רבי חנינא אומר: ישבון באתרא דלא חכימי להו. ומעשה בפרובינציא באחד שהיה טבחו טבוח ויינו מזוג לישא אשת חמיו, ואפסדיה ר"ת לסעודתיה! ואע"ג דשמעתין שרי להו אשת חמיו וחורגו – שמא *אחר כך אסרום. ומיהו בסוף "משוח מלחמה" *מוכיח סוגיא דלא חיישינן למראית העין גבי חורגה הגדילה בין האחין. (סוטה מג:)

אי הכי אשת חמיו נמי. מאם (ה) אם חמיו לא מצי למיפרך דתימא ליה אני מותרת לך כו' – דבעיא היא לקמן אם שניות דרבי חייא יש להן הפסק או לא.

עין משפט נר מצוה

יח א (מיי' פ"א מהל' אישות הלכה ו סמג לאוין קי קלג טור אה"ע סימן טו):

וכ"ה בדרך ארץ רבה פ"א ומסיים ובתה מותרת לו

יט ב מיי' פ"ז מהל' גנבה הלכה יב סמג לאוין קנג טוש"ע ח"מ סימן רלא סעיף יט:

כ ג מיי' פ"א מהל' אישות הלכה ו סמג לאוין קי טוש"ע אה"ע סימן טו סעי' ב:

כא ד מיי' שם טוש"ע שם סעי' ד:

[במסכת דרך ארץ איתא בזה"ל אבל אמרו חכמים אשת חמיו אסורה מפני מראית העין ובתה מותרת לו]

כב ה מיי' שם טוש"ע שם סעיף ו:

כג ו מיי' שם טוש"ע שם סעיף ז:

כד ז מיי' שם טוש"ע שם סעיף ח:

כה ח מיי' שם טוש"ע שם סעיף ט:

כו ט מיי' שם טוש"ע שם סעיף יט:

כז י מיי' שם טוש"ע שם סעיף כ:

כח כ מיי' שם טוש"ע שם סעיף כד:

כט ל מיי' שם טוש"ע שם סעיף יח:

ל מ מיי' שם טוש"ע שם סעיף יח:

מסורת הש"ס

[כילה כט.]

דף כח:

[בשאלתות פ' אחרי סי' נז איתא רב הונא]

[ס"א הגדילהו]

ב"ב דף פח:

עירובין כא:

[עי' פסחים יח. ומ"ש שם על הגליון]

[מ"ק ה.]

[מס' ד"א פ"א ע"ש]

תוספות ישנים

דלא אפשר בתשובה דאין יודע למי משלם ואין להקשות יעשה מהן צרכי רבים דמ"מ אין זה תשובה כתיקונה כיון דאינו משלם לאותו שגזל: הני אפשר בתשובה ובלבד שלא הוליד בן דאם הוליד בן הוי מעוות לא יוכל לתקון: עד שבא שלמה ועשה לה אזנים. וא"ת התם פרק עושין פסין חשיב ערובין ונט"י דקאמר בשעה שתקן שלמה ערובין וידים ואמאי לא חשיב שניות דהכא וי"ל דלא חשיב אלא דבר התלוי בחכמה ובסברת הלב. אבל הכא אין הדבר תלוי בחכמה אלא להחמיר ולעשות סייג לתורה:

הגהות הב"ח

א) רש"י ד"ה ואשת אחי האם מן האב וכו' דהויא נמי שנייה משום דתרווייהו איכא לד אב: ב) ד"ה ד' נשים וכו' אין להם הפסק שלמעלה וכו' הויא נמי שנייה הואיל ואמו מן התורה וכן אשת אבי אביו הואיל ואשת אב הויא דאורייתא וכן אם אביו למעלה מהן וכו' ואם אבי אביו כצ"ל ותיבת אבי נמחק פעמים: (ג) ד"ה וסימן וכו' למעלה מאשת אחי אמו הס"ד: (ד) תום' ד"ה רב יהודה אמר מהכא ואזן: (ה) ד"ה אי הכי וכו' מאם אם חמיו לא. נ"ב [כ]ן הגיה מהרש"ל ועיין בש"ת הב"ח סי' ז:

גליון הש"ס

גמ' ומאי משמע דהאל לישנא דקשה הוא. עי' מדרש רבה פרשה תולדות פ' סד בפסוק את כל האלות האל:

תוספות חד מקמאי

תנו רבנן מה הן שניות אם אמו ואם אביו ואשת אבי אביו ואשת אבי אמו פי' כל הני אין להן הפסק דאם אמו ואם אבי אביו ואשת אבי אביו ואשת אבי (אבי) אמו [אסור] עד סוף כל הדורות. אמר רב [ארבע נשים] יש להן הפסק. ונקט רב בידיה תלת אשת אחי האם מן האב ואשת אחי האב מן (האב) [האם] וכלת בתו אבל כלת בנו וכלת בן בנו עד סוף כל הדורות אין להן הפסק. וזעירי מוסיף אף אשת אבי אמו.

לא א מיי' פ"א מהל' איסורי ביאה הלכה ו טוש"ע אה"ע סימן טו סעיף יט:
לב ב מיי' שם טוש"ע שם:
לג ג מיי' שם טוש"ע שם סעיף ב:
לד ד מיי' שם טוש"ע שם סעיף יח:
לה ה מיי' שם טוש"ע שם סעיף טו:
לו ו מיי' שם טוש"ע שם סעיף יח:

דְּאוֹרַיְיתָא הִיא, דִּכְתִיב °"עֶרְוַת כַּלָּתְךָ לֹא תְגַלֵּה"! אֵימָא: כַּלַּת בְּנוֹ. וְכַלַּת בְּנוֹ יֵשׁ לָהּ הֶפְסֵק? *וְהָא תַּנְיָא: כַּלָּתוֹ – עֶרְוָה, כַּלַּת בְּנוֹ – שְׁנִיָּה, וְכֵן אַתָּה אוֹמֵר [א]בִּבְנוֹ, וּבֶן בְּנוֹ, עַד סוֹף כָּל הַדּוֹרוֹת! אֶלָּא אֵימָא: כַּלַּת בִּתּוֹ. דְּאָמַר רַב חִסְדָּא: הָא מִילְּתָא מִגַּבְרָא רַבָּה שְׁמִיעַ לִי, וּמַנּוּ – רַבִּי אַמִי: לֹא אָסְרוּ כַּלָּה אֶלָּא מִפְּנֵי כַּלָּה. וְאָמְרוּ לִי כַּלְדָּאֵי: מַלְפָנָא הָוֵית. אָמִינָא: אִי גַּבְרָא רַבָּה הָוֵינָא – אַסְבְּרָא מִדַּעְתִּי, אִי מַקְרֵי דַּרְדְּקֵי הָוֵינָא – אֲשַׁיְילָהּ מֵרַבָּנַן דְּאָתוּ לְבֵי כְּנִישְׁתָּא. הַשְׁתָּא סְבַרְתָּהּ מִדַּעְתִּי: לֹא אָסְרוּ כַּלַּת בִּתּוֹ אֶלָּא מִשּׁוּם כַּלַּת בְּנוֹ. אֲמַר לֵיהּ אַבָּיֵי לְרָבָא: אַסְבְּרַהּ לָךְ, כְּגוֹן כַּלָּתָהּ דְּבֵי בַּר צִיתַאי. רַב פַּפָּא אָמַר: כְּגוֹן כַּלָּתָהּ דְּבֵי רַב פַּפָּא בַּר אַבָּא. רַב אַשִׁי אָמַר: כְּגוֹן כַּלָּתָהּ דְּבֵי מָרִי בַּר אִיסַק. § אִיבַּעְיָא לְהוּ: [ב]אֵשֶׁת אֲחִי הָאֵם מִן הָאֵם, מַהוּ? אֵשֶׁת אֲחִי הָאָב מִן הָאֵם, וְאֵשֶׁת אֲחִי הָאֵם מִן הָאָב, דְּאִיכָּא צַד אָב – הוּא דְּגָזְרוּ רַבָּנַן, אֲבָל הֵיכָא דְּלֵיכָּא צַד אָב לָא גָּזְרוּ בְּהוּ רַבָּנַן, אוֹ דִּלְמָא לָא שְׁנָא? אֲמַר רַב סַפְרָא: הִיא *גּוּפָהּ גְּזֵירָה, וַאֲנַן נֵיקוּם וְנִגְזוֹר גְּזֵירָה לִגְזֵירָה?! אֲמַר רָבָא: אַטּוּ כּוּלְּהוּ לָאו גְּזֵירָה לִגְזֵירָה נִינְהוּ? אִמּוֹ – עֶרְוָה, [ג]אֵם אִמּוֹ – שְׁנִיָּה, וְגָזְרוּ עַל אֵם אָבִיו מִשּׁוּם אֵם אִמּוֹ. וְטַעְמָא מַאי? כּוּלְּהוּ "דְּבֵי אִימָּא רַבָּתִי" קָרוּ לֵיהּ. אֵשֶׁת אָבִיו – עֶרְוָה, אֵשֶׁת אֲבִי אָבִיו – שְׁנִיָּה, וְגָזְרוּ עַל אֵשֶׁת אֲבִי אִמּוֹ מִשּׁוּם אֵשֶׁת אֲבִי אָבִיו, וְטַעְמָא מַאי? כּוּלְּהוּ "דְּבֵי אַבָּא רַבָּה" קָרוּ לֵיהּ. [ד]אֵשֶׁת אֲחִי הָאָב מִן הָאָב – עֶרְוָה, אֵשֶׁת אֲחִי הָאָב מִן הָאֵם – שְׁנִיָּה, וְגָזְרוּ עַל אֵשֶׁת אֲחִי הָאֵם מִן הָאָב מִשּׁוּם אֵשֶׁת אֲחִי הָאָב מִן הָאֵם, וְטַעְמָא מַאי – מִשּׁוּם דְּכוּלְּהוּ "דְּבֵי דוֹדֵי" קָרֵי לְהוּ. מַאי? תָּא שְׁמַע: דְּכִי אֲתָא רַב יְהוּדָה בַּר שֵׁילָא אֲמַר: אָמְרִי בְּמַעְרְבָא: כָּל שֶׁבִּנְקֵבָה עֶרְוָה – בְּזָכָר גָּזְרוּ עַל אִשְׁתּוֹ מִשּׁוּם שְׁנִיָּה. וְאָמַר רָבָא: וּכְלָלָא הוּא? [ה]חֲמוֹתוֹ – עֶרְוָה, אֵשֶׁת חָמִיו מוּתֶּרֶת. בַּת חֲמוֹתוֹ – עֶרְוָה, אֵשֶׁת בֶּן חֲמוֹתוֹ מוּתֶּרֶת. בַּת חָמִיו – עֶרְוָה, אֵשֶׁת בֶּן חָמִיו – מוּתֶּרֶת. חוֹרַגְתּוֹ – עֶרְוָה, אֵשֶׁת חוֹרְגוֹ – מוּתֶּרֶת! בַּת חוֹרַגְתּוֹ עֶרְוָה אֵשֶׁת בֶּן חוֹרְגוֹ מוּתֶּרֶת וְהָא דְּרַב יְהוּדָה בַּר שֵׁילָא לְאִיתוּיֵי מַאי? לָאו לְאִיתוּיֵי אֵשֶׁת אֲחִי הָאֵם מִן הָאֵם, דְּכָל שֶׁבִּנְקֵבָה עֶרְוָה – בְּזָכָר גָּזְרוּ *אִשְׁתּוֹ מִשּׁוּם שְׁנִיָּה! מַאי שְׁנָא הָנֵי וּמַאי שְׁנָא הָא? הָא – בְּחַד קִידּוּשִׁין מִקָּרַב לָהּ, הָנֵי – עַד דְּאִיכָּא תְּרֵי קִידּוּשִׁין לָא מִקָּרַב לְהוּ. שְׁלַח לֵיהּ רַב מְשַׁרְשִׁיָּא מִתּוֹסְנַיָּיא לְרַב פַּפִּי: יְלַמְּדֵנוּ רַבֵּינוּ, אֵשֶׁת אֲחִי אֲבִי הָאָב, וַאֲחוֹת אֲבִי הָאָב, מַהוּ? מִדִּלְמַטָּה עֶרְוָה – לְמַעְלָה נַמִי גָּזְרוּ בֵּיהּ, אוֹ דִּלְמָא, הָא אִיתְפְּלִיג דָּרָא? ת"ש: "מַה הֵן שְׁנִיּוֹת", וְלָא קָחָשֵׁיב לְהוּ בַּהֲדַיְיהוּ. *תָּנָא וְשַׁיֵּיר. מַאי שַׁיֵּיר דְּהַאי שַׁיֵּיר? שַׁיֵּיר שְׁנִיּוֹת דְּרַבִּי חִיָּיא*. אֲמֵימָר [ו]אַכְשַׁר בְּאֵשֶׁת אֲחִי אֲבִי אָבִיו, וּבַאֲחוֹת אֲבִי אָבִיו. א"ל רַב הִלֵּל לְרַב אַשִׁי: לְדִידִי חֲזָיָא לִי שְׁנִיּוֹת מָר בְּרֵיהּ דְּרַבָּנָא, וּכְתִיבָן שִׁיתְסְרֵי לְאִיסּוּרָא. מַאי לָאו תְּמָנֵי דְּמַתְנִיתָא וְשִׁית דְּבֵי רַבִּי חִיָּיא, וְהָנָךְ תַּרְתֵּי – הָא שִׁיתְסְרֵי! וּלְטַעְמִיךְ שִׁיבְסְרֵי הָוְיָין, דְּהָא אִיכָּא אֵשֶׁת אֲחִי הָאֵם מִן הָאֵם, דְּפָשְׁטִינַן לְאִיסּוּרָא! הָא לָא קַשְׁיָא, הָנָךְ

תורה אור: ויקרא יח

דְּאוֹרַיְיתָא הִיא. וְהֵיכִי חָשֵׁיב לָהּ רַב בַּהֲדֵי שְׁנִיּוֹת. אֶלָּא אֵימָא כַּלַּת בִּתּוֹ. וְטַעְמָא פָּרֵישְׁנָא לְעֵיל, לְפִי שֶׁאֵין בְּגִלְדָּהּ צַד כַּלּוֹת דְּאוֹרַיְיתָא. לֹא אָסְרוּ כַּלָּה. סְתָם מַשְׁמַע. אָמְרוּ לִי כַּלְדָּאֵי. הַחוֹזִים בַּכּוֹכָבִים. מַלְפָנָא הָוֵית. חָכָם תִּהְיֶה. וְאָמִינָא. אִי הַאי מַלְפָנָא דְּאָמְרוּ לִי גַּבְרָא רַבָּא בַּתַּלְמוּד מַשְׁמַע – אַסְבְּרָא לְהָא דְּרַ' אַמִי דְּלָא אָסְרוּ כַּלָּה מִדַּעְתִּי, וְלָא אֶשְׁאָלֶנָּה בְּבֵית הַמִּדְרָשׁ: וְאִי הַאי מַלְפָנָא מַקְרֵי דַּרְדְּקֵי הוּא – וְלָאו תַּלְמִיד, אֲשַׁיְילָהּ מֵרַבָּנַן – כְּלוֹמַר, אֶהְיֶה צָרִיךְ לִשְׁאוֹל, דְּלָא אֲבִינָהּ מִדַּעְתִּי. לֹא אָסְרוּ כַּלַּת בִּתּוֹ. דְּהָא לֵיתָא בְּבַת צַד כַּלָּה דְּאוֹרַיְיתָא, אֶלָּא מִשּׁוּם כַּלַּת בְּנוֹ, דְּיֵשׁ בְּבֶן צַד כַּלָּה דְּאוֹרַיְיתָא, כְּגוֹן אֵשֶׁת בְּנוֹ. כְּגוֹן כַּלָּתָהּ דְּבַר צִיתַאי. שֶׁהָיְתָה לוֹ כַּלַּת הַבֵּן וְכַלַּת הַבַּת, וְאָתוּ לְאִיחְלוּפֵי, וְכֵן כּוּלְּהוּ. דְּאִיכָּא צַד אָב. וְאִיכָּא לְמִיגְזַר מִשּׁוּם אֵשֶׁת אֲחִי הָאָב מִן הָאָב דְּאוֹרַיְיתָא. אוֹ דִּלְמָא לָא שְׁנָא. אֵשֶׁת אֲחִי הָאֵם מִן הָאֵם מֵאֵשֶׁת אֲחִי הָאֵם מִן הָאָב. הִיא גּוּפָהּ. אֵשֶׁת אֲחִי הָאֵם מִן הָאָב. אַטּוּ כּוּלְּהוּ כו'. הָא כּוּלְּהוּ לָאו דַּוְקָא. אֵם אִמּוֹ שְׁנִיָּה. שֶׁסְּמוּכָה לְעֶרְוָה. וְגָזְרוּ רַבָּנַן עַל אֵם אָבִיו. שֶׁאֵין בָּהּ צַד עֶרְוָה, מִשּׁוּם אֵם אִמּוֹ. וְטַעְמָא מַאי וכו'. אֵשֶׁת אֲבִי אָבִיו שְׁנִיָּיה, שֶׁסְּמוּכָה לְאֵשֶׁת אָב. וְגָזְרוּ רַבָּנַן עַל אֵשֶׁת אֲבִי אִמּוֹ. אע"ג דְּלָא שַׁיָּיךְ בַּהּ אִישּׁוּת אָב דְּאוֹרַיְיתָא לֹא לְמַעְלָה וְלֹא לְמַטָּה מִשּׁוּם אֵשֶׁת אֲבִי אָבִיו: ה"ג. כּוּלְּהוּ דְּבֵי דוֹדֵי קָרוּ לָהּ וְל"ג רַבָּתִי. כָּל שֶׁבִּנְקֵבָה עֶרְוָה. שֶׁאִם הָיְתָה נְקֵבָה הָיְתָה עֶרְוָה לָזֶה, גָּזְרוּ בְּזָכָר עַל אִשְׁתּוֹ. וְכוּלְּהוּ מְפָרֵשׁ וְאָזֵיל לְהוּ: ה"ג. וְאָמַר רָבָא וּכְלָלָא הוּא. בִּתְמִיָּה. בַּת חֲמוֹתוֹ עֶרְוָה. שֶׁהִיא אֲחוֹת אִשְׁתּוֹ. לָאו לְאִיתוּיֵי אֵשֶׁת אֲחִי הָאֵם מִן הָאֵם. דִּבִנְקֵבָה עֶרְוָה, דַּאֲחוֹת הָאֵם מִן הָאֵם עֶרְוָה, דִּכְתִיב "עֶרְוַת אֲחוֹת אִמְּךָ", וְדָרְשִׁינַן בְּ"הַבָּא עַל יְבִמְתּוֹ": בֵּין מִן הָאָב בֵּין מִן הָאֵם, הִילְכָּךְ בְּזָכָר גָּזְרוּ עַל אִשְׁתּוֹ. מַאי שְׁנָא הַאי וּמַאי שְׁנָא הָנָךְ. דִּלְעֵיל אֵשֶׁת חָמִיו וְאֵשֶׁת בֶּן חָמִיו וּבֶן חֲמוֹתוֹ וְאֵשֶׁת חוֹרְגוֹ וּבֶן חוֹרְגוֹ. וְאע"ג דִּנְקֵבָה עֶרְוָה – בְּזָכָר מוּתָּר בְּאִשְׁתּוֹ. הָא אֵשֶׁת אֲחִי הָאֵם בְּחַד קִידּוּשִׁין מִיקַּרְבָא. לְגַבֵּי דְּהַאי, בְּקִידּוּשִׁין שֶׁקִּדְּשָׁהּ אֲחִי אִמּוֹ. אֲבָל כָּל הָנָךְ דִּלְעֵיל – לָא אִיקַּרְבוּ לְגַבֵּיהּ עַד דְּאִיכָּא תַּרְתֵּי קִידּוּשִׁין. כְּגוֹן אֵשֶׁת חָמִיו – בְּקִידּוּשִׁין שֶׁקִּדֵּשׁ (א) אֶת אִשְׁתּוֹ נִתְקָרֵב חָמִיו אֶצְלוֹ, וַעֲדַיִין אֵשֶׁת חָמִיו רְחוֹקָה לָזֶה כָּל זְמַן שֶׁלֹּא קִדְּשָׁהּ חָמִיו. וְכֵן אֵשֶׁת בֶּן חָמִיו, בְּקִידּוּשִׁין שֶׁלּוֹ בְּאִשְׁתּוֹ נִתְקָרֵב בֶּן חָמִיו, וְקִידּוּשִׁין בֶּן חָמִיו בְּאִשְׁתּוֹ, וְכֵן כּוּלָּם. אֵשֶׁת אֲחִי אֲבִי הָאָב מִן הָאָב. דַּאֲמַרַן לְעֵיל: אֵשֶׁת אֲחִי הָאָב מִן הָאֵם יֵשׁ לָהּ הֶפְסֵק, דְּהַיְינוּ הֵיתֵּירָא לְאֵשֶׁת אֲחִי אֲבִי הָאָב מִן הָאֵם, דִּלְמַטָּה דִּידָהּ לָאו עֶרְוָה הִיא אֶלָּא שְׁנִיָּיה. וְכִי קָמִיבָּעֲיָא לֵיהּ – בְּאֵשֶׁת אֲחִי אֲבִי הָאָב מִן *הָאָב, דִּלְמַטָּה דִּידָהּ עֶרְוָה. אֵשֶׁת אֲחִי הָאָב מִן הָאָב, וְכֵן אֲחוֹת אֲבִי הָאָב בֵּין מִן הָאָב בֵּין מִן הָאֵם, דִּלְמַטָּה דִּידָהּ עֶרְוָה, כְּגוֹן אֲחוֹת הָאָב. אִיתְפְּלֵג. נִתְרַחֲקָה קוּרְבָה. מַה הֵן שְׁנִיּוֹת. בָּרַיְיתָא דִּלְעֵיל. שְׁנִיּוֹת דְּרַבִּי חִיָּיא. לְקַמָּן בִּשְׁמַעְתִּין.

הָנָךְ

לא אסרו כלת בתו אלא משום כלת בנו. ותימה: דאמאי לא אסרינן לה משום כל שבנקבה ערוה – בזכר גזרו על אשתו משום שנייה, כדלקמן? דטעם גמור הוא, ולא סימנא בעלמא, מדפריך עלה: מ"ש הני ומ"ש (ב) הני *), הא בחד קדושי מקרב לה כו'! ועוד: מדפשיט מינה אשת אחי האם מן האם, ולא מוקי לה בכלת בתו! ואור"י: דתנא דברייתא לית ליה ההוא טעמא, אבל בדורות האחרונים גזרו, ולהכי, כי פריך מאי שייר דהאי שייר. לא בעי למימר דשייר אשת אחי האם מן האם דפשטנא לאיסור. ואם תאמר: מאי פריך וכללא הוא חמותו ערוה כו'? דלמא בהני נמי גזרו בתר הכי מהאי טעמא? וי"ל: דקים ליה בהנהו – דשרו. והא דפריך לקמן וליטעמיך שבסרי הויין, אע"ג דבתר הכי גזרו, כדפי' – יודע הוא דשניות דמר בריה דרבנא בדורות אחרונים הוה.

רב אשי אמר כגון כלה דבי רב מרי בר איסק. כל חד נקיט אותו שהיה בימיו. וצ"ל דתרי מרי בר איסק הוו: אחד בימי רב אשי, כדמשמע הכא ובפרק "אלו מציאות" (ב"מ דף כב.): אמימר ורב אשי ומר זוטרא איקלעו לבוסתני' דבי מרי בר איסק, ואחד היה בימי רב חסדא, דאמר ב"המפקיד" (שם דף לט: ושם) מרי בר איסק *ואיכא דאמרי חנה בר איסק, אתא ליה אחוה מבי חוזאי, אתא לקמיה דרב חסדא. ורב חסדא נפטר בימי רבא, כדאמר בפ' בתרא דיומא (ד' עה: ושם). וביום שמת רבא נולד רב אשי, כדאיתא בפרק "עשרה יוחסין" (קידושין דף עב:).

אשת אחי אבי האב ואחות אבי האב מהו. הוה מצי למיבעי אחות אם האם, והיא בכלל אחות אבי האב דלמטה דידה ערוה. ואית ספרים דגרסינן לה בהדיא.

מאי שייר דהאי שייר. אף על גב דתרתי נינהו – חדא חשיב להו, כדקאמר בסמוך: הנהו תרתי דדמיין להדדי (ג) חדא חשיב להו. ופירש בקונטרס דהנך תרתי היינו: אשת אחי אבי האב ואחות אבי האב, ולא כמו שפירש רבינו יצחק בן רבינו מאיר דקאי אאשת אחי האם מן האם ואשת אחי האם מן האב – דכולהו אחי אמו קרו להו.

אמימר אכשר כו'. פסק רבינו חננאל דהלכה כאמימר, וכן בשאלתות דרב אחאי*. וכן משמע דסבר רב אשי, דקאמר: השתא נמי דכתיבי לאיסורא – לאו מר בריה דרבנא חתים עלייהו. ולר"י נראה דאין הלכה כאמימר, דסוגיא דגמרא ב"החולץ" (לקמן דף מ: ושם) *דלא כוותיה. (ד) וקאמר נמי: אמימר מוקי לה משום חולץ, וקסבר: גזרו שניות בחלוצה. ואין התלמוד רוצה לפשוט בעיא שלו מדברי אמימר (ה).

[פ' אחרי סי' נ]

שניות

*) נ"ל ומשני הא בחד כו'

תוספות ישנים

אשת אחי האם מן האם מהו. וא"ת אמאי לא קא פשיט ליה דשרי מדלא חשבה בהדי שניות וי"ל דלא חשש לשנותה משום דתנא כבר אשת אחי האם מן האב: **לאתויי** מאי לאתויי אשת אחי האם מן האם. וא"ת אמאי לא קאמר דאתא לאתויי כלת בתו אך לא אשת אחי האם מן האם. וי"ל דפסיקא ליה שנאמר זה הכלל לאחר שנשנית הברייתא דשניות וא"כ לא אתא לרבויי כלת בתו שהרי כבר תנינן לה עם השניות אלא ודאי בא לחדש דבר שלא פירש כגון אשת אחי האם מן האם:

[שם ליתא לפנינו א"ד אבל בכתובות כז: איתא]

תוספות חד מקמאי

אבעיא להו אשת אחי האם מן האם מהו אשת אחי האב מן האם ואשת אחי האם מן האב דאיכא צד אב הוא דגזור רבנן אבל היכא דליכא צד אב לא או דלמא לא שנא ופשיט לאסור דכי אתא רב שילא אמר אמרי במערבא כל שבנקבה ערוה בזכר גזרו על אשתו משום שניה [illegible] לאו בכללא הוא דאילו חמותו ערוה אשת חמיו מותרת. בת חמותו ערוה אשת בן חמיו מותרת חורגתו ערוה אשת חורגו מותר' בת חורגו ערוה אשת בן חורגו מותרת. על כרחין דרב שילא לאתויי אשת אחי האם מן האם. אמימר אכשר באשת אחי [אבי] אביו ובאחות אבי אביו. הר' אלפס לא פסק בשניות כר' חייא. יש להן הפסק או אין להן הפסק ומסתברא לקולא דבשל סופרים הלך אחר המקל

דלא כוותיה דקאמר מאי לאו משום חולץ דהויא לי' אשת אבי אביו לא משום מיתנא דהויא לי' אשת אחי אבי אביו וקאמר נמי והא אמימר מכשיר כו' אמימר מוקי להו כו' בעיא שלו מתוך דברי אמימר משום דלא סבירא ליה כוותיה כו' מהרש"ל

כריתות יד:

ביצה ג. [שבת יח: קא עירובין ז: לט. יומא יא מד: סוכה ו: ע"ז כח. חולי פה: וקד. נדה סז. לקמן קט.]

הגהות הב"ח

(א) רש"י ד"ה הא אש[ת] וכו' שקדש זה את אש[תו] נתקרב חמיו וכו' בקדוש[ין] שלו נתקרב בן חמיו אלו[...] וקידושין: (ב) תוס' ד"ה לא אסרו וכו' מ"ש ה[ני] ומאי שנא הא הא בחד (ג) ד"ה מאי וכו' להדד[י] כחדא חשיב: (ד) ד"ה אמימר וכו' דקאמ[ר] אמימר מוקי כצ"ל ותיב[ת] נמי נמחק: (ה) בא"ד ש[...] מדברי אמימר משום דל[א] סבירא ליה כוותיה הס"[ד]

[נ"ל על אשתו]

[סוכה נג. וש"נ]

(נ"ל האם) לקמן מ:

הָנָךְ תַּרְתֵּי דְּדָמְיָין לַהֲדָדֵי. אֵשֶׁת אֲחִי אֲבִי הָאָב וַאֲחוֹת אֲבִי הָאָב שֶׁהֵן לַד אַחֲוָה דְּאָב, וּלְמַטָּה דִּידְהוּ עֶרְוָה. שְׁלִישִׁי שֶׁבִּבְנוֹ. בַּת בֶּן בְּנוֹ, דְּהָא בַּת בְּנוֹ עֶרְוָה. וְשֶׁבְּבִתּוֹ. בַּת בֶּן בִּתּוֹ, שֶׁהֲרֵי בַּת בִּתּוֹ עֶרְוָה. הִלְכָּךְ בַּת בֶּן בִּתּוֹ שְׁנִיָּה, וְכֵן בַּת בֶּן בְּנָהּ שֶׁל אִשְׁתּוֹ אוֹ בַּת בֶּן בִּתָּהּ. רְבִיעִי שֶׁבַּחֲמִיו. דּוֹר רְבִיעִי שֶׁבַּחֲמִיו, הַיְינוּ אֵם אֵם חָמִיו, וְהוּא דּוֹר רְבִיעִי לְאִשְׁתּוֹ, וְאִשְׁתּוֹ בַּכְּלָל. וְשֶׁבַּחֲמוֹתוֹ. אֵם אֵם חֲמוֹתוֹ. שְׁנִיָּה. דְּאֵם חָמִיו וְאֵם חֲמוֹתוֹ עֶרְוָה, שֶׁהֵן בִּכְלַל אִשָּׁה וּבַת בְּנָהּ אִשָּׁה וּבַת בִּתָּהּ, הִלְכָּךְ אִמּוֹ שְׁנִיָּה. מַאי שְׁנָא לְמַעְלָה. דְּקָרֵי לְאֵם אֵם חָמִיו וְאֵם אֵם חֲמוֹתוֹ רְבִיעִי, וְקָא חָשֵׁיב לְאִשְׁתּוֹ בְּחוּשְׁבְּנָא דְּדָרֵי. וּמַאי שְׁנָא לְמַטָּה. דְּקָרֵי לְבַת בֶּן בְּנוֹ דּוֹר שְׁלִישִׁי, וְלָא חָשֵׁיב אִשְׁתּוֹ, דְּתֶהֱוֵי רְבִיעִי. לָאו מִכֹּחַ אשתו קָאָתֵי. אֶלָּא מִכֹּחַ דִּידֵיהּ, דִּבְנוֹ מֵאֲנוּסָה עָסְקִינַן. לְהַהִיא מַתְנִיתָא. הָא דְּקָתָנֵי לְעֵיל מַה הֵן שְׁנִיּוֹת, בְּהַהִיא אַיְירִי רַב וְאָמַר: אַרְבַּע יֵשׁ לָהֶן הֶפְסֵק וְתוּ לָא, אֲבָל בְּהָנָךְ דְּרַ' חִיָּיא – אִיכָּא. ת"ש. דְּתָנֵי בִּשְׁנִיּוֹת דְּרַ' חִיָּיא שְׁלִישִׁי שֶׁבִּבְנוֹ וּרְבִיעִי שֶׁבַּחֲמִיו וְתוּ לָא, אַלְמָא יֵשׁ לָהֶם הֶפְסֵק. בְּגֵרִים. גָּזְרוּ שְׁנִיּוֹת, שֶׁאִם הָיָה גֵּר נָשׂוּי אֵם אִמּוֹ – יוֹצִיא. מִקְּדוּשָּׁה חֲמוּרָה. שֶׁהַגּוֹיִם מוּזְהָרִין עַל הָעֲרָיוֹת. לֹא גָּזְרוּ בְּהוּ רַבָּנַן. דְּקָטָן שֶׁנּוֹלַד דָּמֵי, וְאֵין לוֹ קוּרְבָה. לֹא יָעִידוּ. לְכַתְּחִלָּה, דְּקוּרְבַת אֵם בְּגֵרִים קוּרְבָה הִיא, דְּהָא וַדַּאי אִמּוֹ הִיא. וְאִם הֵעִידוּ עֵדוּתָן עֵדוּת. דְּקָטָן שֶׁנּוֹלַד דָּמֵי. מְעִידִין לְכַתְּחִלָּה. דְּרַחֲמָנָא אַפְקְרֵיהּ לְזֶרַע מִצְרִי, דִּכְתִיב "וְזִרְמַת סוּסִים זִרְמָתָם" (יחזקאל כג), הִלְכָּךְ קוּרְבַת אָב אֵינָהּ קוּרְבָה. מַאי שְׁנָא. עֵדוּת מֵעֲרָיוֹת, דְּאָמַר לְקַמָּן בְּפֶרֶק "נוֹשְׂאִין" (דף מח.): גֵּר שֶׁהָיָה נָשׂוּי אֲחוֹתוֹ מִן הָאֵם – יוֹצִיא. לַכֹּל מְסוּרָה. הַכֹּל נוֹשְׂאִין נָשִׁים, הִלְכָּךְ אִי שָׁרֵית לְקִיּוּמָהּ – אָתֵי נַמִי לְמִישְׁרֵי עֶרְוָה בְּיִשְׂרָאֵל, דְּכוּלֵּי עָלְמָא לָא יָדְעִי דְּטַעְמָא דְּגֵר מִשּׁוּם דְּקָטָן שֶׁנּוֹלַד דָּמֵי. לְבֵית דִּין מְסוּרָה. וְאִי נַמִי מַכְשַׁרְתְּ עֵדוּת אַחִים גֵּרִים, לָא אָתְיָא לְאַכְשׁוּרֵי אַחִין יִשְׂרָאֵל, דְּבֵית דִּין יָדְעִי דְּגֵר שֶׁנִּתְגַּיֵּיר כְּקָטָן שֶׁנּוֹלַד דָּמֵי.

מתני' אָח מִכָּל מָקוֹם. בַּגְּמָרָא מְפָרֵשׁ. וְאָחִיו לְכָל דָּבָר. מְפָרֵשׁ בַּגְּמָ'. שִׁפְחָה וְגוֹיָה וְלָדָהּ כָּמוֹהָ. וּבַתְרָהּ אָזֵיל, כִּדְיָלֵיף בַּגְּמָ'. עַל מַכָּתוֹ וְעַל קִלְלָתוֹ. אִם הִכָּה אוֹ קִלֵּל אֶת אָבִיו חַיָּיב מִיתָה. גמ' מִדִּלְעִנְיַן יִבּוּם מִיפְּטַר. אֶת אֵשֶׁת אָבִיו מִיִּבּוּם פּוֹטֵר, כְּגוֹן אִם הָיָה לוֹ בֵּן מַמְזֵר, וְנָשָׂא אִשָּׁה וּמֵת, וְלֹא יָלְדָה לוֹ – פְּטוּרָה מִן הַיִּבּוּם בִּשְׁבִיל הַמַּמְזֵר בֶּן בַּעְלָהּ, כִּדְיָלֵיף לְקַמָּן: "בֵּן אֵין לוֹ" – עַיֵּין עָלָיו. מִיזְקַק

הָנָךְ תַּרְתֵּי דְּדָמְיָין לַהֲדָדֵי – כַּחֲדָא חָשֵׁיב לְהוּ, וְהָא שִׁיתְסְרֵי. וְהָא מִכָּל מָקוֹם לְדִידִי חַזְיָין לָן דִּכְתִיבָן לְאִיסּוּרָא! אֲמַר לֵיהּ: וְלִיטַעֲמִיךְ, אִי הֲוָה כְּתִיב לְהֶיתֵּירָא – מִי הֲוָות סָמְכַת עֲלַיְיהוּ? דְּמָר בְּרֵיהּ דְּרַבָּנָא – מִי חָתִים עֲלַיְיהוּ? הָשְׁתָּא נַמִי דִּכְתִיב לְאִיסּוּרָא – לָאו מָר בְּרֵיהּ דְּרַבָּנָא חָתִים עֲלַיְיהוּ. תָּנֵי דְּבֵי רַבִּי חִיָּיא: [א]שְׁלִישִׁי שֶׁבִּבְנוֹ וְשֶׁבְּבִתּוֹ, [ב]וְשֶׁבִּבֶן אִשְׁתּוֹ וְשֶׁבְּבַת אִשְׁתּוֹ – שְׁנִיָּה, [ג]רְבִיעִי שֶׁבַּחֲמִיו וְשֶׁבַּחֲמוֹתוֹ – שְׁנִיָּה. א"ל רָבִינָא לְרַב אַשִׁי: מַאי שְׁנָא לְמַעְלָה, דְּקָחָשֵׁיב לָהּ לְאִשְׁתּוֹ, וּמַאי שְׁנָא לְמַטָּה, דְּלָא קָחָשֵׁיב לָהּ לְאִשְׁתּוֹ? לְמַעְלָה, דְּאִיסּוּרָא מִכֹּחַ אִשְׁתּוֹ קָא אָתֵי, חָשֵׁיב לָהּ. לְמַטָּה, דְּאִיסּוּרָא לָאו מִכֹּחַ אִשְׁתּוֹ קָאָתֵי – לָא קָחָשֵׁיב לָהּ. וְהָא [א]בֶּן אִשְׁתּוֹ וּבַת אִשְׁתּוֹ, דְּאִיסּוּרָא מִכֹּחַ אִשְׁתּוֹ קָאָתֵי וְלָא חָשֵׁיב לָהּ! אַיְּידֵי דְּתָנָא שְׁלֹשָׁה דּוֹרוֹת לְמַטָּה[ב] דִּידֵיהּ, וְלָא חֲשָׁבָהּ, תָּנָא נַמִי ג' דּוֹרוֹת לְמַטָּה דִּידָהּ וְלָא חֲשָׁבָהּ. א"ל רַב אַשִׁי לְרַב כָּהֲנָא: [ד]שְׁנִיּוֹת דְּבֵי רַבִּי חִיָּיא יֵשׁ לָהֶן הֶפְסֵק אוֹ אֵין לָהֶם הֶפְסֵק? ת"ש, דְּאָמַר רַב: ד' נָשִׁים יֵשׁ לָהֶם הֶפְסֵק. וְתוּ לָא. דִּלְמָא, כִּי קָאָמַר רַב – לְהַהִיא מַתְנִיתָא: ת"ש, "שְׁלִישִׁי" "וּרְבִיעִי". שְׁלִישִׁי וּרְבִיעִי – אִין, טְפֵי – לָא! דִּלְמָא מִשְּׁלִישִׁי וְאֵילָךְ, מֵרְבִיעִי וְאֵילָךְ. אֲמַר לֵיהּ רָבָא לְרַב נַחְמָן: חֲזִי מָר הַאי מֵרַבָּנַן דַּאֲתָא מִמַּעַרְבָא וַאֲמַר: בָּעוּ בְּמַעַרְבָא, גָּזְרוּ שְׁנִיּוֹת בְּגֵרִים אוֹ לֹא גָּזְרוּ שְׁנִיּוֹת בְּגֵרִים? אֲמַר לֵיהּ: הָשְׁתָּא, וּמָה עֶרְוָה גּוּפָהּ, [ה]אִי לָאו שֶׁלֹּא יֹאמְרוּ בָּאִין מִקְּדוּשָּׁה חֲמוּרָה לִקְדוּשָּׁה קַלָּה לֹא גָּזְרוּ בְּהוּ רַבָּנַן – [ו]שְׁנִיּוֹת מִיבַּעְיָא?! אֲמַר רַב נַחְמָן: גֵּרִים, *הוֹאִיל וְאָתוּ לְיָדַן נֵימָא בְּהוּ מִלְּתָא: אַחִין מִן הָאֵם לֹא יָעִידוּ, וְאִם הֵעִידוּ – עֵדוּתָן עֵדוּת. אַחִין מִן הָאָב מְעִידִין לְכַתְּחִלָּה. [ז]אַמֵימָר אָמַר: אֲפִילּוּ אַחִין מִן הָאֵם נַמִי מְעִידִין לְכַתְּחִלָּה. וּמ"ש מֵעֲרָיוֹת? עֶרְוָה לַכֹּל מְסוּרָה, *עֵדוּת – לְבֵית דִּין מְסוּרָה, *[ח]וְגֵר שֶׁנִּתְגַּיֵּיר כְּקָטָן שֶׁנּוֹלַד דָּמֵי.§

מתני' [ט]מִי שֶׁיֵּשׁ לוֹ אָח מִכָּל מָקוֹם – זוֹקֵק אֶת אֵשֶׁת אָחִיו לְיִבּוּם, וְאָחִיו הוּא לְכָל דָּבָר, חוּץ מִמִּי שֶׁיֵּשׁ לוֹ אָח מִן הַשִּׁפְחָה וּמִן הַגּוֹיָה. [י]מִי שֶׁיֵּשׁ לוֹ בֵּן מִכָּל מָקוֹם – פּוֹטֵר אֵשֶׁת אָבִיו מִן הַיִּבּוּם, [כ]וְחַיָּיב עַל מַכָּתוֹ וְעַל קִלְלָתוֹ, וּבְנוֹ לְכָל דָּבָר – [ל]חוּץ מִמִּי שֶׁיֵּשׁ לוֹ בֵּן מִן הַשִּׁפְחָה וּמִן הַגּוֹיָה.§

גמ' מִכָּל מָקוֹם לְאַתּוּיֵי מַאי? אֲמַר רַב יְהוּדָה [מ]לְאַתּוּיֵי מַמְזֵר. פְּשִׁיטָא, אָחִיו הוּא! מַהוּ דְּתֵימָא: לֵילַף *אַחֲוָה אַחֲוָה מִבְּנֵי יַעֲקֹב, מַה לְּהַלָּן כְּשֵׁרִין וְלֹא פְּסוּלִין, אַף כָּאן כְּשֵׁרִין וְלֹא פְּסוּלִין – קמ"ל. *וְאֵימָא הָכִי נַמִי! כֵּיוָן דִּלְעִנְיַן יִבּוּם מִיפְּטַר נִפְטַר מִיזְקַק

שניות דרבי חייא יש להן הפסק או לא. תימה: דלעיל תנא דכלת בן בנו אסורה עד סוף כל הדורות, ודומה דכ"ש בת בן בנו עד סוף כל הדורות שהן קורבי עצמו ולא מחמת קדושין! וי"ל: דכלת בן בנו יש (א) לאוסרו, שהן בני ירושה ושכיחא גביה. אבל בת בני בנים – לאו בת ירושה היא ולא שכיחא גביה.

ערוה לכל מסורה. תימה: דלעיל קאמר דטעמא דגרים – שלא יאמרו באנו מקדושה כו', והכא משמע טעמא משום דאתיא לאיחלופי בישראל, כדפי' בקונטרס? וכן בפ' "נושאין" (לקמן דף לז: ושם) משמע דטעמא משום איחלופי, גבי בני יודן אמתא איסתחרור, שרא להו רב אחא בר יעקב למינסב נשי דהדדי, וקאמר: מן האם ולא מן האב כולי עלמא לא פליגי דאסור, [מן האב ולא מן האם – כולי עלמא לא פליגי דמותר. כי פליגי – מן האב ומן האם]. ואי משום "שמא יאמרו" – אמאי שרי התם מן האב ומן האם? אבל אי משום איחלופי – ניחא, דכיון דאיכא נמי לד אב – לא אתי לאיחלופי, דבתר אב שדי להו ומצרים אין להם קורבת אב, דכתיב "וזרמת סוסים זרמתם", ולא שייך למיגזר אטו ישראל! ויש לומר: דהני תרי טעמי צריכין, דבקורבת אב שהיו אסורין קודם לא שייך טעמא לאיחלופי, שהכל יודעים דרחמנא אפקריה לזרעיה, כגון אשת אביו לרבי עקיבא ואחות אביו לרבי אליעזר, דאמר בפ' "ד' מיתות" (סנהדרין דף נח.): "על כן יעזב איש את אביו ואת אמו" ר' אליעזר אומר: אחות אביו, ור"ע אומר: אשת אביו. הוי טעמא שלא יאמרו כו'. אבל אשת אביו לרבי אליעזר, ואחות אביו לרבי עקיבא – שרי, דלא משום שמא יאמרו איכא ולא משום איחלופי איכא. אבל עריות שמצד אם, שלא היו אסורות קודם, יש לאסור משום איחלופי. דמשום "שמא יאמרו" – ליכא. והא דאמר בפרק "ד' מיתות" (ג"ז שם) נשא אחותו מן האם – יוציא, היינו משום איחלופי, ד"שמא יאמרו" ליכא, שלא היו נאסרות בגיותם. ומן האב יקיים – דמשום איחלופי ליכא בצד אב, כדפרישית. והיינו טעמא נמי דאמר אחין מן האם לא יעידו לכתחלה, דלמא אתי לאיחלופי. אבל מן האב – יעידו לכתחלה. **מי** שיש לו אח מ"מ זוקק אשת אחיו. בגמרא מפרש לאתויי ממזר. וא"ת: מרישא שמעינן לה בת ישראל לנתין וממזר דחולצת ולא מתייבמת! ויש לומר: דאי מהתם – הוי אמינא כשניהם ממזרים, אבל כשאחיו המת כשר – אין אחיו ממזר זוקק אשתו. **פשיטא** אחיו הוא. תימה: אמאי פשיטא ליה? הא איצטריך שפיר לאשמועינן דמחייבי כריתות הוי אחיו, ולא ממעטינן ליה למי שיש איסות לאביך בה, כדפריך לקמן (דף כג.) לרבי יוסי בר יהודה, ואימא למי שיש אישות לאביך בה, למעוטי חייבי כריתות! וי"ל: דה"מ לשנויי הכי, אלא דניחא ליה לשנויי דאיצטריך משום דהוה ילפינן אחוה אחוה מבני יעקב, דמשום האי טעמא איצטריך "'בן אין לו' – עיין עליו", דממזר פוטר מן היבום, דלא נימא דנילף אחוה אחוה מבני יעקב דלא זקיק, ומדלא זקיק – מיפטר נמי לא פטר. ועוד אור"י, דהכי פריך: פשיטא, כיון דתני אחיו הוא לכל דבר – פשיטא דזוקק נמי ליבום, ומשני: דס"ד אע"ג דאחיו הוא לכל דבר – ה"א [ליבום] לא זוקק, משום דילפינן אחוה אחוה מבני יעקב. ובתר הכי פריך: ואחיו הוא לכל דבר? דהיינו: ליורשו וליטמא לו – פשיטא, כיון דזוקק ליבום אף על גב דהוה ס"ד למילף מבני יעקב – כ"ש לשאר דברים. מאי

עין משפט נר מצוה

לז א מיי' פ"א מהל' איסות הלכה ו סמג לאוין קי טוש"ע אה"ע סימן טו סעיף יב:

לח ב מיי' שם וטוש"ע שם סעיף יד:

לט ג מיי' שם וטור ש"ע שם סעיף טו:

מ ד מיי' שם טוש"ע שם:

מא ה מיי' פי"ד מהל' איסורי ביאה הלכה יב טוש"ע י"ד סימן רסט סעיף א:

מב ו טוש"ע שם סעיף א:

מג ז מיי' פי"ג מהלכות עדות הלכה ב טוש"ע ח"מ סימן לג סעיף יא וטוש"ע י"ד סימן רסט סעיף י:

מד ח מיי' שם ופי"ד מהל' איסורי ביאה הלכה יא טוש"ע שם:

מה ט מיי' פ"א מהל' יבום הלכה ו סמג עשין נא ולאוין קא טור ש"ע אה"ע סימן קנז סעיף א:

מו י מיי' שם הל' ג טוש"ע שם סי' קנו סעי' ב:

מז כ מיי' פ"ה מהלכות ממרים הל' ט טור ש"ע י"ד סימן רמא סעיף א:

מח ל מיי' שם ופ"א מהל' יבום הלכה ד טוש"ע אה"ע סימן קנו סעיף ב:

מט מ מיי' פ"א מהלכות יבום הלכה ו טור ש"ע אה"ע סימן קנז סעיף א:

תוספות ישנים

מעידין לכתחלה. ומ"ש מעריות ופי' הקונט' דלקמן אמרי' נשא אחותו מן האם יוציא והכא אמרי' מעידין לכתחלה. ותימה לשני שנא ושנא דגבי עדות לא שייך האי טעמא דשמא יאמרו באנו מקדושה חמורה לקדושה קלה ולהכי מעידין אבל גבי ערוה יוציא שלא יאמרו באנו מקדושה חמורה לקדושה קלה. וי"ל דקא בעי משום דאמרינן לקמן טעמא משום דאתי לאחלופי ואם כן היה לנו לגזור בעדות כמו ערוה: **יבום** מפטר פטר. מדאמרינן לקמן ובן אין לו עיין עליו ואיירי הכא תלמודא כאילו ידע הדרשא דלקמן אע"ג דלקמן קאמר מכל מקום לאתויי מאי כן דרך התלמוד בכמה מקומות:

הגהות הב"ח

(א) תוס' ד"ה שניות וכו' לאוסרה יותר שהן בני ירושה:

מסורת הש"ס

הגהות הגר"א

[א] גמ' בן אשתו ובת אשתו. כ"ב גי' הרמב"ם ו ובתו לאיסורא כו' ופי' בת כו' שכל לד מינה אסור (ועמ"ש רבינו באה"ע סימן טו ס"ק כג): [ב] שם למטה דידיה כו' למטה דידה. כ"ב גירסת הרמב"ם להיפך איידי דתני כו' למטה דידה כו' למטה דידיה:

גליון הש"ס

מ' הואיל ואתו לידן. שבת פא ע"ב וש"נ:

[ביצה ה:]

מן מח: סב. לז: בכורות מז.]

[לעיל יז: כ"ב קי:]

תוספות סוטה כו. ד"ה וזו]

מִיזְקַק נַמִי זָקֵיק.§ "וְאָחִיו הוּא לְכָל דָּבָר".§ לְמַאי הִלְכְתָא? [א]לְיוֹרְשׁוֹ וְלִיטַּמֵּא לוֹ. פְּשִׁיטָא, אָחִיו הוּא! סד"א: הוֹאִיל וּכְתִיב °"כִּי אִם לִשְׁאֵרוֹ הַקָּרוֹב אֵלָיו" *וַאֲמַר מָר: [ב]שְׁאֵרוֹ – *זוֹ אִשְׁתּוֹ, וּכְתִיב °"לֹא יִטַּמָּא בַּעַל בְּעַמָּיו לְהֵחַלּוֹ", יֵשׁ בַּעַל שֶׁמִּטַּמֵּא וְיֵשׁ בַּעַל שֶׁאֵין מִטַּמֵּא, הָא כֵּיצַד? [ג]מִטַּמֵּא הוּא לְאִשְׁתּוֹ כְּשֵׁרָה, וְאֵין מִטַּמֵּא לְאִשְׁתּוֹ פְּסוּלָה, ה"נ מִטַּמֵּא הוּא לְאָח כָּשֵׁר וְאֵין מִטַּמֵּא לְאָח פָּסוּל, קמ"ל. *וְאֵימָא ה"נ! הָתָם לְאַפּוּקֵי קַיְימָא, הָכָא – אָחִיו הוּא.§ [ד]"חוּץ מִמִּי שֶׁיֵּשׁ לוֹ אָח מִן הַשִּׁפְחָה וּמִן הַגּוֹיָה".§ •מ"ט? אָמַר קְרָא °"הָאִשָּׁה וִילָדֶיהָ תִּהְיֶה לַאדֹנֶיהָ".§ "מִי שֶׁיֵּשׁ לוֹ בֵּן מ"מ פּוֹטֵר" וכו'.§ מִכָּל מָקוֹם לְאַתּוּיֵי מַאי? אֲמַר רַב יְהוּדָה: [ה]לְאִיתּוּיֵי מַמְזֵר. מַאי טַעְמָא? דְּאָמַר קְרָא °"וּבֵן *אֵין לוֹ" – *עַיֵּין עָלָיו.§ "וְחַיָּיב עַל מַכָּתוֹ",§ אַמַּאי? קְרִי כָּאן °"וְנָשִׂיא בְעַמְּךָ לֹא תָאֹר" – *[ו]בְּעוֹשֶׂה מַעֲשֵׂה עַמְּךָ! *) כִּדְאָמַר רַב פִּנְחָס מִשְּׁמֵיהּ דְּרַב פָּפָּא: בְּעוֹשֶׂה תְּשׁוּבָה – [ז]הָכָא נַמִי כְּשֶׁעָשָׂה תְּשׁוּבָה. וְהַאי בַּר תְּשׁוּבָה הוּא? וְהָתְנַן: *שִׁמְעוֹן בֶּן מְנַסְיָא אוֹמֵר: אֵיזֶהוּ °"מְעֻוָּת לֹא יוּכַל לִתְקֹן", זֶה הַבָּא עַל הָעֶרְוָה וְהוֹלִיד מִמֶּנָּה מַמְזֵר! הָשְׁתָּא מִיהָא עוֹשֶׂה מַעֲשֵׂה עַמְּךָ הוּא.§ תָּנוּ רַבָּנַן: [ח]הַבָּא עַל אֲחוֹתוֹ וְהִיא בַּת אֵשֶׁת אָבִיו – חַיָּיב מִשּׁוּם אֲחוֹתוֹ, וּמִשּׁוּם בַּת אֵשֶׁת אָבִיו. רַבִּי יוֹסֵי *בֶּן יְהוּדָה [נ"ל בר'] אוֹמֵר: אֵינוֹ חַיָּיב אֶלָּא מִשּׁוּם אֲחוֹתוֹ בִּלְבַד, וְלֹא מִפְּנֵי בַּת אֵשֶׁת אָבִיו. מַאי טַעְמַיְיהוּ דְּרַבָּנַן? אָמְרִי: מִכְּדִי כְּתִיב °"עֶרְוַת אֲחוֹתְךָ בַת אָבִיךָ אוֹ בַת אִמֶּךָ" "עֶרְוַת בַּת אֵשֶׁת אָבִיךָ מוֹלֶדֶת אָבִיךָ אֲחוֹתְךָ הִיא" לָמָּה לִי? ש"מ: לְחַיְּיבוֹ מִשּׁוּם אֲחוֹתוֹ וּמִשּׁוּם בַּת אֵשֶׁת אָבִיו. וְרַבִּי יוֹסֵי בְּרַ' יְהוּדָה: אָמַר קְרָא "אֲחוֹתְךָ הִיא", מִשּׁוּם אֲחוֹתוֹ אַתָּה מְחַיְּיבוֹ וְאִי אַתָּה מְחַיְּיבוֹ מִשּׁוּם בַּת אֵשֶׁת אָבִיו – וְרַבָּנַן, הַאי "אֲחוֹתְךָ הִיא" מַאי עָבְדִי לֵיהּ? מִיבָּעֵי לְהוּ לְחַיְּיבוֹ עַל אֲחוֹתוֹ בַּת אָבִיו וּבַת אִמּוֹ, לוֹמַר *שֶׁאֵין מַזְהִירִין מִן הַדִּין. וְרַבִּי יוֹסֵי בְּרַ' יְהוּדָה? אִם כֵּן לִכְתּוֹב רַחֲמָנָא "אֲחוֹתְךָ", "הִיא" לָמָּה לִי – מִשּׁוּם אֲחוֹתְךָ אַתָּה מְחַיְּיבוֹ וְאִי אַתָּה מְחַיְּיבוֹ מִשּׁוּם בַּת אֵשֶׁת אָבִיו. וְרַבָּנַן? אַף עַל גַּב דִּכְתִיב "אֲחוֹתְךָ" אִיצְטְרִיךְ לְמִכְתַּב "הִיא", שֶׁלֹּא תֹּאמַר: בְּעָלְמָא מַזְהִירִין מִן הַדִּין, וְכ"ת: "אֲחוֹתְךָ" דִּכְתַב רַחֲמָנָא לָמָּה לִי – *מִילְּתָא דְּאָתְיָא בְּק"ו טָרַח וְכָתַב לָהּ קְרָא – כָּתַב רַחֲמָנָא "הִיא". וְרַבִּי יוֹסֵי בְּרַ' יְהוּדָה: אִם כֵּן לִיכְתְּבֵיהּ רַחֲמָנָא לַ"אֲחוֹתְךָ הִיא" בְּאִידָךְ קְרָא. וְרַ' יוֹסֵי בְּרַ' יְהוּדָה, הַאי "בַּת אֵשֶׁת אָבִיךָ" מַאי עָבֵיד לֵיהּ? מִיבָּעֵי לֵיהּ: מִי שֶׁיֵּשׁ לוֹ אִישׁוּת לְאָבִיךָ בָּהּ, [ט]פְּרָט לַאֲחוֹתוֹ מִשִּׁפְחָה וְגוֹיָה, שֶׁאֵין אִישׁוּת לְאָבִיךָ בָּהּ. וְאֵימָא: [י]פְּרָט לַאֲחוֹתוֹ מֵאֲנוּסָה? הַהִיא לָא מָצֵית אָמְרַתְּ, מִדְּרָבָא, *דְּרָבָא רָמֵי: כְּתִיב °"עֶרְוַת בַּת בִּנְךָ אוֹ בַת בִּתְּךָ לֹא תְגַלֶּה", הָא בַּת בְּנָהּ דִּידָהּ וּבַת בִּתָּהּ דִּידָהּ – שָׁרֵי, וּכְתִיב °"עֶרְוַת אִשָּׁה וּבִתָּהּ לֹא תְגַלֵּה אֶת בַּת בְּנָהּ וְאֶת בַּת בִּתָּהּ". הָא כֵּיצַד? כָּאן בְּאוֹנְסִין כָּאן בְּנִשּׂוּאִין.
וְאֵימָא

(ויקרא כא; שם; שמות כא; דברים כה; שמות כב; קהלת א; ויקרא יח; ויקרא יח; ויקרא יח)

*) חגיגה ט. ע"ש ב"מ סב. ע"ש ב"ק לח: ע"ש סנהדרין פה. ע"ש

רש"י

מיזקק נמי זקיק. לאשת אחיו ליבום, שאפילו אין כאן אח אלא ממזר זה – זקוקה לחליצה. וליטמא לו. אם כהן הוא, ולו אח ממזר – מיטמא לו. כי אם לשארו. זו אשתו: לאפוקי קיימא הלכך לאו אשתו היא. האשה וילדיה. בשפחה כתיב. גויה. לקמן מפרש בשמעתין מ"כי יסיר את בנך מאחרי". ובן אין לו. מאי למכתב ובן אן לו, כדאמרינן בקדושין (דף ד.) "אן כסף", וכמו "מאן יבמי" (דברים כה) "מאן בלעם" (במדבר כב). ולהכי כתב "אין", למדרש: עיין עליו! דאם יש לו בן בעולם – פוטר. בעושה מעשה עמך. והאי אביו לאו עושה מעשה עמך הוא, שהרי בא על הערוה והוליד ממנה ממזר. כדאמר רב פנחס. בפ' "חומר בקדש". השתא מיהת. הואיל ושב – עושה מעשה עמך הוא. וניהי נמי דעונו גלוי ונזכר כל זמן שממזר קיים – מיהו מתשובה ואילך בכלל "עושה מעשה עמך" הוא. והיא בת אשת אביו. דעל ידי נשואין נולדה לאביו, ולא באנוסין. מכדי כתיב ערות אחותך בת אביך. ובין מן האונסין ובין מן הנשואין משמע, "ערות בת אשת אביך מולדת אביך" למה לי? הא נמי אחותו בת אביו היא! שמעת מינה לחייבו משום שני לאוין הללו, ואם שוגג – חייב שתי חטאות. אחותך היא. בהאי קרא דבת אשת אביך כתיב. לחייבו על אחותו. מן האונסין בת אביו ובת אמו, כגון נולדו הוא והיא מן אנוסה. דמההוא קרא דאונסין לא שמעי' אלא בת אביו שלא בת אמו, דכתי' "בת אביך או בת אמך". והא דכתיב נמי "בת אשת אביך", דמשמע בין אמו בין שאין אמו – באישות הוא דכתיב, אבל באונסין לא שמעינן. להכי כתיב "אחותו" – לרבות בת אביו ובת אמו. מן הדין. מק"ו: אם על בת אביו שלא בת אמו הזהיר – על בת אביו ואמו לכ"ש. שלא תאמר בעלמא מזהירין מן הדין. והוי לאו גמור. ומהכא לא ילפינן למימר, מדאיצטריך "אחותך" – אלמא אין מזהירין מן הדין. דאיכא לשנויי: מילתא דאתיא בק"ו טרח וכתב לה קרא. להכי כתב "היא", כלומר: הכא הוא דאייתר קרא, אבל אזהרת דין ק"ו לאו אזהרה היא. באידך קרא. גבי אחותך בת אביך, דלא הוזכר שם אישות, דנפקי אונסין מיניה. (א) דבנשואין אשמעינן אף בבת אביו ובבת אמו, מדכתיבא הכא – ש"מ למימרא דאע"ג דהיא בת אשת אביו לא מחייב אלא משום אחותו. שאין אישות לאביך בה. בשפחה וגויה לא תפסי בה קדושין. במסכת קדושין נפקא לן מקראי בפ' "האומר לחברו" בסופו (דף סח.): שפחה – עם הדומה לחמור, וגויה, כדכתיב "ואחר כן תבא עליה ובעלתה" (דברים כא), ומעיקרא לא. ואימא פרט לאחותו מאנוסתו. שלא היה אישות לאביך בה. כאן באונסין. ערות בת בנך מאנוסתו לא תגלה, הא בת בנה מאיש אחר – גלה, דלאו אשתך היא. ומיהו, בנו מן האונסין בנו הוא, וכן בתו. הלכך, גבי אחוה נמי אחוה הוא.

תוספות

מאי טעמא. הכא לא פריך פשיטא דבנו הוא, כדפריך לעיל "פשיטא אחיו הוא", אלא אדרבה, בעי מאי טעמא. והיינו משום דשני לעיל נילף אחוה אחוה מבני יעקב כו', ולהכי בעי מאי טעמא לא ילפינן מבני יעקב דלא זקוקה, ואם כן – מיפטר נמי לא מיפטר.

בן אין לו עיין עליו. אע"ג דסתם אח ובן הוי אפילו ממזר, כדפריך לעיל פשיטא, אחיו הוא. והכא נמי לא איצטריך "ובן אין לו" – עיין עליו, אלא משום דלא נילף מבני יעקב. [והא [נ"ל בה"ג] דאיצטריך "וזרע אין לה", עיין עלה – היינו משום] דסתם זרע לא הוי אלא זרע כשר, כדאמר בריש קדושין (דף ד.): אין לי אלא זרע כשר, זרע פסול מנין? ולענין בני בנים הוי איפכא, דזרע משמע •אפי' בני בנים, כדמשמע נמי התם, דקאמר: זרע זרעה לא צריך קרא, דבני בנים הרי הן כבנים. ובן לא משמע אלא בן לבדו, כדאמר ב"יש נוחלין" (ב"ב דף קטו. ושם): אין לי אלא בן(ג), ובן הבן ובת הבן בן בת הבן מנין? ונראה לר"י דמ"עיין עליו" דהכא גבי יבוס אין לדרוש בן הבת ובת הבן שיפטור מן היבוס, כיון דאפקינן לאתויי ממזר. ולהכי איצטריך לאתויי בן הבן ובת הבן לענין נחלה, ולא בעי למילף מדלענין יבוס בן ובן הבן כי הדדי נינהו – לענין נחלה נמי כי הדדי נינהו, כדאמר התם (שם דף קט. ושם) גבי בת. וא"ת: ונדרוש איפכא גבי נחלה לאתויי ממזר, ומ"אין לו" דגבי יבוס נדרוש בן הבן? וי"ל: דגבי נחלה א"צ לאתויי ממזר, דלכל מילי בנו הוא. אלא דלענין יבוס הוה ס"ד למילף מבני יעקב, ולהכי ע"כ ההוא דנחלה אתא לרבות בן הבן. והא דפשיט ליה ב"יש נוחלין" דלענין יבוס בן ובת כי הדדי נינהו – נראה לר"י דיתקא לן מ"לא ימחה" פרט לזה שאין שמו מחוי. א"כ דבת וממזר שקולים, ובת נמי נפקא מ"עיין עליו" דהכא. ומיהו, קשה לר"י: דהיכי נוכל לומר דשקולים הם בת וממזר? הא כיון דמלינו לאוקומי עיין עליו בבת – מהיכי תיתי לאוקומי אף בממזר, כיון דמאחוה אחוה משמע למעוטי ממזר! וי"ל: כיון דאחוה אחוה איצטריך לדרשא אחריתי, לית לן למעוטי מיניה ממזר לענין יבוס, כיון דלכל מילי חשיב בן ואח. ולגבי יבוס נמי מלי לרבויי (ג) בהדיא בת מעיין עליו, הלכך אע"ג דאיצטריך לרבויי בת – לא נניח בשביל כך מלרבויי ממזר. תדע, דהא ריש לקיש דריש לה בריש "החולץ" (לקמן לה: ושם) למילתא אחריתי, ואפ"ה מרבינן מיניה ממזר.

כשעשה תשובה. והא דאמר בפ' "הנחנקין" (סנהדרין דף פה: ושם) לכל אין הבן נעשה שליח לאביו להכותו ולקללו חוץ ממסית כו'! התם כשעשה תשובה. וא"ת: בשלמא מלקות משכחת דמחייב אע"פ שעשה תשובה, אלא לקללו – מי שעשה תשובה אין רשאי לקללו אפילו אחר! ויש לומר: דאם הזכיר שם שמים לבטלה, או עשה דבר שנתחייב בו נדוי, אף על פי שעשה תשובה – חייב, ולא מיפטר.

וכי

עין משפט נר מצוה

נ א מיי' פ"א מהלכות נחלות הלכה ז סמג עשין צו טוש"ע ח"מ סי' רעו סעיף ו:
נא ב ג מיי' פ"ב מהל' אבל הלכה ט סמג עשין כח ולאוין רלה טוש"ע י"ד סימן שעג סעיף ד:
נב ד מיי' שם הל"ג ופ"א מהלכות נחלות הל' ז טוש"ע שם וטוש"ע ח"מ סימן רעו סעיף ו:
לקמן ל:
נג ה מיי' פ"א מהלכות יבום הלכה ג טוש"ע אה"ע סימן קנו סעיף ב:
נד ו ז מיי' פ"ה מהלכות ממרים הלכה יב טור ש"ע י"ד סימן רמא סעיף ד:
נה ח מיי' פ"ב מהלכות איסורי ביאה הלכה ג ד סמג לאוין קה:
נו ט מיי' פ"א מהלכות יבום הלכה ד טוש"ע אה"ע סימן טו סעיף י:
נז י מיי' פ"ב מהלכות איסורי ביאה הלכה ד:

[לקמן לה: ע. קדושין ד. ב"ב קטו.]
[ב"ב ד. ב"מ מח:]
חגיגה ט.

תוספות ישנים

ואימא פרט לאחותו מאנוסה. פי' וגם פרט לאחותו משפחה וגויה דבכולהו אין אישות: **פרט** לאחותו מאנוסה. קשה להר"ס הלא כתיב אחותך בת אביך דמיירי על כרחך באונסים דאי בנשואין תיפוק לי מאשת אביך וי"ל דה"ק ואימא דקרא דאשת אביך ימעט אנוסתו דאינה תחתיו כסדר אישות וקרא דבת אביך מוקים לה בבת שיש לו מן השפחה וגויה שיושבת תחתיו ואע"ג דאף לשפחה וגויה אין לאביו אישות בה מ"מ דרשא דאין לאביך אישות בה אין למעוטי כל אותם שאין בהם אישות אלא אחת לבד וכן משמע בסמוך דבעי קראי אחריני לשפחה ולגויה. וה"נ טוב לנו למעט אנוסתו שאינה כלל תחתיו משפחה ומגויה העומדות תחתיו:

מסורת הש"ס

[פירוש נכון על זה תמ... ברשב"ם ב"ב קטו: קי... וכ"א בשאלתות ריש... אמור שארו זו אש... כדכתיב שארה כסות ועונתה]
[עיין תוספות סוטה ... ד"ה וזו הואיל]
[וגרסת הערוך בערך א... איין עליו וע"ע שם בע... אן א' קלת בארוכות ... עוד שם בערך עין וע... מ"ש הסמ"ע ריש סי... רעו לפרש בלשון אין וא... ע"ש קלת בארוכות והתוי... מ"ה פ"ב דמכילתין מ... עליו ע"ש]

תוספות חד מקמ...

מסקנא דשמעתו דל"ש אחותו מחי... כריתות וכ"ש מחי... לאוין וכ"ש אח... מאנוסתו אסור אח...

הגהות הב"ח

(א) רש"י ד"ה באידך ו... מיניה דהא דהוזאין ו... מדכתביה הכא ש"...
(ב) תוס' ד"ה בן וכו'. לי אלא בן בן הבן ובת... ובן בת הבן מנין כ...
(ג) בא"ד לרבויי ב... בת:

[פסחים כד. מכות ה:]
[פסחים יח: וש"נ]

גליון הש"ס

גמ' מ"ט אמר ... האשה וילדיה לקמן ע"א: **תוס'** ד"ה בן ... לו וכו' אפילו בני ב... כדמשמע נמי התם. סנהדרין פד ע"ב:

לקמן לז.

ואימא פרט לחייבי לאוין? *אמר *רב פפא: [א]חייבי לאוין תפשי בהו קדושין, דכתיב (דברים כא) °"כי תהיין לאיש שתי נשים האחת אהובה והאחת שנואה", וכי יש אהובה לפני המקום ויש שנואה לפני המקום? אלא: אהובה – אהובה בנישואיה, שנואה – שנואה בנישואיה, ואמר רחמנא: "כי תהיין". ואימא פרט לחייבי כריתות – אמר רבא: אמר קרא (ויקרא יח) °"ערות אחותך בת אביך או בת אמך מולדת בית או מולדת חוץ", [ב]בין שאומרים לו לאביך: "קיים", בין שאומרים לו לאביך "הוצא", ואמר רחמנא: "אחותך היא" – אימא: בין שאומר לו אביך "קיים" בין שאומר לו אביך "הוצא", ואמר רחמנא "אחותך היא" – לרבות אחותו משפחה וגויה – אמר קרא "בת אשת אביך", מי שיש לו אישות לאביך בה, פרט לאחותו משפחה וגויה. ומה ראית? מסתברא, חייבי כריתות הוה ליה לרבות, שכן תפסי בהן קדושין לעלמא. אדרבה, שפחה וגויה הוה ליה לרבות, דאי מגיירה – לדידיה נמי תפסי בה קדושין! לכי מגיירה גופא אחרינא היא. ורבנן, למעוטי שפחה וגויה מנא להו? [ג]נפקא להו (שמות כא) °מ"האשה וילדיה תהיה לאדוניה". ורבי יוסי בר' יהודה: חד – בשפחה, וחד – בגויה. וצריכי, דאי אשמעינן שפחה – משום דאין לה חיים, אבל גויה דאית לה חיים – אימא לא. ואי אשמעינן גויה – משום דלא שייכא במצות, אבל שפחה, דשייכא במצות, אימא לא – צריכא. ורבנן, אשכחן שפחה, גויה מנא להו? וכ"ת: נילף משפחה – הנהו מצרך צריכי! *א"ר יוחנן משום ר' שמעון בן יוחי: [ד]אמר קרא (דברים ז) °"כי יסיר את בנך מאחרי", בנך מישראלית קרוי בנך, ואין בנך הבא מן הגויה קרוי בנך, אלא בנה. אמר רבינא, ש"מ: בן בתך הבא מן הגוי – קרוי בנך. *לימא קסבר רבינא *[ה]גוי ועבד הבא על בת ישראל הולד כשר? נהי דממזר לא הוי – כשר נמי לא הוי, ישראל פסול מיקרי. האי בשבעה אומות כתיב! "כי יסיר" לרבות כל המסירים. הניחא לרבי שמעון, דדריש טעמא דקרא, אלא לרבנן מנא להו? מאן תנא דפליג עליה דרבי יוסי ברבי יהודה – רבי שמעון היא.§

[לקמן מה. קדושין סח:]

מתני'

רש"י

פרט לחייבי לאוין. אם נשא אביו ממזרת והוליד בת – לאו אחותו היא, ואימא דלא תפסי בהו קדושי. יש אהובה לפני המקום. לורך היה לו להזכיר שאם זה היה אוהב את זו ושונא את זו אין הבכורה משתנה בכך? פשיטא, שאם זה שונאה – אין המקום שונאה. שנואה בנישואיה. בעבירה. כי תהיינה. דאית בהו הויה. ואימא. דהאי בת אשת אביו פרט לאחותו מחייבי כריתות, דאין אישות בה לאביך, דהא לא תפסי בהו קדושין, דילפינן מאחות אשה שהיא בכרת, וכתיב בה "לא תקח" – אין לך בה ליקוחין, בפ' "האומר לחברו" בקדושין (דף סז:). שפחה אין לה חיים. אין לה יחס, דכתיב "עם החמור" (בראשית כב). וגויה מתייחסת על שם אביה, דכתיב "בלאדן בן בלאדן" (מ"ב כ) *"הדרימן בן טברימון" (מ"א טו). שפחה שייכא במצות. כל מצוה שהאשה חייבת בה – עבד חייב בה, דגמר "לה" "לה" מאשה (חגיגה דף ד.). כי יסיר את בנך. מדלא כתיב "כי תסיר" ש"מ הכי קאמר: בתך לא תתן לבנו כי יסיר בעל בתך את בנך שתלד לו בתך מאחרי, אבל א"בתו לא תקח לבנך" לא קמהדר, ולא קרינן ביה כי תסיר בת הגוי את בנך שתלד מאחרי. אלמא: בנך מן הגוי שילדה לו בתך – קרוי בנך, ואין בנך הבא מן הגויה קרוי בנך. ש"מ. מדכתיב "כי יסיר את בנך", ומוקמינן ליה בבן שתלד בתך לגוי, אלמא: בן בתך הבא מן הגוי קרוי נמי בנך. לימא קסבר רבינא וכו' הולד כשר. ולקמן פליגי בה ב"החולץ" (דף מה.) (א) (ול"נ דהולד ממזר גרסי', דלא הוי כגר שנתגייר, אלא צד ישראלית יש בו, ושייך ביה ממזרות). בשבעה אומות כתיב. ושאר גויות מנלן דולדה כמוה. לרבי שמעון דדריש טעמא דקרא. בפרק "המקבל" בבבא מציעא (דף קטו.): אלמנה עניה אין ממשכנין אותה, אבל עשירה ממשכנין (ב), שאין אתה חייב להחזיר לה, ואין אתה משיאה שם רע בשכנותיה. אלמא דריש טעמא ד"לא תחבול בגד אלמנה" משום שם רע, ומוציא עשירה מן הכלל. והכא נמי לדידיה ניחא, דאי נמי לא מפרש קרא טעמא – הוה דריש טעמא דחיתון משום "כי יסיר את בנך", ולא איצטריך קרא לפרושי טעמא, ואייתר קרא "כי יסיר" לרבות שאר מסירין. אלא לרבנן. איצטריך קרא לפרושי טעמא בז' אומות גופייהו, ולמעוטי שאר אומות, דאינן אדוקין בעבודה זרה כמותן, כדקיימא לן (חולין דף יג:): גוים שבחו"ל לאו עובדי עבודה זרה הן, אלא מנהג אבותיהן בידיהן, ולא איייתר ליה רבויא. ושאר אומות מנלן? ודכוותיה אמרינן בסנהדרין (דף כא.) גבי "לא ירבה לו נשים ולא יסור לבבו", דלר"ש הוי לא יסור לרבויא, דבלאו פירושא דקרא הוה דרשינן ביה טעמא. ולרבנן דלא דרשי טעמא דקרא בעלמא, הכא קרא פירש טעמא.

תוספות

וכי יש אהובה לפני המקום. דפשיטא דבשביל אהבת ושנאת הבעל לא יפקיע המקום זכות בנה. ואם תאמר: ונימא שנואה – היינו רשעה, דהיא שנואה לפני המקום! וי"ל: דמשמע ליה אהובה ושנואה בנישואיה, ואם ברשעה מדבר – בלא נישואיה נמי יש לשנאותה א).

ורבי יוסי ברבי יהודה חד בשפחה וחד בגויה. וא"ת: ולמה לי קרא ד"האשה וילדיה", דמ"בת אשת אביך" נפקי תרוייהו דאין אישות לאביך בה! וי"ל: דהוה מוקמינן קרא בדמסתברא טפי, ואידך הוה מרבינן מ"מולדת חוץ" בין שאומרים לאביך הוצא, כי היכי דמרבינן מיניה חייבי כריתות. ואי אשמועינן גויה משום דלא שייכא במצות. לא הוה צריך להך צריכותא, דגויה לא מפרש בהדיא בקרא ובטעמא קמא סגי. דאי לאו אלא חד קרא – הוה מוקמינן בשפחה, משום דאין לה *חיים. וא"ת: השתא, דאיכא טעמא בגויה ואיכא טעמא בשפחה – למה לי קרא ד"האשה וילדיה" דמ"בת אשת אביך" ממעטי תרוייהו, דהי מינייהו מפקת? וי"ל: דה"א טעמא דלא שייך במצות עדיף, והוה מוקמינן לה בגויה א] ואע"ג דטעמא דגויה לא הוה אתא משפחה, כיון דאיכא בשפחה טעם כל דהו דלא הוי בגויה.

(ג) קסבר רבינא גוי ועבד הבא על בת ישראל הולד כשר. כן גיר' הקונטרס. וכן כתוב ברוב ספרים כאן. אבל בקדושין בסוף פרק "האומר" (דף סח: ושם) ברוב ספרים כתוב: הולד ממזר. וכן גורס התם. וכן נראה עיקר לר"י, דכיון דבתר ישראלית שדינן ליה – הוה טפי ממזר ממאי דהוה שדינן בתר גוי, דאין ממזרות לגוי. וכן משמע לעיל, דקא"ר יוחנן בספ"ק (דף יז. ושם): וכולן לפסול. והדר קאמר: כי אמריתה קמיה דשמואל אמר: אין בנך הבא מן הגויה קרוי בנך אלא בנה, ואין חוששין לקידושיו, דגוי הוא ולא ממזר. והא דאמרינן בפרק "יש בכור" (בכורות דף מז. ושם) גבי לויה שנתעברה מן הגוי בנה פטור מה' סלעים – לא תימא למ"ד אין מזהמין את הולד, אלא אפילו למ"ד מזהמין – לוי פסול איקרי! אומר ר"י דמ"ד אין מזהמין – היינו מ"ד הולד ממזר, דלאו בתר גוי שדינן ליה. ולשון מזהמין על שם גוים שהן מזוהמין, והקונטרס לא פירש שם כן. ההוא בשבעה אומות כתיב. ואע"ג ד"לא תחנם" דכתיב נמי התם מוקמינן בפרק קמא דמסכת ע"ז (דף כ.) בכל אומות, עובדי עבודה זרה הכא לא מוקמינן ליה בז' אומות אלא משום ד"כי יסיר" משמע שבעה אומות, דמסירין טפי. ואי לאו "כי יסיר" – הוה מוקמינן ליה נמי בכל אומות עובדי עבודה זרה לרבנן. ולר"ש דדריש טעמא דקרא, אי לאו "כי יסיר" הוה דרשי' דטעמא דקרא משום הסרה, והוה (ד) מוקי ליה דוקא בז' אומות דמסירין טפי. וא"ת: ד"לא תתחתן בם" דכתיב נמי התם מוקמינן דוקא בז' אומות, אע"ג דאין שייך שם הסרה, דבגירותן איירי, כדאמר ב"הערל" (לקמן דף עו. ושם)! וי"ל: דעל כרחך אי אפשר לאוקומי בכל אומות, דמדאסר גר עמוני ומואבי מצרי ואדומי – מכלל דשאר גרים שרי בישראל. ואם תאמר: והיכי כרת ברית שלמה עם חירם מלך צור, דכתיב "ויכרתו ברית שניהם" (מ"א ה), והכתיב "לא תכרות להם ברית ולא תחנם" (דברים ז) ובכל האומות עובדי עבודה זרה איירי, כמו "ולא תחנם"! וי"ל: דשמא לא אסר אלא כריתת ברית לשם עבודה זרה, כדכתיב באידך קרא "לא תכרות להם ולאלהיהם ברית" (שמות כג) או שמא חירם מלך צור גר תושב היה. ועוד נ"ל: דלא מיתסר כריתת ברית אלא דוקא בשבעה אומות, מדכתיב גבי גבעונים (יהושע ט) "אולי בקרבי אתה יושב ואיך אכרות לך ברית", משמע דבשאר אומות – שרי. ואע"ג ד"לא תחנם" איירי בכל אומות – עובדי עבודה זרה כריתת ברית שאני, דמוכח עניינא דאיירי דוקא בשבעה אומות, כמו "לא תחיה כל נשמה", דדוקא ז' האומות היו מצווים להחרים, דכתיב "שבעה גוים רבים ועצומים וכו' החרם תחרים" (דברים ז) ולוה הכתוב שלא לכרות להם ברית שלום שלא להכותם כדי לכבוש ארץ ישראל. מאן תנא דפליג עליה דרבי יוסי בר' יהודה ר"ש היא. בסוף פ' "האומר" (קדושין סח: ושם) איתא הך סוגיא, ומשני בענין אחר: דאמר קרא "כי תהיינה וילדו לו" כל היכא דקרינן ביה "כי תהיינה" קרינן ביה "וילדו לו", וכל היכא דלא קרינן ביה "כי תהיינה" – לא קרינן ביה "וילדו לו". וקאמר נמי בתר הכי: אם כן "האשה וילדיה" למה לי? ומוקי לה לדרשא אחריתי, ולא קאמר חד בשפחה וחד בגויה וצריכי.

קדמו

עין משפט נר מצוה

נח א מיי' פ"ד מהל' אישות הל' יד סמג עשין מח טוש"ע אה"ע סימן מד סעיף ז:

[בערוך גרס רבא]

נט ב מיי' פ"ב מהלכות איסורי ביאה הלכה א טוש"ע אה"ע סימן טו סעיף י:

ס ג ד מיי' פ"א מהל' יבום הלכה ד:

סא ה מיי' פט"ו מהל' איסורי ביאה הלכה ג סמג לאוין קה טוש"ע אה"ע סימן ד סעיף יט:

[ועיין היטב תוספות סנהדרין פג: סוף ד"ה וטבול יום ותוס' זבחים יז. ד"ה הג"ה וכו' ישוב על זה]

תוספות ישנים

א) ועוד דפשיטא דאין לבני' להפסיד לכך נחלתם: בין שאומרים לאביך הולא והיינו חייבי כריתות דליכא לאוקומי בחייבי לאוין דהא ככבר שמעינן להו מכי תהיינה שהרי קדושין תופסין בהם ועוד ניחא לאוקמי בחייבי כריתות דמשמע הולא משום דהוי אשה דלא תפסי בה קדושין והיינו חייבי כריתות דאילו חייבי לאוין קדושין תופסין: חד בשפחה וחד בגויה וצריכי. ותימה דבפרק האומר משמע דלא צריך רק חד קרא לשפחה וגויה דפריך אלא האשה וילדיה למה לי ולא קאמר חד לשפחה וחד לגויה וי"ל דהכא היינו טעמא דאצטריך תרי קראי משום דחזינן הכא דאף חייבי כריתות דלית בהו קדושין מרבינן מדכתיב מולדת חוץ בין שאומרים לאביו הולא. א"כ אי ליכא תרי קראי לשפחה ולגויה לא הוה ממעטינן רק חד מינייהו שהרי יש לנו לרבות כל מה שנוכל דהא אף חייבי כריתות מרבינן אבל התם אין לחלק ביניהם ותימה כי קאמר הכא אשכחן שפחה גויה מנלן אמאי לא משמע דנפקא מדכתיב כי תהיינה וילדו כל היכא דקרינא ביה כי תהיינה קרינא ביה וילדו לו ושפחה וגויה לא בני הויה נינהו דהכי קאמר תלמודא בפרק האומר וי"ל להא דפרישית ניחא דהכא לא מצי למימר כן משום דאף חייבי כריתות דלא קרינן בהו נמי כי תהיינה מרבינן הכא ממולדת חוץ:

תוספות חד מקמאי

היא. דולדה כמוה ולא תפסי בה קדושין ואפי' בשפחה שטבלה לשם עבדות דשייכא במצות דהא אמר בהא שמעתתא וצריכה דאי אשמעינן בגויה משום דלא שייכא במצות. ואם אנס ופתה אשה מותר לישא בתה ודוקא לאחר מיתת האשה אבל בחיי האשה אסור לישא בתה דתנן הנטען מן האשה אסור באמה ובבתה ובאחותה דנשי לגבי נשי שכיחן דאזלן:

הגהות הב"ח

(א) רש"י ד"ה לימא וכו' ולי נראה נ"ב זה אינו מדברי רש"י: (ב) ד"ה לר' שמעון וכו' עשירה ממשכנין אותה שאין: (ג) תוספות ד"ה לימא קסבר רבינא: (ד) ד"ה ההוא וכו' משום הסרה והוה מוקמי' ליה:

הגהות מהר"ב רנשבורג

א] תוספות ד"ה ואי אשמעינן כו' ואף על גב טעמא דשוכבת כוכבים עדיף לא הוה כו' כנ"ל:

סב א מיי' פ"ט מהל' איסורי ביאה הל"ג סמג עשין מח טוש"ע אה"ע סימן מח סעיף ב:

סג ב מיי' פ"ח מהלכות יבום הלכה א סמג עשין נב טוש"ע אה"ע סימן קטו סעיף א:

סד ג מיי' שם הלכה ב טוש"ע אה"ע שם סעיף ג:

סה ד מיי' פ"ט מהל' אישות הלכה ב סמג עשין מח טוש"ע אה"ע סימן מח סעיף ב וסימן קטו סעיף א:

סו ה מיי' פ"ח מהל' יבום הלכה א.

מתני' *[א]מִי שֶׁקִּידֵּשׁ אַחַת מִשְּׁתֵּי אֲחָיוֹת וְאֵין יוֹדֵעַ אֵי זֶה מֵהֶן קִידֵּשׁ – נוֹתֵן גֵּט לָזוֹ וְגֵט לָזוֹ. [ב]מֵת, וְלוֹ אָח אֶחָד – חוֹלֵץ לִשְׁתֵּיהֶן. הָיוּ לוֹ שְׁנַיִם – אֶחָד חוֹלֵץ וְאֶחָד מְיַיבֵּם. קָדְמוּ וְכָנְסוּ – אֵין מוֹצִיאִין מִיָּדָם. *[ג]שְׁנַיִם שֶׁקִּדְּשׁוּ שְׁתֵּי אֲחָיוֹת, זֶה אֵינוֹ יוֹדֵעַ אֵי זוֹ קִידֵּשׁ, וְזֶה אֵינוֹ יוֹדֵעַ אֵיזוֹ קִידֵּשׁ – זֶה נוֹתֵן שְׁנֵי גִּיטִּין, וְזֶה נוֹתֵן שְׁנֵי גִּיטִּין. מֵתוּ, לָזֶה אָח וְלָזֶה אָח – זֶה חוֹלֵץ לִשְׁתֵּיהֶן, וְזֶה חוֹלֵץ לִשְׁתֵּיהֶן. לָזֶה אֶחָד וְלָזֶה שְׁנַיִם – הַיָּחִיד חוֹלֵץ לִשְׁתֵּיהֶן. וְהַשְּׁנַיִם – אֶחָד חוֹלֵץ וְאֶחָד מְיַיבֵּם. קָדְמוּ וְכָנְסוּ – אֵין מוֹצִיאִין מִיָּדָם. לָזֶה שְׁנַיִם וְלָזֶה שְׁנַיִם – אָחִיו שֶׁל זֶה חוֹלֵץ לְאַחַת וְאָחִיו שֶׁל זֶה חוֹלֵץ לְאַחַת, אָחִיו שֶׁל זֶה מְיַיבֵּם חֲלוּצָתוֹ שֶׁל זֶה וְאָחִיו שֶׁל זֶה מְיַיבֵּם חֲלוּצָתוֹ שֶׁל זֶה. קָדְמוּ שְׁנַיִם וְחָלְצוּ – לֹא יְיַבְּמוּ הַשְּׁנַיִם, אֶלָּא אֶחָד חוֹלֵץ וְאֶחָד מְיַיבֵּם. קָדְמוּ וְכָנְסוּ – אֵין מוֹצִיאִין מִיָּדָם.§ **גמ'** שְׁמַע מִינָּהּ: *[ד]קִדּוּשִׁין שֶׁאֵין מְסוּרִין לְבִיאָה – הָווּ קִדּוּשִׁין! הָכָא בְּמַאי עָסְקִינַן – כְּשֶׁהוּכְּרוּ וּלְבַסּוֹף נִתְעָרְבוּ. דַּיְקָא נַמִי, דְּקָתָנֵי "וְאֵינוֹ יוֹדֵעַ", וְלֹא קָתָנֵי "וְאֵינוֹ יָדוּעַ", ש"מ (א). מַאי קמ"ל? סֵיפָא אִיצְטְרִיכָא לֵיהּ: מֵת וְלוֹ אָח אֶחָד – חוֹלֵץ לִשְׁתֵּיהֶן, הָיוּ לוֹ שְׁנַיִם – אֶחָד חוֹלֵץ וְאֶחָד מְיַיבֵּם. [ה]דַּוְקָא מִיחֲלַץ וַהֲדַר יַבּוּמֵי, אֲבָל יַבּוּמֵי בְּרֵישָׁא – לָא, דְּקָא פָּגַע בַּאֲחוֹת זְקוּקָתוֹ.§ "שְׁנַיִם שֶׁקִּדְּשׁוּ שְׁתֵּי אֲחָיוֹת וכו'".§ שְׁמַע מִינָּהּ: קִדּוּשִׁין שֶׁאֵין מְסוּרִין לְבִיאָה הָווּ קִדּוּשִׁין! הָכָא נַמִי: כְּשֶׁהוּכְּרוּ וּלְבַסּוֹף נִתְעָרְבוּ. דַּיְקָא נַמִי, דְּקָתָנֵי "וְאֵין יוֹדֵעַ" וְלֹא קָתָנֵי "וְאֵין יָדוּעַ", ש"מ. וּמַאי קמ"ל? סֵיפָא אִיצְטְרִיכָא לֵיהּ: מֵתוּ, לָזֶה אֶחָד וְלָזֶה שְׁנַיִם – הַיָּחִיד, חוֹלֵץ לִשְׁתֵּיהֶן. וְהַשְּׁנַיִם, אֶחָד חוֹלֵץ וְאֶחָד מְיַיבֵּם". פְּשִׁיטָא, הַיְינוּ רֵישָׁא! מַהוּ דְּתֵימָא: לִיגְזוֹר תְּרֵי אַטּוּ חַד, קמ"ל. וְדַוְקָא מִיחֲלַץ וַהֲדַר יַבּוּמֵי, אֲבָל יַבּוּמֵי בְּרֵישָׁא – לָא, דְּקָא פָּגַע בִּיבָמָה לַשּׁוּק.§ "לָזֶה שְׁנַיִם וְלָזֶה שְׁנַיִם וכו'".§ הָא תּוּ לָמָּה לִי, הַיְינוּ הָךְ! מַהוּ דְּתֵימָא: לִיגְזוֹר דִּלְמָא מְיַיבֵּם בְּלֹא חֲלִיצָה, קמ"ל. מ"ש מֵהָא דִּתְנַן: *אַרְבָּעָה אַחִין, שְׁנַיִם מֵהֶן נְשׂוּאִין שְׁתֵּי אֲחָיוֹת, וּמֵתוּ הַנְּשׂוּאִין אֶת הָאֲחָיוֹת – הֲרֵי אֵלּוּ חוֹלְצוֹת וְלֹא מִתְיַיבְּמוֹת? הָכִי הַשְׁתָּא?! הָתָם

קדמו וכנסו אין מוציאין מידם. אר"י: דווקא משום דשמא לא פגע באחות זקוקתו, אבל אי ודאי הוה (ב) – זקוק להוציא, אף על גב דגבי שומרת יבם שקידש אחיו את אחותה (לקמן דף מא.) אין צריך לרבנן אפילו להמתין – היינו משום שקדש תחלה, ולא בא עליה באיסור, דכבר נפטרה היבמה [זיקתה ממנו] בקדושי אחותה, אבל הכא, דקני לה בביאה – דוקא במקום ספק הוא דאמרינן קדמו וכנסו אין מוציאין מידם, אבל בודאי – לא.

קדושין שאין מסורים לביאה. פירוש: דע"י קדושין קא מפסדה בביאה. אבל חייבי לאוין ועשה – חשיבי קדושין המסורים לביאה.

דיקא נמי דקתני אינו יודע. וא"ת: א"כ תקשה לאביי, דאמר בפ' "האיש מקדש" (קדושין דף נא. ושם) דהוי קדושין! וי"ל: דאין יודע משמע הכי ומשמע הכי.

ומאי שנא מהא דתנן. פי' בקונט': דפריך אהא דקתני במתני' קדמו וכנסו אין מוציאין מידם. וקשה: דלפי זה ה"ל לאתויי סיפא דמתניתין דד' אחין! ועוד: דבסמוך מייתי סיפא דמתני' אברייתא דשילא! ואר"י: דפריך אהא דקתני במתניתין אחד חולץ וא' מייבם, וגבי ד' אחין שתיהן (ג) חולצות.

מתני' וְאֵין יוֹדֵעַ אֵי זֶה מֵהֶן קִידֵּשׁ. אָסוּר בִּשְׁתֵּיהֶן, דְּכָל חֲדָא וַחֲדָא אִיכָּא לְמֵימַר: זוֹ אֲחוֹת אִשָּׁה. חוֹלֵץ לִשְׁתֵּיהֶן. דְּלָא יָדַע אֵיזוֹ הִיא יְבִמְתּוֹ. וּמִיחֲלַץ חֲדָא וְיַיבּוּמֵי חֲדָא, לָא – דַּאֲחוֹת חֲלוּצָתוֹ אֲסוּרָה לוֹ מִדְּרַבָּנַן בְּחַיֶּיהָ. וְיַבּוּמֵי בְּרֵישָׁא, נַמִי לָא – דְּדִלְמָא לָאו זוֹ הִיא יְבִמְתּוֹ, וְקָפָגַע בַּאֲחוֹת זְקוּקָתוֹ דַּהֲוְיָא כְּאִשְׁתּוֹ. הָיוּ לוֹ שְׁנַיִם אֶחָד חוֹלֵץ. תְּחִלָּה לְאַחַת. וְהַשֵּׁנִי, אִם רָצָה לְיַיבֵּם לַשְּׁנִיָּה – מְיַיבֵּם, דְּאִם זוֹ יְבִמְתּוֹ – שַׁפִּיר, וְאִם אֲחוֹתָהּ הִיא – לָא קָפָגַע בַּאֲחוֹת זְקוּקָתוֹ, דַּחֲלִיצָה אַפְקְעָהּ לְזִיקָהּ. קָדְמוּ וְכָנְסוּ. קוֹדֶם שֶׁנִּמְלְכוּ בְּבֵית דִּין. אֵין מוֹצִיאִין מִיָּדָם. דְּכָל חַד וְחַד אָמַר: אֲנָא שַׁפִּיר נְסֵיבִי. וְאִי נַמִי הֲוָה אִיפְכָא, שֶׁהָרִאשׁוֹן לְיִבּוּם כָּנַס אֲחוֹת זְקוּקָתוֹ – הַהִיא שַׁעְתָּא וַדַּאי הָוְיָא אֲסִירָא, וּמִשֶּׁבָּא אָחִיו וְיִיבֵּם הַשְּׁנִיָּה שֶׁהִיא יְבִמְתּוֹ – פָּקַע זִיקָה מֵאִידָךְ לְמַפְרֵעַ. שְׁנַיִם שֶׁקִּדְּשׁוּ ב' אֲחָיוֹת. וְהֵם נָכְרִים. זֶה חוֹלֵץ לִשְׁתֵּיהֶן וכו'. דְּכָל חַד וְחַד מִינַּיְיהוּ אָסוּר לְיַבּוּמֵי, דְּדִלְמָא בַּאֲחוֹת זְקוּקָתוֹ פָּגַע. הַיָּחִיד חוֹלֵץ לִשְׁתֵּיהֶן. כִּדְפָרֵישִׁית לְעֵיל, שֶׁאִי אֶפְשָׁר לוֹ לְיַיבֵּם לֹא קוֹדֶם חֲלִיצָה מִשּׁוּם אֲחוֹת זְקוּקָתוֹ, וְלֹא לְאַחַר חֲלִיצָה מִשּׁוּם אֲחוֹת חֲלוּצָה. לְפִיכָךְ, הוֹאִיל וְאָסוּר לְיַיבֵּם – יַחֲלוֹץ תְּחִלָּה לִשְׁנֵיהֶם, כְּדֵי לְהוֹצִיא אוֹתָהּ שֶׁהִיא יְבִמְתּוֹ מֵאִיסּוּר יְבָמָה לַשּׁוּק. וְהַשְּׁנַיִם אֶחָד חוֹלֵץ. לְאַפְקוּעֵי זִיקָה מֵאָחִיו אִם זוֹ הִיא יְבִמְתּוֹ, וְתִשְׁתָּרֵי אֲחוֹתָהּ לַשֵּׁנִי מִמָּה נַפְשָׁךְ: אִם יְבִמְתּוֹ הִיא – שַׁפִּיר, וְאִם אֲחוֹתָהּ הִיא – הָא קָפָקְעָה זִיקַת הַיְּבָמָה מִינַּהּ בַּחֲלִיצַת אָחִיו. אָחִיו שֶׁל זֶה מְיַיבֵּם חֲלוּצָתוֹ שֶׁל זֶה. מִמָּה נַפְשָׁךְ: אִם זוֹ יְבִמְתּוֹ – שַׁפִּיר נָסֵיב, שֶׁהֲרֵי אָחִיו לֹא חָלַץ לָזוֹ אֶלָּא לַאֲחוֹתָהּ שֶׁלֹּא הָיְתָה יְבִמְתּוֹ, וְאֵינָהּ כְּלוּם. וְאִי לָאו יְבִמְתּוֹ – שַׁפִּיר נָסֵיב נָכְרִית. דְּאִי מִשּׁוּם אֲחוֹת זְקוּקָתוֹ – לֵיכָּא, שֶׁהֲרֵי חָלַץ אָחִיו לַאֲחוֹתָהּ שֶׁהִיא יְבִמְתּוֹ, וּפָקַע זִיקָה. וְאִי מִשּׁוּם יְבָמָה לַשּׁוּק – הֲרֵי חֲלָצָהּ זוֹ מִן הַיָּחִיד, שֶׁהוּא אַח בַּעְלָהּ. קָדְמוּ שְׁנַיִם. אַחִין שֶׁל אֶחָד וְחָלְצוּ לִשְׁתֵּיהֶן, מִשּׁוּם דְּלָא יָדְעֵי אֵי זוֹ הִיא יְבִמְתּוֹ. לא יְיַבְּמוּ הַשְּׁנַיִם. אִם הָאֲחֵרִים זֶה אֶת זוֹ וְזֶה אֶת זוֹ, דְּקַמָּא דְּנָסֵיב אִיכָּא לְמֵימַר זוֹ הִיא אֲחוֹת זְקוּקָתוֹ. אֶלָּא, אֶחָד חוֹלֵץ תְּחִלָּה לְאַחַת, וְאֶחָד מְיַיבֵּם לַשְּׁנִיָּה, ממ"נ: אִם יְבִמְתּוֹ הִיא – שַׁפִּיר, וְאִי לָאו יְבִמְתּוֹ הִיא – בַּאֲחוֹת זְקוּקָתוֹ לֹא פָּגַע, שֶׁהֲרֵי חָלַץ אָחִיו לִיבִמְתּוֹ. וִיבָמָה לַשּׁוּק נַמִי לֵיכָּא, שֶׁהֲרֵי הִיא חֲלוּצָה מֵאֲחֵי בַּעְלָהּ. ואם קָדְמוּ. אֵלּוּ שְׁנַיִם הָאַחֲרוֹנִים וְכָנְסוּ אַחַר חֲלִיצַת הַשְּׁנַיִם הָרִאשׁוֹנִים, וְלֹא בָּאוּ לִימָּלֵךְ לְבֵ"ד – אֵין מוֹצִיאִין מִיָּדָם, כִּדְפָרֵישִׁית, שֶׁאֵין כָּאן אֶלָּא סְפֵק אִיסּוּר אֲחוֹת זְקוּקָה בַּנְּשׂוּאִין הָרִאשׁוֹנִים. דְּאִיכָּא לְמֵימַר קַמָּא דְּנָסֵיב – יְבִמְתּוֹ הִיא, וְשַׁפִּיר נָסֵיב. וּבַתְרָא נַמִי שַׁפִּיר נָסֵיב נָכְרִית. וְאִי נַמִי הֲוָה אִיפְכָא, דְּקַמָּא פָּגַע בַּאֲחוֹת זְקוּקָתוֹ, כֵּיוָן שֶׁבָּא שֵׁנִי וִיבְמָהּ – פָּקַע זִיקָתָהּ מֵאָחִיו, וְהוּתְּרָה לוֹ אִשְׁתּוֹ, וְאִיסּוּרָא דַּעֲבַד – עֲבַד. **גמ'** שְׁמַעְתְּ מִינָּהּ קִדּוּשִׁין שֶׁאֵין מְסוּרִים לְבִיאָה. שֶׁאֵין סוֹפָן לָבֹא לִידֵי בִּיאָה. דְּקס"ד דְּמַתְנִיתִין בְּשֶׁלֹּא הוּכְּרוּ, בִּשְׁעַת קִדּוּשִׁין לָא הֲוָה יָדַע הֵי מִינַּיְיהוּ, כְּגוֹן דְּאָמַר: הֲרֵי אַחַת מִכֶּם מְקוּדֶּשֶׁת לִי, וְעָשׂוּ שְׁתֵּיהֶן שָׁלִיחַ לְקַבֵּל קִדּוּשִׁין. וְקִדּוּשִׁין אֵלּוּ אֵין סוֹפָן לְבִיאָה, דְּכָל חֲדָא קַיְימָא עֲלֵיהּ בִּסְפֵק אֲחוֹת אִשָּׁה. וּמִדְּקָתָנֵי נוֹתֵן גֵּט לָזוֹ וְגֵט לָזוֹ – מִכְּלָל דַּחֲדָא מִיהָא מְקוּדֶּשֶׁת, וּמִשּׁוּם סְפֵיקָא דְּלָא יָדַע הֵי מִינַּיְיהוּ בָּעֵי לְמֵיתַב גֵּט לְתַרְוַיְיהוּ. אַלְמָא: קִדּוּשִׁין הֵן. וּפְלוּגְתָּא דְּאַבַּיֵי וְרָבָא הִיא, בְּקִדּוּשִׁין. שֶׁהוּכְּרוּ. בִּשְׁעַת קִדּוּשִׁין, וְיוֹדֵעַ הָיָה אֶת מִי מְקַדֵּשׁ. הִלְכָּךְ מְסוּרִים לְבִיאָה נִינְהוּ, וַהֲלוּ קִדּוּשִׁין. וְאֵינוֹ יוֹדֵעַ. מַשְׁמַע: הַשְׁתָּא אֵין יוֹדֵעַ. "אֵין יָדוּעַ" מַשְׁמַע לֹא נוֹדַע הַדָּבָר מֵעוֹלָם. וּמַאי קמ"ל. מַתְנִיתִין, פְּשִׁיטָא דְּתַרְוַיְיהוּ בָּעֵי גִּיטָּא, דְּלָא יָדַע הֵי מִינַּיְיהוּ. סֵיפָא אִיצְטְרִיכָא לֵיהּ. דְּקָתָנֵי: אֶחָד חוֹלֵץ וְאֶחָד מְיַיבֵּם. וְקָא מַשְׁמְעִינַן דַּוְקָא מִיחֲלַץ חַד וַהֲדַר יַבּוּמֵי אִידָךְ, מִמָּה נַפְשָׁךְ, כִּדְפָרֵישִׁית לְעֵיל. אֲבָל יַבּוּמֵי. חַד בְּרֵישָׁא, וַהֲדַר מִיחֲלַץ שֵׁנִי לְאִידָךְ – לָא. דְּקַמָּא דְּיַיבֵּם דִּלְמָא פָּגַע בַּאֲחוֹת זְקוּקָתוֹ. הַיְינוּ רֵישָׁא. דְּהָא אַשְׁמְעִינַן בְּרֵישָׁא: הָיוּ לוֹ שְׁנַיִם – אֶחָד חוֹלֵץ וְאֶחָד מְיַיבֵּם. מהו דתימא. הָכָא לֹא לְיַיבֵּם, כֵּיוָן דְּחַד מִינַּיְיהוּ יֵשׁ לוֹ אָח יְחִידִי – לִגְזוֹר תְּרֵי אַחֵי דְּלָא לְיַיבֵּם חַד מִינַּיְיהוּ אַטּוּ הַהוּא אָח שֶׁאֵין לוֹ אָח שֵׁנִי, וְאָתֵי לְמִפְגַּע בַּאֲחוֹת זְקוּקָה, קמ"ל. וְדַוְקָא מִיחֲלַץ. הָאָח הַיְּחִידִי לִשְׁתֵּיהֶן, וַהֲדַר יַבּוּמֵי חַד מֵהַשְּׁנַיִם אַחַר חֲלִיצַת אָחִיו לַשְּׁנִיָּה. אבל יַבּוּמֵי בְּרֵישָׁא. קוֹדֶם חֲלִיצַת הַיָּחִיד לִשְׁתֵּיהֶן. וַאֲפִילּוּ חָלַץ אָחִיו שֶׁל מְיַיבֵּם לַאֲחוֹתָהּ, דְּלֵיכָּא הַשְׁתָּא אִיסּוּר אֲחוֹת זְקוּקָה – לֹא [מייבם], מִשּׁוּם שֶׁמָּא זוֹ הִיא אֲרוּסַת הַנָּכְרִי וְקָא פָּגַע בִּיבָמָה לַשּׁוּק בְּלֹא חֲלִיצָה. דְּהַיְּחִידִי הוּא הַנָּכְרִי, וְלוֹ הַיְּבָמָה זְקוּקָה, וְהָא מִילְּתָא לָא אַשְׁמְעִינַן בְּרֵישָׁא. אָחִיו שֶׁל זֶה מְיַיבֵּם חֲלוּצָתוֹ שֶׁל זֶה הא תּוּ לָמָּה לִי. הַיְינוּ הָךְ, דְּהָא אַשְׁמְעִינַן בְּרֵישָׁא: הַשְּׁנַיִם, אֶחָד חוֹלֵץ וְאֶחָד מְיַיבֵּם. וה"נ הָכִי הוּא, דְּהָנֵי תְּרֵי – חַד חָלֵיץ וְחַד מְיַיבֵּם, וְהָנֵי תְּרֵי – חַד חָלֵיץ וְחַד מְיַיבֵּם. מהו דתימא. לִיגְזוֹר דִּלְמָא אָתֵי לְיַבּוּמֵי אֶחָד מִשְּׁנַיִם אֵלּוּ וְאֶחָד מִשְּׁנַיִם אֵלּוּ בְּלֹא חֲלִיצָה, וְקָפָגַע כָּל חַד בִּסְפֵק יְבָמָה לַשּׁוּק וּבַאֲחוֹת זְקוּקָה. קמ"ל. דְּלָא גָּזְרִינַן. וְהָא מֵרֵישָׁא לָא שָׁמְעִינַן, דְּהָתָם לָזֶה אֶחָד וְלָזֶה שְׁנַיִם, דְּסוֹף סוֹף לֹא מְיַיבֵּם אֶלָּא חֲדָא. וְכֵיוָן דְּטוֹעֲקִין בַּחֲלִיצָה דַּחֲדָא – מִדַּכְּרֵי נַמִּי וְלָא מְיַיבְּמִי עַד שֶׁיַּחְלוֹץ הַיָּחִיד לִשְׁתֵּיהֶן. אֲבָל הָכָא, כֵּיוָן דִּלְבַסּוֹף תַּרְוַיְיהוּ מְיַיבְּמִין, הָךְ לְהַאי בִּיאָה וְהָךְ לְהַאי בִּיאָה – אָתֵי לְמֵימַר מַה לָּנוּ וְלַחֲלִיצָה. מאי שנא מהא וכו' וְלֹא מִתְיַיבְּמוֹת. וְקָתָנֵי סֵיפָא "אִם קָדְמוּ וְכָנְסוּ יוֹצִיאוּ", וְהָכָא קָתָנֵי "אֵין מוֹצִיאִין מִיָּדָן". חוֹלְצוֹת ולא מתייבמות. וְלָא אָמְרִינַן לֵיחֲלוֹץ חַד מִינַּיְיהוּ וְהָוֵי לִזְוִיקָה דִּידָהּ מֵאָחִיו. וְהַאי מְיַיבֵּם חֲדָא, כִּי מַתְנִי' דְּקָתָנֵי אָחִיו שֶׁל זֶה מְיַיבֵּם חֲלוּצָתוֹ שֶׁל זֶה – כָּל אַחַת לְאַחַר חֲלִיצַת אֲחוֹתָהּ, כִּדְקָאָמַר: אָחִיו שֶׁל זֶה מְיַיבֵּם חֲלוּצָתוֹ שֶׁל זֶה, לֵימָא כּוּלָּן חוֹלְצוֹת כִּי הָתָם, מַאי מַהְדְּרִינַן לְיַבֵּם? הכי השתא. הָתָם זְקוּקוֹת שְׁתֵּיהֶן לָהֶן, אִי לְמ"ד בְּפֶרֶק "ד' אַחִין" טַעְמָא דְּאֵין מִתְיַיבְּמוֹת אֲפִילּוּ אַחַת מֵהֶן מִשּׁוּם דְּיֵשׁ זִיקָה, וּמֵרֵישָׁא מִיתַּסְרָא מִשּׁוּם דְּקָפָגְעָה בַּאֲחוֹת זְקוּקָה, וְכִי חָלֵיץ (מייבם) חַד לַחֲדָא וּפָקַע זִיקָה – לָא מִשְׁתַּרְיָא אֲחוֹתָהּ לְאִידָךְ, דְּכָל יְבָמָה שֶׁנֶּאֶסְרָה שָׁעָה אַחַת עַל יְבָמָהּ, אֲפִילּוּ לְאַחַר נְפִילָה – הֲרֵי הִיא כְּאֵשֶׁת אָח שֶׁיֵּשׁ לוֹ בָּנִים, וַאֲסוּרָה לְעוֹלָם.

וְאִי

[קידושין נח:]

שם

שם

לעיל יח. לקמן כו. כ... עדיות פ"ה מ"ה

תוספות ישנים

מהו דתימא דלמא ייבם בלא חליצה. וא"ת והא ידעינן מלעיל לא גזרינן דלמא ייבם קודם חליצה וי"ל דשאני הכא דכל השתים מתייבמות שהרי זה מייבם חלוצתו של זה וזה מייבם חלוצתו של זה וא"כ יטעו העולם ויאמרו אחר שזה מייבם וזה מייבם ושתיהם מתייבמות מה לנו ולחליצותם אבל לעיל אין חזינן דאיכא אחת דמתייבמת ואחת שאינה מתייבמת יבינו העולם וישימו ללב שלא תתיבם זאת עד שיהא חולץ לאחותה וכן יהי' פוגע באחות זקוקתו:

תוספות חד מקמאי

הא דתנן שנים שקדשו שתי אחיות לזה אחד ולזה שנים היחיד חולץ לשתים והשנים א' חולץ וא' מייבם דוקא מיחלץ היחיד והדר יבומי אחד מן השנים*) והדר מיחלץ היחידי דקא פגע ביבמה

*) אולי צ"ל אבל יבומי אחד מהשנים והדר מיחלץ היחידי לא דקא כו'.

הגהות הב"ח

(א) גמ' ש"מ ומאי קמ"ל: (ב) תוס' ד"ה קדמו וכו' אי ודאי הוה היה זקוק: (ג) ד"ה ומאי שנא וכו' שתיהן חולצות. נ"ב ס"... ומיהו הך פירכא ליתא לר' יוחנן דאמר לאחות אחות אי יודע מי שנתן:

הָתָם אִי לְמ"ד יֵשׁ זִיקָה — יֵשׁ זִיקָה. וְאִי לְמ"ד *אָסוּר לְבַטֵּל מִצְוַת יְבָמִין — אָסוּר לְבַטֵּל מִצְוַת יְבָמִין. הָכָא — כָּל חַד וְחַד, אֵימוּר דִּידֵיהּ קָא מִתְרַמְיָא לֵיהּ.§ "קָדְמוּ וְכָנְסוּ אֵין מוֹצִיאִין כו'".§ תָּנֵי שֵׁילָא: [א]וַאֲפִי' שְׁנֵיהֶם כֹּהֲנִים. מ"ט? [ב]חֲלוּצָה דְּרַבָּנַן הִיא, וּסְפֵק חֲלוּצָה — לָא גָּזְרוּ בְּהוּ רַבָּנַן. וַחֲלוּצָה דְּרַבָּנַן הִיא? וְהָתַנְיָא: *°"גְּרוּשָׁה", אֵין לִי אֶלָּא גְּרוּשָׁה, חֲלוּצָה מִנַּיִן? ת"ל "וְאִשָּׁה"! מִדְּרַבָּנַן הוּא, וּקְרָא אַסְמַכְתָּא בְּעָלְמָא הוּא.§

מתני' [ג]מִצְוָה בַּגָּדוֹל לְיַיבֵּם [ד]וְאִם קָדַם הַקָּטָן — זָכָה.§

גמ' ת"ר: °"וְהָיָה הַבְּכוֹר" — מִיכָּן שֶׁמִּצְוָה בַּגָּדוֹל לְיַיבֵּם, °"אֲשֶׁר תֵּלֵד" — *פְּרָט לְאַיְלוֹנִית שֶׁאֵין יוֹלֶדֶת, "יָקוּם עַל שֵׁם אָחִיו" — לְנַחֲלָה. אַתָּה אוֹמֵר [ה]לְנַחֲלָה, אוֹ אֵינוֹ אֶלָּא לְשֵׁם, יוֹסֵף — קוֹרִין אוֹתוֹ יוֹסֵף, יוֹחָנָן — קוֹרִין אוֹתוֹ יוֹחָנָן? נֶאֱמַר כָּאן "יָקוּם עַל שֵׁם אָחִיו" וְנֶאֱמַר לְהַלָּן °"עַל שֵׁם אֲחֵיהֶם יִקָּרְאוּ בְּנַחֲלָתָם", מַה "שֵּׁם" הָאָמוּר לְהַלָּן — נַחֲלָה, אַף "שֵׁם" הָאָמוּר כָּאן — לְנַחֲלָה. "וְלֹא יִמָּחֶה שְׁמוֹ" — [ו]פְּרָט לְסָרִיס, שֶׁשְּׁמוֹ מָחוּי. אָמַר רָבָא: אע"ג דְּבְכָל הַתּוֹרָה כּוּלָּהּ *אֵין מִקְרָא יוֹצֵא מִידֵי פְּשׁוּטוֹ, הָכָא אֲתַאי גְּזֵירָה שָׁוָה אַפְּקֵיהּ מִפְּשָׁטֵיהּ לְגַמְרֵי. וְאִי לָאו גְּזֵרָה שָׁוָה הֲוָה אָמִינָא "שֵׁם" שֵׁם מַמָּשׁ?! לְמַאן קָמַזְהַר רַחֲמָנָא, לְיָבָם — "יָקוּם עַל שֵׁם אָחִיךָ" מִיבְּעֵי לֵיהּ! אִי לְבֵי דִּינָא — "יָקוּם עַל שֵׁם אֲחִי אָבִיו" מִיבְּעֵי לֵיהּ! וְדִלְמָא הָכִי קָאָמַר לְהוּ רַחֲמָנָא לְבֵית דִּין: אִמְרוּ לֵיהּ לְיָבָם "יָקוּם עַל שֵׁם אָחִיו!". אֶלָּא, אֲתַאי גְּזֵרָה שָׁוָה אַפְּקֵיהּ לְגַמְרֵי. הַשְׁתָּא דְּאָמְרַתְּ קְרָא בְּגָדוֹל כְּתִיב, אֵימָא: בְּכוֹר — לְיַיבֵּם, פָּשׁוּט — לֹא לְיַיבֵּם. א"כ, אֵשֶׁת אָחִיו שֶׁלֹּא הָיָה בְּעוֹלָמוֹ דְּמִיעֵט רַחֲמָנָא — לָמָּה לִי? *פָּרֵיךְ רַב אַחָא: וְאֵימָא לְמַעוּטֵי בּוּכְרָא דְּאִמָּא! הַהוּא לָא מָצֵית אָמְרַתְּ, *דְּיִבּוּם בְּנַחֲלָה תָּלָה רַחֲמָנָא, [ז]וְנַחֲלָה מִן הָאָב וְלֹא מִן הָאֵם. וְאֵימָא: כִּי אִיכָּא בְּכוֹר תִּתְקַיֵּים מִצְוַת יִבּוּם, כִּי לֵיכָּא בְּכוֹר לָא תִּתְקַיֵּים מִצְוַת יִבּוּם! אָמַר קְרָא: "וּמֵת אֶחָד מֵהֶם", מִי לָא עָסְקִינַן דְּמִית בְּכוֹר, וְאָמַר רַחֲמָנָא לְיַיבֵּם קָטָן. וְאֵימָא דְּמִית קָטָן, וְאָמַר רַחֲמָנָא לְיַיבֵּם בְּכוֹר! הָא מִיעֵט רַחֲמָנָא אֵשֶׁת אָחִיו שֶׁלֹּא הָיָה בְּעוֹלָמוֹ. וְאֵימָא: כִּי לֵיכָּא בְּכוֹר — קָדַם קָטָן זָכָה, וְאִי אִיכָּא בְּכוֹר — קָדַם קָטָן לֹא זָכָה! אָמַר קְרָא: °"כִּי יֵשְׁבוּ אַחִים יַחְדָּו" — הוּקְשָׁה יְשִׁיבַת אַחִים זֶה לָזֶה. וְאֵימָא: כִּי אִיכָּא בְּכוֹר — לִיהֲדַר אַגָּדוֹל, כִּי לֵיכָּא בְּכוֹר — אֵין חוֹזְרִין אֵצֶל גָּדוֹל! אַלְמָה תָּנֵי אַבַּיֵי קַשִּׁישָׁא: *[ח]מִצְוָה בַּגָּדוֹל לְיַיבֵּם. לֹא רָצָה — הוֹלְכִים אֵצֶל אָחִיו הַקָּטָן, לֹא רָצָה — חוֹזְרִין אֵצֶל גָּדוֹל! כִּבְכוֹר, מַה בְּכוֹר — בְּכוֹרָתוֹ גָּרְמָה לוֹ, אַף גָּדוֹל — גְּדוּלָּתוֹ גָּרְמָה לוֹ. וְאֵימָא: כִּי מְיַיבֵּם בְּכוֹר — לִישְׁקוֹל נַחֲלָה, כִּי מְיַיבֵּם פָּשׁוּט לָא לִישְׁקוֹל נַחֲלָה! אָמַר קְרָא: "יָקוּם עַל שֵׁם אָחִיו" — וַהֲרֵי קָם. וְאֶלָּא בְּכוֹר דְּקַרְיֵיהּ רַחֲמָנָא — לְמַאי

רש"י

ואי למ"ד. טעמא משום דאסור לבטל מצות יבמין, ואי מייבם האי חדא – דלמא מיית אידך קודם שייבם, ותצא אחותה משום אחות אשה, ונמצא מצות יבמין בטלה על ידינו מיבום ומחליצה הרי נאסרה *משום כך, וכיון שנאסרה שעה אחת א"כ חלץ חד לחדא ואזלא האי השניה – עומדת היא באיסור אשת אח שלא נראית ליבום מתחלה. (א) **אבל הכא**, זו שנאסרה משום אחות זקוקה – לאו יבמה היתה, וכי פקע איסור אחות זקוקה בחליצת אחותה הרי זו מותרת ועומדת, דלאו אשת אח הואי, הלכך, מספיקא לא מפקינן לה, דאימר כל חד וחד דידיה איתרמיא ליה. **ואפילו שניהם כהנים.** וחד מנייהו ודאי חלוצה נסיב, דהא ארוסת הנכרי חלוצה היא מאחד משני אחיו, כדקתני: קדמו שניים וחלצו. **חלוצה.** דאסורה לכהן. **מדרבנן הוא.** והכא, דלכל חד אינה אלא ספק, דשמא זה ייבם את יבמתו גמורה – לא גזור רבנן לאפוקה מספק. **גרושה.** "מאישה לא יקחו". **מכאן שמצוה בגדול.** הכי דריש: "ולקחה לו לאשה ויבמה, והיה הבכור" – המייבם יהיה הבכור. **אשר תלד.** ואותה יבמה תהא ראויה לילד, פרט לאילונית. **יקום.** היבם על שם אחיו לנחול נחלתו, ולא יחלקו אחיו עמו. **אתה אומר לנחלה.** והאי "יקום" ביבם משתעי. **או אינו.** אלא בבן שיולד לו משתעי, שאם היה שם המת יוסי – קורין לזה יוסי. **אין מקרא יוצא מידי פשוטו.** ואע"ג דדרשינן ליה לדרשא – מידי פשוטו מיהו לא נפיק לגמרי. **ואפיקתיה לגמרי.** שאין צריך לקרות לבנו בשם אחיו המת, והכי גמר לה מרביה: ופרכינן ואי לאו גזרה שוה הוה **אמינא** שם ממש בתמיה. **ליבם.** קאמר רחמנא: בן הנולד לך יקום על שם אחיך, מיבעי ליה. **ואי לבית דין.** מודע רחמנא מצות קריית שם הבן. **יקום על שם אחי אביו מיבעי ליה.** אלא ודאי בייבם גופיה משתעי קרא, ולבית דין קאמר רחמנא, שיקום היבם על שם אחיו המת לנחלה. **אמרו לו ליבם.** שיקום בנו על שם אחיו. דכל מצות יבום קא מודע קרא לב"ד, וקאמר להו להזהיר יבמה לבא עליה, והבן אשר תלד לו יקימנו ע"ש אחיו. **אימא בכור.** דוקא קאמר קרא, אבל פשוט – לא לייבם לגמרי, בין איכא בכור בין ליכא בכור. **אם כן.** דפשוט לאו בר יבום הוא, למה לי דמיעט רחמנא אשת אחיו שלא היה בעולמו? תיפוק לי משום דלאו בכור הוא זה שנולד לאחר מיתת אחיו. **ואימא.** האי דמיעט אשת אחיו שלא היה בעולמו – כגון שהיה זה שנולד בכור לאמו ואחיו מאביו, ולהכי אצטריך למעוטי. **בנחלה תלה רחמנא.** ומצילא בכור הנוטל פי שנים הוא דמייבם, אבל בכור לאם – לא. ומדמעטיה – שמע מיניה בכור דקרא לאו דוקא, אלא גדול האחים. **ואימא כי איכא בכור כו'.** כלומר, דלמא לעולם בכור דוקא, והכי קאמר רחמנא: אי איכא בכור קמך – תתקיים מצות יבום או בבכור או בפשוט, דנפקא לן מדאימעיט אשת אחיו שלא היה בעולמו, וכי ליכא בכור – לא תתקיים, ופטורה לגמרי מן הפשוט. **ומת אחד מהם.** משמע שלא היו שם אלא שנים ומת אחד מהן. **מי לא עסקינן.** כלומר, מי לא משתמע נמי מקרא דמת בכור, וקאמר רחמנא לייבם פשוט. **ואימא.** על כרחך קרא דחיק ומתוקם כגון דמית פשוט, וקאמר רחמנא לייבם בכור. דהא כתיב "והיה הבכור". **הא מיעט רחמנא וכו'.** דהכא גבי תרי אחים כתיב מיעוט אשת אחיו שלא היה בעולמו, אלמא דמית גדול משמע, ותו ליכא בכור *קטן. **אימא כי ליכא בכור קדם הקטן זכה.** דהא לא רבי דלייבם פשוט אלא מ"ומת אחד מהם", ומיעוט דאשת אחיו שלא היה בעולמו, דמשמע דמת בכור ואמר רחמנא לייבם פשוט, אבל איכא בכור – לא לייבם פשוט. **הוקשה כו'.** שוין לייבם. **ליהדר אגדול.** אי לא בעו שאר אחיו – נחזור עליו לכופו, דמצוה עליה רמיא ולא על האחרים. אבל כי ליכא בכור – לא רמיא מצוה אגדול טפי משאר אחיו. **הולכין אצל אחיו הקטן.** משמע קטן הימנו, וגדול משאר אחיו, אלמא מהדרינן אגדול, דגדול קודם. ומדקתני חוזרין אצל גדול ליכא לאוקמי, דאיכא למימר: מאי גדול – בכור. דאי לא מצי לשנויי הכי, אדמותיב מדתני אביי – לותיב ממתניתין דקתני בפרק "החולץ" נמי: לא רצה חוזרין אצל גדול. **לא לישקול נחלה.** דהא "בכור" כתיב. אלא

תוספות

אי למ"ד יש זיקה. אר"י: אע"ג דלמ"ד יש זיקה ליכא למיגזר לייבם אחר חליצה משום דלמא אתי לייבם ברישא, כדמשמע בפרק "ד' אחין" (לקמן דף כז: ושם). גבי רבי יוחנן, דאמר: אחיות איני יודע מי שנאן. מ"מ ליכא למימר דליחלץ חד ולייבם חד, כיון דכל אחת נאסרה שעה אחת – אסורה עולמית, אפילו ראשונה, דלית ליה יבמה שהותרה ונאסרה וחזרה והותרה תחזור להתירה, אלא לר' יוחנן, לכך הוצרך לומר אחיות איני יודע מי שנאן. ולמ"ד אין זיקה, אף על גב דלרב דאמר אין זיקה לית ליה לקמן כיון שנאסרה שעה וכו' – מ"מ גזרינן דלא ליחלץ חד ולייבם חד אטו דלמא מייבם ברישא, דכיון דאין זיקה – אתי למטעי ולייבם ברישא, דהא לא מסקי אינשי אדעתייהו דלמא מית אידך. אבל הכא – כל חד וחד אמרינן אימא דידיה מתרמיא ליה, [וליכא למגזר דלמא מייבם ברישא, דאפילו מייבם ברישא אימא דידיה אתרמי ליה, וכי מייבם] שפיר עבד. ומשום מ"ד אין זיקה צריך לומר כל כך.

וספק חלוצה לא גזרו בהו רבנן. הקשה הר"ר משה ברבי יעקב מפיה"ס: דאמר ב"החולץ" (לקמן דף לו:), מת בתוך ל' יום, אם אשת ישראל היא חולצת, ואם אשת כהן היא אינה חולצת. ולמה לא תחלוץ, כיון דספק חלוצה מותרת לכהן? וי"ל דהתם שחולצת לאחר נשואין יאמרו קמו רבנן במילתא דנפל הוה, ולכך הוצרכו חליצה, ואתי למישרי חלוצה לכהן. אבל הכא, כל אחד כשכונס אמרי' קים ליה להאי דלאו חלוצה היא, ולכך כנסה*.

[ע"ש ד"ה הא ולקמן קיט. ד"ה ואם ועי' תוס' ב"ב קלח: ד"ה ולא]

או אינו אלא לשם. ויהא כוליה קרא כפשטיה, ולא נדרוש מבכור דמצוה בגדול לייבם, אלא ה"ק: והיה הבכור. פי': הראשון שתלד היבמה יקרא שמו בשם המת. ויליף בג"ש דלאו שם ממש קאמר אלא לנחלה, וכיון דלנחלה קאמר – ליכא לאוקומי קרא אלא ביבם. דאי על הבכור שתלד היבמה קאמר קרא שיקום על שם המת לנחלה, שאותו בכור יירש את המת – דאם כן יקום על שם אחי אביו מיבעי ליה, דהשתא לא שייך למימר דה"ק: "אמרו ליה ליבם". כדקאמ' בסמוך.

ה"ג ואם לא רצה הולכין אצל אחיו הקטן. פי': אצל קטן ממנו. לא רצה הולכים אצל אחיו – פירוש: שאר פשוטין קטנים ממנו. לא רצו – חוזרין אצל גדול. ויש ספרים דלא גרסי אלא הולכין אצל קטן, ותו לא. וצריך לומר דמשמע דקטן ממנו קאמר, מדלא נקט לישנא דמתני' ד"החולץ" (לקמן דף לט.): מהלכין על כל האחין.

למאי

סז א מיי' פ"ח מהלכות יבום הלכה ב סמג עשין כב טוש"ע אה"ע סימן קעו סעיף ג:
סח ב מיי' פ"א מהלכות אישות הל' ז ופי"ז מהל' איסורי ביאה הל"ז טוש"ע אה"ע סימן ו סעיף א:
סט ג מיי' פ"ב מהלכות יבום הלכה ו סמג עשין נא טור ש"ע אה"ע סימן קסא סע"ד:
ע ד מיי' שם טוש"ע שם סעיף ז:
עא ה מיי' פ"ג מהלכות נחלות הלכה ז סמג עשין נו טוש"ע אה"ע סימן קסג סעיף א:
עב ו מיי' פ"ו מהלכות יבום הלכה ב סמג עשין נא טוש"ע אה"ע סימן קעב סעיף א:
עג ז מיי' פ"א מהלכות נחלות הלכה ו סמג עשין נ טוש"ע ח"מ סי' רעו סעיף ד:
עד ח מיי' פ"ב מהלכות יבום הלכה ד סמג עשין נא טוש"ע אה"ע סימן קסא סעיף ד:

תוספות חד מקמאי

לשוק: **הא** דתני שילא אפי' שניהם כהנים דוקא כשקדמו וכנסו שאין מוציאין אותן מידן אפילו שניהם כהנים אבל לכתחלה לא שרינן אע"ג דחלוצה דרבנן שלא שרינן לכתחלה ואי קשיא הא דגרסינן בפ' החולץ מת בתוך ל' יום ועמדה ונתקדשה אם אשת כהן אינה חולצת ומסקנא משום דאיכא רבנן דפליגי עליה דרשב"ג דאמר אע"ג דלא שהה ולד מעליא הוא אשת כהן דלא אפשר עבדינן כרבנן משמע דלרשב"ג אם אשת כהן היא שמפקינן לה מיניה והא ספק חולצת [היא] איכא למימר שאני הכא שכבר חלצה וכבר כנסה כהן ומשום הכי לא מפקינן מיניה אע"פ שהוא כהן אבל התם לכתחלה הוא דאמר לא תחלוץ ותהוי לכהן והא א) בשלא אקדמו וכנסו קאי אבל לכתחלה לא ב) והתם אי שריא לה השתא לכתחלה למיחלץ אף על פי שהוא כנסה בלכתחלה ואיכא מ"ד שאני הכא שאחת מהן בודאי אינה חלוצה אף על פי שאחת מהן בודאי חלוצה ולאו מילתא היא דהא תינח כהן שני שנשא השניה אבל הראשון ספק חלוצה נשא אמאי לא מפקינן מיניה וכי משום דנסב שני שרי לראשון דאי לא נסב שני הראשון ודאי ספק חלוצה נשא אלא ודאי כדפרישית: **תני** אביי קשישא מצוה בגדול לייבם לא רצה לייבם הולכין אצל קטן אלא בכור דקרייה רחמנא למאי הלכתא מה בכור אינו נוטל בראוי כבמוחזק אף יבם אינו נוטל בראוי

א) נ"ל והא דהכא בשאקדמו וכנסו קאי כו'. ב) אין הלשון מדוקדק ואולי נ"ל והתם אי שרינן לה השתא למחלץ אע"פ שהוא כנסה אתי ג"כ למחלץ ולכנוס אותה לכתחלה ואיכא מ"ד כו'.

מסורת הש"ס: משום כך ושוב אין לה היתר אפילו בדיעבד כל"ל רש"ל
[לעיל יח. וש"נ]
קדושין עח.
לעיל יב.
[לעיל יח: שבת סג.]
[קדושין יג. וש"נ]
[לעיל יז: כ.]
בילה לו. לקמן לט.
אולי נ"ל קמן

הגהות הב"ח
(א) רש"י ד"ה ואי למ"ד וכו' מתחלה מדרבנן אבל הכא זו וכו' וכי פקע איסור אחות זקוקה ביבום אחותה:

תורה אור

למאי הלכתא? לגריעותא, אמה בכור אינו נוטל בראוי כבמוחזק – אף האי אינו נוטל בראוי כבמוחזק.§ **מתני'** *בהנטען על השפחה ונשתחררה, או על הגויה ונתגיירה, הרי זה לא יכנוס. ואם כנס – אין מוציאין מידו. הנטען על אשת איש והוציאוה מתחת ידו, אע"פ שכנס – יוציא.§ **גמ'** הא גיורת מיהא הויא, ורמינהי: אחד איש שנתגייר לשום אשה, ואחד אשה שנתגיירה לשום איש, וכן מי שנתגייר לשום שולחן מלכים, לשום עבדי שלמה – אינן גרים, דברי ר' נחמיה. שהיה רבי נחמיה אומר: אחד *גירי אריות ואחד גירי חלומות, ואחד גירי מרדכי ואסתר – אינן גרים עד שיתגיירו בזמן הזה. בזמן הזה ס"ד?! אלא, אימא: כבזמן הזה. הא איתמר עלה, א"ר יצחק בר שמואל בר מרתא משמיה דרב: גהלכה כדברי האומר כולם גרים הם. אי הכי לכתחלה נמי! משום דרב אסי, *דאמר רב אסי: °"הסר ממך עקשות פה ולזות שפתים וגו'". (משלי ד) ת"ר: *אין מקבלין גרים לימות המשיח. כיוצא בו *דלא קבלו גרים לא בימי דוד ולא בימי שלמה. א"ר *אליעזר: מאי קרא – °"הן גור יגור אפס מאותי מי גר אתך עליך יפול" (ישעיה נד) (א) אבל אידך – לא.§ "הנטען על אשת איש וכו'".§ אמר רב: ובעדים. אמר רב ששת: *אמינא כי ניים ושכיב רב אמר להאי שמעתתא. דתניא: *ההנטען על אשת איש *והוציאוה על ידו, ונתגרשה מתחת ידי אחר, אם כנס – לא יוציא. ה"ד, אי דאיכא עדים – פי אתא אחר ואפסקיה לקלא מאי הוי? אלא לאו דליכא עדים, וטעמא, דאתא אחר ואפסקיה לקלא, הא לאו הכי – מפקינן! אמר לך רב: הוא הדין דאע"ג דלא אתא אחר ואפסקיה לקלא. אי איכא עדים – מפקינן, אי ליכא עדים – לא מפקינן, והכי קאמר: דאע"ג דאתא אחר ואפסקיה לקלא – לכתחלה לא יכנוס. מיתיבי: ובד"א – כשאין לה בנים, אבל יש לה בנים – לא תצא. זואם באו עדי טומאה – אפילו יש לה כמה בנים תצא. רב מוקי לה למתניתין ביש לה בנים ויש לה עדים. ומאי דוחקיה דרב לאוקמי למתניתין ביש לה בנים ויש לה עדים, וטעמא דאיכא עדים – מפקינן, ואי ליכא עדים – לא מפקינן, לוקמה בשאין לה בנים, אע"ג דליכא עדים? אמר רבא: מתניתין קשיתיה: מאי איריא דתני "הוציאוה", ליתני הוציאה, אלא, כל "הוציאוה" בבית דין, ובית דין – בעדים הוא דמפקי. ואי בעית אימא: הני מתנייתא – רבי היא, דתניא: חרוכל יוצא ואשה חוגרת בסינר, אמר רבי: הואיל ומכוער הדבר – תצא. רוק למעלה מן הכילה, אמר רבי: הואיל ומכוער הדבר – תצא.

מנעלים

רש"י

אלא למאי הלכתא קרייה בכור. ליכתוב גדול. **בכור אינו נוטל.** חלק בכורה בנחלה הראויה לבא להם אחר מיתת אביהן, אלא במה שמוחזק ביד אביהן ביום מותו, דכתיב "בכל אשר ימצא לו" (דברים כא), אף יבם הנוטל פי שנים [א] בנכסי אביו – חלקו וחלק אחיו שמת [ב] – אינו נוטל בראוי כבמוחזק. **מתני'** הנטען. חשוד, כלומר: שטוענים עליו דברי לעז. **לא ישאנה.** משום לעז, שלא יאמרו: אמת היה הקול הראשון. **הנטען על אשת איש והוציאוה.** בית דין מתחת בעלה בשביל זה שאסרה עליו, והלך זה ונשאה. **יוציא.** דמדאורייתא אסורה נמי לבועל, דדרשינן "ונטמאה" "ונטמאה" (במדבר ה) שני פעמים, אחד לבעל ואחד לבועל, במסכת סוטה (דף כז:). **גמ' הא גיורת מיהא הויא.** ואע"ג דלא נתגיירה לשם יהדות, אלא בשביל שישאנה זה. **עבדי שלמה.** בעלי שררה היו. **גירי אריות.** °כגון כותים, דכתיב בספר מלכים (ב' יז) "וישלח ה' בהם את האריות" ונתגיירו, כדכתיב התם בגלות שומרון. **גירי חלומות.** בעל חלומות אמר להם להתגייר. **מרדכי ואסתר.** "ורבים מעמי הארץ מתיהדים" (אסתר ח). **בזמן הזה ס"ד.** כל הני מקמי הכי לאו גרים נינהו? כגון נבוזראדן וכיוצא בו. **כבזה"ז.** שלא יעשה מחמת שררה. **אי הכי.** דגיורת מעלייתא היא. **לכתחלה נמי.** יכנוס, ואמאי תני לא יכנוס? **דאמר רב אסי.** טעמא דמתניתין משום דכתיב "הסר ממך עקשות פה ולזות שפתים הרחק ממך", דאתו לאחזוקי לקלא קמא. **הן גור.** הבא להתגייר, "יגור אפס מאותי" – בעוד שאין אני עמכם יתגייר, דהיינו בזמן הזה. **מי גר אתך עליך יפול.** מי גר אתך בעניותך כאשר אמרת. **עליך יפול.** לעוה"ב. יפול = ינוח, כמו "על פני כל אחיו נפל" (בראשית כה) "יפול מצדך אלף" (תהלים צא). **ובעדים.** הא דתנן יוציא זה החשוד שכנסה – כגון שבאו עדים על קול הראשון, שראוה שנייחדה עמו. **להא שמעתתא.** בעדים. **כי ניים ושכיב רב אמרה דתניא.** תיובתא. **ונתגרשה מתחת ידי אחר.** ראובן נטען על דינה אשת שמעון, וגירשה שמעון ונשאה נחשון, וגירשה. אם כנסה ראובן מעתה – לא יוציא. **אי דאיכא עדים.** בזנות קמא – הרי נאסרה עולמית עליו. **ה"ה דאפילו דלא אפסיק אחר לקלא.** וכנסה ראובן מגירושי שמעון לא תצא, הואיל וליכא עדים. והא דנקט מתחת ידי אחר – היא גופה איצטריך לאשמועינן רבותא, דלכתחלה לא יכנוס, כדקתני: אם כנס – אין, לכתחלה – לא. **במה דברים אמורים.** דאם כנס הנטען יוציא – כשאין לה בנים מן הראשון. **אבל יש לה בנים.** מן הראשון – לא תצא. דכי מפקי לה – קא מחזקינן לקלא קמא, ועבדינן להו ממזרים. **ואם באו כו'.** אלמא אין לה בנים – בלא עדים נמי מפקינן. **רב מוקי למתניתין ביש** לה בנים. ומש"ה אמר רב: ובעדים. וב"ד בעדים הוא דמפקי. מבעל ראשון, דאין אשה נאסרת לבעלה משום קול. ואתא רב למימר: דוקא מתני' משום כך יוציא הנטען, הואיל ואיכא עדים. אבל בלא עדים, הואיל ויש לה בנים – לא. **ואבע"א.** בלא בנים לא נפקא בלא עדים, והני מתניתא דאמרי נפקא – ר' אמרינהו, דמפיק אשה מבעלה בקול כל דהו. **רוכל.** מוכר בשמים לנשים להתקשט בהן. **רוכל יוצא.** מן הבית, ומצא זה את אשתו שהיא חוגרת בסינר – מכוער הדבר, שלא התירתו מעליה אלא לזנות. **סינר.** הוא כעין מכנסים, שהיו הנשים חוגרות לצניעות. **רוק למעלה מן הכילה.** ארוכל יוצא קאי, ומצא בעל רוק למעלה בגג הכילה שעל מטתו, מי זרק הרוק למעלה – כ"א השוכב ופניו למעלה, הלכך זינתה זו, ורקקה בשעת תשמיש.

מנעלים

תוספות

למאי הלכתא לגריעותא. פר"י: דהוי מצי למימר לחשיבותא, שאין ירושתו חוזרת ביובל*. **גיורת** מיהא הויא. דמשמע לא יכנוס הוא, אבל אחר – שרי לכנוס לכתחלה. **הלכה** כדברי האומר כולם גרים הם. (ב) הך גירי אריות לא דמי להא דאיכא מ"ד כותים גירי אריות הן, דהתם היו עובדים אלהיהם, כדכתיב בספר מלכים. ולמ"ד גירי אמת הן – קסבר דשוב נתגיירו לגמרי*. **אי** הכי לכתחלה נמי. אי אמרת בשלמא דאינה גיורת גמורה – ניחא דלכתחלה לא יכנוס, משום דספק גיורת היא, דשמא נתגיירה לשם איש. ודיעבד אין להוציא, דאין להחמיר משום חששא זו. **משום** דרב אסי הסר ממך עקשות פה כו'. פר"י: דבנטען על הפנויה אין להחמיר מלכנוס משום לזות שפתים, דאדרבה: מלוה לכונסה, דאנוסה כתיב "ולו תהיה לאשה" (דברים כב). **לא** בימי דוד ולא בימי שלמה. (ג) מאיתי הגיתי *ובת פרעה דבימי שלמה לא קשה, דמידי הוא טעמא – אלא משום שולחן מלכים, והני לא צריכי. אבל קשה, דאמרינן ב"הערל" (לקמן דף עט. ושם) גבי מעשה דגבעונים דבימי דוד נתוספו גרים על ישראל ק"ן אלף! וי"ל: דמעצמן נתגיירו, כדאשכחן גבי מרדכי ואסתר "ורבים מעמי הארץ מתיהדים". ויש ספרים שכתב בהן: לא קבלו גרים לא בימי דוד ולא בימי שלמה, אלא שנעשו גרים גרורים. וההיא דפ"ב דשבת (דף לא.) ההוא דאתא לקמיה דהלל ואמר: גיירני ע"מ לעשות כ"ג – בטוח היה הלל דסופו לעשות לשם שמים. וכן ההיא ד"התכלת" (מנחות מד.) דאתיא לקמיה דרבי: גיירני ע"מ שאנשא לאותו תלמיד. **אמר** רבי הואיל ומכוער הדבר תצא. פר"ת: דתצא מן הרוכל אם נשאת לו, דכל הסוגיא איירי בנטען. דאין לומר תצא מן הבעל – דאין האשה נאסרת על בעלה אלא על ידי קנוי וסתירה, *או שיראו(ד) דרך מנאפין. (כתובות ט.) ועוד: דלגבי בעל הוי קלא דבתר נשואין, דאמר(ה) ב"האשה רבה" (לקמן דף כה. ושם) דלקלא דלבתר נשואין לא חיישינן. °ורוק למעלה בגג הכילה לא עדיף מקלא דלא פסיק, דהא בסמוך אמר דלרבי מפקינן אפי' בקלא דפסיק מכח הך ברייתא. אלא ודאי תצא מן הרוכל אם נשאה. דרוק למעלה בגג הכילה הוי קלא דקמי נישואי רוכל. וכן פר"ת. וכן נראה לר"י, דמתוך ההלכה משמע דאין מוציאין ע"י קול מבעלה, דקאמר: ובית דין בעדים הוא דמפקי. משמע דדבר פשוט הוא דמבעל לא מפקי' אלא בעדים, אע"ג דמנטען קתני בברייתא דמפקי בקול. [אף דקתני הוציאוה הדר רב נחמן דבסמוך הוציאה תנן. דמשמע על ידי בעלה – אפ"ה מבעלה לא מפקינן על ידי קול] באין בנים מן הראשון. והא דאיצטרי' בהנהו עודדי דסוף נדרים (דף צ:) להנהו

טעמי

מכוער אבל מבעל לא מפקינן אלא בעדים ומסתברא כותיה דהא גמרי' דבר דבר מממון מה להלן דבר ברור ולא באמתלא אף כאן דבר ברור ולא באמתלא ולא בדבר מכוער. ובמס' סוטה איבעיא לן עוברת על דת משה ויהודית אם רשאי הבעל לקיימה או לא ולא איפשיטא ומיהו מעוברת על דת ליכא ראיה דהתם [אין] עדים בדבר מכוער של זנות אלא לדבר מכוער של חוצפא ומש"ה איבעי לן אם רשאי הבעל לקיימה ואפילו תימא דבדבר

עין משפט נר מצוה

[ועוד לזה כתבו תוס' בכורות נב: ד"ה בכור]

עה א מיי' פ"ג מהל' נחלות הלכה א סמג עשין צו טוש"ע אה"ע סימן קסג סעיף א:

[וע"ע תוספות חולין ג: ד"ה קסבר]

עו ב מיי' פי"ג מהלכות גירושין הלכה יד סמג עשין נ טור ש"ע אה"ע סימן יא סעיף ה:

עז ג מיי' פי"ג מהל' איסורי ביאה הלכה יד סמג לאוין קטז טוש"ע י"ד סימן רסח סעיף יב:

עח ד מיי' שם הל' טו:

עט ה מיי' פ"ב מהל' סוטה הל' יג טור ש"ע אה"ע סי' יא סע"ב:

[וזה שהתעוררו התוספות מבת פרעה שקיבלה שלמה למידי הוא טעמא אלא משום שולחן מלכים חיזוק קצת מכל זה לשון הר"ן מבואר להדיא בש"ס לקמן עו ע"א מתיב רב יוסף וכו' והא לא קבלו וכו' מידי הוא טעמא וכו']

פ ו שם סעיף ח:

פא ז מיי' שם הלכה טז וטוש"ע שם סעיף ב:

פב ח מיי' פכ"ד מהל' אישות הלכה טו ופ"ב מהל' סוטה הלכה יג טוש"ע שם סעיף ח:

[תוספתא פ"ד]

[נ"ל דרבי חייא]

תוספות חד מקמאי

כבמוחזק: **תניא** אחד איש שנתגייר לשום אשה ואחד אשה שנתגיירה לשום איש וכן מי שנתגייר לשום שולחן מלכים לשום עבדי שלמה אינם גרים דברי רבי נחמיה שהיה ר"נ אומר אחד גרי אריות ואחד גרי חלומות ואחד גרי מרדכי ואסתר אינם גרים עד שיתגיירו שנית ואע"ג דכותים אליבא דמ"ד גרי אריות הן גוים גמורים הן התם לא נתגיירו לגמרי כדכתיב את ה' היו יראים ואת אלהיהם היו עובדים אבל (התם) [הכא] שנתגיירו לגמרי הלכה כולן גרים הן רבינו יעקב ז"ל: **תניא** בד"א שתצא כשאין לה בנים אבל כשיש לה בנים לא תצא. הרב אלפס פירש כשיש לה בנים מן הנטען ור"ש פי' כשיש לה בנים מן הבעל והר"ב כתב כשיש לה בנים מן הבעל לא תצא והא דתניא רוכל יוצא ואשה חוגרת בסינר ואמר רבי הואיל וקיי"ל כותיה בקלא דלא פסיק לבוארה נראה דאבעל קאי וכן נראה מפי' רש"י ז"ל דבדבר מבוער מפקינן לה מבעלה והר"ר אלפס כתב כל דהוא נטען מפקינן מיניה בדבר מבוער אבל מבעל לא

מסורת הש"ס

[לקמן כה: ע"ש]

[קדושין עה: ב"ק לח: סנהדרין פה: חולין ג: נדה נו:]

כתובות כב: [עי' תוס' שם]

[ע"ז ג:]

[לקמן טו.]

[נ"ל אלעזר]

[לקמן לז. קט: ב"ק מז: סה. בכורות כג: נדה ס.]

[נ"ל והוציאוה וכ"כ רש"א]

הגהות הב"ח

(א) גמ' מי גר אתך עליך יפול מי גר אתך בעניותך הוא דעליך יפול אבל אידך לא: (ב) תוס' ד"ה הלכה כדברי האומר כולם גרים הם ואפי' גירי אריות הך גירי אריות: (ג) ד"ה לא וכו' מאיתי הגיתי. נ"ב עיין בפרק בתרא דקדושין דף עו: (ד) ד"ה אמר וכו' או שיראו אותם כדרך המנאפים: (ה) בא"ד באשה רבה. נ"ב דף כה. ועי"ש בתוס' ד"ה כל קלא:

הגהות הגר"א

[א] רש"י ד"ה בכור כו' אף יבם הנוטל כו'. נ"ב אבל ר"ת פי' שאין נוטל חלק אחיו אלא אם מת אחיו קודם לאביו (ועמ"ש ברבינו באה"ע סימן קסג סק"ד): [ב] שם וחלק אחיו שמת. נ"ב חלקו שמת:

גליון הש"ס

רש"י ד"ה גירי אריות כגון כותים. עי' סנהדרין פה ע"ב ברש"י ד"ה גירי אריות: תוס' ד"ה לא בימי דוד וכו' לסופו לעשות לש"ש. עי' לקמן קט ע"ב תד"ה ולעולם: ד"ה אמר רבי כו' ורוק למעלה בגג כו'. עיין לקמן דף כה ע"א תד"ה כל קלא:

מנעלים הפוכים. פיהן למטה, ודאי של נכרי הם, והפכו כדי שלא יכיר הרואה. מקום מנעלים הפוכים. ניכר מקום הפיכתן בעפר שתחת המטה, לשון מורי. לשון אחר: מקום מנעלים מנא הפוך, שבא ומנא את מנעליה במקום שהוא רגיל לתת שלו – ודאי נכרי בא לכאן, ושם מנעליו במקום שלה ושלה במקום בעל. תורה אור

מנעלים הפוכים תחת המטה, אמר רבי: הואיל ומכוער הדבר – תצא. מנעלים הפוכים? ליחזי דמאן נינהו! אלא: מקום מנעלים הפוכים (תחת המטה א"ר: הואיל ומכוער הדבר – תצא). [א]והלכתא כוותיה דרב, [ב]והלכתא כוותיה דרבי. קשיא הלכתא אהלכתא! לא קשיא: [ג]הא – בקלא דפסיק, הא – בקלא דלא פסיק. קלא דלא פסיק וליכא עדים – כרבי, קלא דפסיק ואיכא עדים – כרב. וקלא דלא פסיק עד כמה? *אמר אביי, [ד]אמרה לי אם: דומי דמתא יומא ופלגא. ולא אמרן אלא דלא פסק ביני וביני, אבל פסק ביני וביני – הא פסק. ולא אמרן אלא דלא פסק מחמת יראה, אבל פסק מחמת יראה – מחמת יראה הוא. *ולא אמרן אלא דליכא אויבים, אבל איכא אויבים – אויבים הוא דאפקו ליה לקלא. *תנן התם: [ה]המוציא את אשתו משום שם רע – לא יחזיר. משום נדר – לא יחזיר. שלח ליה רבה בר *הונא לרבה בר ר"נ: ילמדנו רבינו, כנס מהו שיוציא? א"ל, תנינא: הנטען על אשת איש והוציאה מתחת ידו, אע"פ שכנס יוציא. א"ל: מי דמי? התם "הוציאוה" והכא "הוציאה"! ורבה בר ר"נ – מתניתין נמי "הוציאה" תנן. ואכתי מי דמי? הכא – בעל, והתם – בועל! א"ל: שפיר דמי אהדדי: הכא אמור רבנן [ו]לא יכנוס, ואם כנס יוציא – ה"נ אמרי רבנן לא יחזיר, ואם כנס – יוציא. ולא היא, התם – אלומי אלמיה לקלא, הכא אמרינן קם ביה בקלא וליתיה.§ **מתני'** [ז]המביא גט ממדינת הים ואמר "בפני נכתב ובפני נחתם" לא ישא את אשתו. "מת", "הרגתיו", "הרגנוהו" – לא ישא את אשתו. רבי יהודה אומר "הרגתיו" – לא תנשא אשתו, "הרגנוהו" – תנשא אשתו.§ **גמ'** טעמא דממדינת הים – דעליה קסמכינן, אבל מא"י, דלאו עליה קסמכינן, ישא את אשתו, והא מת, דלאו עליה קסמכינן, דאמר מר: *אשה דייקא ומינסבא, וקתני: לא ישא את אשתו! התם ליכא כתבא, הכא – איכא כתבא. דתנן: *מה בין גט למיתה – שהכתב מוכיח.§ "מת", "הרגתיו", "הרגנוהו" – לא ישא את אשתו.§ הוא ניהו דלא ישא את אשתו, [ח]הא לאחר – תנשא. *והאמר רב יוסף: [ט]"פלוני רבעני לאונסי" – הוא ואחר מצטרפין להרגו. "לרצוני" – רשע הוא, [י]והתורה אמרה: °"אל תשת ידך עם רשע להיות עד חמס". וכ"ת שאני עדות אשה דאקילו בה רבנן – והא"ר מנשה: גזלן

רש"י

ראשון עיקר, דא"כ הפוך מיבעי ליה. והלכתא כוותיה דרב. דאמר: אין מחזיקין קלא אלא בעדים. דפסיק. שיצא קול אחר, לומר: שקר הוא הלעז. דומי מתא. חשודי העיר. ל"א: דומי – דלא ידעי ודאי, אלא אמרי בדדמי, לשון מורי. משום נדר לא יחזיר. וטעמא מפרש התם ב"השולח גט": שאם אותה אומר יחזיר, שמא תלך זו אצל חכם לאחר שניסת, ויתיר לה נדרה, ויאמר המגרש: אילו הייתי יודע שיש היתר לנדר שנדרה, אם היו נותנים לי מאה מנה לא הייתי מגרשה, שהיתה חביבה עלי ביותר, ונמצא זה מבטל גיטו למפרע ועוקרו, ובניה מן השני ממזרים. לפיכך אומרים לו מתחלה: הוי יודע שהמוציא את אשתו משום נדר שנדרה – לא יחזיר עולמית, ואם היא חביבה עליך – לא ובקש היתר לנדרה. ואי מגרש לה מהשתא – ודאי שנואה היא עליו, ותו לא מצי עקר (לה) גיטה בדברי שקר. ומשום שם רע. שיצא עליה לא יחזיר, כדפרישית טעמא: שמא תנשא לאחר, ויצא קול על הלעז הראשון ששקר היה, ויתחרט המגרש, ויאמר: אילו הייתי יודע שכן הוא כו'. כנס מהו שיוציא. אם החזירה, מהו שכופין להוציא? תנינא הנטען כו'. והתם נמי מפקיעה מבעלה, דכיון דהוציאה משום שם רע – גילה דעתו שהקול אמת ונאסרה לו, כי היכי דאסרינן לה הכא משום שהחזיק זה הקול כשכנסה. התם הוציאוה. ב"ד, שבאו עדי טומאה ואסורה לבועל מה"ת. הכא הוציאה. והאי דלא יחזיר – דרבנן הוא. ורבה בר נחמן מתני' נמי הוציאה תנן. בלא עדים, הלכך לא אסורה לבועל אלא משום לזות שפתים מדרבנן, ואפ"ה קתני: יוציא. ואכתי מי דמי הכא בעל. החזירה, ואין דבר זה מגונה הוא. התם בועל. כונס, ודבר מגונה הוא. א"ל שפיר דמי להדדי. הכא והכא מדרבנן הוא. ולא היא התם. הוא כשכנס בועל – אלומי אלמיה לקול הראשון, שאמת היה הלעז. אבל הכא, כשהחזירה בעל – בטולי בטליה לקלא, דאמרינן: מדהחזירה – קים ליה בקלא, חזר ובדק בקול ראשון של שם רע, ומצא שאינו. **מתני'** המביא גט ממדינת הים. צריך שיאמר "בפני נכתב ובפני נחתם". וטעמא מפרש בגיטין (דף ב.): לפי שאין בקיאים לשמה. לא ישא את אשתו. הואיל ואדיבוריה סמכינן. מת הרגתיו הרגנוהו לא ישא אשתו. הואיל ועל עדותו היא נשאת – איכא לזות שפתים, שמא עיניו נתן בה והעיד שקר. אבל לאחר – תנשא, דאשה נשאת בעד אחד. ר' יהודה אומר הרגתיו לא תנשא אשתו. אפי' לאחר על פיו, לפי שהוא משים עצמו רשע, והתורה אמרה "אל תשת רשע עד". הרגנוהו תנשא אשתו. לאחר, ובגמרא בעי טעמא.

גמ' אבל מארץ ישראל. המביא גט מארץ ישראל אין צריך לומר "בפני נכתב ובפני נחתם". והא מת דלא עילויה סמכינן. דכי אמר מת בעל, הא דשרו רבנן לאינסובי לאחר – לא עליה סמכינן. דאמר מר. בפרק "האשה" רבה (לקמן דף צג:) היינו טעמא דעד אחד נאמן להשיא אשה, משום דהיא גופה דייקא, עד שיודעת שמת ודאי, ואחר כך נשאת. מה בין גט למיתה. ב"המביא" (וכן לקמן דף קיז.) תנן: אף הנשים שאינן נאמנות לומר מת בעלה, כגון חמותה ויבמתה וצרתה ובת בעלה, נאמנות להביא גיטה, ואף על פי שצריכות לומר "בפני נכתב ובפני נחתם". ומה בין גט למיתה – אלא שהכתב מוכיח, ולאו עלה סמכינן כל כך. פלוני רבעני לאונסי כו' להורגו. את הרובע.

תוספות

טעמי דאיתתא שריא, דאם איתא דעבד איסורא – אירכוסי הוי מירכס, ואם איתא דעבד איסורא – ניחא ליה דליכול. נראה לר"י דהתם באומרת טמאה אני, כי מתני' דהתם דעלה קאי, ואפ"ה שריא מהנהו טעמי. אבל באומרת טהורה אני – שריא בלאו הנהו טעמי דהתם. ואין לתמוה: אמאי שריא כיון שאומרת טמאה, הא שויתה לנפשה חתיכה דאיסורא! דלפי שראו חכמים שנתקלקלו הנשים ליתן עיניהם באחר, ורוב האומרות כן משקרות, לכך נראה להם להתירן*. **הא** בקלא דפסיק. ומיהו, רב גופיה אית ליה ל"ש קלא דפסיק ול"ש קלא דלא פסיק. **ואכתי** מי דמי. בספרים ישנים לא גרסי ליה, אלא גרסי: ורבה בר (א) נחמן הוציאה תני. הכא בעל והכא *בועל, הכא אמור רבנן וכו' ועד ולא היא חד שינויא הוא. והכי פירושו: ורבה ב"ר נחמן הוציאה תני, וכיון דתני הוציאה, והכא בעל והכא בועל הוציאה ולא בית דין. ואפ"ה קתני במתני' "ואם כנס – יוציא", ה"ה דהתם בגיטין (דף מה:) נמי אם כנס מוציא. ויפה פשיט רבה ב"ר נחמן, ומסיק "ולא היא כו' קם ביה בקלא דליתיה". ומה שאסור להחזיר אינו משום שסבורים העולם שאסורה לו משום שם רע, דהא סברי דקם ביה בקלא דליתיה, אלא משום קלקול או משום פריצות, כדאמרינן בגיטין. וקשיא לר"י: דהיאך היה מדמה אותה רבה ב"ר נחמן? וכי לא היה יודע טעם זה, דבהדיא מפרש להנהו טעמי ב"השולח" (גיטין דף מו.) בברייתא! וי"ל: דלא שמיע ליה. א"נ, אומר ר"י, דרבה ב"ר נחמן יודע טעמי דקלקול ופריצות, אבל סובר דכנס יוציא מפני שהעולם אין יודעים הטעם דקלקולא ופריצות, אלא סוברים שמחמת שם רע אסורה לו כיון שגירשה ע"י כן. ולכך, אם כנס – יוציא משום רננה, כמתניתין דהכא. ומסיק: ולא היא, שיטעו העולם בזה, כי יש חילוק גדול בין מתני' דהכא למתני' דהתם – דהכא אלמיה לקלא כו'. **הכא** איכא כתבא דתנן מה בין גט כו'. ואע"ג דלאביי בסוף פ"ב דגיטין (דף כג:) איירי הך משנה בח"ל – מ"מ דייק שפיר מינה דיש לסמוך על הכתב. **מת** הרגתיו הרגנוהו. כיון דאפילו במת לא ישא את אשתו לא הוה צריך למיתני "הרגנוהו", ואפילו בהרגתיו לאחר תנשא, ולא תני ליה אלא משום דר' יהודה מפליג בין הרגתיו להרגנוהו: **הוא** ואחר מצטרפים להורגו. הקשה הר"ר חיים: דבסוף פ"ק דמכות (דף ו. ושם) פריך: הרוג ונרבע יצילו! משמע דהרוג ונרבע פסולים להעיד משום שונא, והכא משמע דכשר! וי"ל: דלא משום שונא פסול נרבע התם, אלא בנרבע לרצונו איירי, ומשום רשע פסול. אפילו לרבא דבסמוך, דסובר דלרצונו נמי כשר – מכל מקום, כשיש עדים שנרבע לרצונו – הוי כנמצא אחד מהן קרוב או פסול. וכי פריך בתר הכי הורג ורובע יציל – פי': יצילו על עצמם, הוה מצי למינקט נרבע דקאי ביה, כיון דאיירי בנרבע לרצונו, אלא משום

פג א ב ג ד מיי' פ"כ מהלכות סוטה הלכה יג יד טוש"ע אה"ע סי' יא סעיף א:
פד ה מיי' פי"ב מהל' גירושין הלכה יב סמג עשין נ' טוש"ע אה"ע סימן י סעיף ג:
פה ו מיי' שם טוש"ע שם סעיף ו:
[וע' טיב תוס' כתובות סג: ד"ה אבל]
פו ז מיי' פ"י מהלכות גירושין הלכה יד טוש"ע אה"ע סימן יב סעיף א:
ס"א בעל
פז ח מיי' פי"ג מהל' גירושין הלכה י טוש"ע אה"ע סימן יז סעיף ז:
פח ט מיי' פי"ב מהל' עדות הלכה ב סמג לאוין ריד טוש"ע ח"מ סימן לד סעיף כו:
פט י מיי' שם פ"י הל' א סמג לאוין ריד טוש"ע ח"מ סימן לד סעיף א:

תוספות חד מקמאי
דבדבר מבוער של זנות מפקינן מבעל בדבר מכוער דחוצפא לא מפקינן והתם אסיקנא דלהפסידה כתובתה צריכה התראה אבל אי הדרא בה תהדר: **תנן** התם המוציא [את] אשתו משום שם רע משום נדר לא יחזיר ואיבעי לן כנס מהו שיוציא ואסיק' אינו מוציא ולא דמי למתני' דנטען דהתם כיון דנסבה נטען אלומי אלמה לקליה הכא אמר קם ביה בקלא וליתא איכא מ"ד (מיהא) דהא מילתא אליבא דלישנא בתרא הוא דקסבר טעמא מאי שלא יהיו בנות ישראל פרוצין בערוות ובנדרים אבל ללישנא קמא דסבר טעמא דמילתא משום קלקולא אם אינו מוציא כ"ש דאיכא קלקולא וכיון דקי"ל כלישנא קמא אם כנס מוציא וכ"כ הראב"ד ז"ל ואני אומר כיון א) דאמרו לה בשעת קדושין המוציא אשתו משום ש"ר לא יחזיר (עלמא) [לעולם] לא אפשר למיהוי בה קלקולא והלכך אם כנס אינו מוציא. וכן נראה מדברי הג' אלפס שפסק כלישנא קמא דאמר דמשום קלקולא הוא ופסק דכנס אינו מוציא:
א) נראה דצ"ל כיון דאמרי' ליה בשעת גירושין דהמוציא אשתו וכו'.

רס"ל מ"ז
מ"ק יח.
[עי' היטב במ"ק יח.]
גיטין מה: כתובות עב:
ב הונא כל"ל. יעב"ץ.
לקמן נג: קטו. קטז:
לקמן קיז. גיטין כג:
סנהדרין ט:
שמות כג

הגהות הב"ח
תוס' ד"ה ואכתי וכו' גרסי' ורבה בר רב נחמן הוציאה:

אגַּזְלָן דִּדְבָרֵיהֶם — כָּשֵׁר לְעֵדוּת אִשָּׁה, גַּזְלָן דְּדִבְרֵי תוֹרָה — פָּסוּל לְעֵדוּת אִשָּׁה. נֵימָא רַב מְנַשֶּׁה דְּאָמַר כְּרַ' יְהוּדָה? אָמַר לָךְ רַב מְנַשֶּׁה: אֲנָא דַּאֲמַרִי אֲפִילּוּ לְרַבָּנַן, וְטַעְמָא דְּרַבָּנַן הָכָא — כִּדְרָבָא, דְּאָמַר רָבָא: *באָדָם קָרוֹב אֵצֶל עַצְמוֹ, וְאֵין אָדָם מֵשִׂים עַצְמוֹ רָשָׁע. לֵימָא רַב יוֹסֵף דְּאָמַר כְּרַבִּי יְהוּדָה?! אָמַר לָךְ רַב יוֹסֵף: אֲנָא דַּאֲמַרִי אֲפִי' לְרַבָּנַן, וְשָׁאנֵי עֵדוּת אִשָּׁה דְּאַקִילוּ בָּהּ רַבָּנַן, וְרַב מְנַשֶּׁה דְּאָמַר כְּרַבִּי יְהוּדָה.§ "הֲרַגְתִּיו" כו' "הֲרַגְנוּהוּ" תִּנָּשֵׂא כו'.§ מַאי שְׁנָא הֲרַגְתִּיו וּמַאי שְׁנָא הֲרַגְנוּהוּ? אָמַר רַב יְהוּדָה: בְּאוֹמֵר "אֲנִי הָיִיתִי עִם הוֹרְגָיו". *וְהָתַנְיָא: *אָמְרוּ לוֹ לְרַבִּי יְהוּדָה, מַעֲשֶׂה בְּלִסְטִים אֶחָד שֶׁיָּצָא לֵיהָרֵג בְּמְגִיזַת קַפּוֹטְקִיָא, וְאָמַר לָהֶם "לְכוּ אִמְרוּ לָהּ לְאֵשֶׁת שִׁמְעוֹן בֶּן כֹּהֵן: אֲנִי הֲרַגְתִּי אֶת בַּעְלָהּ בִּכְנִיסָתִי לְלוּד" וְאָמְרִי לָהּ "בִּכְנִיסָתוֹ לְלוּד" — וְהִשִּׂיאוּ אֶת אִשְׁתּוֹ. אָמַר לָהֶם: *מִשָּׁם רְאָיָה?! *בְּאוֹמֵר: אֲנִי הָיִיתִי עִם הוֹרְגָיו — וְהָא לִסְטִים קָתָנֵי! שֶׁנִּתְפַּס ע"י לִסְטִיּוּת. וְהָא יָצָא לֵיהָרֵג קָתָנֵי! בֵּי דִּינָא דְּגוֹיִם דְּלָא דָּיְיקֵי וְקָטְלֵי.§ **מתני'** גהֶחָכָם שֶׁאָסַר אֶת הָאִשָּׁה בְּנֶדֶר עַל בַּעְלָהּ — הֲרֵי זֶה לֹא יִשָּׂאֶנָּה, *מֵיאֲנָה אוֹ שֶׁחָלְצָה בְּפָנָיו — יִשָּׂאֶנָּה, מִפְּנֵי שֶׁהוּא ב"ד.§ **גמ'** הָא הִתִּירָהּ יִשָּׂאֶנָּה, בְּמַאי עָסְקִינַן? אִילֵימָא בְּחַד — חַד מִי מָצֵי מַתִּיר? וְהָאָמַר *(רַב אָמַר) רַ' חִיָּיא בַּר אָבִין אָמַר רַב עַמְרָם: דתָּנָא, הַתָּרַת נְדָרִים בִּשְׁלֹשָׁה! וְאֶלָּא בִּתְלָתָא — מִי חֲשִׁידִי? וְהָתְנַן: מֵיאֲנָה אוֹ שֶׁחָלְצָה בְּפָנָיו יִשָּׂאֶנָּה, מִפְּנֵי שֶׁהוּא בֵּית דִּין! לְעוֹלָם בְּחַד, *וּכְדַאֲמַר רַב חִסְדָּא אָמַר רַ' יוֹחָנָן: הבְּיָחִיד מוּמְחֶה, והָכָא נַמִי — בְּיָחִיד מוּמְחֶה.§ "מֵיאֲנָה אוֹ שֶׁחָלְצָה וכו'".§ טַעֲמָא דְּב"ד, הָא בִּתְרֵי — לָא. מ"ש מֵהָא *דִּתְנַן: *עֵדִים הַחֲתוּמִים עַל שְׂדֵה מִקָּח זוְעַל גֵּט אִשָּׁה — לֹא חָשׁוּ חֲכָמִים לְדָבָר זֶה! הִיא גּוּפָהּ קָמַשְׁמַע לָן, לְאַפּוֹקֵי מִמּ"ד מֵיאוּן *בִּפְנֵי שְׁנַיִם, קָמַשְׁמַע לָן: מֵיאוּן בְּג'. אִיבַּעְיָא לְהוּ: כָּנַס, מַהוּ שֶׁיּוֹצִיא? רַב כָּהֲנָא אָמַר: כָּנַס — מוֹצִיא, רַב אַשִׁי אָמַר: כָּנַס — אֵינוֹ מוֹצִיא. תָּנֵי לְהוּ רַב זוּטִי דְּבֵי רַב פַּפִּי כְּדִבְרֵי הָאוֹמֵר כָּנַס אֵינוֹ מוֹצִיא. אָמְרוּ לֵיהּ רַבָּנַן לְרַב אַשִׁי: *גְּמָרָא אוֹ סְבָרָא? אָמַר לְהוּ: מַתְנִי' הִיא: *הַנִּטְעָן מִשִּׁפְחָה וְנִשְׁתַּחְרְרָה, מִגּוֹיָה וְנִתְגַּיְּירָה, הֲרֵי זֶה לֹא יִכְנוֹס, וְאִם כָּנַס — אֵין מוֹצִיא. אַלְמָא בִּרְנָנָה

[אגודה דף ע"ה] [שבועות ל"ג:] [ע"ש פ"ג]

רש"י

גַּזְלָן דִּדְבָרֵיהֶם. כְּמוֹ מַפְרִיחֵי יוֹנִים וּמְשַׂחֵק בְּקוּבְיָא. דִּתְנַן (ר"ה דף כב.): כָּל הָעֵדוּת שֶׁאֵין הָאִשָּׁה כְּשֵׁרָה לָהּ, אַף הֵן אֵינָם כְּשֵׁרִים. וַעֲלָהּ אָמַר רַב מְנַשֶּׁה: זֹאת אוֹמֶרֶת גַּזְלָן דִּדְבְרֵיהֶם כו': רָבָא פָּלֵיג עֲלֵיהּ דְּרַב יוֹסֵף וְאָמַר: אֲפִי' אָמַר "פְּלוֹנִי רְבָעַנִי לִרְצוֹנִי" — הוּא וְאַחֵר מִצְטָרֵף לְהוֹרְגוֹ לָרוֹבֵעַ. דְּכֵיוָן שֶׁזֶּה מִתְכַּוֵּין לְעֵדוּת — נֶאֱמָן הוּא אֵצֶל חֲבֵרוֹ, וְאֵין נֶאֱמָן עַל עַצְמוֹ מִמַּה שֶּׁאָמַר "לִרְצוֹנִי", דְּאָדָם קָרוֹב אֵצֶל עַצְמוֹ, וְקָרוֹב פָּסוּל לְעֵדוּת בֵּין לְטוֹבָה בֵּין לְרָעָה. הִלְכָּךְ אֵינוֹ נַעֲשֶׂה רָשָׁע בְּעֵדוּת עַצְמוֹ. וְאֵין אָדָם מֵשִׂים. אֶת (א) עֵדוּתוֹ עֵדוּת אֵצֶל עַצְמוֹ לֵיעָשׂוֹת רָשָׁע. וְהָא דְּקַיְ"ל (ב"מ דף ג:) הוֹדָאַת פִּיו כְּמֵאָה עֵדִים דָּמֵי — הנ"מ לְמָמוֹנָא, אֲבָל לִקְנָסָא וּלְעוֹנֶשׁ מַלְקוֹת וְלִיפָּסֵל — לָא. וְשָׁאנֵי עֵדוּת אִשָּׁה דְּאַקִילוּ בָּהּ רַבָּנַן. הִלְכָּךְ אֲפִילּוּ רָשָׁע נֶאֱמָן. וַאֲנָא לֵית לִי דְּרַב מְנַשְּׁיָא דְּאָמַר הָא דְּדִבְרֵי תוֹרָה פָּסוּל. אֶלָּא רַב מְנַשְּׁיָא דְּאָמַר כְּרַבִּי יְהוּדָה. וְהָכִי מִיתוֹקַם סוּגְיָא: רַב יוֹסֵף מוֹקִים לְרַב מְנַשְּׁיָא כְּרַבִּי יְהוּדָה, וְרַב מְנַשְּׁיָא מוֹקֵי לְרַב יוֹסֵף כְּרַבִּי יְהוּדָה. אֲנִי הָיִיתִי עִם הוֹרְגָיו. אֲבָל לֹא נָגַעְתִּי בּוֹ. ע"י לִסְטִיּוּת. לְפִי שֶׁהָיָה עִמָּהֶן. **מתני'** בְּנֶדֶר. שֶׁנָּדְרָה הֲנָאָה מִבַּעְלָהּ וְלֹא הֵפֵר לָהּ, וּבָאתָה לֶחָכָם לְהַתִּיר לָהּ, וְלֹא מָצָא פֶּתַח לַחֲרָטָהּ. לֹא יִשָּׂאֶנָּה. מִשּׁוּם חֲשָׁד. שֶׁהוּא ב"ד. כְּלוֹמַר, מֵיאוּן אוֹ חֲלִיצָה לֹא עָשָׂה חָכָם זֶה בְּיָחִידִי, דְּקַיְ"ל: חֲלִיצָה וּמֵיאוּן בְּג', וּתְלָתָא לָא חֲשִׁידִי. **גמ'** הָא הִתִּירָהּ. וְאִם מֵת בַּעְלָהּ אוֹ גֵּירְשָׁהּ — יִשָּׂאֶנָּה, שֶׁאֵין כָּאן חֲשָׁדָא. לְעוֹלָם בְּחַד. וּדְקַשְׁיָא לָךְ: מִדְּקָתָנֵי שֶׁאָסַר, מִכְּלָל דְּבַר מִישְׁרֵי הוּא — אִין, בְּיָחִיד מוּמְחֶה, וְכִדְרַב חִסְדָּא בִּנְדָרִי' בְּפֶרֶק "נַעֲרָה הַמְאוֹרָסָה". ב"ד. ג'. לֹא חָשׁוּ חֲכָמִים לְדָבָר זֶה. לוֹמַר: לֹא יִקְחוּ שׂוּב שָׂדֶה זוֹ מִן הַלּוֹקֵחַ, וְכֵן הָעֵד שֶׁל גֵּט לֹא יִשָּׂא אֶת הָאִשָּׁה. הִיא גּוּפָהּ. כְּלוֹמַר, ה"ה דִּתְרֵי נַמִי לָא חֲשִׁידִי. וְהָא דְּקָתָנֵי שֶׁהוּא ב"ד — לָאו מִשּׁוּם לְאַפּוֹקֵי מֵחֲשָׁדָא, אֶלָּא לְאַשְׁמוּעִי' דְּאֵין מֵיאוּן בְּפָחוֹת מִג', וּלְאַפּוֹקֵי מִמַּאן דְּאָמַר בְּפֶ' [ב"ש] (לקמן קז:) מֵיאוּן בִּשְׁנַיִם. כָּנַס מַהוּ שֶׁיּוֹצִיא. אַחֲרָא וְאַחֲרִינָא גֵּט [לָא] קָאֵי. גְּמָרָא אוֹ סְבָרָא. הַאי דְּאָמְרַתְּ כָּנַס אֵין מוֹצִיא. בִּרְנָנָה

תוספות

מִשּׁוּם דְּעַד הַשְׁתָּא אַיְירִי בְּהַלָּכַת הוֹרֵג וְרוֹבֵעַ, מַסִּיק לָהּ. וְהָרוּג נַמִי לָא מִשּׁוּם שֶׁנָּאָה פָּסִיל לֵיהּ הָתָם, אֶלָּא אָמַר רַבֵּינוּ יִצְחָק: דְּמִיפְסַל מִשְׁעָה שֶׁנַּעֲשָׂה טְרֵפָה, דִּטְרֵפָה פָּסוּל לְהָעִיד, כְּדְאָמְרִי' בְּסַנְהֶדְרִין (דף עח. ושם). וה"ר יוֹסֵף מֵאוֹרְלִינ"שׂ מְפָרֵשׁ דְּפָרִיךְ מֵהָרוּג וְנִרְבָּע שֶׁיִּהְיוּ כְּשֶׁהֵם קְרוֹבִים לְהוֹרֵג וְרוֹבֵעַ. וְקָשֶׁה לְרִ"י: דְּאִין ה"נ, דְּנְהִי דְּבַהָרוּג לִיכָּא לְמֵימַר דְּאֵין ה"נ שֶׁיֵּלֵךְ, דְּהָרֵי חִיֵּיב הַכָּתוּב מַכֶּה אָבִיו — מ"מ מִנִּרְבָּע מַאי פָּרִיךְ? וכ"ת: בְּנִרְבָּע נַמִי, דְּהָא דְּרָשִׁינַן בְּסַנְהֶדְרִין (דף נד.) "עֶרְוַת אָבִיךָ" מַמָּשׁ, שֶׁרְבָעוֹ, ה"מ לְעִנְיַן כָּרֵת, אֲבָל מִיתָה — לָא אַשְׁכְּחַן. **רבא** אמר אדם קרוב אצל עצמו. הִקְשָׁה ר' יִצְחָק בֶּן אַבְרָהָם: דִּבְפֶרֶק שֵׁנִי דִּכְתוּבּוֹת (דף יח: ושם) מַסִּיק *רָבָא גּוּפֵיהּ, גַּבֵּי הָא דִּתְנַן הָתָם: אִם אֵין כְּתַב יָדָן יוֹצֵא מִמָּקוֹם אַחֵר הֲרֵי אֵלּוּ נֶאֱמָנִים לוֹמַר אֲנוּסִים הָיִינוּ, לֹא שָׁנוּ אֶלָּא שֶׁאָמְרוּ אֲנוּסִים הָיִינוּ מֵחֲמַת נְפָשׁוֹת, אֲבָל אָמְרוּ מֵחֲמַת מָמוֹן — אֵין נֶאֱמָנִים. וְאַמַּאי אֵין נֶאֱמָנִים? דְּהָוֵה לַן לְפַלּוֹגֵי דִּיבּוּרָא וְלוֹמַר דַּאֲנוּסִים הָיוּ וְלֹא מֵחֲמַת מָמוֹן אֶלָּא מֵחֲמַת נְפָשׁוֹת! וְאוֹמֵר ר"י: דְּלָא פַּלְגִינַן דִּיבּוּרָא כְּדֵי לִפְסוֹל הַשְּׁטָר, דְּמִדְּאוֹרַיְיתָ' עֵדִים הַחֲתוּמִים עַל הַשְּׁטָר נַעֲשָׂה כְּמִי שֶׁנֶּחְקְרָה עֵדוּתָן בְּבֵ"ד. א"נ, הָתָם בְּכָל עִנְיָן שֶׁהֵם אֲנוּסִים, אִם לֹא מֵחֲמַת נְפָשׁוֹת — הָווּ רְשָׁעִים, הִלְכָּךְ לֵית לַן לְמִיתְלֵי בְּאוֹנֶס מֵחֲמַת נְפָשׁוֹת, דְּהָוֵי מִיעוּטָא (א). **ואין** אדם משים עצמו רשע. הַיְינוּ לִפְסוֹל אֶת עַצְמוֹ, אֲבָל נֶאֱמָן הוּא לוֹמַר גַּבֵּי אֲכִילַת חֵלֶב: מֵזִיד הָיִיתִי, כִּדְאָמַר בִּכְרִיתוּת (דף יב. ושם) דְּאֵין לָנוּ לְכוֹפוֹ לְהָבִיא חוּלִּין לָעֲזָרָה לְפִי דְּבָרָיו. וְהָא דְּקָאָמְרִינַן בְּ"הָאִישׁ מְקַדֵּשׁ" (קידושין דף נ. ושם), גַּבֵּי הָבָא לִי מִן הַחַלּוֹן אוֹ מִן הַדְּלוּסְקְמָא, דְּלָא עָבִיד אִינִישׁ דְּמַשְׁוֵי נַפְשֵׁיהּ רְשִׁיעָא לוֹמַר מֵזִיד הָיִיתִי — לָאו מִשּׁוּם שֶׁלֹּא יְהֵא נֶאֱמָן לוֹמַר מֵזִיד הָיִיתִי, דִּפְשִׁיטָא דְּנֶאֱמָן, אֶלָּא כְּלוֹמַר: שֶׁאֵין בְּרָצוֹן אוֹמֵר בְּעִנְיָן דְּמַשְׁוֵי נַפְשֵׁיהּ רְשִׁיעָא. וא"ת: דְּהַשְׁתָּא מַשְׁמַע דְּנִרְבָּע לִרְצוֹנוֹ פָּסוּל לְעֵדוּת, וּבְפֶרֶק "זֶה בּוֹרֵר" (סנהדרין דף כו:) אִיכָּא לְמ"ד דְּחָשׁוּד עַל הָעֲרָיוֹת כָּשֵׁר לְעֵדוּת! וי"ל: דְּהָתָם בְּגוֹמֵל שֶׁהוּא פָּרִיץ, וּמִתְיַיחֵד עִם הָעֲרָיוֹת, וְלָא וַדַּאי בָּא עַל הָעֶרְוָה, כִּדְפֵי' הָתָם בְּקוּנְטְרֵס. וּמַאן דְּפָרִיךְ הָתָם עֲנִי מָרִי אַרְבְּעִים בִּכְתָפֵיהּ וְכָשֵׁר? הַיְינוּ מִשּׁוּם דְּמַלְקִין עַל "לֹא טוֹבָה הַשְּׁמוּעָה". וא"ת: וְכִי וַדַּאי בָּא עַל הָעֶרְוָה אַמַּאי פָּסוּל? הָא רָשָׁע דְּחָמָס בָּעֵינַן, שֶׁיְּהֵא רַע לַשָּׁמַיִם וְלַבְּרִיּוֹת, וְזֶה אֵין רַע לַבְּרִיּוֹת, כְּגוֹן אוֹכֵל נְבֵלוֹת לְהַכְעִיס, דְּכָשֵׁר לְרָבָא בְּפֶרֶק "זֶה בּוֹרֵר" (שם כ"ז.)! וי"ל: דְּהָוֵי כְּמוֹ אוֹכֵל נְבֵלוֹת לְתֵאָבוֹן, דְּפָסוּל לְכוּלֵּי עָלְמָא, אע"פ שֶׁאֵין רַע לַבְּרִיּוֹת, דְּכֵיוָן דְּחָשׁוּד לַעֲבוֹר בִּשְׁבִיל הֲנָאַת עַצְמוֹ — חָשׁוּד נַמִי לְהָעִיד שֶׁקֶר בִּשְׁבִיל מָמוֹן, וְהָכִי נַמִי בָּא עַל הָעֶרְוָה.

לימא רב יוסף דאמר כרבי יהודה. *תֵּימָה: דְּהָכָא לְרַבִּי יְהוּדָה לֵית לֵיהּ פַּלְגִינַן דִּיבּוּרָא, וּבְפֶרֶק "הַחוֹלֵץ" (לקמן דף מז. ושם) אָמְרִינַן: הַהוּא דַּאֲתָא לְקַמֵּיהּ דְּרַבִּי יְהוּדָה וְאָמַר נִתְגַּיַּירְתִּי בֵּינִי לְבֵין עַצְמִי, א"ל: נֶאֱמָן אַתָּה לִפְסוֹל אֶת עַצְמְךָ, וְאִי אַתָּה יָכוֹל לִפְסוֹל אֶת בָּנֶיךָ. אַלְמָא: פַּלְגִינַן דִּיבּוּרָא! וּמִיהוּ, י"ל: דְּהָתָם לָאו מִטַּעַם עֵדוּת נֶאֱמָן, (דְּהָא אָדָם קָרוֹב אֵצֶל עַצְמוֹ, וְעוֹד: דְּאִם נֶאֱמָן לִפְסוֹל עַצְמוֹ — אֵיךְ יִתָּכֵן שֶׁיִּהְיוּ בָּנָיו כְּשֵׁרִים?) אֶלָּא הָא דְּפָסְלִינַן — הַיְינוּ לְאוֹסְרוֹ בְּבַת יִשְׂרָאֵל, דְּשַׁוְּיָא אַנַּפְשֵׁיהּ חֲתִיכָה דְּאִיסּוּרָא. אוֹ אִם נָגַח שׁוֹר שֶׁל יִשְׂרָאֵל אֶת שׁוֹרוֹ — פָּטוּר מִטַּעַם הוֹדָאַת בַּעַל דִּין. וְהַהִיא דְּרַ' יְהוּדָה גּוּפָא קַשְׁיָא, וְשָׁם נִפְרַשׁ בְּעֶזְרַת הַשֵּׁם. **באומר** אני הייתי עם הורגיו. אוֹר"י: דְּאַע"ג דְּאָמַר הֲרַגְנוּהוּ — נַעֲשֶׂה כְּאוֹמֵר אֲנִי הָיִיתִי עִם הוֹרְגָיו. וּכְעִנְיָן זֶה מְפָרֵשׁ ר"ת וְרַבֵּינוּ חֲנַנְאֵל בְּפֶ' "מִי שֶׁאֲחָזוֹ" (גיטין עג: ד"ה "אמר") בְּאוֹמֵר מֵעֵת שֶׁאֲנִי בָּעוֹלָם — נַעֲשֶׂה כְּאוֹמֵר. **במגיזת** קפוטקיא. יֵשׁ סְפָרִים דְּגָרְסִי בְּמְזִיגַת, וְהָוֵי כְּמוֹ בְּמְגִיזַת עַרְבָאֵי*, כְּמוֹ שַׂמְלָה שַׂלְמָה. ר"י. **טעמא** דב"ד הא בי תרי לא. וְאַע"ג דְּאָמְרִינַן בְּרֵישׁ "הַשּׁוֹלֵחַ" (גיטין דף לב: ושם) דִּלְתְרֵי נַמִי בֵּי דִּינָא קָרוּ לְהוּ, מ"מ אוֹר"י דְּדַיֵּיק שַׁפִּיר, דְּמִדְּתָלֵי טַעְמָא בְּבֵית דִּין, וְלָא קָאָמַר מִפְּנֵי שֶׁהָיוּ ב', ש"מ דְּלָא סַגֵּי הָכָא בִּתְרֵי. וְעוֹד: דּוּמְיָא דַּחֲלִיצָה, דְּבִג', אַע"ג דְּאִיכָּא מַאן דְּמַכְשִׁר בְּפֶרֶק "מִצְוַת חֲלִיצָה" (לקמן דף קד.) בְּיָחִידִי — הָךְ תַּנָּא לָא סָבַר לֵהּ כְּוָותֵיהּ, דְּחַד וַדַּאי לָא מִיקְרֵי ב"ד, וְאִיכָּא נַמִי רְנָנָה בְּחַד. **לא** חשו חכמים לדבר זה. וְאַע"ג דְּשָׁרֵי[ג], מ"מ בַּעַל נֶפֶשׁ יִתְרַחֵק, כִּדְתְנִי' עֲלָהּ בְּ"אֵלּוּ טְרֵפוֹת" (חולין דף מד: ושם): דָּן אֶת הַדִּין, זִיכָּה וְחִייֵּב, טִימֵּא וְטִיהֵר, וְכֵן הָעֵדִים שֶׁהֵעִידוּ — כּוּלָּם רַשָּׁאִים לִיקַּח, אֲבָל חֲכָמִים אָמְרוּ: הִתְרַחֵק מִן הַכִּיעוּר וּמִן הַדּוֹמֶה לוֹ. וא"ת: הָא אָמְרִינַן בְּסוֹף "הַמְקַבֵּל" (גיטין דף סז. ושם) גַּבֵּי חַיְישִׁינַן שֶׁמָּא תַּשְׂכּוֹר עֵדִים: דִּיבּוּרָא — אָמְרִי, מַעֲשֶׂה — לָא עָבְדִי! וי"ל: דִּכְשֶׁמְּעִידִים שֶׁקֶר חָשִׁיב נַמִי מַעֲשֶׂה, כִּדְפֵי' בְּקוּנְטְרֵס, כֵּיוָן דְּעַל פִּיהֶם נִגְמַר, וְלָא קָרֵי דִּיבּוּרָא הָתָם אֶלָּא בְּאוֹמֵר: אִמְרוּ, שֶׁאוֹמֵר מִן הַבַּעַל לַסּוֹפֵר וְלָעֵדִים לִכְתּוֹב וְלַחְתּוֹם, דְּלָא נִגְמַר הַדָּבָר עַל יְדֵיהֶם. **אמר** להו מתני' היא הנטען כו'. וְלִנְטְעָן עַל אֵשֶׁת אִישׁ לָא דָּמֵי, דְּהָתָם בְּדִין שֶׁיּוֹצִיא, אִם הוּא אֱמֶת אֲסִירָא לֵיהּ! אֲבָל הָכָא, שֶׁאָסַר אֶת הָאִשָּׁה בְּנֶדֶר אֲפִילּוּ אָסְרָהּ שֶׁלֹּא כַּדִּין, כֵּיוָן שֶׁגֵּירְשָׁהּ בַּעְלָהּ — שְׁרֵיָא לֶחָכָם מִדְּאוֹרַיְיתָא (ג). אגירושין

עין משפט נר מצוה

צ א מיי' פי"ב מהלכות גירושין הלכה יז סמג עשין ג טוש"ע אה"ע סימן יז סעיף ג:

צא ב מיי' פי"ב מהל' עדות הל' ב ופי"ג מהל' גירושין הלכה י סמג לאוין ריד טוש"ע ח"מ סימן לד סעיף כו:

צב ג מיי' פ"י מהלכות גירושין הלכה יד טוש"ע אה"ע סימן יב סעיף ב:

צג ד ה מיי' פ"ו מהל' שבועות הלכה א ה טוש"ע י"ד סימן רכח סעיף א:

ע"ש שהוא רמי בר חמא

צד ו מיי' שם טוש"ע אה"ע סי' יב סע"ב:

צה ז שם סעיף א:

[עי' רש"א]

תוספות ישנים

א) ועוי"ל דשאני הכא שיש לנו לומר פלגינן דבורא דכשאמר פלוני רבעני מעתה נהרג הרובע בין לאונסו בין לרצונו ולא צריך תו לומר לאונסו או לרצונו וא"כ כי אמר אחרי כן לרצונו פלגינן דבורא דמלתא דרבעו חשיבא בפני עצמה היא והוו כתרי דבורי אבל התם כי אמרו אנוסים היינו אין הדבר כלום עד שיפרשו אם מחמת ממון אם מחמת נפשות לכן לא שייך לחלק הדבור שאין זה בלא זה כלום: **באומר** אני הייתי עם הורגיו. יש גורסים בכ"ף פי' כ"ש דמהני כשאומר הרגנוהו כמו אם היה אומר אני הייתי עם הורגיו והוי כדאמרי' בגיטין כאומר מעת שאני בעולם וניחא שלשון נוגע המשנה: **ב)** ולהך פי' צ"ל דכי בעי לעיל כנס מהו שיוציא לא קאי אלא אחכם שאסר וכו' דאי קאי אכולהו כדפ"ה לעיל מאי שנא דלא מפקינן הכא ברננה ובנטען מפקינן אף ברננה. דגם שנאן אשו הרננה אמת שמשקר מהאי דאמר מת הרגתיו אסורה לו מן התורה שעדיין אשת איש היא אלא ודאי לא קאי בעי אלא מחכם שאסר האשה בנדר על בעלה:

תוספות חד מקמאי

מוציא: **אמר** רב מנשה גזלן דדבריהם כשר לעדות הא דדברי תורה פסול לעדות אשה: **הא** דתנן החכם שאסר את האשה בנדר לא ישאנה וקי"ל ביחיד מומחה ולפום הכי אם התירה ישאנה אבל בתלתא אפילו אסרו ישאנה משום שהם ב"ד ובבכורות פרק כל פסולי המוקדשים דכי אמרי' הפרת נדרים בשלשה הדיוטות במקום שאין שם מומחה ורבי יהודה ס"ל התם ואחד מהם חכם ולית הלכתא כוותיה ומקשינן התם מכלל דהנך כל דהו ומשנינן דמסברי להו וסברי: גרסינן בשלהי נדרים ההיא איתתא דכל יומא דמשמש מקדמא ומשיא לגברא יומא חד אייתא ליה מיא לממשא א"ל הא מילתא לא הות האידנא א"ל א"כ חד מהני נכרים דהוו הכא אמר ר"נ עיניה נתנה באחר וכו':

מסורת הש"ס

כתובות יח: סנהדרין ט: כה.

[תוספתא פ"ד]

[שבת כט: וש"נ]

[תוספתא פ"ד ע"ש]

לקמן קח: בכורות לו.

[בכורות לו: ליתא וע"ש היטב]

נדרים עח: ע"ש ב"ב קיג: קכח. בכורות לו.

גיטין סז:

[לקמן קח:]

[לעיל כד: ע"ש]

רש"ל מ"ז

תרגום על כעיי הטבריים במדבר לג פ' מ"ד

הגהות הב"ח

(א) רש"י ד"ה ואין אדם משים את עצמו רשע אין עדותו:

הגהות הגר"א [א] רש"י ד"ה כנס מהו שיוציא אחכם ואמביא גט קאי. נ"ב וכ"כ הרמב"ם ושו"ע. אבל רשב"א כתב דלא קאי רק על מתני' זו על החכם וכ"ה ברא"ש להדיא וכ"מ בתוספתא ועט"ז (ועמ"ש רבינו באה"ע סימן יב ס"ק ב'): [ב] תוס' ד"ה לא כו' מ"מ ב"נ יתרחק. נ"ב אבל לטעם הירושלמי ר"ל דאף לכתחלה מותר ואין כאן הרחק דאל"כ צ"ל שאין שניס כו' אפילו בשביל שניהם כמו במקח ועמש"ש (ע"ש בס"ק ה'):

גליון הש"ס גמ' והאמר (רב) אר"ח בר אבין. נ"ל [רבא] סדר הדורות בהקדמה אות ד: **תוס'** ד"ה לימא רב יוסף דאמר כר"י תימה דהכא וכו'. עיין תשובת רשד"ם חלק י"ד סימן רנד:

בְּרְנָנָה. מִפְּנֵי רִינּוּן וְלַעַז בְּנֵי אָדָם לָא אָמְרִינַן לֵיהּ "הוֹצֵא". וְלָא דָּמֵי לְנִטְעָן עַל אֵשֶׁת אִישׁ, דְּהָתָם הוֹאִיל וְהוֹצִיאָהּ בַּעְלָהּ מִפְּנֵי זֶה, וְהָלַךְ זֶה וּנְשָׂאָהּ – מְכוֹעָר הַדָּבָר. **מתני'** וְכוּלָּם. הֶחָכָם, וְהַמֵּבִיא גֵּט, וְהַמֵּעִיד בָּאִשָּׁה לְהַשִּׂיאָהּ, דִּתְנַן בָּהֶן לֹא יִכְנוֹס. שֶׁהָיוּ לָהֶם נָשִׁים. בִּשְׁעַת מַעֲשֶׂה, וּמֵתוּ לְאַחַר זְמַן – מוּתָּרוֹת אֵלּוּ לִינָּשֵׂא לָהֶם. דְּהַשְׁתָּא לֵיכָּא חֲשָׁד, שֶׁהֲרֵי בְּשָׁעָה שֶׁהֵעִיד בָּהּ הָעֵד אוֹ שֶׁאֲסָרָהּ חָכָם הָיְתָה אִשְׁתּוֹ קַיֶּימֶת, וְלֹא לִישָּׂא אֶת זוֹ נִתְכַּוֵּין. וְכוּלָּן. הַנָּשִׁים הַלָּלוּ. שֶׁנִּישְּׂאוּ. לַאֲחֵרִים, כְּשֶׁאֲסָרָהּ חָכָם אוֹ כְּשֶׁהֵעִיד עֵד בְּמִיתַת בַּעְלָהּ, וּמֵתוּ הַבְּעָלִים הַשְּׁנִיִּים. מוּתָּרוֹת לִינָּשֵׂא. לֶחָכָם, וְלָעֵד, וְלַמֵּבִיא גֵּט. וְכוּלָּן. הַנָּשִׁים הָאֵלּוּ, מוּתָּרוֹת לִבְנֵיהֶם אוֹ לַאֲחֵיהֶם שֶׁל אֵלּוּ הַמַּתִּירִים אוֹתָן, וְאֵין אֲסוּרוֹת אֶלָּא לָהֶן לְבַדָּן. **גמ'** נִתְגָּרְשׁוּ לָא. דְּע"י שֶׁנָּתַן אֶת עֵינָיו בְּזוֹ שֶׁהִתִּיר – גֵּירֵשׁ אֶת אִשְׁתּוֹ. הָא. דְּקָתָנֵי אֲפִי' נִתְגָּרְשׁוּ – כְּגוֹן דְּהָוֵי לְהוּ קְטָטָה מִקַּמֵּי הָכִי, דַּעֲדַיִין לֹא נָתַן דַּעְתּוֹ עַל זֹאת: ה"ג: וְאִיבָּעֵית אֵימָא אִידִי וְאִידִי דְּלָא הָווּ לְהוּ קְטָטָה. הָא. דְּקָתָנֵי נִתְגָּרְשׁוּ לֹא – בִּדְאַרְגִּיל הוּא קְטָטָה, שֶׁהוּא הִתְחִיל לְהַקְנִיט אֶת אִשְׁתּוֹ. וְהָא. דְּקָתָנֵי אֲפִי' נִתְגָּרְשׁוּ – בִּדְאַרְגִּילָה הִיא קְטָטָה, שֶׁהִיא הִקְנִיטַתּוּ תְּחִלָּה. קס"ד מִיתָה אַמִּיתָה. הָא דְּקָתָנֵי וְכוּלָּן שֶׁנִּישְּׂאוּ לַאֲחֵרִים וּמֵתוּ – קָאֵי נַמִי אַרֵישָׁא, דְּקָתָנֵי: מֵת, הֲרַגְתִּיו, הֲרַגְנוּהוּ – לֹא יִשָּׂא אֶת אִשְׁתּוֹ. וְקָתָנֵי דְּאִם נִישֵּׂאת לְאַחֵר עַל פִּיו, וּמֵת הַשֵּׁנִי הַזֶּה – מוּתֶּרֶת לִינָּשֵׂא לָעֵד זֶה. וְאע"פ שֶׁמֵּתוּ ב' בְּעָלֶיהָ – תִּנָּשֵׂא לַשְּׁלִישִׁי, וְלָא אָמְרִינַן הוּחְזְקָה זוֹ קַטְלָנִית, שֶׁהַנּוֹשְׂאָהּ מֵת. וְגֵירוּשִׁין דְּקָתָנֵי נִתְגָּרְשָׁה – קָאֵי אַגֵּירוּשִׁין דִּלְעֵיל, הַמֵּבִיא גֵּט כו'. וְאַשְׁמְעִינַן דְּאִם נִשֵּׂאת לְאַחֵר בְּאוֹתוֹ הַגֵּט וְגֵירְשָׁהּ הַשֵּׁנִי הַזֶּה – מוּתֶּרֶת לִינָּשֵׂא לְמֵבִיא גִּיטָּהּ הָרִאשׁוֹן. בִּתְרֵי זִימְנֵי הָוְיָא חֲזָקָה. לְקַמָּן בְּ"הַבָּא עַל יְבִמְתּוֹ" (דף סד:): נִיסֵּת לָרִאשׁוֹן וּמֵת, לַשֵּׁנִי וּמֵת, לַשְּׁלִישִׁי לֹא תִּינָּשֵׂא – דִּבְרֵי רַבִּי. וּמַתְנִי' דְּלָא כְּרַבִּי. דְּאִי רַבִּי, נְהִי דַּחֲשָׁד לֵיכָּא – מִיהוּ לְכָל הָעוֹלָם אֲסוּרָה, שֶׁהוּחְזְקָה לְהִתְאַלְמֵן אוֹ לְהִתְגָּרֵשׁ. מִיתָה. דְּקָתָנֵי הָכָא שֶׁנִּישְּׂאוּ לַאֲחֵרִים וּמֵתוּ מוּתָּרוֹת – לָאו אַכּוּלְּהוּ דִּלְעֵיל קָאֵי, אֶלָּא אַגֵּירוּשִׁין וְאַמֵּבִיא גֵּט, אוֹ חָכָם שֶׁאָסַר אֶת הָאִשָּׁה. וְגֵירוּשִׁין. דְּהָכָא – אַ"מֵּת" "הֲרַגְתִּיו" "הֲרַגְנוּהוּ". ומש"ה כְּשֶׁנִּתְגָּרְשָׁה מִשֵּׁנִי זֶה – מוּתֶּרֶת לַשְּׁלִישִׁי, שֶׁעֲדַיִין לֹא הוּחְזְקָה בְּחַדָא רֵיעוּתָא תְּרֵי זִימְנֵי. אסור בְּאִמָּהּ וּבִתָּהּ וַאֲחוֹתָהּ. כִּדְמְפָרֵשׁ טַעְמָא לְקַמָּן: שֶׁמָּא לְאַחַר שֶׁיִּשָּׂא אֶת אִמָּהּ אוֹ אֶת בִּתָּהּ תִּזְנֶה זוֹ עִמּוֹ. וּבִזְנוּת קַמָּא לָא הֲוָה מִיתַּסַּר בְּאִמָּהּ וּבִקְרוֹבוֹתֶיהָ, דְּקַיְ"ל (לקמן דף צז.): נוֹשְׂאִין עַל הָאֲנוּסָה וְעַל הַמְפוּתָּה, דְּלָא נֶאֶסְרוּ קְרוֹבוֹת אִשָּׁה עַל הָאִישׁ אא"כ קִדְּשָׁהּ לָרִאשׁוֹנָה, דְּאִישׁוּת כְּתִיב בְּהוּ, וְקִיחָה – *"כִּי יִקַּח אִישׁ אֶת אִשָּׁה וְאֶת אִמָּהּ" (ויקרא כ). אֲבָל מִשֶּׁנָּשָׂא אֶת אִמָּהּ וְאֶת בִּתָּהּ עוֹמֶדֶת – הַנִּטְעֶנֶת הָרִאשׁוֹנָה עָלָיו בְּכָרֵת, דִּתְנַן (שם): הָאוֹנֵס וְהַמְפַתֶּה עַל הַנְּשׂוּאָה – חַיָּיב. וְה"נ אַמַּאי מוּתֶּרֶת לִבְנֵיהֶם? לֵיחוּשׁ שֶׁמָּא עֵצַת זִמָּה הָיָה בֵּינֵיהֶם, לִישָּׂא אֶת בְּנוֹ שֶׁל זֶה, וִיהֵא זֶה רָגִיל אֶצְלָהּ. נָשֵׁי לָא אָסְרוּ. (א) שְׁכִיבַת זְנוּת הַקְּרוֹבָה אֶת אִשְׁתּוֹ גְּמוּרָה עָלָיו, הִילְכָּךְ לָא קָפְדָא אִשְׁתּוֹ וְשָׁתְקָה, וְחָיְישִׁינַן. אֲבָל גַּבְרֵי דְּאָסְרֵי שְׁכִיבָתָן אַהֲדָדֵי, דְּאִשָּׁה הַמְזַנָּה אֲסוּרָה לְבַעְלָהּ – קָפֵיד בַּעַל, וְרָחֵיק הַאי מִינֵּיהּ. א"ה. דִּבְגַבְרֵי לָא חָיְישִׁינַן לִזְנוּת שֶׁיִּזְנֶה קְרוֹבוֹ עִם אִשְׁתּוֹ, לְאָבִיו שֶׁל מַתִּיר נַמִי תִּשְׁתְּרֵי? וְאַמַּאי תָּנֵי לִבְנֵיהֶן וְלַאֲחֵיהֶן, וְלָא תָּנֵי נַמִי לַאֲבִיהֶן? **לא מִיבַּעְיָא לְאָבִיו.** שֶׁל מַתִּיר, דְּמוּתָּרוֹת, וְלָא חָיְישִׁינַן שֶׁמָּא יִזְנֶה מַתִּיר זֶה עִמָּהּ. דְּבָזֵיז מִינֵּיהּ. בּוֹשׁ הוּא מֵאָבִיו, וְאֵימָתוֹ עָלָיו.

אגירושין. אגב מיתה נקט גירושין – דאפי' נתגרשה כמה פעמים שריא לינשא. **אי** הכי אביו נמי. לא הוי לשנויי דנקט בנו לרבותא, אע"ג דאסור באנוסת אביו לר' יהודה* – דהתינח בניהן, אבל אחיהן אמאי נקט אי לאו לדקדק אבל לאביו – לא!

בִּרְנָנָה לָא מַפְּקִינַן, ה"נ בִּרְנָנָה לָא מַפְּקִינַן.§ **מתני'** אוְכוּלָּם שֶׁהָיוּ לָהֶם נָשִׁים וּמֵתוּ – מוּתָּרוֹת לִינָּשֵׂא לָהֶם. בוְכוּלָּן שֶׁנִּישְּׂאוּ לַאֲחֵרִים, וְנִתְגָּרְשׁוּ אוֹ שֶׁנִּתְאַלְמְנוּ – מוּתָּרוֹת לִינָּשֵׂא לָהֶם. גוְכוּלָּן מוּתָּרוֹת לִבְנֵיהֶם אוֹ לַאֲחֵיהֶם.§ **גמ'** מֵתוּ – אִין, נִתְגָּרְשׁוּ – לָא. אֲמַר לֵיהּ רַב הִלֵּל לְרַב אַשִׁי: וְהָתַנְיָא אֲפִי' נִתְגָּרְשׁוּ! לָא קַשְׁיָא; הָא – דַּהֲוַאי קְטָטָה, הָא – דְּלָא הֲוַאי קְטָטָה. וְאִיבָּעֵית אֵימָא: הָא וְהָא דְּלָא הֲוַאי קְטָטָה, וְלָא קַשְׁיָא; דהָא – דְּאַרְגִּיל הוּא, הָא – דְּאַרְגִּילָה הִיא.§ "וְכוּלָּן שֶׁנִּישְּׂאוּ" וכו'.§ קס"ד מִיתָה אַמִּיתָה, וְגֵירוּשִׁין אַגֵּירוּשִׁין, נֵימָא מַתְנִיתִין דְּלָא כְּרַבִּי, דְּאִי כְּרַבִּי – *הָאָמַר: בִּתְרֵי זִימְנֵי הָוְיָא חֲזָקָה! לָא, מִיתָה אַגֵּירוּשִׁין וְגֵירוּשִׁין אַמִּיתָה.§ "וְכוּלָּן מוּתָּרוֹת לִבְנֵיהֶם אוֹ לַאֲחֵיהֶם".§ מַאי שְׁנָא מֵהָא *דִּתְנַן: *הַנִּטְעָן מִן הָאִשָּׁה – אָסוּר בְּאִמָּהּ וּבְבִתָּהּ וּבַאֲחוֹתָהּ! נָשֵׁי לְגַבֵּי נָשֵׁי – שְׁכִיחָן דְּאָזְלָן, גַּבְרֵי לְגַבֵּי – גַּבְרֵי לָא שְׁכִיחָן. אִי נַמִי: נָשֵׁי דְּלָא אָסְרָן שְׁכִיבָתָן אַהֲדָדֵי – לָא קָפְדֵי אַהֲדָדֵי, גַּבְרֵי דְּאָסְרָן שְׁכִיבָתָן אַהֲדָדֵי – קָפְדֵי אַהֲדָדֵי. אִי הָכִי אָבִיו נַמִי! לָא מִיבַּעְיָא קָאָמַר, לָא מִיבַּעְיָא אָבִיו – *דְּבָזֵיז בְּנֵיהּ מִינֵּיהּ, אֲבָל בְּנוֹ דְּלָא בָּזֵיז אָבִיו מִינֵּיהּ – אֵימָא לָא, קמ"ל.§

הדרן עלך כיצד אשת אחיו

הדרן עלך כיצד אשת אחיו

חולצות ולא מתייבמות. פירשתי לעיל (דף יח. ד"ה "דלמא" וכו') ועוד נפרש בגמ' גבי פלוגתא דרב ור' יוחנן. **אי** הכי תלתא נמי. אי אמרת בשלמא יש זיקה ניחא דנקט ארבעה לאשמועינן דאפי' בתרי יש זיקה – אלא אי אין זיקה, וטעמא משום ביטול מצות יבמין – לישמעינן תלתא, דהוי רבותא טפי דאסור לבטל, אע"ג דחדא מינייהו לא חזיא לייבומי. וכל שכן בד', דשתיהן ראויות להתייבם זה אחת וזה אחת, דאסור. ועוד אר"י: דמצי לפרש, דס"ד השתא דחיישינן למיתה דתרי כמו למיתה דחד, ולהכי פריך: א"ה תלתא נמי, כיון דלא אתא לאשמועינן חידוש של חשש מיתה, מדלא נקט חמשה, דהוי רבותא טפי, אלא לאשמועינן דאסור לבטל – זה יכול להשמיענו אפילו בתלתא.

למיתה

אַרְבָּעָה *האַחִין, שְׁנַיִם מֵהֶם נְשׂוּאִים שְׁתֵּי אֲחָיוֹת, וּמֵתוּ הַנְּשׂוּאִים אֶת הָאֲחָיוֹת – הֲרֵי אֵלּוּ חוֹלְצוֹת וְלֹא מִתְיַיבְּמוֹת. וְאִם קָדְמוּ וְכָנְסוּ – יוֹצִיאוּ. *רַבִּי אֱלִיעֶזֶר אוֹמֵר, ב"ש אוֹמְרִים: *יְקַיֵּים, וּב"ה אוֹמְרִי': ויוֹצִיאוּ. *זהָיְתָה אַחַת מֵהֶן אָסוּר' עַל הָאֶחָד אִיסּוּר עֶרְוָה – אָסוּר בָּהּ וּמוּתָּר בַּאֲחוֹת', וְהַשֵּׁנִי אָסוּר בִּשְׁתֵּיהֶן. *חאִיסּוּר מִצְוָה וְאִיסּוּר קְדוּשָּׁה – חוֹלֶצֶת וְלֹא מִתְיַיבֶּמֶת. טהָיְתָה אַחַת מֵהֶן אֲסוּרָה עַל זֶה אִיסּוּר עֶרְוָה, וְהַשְּׁנִיָּה אֲסוּרָה עַל זֶה אִיסּוּר עֶרְוָה – הָאֲסוּרָה לָזֶה מוּתֶּרֶת לָזֶה, וְהָאֲסוּרָה לָזֶה מוּתֶּרֶת לָזֶה. וְזוֹ הִיא שֶׁאָמְרוּ: *אֲחוֹתָהּ כְּשֶׁהִיא יְבִמְתָּהּ – אוֹ חוֹלֶצֶת אוֹ מִתְיַיבֶּמֶת.§ **גמ'** ש"מ: ייֵשׁ זִיקָה. דְּאִי *אֵין זִיקָה, מִכְּדִי הָנֵי מִתְּרֵי בָּתֵּי קָאָתְיָין, הַאי לְיַיבֵּם חֲדָא וְהַאי לְיַיבֵּם חֲדָא! לְעוֹלָם אֵימָא לָךְ: אֵין זִיקָה, וּמִשּׁוּם דְּקָסָבַר *אָסוּר לְבַטֵּל מִצְוַת יְבָמִין; דִּלְמָא אַדְּמְיַיבֵּם חַד – מָיֵית אִידָךְ, וְקָמְבַטֵּל מִצְוַת יְבָמִין. אִי הָכִי, תְּלָתָא נַמִי! – לָא מִיבַּעְיָא קָאָמְרִינַן; לָא מִיבַּעְיָא תְּלָתָא, דְּוַדַּאי בָּטְלָה מִצְוַת יְבָמִין, אֲבָל ד', לְמִיתָה לָא חָיְישִׁינַן – קמ"ל. אִי הָכִי, חֲמִשָּׁה

הדרן עלך כיצד אשת אחיו

אַרְבָּעָה אַחִין. וְלֹא מִתְיַיבְּמוֹת. מְפָרֵשׁ טַעְמָא בַּגְּמָ' מִשּׁוּם זִיקָה. דְּכֵיוָן דְּתַרְוַויְיהוּ זְקִיקָן לְהַאי וּלְהַאי, קַמָּא דִּמְיַיבֵּם פָּגַע בַּאֲחוֹת זְקוּקָתוֹ, דַּהֲוָיָא כְּאִשְׁתּוֹ. אִיסּוּר עֶרְוָה. כְּגוֹן חֲמוֹתוֹ וְאֵם חֲמוֹתוֹ. וּמוּתָּר בַּאֲחוֹתָהּ. דְּלָאו אֲחוֹת זְקוּקָה הִיא, דְּעֶרְוָה לָאו קַמֵּיהּ רָמְיָא לְיַיבּוּמֵי. אִיסּוּר מִצְוָה. רָמְיָא קַמֵּיהּ מִדְּאוֹרַיְיתָא, הִלְכָּךְ אָסוּר בַּאֲחוֹתָהּ, דַּאֲחוֹת זְקוּקָה הִיא. אֲחוֹתָהּ (ב) כְּשֶׁהִיא יְבִמְתָּהּ. אֲחוֹתָהּ שֶׁל עֶרְוָה כְּשֶׁהִיא יְבִמְתָּהּ, אֵשֶׁת אֲחִי בַּעְלָהּ, כְּשֶׁנּוֹפֶלֶת עִמָּהּ לְיִיבּוּם. אוֹ חוֹלֶצֶת אוֹ מִתְיַיבֶּמֶת. דְּלָאו אֲחוֹת זְקוּקָתוֹ הִיא, דְּעֶרְוָה לָא רָמְיָא קַמֵּיהּ. **גמ'** יֵשׁ זִיקָה. כְּלוֹמַר: חוּמְרַת זִיקָה לְשַׁוּוֹיֵי אֲחוֹת זְקוּקָתוֹ כַּאֲחוֹת אִשְׁתּוֹ. וּבְמַסֶּ' נְדָרִים (דף עד.) פְּלִיגִי בָּהּ, אִיכָּא לְמ"ד: זְקוּקָתוֹ כְּאִשְׁתּוֹ לְהַפָרַת נְדָרֶיהָ וְלֶאֱסוֹר קְרוֹבוֹת, וְאִיכָּא לְמ"ד: אֵין זִיקָה. וּבְפִרְקִין דִּלְעֵיל (דף יח:) אִיפְּלִיגוּ בָּהּ רַב הוּנָא וְרַב יְהוּדָה. מִתְּרֵי בָּתֵּי. מִשְּׁנֵי אַחִין נָפְלוּ. מָיֵית אִידָךְ. וְנָפְלָה קַמֵּיהּ דְּהַאי, וְנָפְקָא מִשּׁוּם אֲחוֹת אִשְׁתּוֹ בְּלֹא חֲלִיצָה וְיִיבּוּם. הִלְכָּךְ אָמְרִי' לְהוּ חֲלוֹצוּ, דְּאִי נַמִי מָיֵית אִידָךְ אָח לְבָתַר חֲלִיצָה דְּחַד – הָדַר הַאי חוֹלֵץ וְחָלֵץ לָהּ. תְּלָתָא נַמִי. מַאי שְׁנָא דְּנָקַט ד' אַחִין? אִי אָמְרַתְּ בִּשְׁלָמָא יֵשׁ זִיקָה – אַשְׁמְעִי' רְבוּתָא, דְּאע"ג דִּתְרֵי אַחֵי נִינְהוּ, וְלָא אַלִּימָא זִיקָתוֹ דְּקַמָּא דִּמְיַיבֵּם, דְּמָצֵינוּ לְמֵימַר הַהִיא רָמְיָא קַמֵּיהּ וַאֲחוֹתָהּ קַמֵּי' אָחִיו – וַאפ"ה אָסוּר, וכ"ש שְׁלֹשָׁה אַחִין, ב' מֵהֶם נְשׂוּאִים שְׁתֵּי אֲחָיוֹת, וּמֵתוּ, וְנָפְלוּ שְׁתֵּיהֶן לִפְנֵי זֶה – שְׁתֵּיהֶן אֲסוּרוֹת, דְּתַרְוַויְיהוּ עֲלֵיהּ רָמְיָא, וְזִיקָתוֹ חֲמוּרָה. וְכִי נָסֵיב – הָוֵי פָּגַע בַּאֲחוֹת זְקוּקָתוֹ. אֶלָּא אִי מִשּׁוּם בִּיטּוּל מִצְוַת יְבָמִין – אֲפִי' תְּלָתָא נַמִי, וּמֵתוּ הַשְּׁנַיִם הַנְּשׂוּאִים שְׁתֵּי אֲחָיוֹת – שְׁתֵּיהֶן חוֹלְצוֹת, דְּאִי מְיַיבֵּם חֲדָא – נָפְקָא אִידָךְ בְּלֹא כְּלוּם.

חֲמִשָּׁה

[לעיל ד. לקמן לו.]

צו א מיי' פ"י מהל' גירושין הלכה טו טוש"ע אה"ע סימן יב סעיף ד:
צז ב מיי' שם טוש"ע שם סעיף ג:
צח ג ד מיי' שם והל' עז טוש"ע שם סעיף ד:
א ה ו מיי' פ"ז מהלכו' יבום הלכה א טוש"ע אה"ע סי' קעה סע"ג:
ב ו מיי' שם טוש"ע אה"ע שם סעיף ד:
ג ח ט מיימן שם הל' ב טוש"ע אה"ע שם סעיף ה:
ד י מיי' שם הלכה א טוש"ע אה"ע שם סעיף ג:

לקמן סד: ב"מ קו: [ערכין ל. כתובות מג:]
[נ"ל דתניא]
לקמן מז. [תוספתא פ"ד]
[גיר' הערוך בוזז]
לעיל יח. כג: עדיות פ"ה מ"ה
[ע' תוס' לקמן כח. ד"ה רבי אליעזר]
[לקמן כח.]
[לעיל כ. סנהדרין נג.]
לעיל כ.
[לעיל יח.]
[שם]
נ"ל יקיימו
נ"ל ואיש אשר יקח

תוספות ישנים

ש"מ יש זיקה. וא"ת א"כ לחלוץ לחדא ולייבם לחדא וי"ל גזרה דלמא מייבם והדר חליץ וכי מייבם פגע באחות זקוקתו. ולא נהירא דכיון דקאמר ש"מ יש זיקה א"כ אין לגזור דלמא מייבם ברישא דטעם של זיקה פשוט הוא ולא יטעו כמו שאפרש לקמן בע"ה. וי"ל דטעמא דכיון שנאסרה עליו שעה אחת שוב לא יבא לה היתר עולמית וא"ת לרב דלא סבר כן לקמן מאי איכא למימר. וי"ל דמ"מ מוקים לה להך משנה כר' אליעזר דאמר כיון שנאסרה פעם אחת שוב אין לה היתר אף באיסורא דרבנן כי הכא דאין האיסור רק משום אחות זקוקתו. והא דדייקינן לקמן מדסיפא ר' אליעזר רישא לאו ר' אליעזר זהו לרבי יוחנן אבל רב לא סבר כן א"כ רב לא יסבור האי דיוקא:

תוספות חד מקמאי

ארבעה אחין שנים מהם נשואים ב' אחיות ומתו הנשואין לאחיות הרי אלו חולצות ולא מתייבמות דוקא בדליכא צרות אבל בדאיכא צרות כיון דחליצת צרות מעולה מאחרות חליץ לצרות ולא לאחיות דקי"ל כשמואל דאמר ב' יבמות הבאות מב' בתים חלץ (ליבמות) [לאחיות] לא נפטרו הצרות לצרות נפטרו אחיו' דלא אלימא זיקה לשוויה צרה כערוה ומי' אי חליץ לאחיות אהני למפטר נפשה. אבל לכתחלה אמרינן ליה דיחלוץ לצרות שהיא חליצה מעולה מן האחיות. אבל היכא דליכא צרות לא אפשר דלא למחלץ לאחיות. והוי יודע דאליבא דרב דאמר חליצה פסולה צריכה לחזור על האחין שתי האחיות כל אחת מהן צריכה חליצה משני האחין. ולפי דעתי הלכתא כרב בהא אע"ג דפליג עליה שמואל דקי"ל הלכתא כרב באסורא וראיה לדבר פסק זה ממה שפירש הרב אלפס [גמ"פ ר"ג] גבי פלוגתא דרבי ורבנן כשקדשה לשם יבמות דרבנן כרב ור' כשמואל וקי"ל כרבנן ורב אשי נמי אמר התם דכו"ע חליצה פסולה אינה פוטרת היינו כרב אלמא הלכתא כרב אע"ג דכתב הרב אלפס דכל הני שינויי לא סמכינן עלייהו והרב אלפס כתב דברי רב ודברי שמואל ולא פסק הלכתא כחד מנייהו ואולי סמך על הכלל שבידינו דהלכתא כרב באיסורא: ובמאי

הגהות הב"ח

(א) רש"י ד"ה נשי לא אסרו שכיבתן שכיבת זנות הקרובה לא אסרו את אשתו גמורה: (ב) רש"י ד"ה אחותה של ערוה כשהיא כצ"ל ותיבות אחותה כשהיא יבמתה נמחק:

גליון הש"ס

רש"י ד"ה דבזיז מיניה בוש הוא כו'. עי' נדה טו ע"ב תוד"ה אפילו ילדה:

חמשה – נמי למיתה דתרי לא חיישינן. אמר *רבא בר רב הונא אמר רב: שלש אחיות יבמות שנפלו לפני שני אחין יבמין, זה חולץ לאחת, וזה חולץ לאחת, ואמצעית צריכה חליצה משניהם. אמר ליה רבה: מדקאמרת אמצעית צריכה חליצה משניהם – קסברת יש זיקה, והויא לה חליצה פסולה, *וחליצה פסולה צריך לחזור על כל האחין. אי הכי, קמייתא נמי! – אי דנפול בבת אחת – הכי נמי, לא צריכא דנפול בזו אחר זו נפלה חדא – חלץ לה ראובן, נפלה אידך חלץ לה שמעון נפלה אידך חלץ לה האי מפקע זיקתו, חלץ לה האי מפקע זיקתו. *והאמר רב: אין זיקה! לדברי האומר יש זיקה קאמר. ושמואל אמר: אחד חולץ לכולן. – מכדי שמעינן ליה לשמואל דאמר: חליצה מעליא בעינן, דאמר שמואל: חלץ

חמשה נמי. שנים נשואים שתי אחיות, ומתו השנים ונשארו השלשה, דלמא אדמייבם חד מייתו להו תרי, ובטלה מצות יבמין. לפני שני אחין יבמין. כלומר, לפני שני אחי בעליהן שהן יבמיהן. אמצעית. כלומר, שלישית, ולאו דוקא נקט. צריכה חליצה משניהן. כדמפרש ואזיל: לא גרסינן מדקאמרת זה חולץ כו', אלא ה"ג. מדקאמרת צריכה חליצה משניהם קסברת יש זיקה והויא לה חליצה פסולה וחליצה פסולה צריכה לחזור כו'. כלומר, מדקאמרת צריכה חליצה משניהם, קסברת: אלימא מצות זיקת יבמין למירמי אתרווייהו. והך חליצה על כרחך חליצה פסולה היא, כלומר גרועה, שאם רצה לייבם – אינו יכול, דאחות חלוצתו היא, הילכך לאו מעלייתא היא וצריכה לחזור על כולן, דלא מיפקעא זיקה דתרווייהו בחליצה דחדא, משום דאלימא זיקה ורמיא אתרווייהו. קמייתא. שתים ראשונות נמי ליבעו חליצה משניהם, דחליצתן נמי לאו מעלייתא היא, דאי בעי לייבומי – לא מצי, הואיל ויש זיקה. בבת אחת. כלומר, אם באו לחלוץ כאחת, שלא הספיקה הראשונה לחלוץ עד שנפלה גם השניה והשלישית – הכי נמי דכולן צריכות לחזור אחר כל האחין. הכא דנפלו זו אחר זו. נפילתה של זו אחר חליצתה של זו. נפלה לה חדא חלץ לה ראובן. וחליצה כשרה היתה, שאם רצה – יכול לייבם. נפלה אידך חלץ לה שמעון. וגם זו כשרה, שאם רצה – מייבם. ואין כאן אחות זקוקה, שכבר חלצה אחותה קודם נפילת זו. נפלה שלישית, אי בעי לייבומי – לא מצי, דאחות חלוצת שניהם היא. ובולא כלום נמי לא נפקא, דאחות חלוצה אינה אלא מדברי סופרים, לקמן ב"החולץ" (דף מ:). הלכך, חלץ האי חליצה כל דהו, ולאו מעלייתא היא, שאם חפץ – לא ייבם. ומיהו, חליצתו וזיקתו שוות שתיהן לגרוע, ופקעה זיקתו בחליצתו. חלץ האי מפקע זיקה. והא אמר רב אין זיקה. בפרק "כילד" (לעיל דף יז:): א"ר הונא אמר רב: שומרת יבם שמתה – מותר באמה.

למיתה דתרי לא חיישינן. תימה: דבפ"ק דיומא (דף ב.), גבי הא דאמר ר' יהודה אף אשה אחרת מתקינין לו שמא תמות אשתו, ופרכי לה רבנן: א"כ אין לדבר סוף, ומאי קושיא? הוא רבנן חיישי הכא למיתה דחד ולא דתרי! ואר"י, דהכי פרכי ליה: כיון דחיישת למיתה דזמן מועט, אע"ג דלא שכיחא – תחוש נמי למיתה דתרי אע"ג דלא שכיח, וא"כ אין לדבר סוף?! ומשני התם (דף יג.) דלר' יהודה מיתה דחדא שכיחא, פירוש אפי' לזמן מועט, דתרי – לא שכיחא. והא דקאמרי התם רבנן מיתה לא שכיחא – לאו משום שאין לדבר סוף. דהא דקאמר אין לדבר סוף – היינו משום דלא שכיח, כדפרישי', כי מיתה דחד [דשכיח] יש לדבר סוף, דתרי ודאי לא שכיחי.

מדקאמרת אמצעית צריכה חליצה משניהם קא סברת יש זיקה וחליצה פסולה וכו'. ואית ספרים דגרסי: מדקאמר זה חולץ לאחת וזה חולץ לאחת קא סברת יש זיקה. ופי' בקונטרס דלא גרסי' ליה. ונראה דלא גריס ליה בקונטרס משום דלמ"ד אין זיקה – נמי, זה חולץ לאחת וזה חולץ לאחת, דאי אפשר לייבם אחת משום ביטול מצות יבמין. וליכא למימר נמי דאחד יחלוץ לשתיהן, דלמ"ד אין זיקה – נמי, אין חליצה פסולה של ראובן, שכבר חלץ לאחת, מפקעת זיקת שמעון השתוה. דהא לקמן קאמר: בשלמא צרה דרחל לא תפטר – משום דחליצת רחל חליצה פסולה היא. אלמא, אפי' למ"ד אין זיקה – אין חליצת רחל פוטרת זיקת צרתה השתוה. דהא אוקי דשמואל אליבא דמ"ד אין זיקה קאמר, וה"ה דה"נ לא תפטר חליצת ראובן השניה מאח השני, דהא אכתי לא מסיק אדעתיה לחלק בין מיפטר נפשה בין מיפטר צרה. ולר"י נראה דשפיר גרסי' ליה, דלפי האמת, למ"ד אין זיקה – חליצה גרועה פוטרת השתוה הימנה, דאמרי' בהדיא בפרק "ר"ג" (לקמן דף נא. ושם) דלמ"ד אין זיקה, חלץ לבעלת הגט – נפטרה צרתה, אע"ג דבעלת הגט חליצתה פסולה טפי משל צרה, שהרי חשובה כחלוצה אצלו למיסר בקרובותיה. וע"כ, שמואל דאמר חלץ לאחיות – לא נפטרו צרות, לבעלת הגט לא נפטרה צרה, סבר דיש זיקה. וסוגיא דבסמוך אינה לפי האמת, אלא ה"פ: בשלמא צרה דרחל לא תפטר, כלומר: אפי' אם תאמר דלמ"ד אין זיקה נמי חליצה פסולה צריכה לחזור, והשתא ניחא דצרת רחל לא תפטר, מ"מ צרה דלאה תפטר, דחליצה כשרה היא. תדע דאותה סוגיא אינה לפי האמת, דהא פריך בתר הכי: ואצרה דרחל מי מיפטרא והתנן כו', אלמא בעי למימר דלמ"ד אין זיקה לא מיפטרא רחל בחליצת צרה, אע"ג דלא אסירא צרה אלא מכחה, וכ"ש אם היו שוות. וא"כ איך מדקדק, אפילו לפי גירסת הקונט', דיש זיקה, מדקאמר אמצעית צריכה חליצה משניהם? אלא, על אותה סוגיא אין לסמוך, כדפרישי', דלא קאי הכי. וכי מפרש דשמואל התחיל ולא התחיל קאמר – לא יאמר עוד דשמואל אליבא דמ"ד אין זיקה קאמר, כמו שאפרש, דלדידיה חלץ לאחיות ולבעלת הגט נפטרו צרות, וגרסינן שפיר מדקאמר זה חולץ לאחת כו' קסבר יש זיקה. ומדקאמר אמצעית צריכה חליצה משניהם – קא חדר דחליצה פסולה צריכה לחזור, ואע"ג דתרווייהו יכול לדקדק תסיפא, מ"מ מה שיכול לדקדק מרישא – מדקדק. **וחליצה** פסולה צריך לחזור וכו'. לא [א] כמו שפירש בקונטרס דכל היכא שאינו יכול לייבם חשיבא חליצה פסולה, דהא אמר בפ"ק (לעיל דף יא:) גבי מחזיר גרושתו: או היא או צרתה חולצת, ולא חשיבא חליצת גרושה חליצה פסולה, אע"ג דאין יכול לייבמה. ולקמן נמי קאמר אלא צרה דלאה תפטר, דחליצתה כשרה. אלמא, חשיבא לה חליצה כשרה אע"ג דאסירא ליבמה משום ביטול מצות יבמין. דנהי דלא מבטל מצות יבמין מצרת רחל, דאע"ג דכשייבם לאה יהיה אסור בצרת רחל, כמו שאסור בצרת קרובת חלוצתו – מ"מ, חליצה מיהא בעיא דאורייתא, דאינה צרת אחות אשה לאחר שיבם לאה, [כיון שכבר] לא היתה צרת [אחות אחה] תחתת בעלה. וכשיחלוץ לצרת רחל – לא נייתסרא לאה, דמותר אדם בקרובת צרת חלוצתו, מ"מ איכא ביטול מצות יבמין, אם יבא לייבם לאה – דחיישינן שמא תמות צרת רחל, וקא מבטל מרחל מצות יבמין, וליכא למימר דיש לרחל צרות הרבה דליכא למיחש למיתה דכולהו, אי נמי כשחלץ ללאה קודם נפילת רחל – א"כ בתנם דחק לתרץ מאי לא נפטרו צרות ומאי צרות – צרות דעלמא דה"ל לאוקומי טפי בנפול בבת אחת, ואין כי אם צרה אחת ללאה וצרה אחת לרחל, דאז אסורה לייבם לאה משום ביטול מצות יבמין[ב]. אלא נראה לר"י דלא חשיבא חליצה פסולה אלא אחות זקוקתו למ"ד יש זיקה, או אחות חלוצתו לכ"ע, ובעלת הגט ובעלת מאמר, דבכולהו קלשא זיקה. דאחות זקוקתו דמיא לאחות אשתו דאין בה זיקה, ואחות חלוצתו כאחות גרושתו, ובעלת הגט דמיא לחלוצה, ובעלת מאמר לכנוסה דאין בה זיקה. °וכן סוטה, דרבנן דקרי ליה בירושלמי חליצה פסולה, גבי הא דא"ר שמעון ביאתה כו' דדמיא נמי לסוטה דאורייתא, דאין בה זיקה, דטומאה כתיב בה כעריות. אבל מחזיר גרושתו, ואסור לבטל מצות יבמין – לא נגרעה בהם הזיקה, ולהכי חשיבי חליצה כשרה. **דנפול** בזה אחר זה נפלה חדא חלץ לה ראובן כו'. הקשה ה"ר אברהם מבורגויי"ל: אמאי נקט שלש אחיות? דמידוש זה יכול להשמיענו אפי' בב' אחיות היכא דנפול בבת אחת, דכל אחד ואחד חולץ לשתיהן משום דיש זיקה, וחליצה פסולה צריכה לחזור על כל האחין! ותי': דהתם משכחת לה שמתייבמת אחת, דכשחלץ לשניה הויא ראשונה יבמה שהותרה ונאסרה וחזרה והותרה, דתחזור להיתירה הראשון ומתייבמת לאח השני. אע"ג דגם השני צריך לחלוץ לשניה משום דחליצה פסולה היא – מ"מ אינה אסורה לו הראשונה משום אחות חלוצתו, דכיון דחליצה זו לא עשה אלא משום חיזור, כדמוכח לקמן (דף כז:) דפריך רבי יוסי בר' חנינא לר' יוחנן דאמר: מתה השניה מותר בראשונה, ממתני' דקתני חולצות שתיהן ולא מתייבמות. ואמאי? ליקו חד מינייהו ולחלוץ לשניה כו'. והשיב לו ר' יוחנן: אחיות איני יודע מי שנאן. ואמאי לא שני ליה דחולצות ולא מתייבמות משום דשניה צריכה חליצה משניהם, ולכך אסורה לשניהם הראשונה? אלא ודאי לשני שריא, כיון דלא חלץ לה אלא משום חיזור. ואין ראיה, דאיכא למימר דר' יוחנן לא בעי לשנויי הכי משום דסבר כשמואל דחליצה פסולה אין צריך לחזור, ולפי סברתו היה יכול לומר דבשתי אחיות שריא אפי' שניה לשני, *אם שחלצו לראשונה. דרב לא מפליג לקמן בין ראשונה לשניה, דאמר לקמן: אפי' מתה ראשונה מותר בשניה. ואין נראה לר"י, דלעיל פ"ב (ד' יח.) משמע דלכ"ע, בין למ"ד יש זיקה בין למ"ד אין זיקה – שתיהן חולצות, אי משום ביטול מצות יבמין או משום שנאסרה עליו שעה אחת, כדפי' לעיל. ודוקא ר' יוחנן הוא דאמר אחיות איני יודע מי שנאן, ומתייבמת הראשונה: **נפלה** אידך חליץ לה כו'. והא דקרי לה אמצעית אע"פ שהיא אחרונה – משום דהאחרות כל אחת לא חלצה אלא מן האחד, וזו חולצת משניהם. **לדברי** האומר יש זיקה קאמר. ולא מסתברא ליה למימר דרב סבר יש זיקה, והיא דשומרת יבם – לדברי האומרים אין זיקה קאמר. משום דהתם קמ"ל תרתי: דאין זיקה, ומחייס אסור משום ביטול מצות יבמין, משום הכי סבירא ליה דהיא אליבא דנפשיה:

מאי

וכמאי דאמר שמואל חליץ לאחיות לא נפטרו צרות לצרות נפטרו אחיות פסק הרב כשמואל ואליבא דרב אשי דאע"ג דלא אלימא זיקה לשווי צרה כערוה והוצרך הרב ז"ל למפסק הלכתא כשמואל ואליבא דרב אשי משום דסוגייא קמא בשמעתתא משוי לחליצה צרות כאחיות ופליגא אדרב אשי לפיכך הוצרך ליה למיפסק כשמואל ולעולם בחליצה פסולה דפליגי רב ושמואל הלכה כרב דחליצה פסולה צריכה לחזור על כל האחין. הלכך הא דתנן הכא חולצות האחיות ולא מתייבמות כל אחת ואחת צריכה חליצה משניהם והרב ז"ל ודאי הו"ל (להצריך) [לפרש] כדברי רב שאמר ג' אחיות יבמות וכו' כדאוקימנא בגמ' דנפול בזה אחר זה אבל בבת א' כל אחת צריכה חליצה משניהם אלא שקצר הרב ז"ל דבריו כמנהגו ואי איכא א) מאן דס"ל דמשום דס"ל לרב אלפס הלכתא כשמואל לכך קצר בדברי הרב. ומנ"ל לרב ז"ל דהלכתא כשמואל והא קי"ל כרב באיסורי. ואי משום דתניא כוותיה דרב אשי חליץ לאחיות לא נפטרו צרות לצרות (לא) נפטרו אחיות לא פליג רב אדשמואל בהא מלתא וכל המיקל בו צריך להביא ראיה לדבריו ואין רוח חכמים נוחה הימנו. והוי יודע דמאי דאמרי' בגמ' גבי האי מתני' דילמא אדמייבם חד מיית אידך וקא בטלה מצות יבמין כלומר דאזלא אחותה בלא חליצה דוקא אליבא דמ"ד אין זיקה אבל למ"ד יש זיקה וקי"ל כותיה ג) דלמא אדמייבם חד מיית אידך לא מפטרא אחותה בלא חליצה דתנן בפ' החולץ שומרת יבם שקדש אחיו את אחותה משום ר' יהודה בן בתירה אמרו אומרים לו המתן עד שיעשה אחיך הגדול מעשה מתה היבמה יכנוס את אשתו מת היבם צריכה חליצה ואמר נמי בר"פ כיצד אמר רב הונא אמר רב שומרת יבם שמתה מותר באמה אלמא קסבר אין זיקה ואסיקנא לאחר מיתה אין מחיים לא דאסור לבטל מצות יבמין ופרש"י ז"ל דאזלא יבמה בלא חליצה ג) כדתנן מת יבם מוציא את אשתו בגט ואת אשת אחיו בחליצה וכיון דקי"ל יש זיקה אפי' בתרי אדמייבם חד מיית אידך לא מפטרה אחותה בלא חליצה אמר רבא בר רב הונא אמר רב שלשה אחיות יבמות שנפלו לשני אחים יבמין זה חולץ לאחת וזה חולץ לאחת והאמצעית צריכה חליצה משניהם פירוש אמצעית שלישי' א"ל רבא מדקאמרת אמצעית צריכה חליצה משניהם קסבר יש זיקה ולפיכך חליצה פסולה צריכה לחזור על כל האחין אי הכי קמייתא נמי (לא) צריך אי נפיל בב"א הכי [נמי לא צריכא] דנפיל בזה אח"ז נפל חדא [חליץ] ראובן נפל אידך חליץ שמעון נפל אידך חליץ האי מיפקע זיקתו פירוש נפיל בבת א' בעליהן ששלשתן צריכות חליצה אעפ"י שמתו ג' בעליהן בזה אחר זה השתא מיהת כשבאו לפני ב"ד חליצה פסולה היא שכל אחד אחות וכל א' וא' צריכה חליצה מן האחין אבל בנפול בזה אח"ז שכל א' שמת בעלה באה לב"ד לחלוץ ועדיין לא מתו האחין האחרים וחלץ לה ראובן חליצה כשירה הוא ד) כיון שמת האחד קודם שמת השלישי וחליצה כשרה היא כשמת השלישי חליצה פסולה היא בין למ"ד יש זיקה בין למ"ד אין זיקה דאחות חלוצתו ומיהו למ"ד אין זיקה אין צריכה לחזור על כל האחין. למ"ד יש זיקה לא אלימא חליצה פסולה למפקע זיקה וכ"ת מכדי רב אתא לאשמועינן חליצה פסולה צריכה לחזור על כל האחין למה לי לאשמועינן בנפול בזה אחר זה ובאמצעית (אתא) לאשמועינן בנפול בבת אחת וכל אחת צריכה חליצה משניהם. אין הכי נמי אלא רבותא אשמועינן לא מיבעיא אי דנפיל בבת אחת דזיקה אלימא היא וצריכה לחזור על האחין אלא אפילו חלץ זה לאחת וזה חלץ לאחת דקלשא ליה זיקה משום איסור [אחות] חלוצתו אפ"ה צריכה לחזור על האחין (ליבומי) [אי נמי] לא מיבעיא דנפול בבת א' דכיון דיש זיקה הו"ל חליצה פסולה דאורייתא דהיא זקוקתו ואלא אפי' בזה אח"ז שאין החליצה פסולה משום זיקה אלא משום [אחות] חלוצתו שאינה פסולה אלא מדרבנן [מ"מ] צריכה לחזור על האחין. וחליצה פסולה דאשמועי' משום דאינה ראיה להתייבם. ושמואל אמר א' חולץ לכולן. מכדי שמעינן ליה לשמואל דאמר חליצה מעולה בעיא דאמר (ש"מ) חלץ לאחיות לא נפטרו צרות היכי דקיימא חליצה דשמעון חליצה כשרה חלין לה ראובן חליצה פסולה ומשני מאי אחד חולץ לכולן אאמצעית דהא לא מיפטר לה. והא כולן קאמר כיון דרובא גביה קרי להו כולן ואב"א כי קאמר שמואל חליצה מעולה בעיא למפטר צרה אבל אנפשה פטרה. כתבתי דברי שמואל אע"פ דהלכה כרב לאשמועינן דבמלתא דחלץ לאחיות לא פליג עליה דרב ואיכא למ"ד אליבא דרב כיון דחליצה פסולה צריכה לחזור על כל האחין הכי נמי צריכה לחזור על כל הצרות וכיון דהלכה כשמואל דאמר [חלץ] לצרות נפטרו אחיות שמעינן דלית הלכתא כרב דהא בהא תליא. ולאו מילתא היא דגרסינן בפרק רבן גמליאל נתן לה גט לזו וגט לזו חולץ לראשונה וכו' לימא תהוי תיובתא לשמואל דאמר חלץ לבעלת הגט לא נפטרה צרה והדר פריך לרב דאמר חליצה פסולה צריך לחזור על כל האחין מסיפא דקתני וכן אתה אומר בשני יבמין ויבמה אחת ואילו מרישא לא פריך ליה אלמא לאו מילתא מיתליין אהדדי נינהו וללישנא קמא חלץ לאחיות אף האחיות לא נפטרו וללישנא בתרא חלץ לאחיות נפטרו אחיות ופסק הרב כלישנא בתרא: איבעיא להו בעלת הגט ובעלת מאמר איזה מהן קודמת לחליצה ואסיקנא דכי הדדי נינהו

א) עי' ברא"ש כאן. ב) נראה דצ"ל אפילו אדמייבם חד מייה אידך לא מפטרא וכו'. ג) נראה דחסר כאן וצ"ל והא דתנן דאם מת יבם מוציא את אשת אחיו בחליצה היינו למ"ד דיש זיקה וכיון דקיי"ל דיש זיקה וכו'. ד) נ"ל וכן כשמת השני.

נ"ל רבה. יעב"ץ.

לקמן נא: נג.

לעיל יז: ע"ש

ס"א אחר

הגהות הגר"א

[א] תום' ד"ה וחליצה. כמו שפירש בקונטרס. נ"ב וכ"ד הרמב"ם: [ב] שם אלא נראה לר"י דלא כו'. נ"ב וכן עיקר ועי"ל כ ע"ב וכ"ה בתוספתא פ"ו (ועמ"ש רבינו בא"ה ע"ע סי' ק"ע ס"ק ט"ו וס"ק מ"ה):

גליון הש"ס

תום' ד"ה וחליצה פסולה וכו' וכן סוטה דרבנן דקרי ליה בירושלמי וכו'. ע' לעיל דף יא ע"א תד"ה רש"א:

[א]חָלַץ לָאֲחָיוֹת לֹא נִפְטְרוּ צָרוֹת. הֵיכָא דְּקַיְימָא חֲלִיצָה דְּשִׁמְעוֹן חֲלִיצָה כְּשֵׁרָה, חָלֵיץ לָהּ רְאוּבֵן חֲלִיצָה פְּסוּלָה. מַאי "אֶחָד חוֹלֵץ לְכוּלָּן" נַמִי דְּקָאָמַר – אַאֶמְצָעִית. וְהָא כּוּלָּן קָאָמַר! – כֵּיוָן דְּרוּבָּה גַּבֵּיהּ קָרֵי לֵיהּ "כּוּלָּן". וְאִיבָּעֵית אֵימָא: כִּי קָאָמַר שְׁמוּאֵל חֲלִיצָה מַעַלְיָא בָּעֵינַן – [ב]ה"מ לְמִיפְטַר צָרָתָהּ, אֲבָל מִפַּטְרָא נַפְשָׁהּ – פָּטְרָה. גּוּפָא, אָמַר שְׁמוּאֵל: חָלַץ לָאֲחָיוֹת – לֹא נִפְטְרוּ צָרוֹת, לַצָּרוֹת – נִפְטְרוּ אֲחָיוֹת. *חָלַץ לְבַעֲלַת הַגֵּט – לֹא נִפְטְרָה צָרָה, לַצָּרָה – נִפְטְרָה בַּעֲלַת הַגֵּט. *חָלַץ לְבַעֲלַת הַמַּאֲמָר – לֹא נִפְטְרָה צָרָה, לַצָּרָה – נִפְטְרָה בַּעֲלַת מַאֲמָר. מַאי שְׁנָא לָאֲחָיוֹת דְּלָא נִפְטְרוּ צָרוֹת – דְּהָוְיָא (א) לוֹ אֲחוֹת אִשָּׁה בְּזִיקָה, – חָלַץ לַצָּרוֹת נַמִי לָא לִיפַּטְרוּ אֲחָיוֹת, דְּהָוְיָא לְהוּ צָרוֹת אֲחוֹת אִשָּׁה בְּזִיקָה! – קָסָבַר שְׁמוּאֵל: אֵין זִיקָה. *וְהָא אָמַר שְׁמוּאֵל: יֵשׁ זִיקָה! – לְדִבְרֵי הָאוֹמֵר אֵין זִיקָה קָאָמַר. אִי הָכִי, חָלַץ לָאֲחָיוֹת אַמַּאי לֹא נִפְטְרוּ צָרוֹת? בִּשְׁלָמָא צָרָה דְּרָחֵל לָא תִּיפָּטֵר – דְּכֵיוָן דְּחָלַץ לָהּ לְלֵאָה וַהֲדַר חָלַץ לְרָחֵל – הָוְיָא לָהּ חֲלִיצָה דְּרָחֵל חֲלִיצָה פְּסוּלָה. אֶלָּא צָרָה דְּלֵאָה תִּיפָּטֵר! – מַאי "לֹא נִפְטְרוּ צָרוֹת" נַמִי דְּקָאָמַר – אַצָּרָה דְּרָחֵל, – וְהָא "צָרוֹת" קָאָמַר! – צָרוֹת דְּעָלְמָא. – אִי הָכִי, חָלַץ "לַצָּרוֹת נִפְטְרוּ אֲחָיוֹת", – וְאַצָּרַת רָחֵל מִי מִיפַּטְרָא? וְהָא תְּנַן: *[ג]אָסוּר אָדָם בְּצָרַת קְרוֹבַת חֲלוּצָתוֹ! – שְׁמוּאֵל נַמִי, הִתְחִיל וְלֹא הִתְחִיל קָאָמַר: הִתְחִיל בָּאֲחָיוֹת – לֹא יִגְמוֹר בַּצָּרוֹת, דִּתְנַן: אָסוּר אָדָם בְּצָרַת קְרוֹבַת חֲלוּצָתוֹ, הִתְחִיל בַּצָּרוֹת – יִגְמוֹר אַף בָּאֲחָיוֹת, דִּתְנַן: *מוּתָּר אָדָם בִּקְרוֹבַת צָרַת חֲלוּצָתוֹ. רַב אַשִׁי אָמַר: לְעוֹלָם כִּדְקָאָמְרַתְּ, [ד]וּמִשּׁוּם דְּלָא אַלִּימָא זִיקָה לְשַׁוּוֹיֵי לַצָּרָה כְּעֶרְוָה. תַּנְיָא כְּוָותֵיהּ דְּרַב אַשִׁי: חָלַץ לָאֲחָיוֹת – לֹא נִפְטְרוּ צָרוֹת, הָא לַצָּרוֹת נִפְטְרוּ אֲחָיוֹת – מַאי טַעְמָא, לָאו מִשּׁוּם דְּקָסָבַר יֵשׁ זִיקָה, וְלָא אַלִּימָא זִיקָה לְשַׁוּוֹיֵיהּ לַצָּרָה כְּעֶרְוָה?! א"ר אַבָּא בַּר מֶמֶל: הָא מַנִּי – ב"ש הִיא, דִּתְנַן: *בֵּית שַׁמַּאי מַתִּירִין הַצָּרוֹת לָאַחִין. – אִי הָכִי, יַבּוּמֵי נַמִי תִּתְיַיבֵּם! – כְּרַבִּי יוֹחָנָן בֶּן נוּרִי, דְּאָמַר: *בּוֹאוּ וּנְתַקֵּן לָהֶם לַצָּרוֹת שֶׁיְּהוּ חוֹלְצוֹת וְלֹא מִתְיַיבְּמוֹת. – וְהָאָמַר מָר *לֹא הִסְפִּיקוּ לִגְמוֹר אֶת הַדָּבָר עַד שֶׁנִּטְרְפָה הַשָּׁעָה! אָמַר רַב נַחְמָן בַּר יִצְחָק: אַחֲרָיו חָזְרוּ וְתִקְּנוּ. § אִיבַּעְיָא לְהוּ: בַּעֲלַת

רש"י

חָלַץ לָאֲחָיוֹת. שְׁתֵּי אֲחָיוֹת שֶׁנָּפְלוּ לְפָנָיו מִשְּׁנֵי אַחִים, וְכָל אַחַת צָרָתָהּ עִמָּהּ, וְחָלַץ לָאֲחָיוֹת – לֹא נִפְטְרוּ צָרוֹתֵיהֶן, הוֹאִיל וְאִי בָּעֵי לְיַיבּוּמֵי – לָא מָצֵי. אֶלָּא יַחֲלוֹץ לַצָּרוֹת וְיִפָּטְרוּ אֲחָיוֹת. וְאע"ג דְּצָרוֹת נַמִי, אִי הֲוָה בָּעֵי לָא הֲוָה מְיַיבֵּם – מִיהוּ, קַל אִיסּוּרָם מִשֶּׁל אֲחָיוֹת. הִלְכָּךְ, אַף חֲלִיצָתָם מְשׁוּבַּחַת מִשֶּׁל אֲחָיוֹת, וְהָכִי מְפָרֵשׁ לְקַמָּן. הֵיכָא דְּקַיְימָא חֲלִיצָה דְּשִׁמְעוֹן חֲלִיצָה כְּשֵׁרָה. לַחֲלוֹץ לַשְּׁנִיָּה, שֶׁהוּא לֹא חָלַץ לָרִאשׁוֹנָה. חָלַץ לָהּ רְאוּבֵן חֲלִיצָה פְּסוּלָה. בִּתְמִיָּה, רְאוּבֵן שֶׁחָלַץ לָרִאשׁוֹנָה וְהָוְיָא הָךְ אֲחוֹת חֲלוּצָתוֹ, וְלָא חֲלִיצָה מְעַלְּיָא הִיא כְּדְשִׁמְעוֹן, דְּזִיקָה גְּרֵידְתָּא הִיא. אַאֶמְצָעִית. כְּלוֹמַר, הַשְּׁלִישִׁית, לְאַחַר שֶׁחָלַץ שִׁמְעוֹן לַשְּׁנִיָּה שֶׁהִיא עַל שְׁנֵיהֶן אֲחוֹת חֲלוּצָה, וּשְׁנֵיהֶן שָׁוִין בָּהּ. וְקָסָבַר: חֲלִיצָה פְּסוּלָה אֵין צְרִיכָה לַחֲזוֹר עַל כָּל הָאַחִין. כֵּיוָן דְּרוּבָּה גַּבֵּיהּ. שֶׁהַחוֹלֵץ לַשְּׁלִישִׁית חָלַץ לַב'. לְמִיפְטַר צָרָה. כִּדְקָאָמְרִי': לֹא נִפְטְרוּ צָרוֹת. אֲבָל מִיפַּטְרָא נַפְשָׁהּ פָּטְרָה. בַּחֲלִיצָה דְּכָל דְּהוּ. הִלְכָּךְ אֶחָד חוֹלֵץ לְג', הֵיכָא דְּלֵיכָּא צָרוֹת בַּהֲדַיְיהוּ. לְבַעֲלַת הַגֵּט. ב' יְבָמוֹת מֵאָח אֶחָד, וְנָתַן יָבָם גֵּט לְאַחַת מֵהֶן – שׁוּב אֵין חֲלִיצָתָהּ הוֹגֶנֶת כָּל כָּךְ, דִּקְלִישָׁא זִיקָתָהּ, וְאִם חָלַץ לָהּ – לֹא נִפְטְרָה צָרָה. חָלַץ לְבַעֲלַת מַאֲמָר. עָשָׂה מַאֲמָר בְּאַחַת מִנְּשֵׁי אָחִיו הַמֵּת, וְאח"כ חָלַץ לָהּ – לֹא נִפְטְרָה צָרָה. שֶׁחֲלִיצָה זוֹ אֵינָהּ פּוֹטֶרֶת לְגַמְרֵי, שֶׁעֲדַיִין צְרִיכָה גֵּט לְמַאֲמָרוֹ, כִּדְתְנַן בְּפֶרֶק ר"ג (לקמן דף נ.): עָשָׂה מַאֲמָר וְחָלַץ – צְרִיכָה הֵימֶנּוּ גֵּט. וְאע"ג דְּיָהֵיב לָהּ גֵּט אַחַר דְּחָלַץ לָהּ הוּא דְּמַהַנְיָא, אֲבָל צָרָתָהּ צְרִיכָה חֲלִיצָה, אֲבָל חָלַץ לַצָּרָה נִפְטְרָה בַּעֲלַת מַאֲמָר מֵחֲלִיצָה וְאֵינָהּ צְרִיכָה אֶלָּא גֵּט לְמַאֲמָרוֹ. דְּהָוְיָא אֲחוֹת אִשָּׁה בְּזִיקָה. וְאִי הֲוָה בָּעֵי לְיַיבּוּמֵי לָא מָצֵי, וּלְהָכִי גְּרִיעָה חֲלִיצָתָהּ. לַצָּרוֹת נַמִי. הָא צָרַת אֲחוֹת זְקוּקָה הִיא, וַאֲסִירָא לְיַיבּוּמֵי, דְּצָרָה בִּמְקוֹם עֶרְוָה קָיְימָא. וְהָאָמַר שְׁמוּאֵל כו'. בְּפ"ב. אִי הָכִי. דְּאֵין זִיקָה, חָלַץ לָאֲחָיוֹת שֶׁחֲלִיצָה הוֹגֶנֶת הִיא. בִּשְׁלָמָא צָרָה דְּרָחֵל. דְּחָלְצָה בָּאַחֲרוֹנָה – לֹא תִּפָּטֵר, דַּחֲלִיצָה דְּרָחֵל גְּרוּעָה הֲוַאי, דְּאִי בָּעֵי לְיַיבּוּמֵי – לָא מָצֵי, דַּאֲחוֹת חֲלוּצָתוֹ הִיא. אֶלָּא צָרָה דְּלֵאָה תִּיפָּטֵר. דַּחֲלִיצַת לֵאָה כְּשֵׁרָה הִיא, דְּאִי הֲוָה בָּעֵי מָצֵי לְיַיבּוּמֵי. צָרוֹת דְּעָלְמָא. כְּלוֹמַר, כָּל הֵיכָא דְּמִיתְרְמֵי כה"ג – לֹא נִפְטְרוּ צָרוֹת שֶׁל אַחֲרוֹנָה. אִי הָכִי. דְּצָרוֹת דְּקָאָמַר שְׁמוּאֵל – בְּצָרָה דְּרָחֵל שֶׁחָלְצָה בָּאַחֲרוֹנָה קָאָמַר. חָלַץ לַצָּרוֹת נִפְטְרוּ אֲחָיוֹת. בִּתְמִיָּה, דְּכִי חָלַץ לְצָרַת אֲחוֹת הַחֲלוּצָה נִפְטְרָה אֲחוֹת הַחֲלוּצָה. אַצָּרָה דְּרָחֵל מִי מִיפַּטְרָא. אַחֲלִיצָה דְּצָרָה מִי מִיפַּטְרָה רָחֵל? וְהָא תְּנַן. בְּ"הַחוֹלֵץ". אָסוּר אָדָם בְּצָרַת קְרוֹבַת חֲלוּצָתוֹ. וַאֲפִילּוּ לֹא הָיְתָה צָרָתָהּ מֵאָחִיו אֶלָּא מִנָּכְרִי. וְטַעְמָא הָתָם מְפָרֵשׁ. וְהָכָא נַמִי, אִי הֲוָה בָּעֵי לְיַיבּוּמֵי – לָא מָצֵי. הִתְחִיל בָּאֲחָיוֹת. שֶׁחָלַץ לְלֵאָה, לֹא יִגְמוֹר בַּצָּרוֹת, לֹא פָּטְרָה חֲלִיצַת צָרָה דְּרָחֵל אֶת רָחֵל. דִּתְנַן אָסוּר אָדָם כו'. וכ"ש דְּלֹא יִגְמוֹר בָּאֲחָיוֹת, דַּחֲלִיצַת רָחֵל לָא מִיפַּטְרָה צָרָה, דְּלָאו חֲלִיצָה מַעַלְיְיתָא הִיא, דַּאֲחוֹת חֲלוּצָתוֹ הִיא, אֶלָּא שְׁתֵּיהֶן צְרִיכוֹת חֲלִיצָה. הִתְחִיל בַּצָּרוֹת. שֶׁחָלַץ לְצָרַת לֵאָה. יִגְמוֹר אַף בָּאֲחָיוֹת. אִם רָצָה לַחֲלוֹץ לְרָחֵל – נִפְטְרָה צָרָתָהּ. וְאע"ג דְּרָחֵל קְרוֹבַת לֵאָה שֶׁהִיא צָרַת חֲלוּצָתוֹ – לָא גְּרִיעַ בְּהָכִי, דִּתְנַן: מוּתָּר אָדָם בִּקְרוֹבַת צָרַת חֲלוּצָתוֹ. וְה"נ, כֵּיוָן דְּאֵין זִיקָה, אִי הֲוָה בָּעֵי לְיַיבּוּמֵי לְרָחֵל מְיַיבֵּם, וְכָל שֶׁכֵּן גָּמַר בְּצָרַת רָחֵל וְלֹא בְּרָחֵל, *דִּשְׁכִיחָא מִילְּתָא טְפֵי. לְעוֹלָם. כִּדְאָמַר שְׁמוּאֵל בְּרֵישָׁא, חָלַץ לָאֲחָיוֹת לֹא נִפְטְרוּ צָרוֹת, מִשּׁוּם דְּיֵשׁ זִיקָה, וַחֲלִיצַת הָאֲחָיוֹת גְּרוּעָה, וַאֲפִילּוּ צָרַת לֵאָה לָא מִיפַּטְרָה – חָלַץ לַצָּרוֹת נִפְטְרוּ אֲחָיוֹת, דַּחֲלִיצָתָן מְשׁוּבַּחַת מִשֶּׁל אֲחָיוֹת. וּדְקַשְׁיָא לָךְ: הָוְיָא צָרַת אֲחוֹת אִשָּׁה בְּזִיקָה, וְהָוְיָא כִּי אֲחוֹת זְקוּקָה גּוּפָהּ – לָא הִיא, מִשּׁוּם דְּלָא אֲלִימָא זִיקָה לְשַׁוּוּיֵי לַצָּרָה כִּי עֶרְוָה, וְלָא גָּזְרוּ חֲכָמִים אֶלָּא בַּאֲחוֹת זְקוּקָה. הַצָּרוֹת לָאַחִין. וַאֲפִילּוּ צָרַת אֲחוֹת אִשָּׁה שָׁרֵי לְיַיבּוּמֵי, וְכ"ש צָרַת אֲחוֹת זְקוּקָה. אִי הָכִי. אַמַּאי תָּנֵי חָלַץ? יַבּוּמֵי נַמִי תִּתְיַיבֵּם הַצָּרָה! בַּעֲלַת

תוספות

מאי אחד חולץ לכולן דקאמר **אאמצעית**. תימה: דלקמן מסקינן דשמואל התחיל ולא התחיל קאמר. והתחיל באחיות לא יגמור בצרות, ולא מיפטרא רחל בחליצת צרתה, וכ"ש היכא דשניהן שוין. דבעינן חליצה מתרוייהו. דלהאי שינויא לא מפלגינן בין מיפטר נפשה למיפטר צרה! ואר"י: דההוא דמפרש לקמן דשמואל התחיל ולא התחיל קאמר – סבר כשינויא דבסמוך, דמפלגינן בין מיפטר נפשה למיפטר צרה. ושינויא דהכא דאחד חולץ לכולן אאמצעית – סבר כרב אשי, דאמר לקמן: לא אלימא זיקה לשויי צרה כערוה, וחליצת צרות הויא חליצה כשרה. ולהכי חלץ לאחיות – לא נפטרו צרות. אבל הכא, דשתיהן שוין – אחד חולץ לכולן. **אלא** צרה דלאה תיפטר. דהא חליצה כשרה היא. פי' בקונט': דאי בעי מייבם לה. וא"א לומר כן, דאסירא ליה משום ביטול מצות יבמין. ומ"מ לא חשיב בהכי חליצה פסולה, כדפרישית לעיל.

א"ה חלץ לצרות נפטרו אחיות **ואצרת רחל מי מיפטרא**. פירוש: כיון דאוקמה חלץ לאחיות לא נפטרו צרות דוקא מרחל, ומשום שחלץ ללאה, בענין זה נמי שחלץ ללאה חלץ לצרות נמי לא נפטרו אחיות.

שמואל התחיל ולא התחיל קאמר. השתא לפי המסקנא לית ליה להא דשמואל לדברי האומר אין זיקה [קאמר], דלפי האמת למ"ד אין זיקה חלץ לאחיות ולבעלת גט – נפטרו צרות (ב) אחיות. אלא שמואל אליבא דנפשיה, דאית ליה זיקה, קאמר. והא דלא קאמר "אלא" – לפי שלא הוזכר שם אמורא תחלה. ומיירי כשחלץ ללאה קודם נפילת רחל וצרתה, ולהכי התחיל בצרת לאה – יגמור אף ברחל, דכשנפלה רחל כבר נפטרה לאה בחליצת צרתה, וחליצת רחל חליצה כשרה היא, דלא הויא אלא קרובת צרת חלוצתו. וקצת דוחק הוא, דה"ל לפרש בהדיא דאיירי בנפול זה אחר זה, כיון דעד השתא הוה איירי בנפול בבת אחת. ועוד אמר ר"י: דמצינו לפרש דאיירי אפי' נפול בבת אחת, כדס"ד עד השתא, ואפ"ה – התחיל בצרת לאה יגמור ברחל. ואע"ג דחליצת הצרה הויא חליצה פסולה דהויא לה צרת אחות אשה בזיקה ולא מיפטרה לאה בחליצתה מ"מ חשיב חליצת רחל חליצה כשרה ואפי' אי חלץ ללאה ברישא קודם רחל כיון דלא נשתייר בלאה אלא זיקה מועטת שכבר חלץ לצרתה – חליצה חשובה טפי. ולהכי לא חשיב רחל אחות חלוצתו, כעין שפירש ה"ר אברהם לעיל. ואע"ג דקודם שחלץ לצרת לאה כבר נאסרה רחל, ושמואל סבר ב"החולץ" (לקמן ד' מ:): כיון שנאסרה עליו שעה אחת נאסרה עולמית, מכל מקום הוי חליצת רחל חליצה כשרה, כיון דעכשיו אינה אחות זקוקתו, ואינה אסורה אלא משום שנאסרה עליו כבר.

תניא כוותיה דרב **אשי**. אברייתא לא שייך למימר דהתחיל ולא התחיל קאמר – דא"כ הוה ליה לפרושי הכי בהדיא. אבל שמואל, דאיירי נמי בבעלת הגט ובעלת מאמר – נקט לשון השוה בכולן. **א"ה** יבומי נמי תתייבם. וא"ת: אין ה"נ, ומ"מ נקט חליצה לאשמועינן דחליצה פסולה אינה פוטרת, כמו שמואל ללישנא דהתחיל ולא התחיל ה"מ למינקט יבום! וי"ל: דשמואל לא נקט יבום משום דמתני' היא: מותר אדם בקרובת כו', אבל ברייתא ה"ל למנקט יבום, דעדיפא טפי. אי נמי לשמעינן תרוייהו.

אחריו חזרו ותקנו. דחוק לומר כן, משום דלא מסתבר ליה למימר דלא אלימא זיקה לשווי לצרה כערוה.

בעלת

עין משפט נר מצוה

ה א מיי' פ"ז מהלכות יבום הל' ט סמג עשין נא טוש"ע אה"ע סימן קע סעיף יז יח וסימן קעד סעיף א:

ו ב מיי' שם פ"ה הל' יב סמג שם טוש"ע שם סעיף יט ועי' בטור ובב"י:

ז ג מיי' שם פ"ה הל' טו ופ"ו הלכה כ טוש"ע שם סי' קסב סעיף ה:

ח ד מיי' שם פ"ה הל' יב טוש"ע שם סי' קע סעיף יח:

תוספות ישנים

לדברי האומר אין זיקה וא"ת אמאי חלץ לבעלת הגט לא נפטרה צרה הא אמרינן לקמן פרק ר"ג דלמ"ד אין זיקה חלץ לבעלת הגט נפטרה צרה. וי"ל דהך דלקמן מיירי לפי מסקנא דהכא דסבר שמואל יש זיקה ולכך לא נפטרה צרה. עוד פי' הר"מ דאף כי נמי אמרינן הכא דשמואל איירי אף לדברי האומר אין זיקה היינו דווקא רישא דמלתא דחלץ לאחיות אבל האי דקאמר חלץ לבעלת הגט לא נפטרה צרה מיירי [דוקא] למ"ד יש זיקה. והאי דנקט מלתא כתנאי. י"ל דרישא אשמעינן חדושא דאע"ג דאין זיקה מ"מ חלץ לאחיות לא נפטרו צרות אע"ג דשאר חליצה פסולה פטרה למ"ד אין זיקה פסול דאחיות חמיר טפי וסיפא אשמעינן דלמ"ד יש זיקה חלץ לבעלת הגט לא נפטרה צרה אע"ג דשאר חליצה פסולה פטרה היינו דווקא למ"ד אין זיקה אבל למ"ד יש זיקה לא פטרה:

מסורת הש"ס

לקמן נח.

לקמן נג.

לעיל יח:

לקמן מ:

שם

לעיל יג. עדיות פ"ד מ"ח [לעיל ט.]

[לעיל יג: יד:]

[לעיל טו.]

דשביחא

הגהות הב"ח

(א) גמ' דהויא לה אחות אשה: (ב) תוס' ד"ה שמואל וכו' נפטרו צרות אלא שמואל כצ"ל ותיבת אחיות נמחק:

עין משפט
נר מצוה

ט א מיי' פ"ה מהל' יבום הל' ז טוש"ע אה"ע סימן קע סעיף יז:
י ב ג מיי' פ"ז מהלכות יבום הל' ד סמג עשין נא נב טוש"ע שם סימן קעה סעיף א:

בעלת הגט ובעלת מאמר — איזו מהן קודמת? בעלת הגט עדיפא — (א) משום דאתחיל בה *בחליצה, או דלמא בעלת מאמר עדיפא משום דקרובה לביאה? אמר רב אשי, ת"ש: *ומודה ר"ג שיש גט אחר מאמר, ומאמר אחר גט. אי גט עדיף — לא ליהני מאמר אבתריה, ואי מאמר עדיף — לא ליהני גט אבתריה! אלא לאו ש"מ כי [א]הדדי נינהו, ש"מ. אמר רב *הונא אמר רב: ב' אחיות יבמות שנפלו לפני יבם אחד, חלץ לראשונה — הותרה, חלץ לשנייה — הותרה. מתה ראשונה מותר בשנייה, ואין צריך לומר מתה שנייה שמותר בראשונה, משום דהויא יבמה שהותרה ונאסרה וחזרה והותרה — תחזור להיתירה הראשון. ורבי יוחנן אמר: [ב]מתה שנייה — מותר בראשונה. אבל מתה ראשונה — אסור בשנייה. מ"ט — שכל יבמה שאין אני קורא בה בשעת נפילה "יבמה יבא עליה" הרי זו כאשת אח שיש לה בנים, ואסורה — ורב לית ליה האי סברא? •והאמר רב: *כל אשה שאין אני קורא בה בשעת נפילה "יבמה יבא עליה" הרי היא כאשת אח שיש לו בנים ואסורה! — ה"מ היכא דקאי באפה איסור אחות אשה דאורייתא, אבל הכא — זיקה דרבנן היא. איתיביה ר' יוסי בר חנינא לרבי יוחנן: *ארבעה אחין, ב' מהם נשואים ב' אחיות, ומתו הנשואין את האחיות — הרי אלו חולצות ולא מתייבמות. ואמאי? ליקו חד מינייהו לחלוץ לה לשנייה, ותיהוי ראשונה לגבי אידך כיבמה שהותרה ונאסרה וחזרה והותרה — תחזור להיתירה הראשון! א"ל: [ג]אחיות •איני יודע מי שנאן. — וליפא ליה: מאי "חולצות" נמי דקתני — חולצת חדא! — "חולצות" קתני. — וליפא ליה: מאי "חולצות" (ב) חולצות דעלמא! — "הרי אלו" קתני. — וליפא: דחליץ ליה לראשונה ברישא! — "חולצות" לכתחלה

בעלת הגט ובעלת מאמר. אחיו שמת ולו ג' נשים, ועשה זה מאמר לזו וגט לזו, ושוב אסור לייבם, דקם ליה ב"לא יבנה", כיון שהתחיל לגרש, אי זו מהן הגונה לחלוץ ולפטור צרתה? ומודה ר"ג. דאמר לקמן בפ"ה אין גט אחר גט — מודה הוא שיש גט אחר מאמר. כגון ב' יבמות מאח א', ועשה מאמר בזו ואח"כ נתן גט לזו — מהני גט לפסול הראשונה עליו משום "לא יבנה" ולהאסר בקרובות שנייה כבראשונה, ולא אמרי' מאמר ככנוסה, ואדחאי שנייה מיניה ולא מהני בה גט: ומאמר אחר גט. אם נתן גט לראשונה ואח"כ עשה מאמר בצרתה, לא אמרי': גט קמא במקום חליצה קאי, ותו לא קני מאמר יבמין בצרה; אלא ודאי מהני, וצריכה גט למאמרו, ואסור גם בקרובותיה: כי הדדי נינהו. ותפשוט בעיין שהאחת פוטרת חברתה, ויחלוץ לאיזו שירצה, שחליצת שתיהן גרועה: לראשונה. שנפלה ראשון: הותרה. לשוק: חלץ לשנייה הותרה. לשוק, וה"ה אם חלץ לשנייה ואח"כ לראשונה: מתה ראשונה. בלא חליצה, מותר לייבם את השנייה. ואע"פ שבשעת(ג) נפילתן אחות זקוקתו ראשונה היתה, ואין אני קורא בה "יבמה יבא עליה", כי מתה קמייתא — פקעה זיקה ושריא הך. ולית ליה הא דשנינן בפ' "כילד" (לעיל דף כג:) הך מתני' דהכא אי למ"ד יש זיקה יש זיקה כו', דאוקימנא לעיל דהואיל ונאסרה עליו בשעת נפילה — תו לא משתריא. ואיכא לאותובי מתני' דקתני חולצות ולא מתייבמות, אמאי? ליחלוץ חדא ולישתרי אידך! ולקמן מותבינן ליה מינה ספיקא דמילתיה, ולא מתרץ: ואין צ"ל מתה שנייה. ולא חלצה, שמותר בראשונה. שהיתה ראויה לייבם בשעת נפילתה, אלא שנפלה זו אחרי כן ואסרתה, וכיון שמתה זו — חזרה להיתירה הראשון: ורבי יוחנן אמר מתה שנייה מותר בראשונה. הואיל ובשעת נפילתה היתה ראויה לו: אחות אשה דאורייתא. כגון ג' אחים, ב' מהם נשואין ב' אחיות, ומת אחד מהם, ואח"כ מתה אשתו של ב', דעלה איתמר הך דרב בפרקין (לקמן דף ל.): אסורה יבמתו עליו, הואיל ובשעת נפילה אחות אשתו הואי: דרבנן היא. וכיון דמתה שריא: איני יודע מי שנאן. כלומר, זו אינה משנה: וליפא ליה מאי חולצות חדא. שנייה: חולצות דעלמא. כל היכא דמיתרמי כה"ג — חולצות השניות: הרי אלו. משמע: הנך תרתי דאיירי בהו: לראשונה ברישא. דתו לא משתריא שנייה, שלא נראית בשעת נפילה:
חולצות

בעלת הגט עדיפא. פי': שנעשה בה מעשה עדיף טפי מחברתה. אבל ריב"ן פי': בעלת הגט עדיפא דאתחיל (ד) בחליצה, ולכך יגמור בה חליצתו. ולפירושו לא יהא עדיפא דהכא פירושו כההוא דאי מאמר עדיף או גט עדיף דבסמוך. ומיהו, עדיפא משמע קצת דהיינו קודמת, דקאי אאיזו מהן קודמת דקאמר מעיקרא. **תא** שמע ומודה ר"ג כו'. מדרבנן דשמעינן להו פרק "ר"ג" (לקמן דף נ. ושם) דיש גט אחר גט ומאמר אחר הגט — אין יכול להביא ראיה, דלדידהו דיש גט אחר גט — אפי' עדיף קמא מהני גרוע בתריה לתפוס במה ששייר הראשון. אבל ר"ג, דאית ליה דאין גט אחר גט, סברא הוא דאי עדיף גט ממאמר או מאמר מגט לא מהני הגרוע לתפוס אחר קמא דעדיף, כמו שאין מועיל גט אחר גט ומאמר אחר מאמר. **אי** גט עדיף לא תיהני מאמר בתריה. אע"ג דאפילו אחר חליצה קידושין תופסין — היינו משום דהוי קידושין דאורייתא. אבל ביבמה, דלא הוי מאמר אלא מדרבנן — אין לו להועיל אחר הגט אי גט עדיף. א"נ אומר ר"י: דברייתא' דמודה ר"ג קיימא אמתני' דפ' "ר"ג" (לקמן ד' נ.) דמוקמינן לה כר"ע התם בגמ' (דף נג:), ולא מהני קידושין אחר חליצה, וה"ה דאין להם להועיל אחר הגט אי גט עדיף, דגט במקום חליצה קאי. **אלא** כי הדדי נינהו. ותפשוט דאחת פוטרת חברתה, והיינו כשמואל, וכלישנא דקאמר דאחד הולך לכולן אאמצעי', וכרב אשי. אבל ללישנא דהתחיל ולא התחיל קאמר, היכי דכי הדדי נינהו צריכות שתיהן חליצה, דהא התחיל באחיות לא יגמור אפי' בצרות, ולא מיפטרה רחל החליצת צרתה דעדיפא. והכא הך בעיא על כרחין אליבא דמ"ד יש זיקה איירי דלמ"ד אין זיקה — אפילו חלץ לבעלת הגט נפטרה צרה. **חלץ** לראשונה הותרה. וא"ת: מאי קמ"ל? פשיטא דהותרה! ואר"י: דקמ"ל דהותרה אפי' צרתה, דרב אית ליה אין זיקה, וחלץ לאחיות נפטרו צרות כדפרישית לעיל. **ורב** לית ליה האי סברא והאמר רב כל יבמה כו'. •ממתני' הוה מצי למיפרך, דבהדיא תנן בפירקין (לקמן דף לג.): ב' אחין נשואין ב' אחיות ומת אחד מהן, ואח"כ מתה אשתו של שני — הרי זו אסורה עליו עולמית, הואיל ונאסרה עליו! אלא ניחא להקשות דבהדיא אמר רב אותו לשון עצמו שאמר ר' יוחנן. שכל יבמה שאין אני קורא כו'. ועוד נראה: דממתני' לא הוה מצי לאקשויי, דהתם הוא משום דכבר נפטרה לשוק, ומשום דמתה אשתו אח"כ לא תחשב עוד זקוקה(ה) עדיין זקוקה לחליצה — לא. אבל מדרב פריך שפיר, דרב איירי אפילו היכא דליכא אחין, דלא מידחיא מהאי ביתא *) (לגמרי) כדאמר לקמן (ג"ז שם). **אבל** הכא זיקה דרבנן היא. פר"ח דרב: לטעמיה, דאמר אין זיקה, דאע"ג דאסיר משום ביטול מצות יבמין — לא חשיב הך איסור לאוסרה עולמית אף כשתבא לכלל היתר. אבל למ"ד יש זיקה — ראוי לאסור משום שנאסרה עליו שעה אחת. **איתיביה** רבי יוסי בר חנינא לרבי יוחנן. לעיל פי' בקונטרס דלרב נמי פריך. אבל ריב"ן פירש דלא פריך לרב משום דרב ס"ל חליצה פסולה צריכה לחזור על כל האחים, דהאחת צריכה חליצה משניהן, ושוב השנית א"א לייבם משום דלכל אחד הויא אחות חלוצתו. אבל רבי יוחנן סבר כשמואל, דאינה צריכה לחזור, ולהכי פריך ליה. ואע"ג דרב דאמר צריכה לחזור — היינו אליבא דמ"ד יש זיקה, וליה לא ס"ל — מ"מ מצינו למימר דרב מוקי לה כמ"ד יש זיקה, דפלוגתא דתנאי היא. ואע"ג דלעיל ברים פ' "כילד" (דף יח.) מוקי לה סתמא דהש"ס כר"מ, דאמר אין זיקה — רב לא מוקי לה כוותיה. ולר"ח נמי, דפי' לעיל דרב דלית ליה הואיל ונאסרה עליו שעה אחת, לטעמיה דאמר אין זיקה אתי שפיר נמי דלא פריך לרב, דמוקי למתני' כמ"ד יש זיקה. אבל ר' יוחנן סבר דעל כרחך יש זיקה, דאי אין זיקה, א"כ ב' אחיות שנפלו לפני שני אחין — יתייבמו שתיהן, דהא ר' יוחנן לא חייש למיתה. ומפירכא דפריך רבי יוסי בר חנינא: ואמאי וליקו חד מנייהו כו' — משמע דלא שרי רבי יוחנן לייבם אלא חדא — על כרחך סבר יש זיקה, ואפ"ה שרי לראשונה, ולית ליה הואיל ונאסרה שעה א' שתאסר עולמית, מש"ה פריך לה. ומיהו, נראה לר"י כדפרישית לעיל (דף כד. ד"ה אי) דלרב *דחייש למיתה(ו) משום דלא מסקי אדעתיה דמיית אידך — לא מצי פריך, דגזרי' דלמא אתי לייבם ברישא, אבל לעיל במתה אחת מהן ליכא למיגזר דלמא אתי לייבם בלא מתה אחת מהן, כיון דליכא אלא אח אחד ולא אתי לבטל מצות יבמין להדיא. אבל רבי יוחנן היה יודע רבי יוסי בר חנינא דלא הוי חייש למיתה, להכי *(לא) פריך ליה. *(א"נ, לפי שהיה אצל ר' יוחנן הקשה לו**). **וליפא** ליה דלמא קדים וחליץ לראשונה. פי' ר"י לפי שיטת הקונטר': שכשבאין לפנינו לימלך לא אמרינן להו לחלוץ שניה ולייבם את הראשונה, דגזרינן דלמא אתי למיעבד איפכא באלו [היבמות] עצמן. אבל אם כבר חלץ האחד לשנייה — שרי אידך לייבם הראשונה, כמו במתה שנייה, כיון
דבאלו

*) ס"א איתו
**) שייך לקמן כח ע"א

תוספות ישנים

בעלת הגט עדיפא. פ"ה עדיפא שחליצה תפטור צרתה. ולא נהירא דא"כ מאי קאמר בעלת מאמר עדיפא משום דקרובה לביאה. אדרבה משו"ה הוי חליצה פסולה דאיקלישא לה הזיקה. אלא נראה לפרש איפכא בעלת הגט עדיפא להפטר בחליצת חברתה וניחא הכל: **זיקה** דרבנן היא. פר"ח דרב לטעמיה דסבר אין זיקה אבל אין לפרש דיש זיקה מ"מ לא החמירו כבאחות (זקוקתו) [אשתו] דלקמן בהחולץ משמע דלמ"ד יש זיקה הוי כמו אחות אשתו גמורה. ואין להקשות נהי נמי דאין זיקה מ"מ נאסרה שעה אחת משום ביטול מצות יבמין דלא קרינן אסרה שעה אחת כיון שאין האיסור משום ערוה רק משום גזרה:

תוספות חד מקמאי

נינהו: ופסק הרב אלפס כר' יוחנן בשתי אחיות יבמות שנפלו לפני יבם א' מתה השניה מותר בראשונה אבל מתה ראשונה אסור בשניה ואקשינן לר"י דאמר מותר בראשונה מהא דתנן ארבעה אחין שנים מהן נשואין ב' אחיות ומתו הנשואין את האחיות הרי אלו חולצות ולא מתייבמות ואמאי ליקום חד מינייהו ולחלוץ לשניה ותהוי ראשונה לגבי אידך כיבמה שהותרה ונאסרה ותחזור להיתרה הראשון א"ל ר"י אחיות איני יודע מי שנאן כלומר זו אינה משנה ולימא ליה מאי חולצת חדא חולצות קתני. [ולימא] חולצות דעלמא הרי אלו קתני ולימא ליה דחליץ לראשונה ברישא חולצות לכתחלה קתני. ולימא גזרו דלמא קדם וחליץ לראשונה ברישא ולא מתייבמת קתני דליכא הכא דין יבום כלל ולימא ליה שמא ימות ואסור לבטל מצות יבמין. פירוש וקעבדא חליצה פסולה. ר"י למיתה לא חייש ולימא ליה דלא ידעינן הי נפיל ברישא אי הכי היינו דקתני אם קדמו וכנסו יוציאו. בשלמא ראשון אמרי' [ליה] מאן שרא ליה אלא שני א) אמרי' חבראי שני יבום האיכא ראשון ראשון ש"מ יבמי היינו דקתני אחיות איני יודע מי שנאן:

א) נ"ל אלא שני א' אמר חבראי שנייה ... מייבם והיינו דקאמר אחיות וכו'.

[טעות הדפוס] ס"א ל"ג

מסורת הש"ס

גירסת רש"ל בגירושין
לקמן נא
גירסת הרא"ש יהודה
[לקמן ל. ע"ש קיא: ע"ש]
[לעיל כו. וש"נ]

הגהות הב"ח

(א) גמ' בעלת הגט עדיפ(א) (משום דאתחיל ב)בגירושין) תא"מ ונ"(ב) בתוספות משמע ד(לא) גרסינן ליה: (ב) ש(ם) חולצות דעלמא נ"ב כ(ן) בעמוד א"ו (ג) רש"י ד"(ה) מתה וכו' שבשעת נפילת(ן) (ד) תוס' ד"ה בעלת וכ(ו') עדיפא דאתחיל ב(ה) בגירושין ולכך יגמור ב(ה) (ה) ד"ה ורב וכו' (לא) תחשוב עד זקוקה א(בל) הכא דזקוקה עדיין לחליצ(ה) לא אבל מדרב כל"(ל) (ו) ד"ה איתיביה וכ(ו') דחייש למיתה שפיר מש(ום) דלא מסקי אדעתיהו:

גליון הש"ס

גמ' והאמר רב כל אש(ה) עי' לעיל ב' ע"א תוד"(ה) ואחות אשתו ולעיל יז ע"(ב) תוד"ה אשת אחיו: ש(ם) איני יודע מי שנאן. בב"(ק) נא ע"א ב"ב קטו ע"א ו(ב"מ) קמא ע"ב: תד"ה ו(רב) וכו' ממתני' הוה מ(צי) למפרך וכו'. עי' כתוב(ות) נה ע"ב תוד"ה מתנת שכ(יב) מרע וחולין קטז ע"(א) תוד"ה ומי אמר וקכא ע"(א) תד"ה ומי אמר ויומא (...) ע"ב תד"ה הנ"מ:

דחייש למיתה לא מצי פר(יך) דגזרי' דלמא אתי לייב(ם) ברישא משום דלא מס(קי) אדעתייהו דמיית אידך ו(כו') כל"ל

לְכַתְּחִלָּה קָתָנֵי. [א]וְלֵימָא לֵיהּ גְּזֵירָה דִּלְמָא קָדֵים וְחָלֵיץ לָרִאשׁוֹנָה בְּרֵישָׁא! — "וְלֹא מִתְיַיבְּמוֹת" קָתָנֵי, דְּלֵיכָּא דִּין יִבּוּם הָכָא כְּלָל. — וְלֵימָא לֵיהּ גְּזֵירָה שֶׁמָּא יָמוּת, *וְאָסוּר לְבַטֵּל מִצְוַת יְבָמִין! — רַ' יוֹחָנָן לְמִיתָה לָא חָיֵישׁ. — וְלֵימָא לֵיהּ רַבִּי (א) אֶלְעָזָר הִיא, *דְּאָמַר: כֵּיוָן שֶׁעָמְדָה עָלָיו שָׁעָה אַחַת בְּאִיסּוּר נֶאֶסְרָה עָלָיו עוֹלָמִית! — מִדְּסֵיפָא רַ' אֶלְעָזָר רֵישָׁא לָאו רַבִּי אֶלְעָזָר. וְנֵימָא *לְהוּ דְּנָפוּל בְּבַת אַחַת וְרַבִּי יוֹסֵי הַגְּלִילִי הִיא, *דְּאָמַר: אֶפְשָׁר לְצַמְצֵם! — לָא סָתַם לָן תַּנָּא כְּרַ' יוֹסֵי הַגְּלִילִי. — וְלֵימָא לֵיהּ [ב]דְּלָא יָדְעִינַן הֵי נְפוּל בְּרֵישָׁא! — אִי הָכִי, הַיְינוּ דְּקָתָנֵי "קָדְמוּ וְכָנְסוּ יוֹצִיאוּ"? בִּשְׁלָמָא (ב) רִאשׁוֹנָה אָמְרִינַן לֵיהּ: מַאן שַׁרְיָא לָךְ? אֶלָּא שְׁנִיָּה, אָמַר: חַבְרָאִי שְׁנִיָּה יִיבֵּם, אֲנָא רִאשׁוֹנָה מְיַיבֵּם! — הַיְינוּ דְּקָאָמַר לֵיהּ: אֲחָיוֹת אֵינִי יוֹדֵעַ מִי שְׁנָאָן.§ תְּנַן: *הָיְתָה אַחַת מֵהֶן אֲסוּרָה עַל הָאֶחָד אִיסּוּר עֶרְוָה — אָסוּר בָּהּ וּמוּתָּר בַּאֲחוֹתָהּ, וְהַשֵּׁנִי אָסוּר בִּשְׁתֵּיהֶן. ס"ד דְּנָפְלָה חֲמוֹתוֹ תְּחִלָּה, וְאַמַּאי? לֵיקוּ חָתָן לְיַיבֵּם הַךְ דְּאֵינָהּ חֲמוֹתוֹ בְּרֵישָׁא, וְתֶהֱוֵי חֲמוֹתוֹ לְגַבֵּי אִידָךְ כִּיבָמָה שֶׁהוּתְּרָה וְנֶאֶסְרָה וְחָזְרָה וְהוּתְּרָה — תַּחֲזוֹר לְהֶיתֵּרָהּ הָרִאשׁוֹן. [ג]א"ר פַּפָּא: כְּגוֹן דְּנָפְלָה הַךְ דְּאֵינָהּ חֲמוֹתוֹ בְּרֵישָׁא.§ "ר"א אוֹמֵר: בש"א וכו'".§ תַּנְיָא: *ר"א אוֹמֵר ב"ש אוֹמְרִים: יְקַיְּימוּ, ובה"א: יוֹצִיאוּ. רש"א: יְקַיְּימוּ. אַבָּא שָׁאוּל אוֹמֵר: קַל הָיָה לָהֶם לְב"ה בְּדָבָר זֶה, שֶׁבֵּית שַׁמַּאי אוֹמְרִים יוֹצִיאוּ ובה"א יְקַיְּימוּ. ר"ש כְּמַאן? אִי כְּב"ש — הַיְינוּ ר"א, אִי כְּב"ה — הַיְינוּ אַבָּא שָׁאוּל! — *ה"ק לֹא נֶחְלְקוּ ב"ש וב"ה בְּדָבָר זֶה.§ "הָיְתָה אַחַת מֵהֶם כו'".§ הָא תָּנֵינָא חֲדָא זִימְנָא: *אֲחוֹתָהּ כְּשֶׁהִיא יְבִמְתָּהּ אוֹ חוֹלֶצֶת אוֹ מִתְיַיבֶּמֶת! — צְרִיכָא, דְּאִי אַשְׁמוֹעִינַן הָתָם מִשּׁוּם דְּלֵיכָּא לְמִיגְזַר מִשּׁוּם שֵׁנִי, אֲבָל הָכָא דְּאִיכָּא לְמִיגְזַר מִשּׁוּם שֵׁנִי — אֵימָא לָא. וְאִי אַשְׁמוֹעִינַן הָכָא — מִשּׁוּם דְּאִיכָּא שֵׁנִי דְּקָא מוֹכַח, אֲבָל הָתָם דְּלֵיכָּא שֵׁנִי — אֵימָא לָא, צְרִיכָא.§ "אִיסּוּר מִצְוָה כו'".§ הָא נַמִּי תָּנֵינָא: אִיסּוּר

רש"י

חוֹלְצוֹת לְכַתְּחִלָּה. מַשְׁמַע, כְּלוֹמַר: אֵין כָּאן תַּקָּנָה אַחֶרֶת: ה"ג. וְלֵימָא לֵיהּ גְּזֵירָה דִּלְמָא קָדֵים וְחָלֵיץ לָרִאשׁוֹנָה בְּרֵישָׁא. אִי אָמְרַתְּ לְהוּ חֲלוֹצוּ לַשְּׁנִיָּה וְיַבְּמוּ רִאשׁוֹנָה — גְּזֵירָה דִּלְמָא קָדֵים חַד וְחָלֵיץ לָרִאשׁוֹנָה, וְאָתֵי לְיַיבּוּמֵי אִידָךְ שְׁנִיָּה, דְּסָבְרִי: מָה אִיכְפַּת בֵּין זוֹ לָזוֹ. אֲבָל בְּדִיעֲבַד, שֶׁחָלַץ לַשְּׁנִיָּה תְּחִלָּה, שָׁרְיָא לֵיהּ לְאִידָךְ לְיַיבּוּמֵי קַמַּיְיתָא. דְּמַאן דְּחָזֵי דְּחָלַץ לַשְּׁנִיָּה בְּרֵישָׁא וְחָזַר וְיִיבֵּם קַמַּיְיתָא — אַסֵּיק אַדַּעְתֵּיהּ, וְלָא אָתֵי לְמִחְלַץ לְקַמַּיְיתָא וּלְיַיבּוּמֵי שְׁנִיָּה: וּמְשַׁנֵּי. וְלֹא מִתְיַיבְּמוֹת קָתָנֵי. דְּאִי נַמִּי חָלַץ לַשְּׁנִיָּה אֵין כָּאן יִבּוּם. וְלֵימָא לֵיהּ גְּזֵירָה שֶׁמָּא יָמוּת וְאָסוּר לְבַטֵּל מִצְוַת יְבָמִין. וְה"פ: לֵימָא לֵיהּ רַבִּי יוֹחָנָן, תַּנָּא דְּמַתְנִי' טַעֲמֵיהּ לָאו מִשּׁוּם זִיקָה קָא אָסַר לְיַיבֵּם ב' אֲחָיוֹת, דְּס"ל אֵין זִיקָה. דְּאִי טַעְמָא מִשּׁוּם זִיקָה — מִכִּי חָלֵיץ לַשְּׁנִיָּה וּפָקַע זִיקָתָהּ שָׁרֵי לְיַיבּוּמֵי רִאשׁוֹנָה, כִּדְאָמְרִי אֲנָא. אֶלָּא טַעְמָא מִשּׁוּם שֶׁמָּא יָמוּת, כִּדְאָמַר בְּרֵישׁ פִּירְקִין: דִּלְמָא אַדְּמְיַיבֵּם חַד מָיֵית אִידָךְ כו', וּמשו"ה שְׁקוּל רַבָּנַן דִּין יִבּוּם מֵאֲחָיוֹת לְגַמְרֵי. וַאֲפִילּוּ חָלַץ לַחֲדָא מִינַּיְיהוּ, דְּלָא בָּטְלִי תּוּ מִצְוַת יְבָמִין — כִּי הֵיכִי דְּלָא יַרְגִּילוּ יִבּוּם בַּאֲחָיוֹת, וְאָתֵי לְיַיבּוּמֵי לְכַתְּחִלָּה קַמֵּי חֲלִיצָה, וְאַדְּמְיַיבֵּם חַד מָיֵית אִידָךְ. אֲבָל לְגַבֵּי מִיתָה דִּלְעֵיל, דְּאַיְירֵי בָּהּ ר' יוֹחָנָן — לֵיכָּא לְמִיגְזַר הָכִי. ר' אֶלְעָזָר הִיא. בְּפֶ' ב"ש (לקמן קט.), וַאֲנָא דְּאָמְרִי כְּרַבָּנַן. מִדְּסֵיפָא. דְּמַתְנִי' ר"א, דְּקָתָנֵי: ר"א אוֹמֵר, ב"ש אוֹמְרִים יְקַיְּימוּ (כו'), ב"ה אוֹמְרִים יוֹצִיאוּ. וְלֵימָא לֵיהּ. דְּלָא יָדְעִינַן הֵי נְפוּל בְּרֵישָׁא דְּלֵימָא לֵיהּ חֲלוֹץ לַשְּׁנִיָּה. א"ה. דְּמִשּׁוּם דְּלָא יָדְעִינַן הוּא, הָא אִי הֲוָה יָדְעִינַן — מִתְיַיבֶּמֶת רִאשׁוֹנָה. הַיְינוּ דְּקָתָנֵי. כְּלוֹמַר, הָא דְּקָתָנֵי יוֹצִיאוּ אַמַּאי? בִּשְׁלָמָא לָרִאשׁוֹן אָמְרִי' לֵיהּ. אַפֵּיק, דְּוַדַּאי בְּאִיסּוּרָא אֲתָא לְיָדָךְ. דְּא"נ רִאשׁוֹנָה הִיא, מַאן שַׁרְיָא נִיהֲלָךְ? הֲלֹא אֲחוֹת זְקוּקָה הִיא, וּמִי מֵאַחֶיךָ חָלַץ לַאֲחוֹתָהּ לְאַפְקוּעֵי זִיקָה מִינָּהּ? אֶלָּא שֵׁנִי — לֵימָא: *אַחַר שֶׁיִּיבֵּם רִאשׁוֹן, שְׁנִיָּה אֵירַע לְחֶלְקוֹ, וְהָוְיָא זוֹ רִאשׁוֹנָה יְבָמָה שֶׁהוּתְּרָה וְנֶאֶסְרָה וְחָזְרָה וְהוּתְּרָה. דְּהָכִי אָמַר בְּפֶ' "כֵּיצַד" (לעיל כד.): קָדְמוּ וְכָנְסוּ — אֵין מוֹצִיאִין מִיָּדָם, מִשּׁוּם דְּלֵיכָּא אֶלָּא סָפֵק פָּגַע בַּאֲחוֹת זְקוּקָה, וְהָא נַמִּי לַשֵּׁנִי סָפֵק הוּא. הַיְינוּ דְּקָאָמַר לֵיהּ אֲחָיוֹת אֵינִי יוֹדֵעַ מִי שְׁנָאָן. דְּלָא מָצֵי לְתָרוּצֵי כִּשְׁמַעְתֵּיהּ כְּלָל. אִיסּוּר עֶרְוָה. כְּגוֹן חֲמוֹתוֹ אוֹ עֶרְוָה אַחֶרֶת. דְּנָפְלָה חֲמוֹתוֹ בְּרֵישָׁא. *זוֹ שֶׁאֲסָרָה אֶת הָאַחֶרֶת נָפְלָה תְּחִלָּה. וְהַאי דְּנָקַט חֲמוֹתוֹ — חֲדָא מֵעֲרָיוֹת נָקַט, וְנִיחָא לְמִינְקְטֵיהּ מִילְּתָא דִּשְׁכִיחָא, וּשְׁאָר עֲרָיוֹת טְרִיחָא מִילְּתָא לְאַשְׁכּוּחֵי. אַמַּאי. שֵׁנִי אָסוּר בִּשְׁתֵּיהֶן? לֵיקוּ חָתָן שֶׁל רִאשׁוֹנָה, וּלְיַיבֵּם לַשְּׁנִיָּה דְּאֵינָהּ חֲמוֹתוֹ וְאֵינָהּ אֲחוֹת זְקוּקָה, וְתֶיהֱוֵי חֲמוֹתוֹ לְגַבֵּי אִידָךְ אָח — יְבָמָה שֶׁהוּתְּרָה בִּשְׁעַת נְפִילָה כו'. כְּגוֹן דְּנָפְלָה הָךְ דְּאֵינָהּ חֲמוֹתוֹ בְּרֵישָׁא. וְאִי כִּמְיַיבֵּם לָהּ הָאֵיךְ בְּרֵישָׁא — פָּיְישָׁא שְׁנִיָּה, שֶׁנֶּאֶסְרָה מִשְּׁעַת נְפִילָתָהּ (הוי), הִלְכָּךְ תּוּ לָא מְהַנֵּי לָהּ הֶיתֵּר. קַל הָיָה לָהֶן לְב"ה. כְּלוֹמַר: ב"ה לְקוּלָּא אָמְרִי. ר"ש כְּמַאן. אַלִּיבָּא דְּמַאן. אִי. אָתָא לְמֵימַר בֵּית שַׁמַּאי אוֹמְרִים יְקַיְּימוּ — הַיְינוּ ר"א. וְאִי אַב"ה. קָא מַסְהֵיד — הַיְינוּ אַבָּא שָׁאוּל. וְהָא לֵיכָּא לְמֵימַר דְּטַעְמָא דְּנַפְשֵׁיהּ קָאָמַר, דְּלָאו בַּר פְּלוּגְתַּיְיהוּ דְּבֵית שַׁמַּאי וּבֵית הִלֵּל הוּא. תָּנֵינָא חֲדָא זִימְנָא. בְּפֶרֶק "כֵּיצַד": אֲחוֹתָהּ שֶׁל עֶרְוָה כְּשֶׁהִיא יְבִמְתָּהּ, אוֹ חוֹלֶצֶת כו'. וְהַיְינוּ נַמִּי אָסוּר בָּהּ וּמוּתָּר בַּאֲחוֹתָהּ. הָתָם. הוּא דְּלֵיכָּא אֶלָּא חַד אַחָא לְקַמָּן, וְלֵיכָּא לְמִיגְזַר מִידֵּי. אֲבָל הָכָא דְּאִיכָּא לְמִיגְזַר דִּלְמָא אָתָא שֵׁנִי לְיַיבּוּמֵי *כְּאָחִיו, וְקָא פָּגַע בַּאֲחוֹת זְקוּקָתוֹ, דְּקַמֵּי דִּידֵיהּ הֲווּ רַמְיָין תַּרְוַויְיהוּ — אֵימָא אֲפִילּוּ הַאי דְּלָא רַמְיָא עֶרְוָה קַמֵּיהּ לָא לְיַיבֵּם, קָא מַשְׁמַע לָן. דְּקָא מוֹכַח. דְּמִדְּלָא מְיַיבֵּם הַאי *כְּאָחִיו — אִיכָּא הֶיכֵּירָא דַּאֲחוֹת זְקוּקָתוֹ אֲסוּרָה, וְהַאי דְּיִיבֵּם הַאי — מִשּׁוּם טַעְמָא דְּעֶרְוָה לָא רַמְיָא קַמֵּיהּ, וְלָא אָתֵי לְמִישְׁרֵי אֲחוֹת זְקוּקָתוֹ בְּעָלְמָא. אֲבָל הָתָם. דְּלֵיכָּא אֶלָּא חַד אָח — אֵימָא לָא לְיַיבֵּם, דִּלְמָא אָתֵי לְמִישְׁרֵי אֲחוֹת זְקוּקָתוֹ בְּעָלְמָא. אִיסּוּר

תוספות

דאלו יבמות ליכא שום חששא. והא לא חיישינן שאם נתיר כאן לייבם הראשונה כשכבר חלץ לשניה אתי בעלמא למיעבד איפכא – שאינה חששא גדולה כ"כ, שלא יטעו להתיר השניה שלא הותרה מתחלה בשביל שנתיר הראשונה שהותרה, אבל באו לימלך בפנינו מתחלה – יש לגזור, כיון שהיו *הצרות עצמן יכול לבא לידי קלקול. ומשני: ולא מתייבמות קתני, דליכא דין ייבום כלל, אפי' קדם וחלץ כבר לשניה. ופריך: ולימא ליה שמא ימות וכו', ויעמיד המשנה כמ"ד אין זיקה, דלדידיה ודאי אפילו קדם וחלץ לשניה דליכא למיחש טפי באלו יבמות – מ"מ אסור לייבם ראשונה, שאם נתיר כאן לייבם אחר חליצה – יבוא בעלמא לייבם ברישא, דלא מסקי אדעתייהו טעמא דלמא אדמייבם חד מיית אידך, שאין זה טעם ידוע. ועוד אר"י דיש לפרש בענין אחר: ולימא ליה דלמא קדים וחליץ לראשונה ברישא, ואפי' חלץ כבר מעצמו לשניה – אסרינן ראשונה ליבם, דלמא אתי למישרי בעלמא שניה נמי כשקדם וחלץ לראשונה, אבל במיתת שניה – לא שייך למיגזר כי האי גוונא! ומשני: ולא מתייבמות קתני, דליכא דין ייבום כלל אפילו מתה שניה. ופריך: ולימא ליה גזירה שמא ימות, ולהכי אסרה מתני' אפילו מתה שניה, דאי שריא לייבם בשני יבמים – אחר מיתת שניה יבא להתיר בלא מיתה! אבל ר' יוחנן לא איירי אלא ביבם אחד, דיבם אחד לא אתי להתיר בלא מיתה, דאם כן היה מבטל מיד מצות יבמין, אבל בשני יבמין, דאין מבטל מיד, אלא דגזירה שמא ימות אידך ויבוא לטעות ולייבם. וחזר בו ר"י מפירוש זה, דביבם א' נמי קתני במתני' ולא מתייבמות, דמשמע דליכא דין ייבום כלל, ואפי' מתה שניה. דקתני לקמן: ג' אחין, ב' מהן נשואין ב' אחיות, ומתו הנשואין את האחיות – הרי אלו חולצות ולא מתייבמות. **ולימא** ליה ר"א היא. היינו ר' אלעזר ד"החולץ" (לקמן דף מא. ושם) דתני גבי שומרת יבם שקידש אחיו את אחותה: מתה יבמתו – מותר באשתו, מתה אשתו – אותה יבמה חולצת ולא מתייבמת, ובקונטרס פי': דהיינו ר"א בפרק "ב"ש" (לקמן דף קט. ושם) דתנן: המגרש את אשתו והחזירה – מותרת לייבם, ור' אלעזר אוסר. **לא** סתם לן כר' יוסי הגלילי. לר' יוחנן הוא דמסקינן הכי, אבל רב חסדא מוקי מתניתין ד"שבועת העדות" (שבועות לב. ושם) דכפרו שניהם בבת אחת כר' יוסי הגלילי. ור' יוחנן מסיק התם: אפי' תימא רבנן, והיינו לטעמיה דהכא. ובפ"ק דעירובין (דף ה: ד"ה "וספק") פירשתי דקיימא לן דבידי אדם אפשר לצמצם, ובידי שמים נמי משמע לרבא דאית ליה פרק בתרא דבכורות (דף מ: ושם) דאפשר לצמצם, גבי יצאו שנים בעשירי. ובפרק "בהמה המקשה" (חולין ע. ושם) גבי בעיא אם הלכו באברים אחר הרוב, דמוקי לה שילא אליו ברוב אבר, ואי אמרת דא"א לצמצם – מאי קמיבעיא ליה? דממה נפשך טעון קבורה דשמא יצא רובו. ואין להאריך, כי שם הארכתי. **הך** דאין חמותו ברישא. וא"ת: מ"מ תקשה לרב דשרי אפילו שניה! וי"ל: דרב אית ליה אין זיקה, ולא מיתסר אלא משום ביטול מצות יבמין, וגזרינן דלמא מייבם אידך ברישא:ב) **רבי אליעזר** אומר ב"ש אומרים יקיימו. וא"ת: וכי טעמא דב"ש אתא לאשמועינן?! דהכי פריך בפרק "רבי אליעזר דמילה" (שבת דף קלה.) וי"ל: דאיצטריך הכא לאפוקי מברייתא דאבא שאול, דאמר: קל היה להם לב"ה בדבר זה.

א) [ע"ש היטב וע"ע תוס' שם יז: סוף ד"ה אפשר]. ב) [שייך לעיל במשנה כו.]

מסורת הש"ס

[לעיל יח. וש"נ]

לקמן מח. קט.

ליה יעב"ץ

לעיל יט. בכורות ז. יח. [שבועות לב.]

לעיל כו.

[תוספתא פ"ה]

[שבת מב. קלה. סוכה טו. ב"ק לז.]

לעיל כ.

[בדפו"י אחיו]

[זו שאסורה על האחד נפלה כצ"ל רש"ל]

ס"א כאחות

ס"א כאחות

הגהות הב"ח

(א) גמ' ר' אליעזר היא כצ"ל וכן בכל הענין: (ב) שם בשלמא ראשון אמרינן ליה מאן שרא לך אלא שני אמר:

עין משפט נר מצוה

יא א מיי' פ"ז מהל' יבום הלכה ג סמג עשין נא טוש"ע אה"ע סימן קעה סעי' ה:

נ"א היבמות

יב ב מיי' שם טוש"ע שם סעיף ב:

יג ג מיי' שם הל' ה טוש"ע שם סעיף ה:

תוספות ישנים

דנפלה הך דאינה חמותו ברישא. פ"ה דלאו דווקא נקט חמותו ה"ה ערוה אחרת. א"נ פי' ה"ר ריב"ן דנקט חמותו משום דחמותו הויא ערוה לגבי כללא דכבי חייא דהאחיות לזה מותרת לזה כדקאמר (לקמן) [לעיל דף ט] רב [יהודה] מתרגם מחמותו ואילך.

תוספות חד מקמאי

הדר אקשינן לר"י מהא דתנן היתה אחת מהן אסורה עליו אסור ערוה אסור בה ומותר באחותה והשני [אסור] בשתיהן קס"ד דנפול חמות ברישא ואמאי ליקום חתן ולייבם הך דאינה חמות ותהוי חמות ליבם אידך כיבמה שהותרה ונאסרה וחזרה והותרה תחזור להיתירא הראשון אמר רב פפא כגון שנפל הך דאינה חמות תחילה כך היא הצעת הגמרא. וה"ר אלפס כתב משנתנו כפשוטה. ור"י דקי"ל כוותיה אמר זו אינה משנה וסיפא נמי דקא' השני אסור בשתיהן אוקמה רב פפא אליבא דר"י כגון דנפל הך דאינה חמות תחילה והוא ז"ל לא כתב דברי רב פפא והוא דבר תימה נשוב ונאמר כי דברי הרב ברורים ונכונים וכולה מתני' הלכה היא והא דתנינן ולא מתייבמות משום גזרה דלמא קדים וחליץ בריש הראשונה כדאמרן בהאי פירקא גבי (חזקת) א) יבמין דגזרינן מיבם והדר חליץ דלמא חליץ והדר מייבם הכא נמי לא שנא. ואע"ג דבפרק כיצד אמר קדש א' משתי אחיות ואינו יודע איזה מהן קדש דוקא מחלץ והדר יבומי אבל יבומי והדר מחלץ לא ולא גזרינן דלמא עביד הא אטו הא. שאני התם דספק הוא דהא אם קדמו וכנסו אין מוציאין אותה מידו אבל הכא דודאי אחות זקוקתו הוא גזרינן הא אטו הא ואע"ג דלר"י שנינן ולא מתייבמות קתני למימר דליכא דין יבום כלל. מיהו ר"י מודה דגזרינן דלמא קדים וחליץ לראשונה ברישא והא דקתני בסיפ' אסור בשתיהן אפילו נפלה חמות ברישא ובדין הוא דליקום חתן ולייבם הא דאינה חמות

אלא גזרינן דלמא מייבם הך דאינו חתן ברישא. ורב פפא לא שני ליה הכי דמשמע ליה מדקתני אסור בשתיהן ג) אסור שנה ומשום הכי אוקמוה כגון שנפל הך דאינה חמות ברישא. מיהו מ"מ אפלו נפל חמות בראשונה אסור בשתיהן או משום גזרה דלמא נפל הך דאינה חמות ברישא או משום דגזרינן דלמא קדים ומייבם הך חתן ברישא. וזו אותה סברת הרב שכתב משנתנו כפשטה ודאתו ג) עלה לרב פפא דאמר ג' כגון דנפל דאינה חמות ברישא. דתינח לר"י אלא לרב מתני' היכי מתרצא. איכא מ"ד דלא קשיא מתני' לרב אלא רישא דקתני ולא מתייבמת ולא סיפא דקתני השני אסור בשתיהן דרב לא קאמר אלא במתה. אבל לר"י דאמר אסור בשניה לא שני ליה בין מתה ללא מתה. ואפ"ה מותר בראשונה מפני שהותרה בשעת נפילה ומשום הכי אקשינן ליה ממתני'. ולדידי מסתברא דלא קשיא ממתני' דרב לטעמיה דאמר אין זיקה כדקאמרן לעיל ורב לית ליה האי סברא [illegible] כל יבמה

עין משפט
נר מצוה

יד א מיי׳ פ״ו מהלכות יבום הלכה כה סמג עשין נא טוש״ע אה״ע סימן קעה סעיף ו:

אבל הכא דליכא שני דמוכח. ואם תאמר: הא נמי ידעינן מההיא דפ״ב כדאמרינן לעיל (דף כ.)! ויש לומר: דהתם איכא ערוה דקמוכח שאינה לא חולצת ולא מתייבמת, אבל הכא – שתיהן מתייבמות, וליכא הוכחה. שנעשו צרות זו לזו כו׳. היינו דוקא כשנפלו לפני יבם אחד, אבל כשנפלו לפני שני יבמין – מודה רבי שמעון, כדתניא לעיל: רבי שמעון אומר יקיימו.

אחותה

*איסור מִצְוָה וְאִיסּוּר קְדוּשָּׁה חוֹלֶצֶת וְלֹא מִתְיַיבֶּמֶת! — הָתָם אִיסּוּר מִצְוָה לְחוּדָהּ. הָכָא אִיסּוּר מִצְוָה וַאֲחוֹתָהּ, ס״ד אָמִינָא: לֵיקוּם אִיסּוּר מִצְוָה בִּמְקוֹם אִיסּוּר עֶרְוָה, וְתִתְיַיבֵּם, קמ״ל. וְתִתְיַיבֵּם! — כֵּיוָן דְּמִדְּאוֹרַיְיתָא רַמְיָא קַמֵּיהּ קָא פָּגַע בַּאֲחוֹת זְקוּקָתוֹ, סד״א: מִשּׁוּם מִצְוָה עֲבוּד רַבָּנַן — קמ״ל.§ "הָיְתָה אַחַת מֵהֶן כו׳".§ הָא תּוּ ל״ל? הַיְינוּ הָךְ, מַה לִּי לְחַד מַה לִּי לִתְרֵי! — צְרִיכָא, דְּאִי אַשְׁמוּעִינַן הָתָם — מִשּׁוּם דְּאִיכָּא שֵׁנִי דְּמוֹכָח, אֲבָל הָכָא דְּלֵיכָּא שֵׁנִי דְּקָא מוֹכַח — אֵימָא לָא. וְאִי אַשְׁמוּעִינַן הָכָא — אַדְּרַבָּה, תַּרְוַיְיהוּ מוֹכְחֵי אַהֲדָדֵי. אֲבָל אִידָךְ לָא — צְרִיכָא.§ "זוֹ הִיא שֶׁאָמְרוּ וכו׳" — לְמַעוּטֵי מַאי?§ זוֹ הִיא לְמַעוּטֵי אִיסּוּר מִצְוָה לְזֶה וְאִיסּוּר מִצְוָה לְזֶה. — הָא תּוּ ל״ל? הַיְינוּ הָךְ, מַה לִּי לְחַד מַה לִּי לִתְרֵי! — מַהוּ דְּתֵימָא: כִּי לָא אָמְרִינַן אוֹקֵי אִיסּוּר מִצְוָה בִּמְקוֹם אִיסּוּר עֶרְוָה — הֵיכָא דְּאִיכָּא לְמִיגְזַר מִשּׁוּם שֵׁנִי, אֲבָל הֵיכָא דְּלֵיכָּא לְמִיגְזַר מִשּׁוּם שֵׁנִי — אֵימָא: לְהַאי אוֹקִימְנָא אִיסּוּר מִצְוָה בִּמְקוֹם אִיסּוּר עֶרְוָה וּלְהַאי [אוֹקִימְנָא] אִיסּוּר מִצְוָה בִּמְקוֹם אִיסּוּר עֶרְוָה, וְלַיִיבְּמוּ. קמ״ל אָמַר רַב יְהוּדָה אָמַר רַב. וְכֵן תָּנֵי רַ׳ חִיָּיא: *בְּכוּלָּן אֲנִי קוֹרֵא בָּהֶן הָאֲסוּרָה לְזֶה מוּתֶּרֶת לָזֶה, וַאֲחוֹתָהּ כְּשֶׁהִיא יְבִמְתָּהּ — אוֹ חוֹלֶצֶת אוֹ מִתְיַיבֶּמֶת. וְרַב יְהוּדָה מְתַרְגֵּם מֵחֲמוֹתוֹ וְאֵילָךְ, אֲבָל שִׁיתָּא בָּבֵי דְּרֵישָׁא — לָא. מ״ט? כֵּיוָן דְּבִתּוֹ בְּאוֹנָסִין הוּא דְּמַשְׁכַּחַתְּ לָהּ, בִּנְשׂוּאִין לָא מַשְׁכַּחַתְּ לָהּ, בִּנְשׂוּאִין — קָמַיְירֵי, בְּאוֹנָסִין — לָא קָא מַיְירֵי. וְאַבַּיֵי מְתַרְגֵּם אַף בִּתּוֹ (בָּאָה) מֵאֲנוּסָתוֹ, כֵּיוָן דְּאַשְׁכּוּחֵי מַשְׁכַּחַתְּ לָהּ, אִי בָּעֲיָא בְּאוֹנָסִין — תֶּיהֱוֵי, אִי בָּעֲיָא בִּנְשׂוּאִין — תֶּהֱוֵי. אֲבָל אֵשֶׁת אָחִיו שֶׁלֹּא הָיָה בְּעוֹלָמוֹ — לָא, כֵּיוָן דְּאַלִּיבָּא דר״ש הוּא דְּמַשְׁכַּחַתְּ לָהּ — אַלִּיבָּא דְּרַבָּנַן לָא מַשְׁכַּחַתְּ לָהּ בִּפְלוּגְתָּא לָא קָמַיְירֵי. וְרַב סַפְרָא מְתַרְגֵּם אַף אֵשֶׁת אָחִיו שֶׁלֹּא הָיָה בְּעוֹלָמוֹ, וּמַשְׁכַּחַתְּ לָהּ בְּשִׁיתָּא אַחֵי, וְאַלִּיבָּא דר״ש. וְסִימָנִיךְ: מֵת נוֹלַד וְיִיבֵּם, מֵת נוֹלַד וְיִיבֵּם; רְאוּבֵן וְשִׁמְעוֹן נְשׂוּאִין שְׁתֵּי אֲחָיוֹת, לֵוִי וִיהוּדָה נְשׂוּאִין שְׁתֵּי נָכְרִיּוֹת. מֵת רְאוּבֵן נוֹלַד יִשָּׂשכָר וְיִיבֵּם לֵוִי, מֵת שִׁמְעוֹן נוֹלַד זְבוּלֻן וְיִיבֵּם יְהוּדָה. מֵתוּ לֵוִי וִיהוּדָה בְּלֹא בָּנִים, וְנָפְלוּ לְהוּ קַמֵּי יִשָּׂשכָר וּזְבוּלֻן — הָאֲסוּרָה לְזֶה מוּתֶּרֶת לָזֶה, וְהָאֲסוּרָה לְזֶה מוּתֶּרֶת לָזֶה, — וַאֲחוֹתָהּ שֶׁהִיא יְבִמְתָּהּ. — ל״ל יִיבֵּם יְהוּדָה? בְּלֹא יִיבֵּם יְהוּדָה נַמִּי מַשְׁכַּחַתְּ לָהּ! — מִשּׁוּם צָרָה. — הָא תֵּינַח צָרָה, צָרָה דְּצָרָה מַאי אִיכָּא לְמֵימַר? — כְּגוֹן דַּהֲדַר וְיַבְּמִינְהוּ נַמִּי גָּד וְאָשֵׁר.§ מתני׳ *א שְׁלֹשָׁה אַחִין, שְׁנַיִם מֵהֶן נְשׂוּאִין שְׁתֵּי אֲחָיוֹת, אוֹ אִשָּׁה וּבִתָּהּ, אוֹ אִשָּׁה וּבַת בִּתָּהּ, אוֹ אִשָּׁה וּבַת בְּנָהּ — הֲרֵי אֵלּוּ חוֹלְצוֹת וְלֹא מִתְיַיבְּמוֹת, וְר״ש פּוֹטֵר. הָיְתָה אַחַת מֵהֶן אֲסוּרָה עָלָיו אִיסּוּר עֶרְוָה — אָסוּר בָּהּ, וּמוּתָּר בַּאֲחוֹתָהּ. *אִיסּוּר מִצְוָה אוֹ אִיסּוּר קְדוּשָּׁה — חוֹלְצוֹת וְלֹא מִתְיַיבְּמוֹת.§ גמ׳ *תַּנְיָא: ר״ש פּוֹטֵר בִּשְׁתֵּיהֶן מִן הַחֲלִיצָה וּמִן הַיִּיבּוּם, שֶׁנֶּאֱמַר ׳"וְאִשָּׁה אֶל אֲחוֹתָהּ לֹא תִקָּח לִצְרוֹר" — *"בְּשָׁעָה שֶׁנַּעֲשׂוּ צָרוֹת זוֹ לָזוֹ לֹא יְהֵא לְךָ לִיקּוּחִין אֲפִי׳ בְּאַחַת מֵהֶן.§ "הָיְתָה אַחַת מֵהֶן כו׳".§ הָא תּוּ לָמָּה לִי? הַיְינוּ הָךְ! — לר״ש אִיצְטְרִיךְ: סד״א: הוֹאִיל וְאָמַר ר״ש שְׁתֵּי אֲחָיוֹת לֹא חוֹלְצוֹת וְלֹא מִתְיַיבְּמוֹת — לִגְזוֹר מִשּׁוּם ב׳ אֲחָיוֹת דְּעָלְמָא, קָמַשְׁמַע לָן.§ "אִיסּוּר מִצְוָה כו׳".§

וְהָא

ויקרא יח

תורה אור

אִיסּוּר מִצְוָה. אִם הָיְתָה הָאַחַת אֲסוּרָה עַל הָאֶחָד אִיסּוּר מִצְוָה – אֵינוֹ מוּתָּר בַּאֲחוֹתָהּ, הוֹאִיל וְהִיא מִדְּאוֹרַיְיתָא רַמְיָא קַמֵּיהּ הֲוָאי אִידָךְ אֲחוֹת זְקוּקָתוֹ, הִלְכָּךְ בָּעוּ חֲלִיצָה. הָתָם. בְּפֶרֶק "כֵּיצַד". אִיסּוּר מִצְוָה לְחוּדָהּ. לָא אַשְׁמְעִינַן אֶלָּא יְבָמָה שֶׁנָּפְלָה לְפָנָיו, שֶׁהִיא אֲסוּרָה עָלָיו אִיסּוּר מִצְוָה – חוֹלֶצֶת. וְהָכָא אַשְׁמוּעִינַן אִיסּוּר מִצְוָה וַאֲחוֹתָהּ. שֶׁנָּפְלוּ לוֹ מִשְּׁנֵי אַחִין, דַּאֲחוֹתָהּ לָא מִיַּיבְּמָא. דְּלָא תֵּימָא אוֹקֵי אִיסּוּר מִצְוָה בִּמְקוֹם עֶרְוָה, וְתִתְיַיבֵּם אֲחוֹתָהּ, וְלָא תֶּיהֱוֵי כַּאֲחוֹת זְקוּקָתוֹ. מִשּׁוּם מִצְוָה עֲבוּד רַבָּנַן. שֶׁתִּתְקַיֵּים מִצְוַת יִבּוּם, וְלֹא הֶעֱמִידוּ אִיסּוּר זִיקָה, שֶׁהוּא מִדִּבְרֵיהֶם, לֶאֱסוֹר אֶת אֲחוֹתָהּ הֵיכָא דְּהִיא עָלָיו אִיסּוּר מִצְוָה, קמ״ל. הָכָא לֵיכָּא שֵׁנִי דְּמוֹכָח. שֶׁהֲרֵי שְׁתֵּיהֶן מִתְיַיבְּמוֹת, וְאָתֵי לְמִישְׁרֵי אֲחוֹת זְקוּקָה בְּעָלְמָא, וְאֵימָא לָא לַיַיבְּמָן, קמ״ל. תַּרְוַיְיהוּ מוֹכְחֵי אַהֲדָדֵי. שֶׁזֶּה לֹא יָכוֹל לִישָּׂא אֶת הָאַחֶרֶת אֶלָּא זוֹ, וְכֵן זוֹ – מוֹכְחָא מִילְּתָא שֶׁזּוּ אֲסוּרָה עַל זֶה, וְזוֹ עַל זֶה. לְפִיכָךְ לֵיכָּא אֲחוֹת זְקוּקָתוֹ. הַיְינוּ הָךְ. דְּהָא בְּהֶדְיָא קָתָנֵי לַהּ לְעֵיל: אִיסּוּר מִצְוָה וְאִיסּוּר קְדוּשָּׁה חוֹלֶצֶת. כִּי לָא אָמְרִינַן אוֹקֵי אִיסּוּר מִצְוָה בִּמְקוֹם עֶרְוָה. לְהִתְיַיבֵּם אֲחוֹתָהּ – הֵיכָא דְּאֵין אִיסּוּר מִצְוָה אֶלָּא בְּאַחַת עַל הָאֶחָד, וְלִשְׁנֵי שְׁתֵּיהֶן זְקוּקוֹת. דְּאִי שָׁרֵית לְיַיבּוּמֵי לְהַאי שֶׁהָאַחַת אֲסוּרָה עָלָיו – אָתֵי שֵׁנִי נַמִּי לְיַיבּוּמֵי, וְקָא פָּגַע בַּאֲחוֹת זְקוּקָתוֹ. בְּכוּלָּן אֲנִי קוֹרֵא בָּהֶן. בְּכָל חֲמֵשׁ עֶשְׂרֵה עֲרָיוֹת דְּבְפ״ק, אֶפְשָׁר לָהֶן לִהְיוֹת שְׁתֵּי אֲחָיוֹת נוֹפְלוֹת לִשְׁנֵי אַחִין, וְהָאַחַת אֲסוּרָה עַל זֶה מִשּׁוּם אַחַת מִכָּל הָעֲרָיוֹת הַלָּלוּ, וּמוּתֶּרֶת לָזֶה, וְהַשְּׁנִיָּה אֲסוּרָה עַל זֶה מִשּׁוּם אוֹתוֹ שֵׁם עֶרְוָה עַצְמוֹ, וּמוּתֶּרֶת לָזֶה. וּמִתּוֹךְ כָּךְ נִמְצְאוּ שְׁתֵּי אֲחָיוֹת מִתְיַיבְּמוֹת, וְלֹא הָוְינוּ בַּאֲחוֹת זְקוּקָה. וְכוּלָּן פֵּירַשְׁתִּי בְּפ״א (דף ט:). בְּאוֹנָסִין. בִּבְתּוֹ מֵאֲנוּסָתוֹ, כְּגוֹן: רְאוּבֵן אָנַס אִשָּׁה וְהוֹלִיד בַּת, וּבָא שִׁמְעוֹן וְאָנַס אֲנוּסַת אָחִיו וְהוֹלִיד בַּת, וְנִישְּׂאוּ בַּת רְאוּבֵן וּבַת שִׁמְעוֹן לְלֵוִי וִיהוּדָה אֲחֵיהֶן, וַהֲרֵי הֵן אֲחָיוֹת מִן הָאֵם – בַּת שִׁמְעוֹן מוּתֶּרֶת לִרְאוּבֵן, וּבַת רְאוּבֵן מוּתֶּרֶת לְשִׁמְעוֹן, וְנִמְצְאוּ שְׁתֵּי אֲחָיוֹת מִתְיַיבְּמוֹת. וְכֵן בַּת בִּתּוֹ, וְכֵן כּוּלָּן, אע״ג דְּכָל חֲמִשָּׁה בָּבֵי דְּרֵישָׁא מַשְׁכַּחְתְּ בִּנְשׂוּאִין, הוֹאִיל וּבִתּוֹ לָא מַשְׁכַּחְתְּ שֶׁיְּהוּ שְׁתֵּי בָּנוֹת שֶׁל שְׁנֵי אַחִין אֲחָיוֹת מִן הָאֵם, שֶׁאִי אֶפְשָׁר שֶׁנָּשָׂא יְבִמְתּוֹ שֶׁיֵּשׁ לָהּ בַּת – לָא תָּנֵי בְּהוּ הָאֲסוּרָה לָזֶה כו׳, הוֹאִיל וְכוּלָּן אִיסּוּר שֵׁם בַּת הֵן. דְּאַלִּיבָּא דְּרַבִּי שִׁמְעוֹן הִיא דְּמַשְׁכַּחַתְּ בָּהּ. הָאֲסוּרָה לָזֶה, כִּדְמְפָרֵשׁ רַב סַפְרָא לְקַמֵּיהּ. בִּפְלוּגְתָּא לָא אַיְירֵי. רַבִּי חִיָּיא. הָאֲסוּרָה לָזֶה. אֵשֶׁת לֵוִי הָאֲסוּרָה לְיִשָּׂשכָר שֶׁבָּא וּמְצָאָהּ אֲסוּרָה עָלָיו מִזִּיקַת רְאוּבֵן שֶׁלֹּא הָיָה בְּעוֹלָמוֹ, וּמוּתֶּרֶת לִזְבוּלֻן. שֶׁכְּשֶׁנּוֹלַד כְּבָר נִתְיַיבְּמָה לְלֵוִי, וּכְיִיבֵּם וּלְבַסּוֹף נוֹלַד שָׁרֵי ר״ש. וְאֵשֶׁת יְהוּדָה אֲסוּרָה לִזְבוּלֻן מִשּׁוּם שִׁמְעוֹן שֶׁלֹּא הָיָה בְּעוֹלָמוֹ, וּכְשֶׁנּוֹלַד מְצָאָהּ בְּאִיסּוּר, וּמוּתֶּרֶת לְיִשָּׂשכָר. בְּלֹא יִיבֵּם יְהוּדָה נַמִּי. שָׁרֵי לְיִשָּׂשכָר. וּבַחֲמִשָּׁה אַחֵי מַשְׁכַּחַתְּ לָהּ: מֵת רְאוּבֵן נוֹלַד יִשָּׂשכָר יִיבֵּם לֵוִי, מֵת שִׁמְעוֹן נוֹלַד זְבוּלוּן וּמֵת לֵוִי בְּלֹא בָנִים, וְנָפְלוּ אֵשֶׁת לֵוִי וְאֵשֶׁת שִׁמְעוֹן לִפְנֵי יִשָּׂשכָר וּזְבוּלוּן. אֵשֶׁת לֵוִי אֲסוּרָה לְיִשָּׂשכָר מִפְּנֵי רְאוּבֵן בַּעְלָהּ הָרִאשׁוֹן, וּמוּתֶּרֶת לִזְבוּלוּן, וְאֵשֶׁת שִׁמְעוֹן מוּתֶּרֶת לְיִשָּׂשכָר, שֶׁהֲרֵי בְּעוֹלָמוֹ הָיָה, וַאֲסוּרָה לִזְבוּלוּן. וּמִשּׁוּם צָרָה. הַאי דְּנָקַט יִיבֵּם יְהוּדָה – מִשּׁוּם צָרָה, דְּבָעֵי אַשְׁכּוּחֵי נַמִּי בְּצָרָה הָאֲסוּרָה לָזֶה מוּתֶּרֶת לָזֶה, אִם בָּאוּ יִשָּׂשכָר וּזְבוּלוּן לְיַיבֵּם לִנְשֵׁי לֵוִי וִיהוּדָה הָרִאשׁוֹנָה – אֵשֶׁת לֵוִי אֲסוּרָה לְיִשָּׂשכָר מִשּׁוּם צָרַת אֵשֶׁת אָחִיו שֶׁלֹּא הָיָה בְּעוֹלָמוֹ, וְכֵן אֵשֶׁת יְהוּדָה עַל זְבוּלוּן. וּכְגוֹן שֶׁהָיוּ הַצָּרוֹת אֲחָיוֹת זוֹ לָזוֹ. וְנָכְרִיּוֹת קָרֵי לְהוּ אֶצֶל נְשֵׁי רְאוּבֵן וְשִׁמְעוֹן, דְּאִיכָּא נַמִּי הַשְׁתָּא בְּצָרוֹת הָאֲסוּרָה לָזֶה מוּתֶּרֶת לָזֶה וַאֲחוֹתָהּ כְּשֶׁהִיא יְבִמְתָּהּ כו׳. וְאִי לָא יִיבֵּם יְהוּדָה לָא מִיתּוֹקַם מִילְּתָא דְּרַבִּי חִיָּיא בְּאִיסּוּר צָרָתָהּ, דְּאִם נָפְלוּ שְׁתֵּי נָשִׁים מִשִּׁמְעוֹן – שְׁתֵּיהֶן אֵשֶׁת אָח שֶׁלֹּא הָיָה בְּעוֹלָמוֹ הֵן. צָרָה דְּצָרָה מַאי אִיכָּא לְמֵימַר. הֵיכִי קָרֵית הָאֲסוּרָה לָזֶה מוּתֶּרֶת לָזֶה בְּאִיסּוּר וְצָרוֹת צָרָה? דְּהָא צָרוֹת צָרוֹתֵיהֶן נַמִּי תְּנַן בְּפ״ק. כְּגוֹן דַּהֲדַר יַבְּמִינְהוּ גָּד וְאָשֵׁר. לִנְשֵׁי לֵוִי וִיהוּדָה הָרִאשׁוֹנוֹת, וְלָהֶם נָשִׁים, וְיִיבֵּם גָּד אֶת אֵשֶׁת יְהוּדָה, וְאָשֵׁר יִיבֵּם אֵשֶׁת לֵוִי, וּמֵתוּ גָּד וְאָשֵׁר וְנָפְלוּ לִפְנֵי יִשָּׂשכָר וּזְבוּלוּן. וְאִם בָּאִים לְיַיבֵּם נְשֵׁי גָּד וְאָשֵׁר הָרִאשׁוֹנוֹת – אֵשֶׁת גָּד צָרַת אֵשֶׁת יְהוּדָה שֶׁהָיְתָה צָרַת אֵשֶׁת שִׁמְעוֹן שֶׁלֹּא הָיָה בְּעוֹלָמוֹ אֲסוּרָה לִזְבוּלוּן וּמוּתֶּרֶת לְיִשָּׂשכָר. וְכֵן אֵשֶׁת אָשֵׁר עַל יִשָּׂשכָר, וּמוּתֶּרֶת לִזְבוּלוּן. בְּשָׁעָה שֶׁנַּעֲשׂוּ צָרוֹת זוֹ לָזוֹ. כְּגוֹן (א) הַשְׁתָּא, שֶׁנָּפְלוּ לְפָנָיו וְנַעֲשׂוּ שְׁתֵּי אֲחָיוֹת צָרוֹת זוֹ לָזוֹ בְּזִיקָה. לִיגְזוֹר מִשּׁוּם שְׁתֵּי אֲחָיוֹת דְּעָלְמָא. אע״ג דְּהָא נַמִּי מֵרֵישָׁא שָׁמְעִינַן הָתָם הוּא לְרַבָּנַן לָא גָּזְרִינַן. דְּאִי נַמִּי אָתֵי לְמִישְׁרֵי אֲחָיוֹת דְּעָלְמָא – לֵיכָּא אֶלָּא אִיסּוּר אֲחוֹת זְקוּקָה דְּרַבָּנַן. אֲבָל לר״ש דְּאָמַר אִיסּוּר אֲחוֹת זְקוּקָה עֶרְוָה גְּמוּרָה הִיא, דְּרַחֲמָנָא פַּטְרַהּ, וְקַיְימָא עֲלֵיהּ בְּאִיסּוּר אֵשֶׁת אָח – לִיגְזוֹר הֵיכָא דַּאֲחוֹתָהּ אֲסוּרָה מִשּׁוּם עֶרְוָה וְלֹא זְקוּקָה לֵיהּ, וְנֵימָא לָא לְיַיבֵּם לַאֲחוֹתָהּ, דְּלָא לֵיתֵי לְיַיבּוּמֵי אֲחוֹת זְקוּקָה דְּעָלְמָא, קמ״ל.

וְהָאָמַר

תוספות ישנים

לגזור משום שתי אחיות דעלמא ונהי דלעיל חזינן דלא גזרינן היינו דווקא לרבנן אבל לר״ש דסבר דאלימא כל כך זיקה דאמר דשתי אחיות לא חולצות ולא מתייבמות סד״א ליגזור משום שתי אחיות דעלמא:

תוספות חד מקמאי

יבמה שאין אני קורא לה בשעת נפילה יבמה יבוא עליה הרי היא כאשת אח שיש לה בנים אלמא ס״ל יש זיקה: הא דקתני במתני׳ איסור מצוה או איסור קדושה חולצת ולא מתייבמת פרכינן עלה בגמ׳ הא נמי תנינן אסור מצוה או איסור קדושה חולצת ולא מתייבמת. התם איסור מצוה לחודיה. והכא איסור מצוה ואחותה. ומאי דקתני זו היא שאמרו אחותה שהיא יבמתה חולצת או מתייבמת פרשינן בגמ׳ למעוטי איסו׳ מצוה לזה ואיסור מצוה לזה:

מסורת הש״ס

לעיל כ. [כו.] סנהדרין

לעיל ט.

לעיל יט.

[לעיל כ. וש״נ]

לעיל יט. קידושין נ:

[לעיל יט. ונזכר ר״ש עוד לעיל יח:]

הגהות הב״ח

(א) רש״י ד״ה בשעה וכו׳ כגון הכא שנפלו:

והאמר ר' שמעון: שתי אחיות לא חולצות ולא מתייבמות! — גזירה משום איסור מצוה דעלמא. הא תינח איהי, אחותה מאי איכא למימר? — גזירה אחותה משום לתא דידה. — והא גבי ערוה לא גזרינן! — שאני ערוה דמגמר גמירי לה אינשי, וקלא אית לה.§ **מתני'** *שלשה אחין, שנים נשואים שתי אחיות, ואחד מופנה; מת אחד מבעלי אחיות ועשה בה מופנה מאמר, ואח"כ מת אחיו השני — בש"א: אשתו עמו, והלזו תצא משום אחות אשה. וב"ה אומרים: [א]מוציא את אשתו בגט ובחליצה, ואשת אחיו בחליצה. זו היא שאמרו: *אוי לו על אשתו, ואוי לו על אשת אחיו.§ **גמ'** "זו היא" למעוטי מאי? — למעוטי הך דר' יהושע, דלא עבדינן כוותיה, אלא אי כר"ג אי כר"א. *א"ר אלעזר: לא תימא מאמר לב"ש קונה קנין גמור, דאי בעי לאפוקי סגי לה בגיטא, אלא: מאמר לב"ש אינו קונה אלא לדחות בצרה בלבד. אמר רבי אבין, אף אנן נמי תנינא: בש"א: יקיימו, יקיימו — אין, לכתחלה — לא, ואי

רש"י

והאמר ר' שמעון שתי אחיות לא חולצות ולא מתייבמות. והכא אמאי בעי חליצה? הא כיון דמדאורייתא חזיא ליבומי — זקוקה היא, והוו להו כשאר ב' אחיות שנעשו צרות זו לזו, ור"ש פוטר אחות זקוקה מחליצה. גזירה משום איסור מצוה דעלמא. אי פטרת להו לגמרי, מאן דחזי סבר: טעמא לאו משום אחות זקוקה, אלא משום דאיסור מצוה הויא כערוה ופטורה מחליצה, ואתי למיפטר איסור מצוה דעלמא, דלאו אחיות, מחליצה. תינח איהי. איסור מצוה. אחותה. אמאי חלצה? תיפטר משום אחות זקוקה, דהכא מאי אמרת. משום לתא דידה. משום מזל דידה, דאיסור מצוה. האי "לתא" — יתור לשון הוא. והא גבי ערוה לא גזרינן. דאם היתה אחת מהן אסורה עליו איסור ערוה — אסור בה ומותר באחותה, הערוה יוצאה בלא חליצה, ולא אמרינן תחלוץ ערוה גזירה משום אחותה שאין ערוה וראויה לייבום. והא נמי לרבי שמעון ערוה היא משנעשו צרות, ואמאי מצרכת לה חליצה משום גזרת אחותה? דמגמר גמירי לה אינשי. והכל יודעין שאין צריכה חליצה, ואחותה לאו אחות זקוקה היא, ולא אתי למישרי אחותה בלא חליצה. אבל ערוה דנעשו צרות דר"ש — לא כ"ע גמירי הלכתא דאיסור שתיהן שוות. ואי מפקת לה בלא חליצה — אתי נמי למיפק אחותה שהיא איסור מצוה בלא חליצה, ונפקא מינה חורבה לאיסור מצוה בעלמא: *מגמר גמירי אינשי. וידעי דלא רמיא קמיה, ואחותה לאו אחות זקוקה היא, ולא אתי למישרי אחות זקוקה דעלמא. **מתני'** אשתו עמו. דמאמר ככנוסה דמיא, וכי נפלה אחותה לא מיתסרא הך עליה משום אחות זקוקה. והלזו תצא. אף מן החליצה משום אחות אשה. **גמ'** הך דרבי יהושע. בפרק ב"ש, דקאמר נמי: אי לו על אשתו אי לו על אשת אחיו, ופליגי עלה רבן גמליאל ורבי אלעזר. לא תימא מאמר לב"ש קונה קנין גמור. ותהוי כאשתו, ואי בעי לאפוקי — תיסגי לה בגיטא. אלא מאמר לב"ש אין קונה אלא לדחות בצרה. כלומר: לדחות אחותה שלא תאסרנה לזו משום אחות זקוקה. יקיימו. אם קדמו וכנסו, בריש פירקין. לכתחילה לא. מייבמו, משום אחות זקוקתו. ואי

תוספות

אחותה משום לתא דידה. דאי נפקא בלא חליצה, משום דנעשו צרות זו לזו — אתי לאפוקי מהאי טעמא נמי ההיא דאיסור מצוה, ואתי למישרי נמי איסור מצוה דעלמא, ופרכינן: והא גבי ערוה לא גזרו שתחלץ אלא יוצאה בלא חליצה, ולא חיישינן שמא יסברו דמטעם (א) אחותה יוצאה, ואתי לאפוקי אידך בלא חליצה. **ב"ש** אומרים אשתו עמו כו'. בגמ' גבי השתא ארוסה דעלמא כו' עשה בה מאמר מיבעיא פירש בקונטרס דמאמר יבמין מדרבנן, אפילו לבית שמאי, דמדאורייתא "יבמה יבא עליה" כתיב. ואין נראה לריב"ס, דא"כ אמאי תצא הלזו משום אחות אשה במאמר זה? ומיהו, י"ל: דתצא משום אחות אשה — היינו אחר שיבעול [בעלת המאמר]. אבל קשה, דלעיל פ"ב (דף יח. ושם) דקאמר: הא דקתני מאמר — לאפוקי מב"ש, משמע דלב"ש (ב) יוצאה שניה משום צרת אשת אחיו שלא היה בעולמו. וכן נמי קאמרינן לקמן בפירקין (דף ל.) גבי אחות אשה אלמא מאמר קני דאורייתא לב"ש, וכולה סוגיא דגמרא מוכח הכי. והא דקאמר השתא ארוסה דעלמא כו' עבד בה מאמר מיבעיא — אע"ג דמאמר נמי מדאורייתא, מ"מ קאמר מאמר מיבעיא, משום דהא דמאמר קני — מדאורייתא היינו משום דגמרינן מקידושין דעלמא, הלכך לא עדיף מקידושין. ודיו לבא מן הדין להיות כנדון. **אוי** לו על אשתו כו'. אר"י: דבכל הני דפ' "חרש" (לקמן קיב: קיד:) דתנן מוציא את אשתו בגט ואת אשת אחיו בחליצה לא קתני "אוי לו" כי הכא, משום ד"אוי לו" משמע לשון צער, כלומר: ראוי לו להצטער שהפסיד אשתו בלא פשיעתו. והכא והא דאייתי בגמ' פלוגתא דר"א ור' יהושע דקטנה וגדולה — לא פשע, להכי קתני "אוי לו". אבל התם פשע, שהכניס עצמו בספק חרשות, שלא היה לו לישא חרשת. וכן ההיא ד"ההולך" (לקמן דף מא. ושם) דשומרת יבם שקידש אחיו את אחותה כו' להכי נמי קאמר בגמרא למעוטי דר' יהושע, דשייך התם לשון "אוי לו" כי הכא, ולא קאמר למעוטי כל הני. **אי** כר"ג. דאמר תמתין עד שתגדיל ויבעול ותצא הלזו משום אחות אשה, אע"ג דקדושי קטנה דרבנן — מ"מ הקילו בה מבבעלת מאמר, משום דכנוסה היא אלא קודם זמן גדולה. והא דפריך מינה לעיל בריש פ"ב (דף יח.) אהא דר"מ אוסר לבטל מצות יבמין, ור"ג שרי לבטל מצות יבמין, אע"ג דהכא כנוסה אלא מעיקרא — מ"מ פריך אהא דר"מ חייש לספיקא, ור"ג אפילו לודאי לא חייש. **אי** כרבי אלעזר. דאמר: מלמדין הקטנה שתמאן, ומותר בגדולה לייבם. וא"ת: ואמאי שרי? והא בשעת נפילה נראית כאחות אשה, כדאמרינן לעיל בפ"ק (דף יג.) גבי צרת בתו הממאנת, דבשעת נפילה נראית כצרת בתו, ובשעת נפילה נראית ככלתו! וי"ל: דלא דמי, דהתם, כשהבעל מת, אין דומה כ"כ עוקרת נישואין קמאי כי הכא, שהבעל קייסא). **לא** תימא מאמר לב"ש קונה קנין גמור כו'. אע"ג דאין קונה קנין גמור, מ"מ אמרי' לעיל (ג) ולקמן (דף ל.) גבי אחות אשה דפוטרת [צרתה] לב"ש ע"י מאמר. תימה: מאי קאמר ר"ש לעיל בפ"ב (דף יט.): אם מאמרו של שני מאמר — אשת שני הוא בועל, כי הוי נמי מאמר — אשת שניהם בועל, דהא אפילו לב"ש דמאמר קונה אינו קונה לגמרי, אלא קונה ומשייר! וכ"ת דלר"ש אי קני — קני לגמרי, טפי מלב"ש — א"כ מנא ליה לר' אלעזר דלא קני לגמרי לב"ש כמו לר"ש? **אלא** לדחות בצרה בלבד. פי' בקונטרס: צרה דכולהו שמעתין — אחותה שנופלת עמה. וקשה: לרב אשי דאמר דוחה ומשייר היא ולרתה בעיא חליצה, הא קתני במתני' תצא משום אחות אשה, משמע דיוצאה בלא חליצה! ועוד: אי בעיא חליצה — היאך מקיים את זו? וי"ל: דסבר רב אשי דמהני מאמר להסיר הזיקה, ודחי לצרה לענין שלא תאסור את זו משום אחות זקוקתו, ואחר שיבעול בעלת המאמר — קאמר דתצא אחותה משום אחות אשה. וא"ת: והיכי מייתי לה סייעתא ממתניתין יקיימו — אין, לכתחלה — לא, הא מהני מאמר לרב אשי לכל הפחות דדחי לצרה ושריא בעלת מאמר לכתחלה? וי"ל: דהכי מייתי, דאי ס"ד דבמאמר דהיתירא (ד) דוחה דחייה גמורה לפטור צרתה בלא חליצה — א"כ מאמר דאיסור דחי נמי לצרה לענין שלא תאסור את זו משום אחות זקוקה וזה יעשה מאמר וידחה כו'. ופריך: ואלא הא קתני בש"א אשתו עמו כו' — משמע דדוחה דחייה גמורה, אלא יבמה דחזיא לכולהו כו'. פי': דמאמר דהיתירא — דחי דחייה גמורה. יבמה דלא חזיא לכולהו, דהיינו מאמר דאיסור — לא דחי למקלתה, ולא דחי ההוא מאמר כלל. כן צריך לפרש לפי' הקונטרס. אבל קשה: דצרה דבכל דוכתי היינו — שנופלת עמה מבית אחד. ועוד: שמגיה הספרים אלא יבמה דחזיא לכולהו כו', שלא היה כתוב בספרים "אלא". ועוד: דלמה שינה הלשון יבמה דחזיא כו', ולא נקט לישנא דנקט מעיקרא מאמר דהיתירא קני דאיסורא לא קני! ונראה לר"י: דצרה — היינו שעמה בבית אחד. וה"פ: לא תימא מאמר לב"ש כו' אלא לדחות בצרה בלבד, שאם נתן מאמר לא' מב' יבמות שנפלו מבית אחד, אע"ג דבעלת מאמר לא סגי לה בגט — צרתה מיהו פטורה לגמרי בלא חליצה, דכיון שהתחיל הקנין לעשות בזו, אע"פ שלא נגמר — קרינן ביה בית אחד הוא בונה ואינו בונה ב' בתים. וטעמא דב"ש דסברי דאהני קרא דדרשינן *ביאה גומרת בה ואין כסף ושטר גומרין בה, לענין דאי בעי לאפוקי, דלא סגי לה בגט. ורב אשי סבר דלא מהני מאמר לפטור צרתה בלא חליצה, אלא דוחה הצרה ממנו, שאסור לייבמה, ומשייר קצת זיקה לאוסרה לשוק עד שתחלוץ. ואע"ג דלענין אחותה *דחי מאמר לגמרי לפוטרה לשוק, כדקתני מתני': והלזו תצא משום אחות אשה — התם אחותה נפלה אחר המאמר, כמו שפירשתי בסמוך. וקאמר: אף אנן נמי תנינא, שכשקדמה זיקה למאמר שאין המאמר מפקיע לגמרי — זה יעשה מאמר וידחה כו'. ופריך: אלא הך דקתני בש"א אשתו עמו כו', אלמא ע"י המאמר מידחי אחותה לגמרי, ה"נ תדחה צרתה לגמרי! ומשני: יבמה דחזיא לכולהו, ול"ג "אלא", וה"פ: יבמה דחזיא לכולהו מילי דיבום, כגון ב' יבמות שנפלו מבית אחד, שכל אחת ראויה לחלוץ ולייבם בשעת נפילה, וכן הא דבש"א יקיימו, דבשעת נפילה חזיא כל אחת לכל מילי דיבום מן התורה, דהא חזיא [אף] ליבום מן התורה — חזיא נמי למקצתו, פי': למקצת מילי דיבמה, דהיינו חליצה. דכיון דבהך זיקה איחזיא ליבום — לא מפיק מאמר להסיא זיקה לגמרי, ובעי חליצה. אבל יבמה דלא איחזיא לכולהו מילי דיבום, כגון ההיא דבש"א אשתו עמו, שלא נראית ליבום בשעת נפילה שכבר עשה המאמר באחותה — לא חזיא למקצתו. פי': חליצה, ואידחיא ע"י מאמר חברתה לגמרי. והשתא לא מצי לשנויי כדשני לעיל מאמר דהיתירא דחי כו' — שאפי' במאמר דהיתירא קאמר דלא מפקע הזיקה לגמרי להתיר צרה לשוקב). הקשה ה"ר יעקב דאורלינ"ש: מנא לן דטעמא דב"ש משום דמאמר קונה? דלמא קסברי אין זיקה, ומותר לבטל מצות יבמין, ונקט מאמר משום ב"ה? וי"ל: דלא מסתבר שיהא שום תנא מיקל לבטל בהדיא מצות יבמין. ועוד: דהא אמר לעיל בש"א יקיימו לכתחלה לא. ועוד הקשה: דלמא טעמא דב"ש משום דזיקה ככנוסה? וי"ל: דלא מסתבר ליה למימר דלא נקט מאמר אלא משום ב"ה, כיון שיכול לומר דלב"ש נמי איצטריך.
יעשה

תוספות ישנים

והאמר ר"ש וכו' וא"כ אמאי אמרינן במתני' חולצות. וא"ת ודלמא משום דאיסור מצוה פקעה קצת זיקה. ונראה לר"ס דפריך מאיסור מצוה גופה אמאי חולצת דממה נפשך היה לנו לומר דלא תחלצה דאי איסור מצוה משוי לה ערוה א"כ פטורה היא גם מחליצה ואי לא משוי לה כערוה א"כ יש בכן זיקה כמו שתי אחיות דעלמא דאינן חולצות. והא דקא פריך אחותה מאי איכא למימר אין זה ממה נפשך דהא אי איסור מצוה ערוה היא א"כ מותר באחותה דאינה אחות זקוקתו. אבל מ"מ פריך שפיר דכיון דלא מחזקינן איסור מצוה לערוה ולא אמרי' אלא משום גזרה משום איסור מצוה בעלמא. א"כ אחותה הוי אחות זקוקה: **והא** גבי ערוה לא גזרינן. פי' דאמרינן אסור בה ומותר באחותה ואמאי לא אמרינן דתחלץ גזרה משום אחותה דשמא יאמרו העולם דכי היכי דפטורה איהי תפטר אחותה וזה אינו דהא מותר בה. א"כ לא היה לנו להתיר אחותה היכא דאיכא נמי איסור ערוה גזרה משום שתי אחיות שאין בהם ערוה ומשני ערוה מגמר גמרי אינשי: **שנים** מהם נשואים שתי אחיות וא' מופנה האי דלא נקט הכא וא' נשוי נכרית כמו במשנה דבסמוך. נראה משום דבעי למימר זו היא שאמרו אוי לו על אשתו ועל אשת אחיו לכך מוקים לה דהוי מופנה דהשתא הוי בלא אשה כלל: **אשתו** עמו משום דקסבר ב"ש מאמר קונה ומשמע מדאורייתא הוא מדקאמר והלזו תצא משום אחות אשה ונפקא לן מדכתיב ולקחה לו לאשה כאשה מה אשה בשטר אף יבמה בשטר ודלא כפ"ה דפי' בגמרא עביד בה מאמר מיבעיא. ופ"ה דמאמר אינו אלא מדרבנן ולפי' שפיר י"ל דהוי מדאורייתא וכדפרשתי לקמן דהכי קאמר השתא ארוסה בעלמא דהוו קדושין מפורשים בהדיא בקרא וכו' עביד בה מאמר דלא ידעינן אלא מקדושין מיבעיא: **א)** ועוי"ל דלא דמי ללעיל איירי שמיאנה ביבם לבד ולא בבעל ואינו נראה כעוקרת נשואי המת אבל הכא שממאנת הקטנה בבעלה ורואין העולם שיוצאה מבעלה במיאון יודעין העולם שלא היו נשואיה נשואין ולא היתה אחות אשה: **ב)** והקשה הרב רבינו נתנאל חדא דלפי הך פירושא הך צרה ר"ל באשה אחרת ובזה לא איירי במתני' כי אם באחותה שנפלה מאח אחר. ועוד דפי' דדוחה צרתה משום בית א' הוא בונה קשה אטו מאמר בנין מקרי הא אמרינן בעשרה יוחסין הכל מודים במחזיר גרושתו בקידש ולא בעל דאינו לוקה מאי טעמא דרך ליקוחין אסרה תורה אלמא לא מקרי בנין אלא ביאה. לכן נראה לרבינו נתנאל לפרש שיטה אחרת מרא"ש ועד סוף מאמר אינו קונה אלא לדחות צרה בלבד כלומר לצרתה מאחיו שהיא אחותה של בעלת מאמר לא בעיא חליצה אבל איהי לא סגיא בגט וב"ש לטעמייהו דהכי מפרש בירושלמי אמר ר' אליעזר בן ערך גירש לבעלת מאמר לא תהא צריכה חליצה א"ר הילא בשם ר' אליעזר מודה ב"ש שאם גירש לבעלת מאמר צריכה הימנו חליצה אלמא לב"ש לא סגי לה בגט. וא"ת כיון דלא אליס כח בעלת מאמר לפטור בגט היכי אלימא לפטור צרתה מחליצה י"ל דלא גרע מקדושין דעלמא דהכא נמי כתיב ולקחה זו מאמר ואם קדש אשה ואח"כ מת אחיו נשוי אחותה פשיטא דלא תנא המאורסת הכא נמי הא בעלת מאמר וכו' אע"ג דאליס בעלת מאמר כקדושין דעלמא לענין שלא תהא צרה צריכה חליצה מ"מ הכא לא סגי לה בגט דביאה גומרת בה דכתיב יבמה יבא עליה וזיקה דבהדי מאמר לא פקעה בגט לבד אי ליכא חליצה בהדיה.

עין משפט נר מצוה

טו א מיי' פ"ז מהלכות יבום הלכה ו סמג עשין נח טוש"ע אה"ע סימן קעה סעיף ו:

מסורת הש"ס

לקמן נה: עדיות פ"ד מ"ט

לקמן קט.

לקמן לט: [נדרים עד.]

נ"א ליבנה אחרינא

[לקמן כ. קדושין יד.]

הגהות הב"ח

(א) תוס' ד"ה אחותה וכו' דמטעם אחות אשה יוצאה ואתי: (ב) ד"ה ב"ש וכו' משמע דלב"ש במאמר לחוד יוצאת שניה: (ג) ד"ה לא תימא וכו' מ"מ אמרינן לעיל דפוטר גבי אשת אחיו שלא היה בעולמו ולקמן גבי אחות אשה: (ד) ד"ה אלא וכו' דהיתירא דחיא דחייה גמורה:

מאמר חברתה דחי לגמרי כצ"ל

וְאִי ס"ד מַאֲמָר לְב"ש קוֹנֶה קִנְיָן גָּמוּר — זֶה יַעֲשֶׂה מַאֲמָר וְיִקְנֶה, וְזֶה יַעֲשֶׂה מַאֲמָר וְיִקְנֶה! אֶלָּא מַאי — דּוֹחֶה דְּחִיָּיה גְּמוּרָה? זֶה יַעֲשֶׂה מַאֲמָר וְיִדְחֶה, וְזֶה יַעֲשֶׂה מַאֲמָר וְיִדְחֶה. אֶלָּא מַאי אִית לָךְ לְמֵימַר: מַאֲמָר דְּהֶתֵּירָא — דָּחֵי, דְּאִיסּוּרָא — לָא דָּחֵי — ה"נ: מַאֲמָר, אֲפִילּוּ לְמ"ד מַאֲמָר קוֹנֶה קִנְיָן גָּמוּר, מַאֲמָר דְּהֶתֵּירָא — קָנֵי דְּאִיסּוּרָא — לָא קָנֵי. רַב אַשִׁי מַתְנֵי הָכִי, אֲמַר ר"א: לָא תֵּימָא מַאֲמָר לְב"ש דָּחֵי דְּחִיָּיה גְּמוּרָה, וְצָרָתָהּ חֲלִיצָה נַמִּי לָא בָּעֲיָא, אֶלָּא דּוֹחֶה וּמְשַׁיֵּיר הוּא. א"ר אָבִין: אַף אֲנַן נַמִּי תָּנֵינָא: ב"ש אוֹמְרִים: יְקַיְּימוּ. יְקַיְּימוּ — אִין, לְכַתְּחִלָּה — לָא. וְאִי ס"ד מַאֲמָר לְב"ש דּוֹחֶה דְּחִיָּיה גְּמוּרָה — זֶה יַעֲשֶׂה מַאֲמָר וְיִדְחֶה, וְזֶה יַעֲשֶׂה מַאֲמָר וְיִדְחֶה! — וְאֶלָּא הָא קָתָנֵי, בש"א: אִשְׁתּוֹ עִמּוֹ, וְהַלָּזוּ תֵּצֵא מִשּׁוּם אֲחוֹת אִשָּׁה! — אֶלָּא: יְבָמָה דְּחַזְיָא לְכוּלְּהוּ — חַזְיָא לְמִקְצָתָהּ. יְבָמָה דְּלָא חַזְיָא לְכוּלְּהוּ — לָא חַזְיָא לְמִקְצָתָהּ. *בָּעֵי רַבָּה: מַאֲמָר, לְב"ש, נִישּׂוּאִין עוֹשֶׂה אוֹ אֵירוּסִין עוֹשֶׂה? אֲמַר לֵיהּ אַבַּיֵי: לְמַאי הִלְכְתָא? אִילֵימָא לְיוֹרְשָׁהּ וְלִיטַּמֵּא לָהּ וּלְהָפֵר נְדָרֶיהָ — הַשְׁתָּא אֲרוּסָה בְּעָלְמָא תָּנֵי רַ' חִיָּיא: *אִשְׁתּוֹ [א]אֲרוּסָה לֹא אוֹנֵן וְלֹא מִטַּמֵּא לָהּ, וְכֵן הִיא לֹא אוֹנֶנֶת וְלֹא מִטַּמְּאָה לוֹ, [ב]מֵתָה — אֵינוֹ יוֹרְשָׁהּ, מֵת [ג]הוּא — גּוֹבָה כְּתוּבָּתָהּ, — עֲבַד בָּהּ מַאֲמָר מִיבָּעֲיָא? וְאֶלָּא לְעִנְיַן מְסִירָה לְחוּפָּה, מַאי? נִישּׂוּאִין עוֹשֶׂה — וְלֹא בָּעֲיָא מְסִירָה לְחוּפָּה, אוֹ דִּלְמָא אֵירוּסִין עוֹשֶׂה — וּבָעֲיָא מְסִירָה לְחוּפָּה! א"ל: הַשְׁתָּא, לָא עֲבַד בָּהּ מַאֲמָר כְּתִיב °"יְבָמָהּ יָבֹא עָלֶיהָ", בְּעַל כָּרְחָהּ, עֲבַד בָּהּ מַאֲמָר מִיבָּעֲיָא? א"ל: (א) שֶׁאֲנִי אוֹמֵר *כׇּל הָעוֹשֶׂה מַאֲמָר בִּיבִמְתּוֹ — פָּרְחָה מִמֶּנּוּ זִיקַת יְבָמִין, וְחָלָה עָלֶיהָ זִיקַת אֵירוּסִין. מַאי? ת"ש: *שׁוֹמֶרֶת יָבָם, בֵּין יָבָם אֶחָד בֵּין שְׁנֵי יְבָמִין, ר"א אוֹמֵר: יָפֵר, רַ' יְהוֹשֻׁעַ אוֹמֵר: לְאֶחָד וְלֹא לִשְׁנַיִם, [ד]רַ' עֲקִיבָא אוֹמֵר: לֹא לְאֶחָד וְלֹא לִשְׁנַיִם. וְהָוֵינַן בָּהּ: *בִּשְׁלָמָא ר"ע סָבַר: אֵין זִיקָה אֲפִי' לְחַד, לְרַ' יְהוֹשֻׁעַ: לְחַד — יֵשׁ זִיקָה, לִתְרֵי — אֵין זִיקָה. אֶלָּא לְר"א, נְהִי נַמִּי דְּקָסָבַר יֵשׁ זִיקָה. בִּשְׁלָמָא לְחַד — מֵיפֵר, אֶלָּא לִתְרֵי — אַמַּאי? וְא"ר אַמִּי (*בַּר אַהֲבָה): הָכָא בְּמַאי עָסְקִינַן — כְּגוֹן דַּעֲבַד בָּהּ מַאֲמָר, *וּב"ש הִיא, דְּאָמַר: מַאֲמָר קוֹנֶה קִנְיָן גָּמוּר. אִי אָמְרַתְּ בִּשְׁלָמָא נִישּׂוּאִין עוֹשֶׂה — מִשּׁוּם הָכִי מֵיפֵר, אֶלָּא אִי אָמְרַתְּ אֵירוּסִין עוֹשֶׂה — הֵיכִי מָצֵי מֵיפֵר? וְהָתְנַן: *[ה]נַעֲרָה הַמְאוֹרָסָה אָבִיהָ וּבַעְלָהּ מְפִירִים נְדָרֶיהָ! אֲמַר רַב נַחְמָן בַּר יִצְחָק: מַאי מֵיפֵר — מֵיפֵר בְּשׁוּתָּפוּת. וְלר"א, דְּאָמַר: מַאֲמָר לְב"ש אֵינוֹ קוֹנֶה אֶלָּא לִדְחוֹת לַצָּרָה בִּלְבַד, אַמַּאי מֵיפֵר בְּשׁוּתָּפוּת? אָמַר לָךְ רַ' אֶלְעָזָר: אֵימַר דַּאֲמַרִי אֲנָא אֵינוֹ קוֹנֶה אֶלָּא לִדְחוֹת לַצָּרָה בִּלְבַד — דְּלָא סַגִּי לָהּ בְּגִיטָּא אֶלָּא בָּעֲיָא נַמִּי חֲלִיצָה, לְהָפֵר נְדָרֶיהָ — מִי אָמְרִינַן? וְאִיבָּעֵית אֵימָא, אָמַר לָךְ רַבִּי אֶלְעָזָר: וּלְרַב נַחְמָן בַּר יִצְחָק מִי נִיחָא? מִי קָתָנֵי "יָפֵרוּ"? "יָפֵר" קָתָנֵי. אֶלָּא הָכָא בְּמַאי עָסְקִינַן — (ג) שֶׁעָמְדָה בְּדִין וּפָסְקוּ לָהּ מְזוֹנוֹת מִשֶּׁלּוֹ, וְכִדְרַב פִּנְחָס מִשְּׁמֵיהּ דְּרָבָא, דְּאָמַר רַב פִּנְחָס מִשְּׁמֵיהּ דְּרָבָא: *כׇּל הַנּוֹדֶרֶת — עַל דַּעַת בַּעְלָהּ הִיא נוֹדֶרֶת.§ מתני'

רש"י

וְאִי מַאֲמָר לְב"ש קוֹנֶה קִנְיָן גָּמוּר. זֶה יַעֲשֶׂה מַאֲמָר בְּזוֹ וְיִקְנֶה אוֹתָהּ קִנְיָן גָּמוּר לִהְיוֹת אִשְׁתּוֹ, דְּהָא אֵין אִיסּוּר בְּמַאֲמָר, (ג) וְתֵצֵא אֲחוֹתָהּ מֵעָלָיו, וְלָא הָוְיָא הָךְ אֲחוֹת זְקוּקָתוֹ — וְיִכְנוֹס אֶת אִשְׁתּוֹ. אֶלָּא מַאי כו'. נְהִי נַמִּי דְּלָא קָנֵי קִנְיָן גָּמוּר — הָא אָמַרְתְּ דּוֹחֶה בְּצָרָה. וְתִקְשֶׁה לָךְ נַמִּי: יַעֲשֶׂה מַאֲמָר בְּזוֹ, וְתִדָּחֶה אֲחוֹתָהּ, וְיִכְנוֹס אֶת אִשְׁתּוֹ. דְּהֶתֵּירָא דָּחֵי. מַאֲמָר שֶׁנַּעֲשָׂה בְּהֶיתֵּר, דְּאִי הֲוָה בָּעֵי לְיַיבּוּמֵי בִּשְׁעַת מַאֲמָר הֲוָה מָצֵי לְיַיבּוּמֵי, כְּגוֹן בְּמַתְנִי', דַּעֲדַיִין לֹא נָפְלָה אֲחוֹתָהּ. דְּאִיסּוּרָא. כְּגוֹן דְּנָפְלוּ שְׁתֵּי הָאֲחָיוֹת קוֹדֶם מַאֲמָר. הָכִי נַמִּי. לְעִנְיַן קִנְיָיה. וְצָרָתָהּ. אֲחוֹתָהּ שֶׁנַּעֲשֵׂית לָהּ צָרָה בְּזִיקָה חֲלִיצָה נַמִּי לָא תִּיבָּעֵי (ד) דְּתֵצֵא מִשּׁוּם אֲחוֹת אִשָּׁה. אֶלָּא דּוֹחֶה. אוֹתָהּ מִלֶּאֱסוֹר (ה) אֵשֶׁת בַּעַל הַמַּאֲמָר עָלָיו. וּמְשַׁיֵּיר. דְּבָעְיָא חֲלִיצָה אִם בָּאת לִינָּשֵׂא עַד שֶׁלֹּא כָּנַס הַיָּבָם אֶת בַּעֲלַת הַמַּאֲמָר. וּלְקַמֵּיהּ פָּרֵיךְ לֵיהּ: הָא קָתָנֵי הַלָּזוּ תֵּצֵא מִשּׁוּם אֲחוֹת אִשָּׁה, דְּמַשְׁמַע אַף מֵחֲלִיצָה. זֶה יַעֲשֶׂה מַאֲמָר וְיִדְחֶה. אֶת אֲחוֹתָהּ מֵעָלָיו, וְאַחַ"כ יִשָּׂא אֶת זוֹ. אֶלָּא לָאו מִשּׁוּם דְּלָא דָּחֵי דְּחִיָּיה גְּמוּרָה, וְכׇל כַּמָּה דְּרַמְיָא עֲלֵיהּ לַחֲלִיצָה — זְקוּקָתוֹ הִיא, וְאוֹסֶרֶת אֶת זוֹ עָלָיו: ה"ג. אֶלָּא יְבָמָה דְּחַזְיָא כו'. כְּלוֹמַר, אֶלָּא לְעוֹלָם דּוֹחֶה דְּחִיָּיה גְּמוּרָה, וּדְקַשְׁיָא לָךְ: הָתָם נַמִּי לִידְחֵי — לָא דָּמְיָא לְמַתְנִיתִין דְּהָכָא, דְּכִי נָפְלָה וַעֲבַד מַאֲמָר — הָוֵה חַזְיָא לְכוּלְּהוּ מִילֵּי דִּיבָמָה, לְהִתְיַיבֵּם וְלַחֲלוֹץ, הִלְכָּךְ חַזְיָא לְמִקְנְיַיהּ לְמַאֲמָר, דְּמַאֲמָר דְּחַיָּא אֲחוֹתָהּ לִכְשֶׁתִּפּוֹל. אֲבָל הָתָם, דִּתְרַוַיְיהוּ נָפְלוּ קוֹדֶם מַאֲמָר, וְלָא חַזְיָא לְכוּלְּהוּ מִילֵּי דִּיבָמָה — לָא חַזְיָא לְמִקְנְיָיהּ, לְפִיכָךְ אֵין מַאֲמָר דּוֹחֶה אֲחוֹתָהּ. הַשְׁתָּא אֲרוּסָה. דְּקִידּוּשִׁין דִּידָהּ דְּאוֹרַיְיתָא, תָּנֵי רַבִּי חִיָּיא: אֵינוֹ יוֹרְשָׁהּ וְאֵינוֹ מִטַּמֵּא לָהּ, מַאֲמָר יְבָמִין מִדְּרַבָּנַן הוּא, דְּאִילּוּ מִדְּאוֹרַיְיתָא "יְבָמָהּ יָבֹא עָלֶיהָ" כָּתַב רַחֲמָנָא — מִיבַּעְיָא?! לֹא אוֹנֵן. לֵיאָסֵר בְּקָדָשִׁים (ו). וְלֹא מִיטַּמֵּא. אִם כֹּהֵן הוּא, דְּהָא לָאו שְׁאֵרוֹ הַקָּרוֹב אֵלָיו הִיא. וְכֵן הִיא לֹא אוֹנֶנֶת. לִהְיוֹת אֲסוּרָה בְּקָדָשִׁים. וְלֹא מִיטַּמְּאָה. אֵינָהּ צְרִיכָה לְהִתְעַסֵּק בּוֹ (ז). וְלָאו דַּוְקָא נָקַט וְלֹא מִיטַּמְּאָה, דְּהָא בְּנוֹת אַהֲרֹן לֹא הוּזְהֲרוּ עַל הַטּוּמְאָה. אֶלָּא אַיְּידֵי דְּנָקַט לֹא אוֹנֶנֶת, דְּאִיצְטְרִיךְ לֵיהּ, נָקַט וְלֹא מִיטַּמְּאָה דְּבָעֵי לְמִתְנֵי תַּרְתֵּי, בְּדִידָהּ וּבְדִידֵיהּ. כָּךְ שָׁמַעְתִּי. וְלִי נִרְאֶה: וְלֹא מִיטַּמְּאָה — כְּגוֹן בָּרֶגֶל, שֶׁיִּשְׂרְאֵלִים מוּזְהָרִים עַל הַטּוּמְאָה (ח) מִ"וּבְנִבְלָתָם לֹא תִגָּעוּ", בְּמַסֶּ' ר"ה (דף טז:). גּוֹבָה כְּתוּבָּתָהּ. וּבִדְכָתַב לָהּ מִן הָאֵירוּסִין מִיתוֹקְמָא בִּכְתוּבּוֹת בְּפֶרֶק "הַכּוֹתֵב" (דף פט:). וְלֹא בָּעְיָא מְסִירָה לְחוּפָּה. דְּאִם בָּא עָלֶיהָ בְּעַל כׇּרְחָהּ בְּלֹא חוּפָּה — קָנֵי. וְאִי בָּעֵי תּוּ לְאַפּוֹקֵי בְּגִיטָּא — סַגְיָא לָהּ. בְּעַל כׇּרְחָהּ. דְּקָנֵי לָהּ וְנַעֲשֵׂית כְּאִשְׁתּוֹ לְכׇל דָּבָר בְּבִיאָה בע"כ שֶׁאֵין בָּהּ חוּפָּה. וְחָלָה עָלָיו זִיקַת אֵירוּסִין. וְנִשּׂוּאִין שֶׁל שְׁאָר נָשִׁים. וְאִם בָּא עָלֶיהָ לְאַחַר מַאֲמָר בְּלֹא חוּפָּה – לֹא קָנָה. יָפֵר. אֶחָד מֵהֶן אֶת נִדְרָהּ. לְאֶחָד וְלֹא לִשְׁנַיִם. שׁוֹמֶרֶת יָבָם א' – יָפֵר, אֲבָל שׁוֹמֶרֶת לִשְׁנֵי יְבָמִין – לֹא יָפֵר לֹא זֶה וְלֹא זֶה. אֵין זִיקָה. דְּתֶיהֱוֵי כִּכְנוּסָה. וַאֲפִילּוּ בְּחַד. הֵיכָא דְּלֵיכָּא אֶלָּא חַד, דְּוַדַּאי עֲלֵיהּ רַמְיָא – אפ"ה אֵין זִיקָה. לִתְרֵי אֵין זִיקָה. דְּלָא יָדְעִינַן לְהֵי מִינַּיְיהוּ רַמְיָא, וַאֲפִילּוּ שְׁנֵיהֶם כְּאֶחָד – אֵין הַפָּרָתָן הֲפָרָה, דְּקְלִישָׁא זִיקָתָן. אֶלָּא לִתְרֵי אַמַּאי. נְהִי נַמִּי דְּיֵשׁ זִיקָה אֲפִי' לִתְרֵי, מִיהוּ יָפֵרוּ שְׁנֵיהֶם מִיבָּעֵי לֵיהּ: וַאֲמַר רָמֵי בַּר (ט) חָמָא גָּרְסִינַן. בְּשׁוּתָּפוּת. הוּא וְאָבִיהָ כַּאֲרוּסָה. לִדְחוֹת בְּצָרָה. בַּאֲחוֹתָהּ שֶׁנָּפְלָה לְפָנָיו אַחַר מַאֲמָר זוֹ. דְּלָא סַגֵּי לָהּ בְּגֵט. הָעוֹשֶׂה מַאֲמָר בִּיבָמָה, וּבָא לְהוֹצִיאָהּ – בָּעְיָא חֲלִיצָה וְגֵט, וְלָא אָמְרִינַן כִּכְנוּסָה הִיא, וְסַגֵּי לָהּ בְּגֵט. אָמַר לָךְ רַבִּי אֶלְעָזָר וּלְרַב נַחְמָן מִי נִיחָא. כְּלוֹמַר, נְהִי נַמִּי דְּקוֹנֶה, בִּשְׁלָמָא אִי נִישּׂוּאִין עוֹשֶׂה – שַׁפִּיר. אֶלָּא לְרַב נַחְמָן דְּאָמַר לָא עָבֵיד אֶלָּא אֵירוּסִין – מִי נִיחָא? הָא בְּשׁוּתָּפוּת לֵיכָּא לְמֵימַר דְּיָפֵר קָתָנֵי, יָפֵרוּ מִיבָּעֵי לֵיהּ. אֶלָּא הָכָא בְּמַאי עָסְקִינַן שֶׁעָמְדָה בְּדִין. לְדִידִי [אֲפִילּוּ] בְּלֹא מַאֲמָר. וּלְרַב [אַמִּי] אַחַר מַאֲמָר וְלֹא רָצָה לִכְנוֹס וְלֹא לִפְטוֹר. וּפָסְקוּ לָהּ מְזוֹנוֹת מִשֶּׁלּוֹ. כִּדְתַנְיָא לְקַמָּן בְּ"הַחוֹלֵץ" (דף מא:): עָמַד בַּדִּין וּבָרַח – נִזּוֹנֵית מִשֶּׁל יָבָם, דְּמֵהַשְׁתָּא בַּעְלָהּ הוּא, וְעַל דַּעְתּוֹ נוֹדֶרֶת עַל מְנָת שֶׁיָּפֵר לָהּ.

תורה אור

תוספות

יעשה מאמר ויקנה כו'. ומשום ביטול מלות יבמין ליכא למיחש כדפרישית בפ' שני (לעיל דף יח:) (י).

לא מיטמאה לו. פירוש ברגל שהוזהרו על הטומאה כדאמרינן בר"ה (דף טז:) (כ) ועוד י"ל דאין מטמאה לו היינו דאינה חייבת ליטמא לו למאן דאמר בסוטה (דף ג.) לה יטמא חובה.

עבד בה מאמר מיבעיא. וא"ת דמשמע דלא עדיפא בעלת מאמר מארוסה ובהחולץ (לקמן דף לט. ושם) קאמר רבא גופיה מאמר לב"ש עושה ודאי ארוסה לדחות בצרה וספק נשואה לחלוק בנכסים אלמא מהני ליורשה וי"ל דהכא גרס רבה רבו של אביי דמסיק עלה אמר ליה אביי ולקמן גרס רבא שהוא אחר אביי.

אלא לענין מסירה לחופה. וא"ת: מאי משני? דהשתא נמי תקשי: השתא ארוסה בעלמא בעיא מסירה לחופה, עבד בה מאמר – מיבעיא? וי"ל: דעבד בה מאמר ובא עליה, והביאה עושה אותה ככנוסה.

אביה ובעלה מפירים נדריה. ואם אין לה אב או שאינה ברשות אב – לא מצי מיפר, כדאמרינן בנדרים (דף עא.).

כגון (ל) שעמדה בדין כו'. לפי מסקנא שאיירי דעבד בה מאמר, כדמוכח בנדרים בפ' "נערה המאורסה" (שם עד.) דלר' אליעזר כיון דעביד בה מאמר ופסקו לה מזונות משלו – נודרת על דעתו. ולר' יהושע דוקא בחד יבם, אבל בתרי, כיון דאי בעי אחוה פסיל לה עליה בביאה או בגיטא – אינה נודרת על דעתו. ולר"ע, אפילו ביבם אחד קאמר דלא יפר, אפילו עבד בה מאמר, משום דאין חייבים עליה סקילה כנערה המאורסה. ולא יתכן לפי זה מה שפי' בקונטרס בריש פ"ב (לעיל יז: ד"ה ולימא) דמאן דאמר אין זיקה אפי' בחד – היינו ר"ע. דמאי סבר דיש זיקה, ואפי' הכי לא יפר – משום דאין חייבין עליה סקילה.

שלשה

עין משפט נר מצוה

טז א מיי' פ"ב מהל' אבל הלכה ג סמג לאוין רלה טוש"ע י"ד סימן שעג סעיף ד וסימן שעד סעיף ד וטוש"ע אה"ע סימן נב סעיף ה:

יז ב מיי' פכ"ב מהל' אישות הלכה ב סמג עשין מח טוש"ע אה"ע שם (וסימן נז):

יח ג מיי' שם פ"י הלכה יא סמג שם טוש"ע אה"ע סימן נב סעיף ו:

יט ד מיי' פי"א מהל' נדרים הלכה כג סמג לאוין רמב טוש"ע י"ד סימן רלד סעיף ז:

כ ה מיי' שם הלכה ט טוש"ע י"ד שם סעי' ה:

תוספות ישנים

ואי אמרת מאמר לב"ש קונה קנין גמור זה יעשה מאמר ויקנה אלא מאי דוחה דחייה גמורה זה יעשה מאמר וידחה. פי' המאמר ידחה אחותה שלא תאסר הבעלת מאמר להתייבם ובשלמא אם אינו דוחה אחותה ניחא דאין להקשות זה יבעול וזה יבעול וכו' שהרי היתה ביאה באיסור דהויא או בראשונה אחות זקוקתו. אבל ממאמר פריך שפיר שהרי אין איסור במאמר ולאחר המאמר יכול לייבם שהרי המאמר דחה שאחותה לא תאסר אותה: **בעי** רבא מאמר לב"ש נשואין עושה. לאו לשיטת ר' אליעזר דלעיל בעי דפשיטא לן דלכל תרי ליסני איתו עושה נשואין דהשתא מקדושין גרע דלא סגי לה בגט כקדושין דעלמא ונשואין תהא עושה אלא ודאי בעייתו לאו לשיטה דהכא אלא לשיטת ר' אמי דאמר [לקמן] דס"ל לב"ש מאמר קונה קנין גמור: **אלא** לענין מסירה לחופה. וא"ת ומ"מ הדרא קושיין לדוכתין השתא ארוסה בעלמא בעינן מסירה לחופה עבד בה מאמר מיבעיא וי"ל דמיירי בבא עליה בעל כרחה אחר המאמר ובעילה דבעל כרחה קונה ביבמה. אכן קבעי אי המאמר דקודם הביאה מגרע גרע הביאה לשווייה כאשה בעלמא ובעיא מסירה לחופה: **כל** הנודרת על דעת בעלה היא נודרת. וא"ת א"כ למה אכתבא פרשת נדרים. וי"ל דהא דאמרינן כל הנודרת על דעת בעלה היא נודרת היינו לבתר דאכתבא פרשת נדרים:

תוספות חד מקמאי

ת"ר שומרת יבם בין ליבם א' בין לשנים ר"א [אומר] יפר ר"י אומר לא' ולא לשנים ר"ע אומר לא לאחד ולא לשנים והלכתא כר"א דקי"ל יש זיקה אפילו בתרי והוינן בה לר"א נהי נמי דיש זיקה אפלו בתרי בשלמא לא' מפיר אלא לתרי אמאי מפיר כ"א לבדו ואוקימנא כגון שעמדה בדין עם א' מהן ופסקו לה מזונותיה משלו וכדרבי פנחס משמיה דרבא דאמר כל הנודרת ע"ד בעלה היא נודרת ואיכא דמפרש אע"ג דעמדה בדין

מסורת הש"ס

[נדרים עד:]

לקמן מג: ע"ש כתובות נג. פט: ע"ש בבא מציעא יח. ע"ש סנהדרין כח. [ע"ש היטב]

[לקמן נב.]

נדרים עד

[שם ע"ש]

[בנדרים ליתא]

[לעיל יח. לקמן ל. נח:]

כתובות לט. מו: קדושין ד. נדרים סו:

שבת עג: עד נדה מו:

דברים כה

הגהות הב"ח

(א) גמ' א"ל אין שאני אומר: (ב) שם שעמד בדין ופסקו: (ג) רש"י ד"ה ואי מאמר וכו' אין איסור במאמר והויא לה ככנוסה ותצא אחותה: (ד) ד"ה וצרתה וכו' ותצא משום: (ה) ד"ה אלא וכו' מלאסור את בעלת המאמר: (ו) ד"ה לא אונן ליאסר בקדשים דכתיב לא אכלתי באוני ממנו הס"ד: (ז) ד"ה ולא מיטמאת וכו' ולאו דוקא. נ"ב וכן פרש"י בסנהדרין דף כח ע"ב וע"ל דף מג ע"ב: (ח) בא"ד מובנבלתם לא תגעו: (ט) ד"ה ואמר רמי בר אהבה גרסינן: (י) תוס' ד"ה יעשה וכו' בפ' שני. נ"ב בדף י"ח בד"ה אומרים לו המתן: (כ) ד"ה לא וכו' ועוד י"ל. נ"ב וכן פרש"י בב"מ דף יח ע"ש וכן פרש"י לקמן דף מג ע"ב: (ל) ד"ה כגון שעמד בדין כו' לפי מסקנא זו שאיירי:

מתני' שְׁלֹשָׁה אַחִין, שְׁנַיִם מֵהֶם נְשׂוּאִים שְׁתֵּי אֲחָיוֹת וְאֶחָד נָשׂוּי נָכְרִית. מֵת אֶחָד מִבַּעֲלֵי אֲחָיוֹת, וְכָנַס נְשׂוּי נָכְרִית אֶת אִשְׁתּוֹ, וָמֵת — הָרִאשׁוֹנָה יוֹצְאָה מִשּׁוּם אֲחוֹת אִשָּׁה, וּשְׁנִיָּה מִשּׁוּם צָרָתָהּ. עָשָׂה בָּהּ מַאֲמָר וָמֵת — נָכְרִית חוֹלֶצֶת וְלֹא מִתְיַיבֶּמֶת.§ גמ' טַעְמָא דַּעֲבַד בָּהּ מַאֲמָר, הָא לָא עֲבַד בָּהּ מַאֲמָר — נָכְרִית יַבּוּמֵי נַמִי מְיַיבְּמָה. אֲמַר רַב נַחְמָן: זֹאת אוֹמֶרֶת *אֵין זִיקָה, וַאֲפִילּוּ בְּחַד אַחָא.§ מתני' אשְׁלֹשָׁה אַחִים, שְׁנַיִם מֵהֶם נְשׂוּאִים שְׁתֵּי אֲחָיוֹת וְאֶחָד נָשׂוּי נָכְרִית. מֵת הַנָּשׂוּי נָכְרִית, וְכָנַס אֶחָד מִבַּעֲלֵי אֲחָיוֹת אֶת אִשְׁתּוֹ וָמֵת — הָרִאשׁוֹנָה יוֹצֵאת מִשּׁוּם אֲחוֹת אִשָּׁה, וּשְׁנִיָּה מִשּׁוּם צָרָתָהּ. עָשָׂה בָּהּ מַאֲמָר וָמֵת — נָכְרִית חוֹלֶצֶת וְלֹא מִתְיַיבֶּמֶת.§ גמ' הָא תּוּ לָמָּה לִי? הַיְינוּ הַךְ! הַשְׁתָּא, וּמַה הָתָם דַּאֲחוֹת אִשָּׁה הָוְיָא צָרָה לְנָכְרִית אָמְרַתְּ: נָכְרִית אֲסוּרָה, הָכָא, דְּנָכְרִית הָוְיָא צָרָה לַאֲחוֹת אִשָּׁה — לֹא כ"ש? — תָּנָא הַךְ תָּנָא בְּרֵישָׁא, וְהַךְ (א) חַזְיָא לְהֶתֵּירָא, וְשַׁרְיָא. וַהֲדַר חַזְיָא לְאִיסּוּרָא. וְאַיְּידֵי *דַּחֲבִיבָה לֵיהּ — אַקְדְּמַהּ, *וּמִשְׁנָה לֹא זָזָה מִמְּקוֹמָהּ.§ מתני' בשְׁלֹשָׁה אַחִין, שְׁנַיִם מֵהֶם נְשׂוּאִים שְׁתֵּי אֲחָיוֹת וְאֶחָד נָשׂוּי נָכְרִית. מֵת אֶחָד מִבַּעֲלֵי אֲחָיוֹת, וְכָנַס נְשׂוּי נָכְרִית אֶת אִשְׁתּוֹ, וּמֵתָה אִשְׁתּוֹ שֶׁל שֵׁנִי, וְאַחַר כָּךְ מֵת נְשׂוּי נָכְרִית — הֲרֵי זוֹ אֲסוּרָה עָלָיו עוֹלָמִית, הוֹאִיל וְנֶאֶסְרָה עָלָיו שָׁעָה אַחַת.§ גמ' *אָמַר רַב יְהוּדָה אָמַר רַב: גכָּל יְבָמָה שֶׁאֵין אֲנִי קוֹרֵא בָּהּ בִּשְׁעַת נְפִילָה °"יְבָמָהּ יָבֹא עָלֶיהָ" [דברים כה] הֲרֵי הִיא כְּאֵשֶׁת אָח שֶׁיֵּשׁ לָהּ בָּנִים, וַאֲסוּרָה. מַאי קמ"ל? תְּנֵינָא: הֲרֵי זוֹ אֲסוּרָה עָלָיו עוֹלָמִית, הוֹאִיל וְנֶאֶסְרָה עָלָיו שָׁעָה אַחַת! — מַהוּ דְּתֵימָא: הָנֵי מִילֵּי — הֵיכָא דְּלָא אִיחַזְיָא לָהּ בִּנְפִילָה רִאשׁוֹנָה, אֲבָל הֵיכָא דְּאִיחַזְיָא לָהּ בִּנְפִילָה רִאשׁוֹנָה — אֵימָא תִּשְׁתְּרֵי, קמ"ל. הָא נַמִי תְּנֵינָא: *שְׁנֵי אַחִין נְשׂוּאִין שְׁתֵּי אֲחָיוֹת, מֵת אֶחָד מֵהֶם וְאַחַר כָּךְ מֵתָה אִשְׁתּוֹ שֶׁל שֵׁנִי — הֲרֵי זוֹ אֲסוּרָה עָלָיו עוֹלָמִית, הוֹאִיל וְנֶאֶסְרָה עָלָיו שָׁעָה אַחַת! — מַהוּ דְּתֵימָא: הָתָם הוּא דְּאִידַּחִי לָהּ מֵהַאי בֵּיתָא לְגַמְרֵי. אֲבָל הָכָא, דְּלָא אִידַּחִי לָהּ מֵהַאי בֵּיתָא לְגַמְרֵי, אֵימָא: מִיגּוֹ דְּחַזְיָא לְהַאי נְשׂוּי נָכְרִית חַזְיָא נַמִי לְהַאי, קמ"ל.§ מתני' *דשְׁלֹשָׁה אַחִים, שְׁנַיִם מֵהֶם נְשׂוּאִין שְׁתֵּי אֲחָיוֹת, וְאֶחָד נְשׂוּי נָכְרִית. גֵּירַשׁ אֶחָד מִבַּעֲלֵי אֲחָיוֹת אֶת אִשְׁתּוֹ, וּמֵת נְשׂוּי נָכְרִית, וּכְנָסָהּ הַמְגָרֵשׁ וָמֵת — זוֹ הִיא שֶׁאָמְרוּ: וְכוּלָּן שֶׁמֵּתוּ אוֹ נִתְגָּרְשׁוּ — צָרוֹתֵיהֶן מוּתָּרוֹת.§ גמ' הטַעְמָא דְּגֵירֵשׁ וְאַחַר כָּךְ מֵת, אֲבָל מֵת וְאַחַר כָּךְ גֵּירֵשׁ — אֲסוּרָה. אֲמַר רַב אַשִׁי; זֹאת אוֹמֶרֶת *יֵשׁ זִיקָה, אֲפִילּוּ בִּתְרֵי אַחֵי. — וּלְרַב אַשִׁי קַשְׁיָא דְּרַב נַחְמָן! — אָמַר לָךְ רַב אַשִׁי: יה"ה דְּאַף עַל גַּב דְּלָא עֲבַד בָּהּ מַאֲמָר נָכְרִית — מִיחֲלַץ חָלְצָה, יַבּוּמֵי לָא מְיַיבְּמָה. וְהָא דְּקָתָנֵי מַאֲמָר — *לְאַפּוּקֵי (ג) ב"ש, דְּאָמְרִי: מַאֲמָר קוֹנֶה

קִנְיָן

רש"י

מתני' הָרִאשׁוֹנָה. לִנְפִילָה. גמ' נָכְרִית יַבּוּמֵי נַמִי מְיַיבְּמָה. וְלָא אָמְרִינַן מִשֶּׁמֵּת בַּעַל הָאֲחָיוֹת וְנָפְלָה לְיָיבָם הוּזְקְקָה לִנְשׂוּי נָכְרִית לְבַדּוֹ, דְּהָא עַל בַּעַל אֲחָיוֹת לָא רַמְיָא וְנַעֲשֵׂית (ג) זוֹ צָרָתָהּ בְּזִיקָה, וּכְשֶׁמֵּת תֵּאָסֵר הַנָּכְרִית עַל הַנִּשְׁאָר מִשּׁוּם צָרַת אֲחוֹת אִשָּׁה. וַאֲפִילּוּ בְּחַד אַחָא. כִּדְפָרִישִׁית. דְּאַע"ג דִּתְרֵי אַחִין נִינְהוּ — אֵין זוֹ זְקוּקָה אֶלָּא לִנְשׂוּי נָכְרִית לְבַדּוֹ. מתני' הָרִאשׁוֹנָה. לְנִישּׂוּאִין. גמ' הַיְינוּ הָךְ. וְכ"ש הוּא; דְּהַשְׁתָּא, וּמַה הָתָם דְּנָכְרִית עִיקַּר נְשׂוּאָה הִיא, דַּאֲחוֹת אִשָּׁה נָפְלָה עָלֶיהָ וְנַעֲשֵׂית צָרָתָהּ בְּמַאֲמָר אֲסַרְתָּהּ. הָכָא, דַּאֲחוֹת אִשָּׁה עִיקַּר נְשׂוּאָה הִיא — לֹא כ"ש דְּאוֹסֶרֶת נָכְרִית שֶׁהִיא טְפֵלָה. הָא תָּנָא בְּרֵישָׁא. מִשְׁנָה אַחֲרוֹנָה זוֹ שָׁנָה תְּחִלָּה, וְהַהִיא דִּלְעֵיל לָא הֲוֵי בְּדַעְתֵּיהּ לְמִיתְנֵי מִשּׁוּם דַּחֲזְיָה (ד) לְהֶתֵּירָא, הוֹאִיל וְנָכְרִית עִיקָּר. וַהֲדַר חַזְיָה לְאִיסּוּרָא, מִשּׁוּם דְּמ"מ צָרָתָהּ הִיא, וְתַנְיֵיהּ. וְאַיְּידֵי דְּקָא חֲבִיבָה לֵיהּ. דְּחִידּוּשׁ הוּא. אַקְדְּמַהּ. וְתוּ לָא הֲוָה צָרִיךְ לְמִיתְנֵי סֵיפָא, אֶלָּא הוֹאִיל וְשָׁנִית לֹא זָזָה מִמְּקוֹמָהּ. [מתני'] שָׁעָה אַחַת. בִּנְפִילָה רִאשׁוֹנָה, כְּשֶׁנָּפְלָה מֵאָחִיו הָרִאשׁוֹן. גמ' הֲרֵי הִיא כְּאֵשֶׁת אָח כו'. וְאַע"ג דַּהֲדַר אִיחַזְיָא. בִּנְפִילָה רִאשׁוֹנָה. כָּל זְמַן נְפִילָה רִאשׁוֹנָה הָיְתָה אִשְׁתּוֹ קַיֶּימֶת, שֶׁהִיא אֲחוֹתָהּ. אֲבָל הֵיכָא דְּאִיתְחַזְיָא בִּנְפִילָה רִאשׁוֹנָה. כְּגוֹן שֶׁמֵּתָה אִשְׁתּוֹ אַחַר מִיתַת אָחִיו וְלֹא כְּנָסָהּ נְשׂוּי נָכְרִית. דְּאִידַּחְיָא לָהּ מֵהַאי בֵּיתָא לְגַמְרֵי. (ה) שֶׁנָּפְלָה, וְאֵין כָּאן אַחֵר אֶלָּא זֶה בַּעַל אֲחוֹתָהּ — נִדְחֵית וְנִפְטֶרֶת לַשּׁוּק, וְאֵין עָלֶיהָ צַד זִיקָה עוֹד. אֲבָל הֵיכָא דְּלָא אִידַּחְיָא מֵהַאי בֵּיתָא לְגַמְרֵי. בִּשְׁעַת נְפִילָה, שֶׁהָיָה שָׁם נְשׂוּי נָכְרִית וּזְקוּקָה לְיַיבֵּם. אֵימָא מִיגּוֹ דַּחֲזְיָא לִנְשׂוּי נָכְרִית עֲדַיִין זִיקָתָהּ עָלֶיהָ, וְכִי מֵתָה אֲחוֹתָהּ וְעוֹדָהּ בִּנְפִילָה — תִּתְיַיבֵּם לָזֶה בִּנְפִילָה. קמ"ל. רַב יְהוּדָה דְּלָא. מתני' וּכְנָסָהּ הַמְגָרֵשׁ וָמֵת. מוּתֶּרֶת זוֹ לְהִתְיַיבֵּם, שֶׁהֲרֵי עַד שֶׁלֹּא כְּנָסָהּ גֵּירֵשׁ אֶת הָרִאשׁוֹנָה שֶׁהִיא עֶרְוָה, וְלֹא הָיְתָה צָרָתָהּ מֵעוֹלָם. וְזֶהוּ שֶׁאָמְרוּ. בְּפֶרֶק רִאשׁוֹן: נִתְגָּרְשׁוּ הָעֲרָיוֹת צָרוֹתֵיהֶן מוּתָּרוֹת. גמ' טַעְמָא דְּגֵירֵשׁ. בַּעַל הָאֲחָיוֹת תְּחִלָּה, וְאַחַר כָּךְ מֵת נְשׂוּי נָכְרִית, דַּאֲפִילּוּ בְּזִיקָה לֹא נַעֲשֵׂית צָרָתָהּ מֵעוֹלָם. הָא מֵת נְשׂוּי נָכְרִית, וְהוּזְקְקָה נָכְרִית לְבַעֲלֵי אֲחָיוֹת, וְאַחַר כָּךְ גֵּירֵשׁ וּנְשָׂאָהּ לָזוֹ, הוֹאִיל וְקוֹדֶם שֶׁגֵּירֵשׁ נַעֲשֵׂית צָרָתָהּ בְּזִיקָה — אֲסוּרָה עַל אָחִיו, כְּשֶׁיָּמוּת הַמְגָרֵשׁ, מִשּׁוּם צָרַת אָחוֹת. אִשָּׁה בִּשְׁלָמָא אִי לָא כְּנָסָהּ — הָוְיָא מוּתֶּרֶת לָזֶה מֵחֲמַת זִיקַת אָחִיו הָרִאשׁוֹן, אֲבָל מִשֶּׁכְּנָסָהּ וְעַכְשָׁיו זְקוּקָה לָזֶה מִכֹּחַ בַּעַל הָעֶרְוָה אֲסוּרָה, וְאַע"ג דְּלֹא הָיְתָה צָרָתָהּ אֶלָּא בְּזִיקָה. בִּתְרֵי אַחֵי. כְּגוֹן הָכָא, דְּכִי מֵת נְשׂוּי נָכְרִית קוֹדֶם גֵּירוּשִׁין שֶׁל זֶה — הָיְתָה זוֹ זְקוּקָה לִשְׁנֵי בַּעֲלֵי הָאֲחָיוֹת, וּמְהַנְּיָא בָּהּ זִיקָה זוֹ לְאוֹסְרָהּ עַל הַשֵּׁנִי. קַשְׁיָא דְּרַב נַחְמָן. דְּדָיֵיק לְעֵיל מִסֵּיפָא מַתְנִי': "זֹאת אוֹמֶרֶת: אֵין זִיקָה אֲפִי' בְּחַד אַחָא". אֲמַר לָךְ רַב אַשִׁי. הַהִיא דִּיּוּקָא דִּלְעֵיל לָאו דַּוְקָא, דְּה"ה אַע"ג דְּלָא עֲבַד מַאֲמָר בַּעַל הַנָּכְרִית בַּאֲחוֹת (אשה) אֵשֶׁת אָחִיו כְּשֶׁיָּמוּת — נָכְרִית אִשְׁתּוֹ מִיחַלְּצָא חָלְצָה, וְלֹא מִתְיַיבֶּמֶת, הוֹאִיל וְעֶרְוָה עַל בַּעְלָהּ לְבַדּוֹ הָוְיָת רַמְיָא, (ו) נַעֲשָׂה צָרָתָהּ בְּזִיקָה.

תוספות

שלשה אחין. בהך רישא גרסינן "הראשונה יוצאה משום אחות אשה" וראשונה לנפילה קאמר דומיא דההיא דפרק ב' (לעיל יז.) ובבבא *בתרא ה"ג השניה יוצאה כו'. אמר רב נחמן זאת אומרת אין זיקה. תימה שלא דקדק רב נחמן על מתני' דריש "כילד" (לעיל יז.)? דחביבה ליה אקדמה. בשאר מקומות אין דוחק לומר כן, אלא אמר: זו ואין צריך לומר זו קתני. וכאן (ז) דחק לומר כן, לפי שבבא שלימה דלא צריכה היא. (ח) ונאסרה עליו שעה אחת. בהך בבא הו"מ למינקט ואחד מופנה. אלא נקט הכי, משום דנכרית נמי מתסרא, לפי שהיתה צרת אחות אשה שעה אחת. וקצת קשה: שאינו מזכיר הצרה כלל! וא"ת: לרבי ירמיה דאמר (לעיל דף יג.) דהאי תנא דפירקין סבר נישואין מפילין, אמאי לא נקט דמתה אחת מן האחיות תחלה ואח"כ מת בעלה של שניה, וכנס נשוי נכרית את אשתו ומת — אסורה, שנאסרה עליו שעה אחת, כיון דנישואין מפילין! וכן בבבא דלקמן ב' אחין — ה"ל למתני שמתה אחת מהן תחלה, ואח"כ מת בעלה של שניה! וי"ל: דלא מהני למימר נישואין מפילין אלא לענין שאם היתה צרת ערוה שעה אחת — שוב אין לה היתר, אע"פ שבשעת נפילה כבר אינה צרת ערוה. אבל כאן, משום נישואין מפילין — לא נחשבנה כאילו נפלה בחיי אשתו ויצאה ממנו באותה שעה משום אחות אשה. גירש אחד מבעלי אחיות את אשתו. תימה: אמאי נקט ג' אחין? ה"ל למימר ב' אחין נשואין ב' אחיות וגירש האחד את אשתו ונשא אשה אחרת (ט) ומת! ולרבי ירמיה ניחא, כיון דאיצטריך לאשמועינן דיש זיקה, כדדייק רב אשי בגמרא. ולרבא נמי נקט הכי למעוטי מת ולא גירש, אבל לרב נחמן דקסבר אין זיקה — קשיא: אמאי נקט ג' אחין? וי"ל: דלרב נחמן נקט הכי אגב אורחיה לאשמועינן דאין זיקה, דכר' ירמיה ס"ל דנישואין מפילין ואם יש זיקה — תיתסר, אע"ג דגירש ואח"כ מת. דמקודם שגירשה חשובה נכרית כזקוקה לו משעה שנשאת לאחיו, דנישואין הראשונים מפילין. ורב אשי דדייק מינה דיש זיקה, סבר דלא אסרינן לה, משום דא"א לה ליאסר אא"כ תרי נישואין מפילין. זאת אומרת יש זיקה. וא"ת: והיאך נסבה המגרש? והא הויא לה צרת אחות אשתו בזיקה! וי"ל: דלא חשיב צרת אחות אשתו בזיקה אלא כשמת אחיו ונפלו שתיהן לפניו. אבל כשהוא חי — לא. ומה שכתב בעל ה"ג דאם מת ולא גירש אסירא לתרוייהו — לא בעוד ששניהם חיים, אלא לכל אחד כשימות אחיו — תהיה אסורה.

כתב

עין משפט נר מצוה

כא א מיי' פ"ז מהלכות יבום הלכה ז סמג עשין נא נב טוש"ע אה"ע סימן קעה סעיף ז:

כב ב ג מיי' שם הלכה יא טוש"ע שם סעיף א:

כג ד ה מיי' שם הלכה יב טוש"ע שם סעי' ח:

כד ו מיי' שם טוש"ע שם סעיף ז:

תוספות ישנים

זאת אומרת אין זיקה ואפילו בחד. וא"ת הא מפרק כילד לעיל דייקינן הכי וי"ל דאיצטריך לאפוקי מב"ש דלעיל. וא"ת הא נמי ידעינן בבבא בתרייתא בסמוך. י"ל דתרתי אצטריך למתני כדפרישי' לעיל א) דמסברא אמינא יש זיקה: אבל הכא דלא אדחי לה מהאי ביתא לגמרי אימא לא. וא"ת הא ממתני' דלעיל דארבעה אחין שמעינן לה. וי"ל דשאני התם דנהי דלא אדחי מהאי ביתא לגמרי מ"מ לא איחזיא בנפילה ראשונה אבל היכא דלא אדחי לה מהך ביתא לגמרי ואיחזיא בנפילה ראשונה אימא לא:

א) עי' לעיל י"ח בתוס' ד"ה והאי.

תוספות חד מקמאי

בדין ופסקו לה מזונותיה אינו מפיר אלא א"כ עשה בה מאמר ומ"מ שניהם מפירין ולא הועמדה בדין: הרב אלפס פסק צרת ערוה דכנס ואח"כ גירש מותרת הצרה להתייבם דמיתה מפילה וכיון דבשעת ערוה לא הוי צרת ערוה מותרת וג"כ מתני' דג' אחין שניהן מהם נשואין ב' אחיות וא' נשוי נכרית וגרש א' מבעלי אחיות את אשתו ומת נשוי נכרית וכנסה המגרש פסק דבמת ואח"כ גירש אסור' ויהיב טעמא למילתיה דגזרי' הכא משום זיקה דעלמא. א"נ הכי גבי נכרית כיון דבשעת נפילה באיסור זיקה נפלה קמיה לא מהני לה גרושין אלו דברי הרב ז"ל ויש בהן כמה תמיהות חדא דאם אתמר להני טעמי למה ליה לר' ירמיה לשנויי תברא מי ששנה זו לא שנה זו. ולרבא למה ליה למימר זו ואצ"ל זו קתני לישני ליה דשאני הכא דגזרינן משום זיקה דעלמא. א"נ בשעת נפילה אתסרא ליה למה ליה למימר הכא אליבא דרבא זו היא למעוטי מת ולא גירש ולא כנס לוקמה אפי' דכנס וגירש. ומאי דכתב נמי הכא גבי נכרית כיון דבשעת נפילה באיסור זיקה נפלה קמיה לא מהנו לה גירושין לא ירדנו לסוף דעתו דמאי איסור זיקה איכא בנכרית והרי ב' אחין הנשואין ב' אחיות הוו קיימין בשעת נפילת נכרית ואין כאן איסור [אחות] זקוקתו שהרי שניהם קיימין והרי משנה שלימה שנינו ג' אחין שנים מהן נשואין ב' אחיות וא' נשוי (א') נכרית ומת נשוי נכרית וכנס א' מבעלי אחיות את אשתו וכו' ולא קתני עבר וכנס ועוד אם עבר וכנס מוציא בדקתני רישא בה"א יוצאו אלא ודאי ליתנהו להני טעמי דכתב הרז"ל ומיהו אפשר דרב אשי לית ליה דרבא דאליבא דהאי [תנא] נישואין הראשונים מפילין מת א) ואחד כנס גירש אסורה ואפ"ה הלכתא כת"ק דמתני' דפ"ק דכנס ואח"כ [גירש] מותרת דמיתה מפלת חדא דהא רבא ס"ל דלא פליגי אהדדי. ועוד דתנן נפל הבית עליו ועל אשתו שהיא בת אחיו ואין ידוע איזה מהן [מת] ראשון צרתה חולצת ולא מתייבמת אלמא האי תנא ס"ל מיתה מפלת ועוי"ל דרב אשי לא שמעינן ליה בהדיא דלימא מת ואח"כ גירש אסורה אלא ש"מ זאת אומרת יש זיקה ואפי' בתרי אחי וא"נ ס"ל כרבא דאמר זו היא למעוטי מת דלא גירש ולא כנס ש"מ דיש זיקה אפלו בתרי אחי:

מתניתין

א) נראה דצ"ל ואח"כ גירש או דצ"ל מת וכנס ואח"כ גירש.

מסורת הש"ס

[לעיל יז: כו: לקמן נא. נג.]

[לעיל ב: וש"נ]

[לקמן לב. קדושין כה. ע"ז לה: שבועות ז. חולין לב: קטו:]

לעיל כז: ע"ש לקמן קיח:

[לעיל יז: וש"נ]

[לעיל יח. כט: נח:]

הגהות הב"ח

(א) גמ' חזיא להתירא ושריא. נ"ב עיין בדף יז ע"ב בכתאי סוגיא: (ב) שם לאפוקי מב"ש: (ג) רש"י ד"ה נכרית וכו' ונעשית נכרית זו צרתה: (ד) ד"ה הא תנא וכו' משום דחזיה בדעתיה להתירא: (ה) ד"ה דאידחיא וכו' שנפלה ואין: (ו) ד"ה אמר לך וכו' נעשה צרתה בזיקה: (ז) תוס' ד"ה דחביבה וכו' וכאן דוחק לומר כן: (ח) ד"ה ונאסרה וכו' שנאסרה עליו: (ט) ד"ה גירש וכו' אשה אחרת נכרית ומת:

גליון הש"ס

מתני' הרי זו אסורה עליו עולמית. עי' לקמן דף לב ע"א תד"ה לא פקע:

כה א מיי' פ"ו מהלכות יבום הלכה כב סמג עשין יא טוש"ע אה"ע סימן קעג סעיף ג:
כו ב מיי' פ"ד מהל' אישות הלכה כב טוש"ע אה"ע סי' ל סעיף ה.

קִנְיָן גָּמוּר, קמ"ל דְּלָא כְּב"ש. וּלְרַב נַחְמָן קַשְׁיָא דְּרַב אַשִׁי! וְכ"ת: הוּא הַדִּין דַּאֲפִי' מֵת וְאַחַר כָּךְ גֵּירֵשׁ צָרָתָהּ מוּתֶּרֶת, אֶלָּא "זוֹ הִיא" לְמַעוּטֵי מַאי — לְמַעוּטֵי כָּנַס וְאח"כ גֵּירֵשׁ, — הָנִיחָא אִי סָבַר לָהּ כְּרַבִּי יִרְמְיָה, דְּאָמַר: *תַּבְרָא, מִי שֶׁשָּׁנָה זוֹ לֹא שָׁנָה זוֹ, וְהַאי תַּנָּא סָבַר מִיתָה מַפֶּלֶת, וְהַאי תַּנָּא סָבַר נִישּׂוּאִין הָרִאשׁוֹנִים מַפִּילִים — "זוֹ הִיא" לְמַעוּטֵי כָּנַס וּלְבַסּוֹף גֵּירֵשׁ. אֶלָּא אִי סָבַר לָהּ כְּרָבָא, דְּאָמַר לְעוֹלָם חַד תַּנָּא הוּא, *וְ"זוֹ וְאֵין צ"ל זוֹ" קָתָנֵי — "זוֹ הִיא" לְמַעוּטֵי מַאי? — עַל כָּרְחָךְ כְּרַבִּי יִרְמְיָה סְבִירָא לֵיהּ. וּלְרָבָא, הָנִיחָא אִי סָבַר לָהּ כְּרַב אַשִׁי — "זוֹ הִיא" לְמַעוּטֵי[א] מֵת בְּלֹא גֵּירֵשׁ, אֶלָּא אִי סָבַר לָהּ כְּרַב נַחְמָן, "זוֹ הִיא" לְמַעוּטֵי מַאי? — ע"כ כְּרַב אַשִׁי סְבִירָא לֵיהּ.§

מתני' *[א]וְכוּלָּן שֶׁהָיוּ בָּהֶן קִדּוּשִׁין אוֹ גֵּרוּשִׁין בְּסָפֵק — הֲרֵי אֵלּוּ הַצָּרוֹת חוֹלְצוֹת וְלֹא מִתְיַבְּמוֹת. כֵּיצַד סְפֵק קִדּוּשִׁין? [ב]זָרַק לָהּ קִדּוּשִׁין, סָפֵק קָרוֹב לוֹ סָפֵק קָרוֹב לָהּ — זֶהוּ סְפֵק קִדּוּשִׁין. סְפֵק גֵּרוּשִׁין — כָּתַב בִּכְתַב יָדוֹ וְאֵין עָלָיו עֵדִים, יֵשׁ עָלָיו עֵדִים וְאֵין בּוֹ זְמַן, יֵשׁ בּוֹ זְמַן וְאֵין בּוֹ אֶלָּא עֵד אֶחָד — זֶהוּ סְפֵק גֵּרוּשִׁין.§ **גמ'** וְאִילּוּ בְּגֵרוּשִׁין סָפֵק קָרוֹב לוֹ סָפֵק קָרוֹב לָהּ — לָא קָתָנֵי, מַאי טַעְמָא? אָמַר רַבָּה: אִשָּׁה זוֹ בְּחֶזְקַת הֶיתֵּר לַשּׁוּק עוֹמֶדֶת, וּמִסָּפֵק אַתָּה בָּא לְאוֹסְרָהּ — אַל תַּאַסְרֶנָּה מִסָּפֵק. אָמַר לֵיהּ אַבַּיֵי: אִי הָכִי בְּקִדּוּשִׁין נַמִי, נֵימָא: אִשָּׁה זוֹ בְּחֶזְקַת הֶיתֵּר לַיָּבָם עוֹמֶדֶת, וּמִסָּפֵק אַתָּה בָּא לְאוֹסְרָהּ — אַל תַּאַסְרֶנָּה מִסָּפֵק! — הָתָם לְחוּמְרָא. הַאי — חוּמְרָא דְּאָתֵי לִידֵי קוּלָּא הוּא; זִימְנִין דְּאָזֵיל הוּא וּמְקַדֵּשׁ לָהּ לַאֲחוֹתָהּ קִדּוּשֵׁי וַדַּאי, וְאִי נַמִי זִימְנִין דְּאָתָא אַחֵר וּמְקַדֵּשׁ לָהּ לְדִידָהּ קִדּוּשֵׁי וַדַּאי, וְכֵיוָן דְּאָסַר לָהּ מָר לַצָּרָה לְיַיבּוּמֵי, אָמְרִי: דְּקַמָּא — קִדּוּשִׁין וּדְבַתְרָא — לָאו קִדּוּשִׁין כֵּיוָן

קִנְיָן גָּמוּר. וַאֲפִי' חֲלִיצָה לָא תִּיבָּעֵי נָכְרִית, אֶלָּא תֵּצֵא מִשּׁוּם צָרַת אֲחוֹת אִשָּׁה — קמ"ל חוֹלֶצֶת. ה"ה דַּאֲפִי' מֵת. נָשׂוּי נָכְרִית וְאח"כ גֵּירֵשׁ אֶחָד מִבַּעֲלֵי אֲחָיוֹת אֶת אִשְׁתּוֹ וְכָנְסָהּ, מוּתֶּרֶת לַשְּׁלִישִׁי כְּשֶׁיָּמוּת זֶה, וְלָא אָמְרִי' צָרַת אֲחוֹת אִשְׁתּוֹ שֶׁל זֶה בְּזִיקָה הֲוַאי מֵעִיקָּרָא, קוֹדֶם גֵּירוּשִׁין. **כָּנַס.** הַנָּכְרִית וְאח"כ גֵּירֵשׁ אֶת אִשְׁתּוֹ וּמֵת, דַּאֲסוּרָה נָכְרִית מִשּׁוּם צָרַת אֲחוֹת אִשָּׁה, וְאע"ג דְּהַשְׁתָּא בִּשְׁעַת נְפִילָה לָאו צָרוֹת נִינְהוּ. **הָנִיחָא אִי סָבַר לָהּ.** רַב נַחְמָן כְּר' יִרְמְיָה, דַּאֲמַר בְּפ"ק: כִּי רָמֵינַן הָא מַתְנִי' דְּ"זוֹ הִיא" דִּמְמַעֵט כָּנַס וּלְבַסּוֹף גֵּירֵשׁ אַהַהִיא דְּקָתָנֵי "וְכוּלָּן אִם נִתְגָּרְשׁוּ צָרוֹתֵיהֶן מוּתָּרוֹת", וְאע"ג דְּכָנַס וּלְבַסּוֹף גֵּירֵשׁ, וְאָמַר רַבִּי יִרְמְיָה: תַּבְרָא כו'. **אֶלָּא אִי סָבַר לָהּ כְּרָבָא.** דְּזוֹ וְאֵין צָרִיךְ לוֹמַר זוֹ קָתָנֵי, אַלְמָא כָּנַס וּלְבַסּוֹף גֵּירֵשׁ שַׁרְיָא אֲפִי' לְתַנָּא דְּהָכָא, וְ"זוֹ הִיא" לָאו לְמַעוּטֵי אָתָא. **זוֹ הִיא לְמַעוּטֵי מַאי.** אִי לְמַעוּטֵי מֵת אָחִיו וְאח"כ גֵּירֵשׁ אִשְׁתּוֹ וְכָנַס יְבִמְתּוֹ, הַשְׁתָּא כָּנַס וְאח"כ גֵּירֵשׁ — שַׁרְיָא, גֵּירֵשׁ וְאח"כ כָּנַס מִיבַּעְיָא? וְאִי לְמַעוּטֵי מֵת נָשׂוּי נָכְרִית וְלֹא גֵּירֵשׁ בַּעַל אֲחוֹת אִשָּׁה אִשְׁתּוֹ וּמֵת, דַּאֲסוּרָה נָכְרִית לְיַיבּוּמֵי, מִשּׁוּם דַּהֲוַאי צָרָה בְּזִיקָה לָזוֹ שֶׁנָּפְלָה עַכְשָׁיו בְּעוֹד בַּעְלָהּ חַי, וַהֲרֵי לֹא נִתְגָּרְשָׁה, וּבִשְׁעַת מִיתָה צָרוֹת הֵן, וּבְהָא מוֹדֵי רָבָא — הָא לְר"נ לֵיכָּא לְמֵימַר הָכִי, דְּהָא אֵין זִיקָה סְבִירָא לֵיהּ. וְהִלְכָּךְ, עַל כָּרְחָךְ כְּרַבִּי יִרְמְיָה סְבִירָא לֵיהּ, וּלְמַעוּטֵי כָּנַס וְאח"כ גֵּירֵשׁ, דְּאָמַר נִישּׂוּאִין מַפִּילִין, וְהַאי שַׁעְתָּא צָרַת עֶרְוָה הָוְיָא. **וּלְרָבָא.** דְּאָמַר מִיתָה מַפֶּלֶת, וְכָנַס וְאח"כ גֵּירֵשׁ — שַׁרְיָא. **הָנִיחָא אִי סָבַר [לָהּ] כְּרַב אַשִׁי.** דְּיֵשׁ זִיקָה. **זוֹ הִיא לְמַעוּטֵי מֵת בְּלֹא גֵּירֵשׁ.** וְלָא דָּיֵיק לְמַתְנִיתִין כְּרַב אַשִׁי דְּאָמַר הָא מֵת וְאח"כ גֵּירֵשׁ אֲסוּרָה, דְּהָא רָבָא מִיתָה מַפֶּלֶת סְבִירָא לֵיהּ, וְכֵיוָן דְּגֵירֵשׁ — שַׁרְיָא. אֶלָּא הָכִי דָּיֵיק: טַעְמָא דְּגֵירֵשׁ. דִּבִשְׁעַת מִיתָה לָאו צָרוֹת הֲווּ — זוֹ הִיא דְּנָכְרִית מוּתֶּרֶת. אֲבָל מֵת שֵׁנִי זֶה אַחַר רִאשׁוֹן, וְלֹא גֵּירֵשׁ אֶת אִשְׁתּוֹ, וַאֲפִי' לֹא כָּנַס אֶת הַנָּכְרִית — אֲסוּרָה, דַּהֲוַאי צָרַת אֲחוֹת אִשָּׁה בְּזִיקָה, וַאֲפִילּוּ בִּשְׁעַת מִיתָה. דְּכֵיוָן דְּיֵשׁ זִיקָה הָוֵי כְּאִילּוּ בָּאָה אַף מִכֹּחַ הַשֵּׁנִי. וְא"ת: הוֹאִיל וְזִיקָה חֲשִׁיבָא לִהְיוֹת עָלֶיהָ כֹּחַ הַשֵּׁנִי — הָוְיָא אֵשֶׁת ב' מֵתִים, דִּבְלָאו אִיסּוּר דַּאֲחָיוֹת נַמִי אֲסִירָא! לָא הִיא, דְּזִיקַת שְׁנֵי יְבָמִין דַּאֲסִירָא לֵיתָא מִדְּאוֹרַיְיתָא, וְלָא גְּזוּר רַבָּנַן אֶלָּא הֵיכָא דַּעֲבַד בָּהּ מַאֲמָר, גְּזֵירָה שֶׁמָּא יֹאמְרוּ שְׁנֵי יְבָמוֹת הַבָּאוֹת מִבַּיִת אֶחָד מִתְיַיבְּמוֹת. **אֶלָּא אִי סָבַר לָהּ כְּרַב נַחְמָן.** דְּאֵין זִיקָה, וְהָא שַׁרְיָא — זוֹ הִיא לְמַעוּטֵי מַאי? הָא כּוּלְּהוּ שַׁרְיָין בַּר מִכָּנַס וְלֹא גֵּירֵשׁ, וְהַהִיא פְּשִׁיטָא, דְּהָא בְּהֶדְיָא תָּנֵינָא לָהּ, וְלָא אֲתָא "זוֹ הִיא" לְמַעוּטָהּ. **מתני'** **וְכוּלָּן.** ט"ו עֲרָיוֹת. **שֶׁהָיוּ בָּהֶן.** לְאָחִיו הַמֵּת. **קִידּוּשֵׁי סָפֵק אוֹ גֵּירוּשֵׁי סָפֵק.** הָוְיָא צָרָתָהּ סְפֵק צָרַת עֶרְוָה, דִּלְמָא אִיגַּרְשָׁה עֶרְוָה, וּלְגַבֵּי קִידּוּשִׁין דִּלְמָא לָא מִיקַּדְּשָׁה. **הֲרֵי אֵלּוּ הַצָּרוֹת חוֹלְצוֹת.** וְלָא מִפַּטְרָן בְּלֹא כְלוּם, דִּלְמָא לָאו צָרַת עֶרְוָה הִיא. **וְלֹא מִתְיַיבְּמוֹת.** דִּלְמָא צָרַת עֶרְוָה הִיא. **סָפֵק קָרוֹב לוֹ.** שֶׁהָיוּ ח' אַמּוֹת מְלוּמְצָמוֹת בֵּינֵיהֶן כְּר"ה, וְד' אַמּוֹת קוֹנוֹת שָׁם, וּזְרָקוֹ, סָפֵק בְּד' אַמּוֹת הַקָּרוֹב לָהּ, סָפֵק בְּד' אַמּוֹת הַקָּרוֹב לוֹ. **כָּתַב בִּכְתַב יָדוֹ.** דְּקַיְ"ל (ב"ב דף קעה:): הוֹצִיא עָלָיו כְּתַב יָדוֹ שֶׁהוּא חַיָּיב לוֹ — גּוֹבֶה מִנְּכָסִים בְּנֵי חוֹרִין. אַלְמָא: כְּתַב יָדוֹ בְּלֹא עֵדִים מִילְּתָא הִיא. **יֵשׁ עָלָיו עֵדִים וְאֵין בּוֹ זְמַן.** כָּתוּב, אוֹ יֵשׁ בּוֹ זְמַן וְאֵין בּוֹ אֶלָּא עֵד א' וְאֵינוֹ כְּתַב יָדוֹ שֶׁל בַּעַל — זֶהוּ סְפֵק גֵּירוּשִׁין. דַּאֲמְרִינַן בְּמַסֶּ' גִּיטִּין (דף פו.): ג' גִּיטִּין פְּסוּלִין וְאִם נִשֵּׂאת הַוָּלָד כָּשֵׁר, וְאֵלּוּ הֵן: כָּתַב בִּכְתַב יָדוֹ כו'. וְה"נ חוֹלֶצֶת צָרָתָהּ כֵּיוָן דְּגִיטָּא הוּא. דְּאִם נִיסֵּת — הַוָּלָד כָּשֵׁר וְלֹא מִתְיַיבֶּמֶת, כֵּיוָן דְּלָאו גִּיטָּא מַעַלְיָא הוּא, דְּקָרֵי לְהוּ פָּסוּל לְכַתְּחִלָּה. הִלְכָּךְ, אִי שָׁרֵית לֵיהּ, אָמְרִי אִינָשֵׁי: צָרַת עֶרְוָה מִתְיַיבֶּמֶת. וּבַגְּמָרָא בָּעֵי, אַמַּאי לָא נָקַט נַמִי בְּגֵירוּשִׁין סָפֵק קָרוֹב לוֹ כו'. **גמ'** **וְאִילּוּ בְּגֵירוּשִׁין סָפֵק קָרוֹב לָהּ סָפֵק קָרוֹב לוֹ לָא קָתָנֵי.** דְּהָתָם אֲפִי' חֲלִיצָה נַמִי לָא בָּעְיָא צָרָתָהּ, מ"ט? **אָמַר רַבָּה אִשָּׁה זוֹ בְּחֶזְקַת הֶיתֵּר לַשּׁוּק עוֹמֶדֶת.** קוֹדֶם לָכֵן, אִם יָמוּת בַּעְלָהּ, שֶׁהֲרֵי צָרַת עֶרְוָה הִיא. **וּמִסָּפֵק אַתָּה בָּא לְאוֹסְרָהּ.** שֶׁמָּא נִתְגָּרְשָׁה הָעֶרְוָה. **אַל תַּאַסְרֶנָּה מִסָּפֵק.** אֲבָל בְּהָנָךְ ג' גִּיטִּין לָאו מִסָּפֵק אָסְרִינַן לָהּ, דְּהָא גִּיטָּא הוּא, אֶלָּא שֶׁאֵין מִן הַמּוּבְחָר. **בְּקִידּוּשִׁין נַמִי.** אַמַּאי אָסְרִינַן לָהּ לְיַיבּוּמֵי? לֵימָא: אִשָּׁה זוֹ קוֹדֶם שֶׁקִּידֵּשׁ בַּעְלָהּ אֶת בַּת אָחִיו בְּחֶזְקַת הֶיתֵּר לְיִבּוּם עוֹמֶדֶת כְּשֶׁיָּמוּת, וּמִסָּפֵק אַתָּה בָּא כו'. **לְחוּמְרָא.** שְׁנוּיָא הוּא: וּפָרְכִינַן. **הָא חוּמְרָא דְּאָתֵי לִידֵי קוּלָּא הוּא.** דְּאָזֵיל הַאי מְקַדֵּשׁ בְּסָפֵק וְקָמְקַדֵּשׁ לַאֲחוֹתָהּ שֶׁל זוֹ שֶׁקִּידֵּשׁ בִּסְפֵק קִידּוּשִׁין וַדַּאי. **אִי נַמִי אָתֵי אִינִישׁ אַחֲרִינָא וּמְקַדֵּשׁ לָהּ.** לְהָךְ מְקוּדֶּשֶׁת בְּקִידּוּשֵׁי סָפֵק. קִידּוּשֵׁי וַדַּאי. בְּחַיֵּי בַּעְלָהּ. **וְכֵיוָן דְּקָאָסַר מָר לְצָרָתָהּ לְיַיבּוּמֵי.** לְאָבִיהָ שֶׁל זוֹ, מִשּׁוּם צָרַת הַבַּת. **אָמְרֵי.** אִינָשֵׁי: קִידּוּשֵׁי קַמָּא וַדַּאי הָווּ קִידּוּשִׁין גְּמוּרִין. **וּדְבַתְרָא לָאו קִידּוּשִׁין.** שֶׁאֵשֶׁת אִישׁ קִידֵּשׁ, וְאֵינָהּ צְרִיכָה הֵימֶנּוּ גֵּט. וּלְגַבֵּי קִידּוּשֵׁי אֲחוֹתָהּ נַמִי, דַּאֲמַרַן דְּאָזֵיל הוּא וּמְקַדֵּשׁ לַאֲחוֹתָהּ, אָתוּ לְמֵימַר לְאַחַר מִיתָתוֹ כִּי אָסְרִינַן לַצָּרָה לְיַיבּוּמֵי, אָמְרֵי דְּקַמַּיְיתָא קִידּוּשִׁין [דְּבַתְרַיְיתָא] לָאו קִידּוּשִׁין, שֶׁאֵין קִידּוּשִׁין תּוֹפְסִין בַּאֲחוֹת אִשָּׁה, וְיִשָּׂאֶנָּה אָחִיו מֵאַחַר כְּנָכְרִית בְּעָלְמָא, וּפָגַע בְּעֶרְוָה. כֵּיוָן

כתב בכתב ידו. מפרש ר"י בר' מאיר: אפי' אין כאן אלא חתימת ידו. (א) והא דתנן (ב"ב דף קעה:) הוליא עליו כתב ידו כו' – היינו חתימת ידו, וכן מוכח בפרק שני דכתובות (דף כא. ושם), דאמר אביי: לא ליחוי איניש חתימת ידיה אלא אחספא או אריסא דמגילתא, דלמא משכח איניש דלא מעלי, ותנן הוליא כתב ידו כו'(ב). אר"י: דכתב בכתב ידו ואין עליו עדים – פסול משום זמן, דיכול להקדים זמן כמו שירלה. וא"ת: [מאחר שדעתו לגרשה למה חיישינן לקוניא ועוד]: אם הוא חשוד להקדים זמן ולעשות עם האשה קוניא על הלקוחות בפירות שמכר מזמן הכתוב עד עכשיו, א"כ אנן לא נסמוך על הזמן הכתוב, ואמאי פסול? וי"ל: דאע"פ שבא לגרשה חיישינן לקוניא, כדחיישינן בסוף פרק "שנים אוחזין" (ב"מ דף יט: ושם) גבי שובר, ולא סמכינן אזמן הכתוב בו. ופעמים תפסיד האשה שלא כדין בשלא הקדים הזמן, ואנו חושדין אותו שביום הנתינה כתב והקדים הזמן, ומפסדת האשה שלא כדין פירות שמשעת הזמן עד הנתינה. אבל כשנפסלנו – לא תפסיד שלא כדין, דבדין הוא שלא תטרוף, דהא דאין לבעל פירות משעת כתיבה וחתימה – היינו דווקא בגט כשר. **יש** בו זמן ואין **בו אלא עד אחד וכו'**. הנך ג' גיטין פסולין ואם נשאת הולד כשר, כדתנן בפ' בתרא דגיטין (דף פו. ושם). ולמאן דמפרש התם דכתב ידו ועד אחד שנינו – איצטריך רישא כתב ידו ואין עליו עדים *לאשמועינן דאפילו הכי הולד כשר, וסיפא דאין בו אלא עד אחד אצטריך לאשמועינן דאפ"ה לא תנשא לכתחלה. וא"ת: ולמ"ד דכתב סופר ועד שנינו, ניחוש שמא הסופר כתבו להתלמד וזרקו לאשפה והחתימה עליו האשה עד אחד? וי"ל: שהסופרים חוששים שיבא לידי מכשול ונזהרים בכך. ומ"מ לא חשיב סופר ועד כשני עדים לגרש בו לכתחלה. **אשה** זו בחזקת היתר לשוק עומדת. וא"ת: תינח כנס ואח"כ גירש, שכבר הויא צרת ערוה. אבל גירש ואח"כ כנס – הא לא הויא בחזקת היתר לשוק! ועוד: (ג) לר"י דוקא בגירש ולבסוף כנס איירי! וי"ל: דמ"מ היא בחזקת היתר לשוק, דמוקמינן הערוה בחזקה שלא נתגרשה. וא"ת: דהכא מוקמינן אשה בחזקת היתר לשוק, אע"פ שבשעה שנולד הספק היתה עומדת בחזקת איסור שבעלה עדיין חי, ובפ"ק דחולין (דף ט. ושם) אמרינן: בהמה בחייה בחזקת איסור עומדת, עד שיודע לך במה נשחטה. נשחטה – בחזקת היתר עומדת, עד שיודע לך במה נטרפה. ומשמע: דוקא לענין ריעותא דאתיליד אחר שחיטה הויא בחזקת היתר, כגון בא זאב ונטל בני מעים והחזירם כשהם נקובים, דלא חיישינן שמא במקום נקב נקבו. אבל אם נולד הספק מחיים, כגון ספק דרוסה – לא, משום דבשעה שנולד הספק היתה עדיין בחזקת איסור! ואר"י: דהתם חייש' לספק דרוסה משום דשכיחא, ומוכחא מילתא לאיסורא טפי מדלהיתרא. וכן ההיא דישב לה קוץ בושט דחיישינן שמא הבריא, למאן

רש"ל

[לאשמועינן דהולד כשר וסיפא אתא לאשמועינן כצ"ל רש"ל]

לעיל יג.

[לעיל יג. וש"נ]

גיטין פו:

תוספות ישנים

בחזקת היתר לשוק עומדת ואע"ג דבחזקת אשת איש היתה מ"מ כיון דסופו למות ולבסוף נמי מת קרינן לה שפיר בחזקת היתר לשוק. וא"ת ומאי שנא מספק דרוסה דאסרינן והלא אית לה חזקת היתר דסופה להשחט ואולי דהתם חיישינן דשמא תמות הבהמה: **בחזקת** היתר לייבם. וא"ת התינח היכא שכנס זו קודם הקדושין של ספק אבל היכא שהקדושין של ספק קדמו מאי קאמר בחזקת היתר ליבם הלא לא היתה מעולם בחזקת היתר ליבם דשמא הקדושין גמורים היו וא"כ היתה זו צרת ערוה ואסורה ליבם. וי"ל דמ"מ בחזקת היתר ליבם היא לאוקמה לערוה בחזקת פנויה והויא זו מותרת ליבם:

תוספות חד מקמאי

מתניתין כיצד ספק קדושין זרק לה קדושין ספק קרוב לו ספק קרוב לה כיצד ספק גירושין כתב בכתב ידו ואין עליו עדים וכו' מסקנא דשמעתא דבגירושין נמי זרק לה גטה ספק קרוב לו ספק קרוב לה ל"ש כת אחת ול"ש ב' כתי עדים א' אומר קרוב לו וא' אומר קרוב לה חולצת ולא מתייבמת וקדושין נמי בכתב ידו ואין עליו עדים או אין עליו אלא עד א' לרב כדאית ליה כתב ידו ועד אבל כתב סופר שאינו מובהק ועד הולד פסול ולשמואל אפי' בסופר שאינו מובהק הולד כשר כדאיתא בפ' המגרש וגבי קדושין נמי חולצת ולא מתייבמת כללא

הגהות הב"ח

(א) תום' ד"ה כתב וכו' חתימת ידו וכן הא דתנן: (ב) בא"ד ואר"י דכתב וכו' וא"ת אם הוא חשוד להקדים זמן ולעשות עם האשה קוניא על הלקוחות בפירות שמכר מזמן הכתוב עד עכשיו דאע"פ שבא לגרשה חיישינן לקוניא כדחיישי' בסוף שנים אוחזין גבי שובר א"כ אנן לא נסמוך על הזמן הכתוב ואמאי פסול וי"ל דודאי אינו נאמן ולא סמכינן אזמן הכתוב בו ולכך פסלוהו דלפעמים תפסיד האשה וכו' שמשעת כתיבת הזמן עד כו' כצ"ל. ונ"ב עיין בתוס' פ"ק דגיטין דף ג: (ג) ד"ה אשה וכו' ועוד לר' ירמיה דוקא:

הגהות הגר"א

[א] גמ' מת בלא גירש. נ"ב גירסת הגאונים והרי"ף מת ואח"כ גירש וכ"ש במת ולא גירש וכתב הטור דווקא בלא כנס והרשב"א כתב להיפך דווקא בכנס והרמב"ן אמר (אליבא דהרי"ף) בין בזה ובין בזה (ועמ"ש רבינו באה"ע סי' קעה ס"ק יח):

כֵּיוָן דְּקָא מַצְרְכַתְּ חֲלִיצָה – מֵידַע יָדְעֵי דְּחוּמְרָא בְּעָלְמָא הוּא. – א"ה גֵּירוּשִׁין נַמִּי לִיתְנֵי, ו וְלִיצְרְכָהּ חֲלִיצָה, וּמֵידַע יָדְעֵי דְּחוּמְרָא בְּעָלְמָא הוּא! – אִם אַתָּה אוֹמֵר חוֹלֶצֶת – מִתְיַיבֶּמֶת. – הָכָא נַמִּי: אִם אַתָּה אוֹמֵר חוֹלֶצֶת – מִתְיַיבֶּמֶת! – וְתִתְיַיבֵּם, וְאֵין בְּכָךְ כְּלוּם – אַחֲזָקָה קָא קַיְימָא. אֵיתִיבֵיהּ אַבַּיֵי: *נָפַל הַבַּיִת עָלָיו וְעַל בַּת אָחִיו, וְאֵין יָדוּעַ אֵיזֶה מֵהֶם מֵת רִאשׁוֹן – צָרָתָהּ חוֹלֶצֶת וְלֹא מִתְיַיבֶּמֶת. אַמַּאי? הָכָא נַמִּי נֵימָא: אִשָּׁה זוֹ בְּחֶזְקַת הֶיתֵּר לַשּׁוּק עוֹמֶדֶת, וּמִסָּפֵק אַתָּה בָּא לְאוֹסְרָהּ – אַל תַּאַסְרֶנָּה מִסָּפֵק! וְכִי תֵּימָא: ה"נ לְחוּמְרָא – חוּמְרָא דְּאָתֵי לִידֵי קוּלָּא הוּא, שֶׁאִם אַתָּה אוֹמֵר חוֹלֶצֶת – מִתְיַיבֶּמֶת! – גֵּירוּשִׁין דִּשְׁכִיחִי גָּזְרוּ בְּהוּ רַבָּנַן, *מַפּוֹלֶת דְּלָא שְׁכִיחִי – לָא גָּזְרוּ בְּהוּ רַבָּנַן. אִי נַמִּי: גֵּירוּשִׁין דְּקַיְימָא עֶרְוָה דְּקָא מוֹכַח, וְצָרָתָהּ קָמַצְרְכַתְּ לָהּ חֲלִיצָה – אָמְרִי: קָמוּ בֵּיהּ רַבָּנַן בְּגִיטָּא דְּגִיטָּא מַעַלְיָא הוּא, וְאָתוּ לְיַיבּוּמֵי לַצָּרָה. מַפּוֹלֶת – מִי קָמוּ בְּהוּ רַבָּנַן בְּמַפּוֹלֶת? – וְגַבֵּי גֵּירוּשִׁין מִי לָא תְּנַן? וְהָתְנַן: *א הָיְתָה עוֹמֶדֶת בּרה"ר וּזְרָקוֹ לָהּ, קָרוֹב לָהּ – מְגוֹרֶשֶׁת, קָרוֹב לוֹ – אֵינָהּ מְגוֹרֶשֶׁת. מֶחֱצָה עַל מֶחֱצָה – מְגוֹרֶשֶׁת וְאֵינָהּ מְגוֹרֶשֶׁת. וְאָמְרִינַן: לְמַאי הִלְכְתָא – דְּאִי כֹּהֵן הוּא אֲסוּרָה לֵיהּ, וְאִי עֶרְוָה הִיא – צָרָתָהּ בָּעֲיָא חֲלִיצָה. וְלָא אָמְרִינַן שֶׁאִם אַתָּה אוֹמֵר חוֹלֶצֶת מִתְיַיבֶּמֶת! – הָא אִיתְּמַר עֲלָהּ, *רַבָּה וְרַב יוֹסֵף דְּאָמְרִי תַּרְוַויְיהוּ: הָכָא בִּשְׁתֵּי כִּיתֵּי עֵדִים עָסְקִינַן, אַחַת אוֹמֶרֶת: קָרוֹב לָהּ, וְאַחַת אוֹמֶרֶת: קָרוֹב לוֹ, דַּהֲוָה לֵיהּ סְפֵיקָא דְּאוֹרַיְיתָא. וּמַתְנִיתִין דְּהָכָא בְּכַת אַחַת, דְּה"ל סְפֵיקָא דְּרַבָּנַן. – וּמִמַּאי דְּמַתְנִיתִין דְּהָכָא בְּכַת אַחַת? – דּוּמְיָא דְּקִדּוּשִׁין, מַה קִּדּוּשִׁין בְּכַת אַחַת – אַף גֵּרוּשִׁין בְּכַת אַחַת. וְקִדּוּשִׁין גּוּפַיְיהוּ מִמַּאי דִּבְכַת אַחַת, דִּלְמָא בְּב' כִּיתֵּי עֵדִים? – אִי בְּב' כִּיתֵּי עֵדִים – תִּתְיַיבֵּם, וְאֵין בְּכָךְ כְּלוּם. – קַיְימֵי עֵדִים וְקָאָמְרִי "קָרוֹב לָהּ" וְאַתְּ אָמְרַתְּ תִּתְיַיבֵּם וְאֵין בְּכָךְ כְּלוּם?! וְתוּ: בִּשְׁתֵּי כִּיתֵּי עֵדִים נַמִּי סְפֵיקָא דְּרַבָּנַן הִיא, דְּאָמְרִי': אוֹקֵי תְּרֵי לְבַהֲדֵי תְּרֵי, וְאִשָּׁה אוֹקְמָהּ אַחֲזָקָה. מִידֵי דַּהֲוָה אַנִּכְסֵי דְּבַר שַׁטְיָא. *דְּבַר שַׁטְיָא זַבֵּין נִכְסֵי, אָתוּ בֵּי תְּרֵי וְאָמְרִי: כְּשֶׁהוּא חָלִים זַבֵּין, וַאֲתוּ בֵּי תְּרֵי וְאָמְרוּ כְּשֶׁהוּא שׁוֹטֶה זַבֵּין. וַאֲמַר רַב אַשִׁי: באוֹקֵי תְּרֵי לַהֲדֵי תְּרֵי וְאַרְעָא

רש"י

כֵּיוָן דְּקָמִצְרְכַתְּ חֲלִיצָה לַצָּרָה מֵידַע יָדְעֵי. דְּקִידּוּשֵׁי דְּבַת אָחִיו לָאו קִידּוּשִׁין, וְהַאי דְּלָא מִתְיַיבֶּמֶת צָרָתָהּ – חוּמְרָא בְּעָלְמָא הוּא. לִיתְנֵי. סָפֵק קָרוֹב לוֹ. מֵידַע יָדְעֵי דְּחוּמְרָא בְּעָלְמָא הוּא. כְּלוֹמַר, אִי חָיְישַׁתְּ דְּלָא לֵימְרוּ אִינָשֵׁי מִדְּחָלְצָה וַדַּאי גֵּירוּשִׁין גְּמוּרִין נִינְהוּ, דְּאִי קָדֵישׁ לָהּ לִמְגוֹרֶשֶׁת אִינִישׁ דְּעָלְמָא וַהֲדַר קָדֵישׁ לַאֲחוֹתָהּ, דְּקַמַּיְיתָא (א) קָדֵישׁ, דְּבַתְרַיְיתָא לָאו קִידּוּשִׁין – לָא תֵּיחוּשׁ לְהָכִי. דְּמִדְּלָא מִתְיַיבֶּמֶת צָרָתָהּ, מֵידַע יָדְעִי דַּחֲלִיצָה חוּמְרָא בְּעָלְמָא הוּא. מִתְיַיבֶּמֶת. וְקָמְיַיבֵּם צָרַת עֶרְוָה, דְּאוֹקְמָהּ אַחֲזָקָה, וּפָגַע בְּכָרֵת. הָכָא נַמִּי. גַּבֵּי קִידּוּשִׁין, אַמַּאי חוֹלֶצֶת? הָא אָתֵי לְיַיבּוּמֵי, וְדִלְמָא קִידּוּשֵׁי עֶרְוָה קִידּוּשֵׁי הֲווּ, וְקָמְיַיבֵּם לְצָרַת עֶרְוָה. אַחֲזָקָה קַיְימָא. בְּחֶזְקַת הֶיתֵּר לְיַיבֵּם. וְעַל בַּת אָחִיו. וְהִיא אִשְׁתּוֹ, צָרָתָהּ חוֹלֶצֶת – לָא מִיפַּטְרָא בְּוֹלָא כְּלוּם מִשּׁוּם צָרַת עֶרְוָה, שֶׁמָּא הִיא מֵתָה רִאשׁוֹנָה וְאַחַר כָּךְ מֵת הוּא. וּתְנַן: וְכוּלָּן, אִם מֵתוּ הָעֲרָיוֹת קוֹדֶם לְבַעֲלֵיהֶן – צָרוֹתֵיהֶן מוּתָּרוֹת, בְּפ"ק. וְלֹא מִתְיַיבֶּמֶת. שֶׁמָּא הוּא מֵת רִאשׁוֹן, וְהָוְיָא לָהּ הָךְ צָרַת בִּתּוֹ: ה"ג: חוּמְרָא דְּאָתֵי לִידֵי קוּלָּא הוּא, שֶׁאִם אַתָּה אוֹמֵר חוֹלֶצֶת מִתְיַיבֶּמֶת. גָּזְרוּ בְּהוּ רַבָּנַן. דִּסְפֵק גֵּירוּשִׁין בְּעֶרְוָה לֹא תַּחֲלוֹץ הַצָּרָה, שֶׁאִם אַתָּה אוֹמֵר חוֹלֶצֶת – מִתְיַיבֶּמֶת: דְּקַיְימָא עֶרְוָה. קַמָּן, וְקָמוֹכַחַת, דְּהַכֹּל רוֹאִין שֶׁזּוֹ צָרַת עֶרְוָה הָיְתָה, וְאַתָּה מַצְרְכַתְּ חֲלִיצָה – אָתוּ לְמֵימַר קָמוּ בֵּיהּ רַבָּנַן בְּגִיטָּא, וְגִיטָּא מְעַלְיָא הוּא, וְאֵין זוֹ צָרַת עֶרְוָה – וְאָתָא לְיַיבּוּמֵי. אֲבָל מַפּוֹלֶת. אַף עַל גַּב מַצְרְכַתְּ לָהּ חֲלִיצָה, מִי אָתֵי לְמֵימַר קָמוּ בְּהוּ רַבָּנַן בְּמַפּוֹלֶת? אֵלּוּ הַדַּיָּינִים הַמַּצְרִיכִים אוֹתָהּ חֲלִיצָה, נְבִיאִים הֵם וְיֵדְעוּ שֶׁהִיא מֵתָה רִאשׁוֹנָה, דְּלֵיתֵי לְיַיבֵּם לַצָּרָה? וּמֵידַע יָדְעִי דְּהַאי דְּחָלְצָה – מִשּׁוּם סְפֵיקָא הָיָה. קָרוֹב לוֹ כו'. מְפָרֵשׁ בְּמַסֶּכֶת גִּיטִּין. לְמַאי הִלְכְתָא. קָתָנֵי מְגוֹרֶשֶׁת. דְּהָוֵי לָהּ סְפֵקָא דְּאוֹרַיְיתָא. כֵּיוָן דִּתְרֵי אָמְרִי קָרוֹב לָהּ – לָא מָצֵי לְאוֹקְמִי צָרָה אַחֲזָקָה וּלְמִיפְטְרָא לְעָלְמָא בְּלֹא חֲלִיצָה. וּמַתְנִי' דְּהָכָא בְּכַת אַחַת. עֵד אוֹמֵר קָרוֹב לוֹ וְעֵד אוֹמֵר קָרוֹב לָהּ. הִלְכָּךְ, בְּקִידּוּשִׁין הוּא דְּאִיכָּא לְמִיתְנְיֵיהּ – מִשּׁוּם דִּבְחֶזְקַת הֶיתֵּר לְיַיבֵּם קַיְימָא, וּמִשּׁוּם עֵד אֶחָד דְּאָמַר קָרוֹב לָהּ לָא מַפְקִינַן לָהּ מֵחֲזָקָה, וְחָלְצָה. אֲבָל בְּגֵירוּשִׁין לֵיכָּא לְמִתְנְיֵיהּ דִּבְחֶזְקַת הֶיתֵּר לַשּׁוּק קַיְימָא, וְעֵד א' דְּאָמַר קָרוֹב לָהּ – בָּעֵי לְאַפּוֹקֵי מֵחֲזָקָה, וְכֵיוָן דְּלֵיכָּא עֵדוּת שָׁלֵם – אָזְלִינַן לְקוּלָּא וְקָא מוֹקְמִינַן אַחֲזָקָה, וְלָא בָּעְיָא חֲלִיצָה, שֶׁאִם אַתָּה אוֹמֵר חוֹלֶצֶת – מִתְיַיבֶּמֶת. אַף גֵּירוּשִׁין בְּכַת אַחַת. כְּלוֹמַר, אִי הֲוָה תָּנֵי לְהוּ, דְּע"כ הֲוָה מִיתוֹקְמָא דּוּמְיָא דְּקִידּוּשִׁין, מִשּׁוּם הָכִי לָא תָּנֵי לָהּ: הָכִי גָּרְסִינַן. וְקִידּוּשִׁין גּוּפַיְיהוּ מִמַּאי דִּבְכַת אַחַת דִּלְמָא בִּשְׁתֵּי כִּיתֵּי עֵדִים אִי בִּשְׁתֵּי כִּיתֵּי עֵדִים תִּתְיַיבֵּם צָרָתָהּ וְאֵין בְּכָךְ כְּלוּם קַיְימִי עֵדִים וְאָמְרִי קָרוֹב לָהּ וְאַתְּ אָמְרַתְּ תִּתְיַיבֵּם וְאֵין בְּכָךְ כְּלוּם. וְתוּ, בִּשְׁתֵּי כִּיתֵּי עֵדִים נַמִּי סְפֵיקָא דְּרַבָּנַן הוּא דְּאָמְרִינַן אוֹקֵי תְּרֵי כו'. וְהָכִי פֵּירוּשׁוֹ: אִי בִּשְׁתֵּי כִּיתֵּי עֵדִים לָא הֲוָה תָּנֵי "וְלֹא מִתְיַיבֶּמֶת", אֶלָּא תִּתְיַיבֵּם וְאֵין בְּכָךְ כְּלוּם, דְּהָא אוֹקְמַתְּ אַחֲזָקָה דְּמוּתֶּרֶת לְיַיבֵּם הֲוַאי. וּפָרְכִינַן: קַיְימִי עֵדִים כו' וְהָאָמְרַתְּ שְׁתֵּי כִּיתֵּי עֵדִים סְפֵיקָא דְּאוֹרַיְיתָא הִיא! וְתוּ: בִּשְׁתֵּי כִּיתֵּי עֵדִים נַמִּי סְפֵיקָא דְּרַבָּנַן הוּא. וּבְגֵירוּשִׁין גּוּפַיְיהוּ, אע"ג דְּכַת אַחַת אוֹמֶרֶת קָרוֹב לָהּ – לָא הֲוָה לָן לְאַפּוֹקֵי מֵחֶזְקַת הֶיתֵּר לַשּׁוּק, כֵּיוָן דְּאִיכָּא כַּת אַחֲרִיתִי דְּאָמְרָה קָרוֹב לוֹ, וְאַמַּאי קָתָנֵי חוֹלֶצֶת? וְאִית דִּמְפָרְשֵׁי הָכִי: אִי בִּשְׁתֵּי כִּיתֵּי עֵדִים – מִי הֲוָה אָמְרִינַן לְעֵיל בִּסְפֵק קִידּוּשִׁין תִּתְיַיבֵּם וְאֵין בְּכָךְ כְּלוּם? קַיְימִי עֵדִים וְאָמְרִי קָרוֹב לָהּ וּמְקוּדֶּשֶׁת, וְנַעֲשֵׂית הָרִאשׁוֹנָה צָרַת עֶרְוָה, וְאַתְּ אָמְרַתְּ תִּתְיַיבֵּם? אֶלָּא וַדַּאי בְּכַת א', וּמִשּׁוּם דְּלֵיכָּא אֶלָּא חַד דְּאָמַר קָרוֹב לָהּ – אָמְרִינַן אוֹקֵי צָרָה אַחֶזְקָתָהּ דִּשְׁרְיָא לְיַיבֵּם. וְכָךְ שָׁמַעְתִּי. וְקָשֶׁה בְּעֵינַי: מִשּׁוּם דְּמַיְיתֵי סַיְיעְתָּא לְמִילְּתֵיהּ מִדְּנַפְשֵׁיהּ, דְּהַהוּא "תִּתְיַיבֵּם וְאֵין בְּכָךְ כְּלוּם" דִּלְעֵיל – הוּא גּוּפֵיהּ פֵּירֵשׁ הָכִי. תַּנְיָא

תוספות

למאן דחייש לספק דרוסה. כדאמר בריש "אלו טרפות" (חולין דף מג: ושם), ואדי שנכנס לבין השוורים, ופסק התם אמימר* הלכתא דחוששין לספק דרוסה, אע"ג דאמרינן התם איכא למימר הכי ואיכא למימר הכי, מ"מ מסתברא טעמא לאיסורא טפי מלהתירא. תדע, דהא בספק כלבא ספק שונרא אמרינן התם (דף נג:) אימור כלבא, אפי' לשמואל דחייש לספק דרוסה. **הכא** נמי אם אתה אומר חולצת מתייבמת. תימה: דמעיקרא פריך ואל תאסרנה מספק, ורוצה להתירה ליבם לכתחילה, והשתא פריך דאפילו חליצה לא תיבעי, גזרה שמא תתייבם! ויש לומר: דהכא הכי קאמר: מה מועיל שאתה אוסרה לייבם? וכיון דחולצת יבוא מתוך כך לייבם! ומשני דחולצת ממה נפשך, ואם יבא באקראי בעלמא לייבם – אין בכך כלום. **נפל** הבית וכו'. כאן יש תימה: אמאי חשיב לה טפי בחזקת היתר לשוק מלייבם? דהא קמן ששניהם מתו, וכן יכול להיות שהיא מתה תחלה כמו הבעל! וי"ל: דמשום הכי חשיב לה טפי בחזקת היתר לשוק מלייבם, משום דמיתת הבעל משתריא לשוק, אבל במיתת הערוה אינה ניתרת לייבם עד שימות הבעל עמה. **ואין** ידוע איזה מהם מת ראשונה. קסבר האי תנא דמיתה מפלת.

(ג) **למאי** הלכתא. תימה: דמשנה זו בגיטין ב"הזורק" (דף עח.*) ולא מסיק התם בגמרא למאי הלכתא. **אי** בשתי כיתי עדים תתייבם ואין בכך כלום. פ"ה דחוק הוא: דאיך עלה על דעת המתרץ לומר כן? ועוד, דבספרים ישנים גרס "ודלמא", והוא מוחק וגרס "ותו"! ונראה לר"י דה"פ: דומיא דקידושין, וקידושין משמע ליה דמיירי אף בכת אחת, ואע"ג דבכת אחת דאורייתא מתייבמת, כיון דבב' כיתי עדים הויא ספיקא דאורייתא – גזרו רבנן שלא תתייבם בכת אחת אטו ב' כיתי עדים. ופריך: וקידושין גופייהו, ממאי דמיירי בכת אחת? דלמא דוקא בב' כיתי עדים, אבל בכת אחת – מותרת להתייבם, ולא גזרינן אטו ב' כיתי עדים משום דב' כיתי עדים גופייהו הויא ספיקא דרבנן, ומדאוריית' מתייבמת, דמוקים לה אחזקה. אלא מדרבנן חולצת ולא מתייבמת לחומרא – דווקא בשתי כיתי עדים, אבל בכת אחת – לא החמירו. ומוכיח דשתי כיתי עדים ספיקא דרבנן, כמו שמפורש לבסוף. והשתא קאמר: אי בב' כיתי עדים דוקא אתה רוצה להעמידו, אבל בכת אחת מתייבמת, ולא גזרינן אטו שתי כיתי עדים, דשתי כיתי עדים גופייהו אינה חולצת אלא לחומרא, ואם תתייבם אין בכך כלום, והיכי מלינן למימר דתתייבם ואין בכך כלום(ג)? קיימי עדים ואמרי כו'! ומסיק: ודלמא בשתי כיתי עדים גופייהו הויא ספיקא דרבנן, כמו שהקשה בתחלה. והשתא, לפי מסקנא זו בקידושין בכת אחת – שריא להתייבם. ומיהו ודלמא בעלמא קאמר. ועוד אר"י, דמלינן לפרש: דמשמע ליה דבקידושין איירי בכת אחת, משום דבשתי כיתי עדים לא איצטריך, דפשיטא, שהוא ספיקא דאורייתא, ותנן לה בגיטין (ג"ז שם) גבי ספק גירושין דחולצת. אבל(ד) אי הוה בקידושין מיירי בשתי כיתי עדים – הוה מיירי נמי בגירושין בשתי כיתי עדים, אע"ג דלא איצטריך וכבר תנן לה בגיטין. ולהכי קאמר דומיא דקידושין, דקידושין נמי בכת אחת. ופריך: וקידושין גופייהו דלמא בשתי כיתי עדים, דשתי כיתי עדים נמי ספיקא דרבנן, וכת א' ושתי כיתי עדים הכל הוה שוה, שהכל ספיקא דרבנן, כדמפרש ואזיל. **שתי** כיתי עדים נמי ספיקא דרבנן. וא"ת: וכיון דמסקינן דבשתי כיתי עדים הוי ספיקא דרבנן – למה דחקו רבה ורב יוסף לאוקמי ההיא

תוספות ישנים

שאם אתה אומר חולצת מתייבמת. וא"ת לעיל שאמרנו בפ' כילד חולצת ולא מתייבמת אמאי לא אמרינן שאם אתה אומר חולצת מתייבמת. וי"ל דהתם נמי אינה אסורה לייבם אלא מדרבנן וא"כ תתייבם ואין בכך כלום כדאמר הכא. וא"ת ולר' שמעון דאסר שתי אחיות בזיקה מדאורייתא וכשהאחת איסור מצוה אמרינן לעיל חולצת ולא מתייבמת ואמאי לא גזרינן שאם אתה אומר חולצת מתייבמת דהא מדאורייתא היא וא"א לומר תתייבם ואין בכך כלום. וי"ל דאחיות בזיקה והאחת איסור מצוה מלתא דלא שכיחא היא ולא גזור בה רבנן: **נפל** הבית עליו ועל בת אחיו וכו' ואמאי נימא אשה זו בחזקת היתר לשוק עומדת. וא"ת אדרבה נימא בחזקת היתר לייבם שמתה הערוה מתחלה מספק אתה בא לאוסרה לומר שמת האיש קודם ואל תאסרנה מספק וי"ל דסברא הוא להחזיקה בחזקת היתר לשוק יותר מלייבם משום דלשוק משתרייא במיתת הבעל לבד אבל להתירה לייבם צריך מיתת הבעל והערוה: **ומתניתין** דהכא ממאי דבכת אחת. נראה דאמתני' קפריך אמאי נקט מלתיה בכת אחת ומ"ה גזרינן חליצה אטו יבום והחליצה הוא חומרא בעלמא ליתני בשתי כתי עדים והוי התחלה כדין ולא נגזור אטו יבום ומשני משום דבעי למתני קדושין דמשום גירושין לא תנייה דהא כבר תנינן לה בגיטין אלא משום קדושין תנינן לה וא"כ צריך למתני דומיא דקדושין דמיירי בכת אחת:

עין משפט נר מצוה

כז א מיי' פ"ט מהל' גירושין הלכה יג סמג עשין נ טוש"ע אה"ע סימן קלט סעיף יג:

כח ב מיי' פכ"ט מהל' מכירה הלכה ה סמג עשין פב טוש"ע ח"מ סימן רלה סעיף כא בהג"ה:

מסורת הש"ס

לקמן סז:

[עירובין סג: וש"נ]

גיטין עח.

[שם:]

כתובות כ.

[חולין נג:]

[ועי' תוס' ב"ב קסט: ד"ה בחזקה]

הגהות הב"ח

(א) רש"י ד"ה מידע וכו' דקמייתא קידושין דבתרייתא: (ב) תוס' ד"ה ואמר' למאי הלכתא: (ג) ד"ה אי בשתי וכו' ואין בכך כלום והא קיימי עדים: (ד) בא"ד אבל אי בקידושין הוה מיירי וכו' דכבר תנן לה וכו' דקידושין מיירי נמי בכת אחת:

וְאַרְעָא אוֹקְמָא בְּחֶזְקַת בַּר שַׁטְיָא. אֶלָּא אֲמַר *אַבַּיֵי: °"יַגִּיד עָלָיו רֵיעוֹ" (איוב לו); תָּנָא בְּקִידּוּשִׁין – וְהוּא הַדִּין לְגֵירוּשִׁין, תָּנָא בְּגֵירוּשִׁין – וְה"ה לְקִידּוּשִׁין. א"ל רָבָא: אִי יַגִּיד עָלָיו רֵיעוֹ – מַאי "זֶהוּ" דְּקָתָנֵי? אֶלָּא אָמַר רָבָא: כָּל שֶׁיֵּשׁ בְּקִידּוּשִׁין – יֵשׁ בְּגֵירוּשִׁין, וְיֵשׁ בְּגֵירוּשִׁין מַה שֶּׁאֵין בְּקִידּוּשִׁין. וְ"זֶהוּ" דְּגֵירוּשִׁין לָאו דַּוְקָא, אֶלָּא מִשּׁוּם דְּתָנָא "זֶהוּ" בְּקִידּוּשִׁין – תָּנָא נַמִי "זֶהוּ" בְּגֵירוּשִׁין. וְ"זֶהוּ" דְּקִידּוּשִׁין לְמַעוּטֵי מַאי? – לְמַעוּטֵי זְמַן, דְּלֵיכָּא בְּקִידּוּשִׁין. – וּמִפְּנֵי מָה לֹא תִּקְנוּ זְמַן בְּקִידּוּשִׁין? – הָנִיחָא לְמ"ד מִשּׁוּם פֵּירֵי – [א]אֲרוּסָה לֵית לָהּ פֵּירֵי. אֶלָּא לְמ"ד [ב]מִשּׁוּם בַּת אֲחוֹתוֹ – לִיתְקִין זְמַן! – מִשּׁוּם דְּאִיכָּא דִּמְקַדֵּשׁ בְּכַסְפָּא וְאִיכָּא דִּמְקַדֵּשׁ בִּשְׁטָרָא – לָא תְּקוּן רַבָּנַן זְמַן. א"ל רַב אַחָא בְּרֵיהּ דְּרַב יוֹסֵף לְרַב אַשִׁי: וְהָא עַבְדָּא, דְּאִיכָּא דְּקָנֵי בְּכַסְפָּא וְאִיכָּא בִּשְׁטָרָא, וּתְקוּן רַבָּנַן זְמַן! – הָתָם רוּבָּא בִּשְׁטָרָא, הָכָא – רוּבָּא בְּכַסְפָּא. אב"א: מִשּׁוּם דְּלָא אֶפְשָׁר. הֵיכִי לִיעֲבִיד? לִינְחָה גַּבֵּי דִּידָהּ – מָחֲקָה לֵיהּ. לִינְחָה גַּבֵּי דִּידֵיהּ – זִמְנִין דְּבַת אֲחוֹתוֹ הִיא, וּמְחַפֶּה עֲלָהּ. לִינְחָה גַּבֵּי עֵדִים, (א) אִי דִּזְכִירִי – לֵיתוּ לִיסְהוּד, וְאִי לָא – זִמְנִין דְּחָזוּ מִכְּתָבָא, וְאָתוּ מְסַהֲדִי. [ג]וְרַחֲמָנָא אָמַר: *"מִפִּיהֶם", וְלֹא מִפִּי כְּתָבָם. – אִי הָכִי בְּגֵירוּשִׁין נַמִי נֵימָא הָכִי! – הָתָם לְהַצָּלָה דִּידָהּ קָאָתֵי, הָכָא – לְחוֹבָה דִּידָהּ קָאָתֵי.§ **מתני'** *[ד]ג' אַחִין נְשׂוּאִין ג' נָכְרִיּוֹת, וּמֵת אֶחָד מֵהֶן, וְעָשָׂה בָּהּ הַשֵּׁנִי מַאֲמָר וָמֵת – הֲרֵי אֵלּוּ חוֹלְצוֹת וְלֹא מִתְיַיבְּמוֹת. שֶׁנֶּאֱמַר °"וּמֵת אַחַד מֵהֶן יְבָמָהּ יָבֹא עָלֶיהָ" (דברים כה) (ב) שֶׁעָלֶיהָ זִיקַת יָבָם אֶחָד וְלֹא שֶׁעָלֶיהָ זִיקַת ב' יְבָמִין. רַבִּי שִׁמְעוֹן אוֹמֵר: מְיַיבֵּם לְאֵיזוֹ שֶׁיִּרְצֶה, וְחוֹלֵץ לַשְּׁנִיָּה.§ **גמ'** וְאִי זִיקַת ב' יְבָמִין דְּאוֹרַיְיתָא, חֲלִיצָה נַמִי לָא תִּיבְעֵי! אֶלָּא מִדְּרַבָּנַן, [ה]וּגְזֵירָה שֶׁמָּא יֹאמְרוּ ב' יְבָמוֹת הַבָּאוֹת מִבַּיִת אֶחָד מִתְיַיבְּמוֹת. – וְנִיַיבֵּם לְחָדָא וְנִיחְלוֹץ לְחָדָא! – גְּזֵירָה *) שֶׁמָּא יֹאמְרוּ: בַּיִת אֶחָד, מִקְצָתוֹ בָּנוּי וּמִקְצָתוֹ

תָּנָא בְּקִידּוּשִׁין. סָפֵק קָרוֹב לוֹ כו', וְה"ה בְּגֵירוּשִׁין. וְתָנָא בְּגֵירוּשִׁין. כָּתַב בִּכְתַב יָדוֹ וכו', וְה"ה לְקִידּוּשִׁין: ה"ג. כָּל שֶׁיֵּשׁ בְּקִידּוּשִׁין יֵשׁ בְּגֵירוּשִׁין וְיֵשׁ בְּגֵירוּשִׁין מַה שֶּׁאֵין בְּקִידּוּשִׁין. וְ"זֶהוּ" דְּגֵירוּשִׁין לָאו דַּוְקָא, וּמִשּׁוּם דְּתָנָא "זֶהוּ" בְּקִידּוּשִׁין – תָּנָא נַמִי "זֶהוּ" בְּגֵירוּשִׁין. כָּל שֶׁיֵּשׁ בְּקִידּוּשִׁין. כְּגוֹן סָפֵק קָרוֹב לוֹ וכו' הָוֵי נַמִי סָפֵק בְּגֵירוּשִׁין. וְיֵשׁ בְּגֵירוּשִׁין. שֶׁאֵין סָפֵק לְעִנְיַן קִדּוּשִׁין, כְּגוֹן זְמַן. כִּדְמְפָרֵשׁ לְקַמָּן, דִּבִשְׁטַר קִידּוּשִׁין כְּגוֹן הַמְקַדֵּשׁ בִּשְׁטָר – לֹא תִּקְנוּ זְמַן. וְ"זֶהוּ" דְּגֵירוּשִׁין לָאו דַּוְקָא. דְּמַשְׁמָעוֹ: זֶהוּ דְּהָוֵי סָפֵק בַּגֵּירוּשִׁין, אֲבָל סָפֵק קָרוֹב – לֹא הָוֵי סָפֵק לַגֵּירוּשִׁין. וְאַיְּידֵי דְּתָנָא "זֶהוּ" בְּקִידּוּשִׁין, דְּדַוְקָא זֶהוּ, דְּקמ"ל זֶהוּ סָפֵק קָרוֹב, הוּא דְּשַׁיָּיךְ בְּקִידּוּשִׁין, אֲבָל סָפֵק זְמַן – לֹא שַׁיָּיךְ בְּהוּ. הָנִיחָא לְמ"ד. בְּגִיטִּין בְּפֶ' *"כָּל הַגֵּט" (דף כו:): מִפְּנֵי מָה תִּקְנוּ חֲכָמִים זְמַן בְּגִיטִּין – מִשּׁוּם פֵּירֵי, לֵידַע מֵאֵימָתַי תִּגְבֶּה מִבַּעְלָהּ פֵּירוֹת שֶׁאָכַל מִנִּכְסֵי מְלוֹג שֶׁלָּהּ, דְּקָסָבַר: מִשָּׁעָה שֶׁנָּתַן עֵינָיו בָּהּ לְגָרְשָׁהּ שׁוּב אֵין לוֹ לַבַּעַל פֵּירוֹת. אֲרוּסָה לֵית לָהּ פֵּירֵי. לְפִיכָךְ לֹא תִּקְנוּהוּ בִּשְׁטַר קִידּוּשִׁין, שֶׁאֵין הַבַּעַל אוֹכֵל פֵּירוֹת עַד שֶׁתִּכָּנֵס לַחוּפָּה. דְּכִי תַּקּוּן רַבָּנַן פֵּירֵי לַבַּעַל מִשּׁוּם פִּרְקוֹנָהּ, וּפִרְקוֹנָהּ לֹא קָא מְחַיֵּיב בָּהּ אֶלָּא מִכְּתוּבָּה וְאֵילָךְ, דִּתְנַאי כְּתוּבָּה הוּא: דְּאִם תִּשְׁתַּבַּאי אֶפְרְקִינָךְ, בִּכְתוּבּוֹת פֶּ' "נַעֲרָה" (דף נא.). מִשּׁוּם בַּת אֲחוֹתוֹ. שֶׁמָּא יְהֵא נָשׂוּי בַּת אֲחוֹתוֹ וְתִזְנֶה תַּחְתָּיו, וְיִרְאֶה עֵדִים מְמַשְׁמְשִׁין וּבָאִין, וְיָחוּס עָלֶיהָ וִיגָרְשֶׁנָּה, וְיֹאמַר: קוֹדֶם זְנוּת שֶׁאַתֶּם מְעִידִים – כְּבָר נִתְגָּרְשָׁה. לִיתְקִין זְמַן. נַמִי בִּשְׁטַר קִידּוּשִׁין, שֶׁמָּא תִּזְנֶה, וְיֹאמַר: קוֹדֶם קִידּוּשִׁין הֲוָה. וְהָא עַבְדָּא. מְכִירַת עֶבֶד. וּתְקוּן רַבָּנַן זְמַן. בְּכָל שְׁטָרֵי מְכִירָה [שֶׁל עֶבֶד, כְּדֵי] לֵידַע מֵאֵיזֶה זְמַן יֹאכַל פֵּירוֹת, (ג) שֶׁזֶּה קָנָה נִכְסֵי עַבְדּוֹ: מָחֲקָה לֵיהּ. (ד) לִזְמַן, וְתֹאמַר: קוֹדֶם קִידּוּשִׁין הָיָה זְנוּת זֶה. לִינְחֵיהּ גַּבֵּי עֵדִים. מַאי מְהַנֵּי? אִי דְּכִירֵי אֵימַת הֲוָה קִידּוּשִׁין – אֲפִי' אֵינוֹ כָּתוּב בַּשְּׁטָר מָצוּ לְאַסְהוֹדֵי! אֶלָּא לְהָכִי אָמְרַתְּ דִּמְהַנֵּי, דְּזִימְנִין דְּלָא דְּכִירֵי וְחָזוּ מִכְּתָבָא וְאָתוּ וּמְסַהֲדֵי – וְהַאי לָאו עֵדוּת הוּא, דְּרַחֲמָנָא אָמַר "עַל פִּי שְׁנַיִם עֵדִים" (דברים יט), וְלֹא שֶׁיָּעִידוּ עַל פִּי כְּתָבָם. גַּבֵּי גֵּירוּשִׁין נַמִי. אַמַּאי תִּקְנוּ זְמַן מִשּׁוּם בַּת אֲחוֹתוֹ. גַּבֵּי מַאן נִינְחֵיהּ? לְהַצָּלָה דִּידָהּ קָאָתֵי. וְלֵיכָּא לְמֵיחַשׁ דִּלְמָא מָחֲקָה לֵיהּ. דְּכִי אָתוּ סַהֲדֵי דְּזִינְּתָה, אִי לָא מַיְיתָא שְׁטָרָא דְּאִיגָּרְשָׁה מִקַּמֵּי הָכִי – מוֹקְמִינַן לָהּ בְּחֶזְקַת אֵשֶׁת אִישׁ. וּמִיהוּ, אִי לָא תְּקוּן רַבָּנַן זְמַן – הֲוָה מָצֵי לְאַחְפּוּיֵי עֲלָהּ, וּמִסְּפֵיקָא לָא קָטְלִינַן לָהּ. אֲבָל הַשְׁתָּא דִּתְקוּן רַבָּנַן, (ה) אִי לָא מַיְיתָא לֵיהּ מוֹקְמִינַן לָהּ אַחֲזָקָה וְקָטְלִינַן לָהּ. הָכָא לְחוֹבָה דִּידָהּ קָאָתֵי. זְמַן דְּקִידּוּשִׁין, וְאִי תְּקוּן לָהּ רַבָּנַן זְמַן וְזִינְּתָה – כָּנְשָׁה לֵיהּ לִשְׁטָרָא, אוֹ מָחֲקָה לֵיהּ, וְקָיְימָא אַחֶזְקַת פְּנוּיָה כִּדְמֵעִיקָּרָא. **מתני'** זִיקַת שְׁנֵי יְבָמִין. דְּכָל זְמַן שֶׁלֹּא כְּנָסָהּ זֶה – עֲדַיִין זִיקַת רִאשׁוֹן עָלֶיהָ, וְנִתּוֹסֶפֶת עָלֶיהָ זִיקַת מַאֲמָרוֹ, הֲרֵי כְּשֶׁמֵּת זֶה – נוֹתְרוּ עֲלָהּ זִיקַת שְׁנֵיהֶם, וְאִילּוּ כְּנָסָהּ – הֲוָה פָּקְעָה זִיקָה דְּקַמָּא, וְכִי מָיֵית – לֹא הֲוָה עֲלָהּ אֶלָּא זִיקַת שֵׁנִי. א"נ לֹא עֲבַד בָּהּ מַאֲמָר לֹא הֲוָה עֲלָהּ אֶלָּא זִיקַת רִאשׁוֹן. מְיַיבֵּם לְאֵיזוֹ שֶׁיִּרְצֶה. כִּדְקָתָנֵי טַעְמָא בְּפֶרֶק שֵׁנִי בְּבָרַיְיתָא: אִם מַאֲמָרוֹ שֶׁל שֵׁנִי מַאֲמָר – אֵשֶׁת שֵׁנִי הוּא בּוֹעֵל, וְאִם אֵינוֹ מַאֲמָר – אֵשֶׁת רִאשׁוֹן הוּא בּוֹעֵל. וְחוֹלֵץ לַשְּׁנִיָּה. דְּחָדָא לֹא מִיפַּטְרָא בְּבִיאָה דְּאִידָךְ, דִּלְמָא מַאֲמָר לֹא קָנֵי, וְהָווּ לְהוּ ב' יְבָמוֹת הַבָּאוֹת מִב' בָּתִּים. וְיַיבּוּמֵי תַּרְוַויְיהוּ נַמִי לֹא – דִּלְמָא מַאֲמָר קָנֵי, וְהָווּ לְהוּ ב' יְבָמוֹת הַבָּאוֹת מִבַּיִת אֶחָד. **גמ'** אִי זִיקַת שְׁנֵי יְבָמִין דְּאוֹרַיְיתָא כו'. לְרַבָּנַן פָּרֵיךְ. אֶלָּא מִדְּרַבָּנַן. דְּמִדְּאוֹרַיְיתָא מַאֲמָר לֹא קָנֵי, וְהָווּ לְהוּ שְׁתֵּי יְבָמוֹת מִב' בָּתִּים, וְתַרְוַויְיהוּ מָצֵי לְיַיבּוּמֵי. וְרַבָּנַן הוּא דִּגְזָרוּ, שֶׁמָּא יֹאמְרוּ: ב' יְבָמוֹת הַבָּאוֹת מִבַּיִת א' – מִתְיַיבְּמוֹת. וּמִקְצָתוֹ

ההיא דגיטין בשתי כיתי עדים! י"ל: דלשון מחאה על מחאה דקתני התם במתני' שייך טפי בשתי כיתי עדים. ובפ"ב דכתובות (דף כו: ד"ה "אנן") ובפ' "חזקת הבתים" (ב"ב לג. ד"ה "אנן") הארכתי. **וארעא** אוקמא בחזקת בר שטיא. לא דמי להההיא דאמר בקידושין (דף עט:) ובבבא בתרא (דף קנג: ושם): אם בריא הוא – עליו להביא ראיה שבשכיב מרע היה, ואם שכיב מרע הוא כו'. דהכא, כיון שדרכו להיות עתים חלים ועתים שוטה – לא שייך להעמידו אחזקה כמו שהוא עתה. **אי** יגיד עליו ריעו מאי זו היא דקתני. הוה מצי למיפרך אי יגיד עליו ריעו (ו) ליתני כולהו בחד וליתני חד מינייהו באידך כדפריך בפרק לא יחפור (ב"ב דף יט.). **למעוטי** זמן דליתיה בקידושין. מספקא לר"י: כתב בכתב ידו ואין עליו עדים, אי מהני בקידושין אי לא? דכיון שאין צריך זמן – מה לנו אם אין עליו עדים? **והא** עבדא דאיכא דקני בכספא כו'. פירש בקונטרס: שטר קניית עבד. וקשה לר"י: דא"כ מ"ש דנקט עבד? דהו"מ למינקט שטר מכירת קרקע, וכל שטרי מקח וממכר! ועוד: דהתם לא תיקון רבנן זמן! ונראה דאשטר שיחרור קאי, דתיקון (ז) זמן לידע מתי נאסר בשפחה והותר בבת ישראל. וה"ק: והא עבדא – איכא דקני נפשיה בכספא ואיכא דקני בשטרא. והשתא ניחא הא דמשני התם רובא וכו'. וא"ת: בפ"ק דגיטין (דף ט.) דתנן: בג' דרכים שוו גיטי נשים לשחרורי עבדים, ליתני נמי זמן, ששוו גיטי נשים לשחרורי עבדים וליתיה בקידושין! וי"ל: דכל מילי דחשיב התם ודפריך התם – הוי חד טעמא בגיטי נשים ושחרורי עבדים, אבל [זמן (ח) דשחרורי עבדים – בא] להתירו בבת ישראל, וגיטי נשים – משום פירי*: **דחזן** בכתבא ואתו ומסהדי כו'. קשה לר"י: דב"הגוזל קמא" (ב"ק דף לח. ושם:), גבי השורף שטרותיו של חבירו, פריך: ואי דאיכא סהדי דידעי – ליכתבו ליה שטרא אחרינא, ואמאי? הא אמר "מפיהם ולא מפי כתבם"! ואר"י: דה"נ, אם היו מעידים שכך ראו בשטר – שפיר הוו עדי, דהרי הם כאילו מעידים: ראינו עדות שנתקבל בב"ד, דעדים החתומים על השטר נעשה כמי שנחקרה עדותן בב"ד. אבל חיישינן שמא לא יעידו שכך ראו בשטר, אלא אתא יעידו על המעשה עצמו כאילו הם זוכרים, והם אינן זוכרין אלא על פי הכתב. וכן הא דאמרינן בפ"ב דכתובות (דף כ.): כותב אדם עדותו על השטר ומעיד עליה אפילו אחר כמה שנים, והוא – שזוכרה מעצמו, אבל אין זוכרה מעצמו – לא. התם נמי לא איירי במעיד שכך ראה כתוב, אלא במעיד על מעשה עצמו. ועוד: דהתם לא הוה שטר, אלא שכותב לזכרון דברים בעלמא, ולא שייך למימר נעשה כמי שנחקרה עדותו בב"ד. ואר"י דשמע מר"ת: שנוהגין עכשיו ששולחין העדים עדותן בכתב ידם לב"ד, ולא קרינן ביה "מפיהם ולא מפי כתבם" כיון שהם זוכרין עדותן. והא דתניא ב"מי שאחזו" (גיטין דף עא.) "ואם לא יגיד" – פרט לאלם, שאין יכול לדבר. ופריך: ואמאי? והרי יכול לדבר מתוך הכתב! שאני עדות, דרחמנא אמר "מפיהם ולא מפי כתבם" – שאני אלם שאין ראוי להגיד, כדאמרינן (מנחות דף קו:): כל שאין ראוי לבילה כו'. אבל אחר – מועיל כתב ידו כשזוכר העדות. ומיהו, בפירוש חומש (דברים יט) פרש"י "ע"פ שנים עדים" – פרט שלא ישלחו כתבם לב"ד א). **להצלה** דידה קאתי. פי' בקונט': דהשתא דתיקון זמן, אי לא מייתא שטרא דאיגרשה מקמי הכי – מוקמינן לה אחזקת אשת איש, וקטלינן לה. ואין נראה, דבהדיא אמר בפ' שני דגיטין (דף יז:): גזייה לזמן ויהביה ניהלה – מה הועילו חכמים בתקנתן? ומשני: לרמאי לא חיישינן. אלמא, כי ליכא זמן – לא קטלינן לה! ואר"י: דה"פ: להצלה דידה קאתי, שהגט בא להצילה ולהגיד שהיא מגורשת, ולכך יראה למחוק הזמן כי סבורה שיפסול בכך וגרע כחו טפי. אבל ודאי, אי הוה מחקת ליה – לא הוה קטלינן לה. הכא לחובה דידה קאתי דהקידושין באין להעיד שהיא מקודשת, ומחקה ליה לעולם לזמן. **שלשה** אחין נשואין ג' נשים נכריות. הו"מ למנקט ואחד מופנה. (ט) **מדרבנן** וגזירה כו'. משמע דאשת ב' מתים בשום מקום לא הויא אלא מדרבנן, דאי לאו גזירה דהכא – היתה מתייבמת אפי' בעלת מאמר

א) [וע"ע תוס' ב"ב לג: ד"ה מחאה וכו']

וגזירה דהכא לא אצטריכא משום בעלת מאמר גופה אלא משום נראה דאי לאו גזירה לא חמירא כל כך לאסור גם את הצרה. והשתא נמי האי דקאמר ר' שמעון אם מאמרו של ראשון מאמר ניחא לטעמייהו משום אשת שני מתים:

לא מסרוהו עד שעת העמדה בדין ולא עוד אלא שאומרין לו תנו לו שטרו ויתקיים בב"ד
שטר הזה ראוי למוסרו לידו דלמא מחקא ליה לזמן הלכך ה"ל ההיא שעתא בעדות על
בעיא מפיהם ולא מפי כתבם וההיא שמעתתא דכתובות לא מיפרשא כהאי ענינא

כדפרי' התם וכן עקר בפ' שנים אוחזין כתבתי דעת ר' יעקב ז"ל בענין מפיהם. הא דאמר רבא נתן גט למאמרו הותרה צרתה ואיכא דאמר הותרה אפילו היא א) דוקא ליה ולא לזיקתו והכי איתא

א) נ"ל דוקא דנתן גט למאמרו ולא לזיקתו.

הגהות הב"ח

(א) גמ' גבי עדים אי דכירי ליתו: (ב) שם במשנה אחד מהם יבמה יבא עליה מי שעליה: (ג) רש"י ד"ה ותקון רבנן וכו' מכירה של עבד כדי לידע מאיזה זמן יאכל פירות שדה ויקנה נכסי עבדו: (ד) ד"ה מחקה ליה אם תזנה מחקה ליה לזמן ותאמר: (ה) ד"ה להצלה וכו' דתקון רבנן זמן אי לא: (ו) תוס' ד"ה אי יגיד וכו' ליתנינהו לכולהו בחדא וליתני חדא מינייהו באידך והוא הדין לאידך כדפריך בפ' לא יחפור: (ז) ד"ה והא וכו' דתקון רבנן זמן לידע וכו' עבדא דאיכא דקני וכו' דקני נפשא בשטרא וכו' התם רובא בשטרא וא"ת: (ח) בא"ד אבל זמן לאו חד טעמא דשיחרורי עבדים להתירו בבת ישראל. נ"ב ועיין בתוס' בד"ה מפני מה תקנו זמן בגיטין כתבו לתקון זמן בגט שיחרור דחיישינן שמא ימכור אותו ואח"כ יתן לו והיינו טעמא דמשום פירי ועיין בפ"ק דגיטין דף י' בתוס' ד"ה כי סקסקו קושיא זו דליתני נמי זמן ותירצו מדרבנן כו' לא הויא. נ"ב עיין לעיל בדף יו"ד בד"ה לעולה:

גמרא

וּמִקְצָתוֹ חָלוּץ. — וְיֹאמְרוּ! — אִי דִּמְיַיבֵּם וַהֲדַר — חָלֵיץ הָכִי נַמִי, אֶלָּא גְּזֵירָה *דִּילְמָא חָלֵיץ בְּרֵישָׁא וַהֲדַר מְיַיבֵּם, וְקָם לֵיהּ בְּ"אֲשֶׁר לֹא יִבְנֶה", וְרַחֲמָנָא אָמַר: *כֵּיוָן שֶׁלֹּא בָּנָה — שׁוּב לֹא יִבְנֶה. *אֲמַר רָבָא: נָתַן גֵּט לְמַאֲמָרוֹ — הוּתְּרָה צָרָתָהּ, אֲבָל הִיא אֲסוּרָה, דְּמִחַלְפָא בְּבַעֲלַת גֵּט. [א]אִיכָּא דְּאָמְרִי, אֲמַר רָבָא: נָתַן גֵּט לְמַאֲמָרוֹ — הוּתְּרָה אֲפִי' הִיא, מַאי טַעְמָא? מַאי דַּעֲבַד בָּהּ — שַׁקְלֵיהּ.§

מתני' *[ב]שְׁנֵי אַחִין נְשׂוּאִין שְׁתֵּי אֲחָיוֹת, וּמֵת אֶחָד מֵהֶן, וְאַחַר כָּךְ מֵתָה אִשְׁתּוֹ שֶׁל שֵׁנִי — הֲרֵי זוֹ אֲסוּרָה עָלָיו עוֹלָמִית, הוֹאִיל וְנֶאֶסְרָה עָלָיו שָׁעָה אַחַת.§ **גמ'** פְּשִׁיטָא! הָשְׁתָּא, וּמַה הָתָם דְּלָא מִידַּחְיָא מֵהַאי בֵּיתָא לְגַמְרֵי — אָמְרַתְּ לָא, הָכָא דְּקָא מִידַּחְיָא מֵהַאי בֵּיתָא לְגַמְרֵי — לֹא כ"שׁ?! — תָּנָא הָא תָּנָא בְּרֵישָׁא, וְהַךְ חָזְיָא לְהֶיתֵּירָא (א) וְשָׁרְיָא, וַהֲדַר חָזְיָא לְאִיסּוּרָא. וְאַיְּידֵי *דַּחֲבִיבָה לֵיהּ — אַקְדְּמַהּ, *וּמִשְׁנָה לֹא זָזָה מִמְּקוֹמָהּ. ת"ר: בָּא עָלֶיהָ — חַיָּיב עָלֶיהָ מִשּׁוּם אֵשֶׁת אָח, וּמִשּׁוּם אֲחוֹת אִשָּׁה, דִּבְרֵי רַבִּי יוֹסֵי. רַבִּי שִׁמְעוֹן אוֹמֵר: אֵינוֹ חַיָּיב אֶלָּא מִשּׁוּם אֵשֶׁת אָח בִּלְבַד. וְהָא תַּנְיָא, ר"ש אוֹמֵר: אֵינוֹ חַיָּיב אֶלָּא מִשּׁוּם אֲחוֹת אִשָּׁה בִּלְבַד! — לָא קַשְׁיָא: כָּאן — שֶׁנָּשָׂא חַי וְאח"כ נָשָׂא מֵת, כָּאן — שֶׁנָּשָׂא מֵת וְאח"כ נָשָׂא חַי. ° וְרַ' שִׁמְעוֹן, הֵיכָא דְּנָשָׂא מֵת וְאח"כ נָשָׂא חַי, כֵּיוָן דְּאִיסּוּר אֲחוֹת אִשָּׁה לָא חָיֵיל — תִּתְיַיבֵּם יַבּוֹמֵי! אֲמַר רַב אַשִׁי: אִיסּוּר אֲחוֹת אִשָּׁה מִיתְלָא תָּלֵי וְקָאֵי, אִי פָּקַע אִיסּוּר אֵשֶׁת אָח — אָתֵי אִיסּוּר אֲחוֹת אִשָּׁה וְחָיֵיל, וְהִילְכָּךְ לָא פָּקַע. — וְסָבַר רַבִּי יוֹסֵי אִיסּוּר חָל עַל אִיסּוּר? וְהָא תַּנְיָא: *[ג]עָבַר עֲבֵירָה שֶׁיֵּשׁ בָּהּ שְׁתֵּי מִיתוֹת — נִידּוֹן בַּחֲמוּרָה, רַבִּי יוֹסֵי אוֹמֵר: נִידּוֹן בַּזִּיקָה הָרִאשׁוֹנָה הַבָּאָה עָלָיו. וְתַנְיָא: *כֵּיצַד אָמַר רַבִּי יוֹסֵי נִידּוֹן בַּזִּיקָה הָרִאשׁוֹנָה הַבָּאָה עָלָיו? חֲמוֹתוֹ וְנַעֲשֵׂית אֵשֶׁת אִישׁ — נִידּוֹן בַּחֲמוֹתוֹ, אֵשֶׁת אִישׁ וְנַעֲשֵׂית חֲמוֹתוֹ — נִידּוֹן בְּאֵשֶׁת אִישׁ. אָמַר

רש"י

וּמִקְצָתוֹ חָלוּץ. וְאָתֵי לְמֵימַר בְּב' יְבָמוֹת הַבָּאוֹת מִבַּיִת אֶחָד: חֲדָא מִתְיַיבֶּמֶת וַאֲחֶרֶת חָלְצָה. נָתַן גֵּט לְמַאֲמָרוֹ. אַמַּתְנִיתִין קָאֵי, שֶׁאִם נָתַן זֶה הָעוֹשֶׂה מַאֲמָר גֵּט לְמַאֲמָרוֹ, וְלֹא לְזִיקָתוֹ, וְאח"כ מֵת — הוּתְּרָה אִשְׁתּוֹ הָרִאשׁוֹנָה, שֶׁהִיא צָרָתָהּ, לְהִתְיַיבֵּם לַשְּׁלִישִׁי, דְּמַאֲמָר דַּעֲבַד — שַׁקְלֵיהּ, וְלָאו צָרוֹת נִינְהוּ. וְהָשְׁתָּא לָא אָתֵי לְמֵימַר בִּשְׁתֵּי יְבָמוֹת מִבַּיִת אֶחָד חֲדָא חָלְצָה וַחֲדָא מִיַּיבְּמָא, דְּהָכָא לָאו מִבַּיִת אֶחָד מִיחֲזֵי. אֲבָל הִיא אֲסוּרָה. וְלָא מִשּׁוּם דְּקָם לֵיהּ בְּ"לֹא יִבְנֶה" דְּפוֹסְלָהּ עַל אָחִיו הַנִּשְׁאָר, שֶׁהֲרֵי לֹא נָתַן גֵּט לַזִּיקָה, אֶלָּא מִשּׁוּם דְּאָתֵי לְאִיחְלוּפֵי בְּבַעֲלַת הַגֵּט, הֵיכָא דַּעֲבַד גֵּט לְמַאֲמָרוֹ וּלְזִיקָתוֹ, דְּהַהִיא וַדַּאי מִידַּחְיָא, אֲבָל גֵּט לְמַאֲמָרוֹ — לָא דָּחֵי אֶלָּא מַאֲמָר, וְנִשְׁאֲרָה זִיקָה רִאשׁוֹנָה בִּמְקוֹמָהּ. הוּתְּרָה אֲפִילוּ הִיא. לַשְּׁלִישִׁי, כְּשֶׁיָּמוּת שֵׁנִי. מַאי דַּעֲבַד שַׁקְלֵיהּ. וַהֲוָיָא כְּמוֹ שֶׁלֹּא עָשָׂה בָּהּ מַאֲמָר, וְאָתְיָא וּמִתְיַיבֶּמֶת לַשְּׁלִישִׁי מֵחֲמַת זִיקַת אָחִיו הָרִאשׁוֹן. וְדַוְקָא שֶׁפֵּירֵשׁ לְמַאֲמָרוֹ וְלֹא לְזִיקָתוֹ קָאָמַר, אֲבָל סְתָמָא — קַיְימָא בְּ"לֹא יִבְנֶה" אַכּוּלְּהוּ אַחִין. וְהָכִי מוֹכְחָא מִילְּתָא דְּרָבָא בְּפֶרֶק "רַבָּן גַּמְלִיאֵל" (לקמן ד' נג:) דִּלְמַאֲמָרוֹ וְלֹא לְזִיקָתוֹ קָאָמַר. פְּשִׁיטָא הָשְׁתָּא וּמַה הָתָם דְּלָא אִידַּחְיָא מֵהַאי בֵּיתָא. לְעֵיל (דף ל.), גַּבֵּי שְׁלֹשָׁה אַחִים, שְׁנַיִם מֵהֶם נְשׂוּאִים שְׁתֵּי אֲחָיוֹת וְאֶחָד נָשָׂא נָכְרִית, וּמֵת אֶחָד מִבַּעֲלֵי אֲחָיוֹת, וְכָנַס נְשׂוּי נָכְרִית אֶת אִשְׁתּוֹ, וּמֵתָה אִשְׁתּוֹ שֶׁל שֵׁנִי, וְאח"כ מֵת נְשׂוּי נָכְרִית — הֲרֵי זוֹ אֲסוּרָה עָלָיו עוֹלָמִית מִשּׁוּם אֵשֶׁת אָח, הוֹאִיל וְנֶאֶסְרָה עָלָיו שָׁעָה אַחַת בִּנְפִילָה רִאשׁוֹנָה מִשּׁוּם אֲחוֹת אִשָּׁה. וְאע"ג דְּבְהַהִיא נְפִילָה קַמַּיְיתָא לֹא אִידַּחְיָא לָהּ לְגַמְרֵי, דְּהָא קָאֵי נְשׂוּי נָכְרִית שֶׁזּוֹקְקָהּ לְיִיבּוּם, וְקוֹרֵא אֲנִי בָּהּ בִּשְׁעַת נְפִילָה "יְבָמָהּ יָבֹא עָלֶיהָ" — אֲפִי' הָכִי חָשְׁבִינַן לָהּ לְגַבֵּי בַּעַל אֲחוֹתָהּ כְּאֵשֶׁת אָח שֶׁיֵּשׁ לָהּ בָּנִים לְאִיתַּסּוּרֵי עֲלֵיהּ אֲפִילוּ לְאַחַר מִיתַת אֲחוֹתָהּ. הָכָא. דְּבִשְׁעַת נְפִילָה אִידַּחְיָא מֵהַאי בֵּיתָא לְגַמְרֵי, דְּאֵין כָּאן אֶלָּא בַּעַל אֲחוֹתָהּ, וּמִשָּׁעָה שֶׁנָּפְלָה לְפָנָיו אֵין זִיקַת יִבּוּם עָלֶיהָ — מִיבַּעְיָא?! תַּנָּא הָא. מַתְנִי' דְּהָכָא תָּנָא בְּרֵישָׁא. וְהָךְ. דִּשְׁלֹשָׁה אַחִים, דְּלָא אִידַּחְיָא מֵהַאי בֵּיתָא לְגַמְרֵי, חַזְיָא מֵעִיקָּרָא לְהֶיתֵּרָא, וְשַׁרְיָא, [מִשּׁוּם הָכִי לָא תַּנְיָא]. הֲדַר חָזְיָא לְאִיסּוּרָא. דְּמ"מ לְדִידָהּ לָא קָרֵינָא בֵּיהּ מִשְּׁעַת נְפִילָה "יְבָמָהּ יָבֹא עָלֶיהָ". דַּחֲבִיבָה לֵיהּ. מִשּׁוּם דְּאִידּוּשׁ הוּא. וּמִשְׁנָה הָרִאשׁוֹנָה. שֶׁיְּתֵירָה הִיא מִשֶּׁנִּשְׁנֵית זוֹ, הוֹאִיל וְהָיְתָה שְׁנוּיָה מִתְּחִלָּה. לֹא זָזָה מִמְּקוֹמָהּ. לְעוֹקְרָהּ לְגַמְרֵי. בָּא עָלֶיהָ. בְּחַיֵּי אִשְׁתּוֹ. מִשּׁוּם אֵשֶׁת אָח. דְּהָא רַחֲמָנָא פְּטָרָהּ מִיִּיבּוּם, וְקָמָה עֲלֵיהּ כְּמִי שֶׁיֵּשׁ לוֹ בָּנִים. אֶלָּא מִשּׁוּם אֵשֶׁת אָח. כִּדְמוֹקֵי טַעְמָא לְקַמָּן. בְּנָשָׂא מֵת וְאח"כ נָשָׂא חַי. דְּאִיסּוּר אֵשֶׁת אָח קָדֵים, וְתוּ לָא אָתֵי אִיסּוּר אֲחוֹת אִשָּׁה וְחָיֵיל עֲלָהּ, דְּקָסָבַר: אֵין אִיסּוּר חָל עַל אִיסּוּר. נָשָׂא חַי וְאח"כ נָשָׂא מֵת. אִיסּוּר אֲחוֹת אִשָּׁה קָדֵים, דְּקוֹדֶם שֶׁנְּשָׂאָהּ אָחִיו הַמֵּת הָיְתָה עוֹמֶדֶת עָלָיו בְּאִיסּוּר אֲחוֹת אִשָּׁה. מִיתְלָא תָּלֵי. דְּאִי הֲוָה פָּקַע אִיסּוּר אֵשֶׁת אָח — הֲוָה חָיֵיל אִיסּוּר אֲחוֹת אִשָּׁה. דְּהַאי דְּלָא חָיֵיל מֵעִיקָּרָא — מִשּׁוּם טַעְמָא דְּאִיסּוּר אֵשֶׁת אָח דַּהֲוָה קָאֵי קַמֵּיהּ. הִלְכָּךְ, הוֹאִיל וְאִיסּוּר אֲחוֹת אִשָּׁה מוּכָן וְעוֹמֵד לָחוּל עָלֶיהָ פְּטוּרָה מִן(ב) הַיִּבּוּם — לֹא פָּקַע אִיסּוּר אֵשֶׁת אָח, וְחַיָּיב מִשּׁוּם אֵשֶׁת אָח. שְׁתֵּי מִיתוֹת. כְּגוֹן חֲמוֹתוֹ וְהִיא אֵשֶׁת אִישׁ, דַּחֲמוֹתוֹ שְׂרֵיפָה וְאֵשֶׁת אִישׁ חֶנֶק. נִידּוֹן בַּחֲמוּרָה. בִּשְׂרֵיפָה. חֲמוֹתוֹ וְנַעֲשֵׂית אֵשֶׁת אִישׁ. שֶׁהָיְתָה אַלְמָנָה כְּשֶׁנָּשָׂא בִּתָּהּ. נִידּוֹן בְּאֵשֶׁת אִישׁ. וְאע"ג דְּקִיל הוּא. אַלְמָא: לָא אָתֵי אִיסּוּר חֲמוֹתוֹ וְחָיֵיל אַאֵשֶׁת אִישׁ, דְּאִי חָיְילִי תַּרְוַויְיהוּ עֲלֵיהּ — הֲוָה לָן לְמִדַּיְינֵיהּ בַּחֲמוּרָה. אָמַר

תוספות

מאמר ולא גזרינן לה אטו אשת שני מתים, וא"כ מי שעליה זיקת יבם אחד כו' לא הויא דרשא גמורה אלא אסמכתא בעלמא. וקשה: דבפרק בתרא דגיטין (דף פב: ושם) אמרי': אלא אשת ב' מתים היכי משכחת לה? משמע דהוי דאורייתא, ואפי' בחד דוכתא! וי"ל: דפלוגתא דתנאי היא, כדמוכח לקמן בסוף "האשה רבה" (דף לו:) גבי בן תשע שבא על יבמתו, ומשהגדיל נשא אשה אחרת, ומת, השניה חולצת או מתייבמת, הראשונה שהיא בעלת זיקת שני יבמין — חולצת ולא מתייבמת. ופריך בגמרא: ויעשו ביאת בן תשע כמאמר בגדול ותדחה צרה מיבום. פירוש: כי הכא! ומסיק לרבי יוחנן דעשו ועשו, ופליג תנא דשמעתין אההוא תנא, דהאי תנא דשמעתין גזר משום צרה. פירוש: הא דקא אסר בעלת מאמר משום דאיכא צרה בהדה, כדגזר בשמעתין דלמא חליץ והדר מייבם, כדפירש בקונטרס. אבל משום זיקת שני יבמין — לא מיתסרא, דלאו דאורייתא. ומיהו, כי ליכא צרה בהדה — נמי אסורה אטו היכא דאיכא צרה, כדקאמר התם רבא לעיל, דאפי' היכא דליכא צרה בהדה — מיחלץ חלצה, יבומי לא מייבמא. ותנא דהתם לא גזר משום צרה, פי': הא דקא אסר לבעלת ביאת בן תשע לייבומי — לאו משום צרה, אלא אטו אשת שני מתים, דהוי בעלמא דאורייתא. ודוקא בדידה גזרו, אבל בצרתה לא, דלא רצו להחמיר גם בצרתה אטו אשת שני מתים. וההיא דריש "המגרש" (גיטין פב:) כההוא תנא. וריב"ן פירש שם: דלכולי עלמא אשת שני מתים דאורייתא, ותנא דהכא גזר אף באשת השני משום צרה — דהיינו בעלת מאמר, דקא סבר כיון דבעלמא אשת שני מתים דאורייתא — מחמירי אפי' באידך. ותנא דהתם לא מחמיר כולי האי, ולא גזר באשתו של בן תשע אטו בעלת זיקת שני יבמים. וקשה: דהכא מסיק דטעמא דהך תנא משום הנך גזירות דמפרש הכא! ועוד: דהתם(ג) קרי רבא לאשתו צרה, וקאמר נמי ויעשו ביאת בן תשע כמאמר בגדול ותדחה צרה כו', והכא קרי לבעלת מאמר צרה! וריב"ן הקשה לעצמו שתי קושיות הללו. ופר"י עיקר.

גט למאמרו כו'. הקשה ריב"ן: דתנן בפר"ג (לקמן דף נ.) דיש מאמר אחר מאמר, ואם עשה מאמר בזו ובזו — צריכה ב' גיטין וחליצה, בין יבם אחד לב' יבמות בין ב' יבמין ליבמה אחת, אבל יבומי חד מינייהו — לא, ולרבא, יתן גט למאמרו ולא לזיקתו, וליבומי אידך! ותירץ: דלכתחלה אין לעשות כן, דגזרינן גט למאמרו אטו גט לזיקתו, ודוקא בדיעבד קאמר הכא רבא דהותרה אפי' היא, דכיון דתו ליכא למיגזר בהאי מאמר אטו שאר מאמרות דעלמא — לא גזרינן, דלא שכיחי כולי האי. אבל לכתחלה — גזרינן משום האי מאמר גופיה.

דאידחיא מהאי ביתא לגמרי לא כ"ש. אע"ג דמהאי בבא שמעינן דאסירא, אע"ג דאיחזיא בהך נפילה, דלא שמעינן מבבא דלעיל, כדאמר לעיל (דף ל.) — מ"מ, כיון דאידחיא מהאי ביתא לגמרי פשיטא דאסירא, אע"ג דחזיא בהא נפילה. ולעיל דקאמר טעמא דאיחזיא בהך נפילה (אהאי מתניתין) — משום דאכתי לא אסיק אדעתיה טעמא דאידחיא מהאי ביתא.

שנשא חי ואח"כ נשא מת.(ד) אע"ג דבכי האי גוונא שרו ב"ש צרה לייבומי, לעיל בפ"ק (דף ח.) דכיון דלא חייל איסור אשת אח — חשבי שלא במקום מצוה, ר"ש לית ליה האי סברא, דמכל מקום הרי היא אשת אחיו. **לא** פקע. ואע"ג דלא חייל איסור אחות אשה — אסורה נמי הצרה לייבומי, כיון דלא פקע איסור אשת אח, כמו אילונית דאוסרת צרתה אע"ג דאין בה אלא איסור אשת אח לחודה. וא"ת: לר"ש משכחת לה אשת אח מן האב דפוטרת צרתה, וליחשבה בהדי ט"ו נשים בפ"ק (דף ב. ודף י.) למ"ד בפלוגתא קא מיירי! וכן האי דלעיל דקתני נאסרה עליו עולמית גם היא פוטרת צרתה — וליחשבה! וי"ל: דהני, כיון דמכח אחות אשה אסירא — בכלל אחות אשה נינהו. **ונעשית** אשת איש נידון בחמותו. ואין זה מכח זיקה ראשונה, דבלאו הכי מי שנתחייב ב' מיתות נידון בחמורה. איסור

עין משפט נר מצוה

לד א מיי' פ"ו מהלכות יבום הלכה כט טוש"ע אה"ע סימן קעד סעיף ה:
לה ב מיי' פ"ו שם הל' יב טוש"ע אה"ע סימן קעה סעיף א:
לו ג מיי' פי"ד מהל' סנהדרין הלכה ז:

תוספות ישנים

נתן גט למאמרו הותרה אפילו היא ולא הוי גרושת אחיו כיון שלא נתן גט אלא להפקיע המאמר ומאמר דעבד שקליה ונמצא כאילו לא היתה אשתו מעולם. ודוקא שפירש שנתן גט למאמרו אבל נתן גט סתם אסור ליבמה דכיון שלא בנה שוב לא יבנה. תימה דאמרינן לקמן ובשתי יבמות שנפלו לפני יבם אחד ועשה מאמר בזו ומאמר בזו נותן גט לזו וגט לזו וחליצה אחת לכולן א"כ משמע דלא מצי לייבמה אחר הגט ואמאי לא אמרינן מה דעבד שקליה. וי"ל דלקמן מיירי שנתן הגט סתם ולא פירש למאמרו דלכתחלה לא אמרינן ליה לתת גט להפקיע המאמר. ותימה אמאי לא גזרינן שמא לא יפרש להפקיע המאמר כדאמרינן דמחלפא בבעלת הגט. ונראה להריב"ן דדוקא שנפלו שתי יבמות גזרינן אפילו פירש שהגט להפקיע בעלת המאמר אטו האחרת שיתן לה סתם. אבל הכא דליכא אלא יבמה אחת היכא שפירש בדיעבד שהגט להפקיע המאמר הותרה לייבם. ולא גזרינן מידי כיון דליכא אחרת בהדה: **כיצד** א"ר יוסי נדון בזיקה (שניה) [הראשונה] הבאה עליו חמותו וכו' ומייתי מהא דקאמר אשת איש ונעשית חמותו נדון באשת איש דהאי איסור לא חל על איסור שהרי נידון בחמותו אבל לא מייתי מחמותו ונעשית אשת איש דלאפי' נידון בחמותו דהכא בתרי קטלי לא קטלינן ליה וא"כ נידון בחמותו.

[לקמן מד.] [לעיל י:] [לעיל ל.] [לעיל ב: וש"נ] לקמן נב: [לעיל ל. וש"נ]

הגהות הב"ח

(א) גמ' חזיא להתירא ושריא נ"ב ס"א ושיירא: (ב) רש"י ד"ה מיתלא וכו' מן היבום ולא פקע: (ג) תד"ה (בעמוד הקודם) מדרבנן וגזרה כו' ועוד דהתם לעיל מינה קרי רבא: (ד) ד"ה שנשא וכו' ואע"ג דבכי וכו' לעיל בפ"ק משום דכיון וכו' חשבי לה שלא במקום:

סנהדרין פא. כריתות יד: [תוספתא סנהדרין פי"ב]

כריתות יד:

גליון הש"ס

גמ' ור"ש היכא דנשא מת. עיין בספר המקנה לקידושין דף עז ע"ב בתוס' ד"ה פרט לכ"ג:

עין משפט נר מצוה

לז א מיי' פי"ז מהל' איסורי ביאה הלכה ח ופ"ד מהלכות שגגות הלכה א:

לח ב ג מיי' פ"ט מהלכות ביאת מקדש הל' יב:

לט ד מיי' פי"א מהלכו' מעשה קרבנות הל' ט סמג לאוין שכו:

אָמַר רַ' אַבָּהוּ: מוֹדֶה רַ' יוֹסֵי [א]בְּאִיסּוּר מוֹסִיף. תֵּינַח – הֵיכָא דְּנָשָׂא חַי וְאח"כ נָשָׂא מֵת, מִגּוֹ דְּאִתּוֹסַף אִיסּוּר לְגַבֵּי אַחִים – אִתּוֹסַף אִיסּוּר לְגַבֵּי דִּידֵיהּ. אֶלָּא, הֵיכָא דְּנָשָׂא מֵת וְאח"כ נָשָׂא חַי, מַאי אִיסּוּר מוֹסִיף אִיכָּא? וְכ"ת: מִגּוֹ דְּאִיתַּסַּר בְּכוּלְּהוּ אַחְוָותָא – הַאי אִיסּוּר כּוֹלֵל הוּא! אֶלָּא אָמַר רָבָא: מַעֲלֶה אֲנִי עָלָיו כְּאִילּוּ עָשָׂה שְׁתַּיִם, וְאֵינוֹ חַיָּיב אֶלָּא אַחַת. וְכֵן כִּי אֲתָא רָבִין א"ר יוֹחָנָן: מַעֲלֶה אֲנִי עָלָיו כְּאִילּוּ עָשָׂה ב', וְאֵינוֹ חַיָּיב אֶלָּא אַחַת. מַאי נָפְקָא מִינַּהּ? – *לְקָבְרוֹ בֵּין רְשָׁעִים גְּמוּרִים. וּבִפְלוּגְתָּא, דְּאִיתְּמַר: זָר שֶׁשִּׁימֵּשׁ בְּשַׁבָּת, רַבִּי חִיָּיא אוֹמֵר: [ב]חַיָּיב שְׁתַּיִם, בַּר קַפָּרָא אוֹמֵר: אֵין חַיָּיב אֶלָּא אַחַת. *קָפַץ רַבִּי חִיָּיא וְנִשְׁבַּע: הָעֲבוֹדָה! כָּךְ שָׁמַעְתִּי מֵרַבִּי: שְׁתַּיִם. קָפַץ בַּר קַפָּרָא וְנִשְׁבַּע: הָעֲבוֹדָה! כָּךְ שָׁמַעְתִּי מֵרַבִּי: אַחַת. הִתְחִיל רַבִּי חִיָּיא לָדוּן: שַׁבָּת לַכֹּל נֶאֶסְרָה, כְּשֶׁהוּתְּרָה בַּמִּקְדָּשׁ – אֵצֶל כֹּהֲנִים הוּתְּרָה, לְכֹהֲנִים הוּתְּרָה וְלֹא לְזָרִים, יֵשׁ כָּאן מִשּׁוּם זָרוּת, וְיֵשׁ כָּאן מִשּׁוּם שַׁבָּת. הִתְחִיל בַּר קַפָּרָא לָדוּן: שַׁבָּת לַכֹּל נֶאֶסְרָה, כְּשֶׁהוּתְּרָה – בַּמִּקְדָּשׁ הוּתְּרָה, אֵין כָּאן אֶלָּא זָרוּת. בַּעַל מוּם שֶׁשִּׁימֵּשׁ בְּטוּמְאָה, רַבִּי חִיָּיא אוֹמֵר: [ג]חַיָּיב שְׁתַּיִם, בַּר קַפָּרָא אוֹמֵר: אֵין חַיָּיב אֶלָּא אַחַת. קָפַץ רַ' חִיָּיא וְנִשְׁבַּע: הָעֲבוֹדָה! כָּךְ שָׁמַעְתִּי מֵרַבִּי: שְׁתַּיִם, קָפַץ בַּר קַפָּרָא וְנִשְׁבַּע: הָעֲבוֹדָה! כָּךְ שָׁמַעְתִּי מֵרַבִּי: אַחַת. הִתְחִיל ר"ח לָדוּן: טוּמְאָה לַכֹּל נֶאֶסְרָה, כְּשֶׁהוּתְּרָה בַּמִּקְדָּשׁ – אֵצֶל כֹּהֲנִים תְּמִימִים הוּתְּרָה, לְכֹהֲנִים תְּמִימִים הוּתְּרָה וְלֹא לְבַעֲלֵי מוּמִין, יֵשׁ כָּאן מִשּׁוּם בַּעֲלֵי מוּמִין, וְיֵשׁ כָּאן מִשּׁוּם טוּמְאָה. הִתְחִיל בַּר קַפָּרָא לָדוּן: טוּמְאָה לַכֹּל נֶאֶסְרָה, כְּשֶׁהוּתְּרָה בַּמִּקְדָּשׁ – הוּתְּרָה, אֵין כָּאן אֶלָּא מִשּׁוּם בַּעַל מוּם, זָר שֶׁאָכַל מְלִיקָה, רַ' חִיָּיא אוֹמֵר: [ד]חַיָּיב שְׁתַּיִם, בַּר קַפָּרָא אוֹמֵר: אֵין חַיָּיב אֶלָּא אַחַת. קָפַץ רַבִּי חִיָּיא וְנִשְׁבַּע: הָעֲבוֹדָה! כָּךְ שָׁמַעְתִּי מֵרַבִּי: שְׁתַּיִם. קָפַץ בַּר קַפָּרָא וְנִשְׁבַּע: הָעֲבוֹדָה! כָּךְ שָׁמַעְתִּי מֵרַבִּי: אַחַת. הִתְחִיל רַבִּי חִיָּיא לָדוּן: נְבֵלָה לַכֹּל נֶאֶסְרָה, כְּשֶׁהוּתְּרָה בַּמִּקְדָּשׁ – אֵצֶל כֹּהֲנִים הוּתְּרָה, לְכֹהֲנִים הוּתְּרָה וְלֹא לְזָרִים. יֵשׁ כָּאן מִשּׁוּם זָרוּת, וְיֵשׁ כָּאן מִשּׁוּם מְלִיקָה. הִתְחִיל בַּר קַפָּרָא לָדוּן: נְבֵלָה לַכֹּל נֶאֶסְרָה, כְּשֶׁהוּתְּרָה בַּמִּקְדָּשׁ – הוּתְּרָה, אֵין כָּאן אֶלָּא מִשּׁוּם זָרוּת

בְּמַאי

רש"י

אָמַר רַבִּי אַבָּהוּ מוֹדֶה ר' יוֹסֵי בְּאִיסּוּר מוֹסִיף. שֶׁהוּא חָל עַל אִיסּוּר, כְּגוֹן אִיסּוּר אֵשֶׁת אָח, דְּמוֹסִיף הוּא; שֶׁבַּתְּחִלָּה כְּשֶׁנָּשָׂא זֶה אֶת אֲחוֹתָהּ, וְזוֹ פְּנוּיָה, נֶאֶסְרָה עָלָיו מִשּׁוּם אֲחוֹת אִשָּׁה, וּמוּתֶּרֶת לְכָל אֶחָיו. נִשֵּׂאת לְאֶחָד מֵהֶן – נֶאֶסְרָה עַל כּוּלָּן מִשּׁוּם אֵשֶׁת אָח, וְעַכְשָׁיו נִיתּוֹסֵף אִיסּוּר עָלֶיהָ לְגַבֵּי שְׁאָר אֶחָיו, וּמִגּוֹ דְּחָיֵיל שֵׁם אֵשֶׁת אָח עֲלָהּ לְגַבֵּי שְׁאָר אֶחָיו שֶׁהָיְתָה מוּתֶּרֶת לָהֶם – חָל נַמִּי הַשֵּׁם הַזֶּה לְגַבֵּי דִּידֵיהּ, וְאַע"ג דַּאֲסִירָא עֲלֵיהּ וְקָיְימָא. אֲבָל אֵשֶׁת אִישׁ וְנַעֲשֵׂית חֲמוֹתוֹ, מִתְּחִלָּה הָיְתָה אֲסוּרָה לְכָל הָעוֹלָם מִשּׁוּם אֵשֶׁת אִישׁ, נָשָׂא זֶה אֶת בִּתָּהּ – אֵין אִיסּוּר זֶה רָאוּי לְהוֹסִיף עָלֶיהָ עִם אֲחֵרִים, דְּנֵימָא מִגּוֹ דְּחָיֵיל עֲלַיְיהוּ לֵיחוּל נַמִּי עָלֵיהּ דְּהַאי. דַּחֲמוֹתוֹ וְנַעֲשֵׂית אֵשֶׁת אִישׁ (א) וַדַּאי אִיסּוּר מוֹסִיף הוּא, שֶׁמִּתְּחִלָּה אֲסוּרָה לָזֶה וּמוּתֶּרֶת לְכָל הָעוֹלָם; נַעֲשֵׂית אֵשֶׁת אִישׁ – אִיתּוֹסַף הַאי שֵׁם עֲלָהּ לְגַבֵּי כ"ע, וּמִגּוֹ דְּחָיֵיל עֲלַיְיהוּ חָיֵיל נַמִּי לְגַבֵּי דְּהַאי. וְהַאי דְּקָאָמַר רַבִּי יוֹסֵי נִידּוֹן בַּחֲמוֹתוֹ – מִשּׁוּם דִּבְמִיתוֹת עָסְקִינַן, וְאִי אַתָּה יָכוֹל לַהֲמִיתוֹ בְּב' מִיתוֹת, הוֹאִיל וּשְׁתֵּיהֶן עָלָיו – יִדּוֹן בַּחֲמוּרָה. אֲבָל אִם הָיָה שׁוֹגֵג – הָיָה חַיָּיב ב' חַטָּאוֹת. תֵּינַח **נָשָׂא חַי**. דַּאֲחוֹת אִשָּׁה קָדֵים, וְאח"כ נָשָׂא מֵת, אָתֵי אִיסּוּר אֵשֶׁת אָח חָיֵיל, כִּדְפָרִישִׁית: מִגּוֹ דְּאִיתּוֹסַף אִיסּוּרָא דְּהַאי שֵׁם לְגַבֵּי אֶחָיו כו'. **אֶלָּא הֵיכָא דְּנָשָׂא מֵת**. דְּאִיסּוּר אֵשֶׁת אָח קָדֵים עֲלֵיהּ דְּהַאי, וְאח"כ נָשָׂא אֲחוֹתָהּ, מַאי תּוֹסֶפֶת אִיכָּא עֲלָהּ דְּקַמַּיְיתָא לְגַבֵּי אַחֲרִינֵי דְּנֵימָא מִגּוֹ? וְכִי תֵּימָא **מִגּוֹ**. דִּבְהָנָךְ נִישּׂוּאִין דְּבַתְרַיְיתָא מִתְּסַר הַאי גַּבְרָא בְּכוּלְּהוּ אַחְוָותָא מִשּׁוּם אֲחוֹת אִשָּׁה דְּעַד הָשְׁתָּא הֲווּ שַׁרְיָין לֵיהּ, אִיתְּסַר נַמִּי מִשּׁוּם הַאי שְׁמָא גּוּפֵיהּ עֲלָהּ דְּקַמַּיְיתָא, שֶׁהִיא אֵשֶׁת אָחִיו. הַאי לָאו אִיסּוּר מוֹסִיף הוּא, דְּהָא עֲלָהּ דְּקַמַּיְיתָא לָא אִיתּוֹסַף אִיסּוּר לְגַבֵּי אַחֲרִינָא, אֶלָּא אִיסּוּר כּוֹלֵל הוּא, דְּכָיֵיל לָהּ לְקַמַּיְיתָא בְּשֵׁם אֲחוֹת אִשָּׁה, מִגּוֹ דְּחָיֵיל עַל אֲחוֹתָהּ. **אִיסּוּר מוֹסִיף**. כְּשֶׁהָאִיסּוּר מוֹסִיף עַל הַחֲתִיכָה לְאוֹסְרָהּ עַל מִי (ב) שֶׁמּוּתֶּרֶת עָלָיו. **אִיסּוּר כּוֹלֵל** – שֶׁהָאִיסּוּר חָל עַל חֲתִיכוֹת אֲחֵרוֹת, וְאוֹתָהּ גּוֹרֶרֶת לָזוֹ עִמָּהֶם עַל יְדֵי מִגּוֹ: וְאִית דְּגָרְסֵי הָכָא. **וְתוּ חֲמוֹתוֹ וְנַעֲשֵׂית אֵשֶׁת אִישׁ אִיסּוּר מוֹסִיף הוּא**. וְשִׁיבּוּשׁ הוּא בְּיָדָם. וְאַע"ג דְּוַדַּאי אִיסּוּר מוֹסִיף הוּא – לָאו פִּירְכָא הִיא, דְּוַדַּאי אִית לֵיהּ לְר' יוֹסֵי אִיסּוּר מוֹסִיף, כְּגוֹן אֵשֶׁת אִישׁ חָל עַל אִיסּוּר חֲמוֹתוֹ, וְתַרְוַיְיהוּ אִיסּוּרֵי עֲלֵיהּ. וְהָא דְּקָאָמַר וְיִדּוֹן בַּחֲמוֹתוֹ – מִשּׁוּם דְּזוֹ הִיא הַחֲמוּרָה, דְּאִי אָמְרַתְּ יִדּוֹן בְּאֵשֶׁת אִישׁ – אִם כֵּן אֵין זֶה אִיסּוּר חָל עַל אִיסּוּר אֶלָּא אִיסּוּר מְבַטֵּל אִיסּוּר. **אֶלָּא אָמַר רָבָא**. לְעוֹלָם לֵית לֵיהּ לְר' יוֹסֵי אִיסּוּר חָל עַל אִיסּוּר. וְהָא דְּקָאָמַר לְעֵיל חַיָּיב עֲלָהּ מִשּׁוּם אֵשֶׁת אָח וּמִשּׁוּם אֲחוֹת אִשָּׁה – לָאו בְּשׁוֹגֵג, לְחַיְּיבוֹ שְׁתֵּי חַטָּאוֹת, אֶלָּא בְּמֵזִיד וְלֵיעָשׂוֹת רָשָׁע גָּמוּר וּלְקָבְרוֹ בֵּין רְשָׁעִים (ג) גְּמוּרִים. שֶׁהָרָשָׁע נִקְבָּר אֵצֶל רְשָׁעִים, דִּתְנַן בְּסַנְהֶדְרִין (דף מו.): שְׁתֵּי קְבָרוֹת הָיוּ מְתוּקָּנִין לְבֵ"ד, א' לְנֶהֱרָגִין וּלְנֶחֱנָקִין וְא' לְנִסְקָלִין וּלְנִשְׂרָפִין. וְהָכָא נַמִּי, אַע"ג דְּהַאי לָאו מְחַיְּיבֵי בֵּ"ד הוּא, הוֹאִיל וַעֲבַד תַּרְתֵּי – קָבְרִינַן לֵיהּ גַּבֵּי נִסְקָלִין וְנִשְׂרָפִין. חַיָּיב ב'. ב' אִיסּוּרֵי קָחָשֵׁיב. דְּהָא מִשּׁוּם זָרוּת אֵין כָּאן חַטָּאת, דְּהָא עַל זְדוֹנוֹ מִיתָה בִּידֵי שָׁמַיִם הוּא, וְאֵין חַיָּיב חַטָּאת אֶלָּא עַל שִׁגְגַת כָּרֵת. מֵרַבִּי. רַבֵּינוּ הַקָּדוֹשׁ. כְּשֶׁהוּתְּרָה בַּמִּקְדָּשׁ הוּתְּרָה. סְתָם, הִלְכָּךְ אֵין כָּאן אֶלָּא מִשּׁוּם זָרוּת. שֶׁשִּׁימֵּשׁ בְּטוּמְאָה. דְּקָרְבַּן צִבּוּר קָאָמַר, שֶׁדּוֹחֶה הַטּוּמְאָה. וְכֵן זָר שֶׁשִּׁימֵּשׁ בְּשַׁבָּת וְיֵשׁ כָּאן מִשּׁוּם טוּמְאָה, וְאַזְהָרְתֵּיהּ מִ"וְיִנָּזְרוּ מִקָּדְשֵׁי בְנֵי יִשְׂרָאֵל וְלֹא יְחַלְּלוּ" (ויקרא כב). **אֵצֶל תְּמִימִים** הוּתְּרָה. דִּרְאוּיִם לַעֲבוֹד, דְּיָלְפִינַן מִ"בְּמוֹעֲדוֹ" – אֲפִי' בְּטוּמְאָה (פסחים דף עז.). זָר שֶׁאָכַל מְלִיקַת. הַכֹּהֲנִים. חַיָּיב שְׁתַּיִם. מִשּׁוּם זָרוּת וּמִשּׁוּם נְבֵילָה, דְּקָרְבָּן הַנֶּאֱכָל לְכֹהֲנִים זָר הָאוֹכְלוֹ עוֹבֵר מִשּׁוּם "וְזָר לֹא יֹאכַל כִּי קֹדֶשׁ הֵם" (שמות כט), וְלָאו הַיְינוּ אַזְהָרָה דִּמְעִילָה, דְּכָל שֶׁיֵּשׁ בּוֹ שְׁעַת הֵיתֵּר לְכֹהֲנִים – אֵין בּוֹ מְעִילָה. לְכֹהֲנִים הוּתְּרָה. בְּחַטַּאת הָעוֹף.

בְּאִיסּוּר

תוספות

איסור כולל הוא. וא"ת: ולמא ר' יוסי אית ליה נמי איסור כולל? ואומר ר"י, דקסבר דאשת איש ונעשית חמותו נמי איסור כולל הוא, דמגו דאיתסר בשאר קרובות, וקתני דנידון באשת איש. ומיהו, אר"י, דלהכא לישנא דלקמן דסבר רבי חייא דרבי יוסי מחייב תרתי באיסור כולל – צ"ל דאשת איש ונעשית חמותו לא חשיב איסור כולל, אע"ג דאיתסר בשאר קרובות, כיון שאין (ד) שם אחד – כי היכי דלא תקשה דרבי יוסי אדר' יוסי. והא דחשיב איסור כולל בעל מום ששימש בטומאה, דמעיקרא שרי באכילה ואסור בעבודה, איטמי ליה – מגו דאיתסר באכילה איתסר נמי בעבודה – אכילה ועבודה חשיב נמי שם אחד, דשניהם נאסרו בלשון קריבה. דבעבודה כתיב "כל איש אשר בו מום לא יגש להקריב לחם" וגו' (ויקרא כא) ובאכילה בטומאה כתיב "איש (איש) אשר יקרב מכל זרעכם" וגו' (שם כב) דמיירי באכילה, כדאמרינן בפ"ב דמעילה (דף י:) ובזבחים (דף מה:) ומיהו, איסור מוסיף, אומר ר"י דחשיב אפילו כשאין השמות שוין, כדמוכח בפ' "אמרו לו" (כריתות יד:) גבי הבא על בת בתו חייב משום כלתו כו'. ואין להאריך כאן.

ותו חמותו ונעשית אשת איש איסור מוסיף הוא. בקונטרס לא גרס ליה, דאפילו חייל עליה איסור אשת איש – נידון (ה) בחמורה. וליכא למימר דמשמע ליה נידון בחמותו ולא חל כלל איסור אשת איש, ואם לא התרו בו משום חמותו אלא משום אשת איש פטור – דהא בפרק "הנשרפים" (סנהדרין דף פא. ושם) פריך רב אדא בר אהבה: וליתרו נמי משום איסור אשת איש, דהא א"ר אבהו: מודה רבי יוסי באיסור מוסיף! ומשני ליה התם: אדא ברי, אטו בתרי קטלי קטלת ליה? משמע בהדיא דחל איסור אשת איש, אלא משום דנידון בחמורה. ור"ת אומר: דשפיר גרס ליה, וטעי הכא כדהוה טעי התם רב אדא בר אהבה, והוה סבור דנידון בחמותו משום דלא חייל עליה איסור אשת איש. ולא חש לתרץ, כיון דע"כ צריך לשינויא אחרינא משום קושיא קמייתא.

אלא אמר רבא מעלה כו'. לפי המסקנא דהכא לא איצטריך לר' אבהו למימר דמודה ר' יוסי באיסור מוסיף. מ"מ בהנשרפים (ג"ז שם) מייתי מדרבי אבהו משום דהאמת הוא דמודה ר' יוסי באיסור מוסיף, כדמשמע בפ' "אמרו לו" (כריתות דף יד: ושם) גבי א"ר יוסי: אם עבר זקן ונשאה – חייב עליה משום אשת אב, משום הכי איצטריך ליה לרבי אבהו לאסוקי הכי.

בין רשעים גמורים. פירוש: אצל רשעים כמותו, לפי שאין קוברין רשע אצל צדיק. ולא כמו שפירש בקונטרס לקוברו אצל נסקלים ונשרפין. ור"ש סבר: דאע"פ שיש בעבירה זו שני איסורין, כיון דלא מיחייב אלא חדא – אין קוברין אותו אצל רשעים גמורים.

בעל מום ששימש בטומאה. הא דלא נקט זר כדנקט לעיל – היינו משום דאטומאה לא הוזהרו זרים אלא כהנים, דכתיב "דבר אל אהרן ואל בניו וינזרו" וגו' (ויקרא כב). והא דקאמר טומאה לכל נאסרה – היינו אפי' בעלי מומין.

במאי

[לקמן לג:]

שבועות כו.

הגהות הב"ח

(א) רש"י ד"ה אמר ר' אבהו וכו' אשת איש הא ודאי איסור: (ב) ד"ה איסור מוסיף וכו' על מי שהיתה מותרת עליו: (ג) ד"ה אלא וכו' רשעים גמורים. נ"ב ס"א חמורים: (ד) תום' ד"ה איסור וכו' שאין זה שם אחד: (ה) ד"ה ותו וכו' אשת איש נידון בחמותו החמורה וליכא:

במאי קמיפלגי? באיסור כולל, ואליבא דר' יוסי: רבי חייא סבר, רבי יוסי [א]באיסור כולל מיחייב תרתי; בר קפרא סבר, לא מיחייב אלא חדא. ומאי איסור כולל איכא הכא? בשלמא זר, מעיקרא שרי במלאכה ואסור בעבודה, אתיא לה שבת — מגו דקא מיתסר במלאכה מיתסר נמי בעבודה. בעל מום, מעיקרא שרי באכילה ואסור בעבודה, איטמי ליה, מגו דקא מיתסר באכילה מיתסר נמי בעבודה, אלא מליקה — בבת אחת היא דמשכחת לה, באיסור כולל לא משכחת לה! אלא קמיפלגי באיסור בבת אחת ואליבא דר' יוסי: רבי חייא סבר, רבי יוסי [ב]באיסור בת אחת מיחייב תרתי, ובר קפרא סבר, לא מיחייב אלא חדא. והכא — מאי איסור בת אחת איכא הכא? זר ששימש בשבת, כגון דאייתי שתי שערות בשבת, דהויא להו זרות ושבת בהדי הדדי. בעל מום נמי — כגון דאייתי שתי שערות ואיטמי ליה, דהויא ליה בעל מום וטומאה בהדי הדדי. א"נ: שחתך אצבעו בסכין טמאה. בשלמא לרבי חייא, כי אתנייה לדידיה — אליבא דר' יוסי, כי אתנייה לבר קפרא — אליבא דר"ש, אלא לבר קפרא — °ר' חייא שקורי קא משקר?! אלא: קמיפלגי באיסור בת אחת, ואליבא דר"ש. בשלמא לר' חייא, קא מישתבע לאפוקי לר' שמעון מחזקיה, אלא לבר קפרא — למה ליה לאישתבועי? — קשיא. בשלמא לבר קפרא, כי אתנייה רבי לדידיה — אליבא דר' שמעון, כי אתנייה לרבי חייא — אליבא דרבי יוסי. אלא לרבי חייא, בר קפרא שקורי קא משקר? אמר לך ר' חייא: כי אתנייה רבי לדידיה — תרתי לפטור אתנייה ואיסור

באיסור כולל. לקמיה מפרש מאי איסור כולל איכא. **ואליבא דר' יוסי.** דאמר: בשאר איסורי איסור חל על איסור, ע"י מגו. **באיסור כולל מיחייב תרתי.** דקתני: חייב משום אשת אח ומשום אחות אשה, אפילו נשא מת ואח"כ נשא חי, דליכא איסור מוסיף בהאי בתרא אלא איסור כולל, מגו דמיתסר בכולהו אחוותא כולל גם את זו עמהן. **לא מיחייב אלא חדא.** וכי חייביה רבי יוסי תרתי — בנשא חי ואח"כ נשא מת, דאיסור מוסיף הוא. והא דקתני ר"ש אומר אינו חייב אלא משום אשת אח, דאוקימנא בנשא מת ואח"כ נשא חי — רבי חייא תני לה, בר קפרא לא תני לה. **מעיקרא.** קודם שבת זו. **מגו דמתסרא במלאכה.** משום שבת, כולל את העבודה בכלל האיסור משום שבת. והכא לא שייך מוסיף, שלא ניתוסף איסור על החתיכה דהיינו עבודה. והיכי דמי מוסיף — כגון אי הוה מלינו למימר הכי: עבודה מעיקרא אסורה לזרים ומותרת לכהנים, הוה ליה שבת, מגו דאיתוסף עלה איסור לגבי כהנים משום שבת — איתוסף נמי לגבי דידיה משום שבת. והכי ליכא למימר, דהא משום שבת לא מיתסרי כהנים. **שרי באכילה.** בקדשים, דכתיב "ומן הקדשים יאכל" (ויקרא כא). **מגו דמיתסר באכילה.** משום טומאה, חייל נמי שם טומאה על העבודה. **אלא מליקה.** כולל לא משכחת לה, דהא בשעת מליקה חיילי תרווייהו. דכל זמן שלא נמלקה היה עליה איסור (א) מעילה, ולא זהו איסור זרות האמור בקרבן שניתר לאכילת כהנים. וכשנמלקה ונראית לכהנים פקע מינה איסור אזהרת מעילה, וחייל עליה איסור זרות ד"זר לא יאכל" ואיסור מליקה באיסור בת אחת. **מיחייב תרתי.** דהא דקאמר לעיל חייב שתים — כגון שבא עליו איסור דאשת אח ואחות אשה כאחד, ומשכחת לה כגון (ב) דשוינהו שליח שני אחין לקדש שתי אחיות, והן עשו שליח לקבל קידושיהן, ופגע שליח בשליח. **לא מיחייב אלא חדא.** וכי חייב (ג) באיסור מוסיף — בנשא חי ואח"כ נשא מת, כדמפרש לעיל. **כגון דאייתי שתי שערות.** היום בשבת זו, דהשתא ליכא למימר כדלעיל מעיקרא שרי במלאכה ואסור בעבודה, דהא לא חל שום איסור עליו עד היום, דאיסור זרות ואיסור שבת יחד באו, אבל הביא שתי שערות בחול קדים זרות עליה. **בעל מום נמי כגון דאייתי שתי שערות ואיטמי ליה.** כלומר, דאיטמי קודם (ד) ב' שערות, ובתוך טומאתו ומומו הביא שתי שערות, ובשעת הבאה חלו שניהן, שהרי שניהן היו תלוין עליו. **שחתך אצבעו.** והוא המום, ונטמאה בחתיכתו בסכין. **בשלמא לר' חייא.** מצי לאוקמי גמריה ודבר קפרא הכי. **כי אתנייה.** [רבי] לדידיה כרבי יוסי, ולבר קפרא כר"ש. ובר קפרא הוא דטעה, וסבר דר' אליבא דר' יוסי אתנייה. **אלא לבר קפרא.** דאמר רבי אליבא דר' יוסי אתנייה קולא, א"כ, אליבא דמאן אתנייה לר' חייא חומרא? וכי לבר קפרא שקורי משקר רבי חייא, דלא אתנייה רבי [*לר"י] מחייב שתים? **ואליבא דר"ש.** וה"ק רבי חייא: אע"ג דפליג ר' שמעון ופטר, הנ"מ בכולל, אבל בבת אחת — מודה, הואיל ולא קדים חד לחבריה. ובר קפרא אמר: בבת אחת נמי פליג ר"ש. **לאפוקי לר"ש מחזקיה.** דהוה מחזקינן ליה לרבי שמעון לקולא, ואישתבע לן ר' חייא דבבת אחת מודי. **בשלמא לבר קפרא.** מצי לתרוצי לגמריה וגמריה דרבי חייא ולמימר: כי אתניין רבי פטור — אליבא דר"ש, וכי אתנייה לר' חייא חיובא — אליבא דר' יוסי. ורבי חייא הוא דטעה וסבר דרבי אליבא דר"ש אתנייה. **אלא לר' חייא.** דאמר אליבא דר"ש אתנייה רבי חיובא, אלא פטורא דאתנייה לבר קפרא — אליבא דמאן? וכי שקורי משקר בר קפרא דלא אתנייה ר' פטורא כלל?! **אמר לך רבי חייא.** ודאי בר קפרא לא משקר אלא טעי. דרבי ודאי פטורא אתנייה, ולא בכולהו אלא בתרתי: בזר ששימש בשבת ובעל מום ששימש בטומאה, דמשכחת בין ע"י כולל בין ע"י בת אחת, כדאמר לעיל. ואיסור

*נ"ל דר"י. יעב"ץ.

במאי קמיפלגי באיסור כולל. הו"מ לאקשויי: בשלמא לבר קפרא משתבע לאפוקי ר' יוסי מחזקיה, אלא לר' חייא — למה ליה אשתבועי? דכה"ג דייק בסמוך. אלא כאן לא חש לדקדק, משום דלא קאי הכי (ה). **לא** מיחייב אלא חדא. פי' בקונטרס: והא דקתני ר"ש אומר אינו חייב אלא משום אשת אח בלבד, דאוקימנא בנשא מת ואח"כ נשא חי, דהוי איסור כולל — רבי חייא תני לה ולא בר קפרא. ונראה דבר קפרא נמי תני לה, ולקברו בין רשעים גמורים.

אלא מליקה בבת אחת הוא דמשכחת לה. וא"ת: היכי הויא בבת אחת? והא מיד כי נמלקה הויא לה נבילה, ואיסור זרות לא חייל עד אחר זריקה, שיש היתר לכהנים, כדאמר בפרק בתרא דמכות (דף יח: ושם) דכל היכא דקרינן "ואכלו אותם אשר כופר בהם" קרינן ביה "וכל זר לא יאכל (ו) קודש"! וי"ל: דאיסור נבילה נמי לא חייל עד אחר הזריקה, דנפקא איסור מעילה, דלא חייל איסור נבילה על איסור מעילה דחמיר מיניה, כי היכי דחמיר איסור מעילה מאיסור גיד, כדאמר בפרק "גיד הנשה" (חולין דף קא. ושם). ואע"ג דבר קפרא דשמעתין אית ליה בריש מעילה (ד' ה.) דהיתר זריקה שנינו. ומשנראה לזריקה נפיק מידי מעילה — מ"מ איסור(ז) איכא עד שיזרוק, הלכך לא חייל איסור נבלה עד אחר זריקה. א) ועוי"ל: [דבר קפרא סבר] דר"ש דשמעתין לטעמיה דאית ליה איסור זרות לפני זריקה דאמר התם במכות (דף יז:) דזר שאכל עולה לפני זריקת דמים לוקה חמש, ולא משום זרות דכתיב גבי "ואכלו אותם אשר כופר בהם" — דמשום ההוא לא לקי אפי' לר"ש, כדאיתא בהדיא התם, אלא מההוא קרא ד"לא תוכל לאכול בשעריך" (דברים יב). **באיסור** בת אחת מיחייב תרתי. פי' בקונטרס: דהא דקאמר לעיל חייב שתים — כגון שבא עליו איסור אשת אח ואחות אשה כאחד, ומשכחת לה ע"י שליח, כדלקמן (דף לד.). והשתא הא דפליג עליה ר"ש דאמר אין חייב אלא משום אשת אח בלבד אע"ג דבבת אחת (ח) אשת אח דחמור חייל, דאין לה היתר אחר מיתה אלא במקום יבום, אבל אחות אשה שרי לאחר מיתת אשתו. וברייתא דקתני אינו חייב אלא משום אחות אשה — לא איירי בבת אחת, דא"כ היה חייב משום אשת אח. אלא בנשא חי ואח"כ נשא מת איירי. והא דקאמר ר' חייא דר' יוסי בבת אחת מחייב תרתי — לאו דוקא באיסור בת אחת, אלא אפילו באיסור מוסיף, כדמוכח בפ' "אמרו לו" (כריתות דף יד:).

(ט) **בר** קפרא סבר לא מיחייב אלא חדא. והיא דקתני ר"ש אומר אינו חייב אלא משום אשת אחיו [בלבד, דמשמע] דמחייב ר' יוסי תרתי — היינו לקוברו בין רשעים גמורים ובאידך ברייתא דמיירי בנשא חי ואח"כ נשא מת מודה בה בר קפרא דלר' יוסי חייב שתים דמודה ר' יוסי באיסור מוסיף כמו שפירש בקונטרס כדמוכח ממתני' דפ' אמרו לו וקשה לר"י דמשמע דבאיסור מוסיף חל טפי איסור על איסור מבאיסור בת אחת וכי מסקינן דמיפלגו באיסור בת אחת ואליבא דר"ש, וחייב לר' חייא שתים — באיסור בת אחת לר"ש, ואפ"ה לית ליה איסור מוסיף, דקתני לעיל אין חייב אלא משום אחות אשה! ואר"י: דבודאי איסור בת אחת עדיף, אלא דסבר בר קפרא דדוקא באיסור בת אחת דהכא, כגון אחות אשה, וטומאה, ושבת, ונבילה, (י) דלא חיילא — היינו משום דהותרה בהדי ההיא דלא הותרה, שכן משמע לישנא דקאמר בר קפרא: שבת לכל הותרה, טומאה לכל הותרה — משמע משום דהותרו לא חיילי. ורבי חייא לית ליה האי סברא, כדקאמר: לכהנים הותרה ולא לזרים. הלכך קאמר בסמוך דבבת אחת מחייב ר"ש שתים, אע"ג דבאיסור מוסיף לא מחייב אלא אחת. וכן משמע קצת לקמן דאיסור בת אחת עדיף טפי, דקאמר: השתא משום כולל מיחייב — משום בת אחת מיבעיא! ומאן דמחייב באיסור כולל, היינו משום דמידי דהוה אאיסור מוסיף, כדאמר בפ"ג דשבועות (דף כד: ושם), וא"כ עדיף נמי מאיסור מוסיף. **אצבעו** בסכין טמאה. שהיתה אצבעו תחובה עד משהו אחרון דכשנגע בו הסכין נטמא ונעשה בעל מום. ואיסור

עין משפט נר מצוה

מ א ב מיי' פי"ז מהל' איסורי ביאה הל' ח ופ"ד מהלכות שגגות הל' א ופ"ח מהלכות מאכלות אסורות הלכה ו:

תוספות ישנים

במאי קמיפלגי. דמאי דקאמר כשהותרה וכו' אין זה עיקר טעם דהא אפשר לומר בשני לדדין: **באיסור** כולל מחייב תרתי. וא"כ הא דר' יוסי דלעיל דמחייב באשת אח ובאחות אשה מיירי בין נשא חי ואח"כ נשא מת בין נשא מת ואח"כ נשא חי. וא"ת והא קאמר אשת איש ונעשית חמותו נדון באשת איש ואמאי איסור כולל הוא וא"כ לחייב בחמותו החמורה. וי"ל דלאו כר' חייא אתיא כי אם לבר קפרא. א"נ י"ל דהא דמחייב ר' יוסי באיסור כולל תרתי היינו (כשהיו) [כשהם] משם אחד כמו אשת אח ואחות אשה שהכל משום אחוה הוא. אבל בשני שמות כמו חמותו ואשת איש לא מחייב ר' יוסי. וא"ת והלא קאמר ר' יוסי גבי עבר זקן ונשאה חייב שתים אע"ג דשתי שמות הן וי"ל דהיינו דווקא גבי איסור מוסיף דאין חילוק באיסור מוסיף בין שם אחד לשתי שמות אבל באיסור כולל דגרע מיניה אין חייב שתים רק כשהם משם אחד: **מגו** דמתסר באכילה אתסר נמי בעבודה. ולפי' שפי' נ"ל דשם אחד הוא דעבודה אקרי קריבה דכתיב המקריב ואכילה אקרי קריבה דכתיב איש [איש] אשר יקרב אל הקדשים והיינו אכילה ואי נמי כיון דאיסורא דאית בהו משום טומאה שם אחד הוא [ועי' בתוס' לעיל עמוד ב' ד"ה איסור] ומיירי הכי בקרבן צבור דהותרה בו טומאה ושבת ולהכי הוי איסור כולל ולא איסור מוסיף דלא נוסף בו איסור בדבר שהי' בו היתר אבל בקרבן יחיד היה איסור מוסיף דקודם שבת הותרו כהנים להקריב כי אתא שבת נאסרו הכהנים להקריב מגו דאתוסף בזה איסורא לגבי כהנים שהותרו בו קודם שבת איתוסף נמי איסורא לגבי זר וכן לענין בעל מום ששמש בטומאה אי בקרבן יחיד הו"ל איסור מוסיף דמתחלה אין תמימים מותרים בו. אטמי נאסרו בו אף תמימים שהיו מותרים בו מגו דאתוסף איסורא לגבי התמימים איתוסף איסורא לגבי בעל מום וחייב משום בעל מום וטומאה אלא ודאי בקרבן צבור איירי: **א)** עוד אומר רבינו נתנאל דאף כי אמרינן היתר זריקה שנינו להוציא מידי מעילה היינו דווקא בבהמה דשוחה בחולין שריא משום השחיטה. אבל מליקת שוף דשוחה בחולין אסירא משום נבלה גם הכא לא נפקא מידי מעילה עד לאחר הזאה וכן נמי אמרינן הזה דמה חייבין עליה משום פגול נותר וטמא ואין בה משום מעילה משמע דעד שעת הזאה יש בו משום מעילה: **רבי** חייא סבר רבי יוסי באיסור בת אחת מחייב תרתי [פי' בקונטרס] והא דאמרינן לעיל דמחייב ר' יוסי תרתי באשת אח ואחות אשה מיירי בבת אחת דשוו אינהו ואינהי שליח ופגעו שליח בשליח ואין צריך לומר כן. ונראה דהא דאמרי' לעיל דר' יוסי מחייב שתים היינו לקברו בין רשעים חמורים. וא"ת הלא גבי עבר זקן ונשאה משמע דר' יוסי מחייב שתים באיסור מוסיף וא"כ כ"ש באיסור בת אחת והכא קאמר בר קפרא דלא מחייב ר' יוסי אלא חדא. וי"ל דשאני התם דאיסור חמור הוא דאיכא סקילה. והכא בזר ששימש בשבת לא מחייב רק משום זרות ולא משום שבת אע"ג דאיכא סקילה משום דהותרה מכללה בקרבן צבור. וכן בעל מום ששימש בטומאה מחייב משום בעל מום ולא משום טומאה דהותרה מכללה בצבור. וכן מליקה מחייב משום זרות אבל לא משום נבלה שהותרה מכללה: **שחתך** אצבעו בסכין טמאה. וא"ת מ"מ לא הוי בת אחת דמיד שנגע לסכין אטמי. ובעל מום לא הוי עד שחתך. וי"ל כיון דליכא רק זמן מועט בינתים חשבינן ליה בבת אחת. וכן מפורש גבי דמני לאהדורי ע"י הדחק א) עוד י"מ דמיירי שחתך אצבעו סמוך לעצם הרבה ועתה שחתך העצם בסכין טמאה מיד אטמי ונעשה בעל מום: **באיסור** בת אחת ואליבא דר' שמעון דר' חייא סבר דר' שמעון מחייב תרתי בבת אחת והא דאמר ר' שמעון לעיל אינו חייב אלא אחת ב) אף באיסור בת אחת ולעולם סבר דמחייב על החמור

א) בכתובות דף ל' ע"ב וע"ש בתוס' ד"ה לא צריכא בשם הריצב"א. ב) נראה דחסר כאן וצ"ל אינו חייב אלא אחת מיירי בזה אחר זה ובר קפרא סובר דאף באיסור בת אחת לעולם סבר וכו'.

הגהות הב"ח

(א) רש"י ד"ה אלא וכו' איסור לאזהרת וכו' איסור לאזהרת מעילה: (ב) ד"ה מיחייב וכו' כגון דשוו שני אחין שליח לקדש וכו' שליח בשליח כדלקמן הס"ד: (ג) ד"ה לא מיחייב אלא חדא וכי חייב תרתי באיסור: (ד) ד"ה בעל מום וכו' קודם שהביא ב' שערות: (ה) תוס' ד"ה במאי וכו' דלא קאי הכי. נ"ב ומהר"ר משה תירץ להכי הוצרך ר' חייא לאשתבועי דלא נימא אשת איש ונעשה חמותו איסור כולל הוה ודוחק ע"ל דף לב ע"ב בתוס' ד"ה איסור: (ו) ד"ה אלא וכו' קרינן ביה וכל זר לא יאכל כי קדש הם וי"ל: (ז) בא"ד מ"מ איסור מעילה איכא עד שיזרוק: (ח) ד"ה באיסור וכו' דבבת אחת הן אשת: (ט) ד"ה ובר קפרא וכו' אשת אח דעלמא דמחייב ר' יוסי: (י) בא"ד ושבת ונבילה הוא דלא חיילא ההיא דהותרה בהדי:

גליון הש"ס

גמ' אי נמי שחתך אצבעו. עיין כתובות דף ל ע"ב תד"ה לא צריכא: **שם** ר' חייא שקורי קא משקר. עיין שבועות דף כו ע"א תד"ה את לבך:

עין משפט
נר מצוה

מא א מיי' פ"ד מהל' שגגות הלכה א:

מב ב מיי' פי"א מהל' גירושין הלכה יח סמג עשין נ טוש"ע אה"ע סימן יג סעיף א:

מג ג מיי' פי"א מהל' איסורי ביאה הל' ז סמג לאוין קכא ועשין מח טוש"ע שם סימן ו סעיף יא:

וְאִיסּוּר כּוֹלֵל אַתְנְיֵיהּ, וְאַלִּיבָּא דְּרַ' שִׁמְעוֹן, וְחַזְיָא לְבַר קַפָּרָא לְזָר שֶׁאָכַל מְלִיקָה, וְאַיְּידֵי דְּדָמְיָא לָהּ — עָרְבָהּ בַּהֲדַיְיהוּ, וְעַיֵּין בָּהּ, וְלָא אַשְׁכַּח אֶלָּא בְּבַת אַחַת. וְסָבַר: מִדְּהָא בְּבַת אַחַת — הָא נַמִי בְּבַת אַחַת, וּמִדְּהָנָךְ לִפְטוֹר — הָנָךְ נַמִי לִפְטוֹר. מֵיתִיבֵי: *זָר שֶׁשִּׁימֵּשׁ בְּשַׁבָּת, וּבַעַל מוּם שֶׁשִּׁימֵּשׁ בְּטוּמְאָה — יֵשׁ כָּאן מִשּׁוּם זָרוּת, וּמִשּׁוּם שַׁבָּת, וּמִשּׁוּם בַּעַל מוּם, וּמִשּׁוּם טוּמְאָה, דִּבְרֵי רַבִּי יוֹסֵי. ר"ש אוֹמֵר: אֵין כָּאן אֶלָּא מִשּׁוּם זָרוּת וּבַעַל מוּם בִּלְבַד. וְאִילּוּ מְלִיקָה שַׁיְּירָהּ. לְמַאן שַׁיְּירָהּ? אִילֵימָא לְרַבִּי יוֹסֵי — הַשְׁתָּא רַ' יוֹסֵי בְּאִיסּוּר כּוֹלֵל מִיחַיֵּיב שְׁתַּיִם, בְּאִיסּוּר בַּת אַחַת מִיבַּעְיָא? אֶלָּא לָאו — לְרַ' שִׁמְעוֹן וּבְאִיסּוּר כּוֹלֵל הוּא דְּפָטַר — אֲבָל בְּאִיסּוּר בְּבַת אַחַת מִיחַיֵּיב, תְּיוּבְתָּא דְּבַר קַפָּרָא! תְּיוּבְתָּא. "זָר שֶׁשִּׁימֵּשׁ בְּשַׁבָּת", בְּמַאי? אִי בִּשְׁחִיטָה — שְׁחִיטָה בְּזָר כְּשֵׁרָה, א] וְאִי בְּקַבָּלָה וְהוֹלָכָה — *טִלְטוּל בְּעָלְמָא הוּא. אִי בְּהַקְטָרָה — *וְהָא"ר יוֹסֵי: הַבְעָרָה לְלָאו יָצְאתָה! אָמַר רַב אַחָא בַּר יַעֲקֹב: בִּשְׁחִיטַת פָּרוֹ שֶׁל כֹּהֵן גָּדוֹל, וּכְדִבְרֵי הָאוֹמֵר: שְׁחִיטַת פָּרוֹ שֶׁל כֹּהֵן גָּדוֹל בְּזָר — פְּסוּלָה. — אִי הָכִי מַאי אִירְיָא זָר, אֲפִילּוּ כֹּהֵן הֶדְיוֹט נַמִי! — שֶׁזָּר אֶצְלוֹ קָאָמַר. מַתְקִיף לָהּ רַב אַשִׁי: מִידֵי חַטָּאוֹת קָתָנֵי, אוֹ לָאוֵי קָתָנֵי? אֶלָּא: אִיסּוּרֵי בְּעָלְמָא קָא חָשֵׁיב. לְמַאי נָפְקָא מִינָּהּ — *לְקוֹבְרוֹ בֵּין רְשָׁעִים (א) גְּמוּרִים.§

מתני' אשְׁנַיִם שֶׁקִּידְּשׁוּ שְׁתֵּי נָשִׁים, וּבִשְׁעַת כְּנִיסָתָן לַחוּפָּה הֶחֱלִיפוּ אֶת שֶׁל זֶה לָזֶה וְאֶת שֶׁל זֶה לָזֶה — הֲרֵי אֵלּוּ חַיָּיבִין מִשּׁוּם אֵשֶׁת אִישׁ. וְאִם הָיוּ אַחִין — מִשּׁוּם אֵשֶׁת אָח, וְאִם הָיוּ אֲחָיוֹת — מִשּׁוּם אִשָּׁה אֶל אֲחוֹתָהּ, וְאִם הָיוּ נִדּוֹת — מִשּׁוּם נִדָּה. *ב וּמַפְרִישִׁין אוֹתָן שְׁלֹשָׁה חֳדָשִׁים, שֶׁמָּא מְעוּבָּרוֹת הֵן, *וְאִם הָיוּ קְטַנּוֹת שֶׁאֵינָן רְאוּיוֹת לֵילֵד — מַחֲזִירִים אוֹתָן מִיָּד, וְאִם הָיוּ כֹּהֲנוֹת — נִפְסְלוּ *מִן הַתְּרוּמָה.§ **גמ'** "הֶחֱלִיפוּ", מִידֵי *בְּרַשִׁיעֵי עָסְקִינַן?! וְתוּ: הָא דְּתָנֵי רַבִּי חִיָּיא: הֲרֵי כָּאן שֵׁשׁ עֶשְׂרֵה חַטָּאוֹת. אִי בְּמֵזִיד — מִי אִיכָּא קָרְבָּן? אָמַר רַב יְהוּדָה, תְּנִי: הוּחְלְפוּ. הָכִי נַמִי מִסְתַּבְּרָא, דְּקָתָנֵי סֵיפָא: אִם הָיוּ קְטַנּוֹת שֶׁאֵינָן רְאוּיוֹת לֵילֵד — מַחֲזִירִין אוֹתָן מִיָּד. וְאִי בְּמֵזִיד — מִי שַׁרְיָא? — הָא לָא קַשְׁיָא: *פִּיתּוּי קְטַנָּה — אוֹנֶס נִינְהוּ, גוְאוֹנֶס בְּיִשְׂרָאֵל מִישְׁרָא שָׁרֵי. אֶלָּא דְּקָתָנֵי: מַפְרִישִׁין אוֹתָן שְׁלֹשָׁה חֳדָשִׁים שֶׁמָּא מְעוּבָּרוֹת הֵן, הָא לָאו מְעוּבָּרוֹת — שַׁרְיָין, וְאִי בְּמֵזִיד — מִי שָׁרֵי? אֶלָּא לָאו שְׁמַע מִינָּהּ: הוּחְלְפוּ, שְׁמַע מִינָּהּ. וּמַאן

[לקמן סח:]

וְאִיסּוּר כּוֹלֵל אַתְנְיֵין. כְּלוֹמַר, הֵיכִי דְּאִיתְרַמֵּי עַל יְדֵי כּוֹלֵל אַתְנְיֵין רַבִּי פְּטוּרָא, וְאַלִּיבָּא דְּר"ש, וְהֵיכָא דְּאִיתְרַמּוּ בְּבַת אַחַת — אַתְנְיֵין חִיּוּבָא. אֲבָל מְלִיקָה לָא אַתְנְיֵי' לִפְטוֹר כְּלָל, דְּלָא מַשְׁכַּחַתְּ לָהּ בְּכוֹלֵל אֶלָּא בְּבַת אַחַת, וְהָתָם ר' שִׁמְעוֹן מוֹדֵי. **וְחַזְיָא בַּר קַפָּרָא לְזָר שֶׁאָכַל מְלִיקָה.** דְּדָמְיָא לְהוּ, דְּהָווּ נַמִי כְּקָדָשִׁים: חֲדָא דְּמִיחַיֵּיב עֲלֵיהּ תַּרְתֵּי, וְעָרְבָהּ בַּהֲדַיְיהוּ לִפְטוּרָא. וְכִי עָרְבָהּ — לָא אַסֵּיק אַדַּעְתֵּיהּ דְּהָא לָא מִשְׁתַּכְּחַת בְּכוֹלֵל. **וְעַיֵּין בָּהּ.** לְאַחַר זְמַן, כְּשֶׁנִּתְקַיְּימָה בְּיָדוֹ, וְהָיָה שׁוֹנֶה שְׁלָשְׁתָּן כְּיַחַד, וְאַשְׁכַּח דְּלָא מִיתּוֹקְמָא אֶלָּא בְּבַת אַחַת, וְשָׁכַח דְּהוּא עֲרָבָהּ. וְסָבַר דְּר' אַתְנְיֵיהּ, וְאָמַר: מִדְּהָא בְּבַת אַחַת וּפְטוּרָה — הָנָךְ נַמִי דְּאַתְנְיֵיהּ רַבִּי לִפְטוּרָא — אֲפִי' הֵיכָא דְּמִיתְרַמּוּ בְּבַת אַחַת אַתְנְיֵין. **לְמַאן שַׁיְּירָא.** כְּלוֹמַר, (ב) לְמַאן מִינַּיְיהוּ מוֹדֶה בָּהּ דְּלָא בָּעֵי לְאִיפְּלוּגֵי. **אִילֵימָא ר' יוֹסֵי.** מוֹדֶה בָּהּ, הָשְׁתָּא בְּאִיסּוּר כּוֹלֵל, דְּחַד מִינַּיְיהוּ קָדֵים, א"ר יוֹסֵי אַחֲרוֹן חָל — בְּבַת אַחַת מִיבַּעְיָא? **אֶלָּא לָאו לְר"ש.** וּמִדְּמוֹדֶה בִּמְלִיקָה — ש"מ דְּהָא דְּפָלֵיג בְּהָנָךְ הֵיכָא דְּאִיתְרַמּוּ בְּכוֹלֵל הוּא דְּפָלֵיג, אֲבָל בְּאִיסּוּר בַּת אַחַת — מִיחַיֵּיב תַּרְתֵּי, וּתְיוּבְתָּא דְּבַר קַפָּרָא תְּיוּבְתָּא. **שְׁחִיטָה בְּזָר כְּשֵׁרָה.** וְאֵין כָּאן זָרוּת. **טִלְטוּל בְּעָלְמָא הוּא.** וְאֵין כָּאן א] שְׁבוּת. **אִי בְּהַקְטָרָה.** רַבִּי יוֹסֵי הֵיכִי מִיחַיֵּיב חַטָּאת מִשּׁוּם שַׁבָּת, דְּקס"ד חַטָּאת מִיחַיֵּיב לֵיהּ: **הָאָמַר ר' יוֹסֵי.** בְּפ"ק: הַבְעָרָה לְלָאו יָצְאָה. **בִּשְׁחִיטַת פָּרוֹ שֶׁל כ"ג.** בְּיוֹם הַכִּפּוּרִים. דִּשְׁחִיטָה אַב מְלָאכָה הִיא, וּמִשּׁוּם זָרוּת נַמִי אִיכָּא, כְּדִבְרֵי הָאוֹמֵר בְּיוֹמָא בְּפֶרֶק "טָרַף בַּקַּלְפִּי" (דף מב.): שְׁחִיטַת פָּרוֹ בְּזָר פְּסוּלָה. **אֲפִי' כֹּהֵן הֶדְיוֹט נַמִי.** דְּהָא מַאן דְּפָסֵיל יָלֵיף טַעְמָא מֵאַהֲרֹן, וְחוּקָּה, דִּכְתִיב "וְהִקְרִיב אַהֲרֹן" (ויקרא טז), וּכְתִיב בְּסוֹף הַפָּרָשָׁה "לְחָק עוֹלָם", וְכָל הֵיכָא דִּכְתִיב חוּקָּה — עִיכּוּבָא הוּא, אַלְמָא: אַהֲרֹן דַּוְקָא: הָכִי גָּרְסִי'. **מִידֵי חַטָּאוֹת קָתָנֵי אוֹ לָאוֵי קָתָנֵי.** אִיסּוּרֵי הוּא דְּקָחָשֵׁיב: **מתני' וּמַפְרִישִׁין אוֹתָן ג' חֳדָשִׁים.** שֶׁלֹּא לַחֲזוֹר לְבַעְלֵיהֶן, שֶׁמָּא מְעוּבָּרוֹת הֵן וּבְנֵיהֶם מַמְזֵרִים, וּבָעֵינַן הַבְחָנָה בֵּין זֶרַע כָּשֵׁר לְזֶרַע פָּסוּל, שֶׁלֹּא יִתְלוּ הָעוּבָּרִים בְּבַעֲלֵיהֶן. **אִם הָיוּ כֹּהֲנוֹת.** בַּגְּמָ' מְפָרֵשׁ. **גמ' שֵׁשׁ עֶשְׂרֵה חַטָּאוֹת.** לְכָל אֶחָד אַרְבַּע, וְכֵן לַנָּשִׁים. דְּעַל שְׁנֵיהֶם הוּא אוֹמֵר "וְנִכְרְתוּ הַנְּפָשׁוֹת הָעוֹשׂוֹת" (ויקרא יח). **וְאוֹנֶס בְּיִשְׂרָאֵל מִישְׁרָא שָׁרֵי.** לְבַעְלָהּ, דִּילְפִינַן (כתובות דף נא:) מִ"וְהִיא לֹא נִתְפָּשָׂה", הָא נִתְפְּשָׂה — מוּתֶּרֶת. **מַפְרִישִׁין אוֹתָן שֶׁמָּא מְעוּבָּרוֹת הֵן.** וּלְאַחַר שְׁלֹשָׁה חֳדָשִׁים מוּתָּרוֹת, אַע"ג שֶׁגְּדוֹלוֹת הֵן. וּמַאן

ואיסור כולל אתניין ואליבא דר"ש. אבל לר' יוסי מחייב תרתי באיסור כולל, דלא מצי למימר דאליבא דרבי יוסי נמי אתנייה לפטורא — דא"כ לא הוה טעי בר קפרא לערב מליקה בהדייהו. דבבת אחת פשיטא ליה לבר קפרא דלר' יוסי מיחייב תרתי, ולהכי פשיטא ליה בסמוך דלר' יוסי מיחייב תרתי באיסור כולל, שעל כרחו צ"ל דאליבא דר"ש אתנייה, ולא אליבא דר' יוסי. ופליג רבי יוחנן ארבי חייא ובר קפרא. (ג) **אמר ר' יוסי הבערה ללאו יצאה.** תימה: דאטו מי לא מני לאוי גרידי? והרי זר שאכל מליקה, דליכא אלא לאו דנבלה! וי"ל: דאע"ג דבאיסור מוסיף לר' יוסי חייל איסור קל על איסור חמור, כדפריך רבא אדא בפרק "הנשרפין" (סנהדרין דף פא. ושם): ולידון נמי באיסור אשת איש, דהא מודה רבי יוסי כו', אע"ג דאיסור אשת איש קל מאיסור חמותו, ובפרק "אמרו לו" (כריתות יד: ושם) גבי הא דאמר ר' יוסי אם (ד) זקן נשאה כו', משמע דמודה ר' יוסי דאיסור כרת חייל על חייבי מיתות ב"ד משום איסור מוסיף — מ"מ, באיסור כולל סבירא ליה לגמרא דלא חייל קל על חמור, כדאמר בסוף "גיד הנשה" (חולין קא. ושם): מאן האי תנא דאיסור כולל באיסור חמור אית ליה כו'. ולהכי פריך: והאמר רבי יוסי הבערה ללאו יצאה, ואם כן היכי חיילא אאיסור זרות? הקשה ה"ר יעקב דאורליינ"ש: דאמאי לא מוקי לה בהלכת האליתא, דעבודה היא, ובעיא כהונה, ואין בה מיתה אלא לאו גרידא לפי שאין עבודה תמה, כדאמר בפ"ב דיומא (דף כד:)? דהשתא לא הוי קל על חמור, דתרווייהו לאוי נינהו! ואר"י: דמ"מ איסור שבת קיל, לפי שהותרה במקדש. אבל אי הוה מיתה בהבערה — הוה חשיב איסור חמור, אע"ג דהותר במקדש. ואיסור טומאה נמי, אע"ג דהותר — חל על איסור בעל מום משום (ה) טמא ששימש במיתה, ובעל מום ששימש באזהרה לרבנן דרבי בסוף "אלו הן הנשרפין" (סנהדרין פג.), אע"ג דכולה שמעתין בר קפרא ורבי חייא אליבא דרבי פליגי — מודה רבי דלר' יוסי בעל מום ששימש באזהרה, כרבנן דידיה. ואם תאמר, דאמר בחולין (דף קג.): התורה אמרה יבא איסור נבלה ויחול על איסור חלב, והיינו קל על חמור באיסור כולל! ואר"י: דחלב קל, דהותר מכללו אצל חיה, כדאמר בס"פ "גיד הנשה" (שם). ואע"ג דנבלה נמי הותר במליקה — שאני קדשים, דכהנים משולחן גבוה קזכו, כדאמר ב"העור והרוטב" (שם דף קכ.). ועוד: דיש חומרא בנבלה, שכן מטמאה. ואע"ג דיש חומרא בחלב דליכא בנבלה — אין לחוש בכך, כדאמרינן בפרק "גיד הנשה" (שם דף קא.) מאי חזית דטומאת הגוף חמירא — שכן כרת, דלמא טומאת בשר חמירא דלית לה טהרה במקוה. וא"ת: דאמר לקמן, מאן האי תנא דאית ליה איסור כולל ואיסור מוסיף ואיסור בת אחת, ומשמע דאיסור אחות אשה חייל באיסור כולל אאיסור אשת איש דחמיר מיניה! וי"ל: דאיסור אשת איש קיל, דיש לה היתר בחיי אוסרה, דחשבינן ליה קולא ב"הבא על יבמתו" (לקמן דף נד.). ואע"ג דבפ' "גיד הנשה" (חולין דף קג. ושם) איכא מאן דאמר דאיסור טריפה חל על איסור אבר מן החי, אע"ג דחמיר מיניה, דחשיב משהו בשר גידים ועצמות אע"ג דלית ביה כזית, ונוהג בבני נח, וחייל עלייהו איסור טריפה דקיל אפי' בלא כולל! ואור"י: דיש חומרא בטריפה, דכשנטרפה — שוב אין לה היתר אפי' נשחטה. אבל איסור אבר מן החי — אתיא שחיטה ומפקע ליה. **מידי חטאות קתני או לאוי קתני איסורי בעלמא** קחשיב. וכן גרס ר"ת, דאין כאן לא חטאת ולא לאו, כיון דלא חייל איסור קל על חמור. **לקוברו** בין רשעים כו'. ומ"מ פריך שפיר לעיל לבר קפרא, דמשייר מליקה — מכלל דמודה בה ר"ש. דאין לומר דשיירא לרבי יוסי משום דבהיא חייב תרתי, ולא חשיב אלא הנהו דמעלה עליו כאילו עשה שתים, ולקברו בין רשעים גמורים — דהא חשיב בעל מום ששימש, אע"ג דחייב לגמרי שתים, כיון דקסבר *)רבי חייא דרבי יוסי אית ליה איסור כולל. אם

*) גי' רש"ל בר קפרא

תוספות ישנים

החמור. וא"ת מאי טעמא דאית תנא דתני דקאמר ר' שמעון אינו חייב אלא משום אשת אח ואית תנא דתני דר' שמעון אמר אינו חייב אלא משום אחות אשה. דליכא לתרץ כדמתרץ לעיל כאן שנשא מת וכו' דהא לא מיירי כלל באיסור מוסיף ובאיסור כולל אלא באיסור בת אחת. וא"כ בבת אחת היכי נתרץ הקושיא. וי"ל לעולם סבר דמחייב על החמורה. ובהא פליגי דחד אמר דאשת אח חמירא משום דאסירא אף לאחר מיתה משא"כ באחות אשה דהא שריא לאחר מיתה וחד סבר דאחות אשה חמירא משום דאחות אשה לא הותרה אף בשאין לה בנים ואשת אח הותרה באין לה בנים: **באיסור** בת אחת מיבעיא. וא"ל דלמא באיסור כולל דאיכא תרתי היינו לקברו בין רשעים חמורים אבל באיסור בת אחת ר"ל חיוב גמור דלא מסתבר ליה לחלק. וכן לקמן דקאמר אלמא ר' שמעון באיסור בת אחת מחייב תרתי לא משני לקוברן בין רשעים חמורים. דלא מיסתבר לר' שמעון הך מילתא דלאו לקברו בין רשעים חמורים אפי' באיסור כולל יהיה כן: **מידי** חטאות קתני או לאוי קתני איסורי קתני פ"ה **נשוא בקבלה** והולכה. ואי פרכת טלטול בעלמא הוא. הא לא קשה מידי דהא לא קתני אלא חייב שתים ואיכא למימר איסורי קתני. ולא נהירא דהא אין זה איסורא כיון דאינו אלא טלטול ואסור מדרבנן. לכן נראה דקאי אהא דאמרי לעיל אי בהבערה הא אמר ר' יוסי ללאו יצאת. ועל זה מקשה מידי חטאות קתני או לאוי קתני איסורי קא חשיב. וא"כ נהי נמי דללאו יצאת נימא דאיסורא דמדאורייתא' הוא:

תוספות חד מקמאי

מתניתין שנים שקדשו שתי נשים ובשעת כניסתן לחופה החליפו את של זה בזה ואת של זה בזה חייבין משום א"א ואם היו אחים חייבים אף משום אשת אח ואם היו אחיות חייבים אף משום אשה אל אחותה. ואם היו נדות חייבין משום נדה וכולן מפרישין אותן ג' חדשים שמא מעוברות הן אוקימ' הוחלפו אבל בהחליפו אפילו אינן מעוברות אסורות שהרי זינתה ברצון ואם היו קטנות אפי' ברצון שרו לגברייהו דקטנה היא ואוקימנא שמתני' כר"מ דאית ליה איסור כולל ואיסור מוסיף ואיסור בת

אחת א"נ כר"ש ובאיסור בת אחת ואקשי' בשלמא כולהו משכחת ליה דשוו אינהו שליח ושוו (עלייהו) [אינהי] שליח ופגעו שליח בשליח אלא נדות היכי משכחת לה אמר רב עמרם אמרי בי רב בשופעות מתוך י"ב לאחר י"ב ליחובי אינהי ומתוך י"ג לאחר י"ג לחיובי אינהו וכ"ת אם קדשו בתוך י"ג או ביום סוף י"ג קדושי קטן הוא ואין קדושיו קדושין אפי' גט לא צריכה איכא למימר משכחת לה כגון שקדש לסוף י"ג שהיא מקודשת לאחר י"ג ואליבא דר"מ היא דאמר אדם מקנה דבר שלא בא לעולם ואית דגרם בשופעת מתוך שלשה לאחר שלשה לחיובי אינהו ומתוך י"ב לאחר י"ב לחיובי אינהי פירוש כגון שהיו גדולים וקדשו בנות קטנות פחותות מבת שלשה ונתנו קדושין לאביהן שהן קדושי תורה ושפעו הבנות מתוך שלש [לאחר שלש] דפחותות מבנות שלש אין חייבין עליהן לא משום אשת אח ולא משום חיוב א) וכשהיו אחר ג' הן עליהן חייבן בבת א' וכשהיו הן לאחר י"ג חייבין ז' חטאות הן: אמר

א) נראה דצ"ל ולא משום אחות אשה וא"א ונדה וכשהיו אחר שלש חלו עליהן כולן בבת אחת וכשהיו הן לאחר י"ג חייבין הן ט"ז חטאות.

מסורת הש"ס

[תוספתא פ"ה]

שבת ע. סנהדרין לה: סב. לעיל ו:

[לעיל לב:]

לקמן סט.

[לקמן לה.]

מן הכהונה רש"ל

[יומא ו. כתובות קב. קדושין לג. גיטין לג:]

הגהות הב"ח

(א) גמ' בין רשעים גמורים. נ"ב ס"א חמורים: (ב) רש"י ד"ה למאן שיירא כלומר למאן מינייהו: (ג) תום' ד"ה האמר ר' יוסי וכו' בפ' הנשרפין וליחזו נמי משום איסור אשת איש: (ד) בא"ד ר' יוסי אם עבר זקן ונשאה: (ה) בא"ד משום טמא ששימש במיתה:

הגהות מהר"ן לנדא

א] רש"י ד"ה טלטול בעלמא הוא ואין כאן שבות כצ"ל:

גליון הש"ס

גמ' טלטול בעלמא הוא. עיין סוכה דף מב ע"ב תד"ה טלטול: **שם** והאמר ר"י הבערה ללאו יצאת. עיין ירושל' פ"ב דשבת סוף הל' ה דמשני כיון דהוא רוצה בעיכוס כמבשל הוא: **שם** פיתוי קטנה אונס. עי' כתובות ט ע"א תד"ה והב"א:

הגהות מהר"ב רנשבורג

א] גמ' ואי בקבלה והולכה טלטול בעלמא הוא. נ"ב עי' שער המלך פ"ז מהלכות לולב סוף הלכה כ"ה ד"ה ומלאתי וכו' יעוש"ה דף לא ע"ד:

וּמַאן הַאי תַּנָּא דְּאִית לֵיהּ [א]אִיסּוּר כּוֹלֵל וְאִיסּוּר מוֹסִיף וְאִיסּוּר בַּת אַחַת? אֲמַר רַב יְהוּדָה אֲמַר רַב: ר"מ הִיא. *דְּתַנְיָא: *[ב]יֵשׁ אוֹכֵל אֲכִילָה אַחַת וְחַיָּיב עָלֶיהָ אַרְבַּע חַטָּאוֹת וְאָשָׁם אֶחָד: טָמֵא שֶׁאָכַל חֵלֶב וְהוּא נוֹתָר מִן מוּקְדָּשִׁין בְּיוה"כ. ר' מֵאִיר אוֹמֵר: אִם הָיְתָה שַׁבָּת וְהוֹצִיאוֹ בְּפִיו — חַיָּיב. אָמְרוּ לוֹ: אֵינוֹ מִן הַשֵּׁם. וְר"מ אַלִּיבָּא דְּמַאן? אִי אַלִּיבָּא דְּרַבִּי יְהוֹשֻׁעַ — הָאָמַר: [ג]טָעָה בִּדְבַר מִצְוָה פָּטוּר. אֶלָּא אַלִּיבָּא דְּרַבִּי אֱלִיעֶזֶר. אִיבָּעֵית אֵימָא: לְעוֹלָם אַלִּיבָּא דְּרַבִּי יְהוֹשֻׁעַ, כִּי קָאָמַר רַבִּי יְהוֹשֻׁעַ טָעָה בִּדְבַר מִצְוָה פָּטוּר — הנ"מ גַּבֵּי תִּינוֹקוֹת, [ד]דִּזְמַנּוֹ בָּהוּל. אֲבָל הַאי, כֵּיוָן דְּאֵין זְמַנּוֹ בָּהוּל — לָא. — וַהֲרֵי תְּרוּמָה דְּאֵין זְמַנּוֹ בָּהוּל, וְקָפָטַר! דִּתְנַן: *[ה]הָיָה אוֹכֵל בִּתְרוּמָה, וְנוֹדַע שֶׁהוּא בֶּן גְּרוּשָׁה אוֹ בֶּן חֲלוּצָה — רַבִּי אֱלִיעֶזֶר מְחַיֵּיב קֶרֶן וָחוֹמֶשׁ, וְרַבִּי יְהוֹשֻׁעַ פּוֹטֵר. *הָא אִיתְּמַר עֲלָהּ, אֲמַר רַב בֵּיבָי בַּר אַבַּיֵי: הָכָא בִּתְרוּמָה בְּעֶרֶב הַפֶּסַח עָסְקִינַן, דִּזְמַנָּהּ בָּהוּל. וְאִי בָּעֵית אֵימָא: בְּאִיסּוּר בַּת אַחַת, וְאַלִּיבָּא דְּרַ' שִׁמְעוֹן. בִּשְׁלָמָא *כּוּלְּהוּ — מַשְׁכַּחַת לְהוּ, דְּשָׁוִינְהוּ שָׁלִיחַ, וְשָׁווּ אִינְהוּ שָׁלִיחַ, וּפָגַע שָׁלִיחַ בְּשָׁלִיחַ. אֶלָּא נִדּוּת — הֵיכִי מַשְׁכַּחַת לַהּ? אָמַר רַב עַמְרָם אָמַר רַב: בְּשׁוֹפְעוֹת מִתּוֹךְ י"ג לְאַחַר שְׁלֹשָׁה עָשָׂר לְאַחִיּוּבֵי אִינְהוּ, מִתּוֹךְ שְׁנֵים עָשָׂר לְאַחַר שְׁנֵים עָשָׂר — לְחִיּוּבֵי אִינְהִי.§ "מַפְרִישִׁים אוֹתָן".§ וְהָא אֵין אִשָּׁה מִתְעַבֶּרֶת בְּבִיאָה רִאשׁוֹנָה! אָמַר ר"נ אָמַר רַבָּה בַּר אֲבוּהּ: שֶׁבָּעֲלוּ וְשָׁנוּ. — [א] וְאֶלָּא הָא דְּתָנָא רַ' חִיָּיא: הֲרֵי כָּאן ט"ז חַטָּאוֹת, תְּלָתִין וְתַרְתֵּין הָוְיָין! — וְלִיטַעֲמִיךְ, לְרַ' אֱלִיעֶזֶר, דִּמְחַיֵּיב עַל כָּל כֹּחַ וְכֹחַ, טוּבָא הָוְיָין! אֶלָּא, דִּבְכֹחַ רִאשׁוֹן קָחָשֵׁיב — ה"נ דְּבִיאָה רִאשׁוֹנָה קָחָשֵׁיב. א"ל רָבָא לְרַב נַחְמָן: וְהָא

רש"י

וּמַאן הַאי תַּנָּא. דְּמַתְנִי', דְּאִית לֵיהּ אִיסּוּר חָל עַל אִיסּוּר, בֵּין עַל יְדֵי כּוֹלֵל, בֵּין בְּאִיסּוּר מוֹסִיף, בֵּין עַל יְדֵי בַּת אַחַת, כְּגוֹן אֵלּוּ שֶׁחַיָּיבִין אַרְבַּע חַטָּאוֹת. (א) וּכְשֶׁקִּידֵּשׁ רְאוּבֵן אֶת רָחֵל תְּחִלָּה נֶאֶסְרָה עַל שִׁמְעוֹן מִשּׁוּם אֵשֶׁת אָח וְאֵשֶׁת אִישׁ — וְהַיְינוּ בַּת אַחַת, וְקָמְחַיֵּיב לֵיהּ תַּנָּא דִּידַן אַתַּרְוַיְיהוּ. חָזַר שִׁמְעוֹן וְקִידֵּשׁ לֵאָה, מִיגּוֹ דְּאָסְרִי לֵיהּ הָנָךְ קִדּוּשִׁין בְּכוּלְּהוּ שְׁאָר אַחְוָותָא מִשּׁוּם אֲחוֹת אִשָּׁה, אָסְרִי לֵיהּ נַמִי בְּאֵשֶׁת אָחִיו מִשּׁוּם אֲחוֹת אִשָּׁה, וְאע"ג דַּאֲסוּרָה עֲלֵיהּ וְקַיְימָא, וְהַיְינוּ אִיסּוּר כּוֹלֵל. וַעֲדַיִין רָחֵל זוֹ מוּתֶּרֶת לִרְאוּבֵן בַּעְלָהּ. פֵּירְסָה נִדָּה, מִיגּוֹ דְּאִיתּוֹסַף אִיסּוּר עֲלָהּ לְגַבֵּי בַּעְלָהּ מִשּׁוּם נִדָּה — אִיתּוֹסַף בָּהּ נַמִי אִיסּוּר לְגַבֵּי שִׁמְעוֹן, הֲרֵי אִיסּוּר מוֹסִיף. **אַרְבַּע חַטָּאוֹת.** מִשּׁוּם טוּמְאָה דְּאוֹכֵל קָדָשִׁים בְּטוּמְאַת הַגּוּף בְּכָרֵת, וּמִשּׁוּם חֵלֶב, וּמִשּׁוּם נוֹתָר, וּמִשּׁוּם יוה"כ. וְאָשָׁם מְעִילוֹת, דַּאֲפִילּוּ כֹּהֵן לְגַבֵּי אֵימוּרִים זָר הוּא. **אִם הָיְתָה שַׁבָּת כו'.** אֲבָל מִשּׁוּם יוה"כ לָא הָוֵי מְחַיֵּיב אַהוֹצָאָה, דְּקָסָבַר: אֵין עֵירוּב וְהוֹצָאָה לְיוה"כ. וְהָכִי מְפָרֵשׁ בִּכְרֵיתוֹת. אַלְמָא אִית לֵיהּ לְרַבִּי מֵאִיר כּוּלְּהוּ, דְּהָא הָכָא, מִשֶּׁנּוֹלְדָה בְּהֵמָה זוֹ וְהִיא חוּלִּין — נֶאֶסְרָה חֶלְבָּהּ בַּאֲכִילָה וּמוּתָּר בַּהֲנָאָה. הוּקְדְּשָׁה, מִיגּוֹ דְּאִיתּוֹסַף אִיסּוּר הֲנָאָה עַל הַחֵלֶב מִשּׁוּם [קָדָשִׁים] — אִיתּוֹסַף בֵּיהּ נַמִי אִיסּוּר אֲכִילָה מִשּׁוּם זָרוּת, וְאע"ג דְּאָסוּר וְקָאֵי בַּאֲכִילָה. הָוֵה לֵיהּ נוֹתָר, מִיגּוֹ דְּאִיתּוֹסַף אִיסּוּר לַמִּזְבֵּחַ מִשּׁוּם נוֹתָר — אִיתּוֹסַף נַמִי לַכֹּהֵן מִשּׁוּם נוֹתָר, הֲרֵי הָנָךְ תְּרֵי מִשּׁוּם אִיסּוּר מוֹסִיף. נִטְמָא, זֶה שֶׁעַד עַכְשָׁיו הָיָה מוּתָּר בַּחֲתִיכוֹת בְּשַׂר קֹדֶשׁ וְעַכְשָׁיו נֶאֱסַר בָּהֶן, מִיגּוֹ דְּמִיתְסַר בִּשְׁאָר חֲתִיכוֹת מִשּׁוּם טוּמְאָה — נֶאֱסַר נַמִי בָּזוֹ מִשּׁוּם טוּמְאָה, וְהַיְינוּ אִיסּוּר כּוֹלֵל. ה"ל יוה"כ, מִיגּוֹ דְּמִיתְסַר בְּחוּלִּין מִשּׁוּם יוה"כ — אָסוּר נַמִי בְּקָדָשִׁים מִשּׁוּם יוה"כ, וְהַיְינוּ נַמִי אִיסּוּר כּוֹלֵל. וּמִדִּמְחַיֵּיב לֵיהּ רַבִּי מֵאִיר מִשּׁוּם הוֹצָאַת שַׁבָּת — אַלְמָא אִית לֵיהּ אִיסּוּר בַּת אַחַת חָיֵיל, דִּכְשֶׁקִּידֵּשׁ הַיּוֹם חָלוּ עָלָיו אִיסּוּר אֲכִילַת יוה"כ וְאִיסּוּר שַׁבָּת. **וְר"מ אַלִּיבָּא דְּמַאן.** כְּלוֹמַר, נְהִי דְּסָבַר רַבִּי מֵאִיר אִיהוּ כה"ג אִיסּוּר חָל עַל אִיסּוּר, מִיהוּ הֵיכָא דְּקָא מִתְכַּוֵּין לִדְבַר מִצְוָה לִישָּׂא אִשָּׁה, כְּמַאן מֵרַבּוֹתָיו סְבִירָא לֵיהּ לְרַבִּי מֵאִיר בְּטָעָה בִּדְבַר מִצְוָה וְלֹא עָשָׂה מִצְוָה? אִי אַלִּיבָּא דְּר' יְהוֹשֻׁעַ — הָאָמַר פָּטוּר בְּמַסֶּ' שַׁבָּת, בְּפֶרֶק "ר' אֱלִיעֶזֶר דְּמִילָה" (דף קלז.), דְּתַנְיָא הָתָם בַּגְּמָ': מִי שֶׁהָיוּ לוֹ שְׁנֵי תִינוֹקוֹת, אֶחָד לָמוּל בַּשַּׁבָּת וְאֶחָד לָמוּל בְּא' בַּשַּׁבָּת, וְשָׁכַח וּמָל אֶת שֶׁל אֶחָד בְּשַׁבָּת בַּשַּׁבָּת, דְּהַיְינוּ נַמִי טָעָה בִּדְבַר מִצְוָה וְלֹא עָשָׂה מִצְוָה, שֶׁעֲדַיִין לֹא הִגִּיעַ זְמַנּוֹ — פּוֹטֵר ר' יְהוֹשֻׁעַ. **דִּזְמַנּוֹ בָּהוּל.** שֶׁהָיָה טָרוּד לָמוּל אֶת שֶׁל שַׁבָּת, כְּדֵי שֶׁלֹּא יַעֲבוֹר זְמַנּוֹ. **אֲבָל הָכָא.** גַּבֵּי נִשּׂוּאִין, אֵין זְמַנּוֹ בָּהוּל, דְּאֵין זְמַן קָבוּעַ לַמִּצְוָה, וְה"ל לְמֵידַק. **תְּרוּמָה בְּעֶרֶב הַפֶּסַח** זְמַנּוֹ בָּהוּל. שֶׁלֹּא תִּשָּׂרֵף. **וְאִיבָּעֵית אֵימָא.** כּוּלָּהּ מַתְנִי' לָאו ר' מֵאִיר הִיא, אֶלָּא אֲפִילּוּ לְר"ש דְּמֵיקֵל הָכָא מוֹדֵי, וּכְגוֹן דְּחָלוּ כּוּלְּהוּ בְּבַת אַחַת. **דְּשָׁווּ אִינְהוּ.** שְׁנֵי הָאַחִין שָׁלִיחַ אֶחָד לְהוֹלִיךְ אֶת הַקִּדּוּשִׁין לִשְׁתֵּי אֲחָיוֹת, וְהֵן עָשׂוּ שָׁלִיחַ אֶחָד לְקַבֵּל קִדּוּשִׁין. **וּפָגַע שָׁלִיחַ בְּשָׁלִיחַ.** וְחָלוּ יַחַד זֶה עַל זֶה וְזֶה עַל זֶה, אִיסּוּר אֵשֶׁת אִישׁ, וְאִיסּוּר אֵשֶׁת אָח, וַאֲחוֹת אִשָּׁה. **אֶלָּא נִדּוּת הֵיכִי מָצֵי מַשְׁכַּחַת לַהּ.** בב"א עִם קִדּוּשִׁין? אִי קִדּוּשִׁין קָדְמוּ לְנִדּוּת זֶה — הֲרֵי אֵשֶׁת אִישׁ וַאֲחוֹת אִשָּׁה וְאֵשֶׁת אָח קָדְמוּ, וְתוּ לָא אָתֵי נִדּוּת וְחָיֵיל. וְאִי נִדּוּת קָדֵים תּוּ לָא אָתֵי אִיסּוּר אַחֲרִינָא וְחָיֵיל. **אָמַר רַב עַמְרָם אָמְרֵי בֵּי רַב.** מַשְׁכַּחַת לָהּ ט"ז חַטָּאוֹת בְּאִיסּוּר בַּת אַחַת, **בְּשׁוֹפְעוֹת מִתּוֹךְ** י"ג שָׁנָה לְלֵידַת הַבְּעָלִים, **לְאַחַר י"ג. לְאִיחִיּוּבֵי אִינְהוּ.** כְּלוֹמַר: טַעַם זֶה כְּדֵי לְחַיֵּיב הַזְּכָרִים, שֶׁחָלוּ כּוּלָּן עֲלֵיהֶן בב"א, דְּהָהוּא יוֹמָא אָתוּ לִכְלַל עוֹנָשִׁין. **וּמִתּוֹךְ י"ב לְאַחַר י"ב לְאִיחִיּוּבֵי אִינְהִי.** שֶׁהָאִשָּׁה בָּאָה לִכְלַל עוֹנָשִׁין בַּת י"ב שָׁנָה וְיוֹם אֶחָד, וְהַזָּכָר לְי"ג וְיוֹם אֶחָד. וּמַשְׁכַּחַת לָהּ שֶׁנּוֹלְדוּ הַזְּכָרִים בְּאֶחָד בְּתִשְׁרֵי וְהַנְּקֵבוֹת בְּאֶחָד בְּתִשְׁרֵי לְשָׁנָה הַבָּאָה, וּבְיוֹם אֶחָד מִיטְלָם י"ב לַנְּקֵבוֹת שֶׁהֵן י"ג לַזְּכָרִים. וּמָסְרוּ קִדּוּשִׁין שֶׁיָּחוּלוּ לְיוֹם הַמָּחֳרָת כְּשֶׁהֵן נַעֲשִׂין גְּדוֹלִים, דְּיוֹם אֶחָד בִּשְׁנַת י"ג בָּעֵינַן לַנְּקֵבוֹת, וְיוֹם אֶחָד בִּשְׁנַת י"ד לַזְּכָרִים. וְהִתְחִילוּ שׁוֹפְעוֹת בְּסוֹף י"ב לְלֵידָה עַד לְמָחָר. וְאע"ג שֶׁהַנִּדּוּת קָדַם — לֹא הָיוּ הֵן אֲסוּרוֹת לָאֵלּוּ, לְפִי שֶׁאֵינָן בִּכְלַל מִצְוֹת, וְלֹא אֵלּוּ אֲסוּרִים בָּהֶן, לְפִי שֶׁאֵינָן בְּנֵי מִצְוֹת, נִמְצְאוּ הַקִּדּוּשִׁין וְאִיסּוּר עוֹנֶשׁ נִדּוּת חָל עֲלֵיהֶם כְּשֶׁחָשְׁכָה ר"ה שֶׁל י"ג לַנְּקֵבוֹת, שֶׁהִיא שְׁנַת י"ד לַזְּכָרִים. שֶׁהַקִּדּוּשִׁין וְהַנִּדּוּת קָדְמוּ לְגַדְלוּתָן, וּתְלוּיִין וְעוֹמְדִין לָחוּל כְּשֶׁיִּגְדְּלוּ, וּבְשָׁעָה אַחַת חָלוּ כּוּלָּן. וּלְהָכִי נָקַט שׁוֹפְעוֹת, דְּאִי אֶפְשָׁר לַמְצָא פְּרִיסַת נִדָּה וּתְפִיסַת קִדּוּשִׁין בְּשָׁעָה אַחַת, אא"כ קָדְמוּ שָׁעָה אַחַת בְּקַטְנוּתָן. **תְּלָתִין וְתַרְתֵּין הָוְיָין.** דְּהָא מַתְנִיתִין כְּר' אֱלִיעֶזֶר אוֹקְמִינַן לְעֵיל, וְשָׁמְעִינַן לֵיהּ דְּאָמַר: חַיָּיב עַל כָּל בִּיאָה וּבִיאָה, לְקַמָּן (דף נג.) וּבְמַסֶּכֶת כְּרֵיתוֹת (דף טו.). **עַל כָּל כֹּחַ וְכֹחַ.** שֶׁל בִּיאָה, לְקַמָּן בְּפֶרֶק "הָאִשָּׁה" (דף נג.), וְהָתָם הָכִי תַּנְיָא: בָּא עָלֶיהָ, חָזַר וּבָא עָלֶיהָ — חַיָּיב עַל כָּל אַחַת, דִּבְרֵי רַבִּי אֱלִיעֶזֶר. וְכֵיוָן דְּשָׁמְעִינַן לֵיהּ לְרַבִּי אֱלִיעֶזֶר דִּמְחַיֵּיב אַשְּׁתֵּי בִּיאוֹת בְּהֶעְלֵם אַחַת — עַל כָּרְחָךְ שָׁמְעַתְּ לֵיהּ נַמִי בְּבִיאָה אַחַת כַּמָּה חִיּוּבִין, דְּכָל כֹּחַ וָכֹחַ — הֲנָאָה שֶׁל בִּיאָה בִּפְנֵי עַצְמָהּ הִיא. וּלְרַבָּנַן הוּא דְּלָא מְחַיֵּיב אֶלָּא אַחַת מִשּׁוּם דְּכוּלָּן בְּהֶעְלֵם אַחַת הֵן. וּבִשְׁתֵּי בִּיאוֹת נַמִי לָא הָווּ מִיחַיְּיבֵי אֶלָּא חֲדָא. אֲבָל אִי הֲוָה יְדִיעָה בֵּין כֹּחַ לְכֹחַ — הֲוָה מְחַיֵּיב אַכָּל חַד וְחַד, כְּדִתְנַן בִּשְׁבוּעוֹת (דף יח.) וּבְמַסֶּכֶת (ב) הוֹרָיוֹת *(דף ו): הָיָה מְשַׁמֵּשׁ עִם הַטְּהוֹרָה וְאָמְרָה לוֹ נִטְמֵאתִי, וּפֵירֵשׁ מִיָּד — חַיָּיב, שֶׁיְּצִיאָתוֹ הֲנָאָה לוֹ כְּבִיאָתוֹ, וּלְרַ' אֱלִיעֶזֶר דְּאָמַר בִּיאוֹת מְחַלְּקוֹת — אִית לֵיהּ נַמִי כּוֹחוֹת מְחַלְּקִין. וּמַתְנִי' כְּרַבִּי אֱלִיעֶזֶר אוֹקִימְנָא לְעֵיל, וְהֵיכִי תָּנֵי רַבִּי חִיָּיא שֵׁשׁ עֶשְׂרֵה וְתוּ לָא. וְהָא

תוספות

אם היתה שבת והוציאו כו'. בפרק "אמרו לו" (כריתות דף יד.) רצה לדקדק מכאן דאין עירוב והוצאה ליום הכפורים, מדאיצטריך למנקט אם היתה שבת כו', דהוה ליה למיתני: ואם הוציאו – חייב. ומסיק – דיש עירוב והוצאה ליוה"כ, ולאפוקי חיובי נקט שבת, וחייב משום שבת ויוה"כ. וא"ת: והיכי חשיב רבי מאיר חיובי הוצאה בהדי חיובי דאכילה? מה ענין זה אצל זה! דכמו כן היה יכול לומר אם עשה מלאכה בשבת חייב! וא"ר"י: משום דבשעת בליעה אתי נמי חיוב הוצאה, אע"ג דאכתי לא נח, משום דבליעתן זו היא הנחתן. כדאמר רבא בפרק "המוציא יין" (שבת דף פ.): הוציא ב' אותיות וכתבן כשהוא מהלך – חייב, דכתיבתן זו היא הנחתן*.

והוציאו בפיו חייב. והא דאמר ב"המצניע" (שם דף צב.) המוציא בפיו ובמרפקו פטור, שלא הוציא כדרך המוציאים – במידי דבר אכילה הוי שפיר דרך הוצאה בכך. פי' הקונטרס דאיכא הכא איסור בת אחת, דכשקידש היום חל עליו איסור אכילת יוה"כ ואיסור הוצאת שבת. וקשיא לרבינו יצחק: דמה ענין זה לאיסור חל על איסור? דאפילו למ"ד אין איסור חל על איסור אפילו בבת אחת – הכא חל לכולי עלמא אפילו בזה אחר זה, ואפי' יעשה אכילה והוצאה בזה אחר זה, ואפילו חלו שבת ויום הכפורים בזה אחר זה, שבשביל איסור מלאכת שבת אם הוא תחלה – לא ימנע איסור אכילת יום הכפורים לחול אחריו, שעדיין לא נאסר זה מחמת השבת, וכן איפכא! ואמר רבי יצחק: דאיסור בבת אחת היינו איסור הוצאה דשבת ואיסור הוצאה דיוה"כ, כדפרישית, דנקט שבת לאפוקי חיובי.

טעה בדבר מצוה פטור. וא"ת: והא בפסחים בפרק "אלו דברים" (דף עב. ושם) מוקי רבי מאיר פלוגתייהו בשתי תינוקות, אחד למול בשבת ואחד למול באחד בשבת, דפטר ר' יהושע כשקדם ומל של אחד בשבת בשבת אע"ג דלא עשה מצוה, משום דנתנה שבת לדחות אצל תינוק אחד. אבל בשתי תינוקות, אחד למול בשבת ואחד למול בע"ש, וקדם ומל של שבת בע"ש ושל ע"ש מל בשבת – חייב, אע"ג דעשה מצוה, משום דלא נתנה לדחות. וה"נ גבי שתי נשים – לחייב, דלא ניתנה ערוה לדחות! וי"ל: דהתם לא בדחיה תליא מילתא, אלא משום דטריד בתינוק שיש לו למול בשבת, וטועה בו. וה"נ – הרי טועה באשתו.

בערב הפסח כו'. המ"ל משום דאכילת תרומה איקרי עבודה וטעמא דרבי יהושע משום דכתיב(ג) "ופועל ידיו תרצה" – אפילו חללים, כדאמר פרק "אלו דברים" (פסחים דף עב: ושם).

באיסור בת אחת **ואליבא** דרבי שמעון. ואתי שפיר אפילו כרבי יהושע. דרבי שמעון אית ליה בפרק "אלו דברים" (שם) דלרבי יהושע טעה בדבר מצוה ולא עשה מצוה – חייב.

מתוך שלשה עשר **לאיחיובי** אינהו. כן גירסת הקונטרס. וקשה: דלא הוי בבת אחת, דנדות חל

עין משפט נר מצוה

מד א מיי' פ"ד מהל' שגגות הלכה א:

מה ב מיי' פ"ו שם הלכה ז:

מו ג ד מיי' שם פ"ב הלכה ח:

מז ה מיי' פ"י מהל' תרומות הלכה יב:

מסורת הש"ס

שבת קב. שבועות כד: כריתות יג:

[ל"ל דתנן]

[ועי' תוספות כריתות יד. ד"ה אם ותוספות שבת עא. ד"ה לא יעמוד ותוס' ערובין כ. ד"ה לא]

תרומות פ"ח מ"א פסחים עב: מכות יח:

[פסחים עב:]

[עי' תוספות ב"מ עא: ד"ה כגון]

[ליתא שם] וע"ש פ"ב מ"ה בפי' המשניות להרמב"ם

תוספות ישנים

ומאן האי תנא דאית ליה איסור כולל ואיסור מוסיף ואיסור בת אחת א"ר יהודה אמר רב ר"מ היא. ה"נ הוי מצי למימר רבי יוסי היא דאית ליה איסור כולל וכ"ש דאית ליה איסור מוסיף ואיסור בת אחת אלא נקט רבי מאיר משום דאית ליה בהדיא כל הני יחד כולל ומוסיף ובת אחת:

הגהות הב"ח

(א) רש"י ד"ה ומאן וכו' דכשקידש ראובן: (ב) ד"ה על כל כח וכו' ובמסכת כריתות היה משמש: (ג) תוספות ד"ה בערב וכו' משום דכתיב בכך ה' חילו ופועל ידיו:

הגהות הגר"א

[א] גמ' ואלא הא כו' עד דביאה ראשונה קחשיב תא"מ:

וְהָא תָּמָר בְּבִיאָה רִאשׁוֹנָה אִיעַבְּרָא! א"ל: תָּמָר בְּאֶצְבַּע מָעֲכָה. דְּאָמַר רַבִּי יִצְחָק: כָּל מוֹעֲכוֹת שֶׁל בֵּית רַבִּי תָּמָר שְׁמָן, וְלָמָּה נִקְרָא שְׁמָן תָּמָר? ע"ש תָּמָר שֶׁמָּעֲכָה בְּאֶצְבָּעָהּ. — וְהָא הָווּ עֵר וְאוֹנָן! — עֵר וְאוֹנָן שִׁמְּשׁוּ שֶׁלֹּא כְּדַרְכָּן. מֵיתִיבֵי: כָּל עֶשְׂרִים וְאַרְבָּעָה חֹדֶשׁ דָּשׁ מִבִּפְנִים וְזוֹרֶה מִבַּחוּץ, דִּבְרֵי רַ' אֱלִיעֶזֶר. א"ל: [א]הַלָּלוּ אֵינוֹ אֶלָּא כְּמַעֲשֵׂה עֵר וְאוֹנָן! — כְּמַעֲשֵׂה עֵר וְאוֹנָן, וְלֹא כְּמַעֲשֵׂה עֵר וְאוֹנָן. כְּמַעֲשֵׂה עֵר וְאוֹנָן — דִּכְתִיב °"וְהָיָה אִם בָּא אֶל אֵשֶׁת אָחִיו וְשִׁחֵת אַרְצָה", וְלֹא כְּמַעֲשֵׂה עֵר וְאוֹנָן, דְּאִילּוּ הָתָם — שֶׁלֹּא כְּדַרְכָּהּ, וְהָכָא — כְּדַרְכָּהּ. בִּשְׁלָמָא אוֹנָן — דִּכְתִיב בֵּיהּ "וְשִׁחֵת אַרְצָה", אֶלָּא עֵר מְנָלַן? — אָמַר רַב נַחְמָן בַּר יִצְחָק: דִּכְתִיב °"וַיָּמֶת גַּם אוֹתוֹ", אַף הוּא בְּאוֹתוֹ מִיתָה מֵת. בִּשְׁלָמָא אוֹנָן — מִשּׁוּם "לֹּא לוֹ יִהְיֶה הַזָּרַע", אֶלָּא עֵר מ"ט עֲבַד הָכִי? — כְּדֵי שֶׁלֹּא תִּתְעַבֵּר וְיַכְחִישׁ יָפְיָהּ. ת"ר: °"אוֹתָהּ" פְּרָט לְכַלָּה, דִּבְרֵי רַבִּי יְהוּדָה. וְחכ"א: [ב]פְּרָט לְשֶׁלֹּא כְּדַרְכָּהּ. אֲמַר לֵיהּ הוּן בְּרֵיהּ דְּרַב נַחְמָן לְרַב נַחְמָן: לֵימָא קָא סָבַר רַבִּי יְהוּדָה הַתּוֹרָה חָסָה עַל תַּכְשִׁיטֵי כַּלָּה? — אֲמַר לֵיהּ: לְפִי שֶׁאֵין אִשָּׁה מִתְעַבֶּרֶת מִבִּיאָה רִאשׁוֹנָה. בְּמַאי קָמִיפַּלְגִי? רַבָּנַן סָבְרִי "שִׁכְבַת זֶרַע" פְּרָט [ג]לְהַעֲרָאָה, "אוֹתָהּ" פְּרָט לְשֶׁלֹּא כְּדַרְכָּהּ. וְרַבִּי יְהוּדָה סָבַר: שֶׁלֹּא כְּדַרְכָּהּ וְהַעֲרָאָה — מִ"שִּׁכְבַת זֶרַע" נָפְקָא, "אוֹתָהּ" פְּרָט לְכַלָּה. כִּי אֲתָא *רָבִין א"ר יוֹחָנָן: כָּל שֶׁשָּׁהֲתָה אַחַר בַּעְלָהּ עֶשֶׂר שָׁנִים וְנִשֵּׂאת — שׁוּב אֵינָהּ יוֹלֶדֶת. אָמַר רַב נַחְמָן:: לֹא שָׁנוּ אֶלָּא שֶׁאֵין דַּעְתָּהּ לְהִנָּשֵׂא, אֲבָל דַּעְתָּהּ לְהִנָּשֵׂא — מִתְעַבֶּרֶת. אֲמַר לֵיהּ רָבָא לְבַת רַב חִסְדָּא: קָא מְרַנְּנֵי רַבָּנַן אַבַּתְרִיךְ. — אֲמָרָה לֵיהּ: אֲנָא דַּעְתַּאי עֲלָךְ הֲוַאי. הַהִיא דַּאֲתְיָא לְקַמֵּיהּ דְּרַב יוֹסֵף, אָמְרָה לוֹ: ר', אֲנָא שֶׁהָיִיתִי אַחַר בַּעְלִי עֶשֶׂר שָׁנִים וְיָלַדְתִּי. — א"ל: בִּתִּי, אַל תּוֹצִיאִי לַעַז עַל דִּבְרֵי חֲכָמִים. — אָמְרָה לֵיהּ: לְגוֹי נִבְעַלְתִּי. אָמַר שְׁמוּאֵל: וְכוּלָּן צְרִיכוֹת לְהַמְתִּין שְׁלֹשָׁה חֳדָשִׁים, חוּץ מִגִּיּוֹרֶת וּמְשׁוּחְרֶרֶת קְטַנָּה. אֲבָל קְטַנָּה בַּת יִשְׂרָאֵל — צְרִיכָה לְהַמְתִּין ג' חֳדָשִׁים. וּבְמַאי? אִי בְּמֵיאוּן — וְהָאָמַר שְׁמוּאֵל דְּלָא בָּעֲיָא. וְאִי בְּגֵט — הָאָמְרָהּ שְׁמוּאֵל חֲדָא זִימְנָא. דְּאָמַר שְׁמוּאֵל: *[ד]מֵיאֲנָה בּוֹ — אֵינָהּ צְרִיכָה לְהַמְתִּין שְׁלֹשָׁה חֳדָשִׁים, [ה]נָתַן לָהּ גֵּט — צְרִיכָה לְהַמְתִּין שְׁלֹשָׁה חֳדָשִׁים! — אֶלָּא בִּזְנוּת. וְגָזְרוּ

תורה אור: בראשית לח; שם; ויקרא טו

[כתובות ק:]

וְהָא תָּמָר אִיעַבְּרָא בְּבִיאָה רִאשׁוֹנָה. מִיהוּדָה, כִּדְאָמַר לְקַמָּן דְּעֵר וְאוֹנָן שֶׁלֹּא כְּדַרְכָּן שִׁמְּשׁוּ. **בְּאֶצְבַּע מִיעֲכָה.** קוֹדֶם בִּיאָה, וּפִתְחָהּ פָּתוּחַ, וְהָווּ לֵיהּ כְּב' בִּיאוֹת. **כָּל מוֹעֲכוֹת שֶׁל בֵּית רַבִּי.** הַמְשִׁירוֹת בְּתוּלֵיהֶן בְּאֶצְבְּעוֹתֵיהֶן תָּמָר שְׁמָן. **כָּל כ"ד חֹדֶשׁ.** שֶׁתִּינוֹק יוֹנֵק. **דָּשׁ מִבִּפְנִים וְזוֹרֶה מִבַּחוּץ.** כְּדֵי שֶׁלֹּא תִּתְעַבֵּר, וְתִגְמוֹל אֶת בְּנָהּ, וְיָמוּת. **אֶלָּא כְּמַעֲשֵׂה עֵר וְאוֹנָן.** אַלְמָא, תָּמָר פֶּתַח פָּתוּחַ הָיָה לָהּ. **אוֹתָהּ.** "וְאִשָּׁה (כִּי) [אֲשֶׁר] יִשְׁכַּב אִישׁ אוֹתָהּ שִׁכְבַת זֶרַע וְרָחֲצוּ בַמַּיִם", "אוֹתָהּ" מִיעוּטָא הוּא. **פְּרָט לְכַלָּה.** דְּלָא בָּעֲיָא טְבִילָה מִשּׁוּם טוּמְאַת בִּיאָה רִאשׁוֹנָה, כִּדְמְפָרֵשׁ טַעְמָא לְקַמָּן. **הוּן.** שֵׁם חָכָם. **עַל תַּכְשִׁיטֵי כַלָּה.** כָּחָל וּשְׂרָק שֶׁנּוֹתֶנֶת עַל פָּנֶיהָ, וְאִם תִּטְבּוֹל יַעֲבִירוּם הַמַּיִם. **לְפִי שֶׁאֵין אִשָּׁה מִתְעַבֶּרֶת מִבִּיאָה רִאשׁוֹנָה.** וְלָא "שִׁכְבַת זֶרַע" קָרֵינַן בֵּיהּ, דְּאֵין רָאוּי לְהַזְרִיעַ. וּמִיהוּ, מִיעוּטָא מִ"שִּׁכְבַת זֶרַע" לָא נָפְקָא, הוֹאִיל וְהַאי מָקוֹם רָאוּי לְהַזְרִיעַ הוּא בְּבִיאָה שְׁנִיָּה. וּמִשּׁוּם נוֹגֵעַ בְּשִׁכְבַת זֶרַע נַמִי לָא מִיטַּמְּיָא, דְּטוּמְאַת בֵּית הַסְּתָרִים לָא מְטַמְּאָה, אֶלָּא שֶׁגְּזֵרַת הַכָּתוּב הִיא בְּבִיאָה, וְכֵן הוּא בְּמַסֶּכֶת נִדָּה (דף מא:). **לְהַעֲרָאָה.** שֶׁלֹּא הִזְרִיעַ, אִי לְמ"ד נְשִׁיקָה, אִי לְמ"ד הַכְנָסַת עֲטָרָה. **שֶׁלֹּא כְּדַרְכָּהּ וְהַעֲרָאָה מש"ז נָפְקָא.** שֶׁלֹּא כְּדַרְכָּהּ אֵינוֹ מְקוֹם זֶרַע, הַעֲרָאָה — לָאו שִׁכְבַת זֶרַע הוּא, דְּאֵין כָּאן זֶרַע. הִלְכָּךְ תַּרְוַיְיהוּ מִ"שִּׁכְבַת זֶרַע" מִימְעֲטֵי. **לְבַת רַב חִסְדָּא.** אִשְׁתּוֹ דְּרָבָא. **אַבַּתְרִיךְ.** שֶׁשָּׁהִית עֶשֶׂר שָׁנִים אַחַר בַּעְלֵיךְ הָרִאשׁוֹן, וְרָמֵי בַּר חָמָא הֲוָה. **אָמַר שְׁמוּאֵל וְכוּלָּן.** הַנָּשִׁים שֶׁנִּבְעֲלוּ. **צְרִיכוֹת לְהַמְתִּין.** מִלְּהִנָּשֵׂא שְׁלֹשָׁה חֳדָשִׁים אַחַר בִּיאָתָן, חוּץ מִגִּיּוֹרֶת וּמְשׁוּחְרֶרֶת קְטַנָּה, וְאַע"ג דִּסְתָם גּוֹיוֹת וְשִׁפְחָה זוֹנוֹת הֵן — לָא גָּזְרוּ רַבָּנַן בִּקְטַנָּה לְהַמְתִּין אַחַר טְבִילַת גִּיּוֹרֶת וּמְשׁוּחְרֶרֶת כְּלוּם. **וּמִדְּקָאָמַר שְׁמוּאֵל חוּץ מִגִּיּוֹרֶת קְטַנָּה** — מִכְּלָל דְּכוּלָּן דְּקָאָמַר אַקְּטַנּוֹת נַמִי קָאֵי, דִּקְטַנָּה בַּת יִשְׂרָאֵל צְרִיכָה לְהַמְתִּין. וְאַע"ג דְּלָאו בַּת בָּנִים הִיא, וְאֵין כָּאן הַבְחָנָה בֵּין זַרְעוֹ שֶׁל רִאשׁוֹן לְזַרְעוֹ שֶׁל שֵׁנִי — גְּזוּר בָּהּ רַבָּנַן מִשּׁוּם גְּדוֹלָה. **וּבְמַאי.** נָפְקָא מִבַּעְלָהּ קַמָּא. **אִי בְּמֵיאוּן הָאָמַר שְׁמוּאֵל דְּלָא בָּעֲיָא.** אַמְתּוּנֵי, דְּלֵיכָּא לְמִיגְזַר מִשּׁוּם גְּדוֹלָה דְּאֵין גְּדוֹלָה יוֹצְאָת בְּמֵיאוּן.

חַל עָלָיו תְּחִלָּה שֶׁאֵין יָכוֹל לְקַדֵּשׁ וְלֹא לַעֲשׂוֹת שָׁלִיחַ עַד שֶׁיַּגְדִּיל, דְּאֵין מַעֲשֵׂה קָטָן כְּלוּם. וְאוֹר"ת: דִּבְכָל סְפָרִים קַדְמוֹנִים כֵּן, (א) אֲבָל בְּסֵפֶר "בָּשָׂר עַל גַּבֵּי גֶּחָלִים" גָּרַס בְּשׁוֹפְעוֹת מִתּוֹךְ ג' לְאַחַר ג' לְאִיחוּדֵי אִינְהוּ, דִּלְאַחַר ג' שָׁנִים וְיוֹם אֶחָד חֲזִיא לְבִיאָה, וְאָתוּ כּוּלְהוּ אִיסּוּרֵי וְחָיְילֵי. וּמִתּוֹךְ י"ב לְאַחַר י"ב לְאִיחוּדֵי אִינְהוּ.

וְאִם בָּעֲלוּ כְּשֶׁכּוּלָּן גְּדוֹלוֹת אִיכָּא ט"ז חַטָּאוֹת, וְכֵן לְגִירְסַת הַקּוּנְטְרֵס וְכֵן לְגִירְסָא זוֹ שׁוֹפְעוֹת לָאו דַּוְקָא, אֶלָּא שֶׁרָאֲתָה וְלֹא טָבְלָה בֵּינְתַיִם. וּלְגִירְסַת ר"ת שֶׁרָאֲתָה בְּתוֹךְ ג' וְלֹא טָבְלָה עַד לְאַחַר י"ב. **וְלֹא** כְּמַעֲשֵׂה עֵר וְאוֹנָן דְּאִילּוּ הָתָם שֶׁלֹּא כְּדַרְכָּהּ. מַשְׁמַע דְּאָסוּר לְשַׁמֵּשׁ שֶׁלֹּא כְּדַרְכָּהּ. וּתְמִיהָ: דִּפ"ב דִּנְדָרִים (דף כ:) אָמַר: הַהִיא דַּאֲתִיא לְקַמֵּיהּ דְּרַבִּי וְאָמְרָה לֵיהּ שׁוּלְחָן עָרַכְתִּי לוֹ וְהִפְכוֹ, אָמַר לָהּ: בִּתִּי, הַתּוֹרָה הִתִּירַתֵּךְ לוֹ. וּמַסִּיק דְּהִלְכְתָא הָכִי. וְהִפְכוֹ — הַיְינוּ שֶׁלֹּא כְּדַרְכָּהּ, לְפִי שֶׁמִּצְטַעֶרֶת בְּכָךְ, שֶׁנֶּא' (בראשית לד) "וַיִּשְׁכַּב אוֹתָהּ וַיְעַנֶּהָ" שֶׁעִינָּה אוֹתָהּ שֶׁלֹּא כְּדַרְכָּהּ. וְכֵן "אִם תְּעַנֶּה אֶת בְּנוֹתַי" (שם לא) שֶׁלֹּא כְּדַרְכָּן. דְּאִי הִפְכוֹ הִיא לְמַעְלָה וְהוּא לְמַטָּה — לֹא הָיְתָה קוֹבֶלֶת עַל כָּךְ. וְכֵן בְּפ' "אַרְבַּע מִיתוֹת" (סנהדרין דף נח:) אָמַר: גּוֹי הַבָּא עַל אִשְׁתּוֹ שֶׁלֹּא כְּדַרְכָּהּ — חַיָּיב מִיתָה. וּפָרִיךְ: מִי אִיכָּא מִידֵי דְּיִשְׂרָאֵל לָא מִיחַיַּיב וְגוֹי מִיחַיַּיב? (ב) וְהַיְינוּ הַאי לֹא מְחַיַּיב הַיְינוּ דְּיִשְׂרָאֵל שָׁרֵי. דְּאִי אִיכָּא אִיסּוּר בְּיִשְׂרָאֵל — נִיחָא דִּמְחַיַּיב בְּגוֹי מִיתָה, דְּאַזְהָרָתָן זוֹ הִיא מִיתָתָן כְּמוֹ בְּגָזֵל וּשְׁאָר דְּבָרִים! וְאוֹר"י: דְּהָתָם מַיְירֵי בְּלֹא הוֹצָאַת זֶרַע, דְּשָׁרֵי, דְּכֵיוָן דְּלֵיכָּא הַשְׁחָתַת זֶרַע לָא הָוֵי כְּמַעֲשֵׂה עֵר וְאוֹנָן. עוֹד אָמַר ר"י: דְּלָא חָשׁוּב כְּמַעֲשֵׂה עֵר וְאוֹנָן אֶלָּא כְּשֶׁמִּתְכַּוֵּין לְהַשְׁחִית זֶרַע, וְרָגִיל לַעֲשׂוֹת כֵּן תָּמִיד. אֲבָל דְּאַקְרַאי בְּעָלְמָא, וּמִתְאַוֶּה לָבֹא עַל אִשְׁתּוֹ שֶׁלֹּא כְּדַרְכָּהּ — שָׁרֵי, כִּדְאָמְרִי' בִּנְדָרִים (דף כ:): כָּל מַה שֶּׁאָדָם רוֹצֶה לַעֲשׂוֹת בְּאִשְׁתּוֹ יַעֲשֶׂה, מָשָׁל לְבָשָׂר הַבָּא מִן הַטַּבָּח, וְדָג מִן הַצַּיָּד, רָצָה — אוֹכְלוֹ צָלִי, רָצָה — אוֹכְלוֹ מְבוּשָּׁל, רָצָה — שָׁלוּק. **הַתּוֹרָה** חָסָה עַל תַּכְשִׁיטֵי כַלָּה. שֶׁלֹּא יִפּוֹל שְׂרָק מֵעַל פָּנֶיהָ אַע"ג דְּמִיָּד שֶׁתַּעֲמוֹד תִּפְלוֹט וְתִצְטָרֵךְ לִטְבּוֹל — מ"מ נִיחָא שֶׁהַתּוֹרָה חָסָה כָּל זְמַן שֶׁלֹּא תַּעֲמוֹד, אוֹ שֶׁתִּתֵּן מוֹךְ קוֹדֶם שֶׁתַּעֲמוֹד, כְּדֵי שֶׁלֹּא תִּפְלוֹט. **דַּעְתַּאי** עֲלָךְ הֲוַאי. אָמַר רַבֵּינוּ תָּם: מִשּׁוּם הַהִיא עוּבְדָּא דְּפ"ק דְּב"ב (דף יב:), דְּאָמְרָה בַּת רַב חִסְדָּא: תַּרְוַיְיהוּ קַבְּעִינָא, וְהָיְתָה מְצַפָּה שֶׁתִּתְקַיֵּים נְבוּאָתָהּ. לְפִי שֶׁהָיָה לְרָבָא אִשָּׁה אַחֶרֶת אֲסוּרָה לִינָשֵׂא לוֹ, וְאַפ"ה הָיְתָה מְצַפָּה לוֹ. **אָמַר** שְׁמוּאֵל וְכוּלָּן צְרִיכוֹת כו'. אֲבָל נָשִׁים דִּתְנַן בְּ"הַחוֹלֵץ" (לקמן דף מא.) וּבְבָרַיְיתָא הָתָם בִּגְמָ' (דף מב:) קָאֵי. **אֲבָל** קְטַנָּה בַּת יִשְׂרָאֵל צְרִיכָה לְהַמְתִּין. דְּגָזְרִינַן זְנוּת דִּקְטַנָּה בַּת יִשְׂרָאֵל אַטּוּ גְּדוֹלָה. אֲבָל בְּגִיּוֹרֶת קְטַנָּה לָא שַׁיָּיךְ לְמִגְזַר אַטּוּ גִּיּוֹרֶת גְּדוֹלָה, דִּגְדוֹלָה גּוּפָהּ כֵּיוָן דְּלְדַעְתָּהּ לְאִיגַּיּוֹרֵי מִינְטְרָא נַפְשָׁהּ, כִּדְאָמַר לְקַמָּן, וְלָא אֲסִירָא אֶלָּא אַטּוּ בַּת יִשְׂרָאֵל. וְא"ת: וּשְׁמוּאֵל דְּאָמַר כְּמַאן? בִּשְׁלָמָא בִּקְטַנָּה בַּת יִשְׂרָאֵל — סָבַר לָהּ כר"מ, דְּגָזַר בְּ"הַחוֹלֵץ" (שם דף מב:) בְּבָרַיְיתָא דִּרְדוּפָה קְטַנָּה בְּנִישּׂוּאִין אַטּוּ גְּדוֹלָה, וְקָסָבַר שְׁמוּאֵל דְּה"ה בִּזְנוּת. אֶלָּא בְּגִיּוֹרֶת, כְּמַאן סָבַר לָהּ? אִי כר' יְהוּדָה — אֲפִילוּ גִּיּוֹרֶת קְטַנָּה לִגְזוֹר, כִּדְתַנְיָא בְּסָמוּךְ: הַגִּיּוֹרֶת וְהַשִּׁפְחָה כו', יְתֵירוֹת עַל בְּנוֹת שָׁלֹשׁ שָׁנִים, צְרִיכוֹת לְהַמְתִּין שְׁלֹשָׁה חֳדָשִׁים, דִּבְרֵי ר"י. וְאַע"פ דְּהָכָא בְּרוֹב סְפָרִים לָא גָּרְסִי' יְתֵירוֹת עַל בְּנוֹת שָׁלֹשׁ שָׁנִים, בְּפֶרֶק "אֵלּוּ נְעָרוֹת" (כתובות דף לז.) גָּרְסִינַן לָהּ בְּכָל הַסְּפָרִים. וְאִי כְּרַבִּי יוֹסֵי — אֲפִילוּ גְּדוֹלָה נַמִי תִּשְׁתְּרֵי, דְּר' יוֹסֵי שָׁרֵי אֲפִילוּ בְּגִיּוֹרֶת גְּדוֹלָה לִינָּשֵׂא מִיָּד. דְּהָא בְּאִידָךְ לִישָּׁנָא דִּשְׁמוּאֵל דְּשָׁרֵי גְּדוֹלָה אָמְרִי' הוּא דְּאָמַר כְּרַבִּי יוֹסֵי. וְעוֹד: דִּסְבָרַת שְׁמוּאֵל הֲפוּכָה מִדְּר' יְהוּדָה, דְּהָא בְּבָרַיְיתָא דִּרְדוּפָה לָא גָּזַר ר"י בִּקְטַנָּה בַּת יִשְׂרָאֵל אֲפִילוּ בְּנִישּׂוּאִין, וּבְגִיּוֹרֶת גָּזַר אֲפִילוּ בִּקְטַנָּה, כִּדְקָתָנֵי: יְתֵירוֹת עַל בְּנוֹת ג', וּשְׁמוּאֵל אִיפְּכָא: דִּבִקְטַנָּה בַּת יִשְׂרָאֵל גָּזַר וּבְגִיּוֹרֶת לָא גָּזַר. וּמִיהוּ, לִסְפָרִים דְּגָרְסִי בְּבָרַיְיתָא דִּרְדוּפָה רַבִּי יוֹסֵי וְלָא רַבִּי יְהוּדָה אָתֵי שַׁפִּיר. וּלְקַמָּן *נַמִי נִפְרֵשׁ בְּעֶזְרַת הַשֵּׁם. וְאוֹר"י: דְּלֹ"ג בְּמַתְנִיתִין יְתֵירוֹת, וּבְתוֹסֶפְתָּא לֵיתֵיהּ. וּבִגְדוֹלָה דַּוְקָא אָסַר ר"י, אֲבָל בִּקְטַנָּה שָׁרֵי וּשְׁמוּאֵל כְּרַבִּי יְהוּדָה סְבִירָא לֵיהּ בְּגִיּוֹרֶת.

נָתַן לָהּ גֵּט צְרִיכָה לְהַמְתִּין. הִקְשָׁה ה"ר מֹשֶׁה כֹּהֵן: הָא אָמְרָהּ שְׁמוּאֵל חֲדָא זִימְנָא בְּפֶרֶק "אַע"פ" (כתובות דף ס: ושם), דְּפָסִיק שְׁמוּאֵל הֲלָכָה כְּרַבִּי מֵאִיר בִּגְזֵירוֹתָיו אַבָּרַיְיתָא דִּרְדוּפָה! וְאוֹר"י: דְּעִיקַּר מִילְּתֵיהּ דִּשְׁמוּאֵל לָא אִיצְטְרִיךְ הָכָא אֶלָּא מִשּׁוּם מְמָאֶנֶת, וְעִיקַּר מִילְּתֵיהּ דִּשְׁמוּאֵל דְּהָכָא בְּסוֹף "אַלְמָנָה" בִּכְתוּבּוֹת (דף ק: ושם). וְהָא דְּפָרִיךְ עֲלָהּ הָתָם: כּוּלְּהוּ תְּנֵינָא, וּמְשַׁנֵּי: צְרִיכָה לְהַמְתִּין שְׁלֹשָׁה חֳדָשִׁים אִיצְטְרִיךְ לֵיהּ, דְּלָא תְּנַן — הָכִי פֵּירוּשׁוֹ: דִּין דִּשְׁלֹשָׁה חֳדָשִׁים אִיצְטְרִיךְ לֵיהּ. אֲבָל הִיא גּוּפָהּ לָא אִיצְטְרִיךְ אֶלָּא מִשּׁוּם מְמָאֶנֶת, דְּאֵין צְרִיכָה לְהַמְתִּין, כְּדְפָרֵישִׁית.

חוץ

מח א מיי' פכ"א מהל' איסורי ביאה הלכה יח סמג לאוין קכו טור ש"ע אה"ע סימן כג סעיף א:

מט ב מיי' פ"ה מהל' אבות הטומאה הלכה ט:

נ ג מיי' שם הלכה י:

נא ד מיי' פי"א מהל' גירושין הלכה כב סמג עשין נ טור ש"ע אה"ע סימן יג סעיף ו:

נב ה מיי' שם והלכה כ טוש"ע אה"ע שם סעיף א:

תוספות חד מקמאי

אמר רב נחמן אמר שמואל כל שנשתהה עשר שנים אחר בעלה ונשאת שוב אין נתעברת. ולא אמרן אלא שאין דעתה להנשא אבל דעתה להנשא מתעברת:

[עי' תוס' סוטה כד. ד"ה שאינה]

גליון הש"ס

גמ' והא תמר. עיין פי' רש"י בחומש בראשית יט לז וברא"ס שם בשם מדרש רבה: **שם** באצבע מיעכה. עיין לקמן עו ע"א תד"ה שלא ראה: **שם** אבל דעתה להנשא. עיין כתובות דף סב ע"ב ברש"י ד"ה איעקרה:

הגהות הב"ח

(א) תום' ד"ה (בע') מתוך וכו' דבכל ספ[רים] קדמונים כן אבל בס[פר] נ"ב ס"א וכן בספר [...] (ב) ד"ה ולא וכו' וע[...] כוכבים מיחייב ועל כ[...] האי לא מיחייב:

[דף מב: ד"ה רבי יוס[י]]

וְגָזְרוּ רַבָּנַן קְטַנָּה מִשּׁוּם גְּדוֹלָה. — וּמִי גָּזְרִינַן קְטַנָּה מִשּׁוּם גְּדוֹלָה? וְהָתְנַן: *[א]אִם הָיוּ קְטַנּוֹת שֶׁאֵינָן רְאוּיוֹת לֵילֵד — מַחֲזִירִין אוֹתָן מִיָּד! אָמַר רַב גִּידֵּל אָמַר רַב: הוֹרָאַת שָׁעָה הָיְתָה. — מִכְּלָל דַּהֲוַאי?! אֶלָּא כְּהוֹרָאַת שָׁעָה הָיְתָה, וְחִילּוּף לָא שְׁכִיחַ. לִישָּׁנָא אַחֲרִינָא אָמְרִי לָהּ, אָמַר שְׁמוּאֵל: כּוּלָּן צְרִיכוֹת לְהַמְתִּין שְׁלֹשָׁה חֳדָשִׁים, חוּץ מִגִּיּוֹרֶת וּמְשׁוּחְרֶרֶת גְּדוֹלָה. [אֲבָל] קְטַנָּה בַּת יִשְׂרָאֵל — אֵינָהּ צְרִיכָה לְהַמְתִּין ג' חֳדָשִׁים. בְּמַאי? אִי בְּמֵיאוּן — הָאָמְרָהּ שְׁמוּאֵל חֲדָא זִימְנָא, אִי בְּגֵט — הָא קָאָמַר שְׁמוּאֵל דְּבָעְיָא, דְּאָמַר שְׁמוּאֵל: מֵיאֲנָה בּוֹ — אֵינָהּ צְרִיכָה לְהַמְתִּין שְׁלֹשָׁה חֳדָשִׁים, נָתַן לָהּ גֵּט — צְרִיכָה לְהַמְתִּין שְׁלֹשָׁה חֳדָשִׁים! — אֶלָּא בִּזְנוּת, וּזְנוּת בִּקְטַנָּה לָא שְׁכִיחַ. — גִּיּוֹרֶת וּמְשׁוּחְרֶרֶת, דִּשְׁכִיחַ בְּהוּ זְנוּת, לִיגְזוֹר! — הוּא דְּאָמַר כְּרַבִּי יוֹסֵי. דְּתַנְיָא: *[ב]הַגִּיּוֹרֶת וְהַשְּׁבוּיָה וְהַשִּׁפְחָה שֶׁנִּפְדּוּ וְשֶׁנִּתְגַּיְּירוּ וְשֶׁנִּשְׁתַּחְרְרוּ — צְרִיכוֹת לְהַמְתִּין ג' חֳדָשִׁים, דִּבְרֵי רַבִּי יְהוּדָה. רַבִּי יוֹסֵי מַתִּיר לֵיאָרֵס וְלִינָּשֵׂא מִיָּד. אָמַר רַבָּה: מ"ט דְּרַבִּי יוֹסֵי — קָסָבַר: אִשָּׁה מְזַנָּה מְשַׁמֶּשֶׁת בְּמוֹךְ כְּדֵי שֶׁלֹּא תִּתְעַבֵּר. א"ל אַבָּיֵי: בִּשְׁלָמָא גִּיּוֹרֶת, כֵּיוָן דְּדַעְתָּהּ לְאִיגַּיּוּרֵי — מְנַטְּרָה נַפְשָׁהּ. כְּדֵי לְהַבְחִין בֵּין זֶרַע שֶׁנִּזְרַע בִּקְדוּשָּׁה וּבֵין זֶרַע שֶׁנִּזְרַע שֶׁלֹּא בִּקְדוּשָּׁה. שְׁבוּיָה וְשִׁפְחָה נַמִי, דְּשָׁמְעֵי מִמָּרַיְיהוּ וּמְנַטְּרֵי נַפְשַׁיְיהוּ. אֶלָּא יוֹצֵאת בְּשֵׁן וָעַיִן — הֵיכִי מַשְׁכַּחַתְּ לָהּ? וְכִי תֵּימָא: כָּל דִּמְמֵילָא מוֹדֶה ר' יוֹסֵי — *וְהָתְנַן: אֲנוּסָה וּמְפוּתָּה צְרִיכָה לְהַמְתִּין ג' חֳדָשִׁים, דִּבְרֵי ר' יְהוּדָה. רַבִּי יוֹסֵי [ג]מַתִּיר לֵיאָרֵס וְלִינָּשֵׂא מִיָּד! — אֶלָּא אָמַר *אַבָּיֵי: אִשָּׁה מְזַנָּה מִתְהַפֶּכֶת, שֶׁלֹּא תִּתְעַבֵּר. — וְאִידָּךְ: חָיְישִׁינַן שֶׁמָּא לֹא נִתְהַפְּכָה יָפֶה יָפֶה. § "וְאִם הָיוּ כֹּהֲנוֹת כו'". § כֹּהֲנוֹת — אִין, יִשְׂרְאֵלִית — לָא?! אֵימָא: אִם הָיוּ נְשֵׁי כֹּהֲנִים. — נְשֵׁי כֹּהֲנִים — אִין, נְשֵׁי יִשְׂרְאֵלִים — לָא? וְהָאָמַר *רַב עַמְרָם: הָא מִילְּתָא אֲמַר לָן רַב שֵׁשֶׁת, וְאַנְהֲרִינְהוּ לְעַיְינִין מִמַּתְנִיתִין: [ד]אֵשֶׁת יִשְׂרָאֵל שֶׁנֶּאֶנְסָה, אַף עַל פִּי שֶׁמּוּתֶּרֶת לְבַעְלָהּ — פְּסוּלָה לִכְהוּנָּה! — אֲמַר רָבָא, הָכִי קָאָמַר: [ה]אִם הָיוּ כֹּהֲנוֹת נְשׂוּאוֹת לְיִשְׂרָאֵל — נִפְסְלוּ מִן הַתְּרוּמָה דְּבֵי נְשַׁיְיהוּ. §

הדרן עלך ארבעה אחין

רש"י

וגזרו רבנן קטנה וכו'. וגבי גיורת קטנה לא גזור, משום דלא שכיחא. מכלל דהואי. בתמיה: וכי מעשה כזה אירע בימי חכמים? והא שנים קתני, ולא תני מעשה. אלא כהוראת שעה היתה. (א) ולא גזרינן בה, מ"ט – חילוף לא שכיח. חוץ מגיורת ומשוחררת גדולה. מדקתני בהאי חוץ גדולה, מכלל דצריכות להמתין דקאמר – בגדולות קמיירי. גיורת ומשוחררת גדולה דשכיחא בהו זנות לגזור. שימתינו, כדי להבחין בין זרע שנזרע שלא בקדושה לזרע שנזרע בקדושה. הוא דאמר כרבי יוסי. דלא גזר. דמפרש טעמא, דאשה מזנה מתהפכת כדי שלא תתעבר. ומיהו, בישראלית גזר שמואל זנות אטו נשואין שמתעברת, ולא סבר כר' יוסי דלא גזר בהו, כדאמר לקמן באנוסה ומפותה, אבל בגיורת לא גזור זנות שבנכרית משום נשואין דבנכרית. דאפילו גיורת נשואה, כיון דדעתה לאיגיורי – מתהפכת נמי, כדי להבחין בין זרע קדושה לזרע שלא בקדושה. מנטרא נפשה. ומטעיא מוך בהדה, ומזומן לה. אלא יוצאה בשן ועין. דלא הות ידעה מעיקרא דעתידה להשתחרר, לא מיטרחא ומזדהרא לאתויי מוך בהדה. אנוסה ומפותה. ישראלית. והרי אונס מילא הוא, ואין לה מוך. מתהפכת. ואף יוצאה בשן ועין נמי ליכא השתא למפרך, דכיון דהיפוך קל הוא לה ואין בו טורח – מתהפכת היא, דכל אשה מזנה אינה רוצה להתעבר. כהנות. בנות כהנים. ישראלית לא. בתמיה: הואיל ואשת כהן היא, אפילו בת ישראל נמי אסורה לבעלה כהן! נשי כהנים. אם בעליהן כהנים נפסלו להן, דאשת כהן שנאנסה אסורה לבעלה. נשי ישראלים לא. בתמיה: וכי אם בעליהם של אלו ישראלים – מי לא מיפסלו נמי לכהונה? שאם ימותו אלו – לא ינשאו לכהנים. והאמר רב עמרם כו' ואנהרינהו לעיינין ממתניתין. כלומר: הביא לנו ראיה ממשנתנו. ואותה משנה לקמן ב"הבא על יבמתו" (דף נו.). אשת ישראל שנאנסה אף על פי שמותרת לבעלה. מ"והיא לא נתפשה" (במדבר ה), הא נתפשה מותרת, אפ"ה – פסולה לכהונה אם ימות בעלה. אם היו כהנות. בנות כהנים, ואפילו נשואות לישראל. דלא מהני האי זנות לאסרן לבעליהן. נפסלו מתרומה דבי נשייהו. שאם ימות בעלה וזרע אין לה – אינה שבה אל בית אביה כנעוריה, דפסיל לה האי זנות, כדתניא לקמן ב"אלמנה לכהן גדול" (דף סח.): כהנת לויה וישראלית שבא עליה גר עמוני כו', ויליף טעמא מ"ובת כהן כי תהיה לאיש זר", כיון שנבעלה לפסול לה – פסלה. ואע"ג דמותבינן: ואימא נבעלה לפסול חייבי כריתות? ומשנינן: "כי תהיה" כתיב, הנך דאית בהו הוייה, אלמא זנות דחייבי כריתות לא פסיל מאכילת תרומה – הא הדר מייתינא התם קרא אחרינא "כי תהיה אלמנה וגרושה" – למעוטי כותי ועבד שאין לו אלמנות וגירושין בה, ומההוא קרא נמי נפקא לן חייבי כריתות, דהא אין לו אלמנות וגירושין בה. ומעיקרא פרכינן הכי. ואימא חייבי כריתות ולא חייבי לאוין.

הדרן עלך ארבעה אחין

תוספות

חוץ מגיורת ושפחה משוחררת גדולה. והא דתניא ב"החולץ" (לקמן דף מב.) לפיכך גר וגיורת צריכין להמתין שלשה חדשים – כר' יהודה אתיא, דחייש שמא לא נתהפכה יפה יפה. א"נ, אפילו כרבי יוסי, וה"ק: לפיכך גר וגיורת צריכין להמתין, אם ידוע שנבעלה ולא נתהפכה. ועוד אר"י, דיש לחלק: דלא מינטרא נפשה כלל – כשמתגיירת עם בעלה, כיון שכל הזרע מאותו איש ואין חוששת להבחין בין זרע שנזרע מבעלה זה בקדושה לשלא נזרע בקדושה.

גיורת ומשוחררת דשכיחא (ב) לגזור. פירוש: לגזור שיהיו צריכות להמתין. ולא לגזור אטו בת ישראל קאמר, דמהא לא הוה משני מידי.

אשה מזנה מתהפכת. וכן גיורת ומשוחררת, כיון דדעתה לאיגיורי. אבל יוצאה בשן ועין – מודה בה רבי יוסי.

כהנות אין ישראלית לא. ובכתובות (דף נא.), גבי הא דתנן: ובכהנת אהדרינתיך למדינתיך, לא דייק הכי. אלא דוקא הכא, משום דכי משני אימא נשי כהנים – אכתי אית ליה פירכא אחריתי: נשי כהנים – אין, נשי ישראלים – לא.

אע"פ שמותרת לבעלה פסולה לכהונה. פי' בקונט': טעמא דשמעתין משום "ובת כהן כי תהיה לאיש זר". ולר"י נראה דמ"בת איש כהן" לא שמעינן אשת איש וכל חייבי כריתות הנאסרות ע"י קדושין, משום דלא הוי זר אצלה מעיקרא. והכי משמע ב"הבא על יבמתו" (לקמן דף נו:) דקאמר רבא: אשת כהן שנאנסה ובא עליה – לוקה משום זונה ומשום טומאה. ואי מ"בת כהן כי תהיה לאיש זר" שמעינן נמי אשת איש, א"כ יהא לוקה נמי מהאי קרא, דלכהונה נמי אסורות מק"ו דלקמן בפרק "אלמנה" (דף סח: ושם) דלא חשיב לה התם אזהרה מן הדין, אלא גילוי מלתא בעלמא הוא. וה"נ משמע כן קצת מדקאמר: אף על פי שמותרת לבעלה – פסולה לכהונה. ואי פסולה מקרא דבת כהן – פשיטא, דאין לחלק בין אונס לרצון. ואי היא גופה אתא לאשמועינן דשייך קרא דבת כהן בחייבי כריתות דע"י קדושין, כיון דשייך בהו ממזרות, אע"ג דלא הוי זר אצלה מעיקרא – אם כן לישמעינן הכי בהדיא וממילא ידענו דלא שייך בהאי קרא לפלוגי בין אונס לרצון באשת איש טפי מבשאר [פסולי כהונה]. אלא (ג) לר"י נראה דפסולה מן הכהונה מטעם טומאה וזונה, כדאמר ב"הבא על יבמתו" (לקמן דף נו: ושם). וללישנא דאמר התם דכל באונס לא מיקריא זונה – פסולה לכהונה משום טומאה גרידא. ומיהו, קשה לר"י: (ד) כיון דלא חשיב טומאה אאשת ישראל שנבעלה באונס, דכתיב "והיא לא נתפשה", הא נתפשה מותרת, אם כן, אמאי פסולה לכהונה? דבכלל איסור טומאה הוי בעל ובועל ותרומה וגם כהונה, וכי שרי לבעלה – תשתרי נמי לכהונה! ואמר ר"י: דההוא קרא ד"לא נתפשה" לא איירי אלא בטומאה דבעל גרידא, דנטמאה קמא אית לן לאוקמי לבעל, ולענין בעל שרי אונס בישראל. אבל ונטמאה בתרא, דנפקא לן מינה איסור תרומה וכהונה – לא מפליג בה בין אונס לרצון. בין אשת כהן לאשת ישראל, ויש לאסור בכל ענין. דכיון דאשכחן באשת כהן דאפילו באונס – אסורה – אין לנו לחלק בין אונס לרצון לענין תרומה וכהונה אפילו באשת ישראל. ומיהו, גבי בועל אע"ג דלא כתיב ביה "לא נתפשה" יש לחלק בין אונס לרצון באשת ישראל, דסברא הוא דלא נאסרה על הבועל. אלא כשנאסרה על הבעל. ולפי פר"י אין פסולה זונה לתרומה מקרא ד"בת כהן", אלא שמא מטעם דכלליה קרא בהדי חללה – פסולה לתרומה כמו חללה, ובפרק "החולץ" (לקמן דף מד: ד"ה הכא) כתב ר"י מזה:

הדרן עלך ארבעה אחין

עין משפט נר מצוה

נג א מיי' פי"א מהל' גירושין הלכ' כ סמג עשין נ טוש"ע אה"ע סימן יג סעיף יא:

נד ב מיי' שם הלכה כא טוש"ע אה"ע שם סעיף ה:

נה ג מיי' שם הלכה כב טוש"ע שם סעיף ו:

נו ד מיי' פי"ח מהלכות איסורי ביאה הלכה ז סמג לאוין קכח טוש"ע אה"ע סימן ו סעיף יא:

נז ה מיי' פי"ו מהלכות תרומות הל' ז והל' י:

מסורת הש"ס

[לעיל לג:]

כתובות נ. כל הסוגיא ע"ש

[נ"ל והתניא]

[שם איתא רבה וברב אלפס הגירסא איתא רבא]

[לקמן נו.]

הגהות הב"ח

(א) רש"י ד"ה אלא וכו' היתה (ולא היתה) תא"מ ונ"ב ס"א אין זה: (ב) תוס' ד"ה גיורת ומשוחררת דשכיחא בה זנות לגזור: (ג) ד"ה אע"פ וכו' אלא נראה לר"י: (ד) בא"ד ומיהו קשה לר"י כו' אאברהם כיון דלא כתיב:

גליון הש"ס

גמ' והאמר רב עמרם. הא מילתא אמר לן רב ששת ואנהרינהו לעיינין. עיין לקמן דף נו:

תוספות ישנים

אבל קטנה בת ישראל אינה צריכה להמתין. פי"ה מדקאמר חוץ מגיורת ומשוחררת גדולה מכלל דהאי דקאמר דבת ישראל צריכה להמתין מיירי בגדולה...

תוספות חד מקמאי

אמר שמואל כולן צריכות להמתין שלשה חדשים חוץ מגיורת ומשוחררת גדולה וקטנה בת ישראל בזנות דזנות בקטנה [לא שכיח] אבל קטנה יוצאה בגט או במיאון...

לאגיורי מנטרא נפשה בין זרע כשר לזרע פסול כך פרש"י ז"ל והראב"ד פי' דבגיורת ומשוחררת איכא תרי ספיקא ספק זינתה ספק לא זינתה ואת"ל זינתה שמא נתהפכה יפה יפה אבל באנוסה ומפותה ליכא אלא חד ספק ולפום האי טעמא יוצאה במיאון צריכה להמתין ג' חדשים ומאי דאמר שמואל דאמר כר' יוסי סבר לה כוותיה בחדא ופליג עליה בחדא ס"ל כוותיה בחדא בגיורת ומשוחררת גדולה ופליג עליה בחדא בבת ישראל ומסתברא דלית הלכתא לא כר' יהודה ולא כר' יוסי אלא כשמואל... עקרות ואפילו איילונית לא ינשאו ולא יתארסו דגזרינן הא אטו הא. הא דתנן כהנות פסולות מן התרומה ה"ה לישראלית וה"ה לנשי ישראל שאנוסה אע"פ שמותרת לבעלה פסולה לכהונה אלא הא"ק אם היו

מאנוסה ומפותה נימא כדמתרץ תלמודא דודאי מתהפכת היא שלא תתעבר ואין טורח גדול בדבר: **אע"פ** שמותרת לבעלה פסולה לכהונה דכתיב ובת איש כהן כי תהיה לאיש זר כיון שנבעלה לפסול לה פסלה. ואע"ג דאמרינן לקמן ואימא בחייבי כריתות אמר קרא כי תהיה בהנך דאית בהו הויה ולא למעט חייבי כריתות אתא דגלי קרא (בזר) [דכי תהיה לאיש זר] הכא ובת כהן כי תהיה אלמנה וגרושה מי שיש לו אלמנות וגירושין בה ומחייבי כריתות לית בהו אלמנות וגירושין אלא ה"ק ואימא חייבי כריתות ולא חייבי לאוין:

תלמוד בבלי

הוצאת קורן ירושלים

— מהדורת נאה —

מסכת יבמות
דף יז. עד דף לה.

COMMENTARY BY

Rabbi Adin Even-Israel
Steinsaltz

EDITOR-IN-CHIEF

Rabbi Dr Tzvi Hersh Weinreb

EXECUTIVE EDITOR

Rabbi Joshua Schreier

•

STEINSALTZ CENTER
KOREN PUBLISHERS JERUSALEM

Please note that the number ranges that appear at the bottom of each daf of the Vilna pages indicate the corresponding pages of the Koren Talmud Bavli translation and commentary.

תלמוד בבלי

— מהדורת נאה —

יבמות חלק ב

Steinsaltz Center

KOREN